Collaborating with Parents to Reduce Children's Behavior Problems

A Book for Therapists Using the Incredible Years® Programs

CAROLYN WEBSTER-STRATTON, PH.D.

www.incredibleyears.com

Collaborating with Parents to Reduce Children's Conduct Problems
A book for Therapists using the Incredible Years® Programs

Some chapters were updated and substantially revised from the book *Troubled Families—Problem Children, Working with Parents: A Collaborative Process*, by Martin Herbert and Carolyn Webster-Stratton and Martin Herbert, published in 1994 by John Wiley & Sons, Ltd.

Book design by Janice St. Marie
Cover photos www.istockphoto.com

Webster-Stratton, Carolyn
Collaborating with Parents to Reduce Children's Conduct Problems
A book for Therapists using the Incredible Years® Programs

Includes bibliographical references.
ISBN 978-1-892222-11-4

Publisher:
Incredible Years®, Inc.
1411 8th Avenue West
Seattle, WA 98119 USA
206-285-7565
www.incredibleyears.com

Printed in USA

For all those professionals—nurses, teachers, social workers, psychologists, psychiatrists, physicians, and others—who collaborate with families and support each other in order to alter the future for these children.

ACKNOWLEDGEMENTS

I owe a great deal to the many families from the Parenting Clinic at the University of Washington who permitted us to videotape or audiotape intake appointments and therapy sessions in order to make these qualitative analyses possible. These families have taught us so much and will continue to do so if we listen carefully.

I am particularly indebted to Ada Spitzer, who was a doctoral student here at the clinic more than 20 years ago when she worked with me on the qualitative analyses of the data that provided the bases for Chapters Three and Ten. She taught me most of what I know about qualitative analysis and gave me a new lens from which to view and understand these families. Secondly, I am indebted to those incredible therapists who have worked with me since 1982 to deliver these programs to families. Over those years we met weekly to review videos of group sessions, to plan subsequent sessions, to try out and practice new therapeutic ideas, and to refine our protocols and methods. These therapists supported each other as well as myself to continue to work with these families who were at times difficult, in order to in turn motivate and encourage them to persist with the hard work of parenting their children.

Contents

PREFACE

Many years ago in the course of interviewing the parent of a child with severe conduct problems, I asked her whether she had made any prior attempts to get help for her child. The account she gave me was a chilling one; one that I have never forgotten. She told me she had first gone to see her pediatrician to discuss her frustration over her four-year-old son's problems: he was aggressive, defiant, and noncompliant, and her attempts to toilet train him had been entirely unsuccessful. Her doctor attempted to reassure her, saying that her son would eventually outgrow these problems. He advised her to just "loosen up," "be patient," and wait calmly for the better times that would come as her son matured.

A year later, her son's behavior problems had escalated. He had repeatedly tried to run away from home. His teachers were threatening to expel him from school for hitting other children, for his generally non-cooperative behavior, and for his habit of soiling in his underpants. This time the mother went to a child psychologist for help. The psychologist told her she was too "laissez-faire" in her parenting; she needed to be firmer and more consistent in setting limits with her child. He recommended a book on Time Out techniques. Over the next six months, she said, she disciplined her son constantly, but his aggression only worsened—as did her own frustration.

When her child's teachers finally asked her to find another school for her son because they couldn't manage him in the classroom, she sought the help of a psychiatrist. She told me, "I hoped the psychiatrist would give us some medicine like Ritalin that would help him behave better. But instead she told me I needed to work on my own marital problems, and then my son's behavior would improve." However, her husband was against any kind of marital counseling. "So," she said, "what was I to do?"

At the point when this mother came to our Parenting Clinic at the University of Washington for help, her now 8-year-old son had no friends and had been rejected from five different schools. She herself was depressed, and her marriage was in considerable turmoil. She felt hopeless about the possibility of getting any real help for her child. She had experienced stigmatization and isolation from parents of "normal" children. She felt blamed for her child's problems—not only by other parents and her son's teachers, but also by the professionals to whom she had turned for help. Moreover, she felt hopelessly confused about which approach to take toward her son's behavior problems.

Over the past 30 years I have heard countless similar stories from parents of more than 1000 children with oppositional defiant and conduct disorders who have come through our Parenting Clinic. What this mother experienced in her attempts to get professional help is, unfortunately, all too common. These parents' stories highlight two unhelpful attitudes of professionals in our field: on the one hand, the tendency to minimize the child's problems and the family's level of distress and, on the other hand, pathologizing the family itself by labeling or diagnosing its members as "antisocial," "personality disordered," "depressed," "resistant," or "unattached," implicitly or explicitly blaming the parents for the child's problems. Such attitudes on the part of professionals, as reflected through the eyes of parents of children with conduct problems, imply a lack of empathy. These parents feel that professionals simply do not understand their situation; we psychologists, nurses, social workers, pediatricians, teachers, psychiatrists and other professionals are unable or unwilling to grasp the extent to which these parents are experiencing a kind of private hell. Even the research literature concerning conduct disorders tends to contribute to this perception by describing parents of children with conduct disorders as having "parenting skills deficits"; for, in shifting the focus from the child's behavior to the parents' lack of skills, this model implicitly blames the parents for the child's problems.

The "parenting skills deficit" model has had tremendous research as well as clinical value for professionals: it has led to greater refinements in intervention, forcing us to identify precisely which behavior management skills to target in treatment programs for parents of children with conduct disorders. Nevertheless, adherence to the deficit model can lead us to consciously or unconsciously attribute blame to the parents, ignoring all the stressful factors in the family's situation which have led to the breakdown in parenting skills; factors over which parents have little or no control. This is ironic, for the deficit model has spawned our most effective interventions to date. Yet it short-circuits our understanding of these families. It does not help us empathize with what it is like to be the parents of a child with conduct problems. And we need to know this if we are going to be effective practitioners.

It is this mother's story and the many others like it that lie beneath my determination to write about these parents. For very little has been written about the experience of living with a child with conduct disorders from the parents' perspectives. What do these parents experience in a typical day with their child? What kinds of feelings come up for them? How do they perceive their child's problem, and what do they think about it? What are their attributions? How do they "process" their experience of living with a child with conduct problems? How is their marital relationship affected? What impact does their child's behavior have on their relationships with other parents and their adult friendships? What are the effects on their relationships with their own parents (the grandparents), their extended family, and with schools? My hope is that a better understanding of these parents' feelings, experiences, and perceptions will help us refine our assessment and treatment approaches. For instance, if we know what these families have experienced in their homes and communities prior to seeking treatment, we may be able to better understand what factors will make it difficult or easy for them to benefit from a particular treatment strategy. Moreover, we may be able to offer help earlier, before they have reached such levels of despair. In any case, an increased understanding should help us avoid those twin professional pitfalls of either minimizing the experience of these parents or pathologizing the family.

In addition to describing what it is like for parents to live with a child with conduct disorders, a second goal for this book was to describe what it is like for families with children with conduct problems to undergo treatment. How are parent intervention and therapy programs experienced by the parents in them? What is the process like for them? What are their perceptions about their own progress or lack of it? Which aspects of treatment are especially difficult? When treatment is successful, what makes it so? How do they feel about the ways they are treated, and are there ways they would change their treatment, if they could? Again, there has been very little attempt in the literature to describe the therapy process from the parents' perspective. Yet the usefulness of this knowledge seems obvious. By understanding how families perceive and experience therapy during the different phases of parent training, therapists can be better prepared for the resistance and the regressions, and to some extent can prepare parents for the difficulties they are likely to encounter while in therapy, and can anticipate and predict the families' eventual acceptance and use of effective coping strategies.

Parents' experiences of therapy are strongly affected (though not determined) by what I will refer to as the therapy process: therapeutic philosophy, therapeutic aims and methods, the group dynamics (if it is group therapy), the role the therapist (or group leader) assumes in relation to them, even the physical environment in which the therapy takes place. Thus, in addition to describing what we have learned about how parents experience therapy, it seemed important to provide a qualitative account of the *process* of our own intervention with families. Surprisingly, in spite of the documented effectiveness of various types of parent training programs, the literature contains comparatively little discussion of the actual therapeutic processes utilized in such intervention programs.

In contrast, there is a rather large body of literature describing the *content* of parent training programs. For example, behavioral principles such as Time Out, Beta Commands, Praise, Differential Attention, Response Cost, and the accompanying parenting strategies have been carefully outlined in detail over the past 3 decades (Eyberg, 1988; Forehand & McMahon, 1981; Kazdin & Weisz, 2010; Patterson, 1975a, 1982; Webster-Stratton, 1984; 2001; 2007). But descriptions of the content of parenting programs do not elucidate the mechanisms of parent training or the ongoing processes of therapy; that is, how exactly do the therapists go about trying to modify parents' behavior, emotions, cognitions, and practices in parent training? There are many questions to be answered concerning the "how" of parent training, such as: How do therapists handle parents' resistance to new concepts and behaviors? How do they teach new skills without making parents feel inadequate or guilty? How do they answer parents' questions about such things as the advantages of hitting or disadvantages of praise and tangible rewards? How do they ensure that homework is carried out? When and how do they use confrontation? How do they promote parents' feelings of self-confidence and effectiveness? How do they teach new skills to parents with low self-esteem without exacerbating their feelings of incompetence? How do they make their training program culturally sensitive? And, more generally, which teaching/training methods and strategies are best with particular populations? Perhaps some approaches that are effective in other situations are counterproductive with these families. Perhaps some methods actually perpetuate the distress, guilt, and incompetence typically felt by these families. For example, it is possible that if families appeared to be "difficult" or "resistant" in treatment, perhaps it is due to the nature of the therapy process. This book explores typical parent questions and concerns about our parenting intervention and discusses possible therapist responses.

The parent population that served as the data base for the qualitative studies described in this book was over a thousand families who attended the Parenting Clinic at the University of Washington, School of Nursing or were involved in parent groups offered in the community. The University of Washington Parenting Clinic, funded by the National Center for Nursing Research and the National Institute of Mental Health, was founded in 1981 to develop and evaluate prevention and treatment programs for young children, ages 3 to 8 years, with conduct problems. The families we have treated in our clinic are representative of many families of young children with conduct problems: One-third were on welfare, one-third were middle-class, and one-third were upper-class families. Their family structure also was also representative: One-third were single-parent families and two-thirds were married, with half of the married couples experiencing significant marital turmoil. Study children included four boys for every girl treated, with a pre-treatment average of 21.3 behavior problems according to the Eyberg Child Behavior Inventory (ECBI), indicating that the children were clearly in the clinic range according to Eyberg and Ross (1978) (Boggs, Eyberg, & Reynolds, 1990; Eyberg & Pincus, 1999; Robinson, Eyberg, & Ross, 1980).

Quantitative accounts of the Parenting Clinic's intervention programs in numerous randomized controlled trials by our own research team as well as independent investigators have shown that the Incredible Years programs are effective in promoting more nurturing parenting interactional behaviors (academic, persistence, social and emotion coaching, praise, effective limit setting, predictable routines, proactive discipline, and problem solving), increasing children's social and emotional competence and school readiness, and reducing child conduct problems in comparison to untreated control families. These findings have been replicated numerous times in prevention studies with high-risk populations and in treatment studies with children diagnosed with ODD and ADHD. In deciding to present some qualitative accounts of our programs, I had an enormous amount of data to draw from, since our clinic had videotaped all intake and group therapy sessions as well as individual consultation and feedback sessions. This data provides a window into the experience of parents both prior to and during therapy. I was able to use these data to conduct qualitative analyses of how parents experienced life with a child with conduct problems, how they perceived and reacted to the group-based, video modeling parenting program, what their questions and unique needs were while participating in the program, and what they felt was missing from the program. I also analyzed the therapists' interactions with parents, looking specifically at how they tailored the video program to better fit the needs of these families.

—Carolyn Webster-Stratton
Professor Emeritus
University of Washington

OVERVIEW OF CHAPTERS

Part 1 is focused on understanding the problem of child conduct problems, including those diagnosed with Oppositional Defiant Disorder (ODD), Conduct Disorder (CD) and Attention Deficit Disorder (ADHD). We begin in Chapter One and Two with a general discussion of child conduct problems, looking at behavioral characteristics, causal factors, the course of the disorders, a brief overview of the underlying theories for intervention and research regarding family behavioral approaches for treating this disorder. Chapter Three provides a description of the child's characteristics from the parents' perspective and a discussion of the impact of the child's problems on the family, extended family members, and community. I present a series of cognitive/emotional phases, which appear to describe the typical experience of parents living with a child with conduct problems.

Part 2 is focused on treatment of child conduct disorders. Chapters Four and Six describe the content of the parenting programs focusing on the parenting tools using the Incredible Years Parenting Pyramid as the architectural framework. Chapters Five and Seven present typical questions and objections parents raise about the content and the key themes and processes that contribute to therapists' responses. Chapters Eight and Nine describe the collaborative therapy process and methods of helping families as delivered in the Incredible Years programs. In Chapter Ten I discuss parents' experiences while being involved in Incredible Years parenting groups at the Parenting Clinic. I define a predictable sequence of phases that most parents experience with the hope that therapists knowing what these phases are can help them guide and support these parents through therapy.

Part 3 focuses on ways to maximize results. Chapter Eleven focuses on special considerations for working with multicultural families and Chapter Thirteen for tailoring the program when delivered to child welfare referred families. Chapter Twelve discusses the child and teacher programs that are designed to be used in conjunction with the parent programs. Chapter Fourteen presents a case study, which illustrates how to bring all the intervention components together for one family. Finally, Chapter Fifteen, the epilogue, summarizes my thoughts and presents some future directions for working with families and for preventing and treating conduct problems in young children.

A NOTE OF CAUTION

This book does not attempt to provide a comprehensive review of all the assessment procedures, theories, therapeutic approaches or treatment research regarding conduct disorders. These areas have been well described in other books and articles (Kazdin & Weisz, 2010; Murrihy, Kidman, & Ollendick, 2010). Rather, this book represents an in-depth qualitative analysis of the experience of parents with children with conduct problems, before, during, and after they are in therapy, and a qualitative analysis of the therapist's role, using one particular type of intervention program as a model (The Incredible Years Parenting Curriculum delivered at the Parenting Clinic). Undoubtedly, other therapists doing family behavioral therapy, whether with individuals or groups, may be using similar processes. However, I believe it is important to detail these processes in order to illustrate that there is much more to a successful parent program delivery than merely conveying behavioral techniques or skills. Moreover, greater discussion among therapists of the precise therapeutic processes utilized in different parent intervention programs could bring to light differences and similarities among programs, suggesting new avenues for research regarding intervention strategies and family change processes.

I also want to note that the family behavioral change processes and examples that I describe in this book are based primarily on families with young children ages 3 to 8 years. I do not discuss issues related to adolescents with conduct disorders. My focus on this young age group is due my strong belief that one strategic point in the child's emotional and social development for intervention is the Piagetian cognitive developmental stage of "preoperational thinking," that is the transition period between children (ages 3-8 years) and the early school-age period when children enter the "operational" cognitive phase of development. My decision to focus interventions at this age period are based on the evidence that ODD and CD children are clearly identifiable at an early age. Studies have revealed that even children as young as age 4 have already been expelled from two or more preschools and have experienced considerable peer and teacher rejection. I believe that if we can socialize very young children with early onset ODD or high risk symptoms with positive, rather than antisocial interactions then it may be possible to disrupt and prevent the developmental trajectory from early onset conduct problem to well established negative reputations, peer rejection, low self-esteem and spiraling academic failure. In other words, optimal parenting nurtures healthy brain development and immunizes children against negative risk factors and a firm family foundation is established for future social and emotional development.

Our final cautionary note is that this book addresses only the parents' point of view and interventions for parents; it does not focus on the child's perspective and only briefly on the IY child treatment program and school intervention. This perspective is not meant to imply that I do not acknowledge or value the role that child factors or school factors play in the development of conduct disorders. In fact our research has indicated that training teachers in the Incredible Years Teacher Classroom Management program and the child Dina Dinosaur Social, Emotional and Problem Solving Skills curriculum substantially improves our outcomes. The most effective interventions will ultimately be those that involve parents, teachers, and children as agents of change, as well as those that promote positive bonds and continuity in efforts between the home and school environments. However, space limitations require that I leave the qualitative descriptions of these approaches to another book.

FOOTNOTE

* The words "therapist," "group leader," and "clinician" are used in this book interchangeably to refer generically to any professional involved in therapeutic work with families—such as nurse clinicians or practitioners, physicians, psychologists, social workers, psychiatrists, and others.

PART ONE

Understanding the Problem of Child Conduct Problems

Introduction to Child Conduct Problems

Clinicians or therapists working with families typically encounter children who exhibit persistent patterns of aggressive and hostile behavior. These behaviors manifest in significant impairment of everyday functioning at home or school, or conduct considered unmanageable by parents or teachers. The terms "externalizing", "disruptive behavior disorder", or "conduct problems" have generally been used to summarize a set of negativistic behaviors that commonly co-occur during childhood. In the preschool years, typical "externalizing" behaviors include noncompliance, aggression, tantrums, and oppositional-defiant behaviors. In the school-age years aggressive and oppositional behaviors continue with the addition of more serious violations of classroom and adult authority such as lying, cheating, and bullying. By adolescence these behaviors have escalated to antisocial ones that include violations of the law or of community authority, such as shoplifting, truancy, drug and alcohol use, and involvement with deviant peer groups. These problems are widespread; disruptive behavior disorders are the most common reason for mental health service referrals in children and youth (Kazdin, 2003). These children and their families utilize multiple social and educational services, sometimes on a daily basis. Moreover, the prevalence of disruptive behavioral disorders is increasing, creating a need for service that far exceeds available resources and personnel (Snyder, 2001a). Projections suggest that fewer than 10% of children who need mental health services actually receive them (Egger & Angold, 2006), and even fewer of those who get treatment receive an evidence-based treatment.

Fewer than 10% of children who need mental health services actually receive them.

"Externalizing" childhood behaviors are by no means abnormal. At one time or another, most children lie, cheat, take things that belong to others, hit when they are angry, tantrum, and refuse to do as their parents say. The distinction between typical difficult behaviors and the behaviors exhibited by children diagnosed with Oppositional Defiant Disorder (ODD) is the severity and the extent to which their behaviors interfere with normal functioning. The degree of the destruction and disruption, the occurrence of the behaviors in more than one setting (e.g., at home and at school), and the persistence of these behaviors over time, beginning at an early age, are what cause concern for families and clinicians alike.

This chapter details the features characterizing children to whom the labels of "oppositional defiant disorder" and/or "conduct disorder" are frequently applied. These children typically exhibit a "complex" or pattern of disruptive behaviors (i.e., lying, cheating, stealing, hitting, and noncompliance to parental requests) and, to a lesser extent, violations of social rules. In addition to diagnostic issues, I discuss the prevalence, course and prognosis for the disorder, as well as some theories regarding the risk factors underlying the development of the problem.

The following two case descriptions illustrate the type and the severity of problems represented by the child with conduct problems.

ROBBIE

Robbie is a 4-year-old boy living at home with his father, mother, younger sister, and 10-month old brother. Robbie has developmental and speech delays in combination with ODD and possible Attention Deficit Hyperactivity Disorder (ADHD). At the onset of therapy he was difficult to understand and had limited ability to express his needs verbally. He exhibited considerable oppositional behavior and frequent temper tantrums, often at times when he was unable to find the words to express his wishes or needs. Robbie's parents were very concerned because he made frequent threats of violence towards both younger siblings. Robbie's history reveals an escalation in aggressive activity, including the initiation of physical fights with peers, destruction of household property and refusal to do what his parents request. Robbie's parents express exasperation and exhaustion in dealing with Robbie, and no longer feel able to handle his behavior, which has become increasingly difficult since he was a toddler. Although they were initially told by professionals he would "outgrow" these problems, they have found that he has become increasingly aggressive and defiant. Robbie has been expelled from two preschool classrooms. His teachers report that he is one of the most challenging children they have worked with and feel that the other children in the class are not safe around him because his aggression is unpredictable. His teachers expressed to the therapists that they feel his parents don't understand the extent of his problems and don't care enough to get help. The parents report that they have tried every discipline strategy they can think of—such as Time Out, yelling, hitting and spanking, taking away privileges, and grounding him. They feel that none of these approaches have worked. The parents feel isolated and stigmatized by other parents with more "normal" children, and also feel that his teachers blame them for his misbehaviors.

Robbie's home life includes a mother with moderate depression who is struggling to manage Robbie and his two siblings.

She reports avoiding calls from the preschool and meetings with his teacher because of fears about what she will hear. Robbie's father works long hours and gets home late at night. On the weekends, he sometimes drinks heavily, and then loses his temper with his wife and the children. Although he has never physically hurt any of them, his outbursts are verbally aggressive. He admits that he is remorseful about this, and would like to stop drinking, but he feels that he needs the alcohol to cope with the stressful household. When he is not drinking, he attempts to be engaged and involved with Robbie, but these interactions frequently end in conflict when Robbie does not meet his expectations.

MELINDA

Melinda is a 5-year-old girl who screams and tantrums when she doesn't get her own way at kindergarten. She also behaves impulsively and can be hyperactive in the classroom. Her teachers have threatened to kick her out of kindergarten for these behaviors. Her mother reports that at home she throws chairs and threatens her with knives. She whines incessantly to get what she wants and refuses to brush her teeth, get dressed, or go to bed. Her mother feels unable to go out in public with Melinda because of her emotional outbursts. She reports that every request involves a series of intensive negotiations and cajoling. The mother says Melinda has been difficult since she was 8 months old. She reports feeling exhausted and trapped, isolated from other adults by her situation and unable to invite friends over socially. She feels that her daughter "blackmails" both her parents and her teachers to get what she wants by means of her aggressive outbursts, which sometimes last for over an hour.

Melinda's mother says she feels her own temperament is similar to Melinda's in that as a child she had similar emotional outbursts until she was in grade 5 or 6. At that point, she gained some control over her angry outbursts, but continued to engage in some risk-taking behavior as an adolescent. Currently she reports that she is still inclined to react emotionally when she is stressed. She separated from Melinda's father a year ago after 7 years of marriage. Although a number of factors led to the separation, Melinda's mother states that their different parenting styles and responses to Melinda's behaviors contributed to their marital distress. While Melinda's mother was frustrated by her husband's hands-off approach, he felt that she micro-managed and overreacted to Melinda's behaviors. They have joint custody, and Melinda goes to stay with her father every other weekend as well as one night a week.

Melinda's mother obtained her Master's degree in Nursing and is currently working full time and managing to support herself and her daughter on this income. Melinda's father is an accountant, but has recently lost his job and is unable to pay child custody support.

The family background reveals that Melinda's mother had a close relationship with her own mother, who was a social worker and died shortly after Melinda was born. Melinda's mother described her own father as cold, non-supportive, paranoid, and prone to emotional outbursts. Melinda's paternal grandmother was seriously depressed when Melinda's father was a child and spent much of her time in the hospital. Melinda's paternal grandfather was a warm and supportive parent, although he worked long hours to keep the family financially stable and so Melinda's father's primary care was often provided by a live-in care giver.

DIAGNOSTIC ISSUES

DSM-IV

According to the DSM-IV (American Psychiatric Association, 2000), externalizing behavior problems are referred to collectively as "Attention Deficit and Disruptive Behavior Disorders." There are three subgroups related to this larger category: Oppositional Defiant Disorder (ODD), Attention Deficit Hyperactivity Disorder (ADHD) and Conduct Disorder (CD). As Conduct Disorder is rarely diagnosed before age 6, most young children with externalizing symptoms fit the criteria for ODD, ADHD, or a combination of the two disorders. The primary features of conduct disorder are conduct problems and violations of the rights of others and of rules. A diagnosis of Conduct Disorder requires a disturbance lasting for at least 6 months during which three of the following symptoms are present: physical cruelty towards people or animals, stealing or breaking and entering, lying and cheating in games or in schoolwork, aggression towards others often including a weapon, destruction of property, truancy from school, and running away from home (APA, 2000). The DSM-IV (APA, 2000) mentions three subtypes of Conduct Disorder—Childhood onset, Adolescent onset and Unspecified onset.

Co-morbidity

There seems to be considerable diagnostic ambiguity regarding ODD, CD and ADHD in young children as well as true co-morbidity (i.e., hyperactive, impulsive, inattentive children have externalizing problems)(Loeber, Lahey, & Thomas, 1991). Current reports suggest that as many as 50% of children who are diagnosed as having attention deficit disorder with hyperactivity (ADHD) can also be identified as having ODD or CD (Beauchaine, Hinshaw, & Pang, in press; Kazdin & Whitley, 2006; Webster-Stratton, Reid, & Beauchaine, 2011). It has been proposed that hyperactivity may influence the emergence of conduct disorder, and even that hyperactivity may be inherent in children with CD (Loeber & Farrington, 2000). However, careful assessment of the child may reveal that the child actually meets the criteria for one but not the other. The criteria for ADHD and ODD and CD, while similar, are not identical. It is important that ODD and ADHD be differentiated, if possible, for both clinical and empirical reasons. Furthermore, those children who display concurrent ODD and ADHD appear to be at heightened risk for development of severe antisocial behavior or CD when compared to children with only one of these disorders (i.e., ODD or ADHD, but not both) (Loeber & Farrington, 2000; Walker, Lahey, Hynd, & Frame, 1987). Finally, many children with ODD and CD also experience depression (Webster-Stratton & Herman, 2008) but their diagnosis is frequently masked as disruptive behavior due to their lack of emotional language skills (Garber & Horowitz, 2002).

Developmental Progression from ODD to CD

A number of theorists have shown high continuity between disruptive and externalizing problems starting in the preschool years and externalizing problems occurring in adolescence (Loeber, 1990; Rutter, 1985). Recently, developmental theorists have suggested that there may be two developmental pathways related to conduct disorders: the "early starter" versus "late starter" model (Patterson, Capaldi, & Bank, 1991). The hypothesized early onset pathway begins formally with the emergence of oppositional disorders (ODD) in early preschool years and progresses to aggressive and nonaggressive (e.g., lying, stealing) symptoms of conduct disorder in middle childhood (CD), and then to the most serious delinquent acts in adolescence (Lahey, Loeber, Quay, Frick, & Grimm, 1992). In contrast, the "late starter" pathway first begins with symptoms of CD during adolescence after a normal history of social and behavioral development during the preschool and early school years. The prognosis for "late starter" adolescents appears to be more favorable than for adolescents who have chronic histories of disruptive behavior problems beginning during their preschool years. Adolescents who are most likely to be chronically anti-social are those who first exhibited symptoms of ODD in the preschool years (Snyder, 2001b; Tremblay et al., 2000; White, Moffit, Earls, & Robins, 1990). Thus, early onset ODD is a sensitive predictor of subsequent CD; indeed, the primary developmental pathway for serious

The primary developmental pathway for serious conduct disorders in adolescence appears to be established in the preschool period.

conduct disorders in adolescence and adulthood appears to be established in the preschool period (Tremblay, Mass, Pagani, & Vitaro, 1996).

Course of the disorder. Research has indicated that a high rate of childhood aggression, even in children as young as age 3, is fairly stable over time (Campbell, Ewing, Breaux, & Szumowski, 1986; Robins, 1981). Richman, Stevenson, and Graham (1982) found that 67% of children with externalizing problems at age 3 continued to be aggressive at age 8. Other studies have reported stability correlations between .5 and .7 for externalizing scores (Rose, Rose, & Feldman, 1989; Tremblay, et al., 2000). Loeber (1991) contends that the stability may actually be higher than these estimates, because manifestations of the problems are episodic, situational, and change in nature (i.e., from tantrums to stealing). Early onset of ODD appears to be related to later aggressive and antisocial behavior, as well as to the development of severe problems later in life (e.g., school dropout, alcoholism, drug abuse, juvenile delinquency, adult crime, marital disruption, interpersonal problems, and poor physical health (Snyder, 2001a). However, it is important to note that not all children with CD incur a poor prognosis as adults. Data suggest that fewer than 50% of the most severe children with CD become antisocial as adults. The fact that fewer than one-half of children with CD continue into adulthood with significant problems, whereas almost all adolescents diagnosed with conduct disorders had ODD earlier in childhood, means that early onset of ODD is a necessary but not sufficient condition for the development of antisocial conduct in adulthood.

Although not all ODD children become CD and not all children with CD become antisocial adults, certain risk factors contribute to the continuation of the disorder:

(a) *early age of onset* (preschool years) of ODD and CD. Those children with conduct symptoms prior to age 6 are at greater risk for developing antisocial behavior as adults than those whose problems start after age 6.

(b) *breadth of deviance* (across multiple settings, such as home and school). The children most at risk for continuing antisocial behavior as adults have conduct problems that occur not only in the home, but also at school and in other settings.

(c) *frequency and intensity of antisocial behavior.* The likelihood of becoming an antisocial adult increases in direct proportion to the number of different behavior problems evidenced as a child. 18% of adolescents with a minimum of three conduct problems were later diagnosed as antisocial, whereas 46% of those youngsters exhibiting at least six conduct behavioral indices were so diagnosed as adults (Robins, Tipp, & Przybeck, 1991).

(d) *diversity of antisocial behavior* (several versus few) and covert behaviors at early ages (stealing, lying, fire setting). The greater variety of both covert and overt behavior problems, the greater the likelihood of becoming an antisocial adult, although aggressive behavior is probably the most stable behavior over time.

(e) *family and parent characteristics*. Children whose biological parent have an antisocial personality are at greater risk for conduct problems (Loeber & Farrington, 2000).

(f) *teacher classroom management skills and classroom level of antisocial behavior.* Children with teachers who have ineffective management skills and classrooms with high numbers of children with ODD are at a greater risk of continuing to be aggressive (Kellam, Ling, Merisca, Brown, & Ialongo, 1998).

However, a delineation of contributing risk factors does not convey a complete understanding of the complex nature of variables involved, nor the relationship of the variables with one another. It appears to be the combined interactive or synergistic effects of these risk factors, as well as the number of risk factors, that contributes most to the child's risk of ongoing development of CD.

CAUSES OF THE DISORDER

It is widely accepted that multiple factors contribute to the development and maintenance of child conduct disorder (Hawkins et al., 1998). It is important to briefly review these risk factors because of their implications in designing interventions. These factors include: child, parent, and school-related risk factors.

Child Factors

Child Factors ~ Temperament. The "child deficit" hypothesis argues that some abnormal aspect of the child's internal organization at the physiological, neurological, and/or neuropsychological level (which may be genetically transmitted) is at least partially responsible for the development of disruptive behavior disorders. The contribution of temperament has perhaps been the most researched factor with regard to the development of behavior problems (Bates, 1990; Blair, Denham, Kochanoff, & Whipple, 2004; Webster-Stratton & Eyberg, 1982). Temperament refers to individual biologically based aspects of the personality that show consistency over time and across situations, and are identified as constitutional in nature (Thomas & Chess, 1977). Some commonalities in defining early child temperament styles have emerged including negative and/or positive emotionality, effortful control, attentional focusing, and social adaptability (Rothbart, Ahadi, Hershey, & Fisher, 2001). Research has indicated that there are links between specific temperament dimensions and externalizing or internalizing problems. For example, lack of adaptability and overt negative emotionality, in particular, appears to frequently predict later aggressive behavior problems (Bates, 1990; Rothbart & Bates, 1998; Seifer, 2000). In one longitudinal study, mothers' reports of infant difficultness (at 6 months) and infant resistance to control (at 1 year) proved to be significant predictors of externalizing problems at ages 6 and 8 years (Bates, Bayles, Bennett, Ridge, & Brown, 1991).

Parenting and family factors moderate a genetic vulnerability factor.

Although studies have shown that early assessments of temperament predict later behavior problems, the amount of variance in terms of behavior problems accounted for by temperament is in fact relatively small. Factors such as degree of family conflict, level of support, and quality of parent and teacher management strategies and socialization practices appear to interact with temperament to influence social and emotional outcomes. Several studies have shown that in the context of favorable family conditions and positive parenting, extreme (difficult) infant temperament is not likely to increase the risk of disruptive behavior disorder at age 4 (Maziade, Cote, Bernier, Boutin, & Thivierge, 1989). In general, the findings on temperament clearly support the notion of Thomas and Chess (1977) that "*no temperamental pattern confers an immunity to behavior disorder, nor is it fated to create psychopathology*" (p. 4). In other words, parenting and family factors moderate a genetic vulnerability factor (Brody, Beach, Philibert, Chen, & Lei, 2009).

Child Factors ~ Other Neurologic Difficulties. Neurological abnormalities are inconsistently correlated with conduct disorder. An association exists more generally with childhood dysfunction, rather than with conduct disorder in particular (Blair, 2002; Blair et al., 2004). There is much speculation, and some evidence, that deficits in verbal functioning, language comprehension, reading difficulties, impulsivity, and emotional regulation in aggressive children may be based in the left frontal lobe and its relationship to the limbic system (Bennett, Brown, Boyle, Racine, & Offord, 2003; Gorensten & Newman, 1980; Lahey, Hart, Pliszka, Applegate, & McBurnett, 1993). However, it is important to note that children with CD have an increased likelihood of a history of physical abuse, including head and facial injuries, and neglect, which may contribute to some of their neurological abnormalities (e.g., soft signs, EEG aberrations, seizure disorders). Moreover, research on the brains of children exposed to maltreatment have shown that brain development is adversely affected by such experience (Belsky & de Haan, 2011).

Research on the brains of children exposed to maltreatment have shown that brain development is adversely affected.

Biobehavioral systems are also implicated in the expression of impulsivity and aggression (Fowles, 1988; Milich, Hartung, Martin, & Haigler, 1994; Quay, 1993). These include basic approach, avoidance, and emotional regulation systems. Children and adolescents with ADHD appear to suffer from chronic dysregulation of the behavioral inhibition systems, reflected in impulsivity. Children and adolescents with CD suffer from additional deficiencies, including sympathetic underarousal and dysregulated fight or flight responses. There is some evidence of a low resting heart rate (lower vagal tone) among antisocial youth (Beauchaine, 2001; Beauchaine, Neuhaus, Brenner, & Gatzke-Kopp, 2008; Raine & Venables, 1984; Raine, Venables, & Mednick, 1997). Skin conductance responses have been found to differentiate between conduct-disordered youth and non-conduct-disordered controls in both adolescents and younger children (Scarpa, Raine, Venables, & Mednick, 1997; Schmidt, Solanto, & Bridger, 1985). While one cannot determine cause and effect from correlation data, these data do suggest a possible autonomic arousal system deficit in some of these children.

Child Factors ~ Cognitive and Social Skills Deficits. In addition to temperament, other organic and cognitive factors have been implicated in child conduct disorders and antisocial behavior. It has been suggested that children with conduct disorders distort social cues during peer interactions (Milich & Dodge, 1984), including attributing hostile intent to neutral situations (Dodge, Price, Bachorowski, & Newman, 1990). Aggressive children search for fewer cues or facts when determining another's intentions (Dodge & Newman, 1981) and focus more on aggressive cues (Goetze, 1981). The child's perception of hostile intentions from others may, in turn, encourage the child to react aggressively. There are also data indicating that deficits in social problem-solving skills and information processing contribute to poor peer interactions (Asarnow & Callan, 1985; Crick & Dodge, 1994; Dodge & Crick, 1990). These children may define problems in hostile ways, seek less information, generate fewer alternative solutions to social problems, and anticipate fewer consequences for aggression (Richard & Dodge, 1982; Slaby & Guerra, 1988).

Research examining the relationship between empathy and aggression also reveals some interesting information about children's development. Aggressive behavior in children is correlated with low empathy across a wide age range (Decety & Meyer, 2008; Feshbach, 1989). In other words, aggressive children, lacking empathy, have difficulty perceiving or understanding another person's point of view or feelings, which may explain their lack of interpersonal competencies and their antisocial behavior. Researchers have hypothesized that empathy and sympathetic concern for others are essential factors in inhibiting aggression toward others (Eisenberg, 2005; Frick, Stickle,

Dandreux, Farrell, & Kimonis, 2005; Lahey & Waldman, 2003). It is unclear whether aggressive children's cognitive processing of social information is a result of negative experiences with parents, teachers or peers, or is defective a priori.

Child Factors ~ Academic Deficits and Developmental Delays. Academic performance has been implicated in child conduct disorder. Low academic achievement and a lack of social skills often manifest themselves in children with conduct disorders early on, during the elementary grades, and continue through high school (Caprara, Barbaranelli, Pastorelli, Bandura, & Zimbardo, 2000; Frick et al., 1991; Hinshaw, 1992; Malecki & Elliott, 2002). Reading disabilities and language delays in particular are associated with conduct disorder (Bennett et al., 2003; Kaiser, Hancock, Cai, Foster, & Hester, 2000; Menting, Van Lier, & Koot, 2011; Sturge, 1982). One study indicated that children with CD exhibited reading deficits defined as a 28-month lag in reading ability behind that of normal children (Rutter, Tizard, Yule, Graham, & Whitmore, 1976). The fact that this relationship between academic performance and conduct disorder is considered bi-directional complicates this association because it is unclear whether disruptive behavior problems precede or follow the academic difficulties, language delay, or neuropsychological deficits. However, there is some evidence that cognitive and linguistic problems or delays may precede disruptive behavior problems (Kaiser et al., 2000; Menting et al., 2011; Schonfeld, Shaffer, O'Connor, & Portnoy, 1988). Moreover, children who enter school with poor school readiness skills, cognitive deficits, language and developmental delays, are more likely to have behavior problems, further exacerbating any preexisting learning problems (Duncan et al., 2007; Malecki & Elliott, 2002; Menting et al., 2011).

Children who enter school with poor school readiness skills are more likely to have behavior problems.

Heredity versus Environment. Longitudinal studies suggest that conduct disorder is stable across generations. This suggests the role of a genetic and biological vulnerability risk factor for child conduct disorder, as discussed above. For example, twin studies have shown greater

Environmental family risk factors in conjunction with genetic influences, contribute to risk for conduct problems.

concordance of antisocial behavior among monozygotic rather than dizygotic twins (Edelbrock, Rende, Plomin, & Thompson, 1995; Kazdin, 1987). Adoption studies, where the child is separated from the biological parent, indicate that offspring of antisocial parents show a greater risk of antisocial behavior. The increased risk due to antisocial behavior in the biological parent establishes some credence for the inclusion of genetics in accounting for a portion of the variance in conduct disorder. However, it has also been established that genetic factors alone do not account for the emergence of the disorder. Rather, these studies affirm that environmental family risk factors, such as adverse conditions in the home (e.g., marital discord, psychiatric dysfunction), ineffective family problem-solving and coping strategies, and harsh parenting skills, in conjunction with genetic influences, contribute to risk for conduct problems (Brody et al., 2009; Cerda, Sagdeon, Johnson, & Galea, 2010; Feinberg, Neiderhiser, Howe, & Hetherington, 2001; Loeber & Farrington, 2000; Webster-Stratton, 1985a).

Parent Factors

Parent Factors ~ Parent Skills Deficits. Parenting interactions are clearly the most well researched and most important proximal cause of conduct problems. Research has indicated that some parents of children with ODD/CD lack certain fundamental parenting skills. Parenting behaviors consistently associated with poor social and emotional competence and aggression in children include low levels of parenting competence (e.g., critical, hostile, unpredictable, inconsistent) (Deater-Deckard, Dodge, Bates, & Pettit, 1996; Ostrander & Herman, 2006), permissive, neglectful, and abusive discipline (Barth et al., 2005; Fantuzzo, DelGaudio, Atkins, Meyers, & Noone, 1998; Jaffee & Maikovich-Fong, 2011; Knutson, DeGarmo, Koeppl, & Reid, 2005), and lack of parental support, praise and a nurturing relationship (Pettit, Bates, & Dodge, 1997). For example, parents of children with disruptive behavior problems have been shown to be more likely to reinforce their inappropriate behaviors and to ignore or punish prosocial behaviors (Dishion, Patterson, Stoolmiller, & Skinner, 1991; Frick et al., 1992; Najaka, Gottfredson, & Wilson, 2001). The most influential developmental model for describing the family dynamics that underlie early antisocial behavior is Patterson's theory of the "coercive reinforcement process" (Patterson, 1982; Patterson & Capaldi, 1991; Patterson & Fisher, 2002). Patterson's theory describes a process whereby children learn to escape or avoid parental criticism by escalating their negative behaviors, which in turn lead to increasingly aversive parent interactions. The negative responses, in turn, directly model and reinforce the child's deviant behaviors.

Other researchers have emphasized the attachment or affective nature and strength of the parent-child bond as a key parenting factor effecting children's outcomes (Belsky & Fearson, 2002; Greenberg, Speltz, & DeKlyen, 1993). There is considerable evidence that a warm, positive attachment between parent and child leads to increased positive communication, nurturing parenting strategies and a more socially competent child (Baumrind, 1995; Belsky & Fearson, 2002). Nonetheless, the parenting difficulties faced by parents of a child with ODD/CD could also stem from having to cope with a biologically more difficult child who is unresponsive to the usual parenting approaches (Kim-Cohen, Caspi, Taylor, Williams, & Newcombe, 2006). Children with conduct disorders engage in higher rates of defiant, impulsive behaviors and noncompliance with parental commands than do typical children (Webster-Stratton, 1985b). When interacting with their mothers, children with ODD/CD exhibit fewer positive verbal and nonverbal behaviors (smiles, laughs, enthusiasm, praise) than do other children. In addition, children with conduct disorders exhibit more negative nonverbal gestures, expressions, and tones of voice in their interactions with both mothers and fathers. These children have less positive affect, seem depressed, and are less reinforcing to their parents, thus setting in motion the cycle of aversive parent/child interactions. These parenting risk factors interact synergistically with the child's genetic, biological and developmental risk factors noted earlier.

Parent Factors ~ Interpersonal. Parent psychopathology places the child at considerable risk for conduct disorder (Ashman, Dawson, & Panagiotides, 2008). Specifically, depression in the mother has been shown to increase the child's risk for conduct disorder. For example, in a recent community study, maternal depression when the child was 5 was related to parent and teacher reports of behavior problems at age 7 (Williams, Anderson, McGee, & Silva, 1990). This correlation is complicated by the fact that maternal depression is associated with misperception of a child's behavior; e.g., mothers who are depressed are more likely to perceive their child's behavior as maladjusted or inappropriate.

Depression also influences the parenting behavior directed toward a child's misbehavior (Ashman et al., 2008; Fergusson & Lynskey, 1993; Levendosky, Okun, & Parker, 1995; Webster-Stratton & Hammond, 1988). For example, depressed mothers often increase the number of commands they give their children. In response the child displays an increase in non-compliance or defiant child behavior. Depressed mothers also give an increased number of criticisms, a form of negative attention. It is hypothesized that maternal depression and irritability indirectly lead to behavior problems as a result of negative attention, reinforcement of inappropriate child behaviors, inconsistent limit-setting, emotional unavailability, and neglect.

Maternal insularity is another parental factor implicated in child conduct disorder. Insularity is defined as "a specific pattern of social contacts within the community that are characterized by a high level of negatively perceived social interchanges with relatives and/or helping agency representatives and by a low level of positively perceived supportive interchanges with friends" (Wahler & Dumas, 1984, p. 387). This definition is important because it appears that rather than the number or the extent of social contacts, it is the individual's perception of the social contact as supportive or positive that makes the social contact advantageous. Mothers characterized as "insular" are more aversive, indiscriminate in their mothering, and use more negative consequences with their children than "noninsular" mothers (Dumas & Wahler, 1985; Wahler & Sansbury, 1990). Insularity and lack of parental support have also been reported to be significant predictors of a family's relapse or failure to maintain treatment effects (Webster-Stratton, 1985).

As might be expected, the presence of antisocial behavior in either parent places the child at greater risk for conduct disorders. In particular, criminal behavior and alcoholism in the father are consistently demonstrated as parental factors increasing the child's risk (Frick, Lahey, Christ, Loeber, & Green, 1991). Grandparents of children with conduct disorders are also more likely to show antisocial behavior compared to grandparents of children who are not antisocial. How much of the child's conduct disorder is due to the inappropriate modeling of antisocial behaviors by the parent? How much is it due to a genetically transmitted predisposition? This question is, as of yet, difficult to unravel (Collins, Maccoby, Steinberg, Hetherington, & Bornstein, 2000).

Parent Factors ~ Interparental. Specific family characteristics have been found to contribute to the development and continuation of child conduct disorder. Interparental conflict leading to and surrounding divorce is associated with, but is not a strong predictor of, child conduct disorder (Brown, Green, & Druckman, 1990; Cowen, Pedro, & Alpert, 1990; Forehand, Thomas, Wierson, Brody, & Fauber, 1990; Webster-Stratton & Hammond, 1999). In particular, boys appear to be more apt to show significant increases in antisocial behaviors following divorce. However, there is considerable variation: After a separation or divorce, some single parents and their children appear to do relatively well over time, whereas others are chronically depressed and report increased stress levels (Fincham, 1994). One explanation for the poor child outcomes in some single-parent families might be that, for some, the stress of divorce sets in motion a series of stages of increased depression and increased irritability that, in turn, leads to a loss of friendships and social support, placing the parent at increased risk for more irritable behaviors, ineffective discipline, and poor problem-solving outcomes. The poor problem-solving of these parents, in turn, results in increased depression and stress levels and negative parenting, completing the spiraling negative cycle. This irritability and negative emotion simultaneously sets in motion a process whereby the child also becomes increasingly antisocial (Davies & Cummings, 1994; Forgatch, 1989).

The amount and intensity of parental conflict, negative emotion and violence is a more important risk factor than family structure per se.

Once researchers began to differentiate between parental divorce, separation, and discord, they began to understand that the divorce per se was not the critical factor in shaping the child's behavior, but rather the amount and intensity of parental conflict, negative emotion and violence (Brown et al., 1990; Grych & Fincham, 1990; O'Leary & Emery, 1982). For example, children whose parents divorce but whose homes are subsequently conflict-free are less likely to have problems than children whose parents stay together but experience a great deal of conflict. Children whose parents continue to have conflict during and after divorce have more conduct problems than children whose parents experience conflict-free divorce. In our own studies of families with children with ODD, half of the married couples reported experiences with spouse abuse and violence and half reported warm and supportive marriages (Webster-Stratton, 1989; Webster-Stratton & Hammond, 1999). Taken together, these findings highlight the importance of parents' marital conflict and violence, rather than family structure per se, as key factors influencing children's externalizing problems.

Marital conflict is associated with more negative perceptions of the child's adjustment, inconsistent parenting, increased use of punitive measures, decreased reasoning, and fewer rewards for children (Jouriles, Murphy, Farris, & Smith, 1991; Webster-Stratton, 1989). Conflictual, unhappy marriages where aggressive behavior is displayed, contributes to the formation of conduct disorder. It is consistently demonstrated that if aggressive behavior is present in the marital relationship, the likelihood of conduct disorder is greater than if marital conflict alone is present without overt aggression (Jouriles, Murphy, & O'Leary, 1989). This provides another explanation for the increased incidence of conduct disorders in maritally distressed families: namely, the child models the aggressive behaviors observed in the marital interactions.

Frick and colleagues (Frick, Lahey, Hartdagen, & Hynd, 1989; Frick et al., 1992) have proposed two models to help explain the correlation between marital distress and child conduct disorders. One model proposes a direct and indirect path from marital satisfaction to child conduct disorders, suggesting marital satisfaction or dissatisfaction directly influences the development of conduct disorders (i.e., negative parental affect and conflict disrupts the child's emotional regulation). The second model proposes that the significant correlations between marital satisfaction and child conduct problems are chiefly an artifact of the common effects of maternal antisocial personality and social class. Frick and colleagues (1992) found that the relationship between marital satisfaction and child conduct problems was based primarily on the common association with maternal antisocial personality, and that social class did not play an important role as a third variable. These findings seem to argue for the importance of parents' psychological adjustment (e.g., marital distress, depression) as a primary determinant of the effects of stress on parent-child interactions, rather than environmental factors such as poverty or low social status.

Family Factors ~ Environmental Stress. Research suggests that life stressors such as poverty, unemployment, crowded living conditions, and illness have deleterious effects on parenting and are related to a variety of forms of child psychopathology, including conduct disorders (Evans, 2004; Hashima & Amato, 1994). Families with children with ODD/CD report major stressors at an incidence two to four times greater than for families with typically developing children (Webster-Stratton, 1990). These parents also indicate that they experience more day-to-day hassles and major crises than non-referred families (Crnic & Greenberg, 1990; Sedlar & Hansen, 2001). An accumulation of minor day-to-day chronic life hassles is related to more aversive parenting interactions, such as higher rates of coercive behavior and irritability in the mother's interactions with her children. Recent reports have also shown maternal stress to be associated with inept discipline practices, such as explosive discipline and "nattering" with children (Forgatch, Patterson, & Skinner, 1988; Webster-Stratton, 1990). Thus, a cascading pathway may occur where environmental stressors result from poverty, marital conflict, or mental illness, resulting in inconsistent, neglectful, or abusive parenting and poor parent-child attachment. This disrupted parenting models emotional dysregulation for the child, contributing to the child's disrupted brain

Environmental stress disrupts parenting and attachment, which in turn disrupts children's brain development and leads to behavior problems, which in turn exacerbates parents' ability to socialize their children.

development, developmental delays, and behavior problems, which in turn contributes to further parenting difficulties in socializing the child.

School Risk Factors

Peer and teacher rejection. Once children enter school, negative school and social experiences further exacerbate the adjustment difficulties of children with conduct problems. Children who are aggressive and disruptive with peers quickly become rejected by their peers (Ladd, 1990), and this rejection can extend through the school years. Over time, peers become mistrustful of aggressive and disruptive children, rejecting them and responding to them in ways that increase the likelihood of reactive aggression (Menting et al., 2011). Because of their noncompliant, disruptive behavior, aggressive children also develop poor relations with teachers and receive less support and nurturing in the school setting (Campbell & Ewing, 1990). There is some evidence to suggest that teachers retaliate in a coercive process cycle similar to parents and peers. Studies have indicated that antisocial children are much less likely to get encouragement from teachers for appropriate behavior and more likely to get punished for negative behavior than more socially competent children (O'Connor, Dearing, & Collins, 2011). Frequently, these children are "expelled" from preschools and classrooms. At the Parenting Clinic, I found that during my studies with children with ODD, ages 3-7 years, more than 50% of the children had been asked to leave two or more schools.

Classroom Environment. The school setting has been studied as a risk factor contributing to the development of conduct disorders. Quality of teacher-student-family relationships and use of evidence-based classroom management practices are key protective factors related to child outcomes. Poor home-to-school relationships and ineffective classroom management are linked with the development of children's social and emotional difficulties, conduct problems and academic underachievement (Brophy, 1996; Conroy & Sutherland, 2008; Doll, Zucker, & Brehm, 2004; O'Connor, Dearning, & Collins, 2011; Walker, Colvin, & Ramsey, 1995). Low rates of praise, harsh discipline, negative relationships between teachers, students and parents, failure to focus on social-emotional curriculum, and low emphasis on home and school collaboration are all linked to risk for poor academic performance, escalating aggression, rejection (Kellam et al., 1998; Simonsen & Fairbanks, 2008), and poor long-term adjustment for students (Hawkins, Smith, & Catalano, 2004; Reinke & Herman, 2002). Research has shown that teachers with students that exhibit disruptive behavior problems in their classroom find that these coercive behaviors tend to dominate their interactions, making teaching difficult and unpleasant (Shores et al., 1993). This results in teachers' providing these children with less instruction and easier tasks than those given to children who do not exhibit such difficult behaviors (Carr, Taylor, & Robinson, 1991). Moreover, teacher reinforcement for such students' positive behavior is infrequent and reprimands are often non-contingent upon student behavior (Bierman et al., 1992; Stormont, Smith, & Lewis, 2007). As Patterson and colleagues (Patterson, Reid, & Dishion, 1992) have described, these patterns of negative or coercive interactions at school as contributing to a cascade of negative outcomes for children with conduct problems including peer rejection, negative school reputations, academic failure, and further escalation of antisocial problems. Furthermore, parent-teacher relationships are often strained due to a failure to develop supportive partnerships that promote home-school consistency and collaboration (Christenson & Sheridan, 2001).

The child's "bonding" to social institutions (both family and school) as well as the family's bonding to the child and school are believed to be critical features in prevention of conduct problems.

School and Home Connections as Factors. Bronfenbrenner (1979) has not only elucidated the importance of interactions that children have in their growing fields such as family, peers and school (microsystems), but also of the connections between these social fields (exosystems). The child's "bonding" to social institutions (both family and school) as well as the family's bonding to the child and school are believed to be critical features in prevention of conduct problems. For example, many parents of children with ODD and CD have had negative encounters with teachers concerning their children's

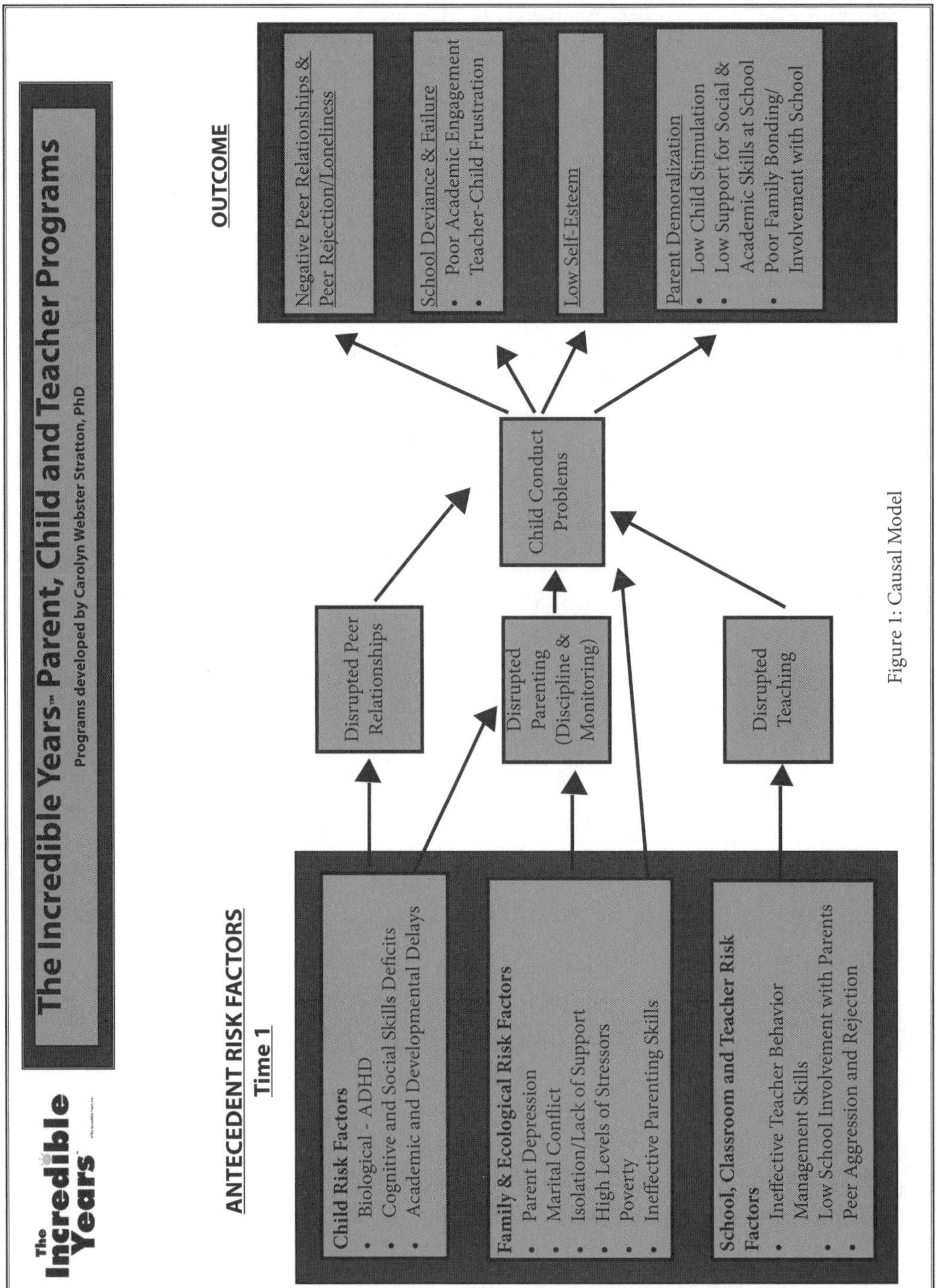

The Incredible Years

The Incredible Years™ Parent, Child and Teacher Programs

Programs developed by Carolyn Webster Stratton, PhD

ANTECEDENT RISK FACTORS
Time 1

Child Risk Factors
- Biological - ADHD
- Cognitive and Social Skills Deficits
- Academic and Developmental Delays

Family & Ecological Risk Factors
- Parent Depression
- Marital Conflict
- Isolation/Lack of Support
- High Levels of Stressors
- Poverty
- Ineffective Parenting Skills

School, Classroom and Teacher Risk Factors
- Ineffective Teacher Behavior Management Skills
- Low School Involvement with Parents
- Peer Aggression and Rejection

Disrupted Peer Relationships

Disrupted Parenting (Discipline & Monitoring)

Disrupted Teaching

Child Conduct Problems

OUTCOME

Negative Peer Relationships & Peer Rejection/Loneliness

School Deviance & Failure
- Poor Academic Engagement
- Teacher-Child Frustration

Low Self-Esteem

Parent Demoralization
- Low Child Stimulation
- Low Support for Social & Academic Skills at School
- Poor Family Bonding/ Involvement with School

Figure 1: Causal Model

behavior problems. Such encounters only add to parents' feelings of incompetence, sense of helplessness regarding strategies to solve the problems, and their alienation from the school. A spiraling pattern of child negative behavior, parent demoralization and withdrawal, and teacher reactivity can ultimately lead to a lack of coordination and support between the socialization activities of the school and home: a weak exosystem, to use Bronfenbrenner's term. This suggests that an intervention model requires both the development of appropriate social, cognitive and behavioral skills in the child and parent, as well as healthy bonds or connective relationships between parents and school, child and school, and parents and teachers. The child benefits from a strong family-school bond, because of the parents' increased expectations, interest in, and support of the child's social and academic performance (Battistich, Schaps, & Wilson, 2004; Epstein, 1992; Hawkins & Weiss, 1985; Webster-Stratton & Reid, 2010).

PART TWO

Helping Families with Children Who Have Conduct Problems

Overview of Treatment Approaches and Research

FAMILY-BASED INTERVENTIONS

Over the past three decades numerous parent training programs have been developed to address family risk factors related to the development of conduct problems (ODD/CD) as discussed in Chapter One. The central assumption for a parent-based intervention approach is a model that suggests parents' skills deficits and relationship difficulties are a major factor in the development and maintenance of conduct problems. Another important reason for focusing on strengthening the quality of parenting interactions is that parenting behaviors, emotions and relationships are perhaps more malleable than some biological and environmental intervention targets and risk factors. Intervention approaches based on this parenting model aim at the parents of the child with conduct problems rather than at the child himself/herself. The goal is to change the child's emotional and social behaviors by changing the parents' behavior and emotional responses, essentially to teach parents to use more effective parenting techniques and to strengthen positive attachment. Evidence-based parent program interventions have many similarities but differ somewhat in the specific aspects of parenting that are emphasized, the methods of intervention delivery, the length of the program, the age group or risk level of population addressed, and level of emphasis placed on the cognitive, affective, attachment relationship, child development or behavioral components. For example, some parenting programs primarily focus on changing the negative reinforcement coercive cycle that is eliciting and maintaining the child's negative behaviors, as well as identifying and rewarding children's pro-social behaviors. Other programs place more emphasis on building positive, nurturing parent-child relationships and attachments, or helping parents to create realistic expectations and build understanding and knowledge related to children's normal developmental tasks and home safety planning. Still other programs place more emphases on the cognitive and emotional aspects of parenting versus the behavioral changes targeted. Others may be more concerned with how wider systems, such as family poverty, the school or neighborhood, can influence a child's development. Some of these programs are offered in one-to-one settings at home, or in a mental health setting or school, others in a group format. Some parenting programs target specific developmental age stages such as toddlers, preschoolers, or school age children, while others mix parents of children of all ages together. Some programs offer interventions targeted at specific populations such as child welfare referred families, foster care parents, particular cultural groups, families whose children have certain diagnoses (ODD/CD, ADHD, depression), or families with specific risk factors (such as poverty or drug abuse).

Reviews of the efficacy of a number of parent training prevention programs (Kazdin, 2010; Sandler, Schoenfelder, Wolchik, & MacKinnon, 2011) and treatment programs have shown these programs to be highly promising for changing maladaptive parent and child behavior in younger children (Brestan & Eyberg, 1998; Eyberg, Nelson, & Boggs, 2008; Kaminski, Valle, Filene, & Boyle, 2008; Kazdin, 2010; Sandler et al., 2011). However, treatment-outcome studies suggest that interventions for

CD are of limited effect and more costly when offered in adolescence, after delinquent and aggressive behaviors are entrenched, and secondary risk factors such as academic failure, school absence, and the formation of deviant peer groups have developed (Dishion & Piehler, 2007; Offord & Bennet, 1994). In fact, group-based interventions targeting adolescents with CD may result in worsening of symptoms through exposure to delinquent peers (Dishion & Andrews, 1995; Dishion, McCord, & Poulin, 1999). This increased treatment resistance in older CD probands results in part from delinquent behaviors becoming embedded in a broader array of reinforcement systems, including those at the family, school, peer group, neighborhood, and community levels (Lynam et al., 2000). In contrast, there is evidence that the younger the child is at the time of intervention, the more positive the behavioral adjustment at home and at school. This seems to suggest that early intervention during the critical transitional period from preschool to school, when the parents are still the primary socialization agents in the child's development (as opposed to peers and teachers), offers promise for preventing the trajectory from ODD to CD and delinquency. Even with the younger children, there is evidence that the more risk factors that are targeted for interven-tion (such as poverty, school factors, parenting), the more sustained the outcomes.

The younger the child is at the time of intervention, the more positive the behavioral adjustment at home and at school.

It is not the intent of this chapter to review all evidence-based parenting programs available. Rather the focus of this book will be the content, methods, process, and research related to the Incredible Years Programs. Please see existing reviews regarding prevention parenting programs (Sandler et al., 2011) and treatment programs for conduct problems (Eyberg et al., 2008) and the Internet for lists of exemplary programs. For example, *Blueprints for Violence Prevention* web site

http://www.colorado.edu/cspv/blueprints/

lists programs selected as "exemplary" or "promising" depending on research evaluations standards such as: (1) intervention research design (control group), (2) statistically significant effects, (3) evidence of sustained results for at least one year and (4) replication by independent investigators.

The rest of this chapter will briefly highlight a few parent programs targeting parents of younger children with disruptive behavior problems (ages 3-8 years) and will describe in more detail research regarding the Incredible Years programs.

Three of these programs, *Parent-Child-Interaction Therapy* (PCIT) (Brinkmeyer & Eyberg, 2003; Eyberg, Boggs, & Algina, 1995), *Triple P-Positive Parenting* (Sanders, 2008; Sanders, Markie-Dadds, Tully, & Bor, 2000), and the *Incredible Years Toddler, Preschool* and *School-Age programs* (Webster-Stratton & Reid, 2010) all have similar underlying theoretical frameworks and content and have been shown in randomized control group trials to bring about significant improvements in positive parenting, reductions in harsh discipline, and decreases in parents' reports of child behavior problems (Sanders et al., 2000; Webster-Stratton & Reid, 2010; Zisser & Eyberg, 2010). Independent home observations have also indicated that parents can reduce children's levels of aggression by 20-60% and that generalization of behavior improvements from the clinic setting to the home are sustained over reasonable follow-up periods (1 to 4 years) (Brestan & Eyberg, 1998; Eyberg et al., 2001; Sanders et al., 2000; Webster-Stratton, 1990c; Webster-Stratton, Rinaldi, & Reid, 2010). Most parent-training programs have received high ratings from parents in terms of acceptability and consumer satisfaction. However, improved child behavior at home does not necessarily generalize to the preschool or school setting. Across many parenting programs studies have indicated that although a child's behavior improves at home, teachers or child care providers do not necessarily report improvements in conduct problems and peer relationships at school (Breiner & Forehand, 1982; Brestan & Eyberg, 1998; Forehand et al., 1979).

Parents can reduce children's levels of aggression by 20-60%.

Despite the general success of a variety of comprehensive parent training programs in producing statistically significant changes in parent and child conduct problems, there is also evidence that some families do not respond to treatment and continue to report clinically significant behavior problems in their children even after treatment. If one defines the criterion for treatment response by the extent to which parents and teachers report children's adjustment within the normal or the non-clinical range of functioning on standardized measures, then the results of these interventions look less robust. Long-term follow-up studies suggest that 30% to 50% of treated parents and 25-50% of teachers report that children continue to have behavior problems in the deviant or clinical range (Schmaling & Jacobson, 1987; Forehand, 1984; Webster-Stratton, 1990a,b).

A Broad-Based Family Training Model

Research has suggested that not only are parent programs more effective at reducing conduct problems when children are young, but also when programs are combined with strategies that address other family interpersonal issues and maximize family engagement and problem solving. Researchers have convincingly demonstrated that parental family and personal risk factors, such as depression, marital discord, lack of social support, environmental stressors, and poverty, disrupt parenting behavior and predict parent training treatment relapses (Dadds & McHugh, 1992; Lochman, Lampron, Burch, & Curry, 1985; Webster-Stratton, 1985a, 1985b; Webster-Stratton & Hammond, 1990; Webster-Stratton et al., 2010). As a result, broader-based expansions of family training have been developed to focus on adjunctive strategies to address these family interpersonal issues (e.g., marital communication, stress and depression management, and anger control). In this expanded model, broader-based interventions are hypothesized to mediate the negative influences of family stressors on parenting skills and also to promote increased maintenance and generalizability of treatment gains (Webster-Stratton, 1990b, 1994). Unfortunately, few studies have specifically assessed the relative contribution of treatment adjuncts and differentiated their effects from those of parenting interventions. However, studies have demonstrated promising results in terms of more effective problem solving, reduced depression, and enhanced support (Sanders et al., 2000; Webster-Stratton, 1994; Webster-Stratton, Reid, & Hammond, 2004; Forehand et al., 1979).

Regarding the Effects of the Incredible Years Basic Parent Training Programs

The Incredible Years (IY) Training Series promotes research-based parenting and teaching practices that positively and effectively reduce conduct problems and strengthen children's social and emotional competence. The BASIC parent series has 4 core curricula addressing various age groups: Baby Program, Toddler Program, Preschool Program and School-Age Program. The content of the Incredible Years Parent programs is described in detail within Chapters Four and Six. With the exception of the recently developed IY Baby program, all of the BASIC series programs have received numerous randomized control group trials (RCTs) by the developer and other independent investigators. (Webster-Stratton & Reid, 2010). These group trials (RCTs) were conducted both with prevention and treatment populations. The IY Baby program is currently under evaluation. The following section provides a review of these studies. Additional information about the individual research studies can be found in the library of the IY web site.

www.incredibleyears.com/Library/default.asp

Evidence for the Effects of IY Studies with Treatment Populations

The efficacy of the IY parent treatment program for children (ages 3–8 years) diagnosed with ODD/CD has been demonstrated in eight published RCTs by the program developer and colleagues at the University of Washington Parenting Clinic (Reid, Webster-Stratton, & Hammond, 2007; Webster-Stratton, 1981; Webster-Stratton, 1982, 1984, 1990a, 1992, 1994, 1998; Webster-Stratton & Hammond, 1997; Webster-Stratton, Hollinsworth, & Kolpacoff, 1989; Webster-Stratton, Kolpacoff, & Hollinsworth, 1988; Webster-Stratton, Reid, & Beauchaine, 2011; Webster-Stratton et al., 2004) and replicated in six RCTs by independent investigators in mental health clinics (Drugli & Larsson, 2006; Larsson et al., 2009; Lavigne et al., 2008; Posthumus, Raaijmakers, Maassen, Engeland, & Matthys, in press; Scott, Spender, Doolan, Jacobs, & Aspland, 2001; Spaccarelli, Cotler, & Penman, 1992; Taylor, Schmidt, Pepler, & Hodgins, 1998).

Summary of outcomes for which significant findings were found in one or more studies across RCTs that used IY Parent Programs with parents of children with ODD/CD and ADHD:

- Increases in positive parenting including child-directed play, coaching, praise and reduced criticism and negative commands
- Increases in parent use of effective limit setting by replacing spanking/hitting and harsh discipline with proactive discipline techniques and increased monitoring
- Reductions in parental depression and increases in parental self-confidence and self-efficacy
- Increases in positive family communication and problem solving
- Reductions in conduct problems in children's interactions with parents and increases in children's positive affect, compliance to parental commands and social competence
- 2/3 of children of participating families in normal range for behavior problems and social competence at 3-year and at 10-year follow-up

Families who received the ADVANCE treatment showed significantly better results for children's prosocial problem solving.

Treatment component analyses of one of the developer's earlier studies indicated that the combination of group discussion with a trained therapist and video modeling produced the most lasting results in comparison to treatment that involved only one component (such as the group discussion only or self-administered video modeling component) (Webster-Stratton et al., 1989; Webster-Stratton et al., 1988). In the developer's fourth RCT study, the effects of adding an ADVANCE intervention component to the BASIC intervention were studied (Webster-Stratton, 1994). This ADVANCE intervention provided content on parental problem solving with partners and children, parental anger and depression management, and methods for giving and getting support. In addition to the positive outcomes for parents and children mentioned above, families who received the ADVANCE treatment showed significantly better results for children's prosocial problem solving, observed couple problem-solving, communication, and collaboration skills compared to families who received BASIC parenting only.

Overall, these results suggest that helping families to manage personal distress and interpersonal issues through a video modeling group discussion treatment (ADVANCE) adds to treatment outcomes for the BASIC program. Consequently a 20-24 week program that combines the BASIC parenting program plus ADVANCE (parental problem solving, communication, and stress management) became the IY core treatment parent protocol for the remainder of the studies for children with conduct problems.

The Basic parent program plus Advance is the core treatment program for children with ODD.

In the developer's sixth and seventh studies respectively, the additive effects of combining the IY child training intervention (Dinosaur School) and IY teacher classroom management training program with the parent training program (BASIC + ADVANCE) were examined. Both studies replicated results from the prior ADVANCE study and provided data on the advantages of training children and teachers as well as parents (Webster-Stratton & Hammond, 1997; Webster-Stratton et al., 2004). See descriptions of study results below in the sections on child and teacher training results.

Parent training treatment: Who benefits and who does not? Families who were treated with the IY parent programs were followed longitudinally (1, 2, and 3 years post treatment), and a subset of children were followed for 10- to 15-years post treatment. Both the "statistical significance" of treatment effects, and also their "clinical significance" were assessed. Clinical significance was defined by the degree to which parent and teacher reports indicated that the children were within the normal or nonclinical range of functioning or showed a 30% improvement if there were no established normative data, and by whether families requested further therapy for their children's behavior problems at the follow-up assessments. A 3-year follow-up of 83 families treated with the BASIC program, indicated that approximately two-thirds of children showed clinically significant behavior improvements. Twenty-five to forty-six percent of parents and 26% of teachers still reported child behavior problems (Webster-Stratton, 1990c). Families whose children had continuing externalizing problems (according to teacher and parent reports) at the 3-year follow-up assessment were more likely to be characterized by maritally distressed or single-parent status, increased maternal depression, lower social class, high levels of negative life stressors, and family histories of alcoholism, drug abuse, and spouse abuse (Webster-Stratton, 1990c; Webster-Stratton & Hammond, 1990).

Hartman (Hartman, Stage, & Webster-Stratton, 2003) examined whether children comorbid for ADHD symptoms (i.e., inattention, impulsivity, and hyperactivity) predicted poorer results from parent training treatment than children with simple ODD/CD. Contrary to Hartman's hypothesis, analyses suggested that the children with ODD/CD who had higher levels of attention problems showed greater reductions in conduct problems than children with no attention problems. Similar findings for children with ADHD were reported in a UK study (Scott et al., 2001). In the developer's 8th treatment study, the 20-week parent program with the small group child program was evaluated for children whose primary diagnosis was ADHD. Half of the 99 children in the sample were also comorbid for ODD/CD. Results indicated significant effects for children's externalizing, hyperactivity, inattentive, oppositional behaviors, emotional regulation and social competence. There were also significant effects for children's emotion vocabulary and problem-solving ability. At school, teachers reported treatment effects for externalizing behaviors, and independent classroom observations indicated improvements in social competence compared with control students (Webster-Stratton et al., 2011). Follow-up data determined the short-term positive changes were sustained.

10- to 15-year follow-up indicated 75% of teenagers where parents received IY treatment were typically adjusted with minimal behavioral and emotional problems.

Rinaldi (2001) conducted an 8- to 12-year follow-up of families who received the BASIC plus ADVANCE interventions. She interviewed

83.5% of the original study parents and adolescents (ages 12–19 years). Results indicated that 75% of the teenagers were typically adjusted with minimal behavioral and emotional problems. Furthermore, parenting skills taught in the intervention had lasting effects. Predictors of long-term outcome were mothers' post-treatment level of critical statements and fathers' use of praise. In addition, the level of coercion between the children and mothers immediately post-treatment was a predictor of later teen adjustment (Webster-Stratton et al., 2010).

Evidence for Effects of IY Parent Programs as Prevention

The developer also evaluated a prevention version of the IY BASIC parent program in 4 RCTs with high risk, multi-ethnic populations (e.g., Head Start, parents of children with symptoms, and primary schools that serve high numbers of families living in poverty). Results showed significant improvements in positive parenting and school involvement, reductions in harsh discipline and aggressive behavior problems, and increases in social competence. Additionally, there have been at least 6 RCTs by independent investigators with indicated and selective multiethnic, socioeconomically disadvantaged families (e.g., Sure Start) (Brotman et al., 2005; Gardner, Burton, & Klimes, 2006; Gross et al., 2003; Hutchings & Gardner, 2006; Hutchings, Gardner, et al., 2007; Miller Brotman et al., 2003; Scott et al., 2010; Scott et al., 2009). One study reported on the effectiveness of the IY parent program with foster parents (Linares, Montalto, MinMin, & Vikash, 2006), another evaluated the self-administered version of the program (Ogg & Carlson, 2009), and another was conducted in doctors' offices (Lavigne et al., 2008). These replications were "effectiveness" trials done in applied mental health settings, not a university research clinic, and the therapists were typically therapists at the centers. Several of the independent replications mentioned above were conducted in England, Wales, and Norway. This illustrates the transportability of the BASIC parenting program to differing cultures.

Results of all these studies suggest the program's effectiveness as a method of preventing the development of conduct problems and strengthening social competence in preschool children. These studies also showed that programs were equally effective for families from diverse cultural and ethnic backgrounds including Latino, Asian, and African

American families. (Reid, Webster-Stratton, & Beauchaine, 2001). A more recent study (Reid et al., 2007) with primary school children in an indicated, culturally diverse population, also showed the program's effectiveness in reducing externalizing problems, improving emotion regulation, and building stronger parent–child bonding than control children. Mothers in the intervention group showed more supportive and less coercive parenting than control mothers.

Summary and significance. Over the past 30 years studies have shown that parent training is a highly effective therapeutic method for producing significant behavior change in children with conduct problems and with high-risk, multi-ethnic populations (i.e., socioeconomically-disadvantaged). These findings provide support for the notion that parenting practices play a key role in children's social and emotional development and also that parenting practices can be changed by training programs.

CHILD-FOCUSED INTERVENTIONS

The failure to acknowledge the role played by children's biological, developmental and school risk factors in the development of conduct disorders, may be one reason for the reduced effectiveness of parent programs in modifying some children's behavior. As noted in Chapter 1, children with a chronic history of early onset conduct problems are more likely to be comorbid for other neurological, language, developmental, social and emotional regulation difficulties, attention-deficit/hyperactivity disorder (ADHD), or depression. As a result of this research, a variety of innovative child training programs have been developed for use in schools and mental health settings to promote social and emotional learning. These studies generally show promising results, but more research is needed to confirm the durability and generalization of the programs. The reader is referred to review articles for more information about other child programs and their research base (e.g. Durlak, Weissberg, Dymnick, Taylor, & Schellinger, 2011; Elias & Tobias, 1996; Greenberg, Domitrovich, & Bumbarger, 2001; Wilson & Lipsey, 2007).

The next section of this chapter presents a few brief examples of types of child programs, followed by a detailed review of research related to the Incredible Years *Dina Dinosaur Social, Emotional and Problem Solving Skills Program* designed for children ages 4-8 years.

Historically, there have been two basic types of child skills training approaches. The first approach focused on training the child in *target social behaviors* and was based on the hypothesized social skills child deficits such as play skills, friendship, and conversational skills (Durlak, Weissberg, & Pachan, 2010; Gresham, 1998; Ladd, Price, & Hart, 1990; Mize & Cox, 1990; Walker, Schwartz, Nippold, Irvin, & Noell, 1994), as well as academic and social interaction delays, (Coie & Krehbiel, 1984), and behavioral control (Bierman, Miller, & Stabb, 1987). A second type of child training approach focused on training in *cognitive processes* and emotional competence and was based on the hypothesized cognitive deficits in problem solving, attributions of self-regulation and empathy or perspective taking (Camp & Bash, 1985; Kazdin, 2002; Kazdin, Esveldt-Dawson, French, & Unis, 1987; Kendall, 1993; Lochman, 1990; Lochman, Burch, Curry, & Lampron, 1984; Shure, 1997). Research evidence for these programs is encouraging, particularly for a cognitive program called the *Coping Power Program* (Lochman & Wells, 2002). This program was developed as a multi-component preventive intervention that includes a parent component as well as a classroom-based curriculum to improve preadolescent children's social cognitions, prosocial behavior, anger management, and academic behaviors. Studies have shown that the child component increased the program effects on child behavior more relative to the parent component. Results have indicated improved social competence and appropriate behavior at school and reduced externalizing and delinquent behavior and substance abuse at 1-year follow-up (Lochman, Boxmeyer, Powell, Roth, & Windle, 2006; Lochman & Wells, 2004). In general, the findings of multiple randomized trials regarding school-based social and emotional learning programs, some of which include parenting components, indicate significant improvements mainly for preadolescents on a broad range of outcomes including targeted prosocial behaviors, reduced conduct and internalizing problems, and improved academic performance (Durlak et al., 2010). Most of these child programs are school-based, prevention oriented and time limited, and the majority of programs have not specifically targeted young children with early onset ODD/CD. Those that have targeted children with ODD/CD for child interventions have tended to intervene during the preadolescent age (ages 8 and older) and adolescent delinquents rather than young preschool aggressive children. The most effective programs have combined child programs along with parent programs. Few studies have dismantled the specific effects of the child adjunct component from the parenting component or the additive effects of other components (West & Aiken, 1997).

Evidence for the Effects of the Incredible Years (IY) Social, Emotional and Problem Solving Skills Program (aka Dinosaur School)

IY Child Treatment Program

In 1990 the IY child treatment program (Dinosaur School) was developed to focus directly on the social, emotional and cognitive learning deficits of children diagnosed with ODD or CD (ages 4–8). The 22-week program (revised 2005) consists of a series of DVD programs (over 180 film vignettes) delivered in an interactive group format. Content of the program is organized to dovetail with that of the parent training program. The program consists of seven main topic areas: Introduction and Rules; Empathy and Emotion; Problem Solving; Anger Control; Friendship Skills; Communication Skills; and School Success Skills. The details of this program will be described in Chapter Twelve.

To date, the effectiveness of the IY child small group treatment program for reducing conduct problems and promoting social and emotional competence in children diagnosed with ODD/CD has been evaluated by three randomized treatment studies by the developer (Webster-Stratton & Hammond, 1997; Webster-Stratton et al., 2011; Webster-Stratton et al., 2004) and one by an independent evaluator (Drugli & Larsson, 2006). In the first study by the developer and a second by an independent investigator (Drugli & Larsson, 2006; Webster-Stratton & Hammond, 1997), clinic-referred children (with ODD) and their parents were randomly assigned to one of four groups: a parent training group (PT), a child training group (CT), a child and parent training group (CT + PT), or a wait-list control group (CON). Post-treatment assessments indicated that all three treatment conditions resulted in significant improvements in parent and child behaviors in comparison to control groups. Comparisons of the three treatment conditions indicated that the conditions that combined child and parent training produced significant improvements in problem solving as well as conflict management skills, as measured by observations of child interactions with a best friend. Differences among treatment conditions on these measures consistently favored the child training condition (CT) over the parent training (PT) condition alone. On measures of parent and child behavior at home, PT and CT+ PT parents and children had significantly more positive interactions in comparison to CT parents and children.

Combined child and parent training condition produced the most significant and sustained improvements in child behavior at 1-year follow-up.

One-year follow-up assessments indicated that all the significant changes noted immediately post-treatment were maintained over time. Moreover, child conduct problems at home significantly decreased over time. Analyses of the clinical significance of the results suggested that the combined child and parent training condition (CT + PT) produced the most significant improvements in child behavior at 1-year follow-up. However, children from all three treatment conditions showed increases in behavior problems at school one year later, as measured by teacher reports (Webster-Stratton & Hammond, 1997). The next study evaluated the effects of adding the IY teacher classroom management training component to the parent and the child training conditions (Webster-Stratton et al., 2004). This study aimed to determine the added effects of involving teachers in the treatment plan. The findings of this study are described in the teacher section below.

In a recent study (Webster-Stratton et al., 2011) children diagnosed with ADHD received both the IY parent and child interventions. Results indicated significant changes in children's emotion vocabulary, problem solving ability, social competence at school and externalizing behaviors at home. However, in this study the effects of the child treatment program and the effects of the parent intervention cannot be parceled out separately because all children in the treatment condition received both interventions. However, the prior two studies with children diagnosed with ODD/CD (half of whom also had ADHD) indicated that the combined parent and child approach was most effective for improving child behavior improvement with teachers in the classroom and with peers (Webster-Stratton et al., 2004).

Who benefits from Dinosaur child training? Analyses conducted on 99 children diagnosed with ODD/CD who received the child treatment program examined the effects of child hyperactivity, parenting style, and family stress on treatment outcomes. The hyperactivity or family stress risk factors did not have an impact on children's treatment response. On the other hand, negative parenting risk factors did negatively impact children's treatment outcome. Fewer children of parents with one negative parenting risk factor (high levels of criticism or physical spanking) showed clinically significant improvements compared to children of parents without a negative parenting risk factor. This finding suggests that for children whose parents exhibit harsh and coercive parenting styles, it is important to offer a parenting intervention in addition to a child intervention (Webster-Stratton, Reid, & Hammond, 2001). Our studies also suggest that child training significantly enhances the effectiveness of parent training treatment for children with pervasive conduct problems (home and school settings).

IY Child School-based Prevention Program

A fourth study evaluated the Incredible Years Child School-based Prevention Program with an economically disadvantaged population including Head Start and primary schools that had more than 60% of students receiving free and reduced lunch. Teachers paired with research interventionists to deliver the program in the classroom twice a week throughout the year with weekly dinosaur home activities to encourage parents' involvement. Classroom observations of 153 teachers and 1,768 students indicated that intervention classroom students had more social competence and emotional self-regulation and reduced conduct problems compared with control classrooms (Webster-Stratton, Reid, & Stoolmiller, 2008). To date, there has been no replication of the classroom delivery of the program by an independent investigator.

Summary of outcomes for which significant findings were found across studies that used IY Child Training Program:

- Increases in children's emotional language, emotional self-regulation, social competence, positive affect and appropriate cognitive problem-solving strategies with peers
- Reductions in conduct problems at home and at school
- Reductions in hyperactivity and inattention

TEACHER-FOCUSED INTERVENTIONS

Although robust positive effects on prosocial behaviors with peers have been found for the IY child intervention, effect sizes for children's oppositional behaviors with parents and teachers were smaller for the child program than for the parenting programs. The exclusive focus on child skills as the locus of change and the failure to acknowledge such school risk factors as teacher classroom management skills and the role these have in the reduction or development of conduct disorders, may be one explanation for this. As noted above, ineffective teacher classroom management skills and failures to focus on social-emotional curriculum or collaboration with parents are linked to risk for escalating aggression in the classroom as well as poor academic achievement (Kellam, Ling, Merisca, Brown, & Ialongo, 1998; Simonsen & Fairbanks, 2008).

Considerable research has demonstrated that teachers' use of effective classroom management strategies can reduce disruptive behavior (Conroy & Sutherland, 2008; Doll, Zucker, & Brehm, 2004; Hawkins, Catalano, Kosterman, Abbott, & Hill, 1999; Kellam et al., 1998; Walker, 1995), enhance academic achievement (Brophy, 1996), and increase children's emotional and social competence and school readiness (Webster-Stratton et al., 2004; Webster-Stratton et al., 2008). Well-trained teachers can help children who are aggressive, disruptive, and uncooperative to develop the appropriate social behavior and emotional self-regulation that is a prerequisite for their success in school (Walker et al., 1994; Webster-Stratton et al., 2004; Webster-Stratton et al., 2008).

Unfortunately, many teachers simply are not adequately supported to manage the escalating number of behavior problems in the classroom; some even enter the workforce without having taken a single course on behavior management, child development or cognitive social learning theory (Barrett & Davis, 1995; Evertson & Weinstein, 2006; Houston & Williamson, 1992). Very few teachers in the United States have been trained to deliver evidence-based curricula on social and emotional literacy, social skills, and problem solving. Surveys indicate that many schools do not use evidence-based social and emotional curricula, or use them with poor fidelity (Gottfredson & Gottfredson, 2002).

In a recent survey of elementary school teachers, teachers reported that managing behavior in the classroom was their greatest challenge as well as the area in which they felt they needed the most additional training (Reinke, Stormont, Herman, Puri, & Goel, 2010). Teachers today are presented with increasingly complex classrooms. Growing numbers of students with English as a second language (National Clearinghouse for English Language Acquisition, 2009) and emotional and behavioral problems are entering school (Walker, Colvin, & Ramsey, 1995). Increased classroom sizes and the addition of students receiving special education services in general education classrooms, present challenges for teachers who must provide instruction and manage classroom behaviors among diverse learners at different developmental stages. In fact, nearly half of new teachers leave the profession within five years, many citing student misbehavior as a primary reason for their leaving (Ingersoll, 2002). Thus, in order to achieve the goal of promoting social and emotional competence and reducing conduct problems, it is key that teachers are supported and trained to provide evidence-based classroom management practices that nurture, encourage, and motivate students with varying developmental abilities and cultural backgrounds.

Nearly half of new teachers leave the profession within five years, many citing student misbehavior as a primary reason.

Given the teacher risk factors noted earlier and the parent program's inconsistent results in achieving child behavior improvements beyond the home environment into the classroom, it was hypothesized that involving teachers in the intervention would result in better outcomes. In 1995, a 6-day (42-hour) IY teacher training classroom management program was developed (revised 2011). The goal of the program was to promote teacher competencies and strengthen home–school connections by doing the following: (a) improving teachers' classroom management skills, including proactive teaching approaches and effective discipline; (b) increasing teachers' use of persistence, social, emotional and academic coaching with students; (c) strengthening teacher–student bonding; (d) improving home–school collaboration and parent–teacher bonding; and (e) increasing teachers' ability to teach social skills, anger management, and problem-solving skills in the classroom. A complete description of the content included in this curriculum is described in the teacher program book, titled *Incredible Teachers: Nurturing Children's Social, Emotional and Academic Competence* (Webster-Stratton, 2012). See Chapter Fourteen for a brief description of IY teacher program.

Evidence of Effects of IY Teacher Classroom Management (IY TCM) Program

Treatment Studies

IY TCM program has received one RCT by the developer for children diagnosed with ODD/CD (Webster-Stratton et al., 2004). The developer's study compared the additive effects of different combinations of IY parent, child, and teacher training programs. Families with a child diagnosed with ODD were randomly assigned to one of six groups: (a) Parent training only; (b) Child training only; (c) Parent training plus teacher training; (d) Parent training plus teacher training plus child training; (e) Child training plus teacher training; or (f) Waitlist control.

As expected, results for the IY parent training component replicated earlier studies with parents in all three parent training conditions showing significantly less negative parenting and significantly more positive parenting than parents in conditions that did not receive parent training (Webster-Stratton & Reid, 1999). Children in all five treatment conditions showed reductions in aggressive behaviors with mothers at home, and at school with peers and teachers, compared with controls. Treatment effects for children's positive social skills with peers were found only in the three conditions that included child training and/or teacher training compared with controls. Trained teachers were rated as less critical, harsh, and inconsistent, and more nurturing than control teachers. Most treatment effects were maintained at 1-year follow-up. In summary, this study replicated our previous findings about the effectiveness of the combined parent and child training programs as well as indicated that teacher training significantly improved classroom atmosphere, teachers' classroom management skills and children's aggressive behavior in the classroom. In addition, treatment combinations that added either the child training or the teacher training to the parent training were most effective in strengthening academic and social skills as well as positive peer relationship skills. It is unclear from this study what classroom results are attained when the IY TCM is offered alone without the parent or child treatment components.

Treatment combinations that added either the child training or the teacher training to the parent training were most effective.

Prevention Studies

There have been two prevention studies using IY TCM by the developer and six replications by independent investigators. In the first RCT prevention study, regular Head Start classrooms were compared with Head Start classrooms with teachers trained in the 6-day IY TCM program and parents (N=272 children) trained in the group-based parent program(Webster-Stratton et al., 2001). In classrooms where teachers received training, children were observed to have higher school readiness scores (engagement and on-task behavior) and increased prosocial behaviors, as well as significantly reduced peer aggression. Teachers' reports of children's social competence and parent bonding and involvement in school were also significantly higher for trained teachers than for untrained teachers. In the second prevention study by the developer (Webster-Stratton et al., 2008) teachers received training in the IY TCM program plus training in the classroom prevention version of the dinosaur program. Results of intervention classrooms compared to control classrooms showed that teachers who received the training used more positive classroom management strategies and had more positive involvement with parents. Again, it is not possible to separate the individual impact of the IY teacher classroom management program from the training for the delivery of the Dinosaur classroom social, emotional and problem solving curriculum.

Two independent evaluations used the IY TCM program as a single component group training approach (that is without parent or child components) in combination with a mental health consultation approach in low-income, high-minority Head Start classrooms in Chicago and North Carolina (Raver et al., 2008; Williford & Shelton, 2008). Both studies provided support for the efficacy of this group training approach with preschool and elementary grade teachers and children. Findings indicated higher levels of positive classroom climate, teacher sensitivity, and behavior management than control classrooms.

The IY TCM program has also been evaluated in Wales as a stand alone program (without coaching or consultation) with similar results (Hutchings, Daley, et al., 2007). A fourth study was conducted in Jamaica (Baker-Henningham, Walker, Powell, & Meeks Gardner, 2009) with teachers of 24 preschools in inner-city, high poverty areas of Kingston. Schools were randomized to intervention or control conditions. All teachers in the intervention schools were trained in 8-9 full day workshops. A longer training time was applied due to the baseline skill level of the teachers. Large benefits were found for teacher classroom management practices, improved classroom atmosphere, and child behaviors. A fifth study evaluated the recently updated IY TCM program, which is offered in weekly 4-hour session rather than monthly day-long workshops. The study evaluated the program with one of the lowest income and highest unemployment counties in Michigan. Follow-up data found sustained improvements in teachers' perceptions of positive management strategies and their use (Carlson, Tiret, Bender, & Benson, 2011). The IY TCM has also been investigated as a stand-alone self-administered training program with preschool teachers (Shernoff & Kratochwill, 2007) compared with self-study plus consultation model. Results from this study indicated improvements in favor of the self-study plus consultation model in terms of greater teacher confidence, use of positive instructional practices and teacher reports of program acceptability. Positive trends also favored the combined self-study plus consultation model in terms of students' increased social competence. In all but the last one of these studies the intervention was delivered in a group format. Training time varied from 4-9 days (32-56 hours).

Summary of outcomes for which significant findings were found across studies that used IY TCM:

- Increases in teacher use of praise and nurturing and reduced use of criticism and inconsistent and harsh discipline
- Increases in child prosocial behaviors, cooperation with teachers, positive interactions with peers, school readiness, academic competence, emotional self-regulation and engagement with school activities
- Reductions in peer aggression in the classroom
- Increases in positive classroom atmosphere

SUMMARY

In order to more effectively prevent and treat behavior problems when they first begin (infant-toddler through elementary school) and to intervene in multiple areas of risk, the Incredible Years Parents, Teachers, and Children's series of programs have been designed, revised, and improved upon over the past 30 years. Research suggests that delivering interventions as early as possible can counteract risk factors and strengthen protective factors, thereby helping to prevent a developmental trajectory of increasingly aggressive and violent behaviors.

Our early research with the IY parent programs indicated that while the majority of children originally diagnosed with ODD/CD improved their social and emotional behavior at home and their relationships with their parents after receiving the parent program, 30-50% of the children continued to have significant school problems such as social acceptance, conduct problems, and academic under achievement. The addition of the IY child dinosaur training program and/or the IY teacher classroom management training program improved child outcomes across settings (with peers and teachers as

Research suggests that delivering interventions as early as possible can prevent a developmental trajectory of increasingly aggressive behaviors.

well as with parents.) Furthermore, contemporary research indicating documented links between children's under achievement, developmental delays, reading disabilities and conduct disorders, shaped enhancements of the IY parent programs including additions of parent training methods that promote children's reading skills, language skills and help children with their academic difficulties. Program components also teach parents to collaborate and problem solve with teachers and schools in order to foster a supportive relationship between the home and school settings. The IY TCM program provides teachers with strategies for partnering with parents to develop behavior plans and to promote parent involvement in their children's learning. Such coordinated efforts between the home and school regarding social, emotional and academic goals seem to improve generalization of child improvements across settings.

The review of the research indicates that many creative interventions have been developed, offering much hope for effectively treating families with children with conduct problems. Such programs also hold promise as prevention programs to be offered early with high-risk populations, before the disorder develops in the first place.

I have also noted that early intervention is strategic to facilitating babies' and preschool children's social and emotional development. If behavior problems persist, it is useful to involve schools, teachers, and peer groups in the intervention plan as well as to help families with other personal issues. For example, in the case examples outlined at the beginning of chapter 1, it will be necessary for Robbie and Melinda's parents to have help with their depression, social isolation, and interpersonal communication as well as with their parenting skills. The teachers of both children will need support to develop positive classroom behavior plans and to learn ways to reach out to these isolated and struggling parents. Both Robbie and Melinda will benefit from a supportive home-school network where parents and teachers are talking and coordinating positive goals across settings. Lastly, because both of these children are also experiencing peer difficulties, direct intervention in the form of a child emotion and social skills group would benefit both children by helping them to learn new strategies for regulating their emotions and for engaging prosocially with peers. Thus, effective intervention programs need to encompass various levels of the microsystems and ecosystems—family, community, school, peer, and child.

Moreover, the importance of developing programs designed to identify children with conduct problems in their early preschool years cannot be over-emphasized. Robbie and Melinda's problems began in infancy and the toddler years, and these families should have been offered support long before their child was faced with expulsion from school. Program design must also consider that conduct disorder is a chronic problem transmitted across generations. Therefore, successful intervention necessitates periodic training and support for parents within a variety of contexts at critical stages of the child and family's development.

Effective intervention programs need to encompass various levels of the microsystems and ecosystems.

Parenting a Child with Conduct Problems: "Families Under Siege"*

As increasing numbers of children are diagnosed with conduct problems at younger ages, growing emphasis has been placed on understanding the factors that contribute to conduct disorder development. Parenting style in particular has received much attention, and there are documented associations between highly coercive styles of parental discipline and child conduct disorders. However, literature published on children with conduct problems has given comparatively little discussion to the impact of the child on the parent and family system. While there is research to indicate that families of children with conduct disorders experience high rates of major and minor life stressors (Campbell, 1994; Dodge, Pettit, & Bates, 1994; McLoyd, 1990;

* *This chapter is derived from a paper co-authored by Dr. Webster-Stratton and Dr. Ada Spitzer, Dean, A. Yelin School of Nursing, Haifa, Israel.*

Webster-Stratton, 1990), marital stress (Cummings, 1994; Forgatch, Patterson, & Skinner, 1988; Sedlar & Hansen, 2001; Webster-Stratton, 1989), and social isolation or lack of social support (Wahler, 1980; Webster-Stratton, 1985), it is unclear exactly how child conduct disorders contribute to these stresses, how they may affect relationships within the family (e.g. between parents, or between parents and their other children), and relationships between the family system and outside systems or agencies (e.g. with grandparents or teachers). Unfortunately, little information has been collected from the parents' point of view about the difficulties and stresses encountered while coping with a child's conduct problems.

This chapter will examine the experience of having a child with conduct problems from the parents' point of view. We will discuss four major domains of this experience: the child's profile, the impact on the family system, the impact on the family's relationships with the community, and the dynamics of living with a child with conduct problems. These dynamics and themes were derived after analyzing the transcripts and videotapes of over 70 intake interviews with mothers and fathers who participated in the University of Washington Parenting Clinic programs.

THE CHILD'S PROFILE

In order to understand the meaning of living with a child with conduct problems, it was crucial to understand how children with conduct problems are perceived by their parents. We had a wealth of data on the behavior of these children, as reported by their parents and teachers as well as by independent observers. But what did their parents feel? Did they experience anger, guilt, embarrassment, empathy, apathy, sympathy, rage, indifference, and/or sadness? What did these parents think about the behavior: what were their cognitive responses? Did the parents cope using denial, rationalization, projection, and/or distortion? We wanted to know whether certain emotional, psychological, and cognitive reactions are typical of parents of children with conduct problems. Insight and awareness of perspective is crucial for therapists who are working with these parents. A parent's perceptions of their child, the meanings they attribute to the child's behavior, and the feelings they have as a consequence of those attributions, shape their reactions to the child in general and the conduct problems in particular, as well as their attitude toward parenting and intervention.

Child as Tyrant, Parent as Victim

When asked to name their child's dominant characteristic, parents who we interviewed specified *aggression*. Children with conduct problems were described by their parents as both verbally and physically aggressive toward family members as well as abusive toward pets. Parents reported that their children intentionally harmed these targets with no evidence of remorse or regret.

> **Mother:** *I don't know if you have suffered the physical abuses—I have. Just a few weeks ago, he threw his booster seat in my face and hit my jaw. And he thought it was funny! … He was acting up, and I think he had already had one Time Out for yelling and screaming and interrupting us at the table. And I said, "Fine, you are going upstairs now. You are not having dessert." And he just flew into a rage. He picked up a metal fork and threw it with all his force, and hit me—barely missed my eyes. There was blood on my forehead. I was screaming, I was hysterical. And I was terrified, I mean, to see that type of behavior, that type of rage.*

> **Mother:** *She tells me she is going to run away from home and that she wants to leave. She told her father she wished he was dead so that way he won't wake up…*

> **Father:** *One of the things that really bothers me is that she says, "I hate you. Why don't you move out?"*

> **Mother:** *He is just real violent with animals. And I have repetitively taught him how to stroke animals nicely. He can't help himself. I caught him holding the cat in the toilet with the lid shut.*

This aggression extended outside of the family as well. Parents reported that their children were aggressive toward other children in day care settings, at friends' homes, and toward strangers in public places. Sometimes this aggression was sexual in nature: pulling down other children's underwear, touching children in their genital areas, or using sexually provocative language. Parents described having to be always on guard, for their own sake and to ensure other children's emotional and physical safety.

> **Mother:** *He is aggressive around other children. We can't really trust him not to walk up and wallop the smaller ones. He pokes them in the eyes or pushes them down... I understand a lot of children go through this thing with aggression—but again, it seems so exaggerated, it's almost like he seeks out other children to hurt them. If you take him to the zoo, here we are in a situation where we could be having fun, talking about animals, walking...and he's seeking out little children in strollers and picking up handfuls of sand and throwing it in their faces.*

> **Mother:** *He is so violent with his sister. He split her lip a couple of times. And he almost knocked her out once when he hit her over the head with a five-pound brass pitcher. He's put plastic bags over her head. Even things that you wouldn't think could be dangerous, you have to make sure and keep out of his reach.*

They were also concerned that younger siblings would develop similar patterns of aggressive problems by watching their older brother or sister. In the face of this verbal, emotional, and physical aggression, parents reported feeling victimized and tyrannized. The ever-present possibility of abuse left them feeling deeply insecure when around their children. Clearly, these parents experienced their child as the one in charge, the family member who "called the shots."

Such repeated episodes of verbal and physical aggression towards other children led to these children to be disliked, rejected, and ridiculed by other children. Moreover, parents of other children did not want their child to associate with the aggressive child. Consequently, these children with conduct problems were rarely invited to birthday parties or for after-school play times. Frequently parents reported that their child had no friends and was lonely. This feedback from teachers and other parents was an important indicator to parents that their child was not like other children. It was also a key component of tensions with parents of other "typical" children, contributing to feelings of rejection, humiliation and isolation in the parents of children with conduct problems.

Parents felt "held hostage" by their child.

Dismantling the house. Frequently parents recounted incidents in which their children had been destructive to the house or household objects.

> **Mother:** *I have really tried to value our child more than I value the house, but it's been incredibly painful to watch our brand new house—brand spanking new—be destroyed. And we've told ourselves, it's all fixable, but he has caused an incredible amount of destruction which has been painful to watch. When you work and personally invest yourself in your home, when other people don't respect it or take care of it, it's painful.*

In summary, parents uniformly portrayed their child's behavior in terms of verbal and physical aggression towards parents, siblings, animals, other children and adults, and towards physical property. Overwhelmingly these parents conveyed the feeling that they did not have control over these aggressive acts; that they were held hostage by their child.

Child's Non-Compliance and Defiance

Another well-known characteristic of children with conduct problems is their non-compliance and defiance. Parents gave vivid descriptions of the arguments they had with their children, which frequently ended up in screaming fights. Parents reported that they could only get their children to comply by extending an enormous amount of energy.

> **Father:** *He's the most stubborn child or person I have ever met, because he won't stop. His power is he won't stop. He usually ends up crying and he gets like a mule—he kind of digs his heels in, and doesn't want to do it.*

> **Mother:** *He just digs his heels in, "That's it, I am not wearing these socks! Forget it, I'm not going!" And he is right. He's gone to school in his pajamas, without lunch, in the pouring rain without any coat. "I've made up my mind Mom, that's it!" and he'll say to me, "Mom we are done." He will explain to me, "Mom, we are done with this discussion"... He doesn't have an easy-going bone in his body. He is not ever going to say, "Okay, I'll put that turtleneck on." It's going to be, "I will do something but only on my terms... I will do nothing that you want me to do and furthermore I'll throw such a tantrum and throw this cereal bowl all over the wall, so you will be late, and mad at me when you clean it up..." He enjoys that power.*

Perpetually faced with these defiant reactions, these parents often felt exhausted. In short, these children controlled the entire family by virtue of the power commanded through their resistance.

Hyperactivity, distractibility, high intensity

A third well-known trait of children with conduct problems is their hyperactivity and distractibility. Many of the parents interviewed talked about their child's high intensity temperaments. They described their children as highly active, easily "wound up," overexcited, loud, wild and out-of-control since birth.

> **Father:** *He's mentally fine, but his emotions are twisted in some ways—he doesn't seem to have the normalities that a lot of kids have. I look at my nieces and nephews and, while they have their moments, most of the time they can listen and talk. But with Keith he goes off into outer space and won't come back—he's not even on this planet! He's crazy, running around the house screaming, jumping on the bed, and goes into a fit of hyperactivity trying to*

accumulate as many things wrong as possible in that time. To get him under control we have to restrain him until he's so worn out, he's exhausted.

Moreover, these parents felt that their children had trouble listening and concentrating even for brief periods of time. They reported that when they made requests of their children, their children often "tuned them out" or got so distracted by their surroundings that they forget what the parents had requested. Parents described their children as unable to sit still to play on their own, constantly demanding attention. The consequences for the parents were twofold: exhaustion and anxiety. These parents never had a break or quiet moment during the day. Furthermore, because their children's activity level is so high, the child's safety and even survival is a major parenting issue.

Mother: *From 15 months he started running and destroying everything in sight and has not stopped since then. Keeping him alive became paramount. Once he crawled out of his car seat and over the seat when I was going 50 miles an hour and he hit the door and it flew open. He was so reckless that I could not shower unless he was in his crib asleep. I could not have him out of my sight for a minute. Life with him was a nightmare. One time I put him in his room for a nap, and turned on the shower. And I hear this frantic banging on my door, and it was my neighbor telling me that my son's second floor window was open—he had thrown a book on the roof and was going to get it. And so from 25 months to 3, it was this incredible desire to keep him alive. We couldn't afford one mistake.*

Many parents were concerned about their child's inability to learn from their experiences. Too often, they had seen their child suffer the negative consequences of a particular behavior, yet go on to repeat the same self-defeating behaviors later.

Father: *I am concerned because he is so experimental. If you tell him (or explain to him) not to do something, that guarantees he will try it at least one more time. He's so impulsive he doesn't think out the*

> *consequences of what he does. He has a kind of destructive curiosity which will get him into big trouble if he is still doing that as a teenager.*

> **Mother:** *I'm concerned because he makes a mistake and we talk about it, but there is no carryover to the next situation. He still makes the same mistake. Then when I try to talk about it with him, he has this blank face with rolling eyes and I get scared that a kid this young is tuning me out.*

Similarly, they would describe having tried to help the child understand a problem, only to be met with either a blank expression or a deliberately defiant continuation of the troublesome behavior. This led parents to worry about their child's future.

Developmental Problems

Parents of children in the 3-8 year old age range commonly report a number of developmental difficulties related to sleeping, eating, and toilet training. Among children with conduct disorders, the intensity with which children experienced these problems made their parents' experiences far from normal or typical.

> **Mother:** *I notice he's going through the potty language stage. And I'm hoping it's just a stage—and believe me, every negative stage that a child may or may not go through, he's gone through.*

Many parents described bedtime as a particularly difficult time. They expressed difficulty getting their children to cooperate with set bedtimes. When these parents tried to enforce bedtime, their children would be become excessively noncompliant and defiant. Parents also reported that their children did not seem to need a lot of sleep. Even if they could get their child in his bedroom, he would not be able to fall asleep and would stay awake until midnight or later.

> **Mother:** *One day we tried just to wait him out (at bedtime). At 6:00 I said, "We've got to go to bed." Six a.m.! We waited all night and he never did go to sleep.*

Father: *You have to follow them every step of the way to get them to go to bed. And then, once they are in bed, they're either turning on the light and getting up and playing with their toys, or else sneaking around the house. They won't stay put. I found the only thing that I can do to really control that is: I take a chair down at the end of the hall, park it in front of their door, and sit and read a book. Then they'll settle down and go to sleep.*

Normal eating problems were exacerbated by the child's high activity level, lack of concentration, and inability to sit in the same place for a long period of time.

Father: *A meal at our house is like a circus. It's like two rats out of a sack. One goes one way and one goes the other. He'll run around the table. He'll take a bite of food, he'll sit down half on the chair, take another bite of food and then run off and chew it and run around.*

They also described resorting to various extreme measures in order to achieve some semblance of family meal times.

Mother: *He is so hyperactive at meals that even at age 4 we keep him strapped in a high chair to get him to eat. We joke about how we have to break his legs to get him in the high chair. We are just so determined to have a family meal where he is not running and around and causing havoc.*

Transitions are difficult for many children between the ages of 3 and 8 years. Yet for children with conduct problems, this common developmental problem is extreme. Almost any change in routine was reported by the parents to result in defiant behavior. At the root of this problem is the child's inability to adapt.

Mother: *Transitions are really hard for him. We try to give him warning like, bed time is in 10 minutes. And then sometimes you get a temper tantrum getting his teeth brushed. Because even though he's*

> *had warnings, he hasn't assimilated that we mean, "you are going to bed, we're going to turn the light off." He thinks he can still play.*

A fourth developmental problem reported by these parents is concern with fears. Whereas it is commonly believed that children with conduct problems exhibit externalizing but not internalizing behaviors, interviews with parents indicated that these children also exhibited many internalizing problems such as fears and suicidal thoughts.

> **Father:** *He has night fears. It's been awful. It started about a year ago but it got really bad about 4 months ago. The toys started moving their heads, and the stuffed animals...and then I had this long conversation with him in the bathtub the other day and he is scared of thunder and lightning and it comes every night. He thinks that the thunder and lightning can throw bowling balls down from the roof and they can come and get him...it took about 20 minutes to get through that conversation. He has anxiety in his room—he lays awake for hours. We give him flashlights—sometimes he'll be awake at 2 or 3 in the morning from anxieties.*

> **Father:** *He often talks about wanting to die and how he wants to kill himself. Like the other day he was angry because he got pulled out of swim lessons for not keeping his hands to himself and he said, "It's so terrible, I should just die."*

Unpredictability: Child as "Jekyll and Hyde"

Along with reporting the negative aspects of their children's behaviors, most parents talked about their children's personalities as having positive aspects. For instance, parents often portrayed their children as particularly sensitive and reactive to others' moods.

> **Mother:** *He doesn't like to see anybody upset. It really bothers him. He just becomes very emotional. Say if I'm upset, he really catches on to it. Or if my husband and I are having a disagreement, he'll immediately start hollering at my husband to side with me, to get him to stop screaming.*

While this sensitivity presented a challenge for parents, it was also seen as a positive characteristic or a special gift. Many parents described their children as having unique cognitive abilities and being more developmentally advanced than other children in their age group.

> **Father:** *She amazes me—the intelligence she has. The things she says, and thinks, and the rationale that she uses are junior high [level]. She has an incredible memory.*

One parent characterized her child as a "Jekyll and Hyde," an apt label for the child who is at times highly tyrannical, destructive and defiant, and at other times loving, intelligent, understanding and sensitive to parents' emotions.

> **Mother:** *He is like a "Jekyll and Hyde." Sometimes he can be sweet, charming, loving, easy to get along with, he's a very good-natured child. But then there's the other side of him which emerges—an angry, hostile, aggressive, hurting child, who will do violent things to try to get his way. He is rough with animals and mean with little children, and he is very noncompliant. By the time he is ready to be loving again, you are fed up.*

> **Father:** *He has three personalities—I'd give the hyper episodes a couple times a week, the disobedience about 60-70% of the time and the part where you can actually talk to him about 20% of the time and I don't know about the rest.*

Although the personality profile that emerged from our interviews with parents described a child with conduct problems with a mixture of negative and positive characteristics, the negative certainly predominated. The unpredictability of the negative behaviors also seemed to cause parents additional stress. Behavior problems might arise any time, any place; parents always had to be on their guard. Thus, ironically, the child's positive characteristics contributed to the parents' stress, since without a positive side there would have been no unpredictability. A "Jekyll and Hyde" child was harder to cope with than a mere "monster" child would have been.

> **Father:** *We have these stressful times where he is very defiant and argumentative, we all lose our temper and perhaps he finally gets a swat. Then there is this emotional breakdown followed by big make-up sessions where he tells us he loves us. It is an emotional roller coaster.*

In summary, it is evident from these descriptions that children with conduct problems are not only non-reinforcing to their parents, but also physically and emotionally punishing. Parents' feelings of victimization were also amplified by their uncertainty about how their children might respond at any moment.

IMPACT OF THE CHILD ON THE FAMILY SYSTEM: "THE RIPPLE EFFECT"

Our quantitative research had informed us about the high level of family stress, particularly marital stress, found in families of children with conduct problems. However, because quantitative measures do not reveal anything about the parents' perceptions of the stress, we did not know how the stress was related to their experience of living with a child with conduct problems. Our qualitative data revealed that a child's conduct problems introduces significant stresses into his or her family system and, moreover, that these stresses have a cumulative effect on the parents. Parents' descriptions of the impact of their child's conduct problems on their lives evoked an image of ripples in a pond that widen, eventually affecting the whole pond. The child's behavior had consequences that radiated outward from the child in ever-widening circles, affecting first the parents, then the marital relationship, then other siblings, then the extended family, and then the family's relationships with the community.

Impact on Marital or Couple Relationships

We have already described the impact of the child's behavior on his or her parents individually; namely, the experience of being tyrannized or victimized. But the couple's relationship also is affected. In the case of parents of children with conduct problems, the relationship between parents is dominated by the need to continually monitor and discipline the child. Very little time and energy remains for parents to devote to themselves or to each other.

> **Mother:** *One of the things that is so frustrating is that he has consumed our lives. Since he's been born, 99% of our conversation is about Matthew and what we are going to do to deal with his behavior problems. We don't have a life—everything revolves around Matthew.*

In the majority of our families the mother was the primary caretaker who spent the most hours "under siege" with the child. Furthermore, the mothers often took on a disproportionate sense of responsibility for the child. Typically, this imbalance created a situation in which mothers were exhausted and beleaguered, desperate for some time alone, with little energy to spare for husbands. However, at the end of a long day with a child with conduct problems, mothers needed to share these feelings with their partners, especially when they blamed themselves for the day's problems.

The father, on the other hand, typically spent less time with the child and therefore tended to have a less intense, somewhat easier relationship with the child. The difference between the mother-child and father-child relationship was potentially a source of relief and perspective but more typically created conflict within the parents' own relationship. Observing their partner engaged in long episodes of cajoling and yelling at the child, fathers often questioned these approaches and were critical of the mothers' discipline or any inconsistency.

> **Father:** *On a micro level if my son gets my wife upset, she doesn't distinguish between him and me. If it's a weekday and I've had a hard day at work, I have limited resources when I get home at night.*

> *I may try to smooth the waters a little but I'm often not successful and sometimes I get concerned about the way he is treated. I feel real angry about it but I haven't done anything.*
>
> **Father:** *I'll come home and she [my wife] will tell me what the children did to her today. And I'll get mad, and then the first time they do something I'm set for it. I'm primed to discipline them for her, or whatever. And so the first thing they do, that sets me right off.*

We commonly heard fathers express the belief that their wives were "too easy" and "not tough enough." These criticisms were bolstered by the fathers' awareness that they did not experience the same kinds of problems with their children that their partners did. Mothers, in turn, felt resentful if fathers had an easier time with the child. Fathers often reported feeling left out and unsure how to contribute. Their subsequent guilt and confusion discouraged, rather than encouraged, communication between the couple. Frequently, fathers' distress was so great that they withdrew from the situation or avoided discussions with their partners about the children. Of course, these kinds of responses from fathers exacerbated the mothers' anger and frustration, thereby undermining the potential support system in the couple's relationship. The result of this dynamic was a polarization of the couple:

> **Mother:** *I always feel that if you (looking at husband) took a bigger role in parenting we could do it together and share the role. I feel it is you against "us" (mom and the children). I want it to be "us" and "them."*
>
> **Father:** *Since our son was born, you (looking at his wife) have become really obsessed with parenting. Even during the pregnancy you were always reading really big books about how to parent and trying to be supermom. I am not willing to put my mind, body, and soul into parenting all day and night. I'm going to have walls and boundaries. You are constantly attached—even when we go out for time alone, what do you talk about? Nothing but the kids! I finally*

made it a rule when we are out with friends not to talk about the children. The separation in our relationship began when he was born.

In this last example, the father's experience of parenting a child with conduct problems has distorted his thinking about the relationship. The normal estrangement a husband feels at birth (feeling outside the mother-child bond) becomes, upon reflection, a permanent condition. He projects onto the past what he feels now, a "rewriting" of the couple's history that only increases the emotional estrangement. Consequently, this couple experiences a loss of intimacy not only to the practical constraints of limited time and privacy for a meaningful and close adult relationship, but also to the intense feelings of guilt, anger, frustration, and resentment that resulted from perceiving the relationship in terms of estrangement. For many parents, the child also had an impact on their energy and privacy for a satisfying sexual relationship:

Mother: *He [child] comes into our room every night. He would never tolerate our door being locked or he would go to pieces and tantrum. Consequently we have a nonexistent sex life.*

The sense of loss of control that parents felt in their parenting role seemed to spill over into their own relationship. Instead of the relationship being a protective factor, a zone of relief from the stress of parenting a child with conduct problems, it was permeated by that stress and developed its own stressful dynamics.

Mother: *She [child] doesn't allow us to talk together—with the kids we don't get enough time together. As far as a romantic sexual type relationship, for the past 4 years, it's been shot to hell! We don't have time to talk, we don't have time to pull in together, and you know, just have a relationship.*

Some mothers reported feeling guilty not only for their failure to manage the children well and their preoccupation with parenting (guilt that was often reinforced by their husbands' criticisms) but also for failure in their marriage. The mothers' sense of incompetence seemed to extend from the parenting role into other aspects of their marital relationship, resulting in paralyzing depression and a sense of hopelessness.

> **Mother:** *Once we had kids I put the focus there. Then our son took so much of my attention. You see, I'm the emotional one and I get bothered by things that bother the children and my intensity goes into the children. Well, we started taking one night out a week because we were getting lost in caring for the children. I know I get so emotionally involved with the kids that I haven't given as much to the marriage as I should have.*

Impact on Siblings

As described by these parents, living with a child with conduct problems has both a direct and an indirect impact on siblings. The direct impact lies in the child's aggressive behavior, which is often directed toward siblings. The indirect impact lies in parents' relationships with the siblings', and especially in the parents' expectations of them. Most parents felt that the constant, extraordinary degree of attention required to manage a child's behavior problems left them with very little time or energy to attend to the other siblings. Stretched to the limits, parents felt unable to tolerate misbehavior from more than one child. Often parents expected siblings to be model children who always acted responsibly and under control.

> **Mother:** *Our life is such a nightmare when both children are there that almost every weekend his older brother goes away for the weekend to a friend's house. I feel so guilty, but I can't take them both at home.*

> **Mother:** *What happens in our family dynamic is that our non-problem child always has to be responsible. Wrongly, but you know, because life with his brother is so incredibly complicated, he is expected to act like a 40-year-old and think like a 40-year-old. The consequences for him are great. I expect too much of him, I expect him to act, to use his head every minute of every day about dangers for his brother—that's more than an 8-year-old should have to contend*

> *with. Because life with his brother is so dangerous for everybody and because we try to control his brother's behavior, we are constantly on him to control his. And that is hard...he never gets to have a bad day, he never gets to throw a tantrum, he never gets to do anything because we are so maxed out on his brother, there's nothing left for him. He has to shut up, behave, and not talk to us about any of his concerns and problems.*

Because these parents felt so beleaguered, they sometimes placed the siblings in a shared parenting role, expecting them to care for the child with conduct problems. When siblings are expected to act as adults and sometimes as parents, normal familial roles are distorted. The normal balance of power is further shifted when a child becomes a tyrant and parents become victims; the family system is turned on its head.

It is obvious that these parental expectations place an unfair burden on the sibling in terms of age-inappropriate responsibilities. Moreover, these expectations are likely to create siblings' feelings of resentment towards the misbehaving child. In many of these families, the "good sibling" became increasingly difficult by mimicking the problematic behaviors—a predictable result of the excessive parental attention given to the problem child.

> **Mother:** *He definitely requires a lot of attention. And basically what we are feeling now is a backlash from giving him so much attention, that my older one, who used to be my "great kid," is now acting up and being sneaky and starting to get that way.*

Impact on the Extended Family

These parents also reported that their children's conduct problems had become a source of tension between themselves and their parents and/or siblings (i.e., between the parents and grandparents or between the parents and aunts and uncles). It seems that grandparents attributed the child's misbehaviors to a lack of good parenting. Many parents reported that their parents (the child's grandparents) were always giving advice about how they "should" handle the problems. Typically, they advocated a stricter approach to misbehavior.

> **Mother:** *When Grandma comes to visit about once a month, he [child] just goes ape. He starts terrorizing the cats, he starts throwing his toys. He starts going ape. And he has a real hard time when Grandpa is there and Grandpa likes him. But Grandma thinks we should "nail the little sucker a good plant a couple of times on the rear end."*

Conversely, some children did not behave as badly with grandparents as they did with their own parents, a fact that parents interpreted as further evidence of their own failure as parents.

IMPACT OF THE CHILD ON FAMILY'S RELATIONSHIPS WITH THE COMMUNITY: "MORE RIPPLES"

Eventually the child's problems "rippled outward" to affect the family's relationships with professionals, teachers, and other parents in their community. In general, these relationships became characterized by negative feedback to the parents: stigmatization, social isolation, and rejection.

Parents felt rejected and isolated by the reactions of teachers and day-care providers to their children's misbehaviors. The aggression and defiance displayed by their child created problems with their peer group at school, causing other children to cry or misbehave, and generally increasing the level of aggression in the classroom. Understandably, teachers became increasingly disapproving and punishing toward these children. Parents frequently reported that they had been asked by teachers to find another day-care or school for their child because their child was unmanageable and consumed too much of the teacher's time. Some families had been asked to leave half a dozen day care centers by the time their child was 5 years old.

Parents felt rejected and isolated by teachers and day-care providers.

Mother: *It started when he was 18 months old. He was always the most aggressive, the most outgoing, the loudest child in every group he's ever been in. And I remember after his first day at day care—I picked him up and I got a phone call. It was on my answering machine—I mean the teacher never confronted me in person and she just said she didn't think it was going to work—he was terrorizing other children and really being a disruptive force to her preschool. And I had to drop that day care. So you know, no notice—and it's just been like that from that point. I remember getting a phone call on my answering machine, and with it one of the teachers asking me to call back—I was just holding my breath, wondering if she was going to tell me to take him out...I would come back after 3 hours and just the expression on her face—it was this horrified, painful expression.*

Mother: *He's 3 years old and he's always on probation. The teacher just greeted me with one of those really painful expressions I'm so familiar with: "Your son did this." Then you would hear stories of how your son had to have two people release him from a choke hold on another child or how he was pouring water on someone's head. They told me not to bring him back. I was just so embarrassed.*

Moreover, as children's antisocial identity became more established, they frequently became targets of other children's ridicule and rejection.

A further "ripple effect" was that the disproportionate amount of teacher time devoted to the child's problems, often resulting in resentment by parents of other children and complaints to teachers and principals.

Mother: *I've never been to a school meeting when I haven't been trashed. I can't stand to go to one more meeting and have them tell us what they are not going to do for us. After they got rid of us—well it was like we were disposable and we've never heard from them again.*

This intense negative feedback compounded the parents' feelings of isolation and lack of support.

Mother: *The principal came up to me and said: "your boy is a very sick boy and is going to need many years of psychoanalytic counseling"—I feel all the teachers knew this and set us up in the school so we couldn't win. I felt everyone else in this kindergarten were on this raft while we were swimming around trying to clutch to get on. We said we'll pay for books, and I'm helping out twice a week in class and I'm offering to be a personal aid and we'll pay for a social skills teacher—and everywhere we'd go around the raft and try to get on, someone would step on our fingers.*

Yes, and we even sent away for literature to provide ADHD handbooks for the teachers which were never read. By the end of the school year we started realizing that the kindergarten raft was sailing away, and when they told us not to come back, we felt we were left drowning in the water.

Faced with this stigmatization and confused by their child's behavior, these parents sought help from a variety of professionals, such as pediatricians, psychologists, counselors, and psychiatrists. In general, they were frustrated with this quest. Parents had received multiple diagnoses for the child's problems, conflicting opinions regarding the seriousness, and contradictory advice about how to deal with them. Many parents reported being told that their child was "normal," that s/he would soon "outgrow" the problems, and that they should just "loosen up" and "be patient." Far from being reassuring, this advice caused parents to blame themselves for overreacting to the problem behaviors, or caused them to feel confused, since in their experience the behavior was not normal.

Mother: *I've talked to our pediatrician about it. I went and saw a counselor, and I've talked to him about it. And everyone basically told me, "Oh, he's just a normal kid." Well, I mean our life at home is not normal...and they say, "he is just like a normal 4-year-old...nothing is wrong with your child." And he [says], "I wouldn't worry about it." And he kept telling me, "I wouldn't worry about your kid, I would worry about the ones that are quiet and compliant and do everything they're told." So you know I was just pulling my hair out—while they are trying to make you happy and realize that you don't have a weird*

> *child—but that's not what I wanted to hear. I wanted to hear step one, two, three, four...and I really don't know what to do.*

Other professionals would tell parents to "be more consistent and get stricter control" of their children's problems. The net result, regardless of the type of advice given, was that parents were made to feel at fault and confused about how to cope with the situation.

As the "ripples" spread, these parents experienced increasing isolation from other parents in their neighborhoods and in their schools. Parents felt a lack of connection and support from parents of "normal or typical" children. They thought if they were honest about their difficulties, they would encounter indifference.

> **Mother:** *Basically I feel I am really in a minority. Because of all the other mothers I've talked to...they've never been hit. I mean to me it's unimaginable not to be slapped and kicked. And I have a friend. I was telling her about it and she says, "What? Your son hits you? My daughters never hit me." I mean other parents look at me like I just walked off another planet. So I feel very isolated. I feel like no one is like me! No one has my situation.*

> **Mother:** *There's always the fear that if you share with somebody what your child is like, somebody will assume it's your fault, and think you screwed up as a parent. Or they'll reject you and say, "God, I don't want to hear about this!"*

Worse yet, some parents feared the reprisals this information could have on others' perceptions of them or their child. The tremendous amount of negative feedback these parents received from other parents bred feelings of stigmatization. The lack of empathy displayed to them was often perceived as rejection or condemnation. When these parents invited other children to come over to their house to play with their child, they were turned down. Their children seldom received invitations to attend birthday parties or to play at another child's house. Typically, after one experience with their child, a babysitter would not want to come back.

Mother: *She has run off three babysitters. No one wants to babysit her. I mean, one day she was jumping on the bed, pulled down the curtains, threw pillows all over the place, wouldn't mind the babysitter. We came home, everything was trashed. And the babysitter said, "Look what this child did."*

Parents even felt rejection from strangers in grocery stores, parks, and restaurants.

Mother: *There have been times when he has been aggressive enough that I've seen a look in other people's eyes that just makes me feel horrible to the core. One day I took him to the Children's Museum by myself, and by the time we left, maybe 45 minutes later, I was really an emotional wreck because I'd seen a look and posture in the other parents there that showed repulsion on their part. And I felt that we were really being rejected. And I literally saw other people come into a play area and, seeing we were there, just turn their own child away.*

As a result, parents reported becoming more and more insular. Frequently, they reported that they stopped taking their children to grocery stores and restaurants in order to avoid dealing with possible tantrums and negative behavior in public places.

Mother: *I won't take him shopping with me because he throws temper tantrums, and with child abuse laws the way they are now you can't discipline him in public any more. So I won't take him. I won't even take him to a restaurant.*

This apprehension of blame and rejection from extended family members and from the community led parents to feel more and more isolated.

Mother: *There is huge isolation. My mother doesn't understand, my stepfather is hypercritical and other parents think it's awful—rarely do we get support. Other parents walk in our house and look at the holes and think, "My God what kind of children live here, obviously these* *parents are letting things run amok." Isolation has been a huge issue for me. I don't think anyone else understands. Nobody has a child like him.*

In sum, these parents felt stuck with a child who was noncompliant and aggressive—a tyrant at home, a terror at school and in the community—with no support or understanding from others.

LIVING WITH A CHILD WITH CONDUCT PROBLEMS: AN EXPERIENCE OF LEARNED HELPLESSNESS

When professionals and lay people look at families of children with conduct problems certain judgments are commonplace: parents are at fault for the child's misbehaviors and parents might resolve the child's problems if only they were more committed or effective in their discipline strategies. These judgments are off base. People outside these families of children with conduct problems are likely to have only a superficial view of what the families experience and the cumulative effects of the child's behaviors. Often outsiders view the situation within the context of their own generally positive experiences of child rearing. Such an approach is insensitive to the disruptive process that parents of children with conduct problems endure. Parents of 'typical' children have never experienced what it is like to feel "held hostage" by a tyrannical child. Nor have they experienced the complexities of the "ripple effect."

Unfortunately, research has done little to correct these misperceptions. Quantitative data such as mean scores of parental critical statements toward their children, number of spankings per day, as well as mean scores of depression or marital scores do not help us understand subjective realities nor the context of the phenomenon. Such data may even bolster common misperceptions of these parents as incompetent and blameworthy.

Findings from our study indicate that the experience of parenting a child with conduct problems is a process of learned helplessness. This process contains three phases that are influenced by first, the chronicity of the child's problems, second, the futility of the search to understand the cause of the problems, and third, the experiences they underwent in their attempt to discipline the child— experiences that often convince the parent that the situation is inalterable and they are inept.

Phase I: "Treading Water"

Most parents in this study told us that they felt their child's problems started at birth. Many described infants who were not cuddly and who reacted to physical affection by withdrawing, becoming rigid or escalating anger.

> **Father:** *Since he was born, he has never liked to be touched or to be held—he didn't want to be constricted in any way even as a baby. It was so frustrating because you know how you want to be close to a baby—well, not with him. It made bonding difficult. He just wanted to be left alone. It's a privilege now to get a sincere hug or for him to sit still with physical contact—that's a major thing.*

Clearly, these infants did not reinforce their parents' efforts to comfort them in time of distress. As toddlers, they had more than their share of tantrums and defiance. The initial reaction of these parents was to wait for the toddlers' irritability, defiance, noncompliance, and tantrums to disappear with maturity. Typically, parents anticipated that by age 3 their child would grow out of such problems. This belief led them to focus less on the child's problems and more on the hope that soon they would not have to deal with the problems.

The parents' hope that the problem would disappear with age was also manifested in these parents' efforts to ensure the child's physical safety without putting forward consistent effort to alter the child's misbehaviors through parenting skills.

> **Mother:** *Even though my personal life was a shambles, from 15 months till 3, I got through it because it was like, this is part of having a busy toddler. Keeping him alive became paramount. But we went through it all because that's what you do when you have little kids...*
>
> *My expectation was that we would get through this—every other family does. Our older child stopped at 3. He could walk in a room*

> *and stop making messes. So my expectation was that at 3 no matter how bad it is, it would calm down. But at 3 nothing happened. In fact, it got worse, because he got bigger and it was harder to contain him. And as he got bigger and more things were available to him, his destruction level went up.*

Professionals, such as pediatricians and nurses, also reinforced this belief that the child's problems would decrease with age by reassuring parents that nothing was wrong and that soon their child would "outgrow" the problems.

Phase II: Problem Recognition

It is not easy for parents to admit that they have a child with serious behavior problems or a child who is different from other children. However, after 3 years of disruptive behaviors, with no relief as the child matured, most parents realize that their child is different from other children. Three categories of problem recognition were identified: grasping the problem, searching for reasons, and mounting self-blame.

Grasping the problem. As the children grew older and their behavior problems escalated, parents began to realize that their children's behavior problems were not going to disappear. This awareness came gradually, as parents made comparisons between their problem child and other children of the same age, or other siblings in the same family.

> **Mother:** *I took him to parent-toddler classes. And he was always the one that wouldn't sit for the story time, he never did the art projects, he was always racing around.*

Searching for reasons. Why? Why? Why? As parents began to realize that their child's behavior was different from other children's, they started to search for the reasons behind these behavior problems. This search for reasons can be seen as a coping process; it contains elements of problem solving and of emotional regulation.

The problem solving was characterized by parents' attempts to identify factors influencing the child's misbehaviors in the hope that these factors could be eliminated, thereby alleviating the behavior problems.

Typical external factors that parents identified included nutrition and sleep. Many parents reported trying different fad diets. Many reported eliminating sugary foods, food additives, milk, or other elements from the child's diet in order to bring about improvement in the child's behaviors. Many reported being continually concerned that their child sleep enough at night to ensure that the child was not misbehaving due to fatigue. Mothers searched their memories for things they might have done wrong during their pregnancy and for birth and postnatal difficulties which could possibly have contributed to the child's problems.

> **Mother:** *He was premature and came home after 5-1/2 weeks. So initially I remembered feeling there was not that bonding you are supposed to have within hours of birth.*

Parents also searched for external factors in the children's schools or the approaches of teachers that might contribute to the child's difficulties. Frequently, parents sought out new schools, hoping to find one that was more sensitive to their child's specific learning style, intelligence, and temperament.

> **Mother:** *He was in day care where he was the youngest, and it didn't seem he was watched out for. It could have been he was overlooked, and there were some occasions perhaps where he was picked on. And when I realized what was going on, then I changed situations.*

They searched for clues in their own family histories, lives and marriages that could be contributing to the child's problems.

> **Father:** *A lot of the problem is when we moved into my mother's house. There were too many authoritarian figures over him and he didn't know exactly who to listen to. He was only 3-1/2 and there were all these authority figures, my brother, my mother, my sister, me and my wife, and sometimes my sister's husband.*

The search for reasons also served the function of emotional regulation—that is, trying to modulate and de-escalate angry and/or depressive feelings. Typical emotional regulation strategies of coping involved parents' analyzing their own childhoods. Often fathers told stories of having similar problems with aggression when they were children. Parents also spoke of being hit or otherwise abused by their parents, as well as rejected by their peer group at school.

> **Father:** *Perhaps some of it is genetic. I mean, I had some problems when I was a kid. I was very aggressive. I almost got kicked out of preschool. I bit kids and hit kids and I was somewhat of a terror as well. I would want toys and if someone tried to get the toys from me, I'd throw a block at them.*

While these painful memories allowed them to identify with their children's difficulties and therefore feel less alienated from them, there was a negative aspect as well: they became more discouraged because they felt the family pattern was repeating itself.

> **Father:** *Well I was always in trouble as a child—always in the principal's office—and my Dad, he whipped me constantly. Now my son has the same problems I did and as a parent I want to respond differently, but I see myself doing the same things.*

Adoptive parents were inclined to search for the roots of the child's problems in the genetic backgrounds of the biological parents as well as question their own motivation, attachment, and readiness for adoption, feeling that perhaps these factors contributed to the child's insecurities and misbehaviors.

> **Father:** *He was adopted and we got him at 4 weeks. He came suddenly and I don't think we were prepared to deal with it. It has been a series of stressful changes.*

Self-blame. For most parents, the process of looking for reasons for the child's problems involved looking internally as well as externally. This acknowledgement of their own limitations promoted feelings of self-blame and guilt. Parents' hypotheses regarding their own contribution to their child's problems included moves to new neighborhoods, ineffective parenting approaches, lack of time to attend to their children's needs, unemployment, too much time devoted to their jobs, medical problems, use of drugs during pregnancy, divorce or death in the family, poor housing accommodations, and personal inadequacies or health problems.

Mother: *The reason we're having so much trouble disciplining him is because I don't like conflict. It's almost like sometimes I'm trying not to start any conflict—but that's not helping him.*

Father: *I think a lot of his playing rough could be partially due to me, because when I play with him I like to play rough. We tumble around, and roll around and punch each other—so a lot of it could be my fault.*

Father: *We moved and my wife was on bed rest for 5 months with our second child—she couldn't pick him up. It's kind of like he got hit with a lot in a short period of time. We put him in day care. All of a sudden there is competition for affection...so he's learned that by being uncooperative and bad he definitely gets attention. Let's assume my wife never was on bed rest and he never ended up in day care, and we did all this when he was 5 instead of 2—it would have been totally different.*

Mother: *He screams really violently if he doesn't get his way. I know why he does that—because when I was having a lot of bad headaches a few months ago, whenever he'd scream, I'd usually give in to him. So now it's become a habit.*

Father: *I feel like I lack the skills to help him become a mature person primarily because the environment I grew up in there was no training—I don't really know how to do it. I worry about my responses to his behavior—whether I provide a model or a way to do things positively. My father died when I was young, so I'm not sure about myself as a father or a parent in general. I know that I love him and want the best, but I'm not sure I'm helping him. You know,*

I feel that I express love, but when things get tough I feel that I have a tendency to withdraw from everybody.

Sometimes professionals' theories regarding the causes of misbehavior in children reinforced these feelings of self-blame for the child's problems. However, because most of these parents consulted a variety of professional sources, they encountered conflicting explanations, which contributed to a sense of bewilderment.

Mother: *Well I went to the pediatrician who told me to "loosen up" and said he was normal. I tried that for a while but things just got worse. Then I went to a psychologist who said I wasn't strict enough with him—well, clamping down didn't seem to work either. Finally I went to a psychiatrist who said if I'd only get my marriage together my son would be okay. But my husband didn't want marriage counseling, so what was I to do?*

Phase III: Learned Helplessness

This phase is characterized by a transition from desperate attempts to understand and cope with problems to a mode of giving up. Three categories were identified as elements of learned helplessness: "nothing works," "mounting anger and loss of control," and the "paradoxical investment."

Nothing works. As parents came to realize that their child's behavior problems were not going to disappear, they coped with feelings of self-blame by launching into a variety of discipline approaches. Parents reported seeking help from books, courses and various professionals. They tried a range of discipline strategies such as teaching, yelling, criticism, spanking, Time Out, taking away privileges, tough love, and bribes. Although the parents' broad use of a range of strategies may seem positive, their inconsistent choice of strategies and low confidence about when to use a particular strategy with a specific problem indicated how desperate they were.

After several years of struggling to control the child's behavior problems with limited, if any, success parents began believing that they were doomed to be ineffective in changing their child's behavior. In fact, it was typical that the child's misbehaviors gradually escalated under what parents perceived as their own best efforts. Parents reported reaching a point when they believed that "nothing worked."

> **Father:** *I get agitated easily, I mean, this has been 4 years of this. And I am 42 years old, and I've just about had it. So now I'm kind of at my wit's end, like what to do. Because nothing is working. Time Outs don't work. If I put her in her room, she'll go and start kicking the door, or throwing toys—so then I'll lose it, I'll go in and I'll spank her.*

> **Mother:** *We've done a lot of parenting. Both of us are professionals and we work with people a lot and we've had a lot of resources. We've been in counseling since he was 3 years old and seen several psychologists and psychiatrists, and we've worked very hard, but haven't gotten very far. He's still got the same traits and that's scary.*

> **Mother:** *I'm stuck here—it will never get any better, this child is going to be a delinquent, I know it. I'm going crazy and I need help. Maybe I should give up because I'm going down on a sinking ship.*

Parents felt helpless and inadequate in their parenting roles, and more generally, as human beings. Moreover, their extended family members, teachers, professionals and other parents seemed to confirm these feelings of ineptitude.

Mounting anger and loss of control. The basic premise of the learned helplessness theory (Seligman, 1975) is that during contact with an uncontrollable situation, an organism learns that outcomes and responses are non-contingent (Abramson et al., 1978; Maier & Seligman, 1976; Seligman, 1975). Transition from intense feelings of inadequacy to learned helplessness was evident in parents' reports of feelings of being overwhelmed, even paralyzed, by their children's problems. Parents frequently spoke as though they believed their children were "out to get them." As the embattled parents felt increasingly helpless, they began seeing their children as the powerful ones. In an inversion of the usual power structure, the children controlled their parents' lives. Thus, the parents became victims and the children the oppressors. In response to their sense of victimization, the parents' anger increased, as if in an effort to regain control and power in the relationship. These powerful feelings of anger were coupled with fears of losing control of their own behavior and sanity. Furthermore, many parents reported fantasies of getting rid of their child or running away themselves.

> **Mother:** *I was ready to just walk away from everybody. It was just too much—his screaming, the temper tantrums all day. And I thought I was completely loony bins. I felt like a real failure as a human being...There are times when he just drives me to destruction...*

Sometimes parents reported losing control and using excessive physical punishment or locking their children in their room for hours. Such out-of-control reactions further inflamed their self-blame, setting in motion a vicious cycle of anger, loss of control (ineffective parenting) and guilt. These reactions and feelings further aggravated the child's aggressive responses. Eventually, the parents' fear of their own angry responses led them to give up on disciplining and to withdraw, which in turn, brought on depression.

> **Mother:** *It's like he pushes, and pushes, and pushes me...I feel real helpless...and what I do is, rather than react appropriately, I shut down. I mean it's like I'm in shock. That's when I feel really incompetent...I have truly never questioned my own sanity, as I have with the kind of episodes I told you. It really overwhelms me —it scares me.*

> **Mother:** *Every time I've gotten to the point where I've just felt like I'm losing control, because nothing is working, and I'm spanking, I tried in the past to get on the phone and call a crisis clinic, a parenting group, somebody to provide help. And there really isn't any help out there. You try calling somebody in a crisis situation and what you get is an answering service or a disconnected number. Or you get a recording, you know, leave your name and number. "I'm hurting my child now, call me back when I am sane." People beat their children. I understand their frustration.*

Paradoxical Investment. Another characteristic of the learned helplessness that was difficult for parents to accept was a sense of having invested so much in their child with little or no "return" in terms of joy and pleasure in the parent-child relationship. This situation, in which parents experienced few rewards for the difficult work of parenting, created a sense of despair in parents who felt that the discrepancy between what they were "putting in" and what they were "getting out" was just too great.

> **Mother:** *I've noticed other mothers and families, and they really enjoy their little girls and their little boys, because it's a real different situation for them. And it's not like that for me. I don't have that real enjoyment. What's wrong with me?*

In sum, these parents felt stuck with an unresponsive and aggressive child, with no support or understanding from others. They felt afraid that their child would never improve and would have escalating problems in the years to come.

SUMMARY

Qualitative analyses of the interviews of these parents indicated that the process of parenting a child with conduct disorders involved three phases: treading water, problem recognition, and eventual learned helplessness. As mentioned earlier, the cornerstone of the learned helplessness hypothesis is that individuals who experience situations in which they have no control over what happens, often develop certain motivational, cognitive, and emotional deficits. The motivational deficit that occurs is characterized by retarded initiation of voluntary responses. The cognitive deficit is a belief or expectation that outcomes are uncontrollable. The emotional deficit is characterized by depressed affect (Abramson, Seligman, & Teasdale, 1978; Ashman, Dawson, & Panagiotides, 2008; Dweck, 1975; Seligman, 1975).

Parents of children with conduct disorders learn through repeated experiences that regardless of the parenting strategy used (e.g., Time Out, spanking, explanation, positive reinforcement), the child's aversive behavior will remain constant. In other words, the outcome is not affected by the actions. Moreover, even when these parents were able to influence their child's behavior, they felt that there was no relationship between the parenting strategy used and the outcome. For example, Time Out might be effective at one time, but not at a different time—even in response to the identical problem behavior. Thus parents felt that there was no discernible relationship between their actions and the outcome.

According to the learned helplessness hypothesis, the attribution a person makes about an event is crucial. Abramson et al. (1978) distinguishes between universal and personal helplessness. In universal helplessness, a person believes that neither s/he nor anyone can solve the problem, whereas in personal helplessness a person believes that while the problem is solvable, s/he lacks the skills to solve it (i.e., low self-efficacy expectations). Analysis of the attributions by the parents of children with conduct problems in our study revealed that these parents developed a sense of personal helplessness. Parents constantly compared their childrearing skills to those of other parents and came to believe that unlike other parents, they were incapable of controlling their child's behavior. These internal comparisons were reinforced by feedback from family members, teachers, and other professionals, who also attributed the child's misbehaviors to the parents' lack of parenting skills. This, in turn, increased the parents' sense of personal helplessness.

Our findings also indicated that these parents reported very low self-esteem and/or high depression. These findings are explained by the learned helplessness theory, which asserts that people who feel personally helpless show lower self-esteem than do those who experience their helplessness as universal (Abramson et al., 1978).

A related hypothesis advanced by Bandura (1982, 1985, 1989) may also help explain this finding. Bandura proposes that self-efficacy beliefs are central to an individual's transactions with environment. For example, a parent may believe they understand how to do Time Out with an aggressive child, but be unable to do it because of self-doubts. In addition, Bandura (1989) has suggested that the relationship between self-efficacy and performance is bidirectional. Self-efficacy beliefs are enhanced or decreased, respectively, by success or failure experiences. The parents in our study reported feeling ineffective due to their repeated experiences of failure while trying to parent their difficult children. Thus, they stopped trying.

According to the theory, learned helplessness varies in terms of generality, chronicity, and intensity of the problem (Abramson et al., 1978; Kofta & Sedek, 1989; Mikulincer & Casopy, 1986; Miller & Norman, 1979). The helplessness felt by these parents was extreme in all three respects. With regard to generality, parents of children with conduct problems felt inadequate in areas of their lives beyond childrearing, including their marital relationship and relationships with teachers, other parents, and professionals in the community. Many felt isolated, stigmatized, and even rejected. Thus, the sense of helplessness experienced by these parents became somewhat globalized, rather than remaining specific to the child. With regard to chronicity, these parents reported waiting endlessly for their child's problems to disappear before attempting to control them. Furthermore, when they did try to handle the problems, they were usually unsuccessful. Therefore, most parents had experienced chronic helplessness for several years. With regard to intensity, the high intensity at which the parents experienced these problems evolves from the importance our society places on successful childrearing and a harmonious family. Abramson et al. (1978) has suggested that the intensity of helplessness will be higher according to how highly preferred or valued the person perceives the event to be. It is not difficult to understand the intense feelings of helplessness that can occur when parents develop the conviction that they lack the skills for rearing behaviorally normal children.

Teaching, coaching and supporting parents' use of evidence-based behavior management skills undoubtedly starts a reversal process and builds self-confidence.

This parental perception, formulated by parents of children with conduct problems, has important implications for treatment, because learned helplessness and low self-efficacy beliefs can be reversed by experiences of success. Teaching, coaching and supporting parents' use of evidence-based behavior management skills undoubtedly starts a reversal process; it begins to give parents some expectation that they will eventually be able to control outcomes (i.e., their children's behaviors). However, because of the global nature of the helplessness, it is also important to modify any unrealistic expectations and substitute realistic plans about their child's developmental abilities and the nature of their temperament. This in turn, promotes revised parent self-efficacy, both in the context of dealing with their child's misconduct and also more generally in parental relationships, problem-solving and coping skills. These findings also reveal the importance of enhancing social support, reversing these parents' experience of stigmatization and isolation by involving partners and, if possible, teachers in the intervention. Indeed, these findings indicate that group-based approaches may be particularly helpful for these parents because the group experience with other parents counteracts their isolation, normalizes some of their experiences and provides a support network.

The group experience counteracts their isolation, normalizes some of their experiences and provides a support network.

Content of the Incredible Years® Parenting Pyramid™ Foundation~ Building Children's Social and Emotional Competence

OVERVIEW

The BASIC Incredible Years (IY) parent training series is the "core" Incredible Years training series. BASIC IY parent training is considered a necessary and essential part of program delivery for treating conduct problems in young children. Other IY programs, such as the teacher or child programs, are recommended as adjuncts for populations according to their particular risk levels. The BASIC parent training series has 4 different BASIC curricula designed to address different age groups: Baby Program (6 weeks to 1 year), Toddler Program (1- 2 ½ years), Preschool Program (3-5 years) and School-Age Program (6-12 years). Each curriculum emphasizes developmentally appropriate parenting skills proven to promote children's social competence and emotional regulation and to reduce behavior problems.

Goals of the IY parent programs

While each curriculum focuses on specific parenting skills that relate to the developmental stage of the child, the overall goals of the BASIC IY series are as follows:

- Increase positive parenting, self-confidence, and parent-child bonding/attachment
- Teach parents to coach and support children's language development, persistence and sustained attention, and social, emotional and cognitive development
- Decrease parents' harsh discipline and increase proactive age appropriate discipline strategies
- Improve parents' problem solving, anger and depression management and communication skills
- Increase family support networks and school involvement/bonding
- Help parents and teachers work collaboratively
- Increase parents' involvement in supporting children's academic-related activities at home

Theoretical Framework

The underlying theoretical backgrounds for all the Incredible Years Series include the following:

- Cognitive social learning theory, and in particular Patterson's coercion hypothesis about negative reinforcement and the development and maintenance of deviant behavior (Patterson, Reid, & Dishion, 1992)
- Bandura's modeling and self-efficacy theories (Bandura, 1986)
- Piaget's cognitive development stages and interactive learning methods (Piaget & Inhelder, 1962)
- Cognitive strategies and attribution theory about challenging angry, negative, helpless and depressive self-talk and increasing parent self-esteem and self-confidence (Abramson, Seligman, & Teasdale, 1978; Beck, 1979; D'Zurilla & Nezu, 1982; Jacobson & Margolin, 1979)
- Attachment and relationship theories (Bowlby, 1980, 1988; Grossmann, Grossmann, & Waters, 2005)

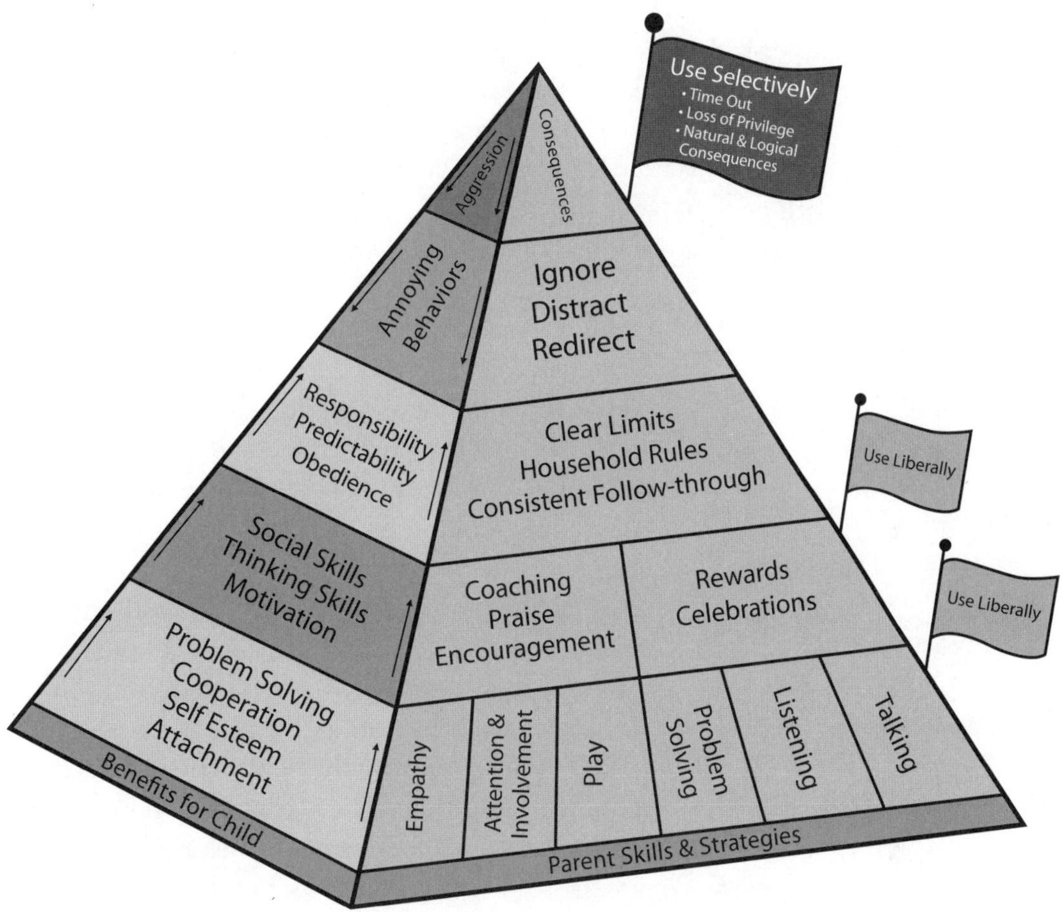

Parenting Pyramid™

The Parenting Pyramid

The IY Parenting Pyramid™ serves as the architectural plan for delivering the parenting content. It helps parents conceptualize effective parenting tools and learn how to use these tools to help achieve their goals. The bottom of the pyramid depicts parenting tools that should be used liberally, as they form the relationship foundation for children's emotional, social, and academic learning. These foundational tools include positive parent attention, sensitive responding and communication, and child-directed play interactions designed to build secure, loving and trusting relationships. Parents also learn how to use specific academic, social, emotional and persistence coaching tools to help their children manage feelings, persist with learning despite obstacles, and develop social interactions. The second tier of the pyramid describes the incentive systems, celebrations and behavior-specific praise for targeted prosocial behaviors that parents study after learning about the foundational tools. As parents continue to move up the pyramid, they learn tools that reduce specific targeted negative behaviors and are used more sparingly.

The IY Parenting Pyramid™ serves as the architectural plan for delivering the parenting content.

The middle layer of the pyramid describes scaffolding practices that build clear boundaries and structure for children's exploratory behaviors and drive for autonomy, assuring their safety. Such practices include predictable routines, rules, and respectful limit setting. The least intrusive proactive discipline tools, such as ignoring inappropriate behaviors, distractions, and redirection, follow this tier. Finally, at the very top of the pyramid, parents will find the strategic and sparing use of proactive and respectful discipline tools (such as Time Out) for aggressive behaviors and logical consequences. It is only after studying the bottom tiers of the pyramid that parents of children older than three years learn how to use these discipline tools. After the top of the pyramid is reached, the final part of the curriculum focuses on how parents can return to the base of the pyramid. This refocuses parents on integrating positive and proactive strategies for teaching children to problem solve, self regulate, and manage conflict. At this point parents have all the necessary tools to navigate some of the uncomfortable, but inevitable, aspects of their parenting interactions with their children. The basic premise of the model is twofold: first, a positive relationship foundation precedes clear and predictable discipline strategies, and second, attention to positive behaviors should occur far more frequently than attention to negative behaviors. Parenting tools found higher up on the pyramid only work when a positive foundation has been solidly constructed with secure scaffolding.

Group leaders/therapists use the pyramid building metaphor with parents to explain the program and illustrate the "construction plan" so that parents can see where each parenting tool fits into the program process. Group leaders teach parents the foundational tools necessary to address their individual goals and understand how to support their child's learning, motivation, and developmental progress. After learning these basic parenting skills, therapists introduce parents to the tools needed for reducing misbehavior, making corrections, and repairing mistakes. By the time parents complete the program they will understand how to select parenting tools that are appropriate to their child's developmental abilities and specific to different kinds of problems. Certain tools are used more frequently than others at different developmental stages of children's cognitive, emotional, and social development.

A positive relationship foundation precedes clear and predictable discipline strategies.

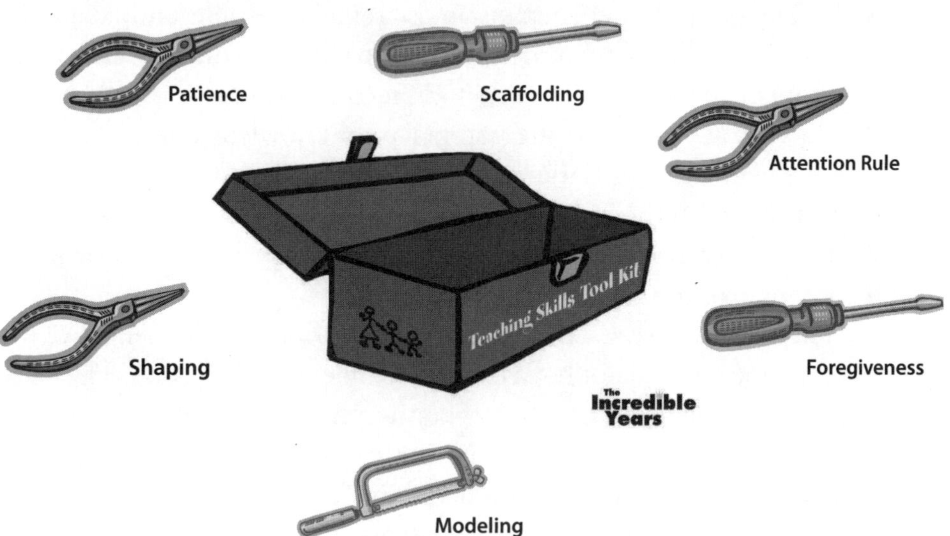

Timing of the Parenting Pyramid Construction

A recommended minimum number of session protocols is provided for each of the parenting programs. Depending on the specific age level of children for whom the program is to be delivered, the risk status of the population, and whether the program is prevention or treatment in focus, these session protocols will range from 12 to 26 weekly, 2-hour

The group leader/therapist must remain flexible and adapt the timing and pacing of the program.

sessions. If the population is high risk, including child welfare families referred for abuse or neglect, utilizes interpreters, or is a treatment group for children diagnosed with ODD/CD and/or ADHD, more sessions are necessary to complete the program. The lengthened program protocol provides parents with sufficient time to learn new concepts and understanding about child development, practice new behaviors and get feedback, change negative cognitions and to develop trusting relationships. During the treatment process therapists offer parents substantial support, as well as the scaffolding and time necessary for parents to solidify their new thoughts, feelings and behaviors and achieve their goals. The group leader/therapist must remain flexible and adapt the timing and pacing of the program. The specific parenting tools taught, the number of vignettes shown, and practices needed in each session should vary according to the parents' prior knowledge of the content, baseline familiarity with the behavioral principles and the nature of the relationship with their child. It may be necessary to add sessions to the minimum recommended number in order for parents to learn and incorporate all the tools in the series.

Therapists who have tried to reduce the recommended length of the program find they do not have time to complete all the topics. They also tend to lecture in a didactic fashion rather than engage in collaborative, experiential, reflective, and therapeutic learning. These interactive leadership methods, discussed in detail in Chapter Eight are key to parents' effective learning of new behaviors, thoughts, and feelings.The recommended minimum number of sessions for the prevention and treatment versions of the program are based on numerous RCTs with prevention and treatment studies over 30 years which have resulted in improvements and updates. In order to deliver the program with fidelity and to achieve results similar to the research studies, the recommended delivery cannot be shortened. Like any construction project, the process of building parenting skills usually takes longer than anticipated due to unforeseeable circumstances that must be addressed along the way.

Summary of the Four Basic Parenting Programs

The *Incredible Years Baby and Toddler Programs* place parental focus on helping their babies and toddlers successfully accomplish three developmental milestones: secure attachment with their parents; language and social expression; and beginning sense of self. The baby program topics

include: baby safety alerts; developmental principles regarding feeding, sleeping, and bowel movement patterns; ways to cope with babies' crying and fussy periods; speaking "parentese"; providing physical, tactile, and visual stimulation; and how to get support from others. The toddler program topics include: child-directed play; social and emotion coaching; nurturing parenting, rich with language and positive communication; understanding toddlers' drive for exploration and need for predictable routines and clear boundaries; separation and reunion strategies; clear limit setting and toddler-proofing the home to assure safety. Each program uses a textbook and journal entitled *Incredible Babies* or *Incredible Toddlers* (Webster-Stratton, 2011a, 2011b).

The *Preschool Program* places parental focus on the following developmental milestones: encouraging school readiness skills (prewriting, prereading, discovery learning), emotional regulation, and beginning social and friendships skills. Program topics include a continuation of toddler topics as well as: academic, persistence, and self-regulation

coaching; effective use of praise and encouragement; proactive discipline; and teaching children beginning problem-solving skills and calm down strategies. The text for both the Preschool and the School Age programs is *The Incredible Years: A troubleshooting guide for parents of children aged 2-8 years* (Webster-Stratton, 2005).

The *School Age BASIC Program* places parental focus on the developmental milestones of: encouraging children's independence; motivation for academic learning; and development of family responsibility, emotional security, and empathy awareness. Program topics continue to build on core relationship skills through special time with parents, and provide

age-appropriate information on reward systems for difficult behaviors, clear and respectful limit setting, encouragement of family chores and sense of responsibility, predictable home work routines, and logical consequences. There is a middle childhood (children ages 6-8 years) protocol and a preadolescence (children 9-12 years) protocol for this program. The content of the preadolescence protocol includes all the younger school age content plus additional information regarding ongoing monitoring of children's afterschool activities, and discussions regarding family rules including TV and computer use, as well as drugs and alcohol. Finally, the School Age BASIC program teaches parents methods for developing successful partnerships with teachers and strategies for supporting their children's curiosity for learning, such as reading time and the development of predictable and supportive homework routines.

> The preadolescent program adds focus to monitoring after school activities, family discussions regarding technology usage, drugs, alcohol and homework.

THERAPISTS HELPING PARENTS LEARN THE FOUNDATIONAL PARENTING BUILDING BLOCKS

While many parents will want to begin parent sessions by talking about their children's behavior problems, it is important for therapists to help parents understand why beginning with building their relationship foundation is key to their eventual success in achieving their goal for improved misbehavior. Through child-directed play, or "special time," parents learn how to encourage children's cooperation, foster their creativity and curiosity, build their self-esteem, strengthen their prosocial behavior and self-regulation, and keep them safe. By beginning with these positive goals therapists achieve several advantages by:

- Emphasizing the positive aspects of building the parent-child relationship and attachment rather than focusing on behavior problems.

- Introducing parents to the idea that their responsive and sensitive interactions with their children make a difference to what behaviors and brain neuron connections will be strengthened and build a strong foundation for future social, emotional and academic development.
- Helping parents and children feel good about their responses to each other and promoting bonding.
- Helping parents give children consistent attention, coaching, approval, and praise for prosocial behavior rather than negative attention and criticism for misbehavior.
- Promoting parents' empathy for their children and understanding of developmental milestones and how temperament and biological differences can impact behavior.

Child-directed play helps children feel deeply loved and valued, thereby fostering a secure attachment base for their ongoing emotional and social development.

Child-Directed Play & Special Time Programs

All the BASIC programs begin with therapists helping parents to understand the value of child-directed and responsive parent play interactions. These forms of play strengthen attachment, promote optimal brain development, build children's self-confidence and curiosity about learning; however, many parents, particularly parents of children with behavior problems, seldom play with their children. This is often because parents do not understand the value of play for promoting their children's development nor have they ever experienced it themselves as children, or because their lives are so stressful and chaotic that there seems to be little time to play. Parents with children who have conduct problems, ADHD, or difficult temperaments also may not play because these interactions are simply too stressful. Typically there is negativity on both sides: parents feel anger and frustration related to their children's misbehavior, and their children, in turn, model this behavior and respond with negativity towards their parents. The first step in breaking this coercive cycle of behaviors and feelings is therefore an infusion of positive feelings into the relationship through child-directed play. For parents of highly aggressive children, these child-directed play times can be the first pleasurable times they have had with their children in months or even years.

Regular child-directed play times, where parents provide focused attention on their children's activities, help build warm relationships between family members. These play times in turn build a "bank account" of positive feelings and experiences that can be "drawn upon" in times of conflict. This is particularly important for parents of children with conduct problems who may be feeling resentful, angry, distant, or hopeless about their relationship. Child-directed play with parents helps children feel deeply loved and valued, thereby fostering a secure attachment base for their ongoing emotional and social development. Just as important, it also promotes parents' feelings of attachment and warmth towards their child.

Academic, Persistence, Social and Emotion Coaching Programs

Next therapists teach parents about the importance of talking to their babies and children in developing their language skills. In the Babies Program parents learn how to speak "parent-ese," a language of single vowels or words spoken slowly in a high pitched, melodious, and playful voice. In the Toddler Program this language becomes more elaborate as sentences become longer, more detailed, and complex. Parents learn descriptive commenting, which is the practice of describing objects, actions, or positions of things they see in their day-to-day life. Parents learn to talk about what the toddler shows interest in and point to the object as he or she names it. For example: "Yes, the kitty is furry and brown. You can touch the kitty gently," or "We need some apples today. There's a red apple going into the basket." This communication is child-directed and non-directive so as not to interfere with the toddler's curiosity and drive to explore and discover. This approach also promotes toddler's learning of the vocabulary needed for communication.

Academic Readiness Coaching. Once toddlers begin to learn the names for objects and actions, therapists help parents learn something called *academic readiness coaching*. This is when parents describe things that will contribute to their children's preschool readiness. This can include naming numbers, letters, shapes, or colors. Parents are encouraged not to ask questions of their children, because questions are parent-directed and may pressure children into providing answers before they are ready. Instead parents just familiarize their toddler with the concepts by naming them as part of toddler-directed descriptive commenting. When the child repeatedly hears the vocabulary at the same time that she is exploring and playing with the objects, she will begin to link the ideas with words long before she can produce the words herself. Parents are also encouraged to use this form of communication while reading picture books to babies and toddlers.

Persistence coaching provides the scaffolding that a child needs to be able to stay calm and persist through a difficult activity.

Persistence Coaching. Therapists also teach parents of preschoolers and school age children about persistence coaching. *Persistence coaching* is the practice of naming the child's internal cognitive state when she is being patient, trying again, staying calm, concentrating, focusing, persisting, or working hard with a difficult task. This type of coaching is beneficial for all children but is particularly important for inattentive, impulsive, and hyperactive children. It helps them recognize when they are focused and attentive, what it feels like to be in that cognitive state, and to put a word to it. This coaching provides the scaffolding that a child needs to be able to stay calm and persist through a difficult activity for a few minutes longer than he might have otherwise. This skill of patience and persistence is an important life lesson that contributes to emotional regulation. Children begin to learn that it is normal to struggle to learn something new, but that with patience, persistence, repeated practice and parental support, they can eventually accomplish the task and feel proud of it.

Social Coaching. The Toddler, Preschool, and School Age BASIC Programs all teach parents ways to use social coaching with their children. Therapists help parents understand how to target this coaching according to their child's developmental ability and temperament. Before the age of 2 or 3, children's play is egocentric, solitary, and non-cooperative. Toddlers have very few prosocial skills, especially with their peers.They rarely share, wait, or take turns. This is the age of curious exploration, "mine–mine–mine," and "I want what I want when I want it!" Moreover, when toddlers play with peers, they usually engage in what is called "parallel play." Parallel play occurs when children are playing next to each other but are not initiating interactions with one another. When toddlers do this, they are probably unaware of what the other is doing because they are so absorbed in their own discoveries. This may also be true for many preschool children and some early school-age children, especially for those with autism or ADHD. While therapists help parents of young children or developmentally delayed children to understand that this parallel play is quite normal, they also help parents learn how to use social coaching to teach the language and concepts of social skills, such as what it means to share, take turns, help, or use words to ask for what they want. Therapists also teach parents how to model and prompt these behaviors and words in their one-on-one child-directed play interactions.

The Preschool and Early School Age Programs expand the use of social coaching to peer-play interactions. Parents learn to coach several children playing together by describing skills such as waiting, being polite, listening, being cooperative, and acting like a good team player. The therapist helps each parent target their child's specific social skills goals according to their developmental play abilities. For example, parents of children who seldom initiate social interactions with peers or seem unaware of peers are coached to prompt their children to initiate an interaction using friendly words. Parents of children who are interacting with other children in inappropriate ways might learn to prompt such targeted behaviors as asking, waiting for a turn, accepting no, and staying calm. In addition to commenting on and prompting targeted skills, parents are taught to model the skills with their own behavior or through the use of a puppet in imaginary play. For example, the parent or puppet might say: "I'm going to share this truck with you" or "I'll wait my turn for

Parents are encouraged to strategically attend to targeted social behaviors they want to see more of, while giving little or less attention to behaviors that they want to decrease.

a chance with that doll." Throughout this unit, parents are taught to think about the power of their attention in maintaining children's behavior. They are encouraged to strategically attend to targeted social behaviors they want to see more of, while giving little or less attention to behaviors that they want to decrease.

Emotion Coaching. Another type of coaching is called *emotion coaching*. This approach starts in infancy when parents tell babies they are loved and respond to their emotional states with appropriate reciprocal interactions and care. For example, parents may smile and giggle when their baby is calm and happy, give cuddles when their baby is sleepy, and comfort and care when their baby is upset. In toddlerhood parents continue to help children understand emotions by labeling their feelings and behavioral reactions. By naming children's feelings when they are excited, curious, proud, brave, disappointed, frustrated, or angry, parents teach feelings literacy; that is, the vocabulary needed for recognizing and expressing their own feelings and eventually to understanding emotions in others. Children who have a rich feeling vocabulary can more easily regulate their emotional and behavioral responses. Research has shown that many preschoolers only know 2.5 feeling words: mad, sad, and sometimes happy. The goal is to expand children's feeling vocabulary, to recognize and experience more positive feelings than negative ones, and to learn how they can cope with their negative feelings. This understanding will eventually lead to empathy, as older children are able to recognize feelings not only in themselves, but also in others. Therapists also teach parents how to express their joy and playfulness with their children by encouraging parents to enter into their child's imaginary and pretend worlds and use of puppets and toy characters.

Therapists teach parents to support their children when they are feeling an unpleasant or uncomfortable emotion. This will help to build a child's attachment to a parent as well as the child's feelings of security, self-confidence, and ability to self-regulate when upset. This approach helps children to understand another person's perspective when distressed. Coaching children's negative or unpleasant emotions is tricky because excessive attention to negative emotions can make children more frustrated, angry, or sad. If done skillfully, parent coaching of unpleasant emotions can make their child feel validated, understood, and can help regulate a child's mood and understanding that unpleasant feelings change with time. Parents learn the importance of pairing their comments about their child's negative feelings with positive coping statements. For example, if a school age child is having trouble reading, the parent might say, "That is frustrating and hard work, but you are staying so patient and you keep trying. I think you're learning to read." Or, if a child is disappointed because he wanted to go to the park and something prevents the parent from taking him, the parent might say, "I know this is very disappointing for you. I'm really sorry. Even though you are mad, you are staying calm. Let's think of something else to do now that will be fun and then you will feel happier." In this way, the parent avoids giving too much attention to negative behaviors, focusing instead on a coping response to the negative feelings and a prediction of eventual positive change in the negative feeling. This may even pre-empt a negative response, such as an angry tantrum or giving up in frustration.

However, therapists must also help parents understand that sometimes a child will be too dysregulated to listen to a parent's coaching. If a parent has labeled the unpleasant emotion once and provided the coping strategy, and the child is still crying hard or becoming argumentative, then it is a good idea for the parent to back off, ignore, and give the child some space to calm down before talking again. Additional attention or talking when the child is dysregulated will likely prolong the anger. When the child has finally calmed down, the parent can then label that emotion. "I'm proud of you. Your body is looking much calmer now. You really tried hard and now you are calm!" This approach also helps children develop a sense of optimism about their ability to take responsibility for their own behavior.

Parents learn the importance of pairing their comments about their child's negative feelings with positive coping statements.

Summary of Child-Directed Play and Coaching

These child-directed play and parent coaching methods can take 5 or more sessions to complete. Some parents, like Robbie's father, find this type of coaching to be a completely new language. Like learning a new language, some parents find the process awkward and difficult and require a lot of practice and scripting. Parents may have difficulty because their more natural communication style is to ask questions, correct, instruct, compete with their child, criticize his or her actions, or interfere with their child's discovery process. Parents may also give only divided attention to their child because they are also trying to text, talk on the phone, or do chores. Other parents may have limited language skills themselves; perhaps they don't use emotion language and don't have a broad repertoire of emotion words, or have difficulty knowing how to describe the positive social skills that they want to replace their child's negative behaviors. Therapists will help parents develop these new scripts and ask them to practice these coaching methods at home with their children, as a weekly home activity. Parents also receive refrigerator notes that summarize key points learned in the session.

Based on the parents' experiences at home and feedback about the home activities, therapists determine the need for further practice sessions and additional video vignette viewings, pacing the program content accordingly.

On the following pages are two examples of these weekly refrigerator notes given to parents. Others may be found on the web site .

Children who receive little parental attention for positive behaviors learn that misbehavior is a sure way to get their parents' attention.

Positive Attention, Encouragement and Praise Programs

The goal of the praise and encouragement programs is to increase parents' attention toward targeted positive behaviors. Parents of children with conduct problems often find it hard to praise their children. While some parents believe they should not have to praise their children for everyday behaviors, many others simply do not know how or when to give praise and encouragement. Perhaps they received very little praise from their parents when they were young, or are unaccustomed to hearing praise and the words seem awkward or

Points to Remember about

Promoting Your Toddler's Emotion Self-regulation Skills

- Try to understand what your toddler is feeling and wanting.
- Describe your toddler's feelings (don't ask him what he is feeling because he is unlikely to have the words to tell you).
- Label your toddler's positive feelings more often than his negative feelings.
- When naming negative feelings such as frustration or anger, point out the coping strategy your child is using: *"You look frustrated, but you are staying calm and trying again."*
- Praise your child's self-regulation skills such as staying calm, being patient, trying again when frustrated, waiting a turn, and using words.
- Support your toddler when he is frustrated, but recognize when he is too upset to listen and just needs space to calm down.
- Model and give your toddler the words to use to express his needs (e.g., You can say, "can I have the truck").
- Help your toddler learn ways to self-soothe such as using a pacifier or blanket or special stuffed animal.
- Praise and encourage your toddler when he stays calm in a frustrating situation.
- Cuddle and soothe your toddler when he is hurt or frightened. Stay calm yourself to provide extra reassurance.

artificial. Parents may also be so angry with their children for their misbehaviors that they cannot see any praiseworthy behavior, even when it does occur. Research indicates that a lack of praise and attention for appropriate child behaviors can actually lead to an increase in misbehavior. This is likely because children who receive little positive attention learn that misbehavior is a sure way to get their parents' attention. In

Points to Remember about
Promoting Your Toddler's Social Competence

One-on-One Parent-Toddler

- During play, model social skills for your toddler such as offering to share, waiting, giving a compliment, taking turns, asking for help.
- Prompt your toddler to ask for help, take a turn, share something, or give a compliment and then praise if it occurs. Let it go if your toddler does not respond to your prompt.
- Praise your toddler any time s/he offers to share with you or help you.
- Participate in pretend and make-believe play with your child by using a doll, action figure, or puppet to model skills such as asking to play, offering to help, taking a turn, giving a compliment, calming down with a deep breath and waiting.
- Model and prompt your child with a suggestion of the appropriate words to use.
- Try to give enough help so children are successful but not so much help that you take over.

Peer Social Coaching

- Occasionally prompt your child to notice what another child is doing or to help him or her in some way.
- Help your toddler understand that when he shared, the other person felt happy so he can see the connection between his behavior and another's feelings.
- Encourage play dates with friends.
- Praise and encourage children's ideas and creativity; avoid criticism.
- Use descriptive comments instead of asking questions.
- Prompt, coach, and praise children's friendly behaviors whenever you see them (e.g., sharing, helping, taking turns, being polite).
- Laugh and have fun.

fact, praise and encouragement can be used to guide children through the many small steps it takes to master new skills, to help them develop a positive self-image, and to provide the motivation they need to persist through a difficult task. Unlike tangible rewards such as money or privileges, there can be an almost endless supply of praise and other social rewards. It takes very little time to encourage positive behaviors in children. A simple statement such as, "I like the way you are playing quietly—what a patient girl!" or a well-timed hug is all that is required.

Teaching parents how to praise and encourage their children begins in the Baby and Toddler Programs and continues throughout the subsequent programs. Parents are encouraged to have their positive statements outnumber their criticisms or corrections by ten to one. In other words, parents are taught to spend more time praising, describing, and strengthening the "positive opposite" behaviors in their children with their attention, coaching and praise than giving attention to negative behaviors. They learn to give praise that is genuine, specific, and focused on the child's efforts or small steps toward the age appropriate goals parents have set for their children. Sometimes parents will say their child is so "bad" that they can find nothing to praise. This is especially true for parents who suffer from depression. Therapists will need to help these parents list positive behaviors that can be praised and give them practice first looking for them on the video vignettes and then rehearsing the positive language. It might not occur to some parents the children are working hard when they are struggling to put on their shoes or shirt, or waiting to eat breakfast, or listening to their instructions and complying to them. Without praise these efforts toward the positive behaviors are likely to disappear or be replaced with misbehavior, which is more likely to get a response.

Remember to Build Up Your Child's Social Bank Account

Self-Praise. Parents who don't praise their children often don't praise themselves. If they listened to their internal self-talk, they might find that they rarely or never say things to themselves like, "I handled

Remember to Build Up Your Self Confidence Bank Account

that conflict calmly and rationally," or "I've been very patient in this situation." Instead, parents are quick to criticize themselves for every flaw or mistake they make. Therapists help self-critical parents learn to stop these negative thoughts and focus instead on "positive opposite" thoughts. Parents learn to self-praise by focusing on their successes and solutions to problems rather than their mistakes, and also by creating positive experiences and expectations for themselves. When parents are able to do this, they are more likely to do the same for their children. Therapists help parents in groups to praise themselves by doing a buddy check-in with another parent. During the buddy check-in parents share a success they have had that week doing the home activities or using something they learned in the class. These successes are then shared with the whole group and can be written on a gold coin and added to their personal bank account to illustrate how investing in themselves helps their children too.

Motivating Children Through Incentives (Preschool and School-Age BASIC Programs)

Content related to incentives and rewards is started in the Preschool Program with spontaneous, surprise rewards, and celebrations for positive behaviors or accomplishments. For instance a child might receive a sticker for sitting on the potty or get an extra bedtime story for putting on her pajamas cooperatively. Incentives are covered more extensively in the School Age Program where parents plan the reward in advance with the child, as in a contract or reward system. Research indicates that with new and difficult behaviors, parental praise is sometimes not sufficient reinforcement to change a child's behavior. This is particularly true for children with conduct problems or those who have experienced neglect or abuse in the past. In these cases, a combination of tangible and non-tangible incentives can be used as motivation. Some examples of incentives might be a small toy, playing a favorite game with a parent, having a friend over, a sticker, additional special time with a parent, baking cookies, renting a movie, or getting to plan a favorite dinner menu. During parenting sessions parents brainstorm a list of low or no-cost incentives that they believe will motivate their children (particular emphasis is placed on incentives that involve a parent-child activity). When teaching parents about using incentives, therapists stress the importance of continuing to provide coaching, positive attention, and praise to build their relationship and strengthen their attachment. Of course, time with the parent will only work as a reward if this foundational work has been and continues to be done. Once children are successful at achieving the desired behavior, the therapist helps parents learn how to gradually phase out the tangible rewards and use their coaching, praise and encouragement to maintain the newly learned behaviors.

It is important that the therapist help parents develop incentive plans that are developmentally appropriate for their children. All parents pick behaviors that they want to see more of (often these are the "positive opposites" of their identified problem behaviors). Therapists help parents to make these positive behaviors specific and obtainable. For instance the goal of "being good in the grocery store" would be further explored, clarified and stated as "stay near cart, use inside voice, and keep hands to self." Young children receive immediate small rewards while older children may be working for slightly longer term rewards that can be earned over several days or even a week. Parents work to involve their children in the plan, while also learning to maintain parental control over the process. It is a typical mistake for parents to put too many behaviors on a reward chart or to list a lack of negative behavior, such as no hitting, rather than the positive opposite behavior such as gentle touch. For older children, especially those with conduct problems, reward charts can lead to fights over whether the child earned the reward or not; it is important that therapists help parents to make these contracts simple, clear, and achievable, so that parents are able to keep control of them.

Make these contracts simple, clear, and achievable.

Self-Rewards. Parents also create a list of incentives or rewards for themselves for following through with their goals, incentive systems, charts, child-play times, and parenting work each week. These rewards might include a bubble bath; 30 minutes of uninterrupted time to exercise, read, or meditate; time visiting with a friend, in person or on the phone; movie night at home or in the theater. Parents who have partners are encouraged to work on these rewards together, either by taking turns caring for the children, or getting a babysitter and spending the time together. Parents without partners brainstorm other ways that they can get support to refuel their energy. Sometimes parents in the group pair up with a buddy to give each other the reward of a break from parenting. Within the group therapists help parents celebrate their successes and efforts by giving out special prizes. Prizes for this content include things the children might enjoy (e.g, play dough, crayons or markers, stickers) and items parents might like for themselves such as lotion, special tea, chocolate, or an award certificate.

SUMMARY OF FOUNDATION OF PYRAMID

Depending on the age and developmental level of the children and the parents' prior knowledge and cultural experiences, the topics and parenting tools covered in the first 7-9 weeks include: child-directed play, academic, persistence, social and emotion coaching, physical warmth, labeled praise, tangible rewards, self-praise and rewards, and incentives and behavioral principles such as the "attention rule" (i.e. giving more attention to positive behavior than negative behavior), modeling, shaping behavior, prompting social interactions, redirection, practice and the fun principle. The Baby Program spends more time on building positive parent-baby attachment through sensitive and nurturing responding in baby-led play interactions. The Toddler Program provides more emphasis on various coaching methods while the School Age Program includes coaching during "special time" and a focus on reward and incentive systems charts. The objective of this first half of the BASIC training is to foster positive relationships and bonding between parents and children and to help parents know how to promote their children's language and social skills, as well as emotional literacy, and academic readiness. In essence, parents are building the positive skills needed to replace the inappropriate behaviors that they want to decrease. Behavior problems often improve in this part of the program even though discipline has not been directly discussed. Therapists frequently refer to the pyramid (see earlier figure of parenting pyramid) at the start of the next phase of the parenting program in order to remind parents of all the tools they have already learned to build a stable relationship with their child (play, coaching, positive reinforcement). Doing this also reinforces how important positive scaffolding is for developing this foundation that further parenting tools will rest upon in future sessions.

Parents are building the positive skills needed to replace the inappropriate behaviors that they want to decrease.

Content of the Incredible Years® Parenting Pyramid™ Foundation~ Typical Parent Questions

This chapter presents a number of questions and objections that parents frequently raise when discussing the foundational tools of the parenting program pyramid. The intention of this chapter is to help therapists prepare for parent group discussions. Therapists who provide a clear rationale for the parenting tools in discussion and who explain how they address parents' personal goals are more successful at enhancing parents' intrinsic motivation to change. If parents do not ask these questions, the therapist should raise some of these issues to foster deeper discussion and problem solving. Therapists may probe more deeply by asking open-ended questions, listening reflectively, and promoting self-reflection. The details of each major content area are described earlier in Chapter Four. The therapy process and methods are described in Chapter Eight.

CHILD-DIRECTED PLAY SKILLS

Beginning with the first parent group session, parents are given a home assignment to play with their child for at least 10 minutes every day using a child-directed approach. During the first session, the therapist and parents brainstorm the benefits of child-directed play rich with language descriptions. During the subsequent session, the therapist and parents discuss their success in doing the home play activity and explore most common obstacles or pitfalls parents encountered when doing this play assignment.

Questions Parents Ask About Child-Directed Play with Children

Questions from parents fall into different categories. Typically, some parents will question the importance of taking time to play with their children, either out of genuine curiosity or a worry that playing will not help their identified problems. Others will grant the importance of playing with their children, but will raise questions about the recommended approach—either questioning the approach based on its divergence from their assumptions about the value of structured parent-directed play, or based on their experience encountering problems when they tried the child-directed approach. Some parents will raise objections that reflect a fear of exacerbating the child's ongoing behavior problems, worrying that following their child's lead means losing their ability to control their child even further. Such parents may be somewhat hostile or resistant to talking about child-directed play because they want to learn about discipline strategies to control their child's behavior problems and feel play interactions are not focusing on their goals. Therapists must expect to hear some of these objections and worries from parents and be prepared to listen to them and carefully explain the rationale for the approach and how it addresses the parents' goals. This questioning

Questioning is a healthy sign that parents feel safe in the group.

is a healthy sign that parents feel safe in the group and are engaged in the collaborative process of learning. The following is a representative sample of some of the questions a therapist may encounter.

Shouldn't we be talking about discipline?

"I don't get it! I came here for help with my child's behavior problems, and we're talking about child-directed play. What does this have to do with helping my child improve his behavior? He already has too much control; won't this make him worse? Besides, my child has been so impossible that, to tell you the truth, I don't feel like playing with him. Not only that, he doesn't seem to want to play with me either!"

Child-directed play is a highly effective and positive way to foster young children's major developmental milestones.

When talking about child-directed play we are also, in a roundabout way, discussing a discipline approach. The root of the word "discipline" means "to learn," and in this program discipline is defined as "training that develops self-control and efficacy." The child-directive approach to play provides children with opportunities for legitimate control and power to use appropriate social behaviors. During effective child-directed play, appropriate social behaviors and emotional regulation receive parental attention, while inappropriate behaviors are ignored or redirected. This results in decreased behavior problems and increased social and emotional competence. Child-directed play is a highly effective and positive way to foster young children's major developmental milestones such as secure attachment with parents, language skills, and social relationship skills. Child-directed play also promotes children's unique sense of self, while scaffolding their intense drive for exploration.

The basic principle behind the development of many common behavior problems is a child's need for attention. Children will work for attention from others, especially their parents, whether it is positive (praise and reward) or negative (criticism and punishment). If children do not get positive attention for appropriate social behavior, then they will work to gain negative attention by misbehaving. If parents actively participate in child-directed play, thereby giving their child positive attention, the child will have less need to resort to negative behavior in order to gain their parents' attention. In fact, many parents reported that when they began giving their child a regular dose of child-directed play each day, their children were better behaved. Furthermore, many parents reported that their children eventually began to play more independently, and so parents in turn found more personal time for themselves.

Therapists encourage parents to move beyond the helplessness or resentment they feel and energized to take the first step towards changing the negative dynamic.

As for parents who do not want to play with their difficult child, or feel their child does not want to play with them, it is important to note that it may be genuinely difficult for parents to make time to play positively with their children if they are angry at them for breaking a window, biting another child or displaying other undesirable behaviors. Parents may also be depressed about how their child is making family life miserable or find their child's hyperactive and impulsive play interactions intolerable; however, children will detect these negative feelings and may in turn display a lack of interest in playing with their parents. This is a negative stalemate situation. It can be helpful to let parents express their negative feelings towards spending time with their children. Many parents will feel guilt and embarrassment at having these feelings and will find reassurance in the fact that these are normal responses, they are not alone and that they are not "bad" parents. The next job for the therapist is to help parents move beyond the helplessness or resentment they feel and to energize them to take the first step towards changing the negative dynamic with their child. It is a mistake for a parent to wait for the child to break the negative cycle. Someone has to end the negative interactions, and it is not likely to be the child: it is up to the parent. The parent needs to watch for moments of positive interaction and capitalize on these opportunities by engaging in child-directed play. As these playtimes become more frequent, comfortable and positive, children will look forward to them, as will parents. Therapists can predict these positive outcomes for parents, letting them know that if they consistently work at these child-directed interactions, they are likely to feel a shift in their relationship with their children.

But playing with my child is a waste of time.

"Let's get real. Sure, my child behaves better if I play with him, but I can't be expected to just sit around and play all day! I've got a lot of other things to do! Isn't play with friends just as good?"

Parents, especially parents of oppositional and highly aggressive children, may find it difficult to see the value in taking precious time out of their busy and stressful lives for something as seemingly frivolous as play. Therapists need to be realistic in their expectations and help parents establish goals that they can be successful in achieving. At the UW Parenting clinic, we generally asked parents to do a minimum of 10 minutes of child-directed play with their child each day. The therapist helped parents to see this time as an investment in their child's future, not unlike regularly putting a deposit in the bank. If parents work to build up their child's psychological "bank account" through regular play times, they will experience behavioral "payoffs." In other words, as their child becomes secure in the knowledge that he will have regular play time with his parents and the parents' time with him is valued, he will have less need to devise inappropriate ways of getting attention. Parents may be persuaded to invest that time if it is pointed out to them some extra attention now may even buy some additional personal time later.

For some parents, particularly those with a child whose hyperactive, impulsive, or oppositional temperament clashes with their own temperament, even 10 minutes a day is more than is achievable at first. If this is the case, they are encouraged to play in 2-3 minute intervals at various times during the day when they notice their child is playing calmly. Over time they will gradually build their children's focus and concentration on an activity and slowly increase their own time playing with them. For other

A predictable routine for play with a parent helps the child feel secure.

parents who have busy schedules and never seem to have time to play, it can be helpful for the therapist to work with them to choose a specific time of day to schedule play, such as just before bedtime. Setting up a predictable routine for play helps the child feel secure because he knows when he is going to receive some attention.

As for the question of whether peer play can replace parent child-directed play: both types of interactions are important for children's social, emotional and cognitive development. In peer play toddlers and many preschoolers engage in parallel play, each child playing independently with little awareness of the other. As children develop socially, they typically become more interested in other children and start to initiate play with peers and gradually become more cooperative and more competitive. During the preschool and school-age developmental phase, peer interactions help children to gradually learn important relationship skills such as how to resolve disputes, help, share, take turns, and to communicate feelings. For many typically developing children, social skills are learned through trial and error, feedback from peers, and some guidance from parents and teachers. However, some children have more difficulties with peer play, such as children with conduct problems, ADHD, or developmental and language delays. These children are more impulsive, more aggressive, less cooperative and friendly, and thus are more likely to experience peer rejection and isolation.

While all children need child-directed play with their parents, children with more social difficulties particularly need this parent-child play time because the benefits of child-directed play with parents are quite different from the benefits of peer play. When children play together, each child is operating at his or her own developmental level, and children are naturally self-centered. A child with good social skills may share, take turns, or wait, but if the peer does not respond in kind, the child is likely to give up, lash out, or refuse to continue playing. Thus, children with social difficulties frequently frustrate their peers, and consequently do not get the support and scaffolding they need to learn more appropriate behaviors. During child-directed play times, the parent focuses his or her attention entirely on the child. During this time the parent can help nurture and support the child's exploration and discoveries as well as efforts to solve problems and communicate feelings. A parent can also model positive behavior, respond positively to any prosocial attempts (however clumsily), and redirect inappropriate behavior without giving it attention. This builds the parent-child relationship and strengthens the child's self-esteem and self-confidence. These benefits are unlikely to occur during peer play between typical children, and even less likely during peer-play with a child with behavior problems or developmental delays.

But play with children is boring!

"Play with my child is so boring—she keeps doing the same things over and over again. Should I structure her play to make it more stimulating?"

When babies and young children are playing, they tend to repeat the same activity over and over again. Remember the baby who kept dropping her spoon on the floor to see where it went? Or the toddler who kept repeatedly filling and emptying a box? How often have you groaned inwardly when asked to read the same story yet again? Certainly, repetitive play soon comes to bore most parents. It is often tempting for parents to quicken the pace by introducing a new idea or a more sophisticated way of using a toy, however therapists should caution parents that this temptation arises from the parent's need, not the child's. It is the parent who feels a need for more stimulation. Children need to take the time to explore, think, rehearse, and practice an activity over and over in order to discover how it works, master it, and to eventually feel confident about their abilities. If they are shortchanged in this repetition and pushed too quickly into a new activity, they may feel frustrated and give up playing because they feel incompetent. Children may also feel that they're not able to meet their parents' expectations, or the challenge of the task. The end result is that the child's important cognitive learning process of exploration and discovery is interrupted, resulting in less learning, decreased self-esteem, and a lack of confidence.

Engaging in child-directed play means parents must pace their play interactions according to their child's tempo. The therapist can encourage parents to slow down and allow plenty of time for their children to practice an activity and to use their imagination. Caution parents not to push a child simply because they are bored. Parents should wait to change the play until the child decides to explore something different. Remind parents that many children move much more slowly from one idea to another than adults.

On the other hand, some children are impulsive, hyperactive, inattentive, and cannot concentrate on one activity for more than a few minutes. They rapidly go on to one new activity after another. This can be exhausting for parents and also does not provide the child with the experience of focusing and exploration. If the parent tries to match the child's frenetic speed in this case, the interaction can spiral out of control. Parents of such children should be encouraged to stay calm and keep their own pace controlled. They should still try to follow their child's lead (without forcing their child to attend to one activity) but their calm and patient interest in each object that the child explores may help the child to focus. When the idea of academic and persistence coaching is explained, parents will be encouraged to coach their active child's persistence and focus, with the eventual goal of extending the child's attention span.

But don't children *need* structure in their play?

"I always thought that you should use play times to teach your children things like colors, shapes, and rules. How will children learn if you don't structure their play and correct their mistakes?"

Some parents believe it is important to structure their child's play by turning it into a lesson: how to build the castle the *right* way, how to make the perfect valentine, how to complete a puzzle correctly. Perhaps they believe that they are more effective as teachers or make play a worthwhile activity in this way, however this emphasis on the "right" or "best" way to do something produces a string of commands, instructions, and corrections that usually make the experience unrewarding for both the child and the adult.

Consider, for instance, what happens when Lisa, a 4-year-old girl and her mother settle down to play with Lisa's new dollhouse. Mom says, "First let's put the fridge and stove in the kitchen." Lisa suggests a place for the kitchen, and her mother responds, "Okay, and now all these other kitchen things must go over there too." She then goes on to say, "And the living room furniture must go here." As Lisa begins to put some of the furniture in the living room, her mother shows her where to put the bathroom items. Soon Lisa will either start refusing to comply out of a need to establish her own individuality or she will stop playing, sit back, and watch her mother organize everything in the correct rooms. By now, Lisa's mother is doing all the playing. She has given Lisa little opportunity for thinking about how to organize the furnishings, whether conventionally or creatively. Further, she has missed the opportunity to learn about her daughter, to discover what Lisa might have wanted to do with the dollhouse. Had she waited, she might have found that Lisa's play was highly imaginative, with beds paced outside for "camping" or living room furniture in every room.

Therapists help parents to imitate their child's actions, and do what they request.

The first step to effective play with children is for parents to recognize the importance of following the child's lead. Letting the child explore their own ideas and imagination, rather than imposing a structure by giving commands, rules or instructions is paramount. The therapist can suggest to parents that they try not to teach their children anything in play. Instead, parents should try to imitate their children's actions and do what the child requests. It can be especially hard for the parent of a child with behavior problems to let go of control during play, for fear that the child will become disruptive. The therapist must explain to parents that by accepting and going along with their children's rules and ideas, they are actually modeling compliance for their children. On the other hand, if parents try to impose their own ideas on their child's play, they are actually modeling non-cooperative behavior. Parents quickly discover that when they sit back and give their child a chance to exercise their imagination, their child becomes more involved and interested in playing, as well as more creative and cooperative. This approach not only strengthens friendly play interactions, but also helps the child become more compliant outside of the play situation when the parent really does need to enforce some structure on what they can and can't do.

What if children want parents to structure their play?
"Usually he insists on my leading the play or else he doesn't seem to know what to do. What can I do? "

When parent-child play has typically been structured by the parent, it may be difficult and frustrating for the child when the parent begins to take a less directive approach. If a child is used to playing according to her parents' rules, suddenly being expected to come up with her own ideas for play may leave her feeling insecure, unsure what to do, and anxious about making mistakes. Most likely, the child will try to get the parent to respond as usual by asking, "Dad, you show me how," "Mom, I can't do it. I need your help to do it, " or "Mom, I don't know what to do." If this is the case, the therapist may suggest that the parent begin by complying to the child's request and offering some assistance, but gradually withdraw parent control while simultaneously reinforcing the child's independent activities and creativity. For example, the parent might start by saying, "I can help you. How about I hold the bottom in place while you add the blocks." Then, at the child's next request, the parent might say, "I'm happy to help. Can you tell me where I should put these?" With time and parental support and reinforcement, the child will become confident of her decisions and ability to play more independently.

On the other hand, sometimes children ask parents to help them because they are worried that if they don't engage them in the activity they will not continue to play with them. As soon as a child sees that their parent is genuinely interested in their play explorations, allowing them to take the lead while still giving them undivided attention, the child relaxes and enjoys sharing their discoveries.

Should parents play anything the child wants?
"All my child plays with is guns. I hate that aggressive stuff! Are you saying that I need to go along with this and pretend to shoot people too? I'm not comfortable with that."

In following the child's lead, there are times that the parent will be asked to play something that s/he objects to or isn't comfortable playing. For example, typically we hear mothers who don't want to play aggressive shooting games and fathers who don't want to play dress up baby dolls with their children. Because a child will pick up easily on a parents' discomfort or inability to enjoy the playtime, a good rule of thumb is that if the child's suggested play activity makes the parent very uncomfortable, it is probably a good idea to play something else. In the gun example above the parent might say matter-of-factly, "I would like to play something other than guns. Do you have some ideas?" If the child cannot think of anything else, the parent might suggest several things that the child usually likes to do, such as "How about that Lego model you were working on?" or "How about that new puzzle you got for your birthday?" It is important in these instances not to engage in a power struggle or argument with the child about guns. The parent should try to divert and distract the child to something else. If the child is persistent, it may even be necessary for the parent to start independently playing with something else as if it were a very enjoyable activity. Soon the child will want to play along and the parent can gradually become less directive.

What if children want to engage in aggressive play? Should parents follow their lead?

"My child only wants to wrestle with me or run around shooting guns. Will this make him more aggressive?"

Certainly aggressive toys bring out children's aggressive behaviors, but even if parents do not allow their children to have guns or aggressive toys, frequently children, especially boys, will act them out in their fantasy play. Whether parents actively promote aggressive behaviors by giving children aggressive toys or merely play along with an aggressive fantasy, they are reinforcing aggressive play. If parents are uncomfortable with this kind of play and want to decrease it, they should minimize the amount of attention and reinforcement their children get for aggressive behavior through their use of differential attention. For the child who is highly aggressive in play, the parent can begin by giving attention to and praising nonaggressive play behaviors such as talking quietly, being gentle, helping, and walking slowly. If the child begins to yell, shoot or be aggressive with a toy, the parent can withdraw her attention by not commenting or playing with something else. It is very important for the parent to return attention to the child as soon as he/she discontinues the aggressive behavior. This low-key differential attention is usually much more effective at minimizing and redirecting aggressive behavior than trying to make children stop their pretend play with guns.

Wrestling is another matter. Many fathers especially enjoy wrestling with their children. This is usually a good time for both the children and parents and does not need to be omitted out of fear of encouraging aggression. However, parents of children with aggressive behavior need to exercise caution, as their children may become so over-excited or dysregulated during wrestling, putting them at risk of hurting themselves or others. Parents will need to monitor this and de-escalate wrestling play before it gets out of control.

Don't children need to learn how to lose?

"I get into such battles with him when we play board games. He cheats and makes up rules, and then falls apart when he doesn't win. Don't I need to teach him how to lose? What's going to happen when he plays games with other children? I really feel I need to teach my child how to follow the rules so that he doesn't run into problems thinking he can change the rules whenever he wants with others."

Most parents occasionally find themselves in a power struggle with their children over who won a game and what the rules are. To some extent this is inevitable, but many parents unwittingly set up a competitive relationship with their children. For instance, when playing board games parents may feel it is necessary to teach their children to play by the rules and to be good losers. Or parents may simply do their part of an activity or game so well that their children feel incompetent. Consider a mother and son playing with building blocks. For a few minutes the child is happily absorbed in getting the first wall of his house to stay up. When he finishes the wall, he looks to his mother for approval only to find that she has completed a whole house. Besides feeling less competent, the child also feels he is somehow involved in a competition with his mom, and one he is not equipped to win. At this point, the child may give up playing or may try to gain control of the situation in other ways, such as having a tantrum or knocking down the house his mother built.

Therapists may find it helpful to teach parents about some of Piaget's discoveries about children's cognitive development (Piaget, 1962). Young children, ages 2-6 years, who are in the "preoperational stage" of cognitive development, do not understand the permanency of rules and sequences of board and card games. They frequently confuse fantasy and reality. It is not until children are in the "concrete operational" stage of cognitive development (ages 7 to 8) that they begin to show signs of true cooperative interaction. Even then, some children's understanding of rules may still be somewhat vague. Every child's developmental progress is unique. Nonetheless, young children can enjoy playing a structured game with adults as long as excessive competition or concern with rules is avoided. If young children come up with different rules for a game that allow them to win, this should be permitted. Parents don't need to worry about their children not learning to lose; many other aspects of their lives will teach them that. If parents cooperate with children's rules and model acceptance, children are then more likely to go along with parents' rules in other situations. Finally, therapists should encourage parents of children with behavior problems to initially avoid competitive games with their children, and instead play unstructured activities. For early school-age children (ages 6-8), when playtimes are going well, parents might want to try some board games, as long as they can avoid power struggles. The key point is for the parents and children to be having fun together.

Isn't this unfair to my other children?

"I'm a single parent with several children. I try to play with one child, and my other children act up for attention."

Children in a family watch to see who is getting attention for what. If children notice that one sibling is getting special daily playtimes with a parent, it is inevitable that they will want the same treatment. If at all feasible, the parent should have separate playtimes with each child. This fosters children's sense of uniqueness and individuality in their relationships with their parents. If this is not feasible due to the number of children or the lack of a parenting partner to help, it is still possible to use these child-directed play strategies while playing with several children at once. During the play sessions the parent must go back and forth between the children, giving attention and praise to each child individually.

Do I need fancy toys for my child?
"I don't have the money to buy Duplos or bristle blocks."

The therapist should help the parent understand that playing effectively with their children is not about having fancy or expensive toys. In fact, children seem to like common household objects better than anything else. For example, cups, pots and pans, cereal boxes, wooden spoons, a bucket of water, and some home made play dough (or sand and mud), old shoes, clothes and hats, or a broken phone or piece of technology will do the trick. The value of the play experience for the child has to do with the parents' child-directed approach and warm, supportive attention; the parent is the real toy.

If I let my child tell me what to do during play, am I training him to be bossy?
"I'm afraid that if I let my child take the lead in play I will be reinforcing his obnoxious, bossy behavior. He'll say, 'Don't put that there!' or he'll grab something out of my hand and say, 'Give me that!' He's always told me what to do so I don't see how this will help him be more compliant, quite the opposite!"

Some parents are worried that if they follow their child's lead during play, they will encourage them to be bossy and manipulative. The truth is that children are not made bossy by such an approach. In fact, the opposite is true: parents who decrease their own bossiness in play interactions, going along with their children's ideas, are modeling compliance and acceptance of others' requests and ideas. This parental support for children's ideas not only increases children's self-esteem and confidence, but also is likely to be imitated by children. In fact, a child whose parents demonstrate a sharing and respectful attitude is more likely to be compliant and accepting of their parents' requests in other situations including with their peers.

How should I end the play session?

"My child doesn't want to stop the play! Every time we end, it's a real hassle with screams and protests; so much so that I don't even want to start the play for fear of the ending."

Sometimes parents are reluctant to play with their children because they fear that there will be a big tantrum when they stop. The therapist should help parents to prepare their child for the end of a play session. Five minutes before the end of a play period a parent may say, "In a few minutes it will be time for me to stop playing with you." Parents need to be prepared to ignore any protests or arguments, and do their best to distract their child by focusing on something else. When 5 minutes have passed the parent may simply state, "Now it's time for me to stop playing. I had fun playing with you. We'll play again tomorrow." The parent should walk away and ignore any pleading.

Once children find out that they cannot manipulate their parents into playing longer, their protests will subside. Therapists should share this with parents and prepare them to ignore protests or arguments. Moreover, when the child realizes that there is a regular play period with their parent every day, they'll feel less of a need to protest because they know there will be another opportunity to play with a parent tomorrow. The therapist should also remind the parents that a child who protests at the end of their play time is giving the signal that he had such fun that he doesn't want to stop! Because children are still working on emotional regulation skills, it is natural for them to protest more loudly when they are asked to stop doing something they find fun.

ACADEMIC, PERSISTENCE, SOCIAL AND EMOTION COACHING

Once parents become familiar with the value of child-directed play, they learn next about the ideal kind of communication to use during these play times. As we described in Chapter Four, parents learn four types of coaching methods in roughly 4-5 group sessions. Academic and persistence coaching helps strengthen children's language development, persistence and patience with a frustrating activity, ability to sustain focus, and some school readiness skills such as numbers, colors, shapes and reading skills. Social coaching helps children learn friendship skills such as sharing, helping, taking turns, waiting, and teamwork. Emotion coaching helps children learn emotional literacy in the form of expressing their own feelings, beginning to take the perspective of others, and regulating their own emotions. Using these coaching methods helps children achieve the major developmental milestones as well as strengthen their relationships with their parents.

This is a new language for most parents, and at first it may seem awkward, artificial and uncomfortable. Therapists need to help parents to understand the tremendous value of coaching for their children as part of the core foundational piece of the parenting pyramid.

Questions Parents Have about Coaching Methods

Isn't Descriptive Commenting just psychological jargon?

"Descriptive commenting seems pretty weird to me, it feels artificial and phony. Even my child asks me to stop talking so funny. I don't really understand why I should do this. When I ask my child questions, I feel I know what he has learned. I don't see how descriptive commenting is more helpful than question-asking in helping my child learn."

Descriptive commenting is a running commentary on a child's behaviors, actions and feelings and can often sound like a sports announcer's play-by-play description of a game. Because this is a novel way of communicating for most people, parents often feel uncomfortable and artificial when they first attempt to interact with their child in this way. However, this is merely the awkwardness anyone feels whenever attempting something unfamiliar. Remember learning a different language, or learning to drive a car? The discomfort of using descriptive commenting will diminish as parents practice using this new language in a variety of situations. If parents are persistent in learning to use descriptive commenting, they will find that their children come to love this kind of attention.

When parents start using descriptive commenting, many children notice that their parents are talking to them differently. Children who have difficulty accepting change may ask their parents to "stop talking so weird." Parents should not be deterred by this negative response. After all, when a family member behaves differently, often times the rest of the family will initially resist the change in an effort to revert back to what is familiar and safe. However, over time, this form of communication will become the status quo in parent-child interactions and may also be imitated by the children in their communication with siblings and friends.

Descriptive commenting is also more effective than question asking at teaching vocabulary and actively encouraging language development. For instance, a parent might say, "You're putting the red truck in the blue garage. Now it's getting gas." Soon parents will find that their children are spontaneously imitating their commenting and narrating the color of things they are using. Parents can then praise their knowledge and their children will feel excited about their accomplishments. Occasionally parents have a tendency to ask a string of questions while playing: "What animal is that?" "How many spots does it have?" "What shape is that?" "Where does it go?" Through such questions, parents usually intend to help their children learn. But all too often it has the reverse effect, causing the child to become defensive, to retreat into silence, and to be reluctant to talk freely.

Providing parents with language cue cards and scripts for the specific social, emotional academic goals of their child is especially useful.

In fact, when parents already know the answer, question asking is a command because it requires the child to perform. Queries that ask children to define what they are doing or making are in a special category —they often occur before the child has even thought about the final product or had a chance to explore his/her ideas. By asking the question, the parent puts the emphasis on the product rather than the process of play. Descriptive commenting, on the other hand, is a nonthreatening way of communicating with children and giving them attention that follows the process of play without demanding performance.

I find I keep wanting to ask my child questions, and when I stop I don't know what else to say.

"I hear myself asking a lot of questions but find it difficult to know what else to say. I don't know what social behaviors or emotions to talk about."

The therapist should explain to parents that it is quite normal to find this new communication approach awkward at first; it is a new language. Helping parents to brainstorm scripts for each type of coaching can be helpful. Tailoring parents' language cue cards for the specific social, emotional academic goals of their child is especially useful. For example, the parent of a child who is withdrawn, fearful, and anxious may use emotional language focused on bravery and courage or social coaching to help her initiate interactions with peers. The parent of a child who is angry and aggressive may use emotion coaching focused on times when he is calm and patient or social coaching when he is gentle and willing to share. These scripts can be written down and taken home for parents to practice. There are also coaching scripts that can be used by parents in practice sessions and at home.

I don't understand why I should coach more positive emotions than negative emotions. Won't that lead to children who are afraid to talk about negative emotions?

"In my family I could never talk about negative emotions. We could only talk about positive things. Now I have trouble bringing up any conflict situation with anyone. I want it to be all right for my children to talk about their worries and problems."

Actually, helping children to be comfortable talking about all their feelings, both comfortable and uncomfortable is exactly the goal of emotion coaching! Emotion coaching will help the parent with the above concerns to meet his or her goals. It is important for the therapist to help parents think about what emotion language their child already uses (if any) as well as the emotion language they model for their child. The task for parents is to build a rich and varied bank of emotion vocabulary. The therapist begins by having parents work in their groups to come up with a list of positive emotion words such as: confident, brave, calm, patient, forgiving, caring, loving and loved, happy, pleased, excited, and joyful. Next parents work on their list of negative or uncomfortable emotion vocabulary such as: angry, frustrated, sad, fearful, worried, hurt, anxious, insecure, embarrassed, or mean. The value of children developing this emotion literacy is that they can articulate their feelings to others rather than act them out in inappropriate ways. The focus on labeling positive feelings is suggested because people are usually more adept at labeling negative ones. In this case children often learn that they will get more parental attention for angry feelings than calm ones. In most cases, children rarely have their positive feelings labeled (e.g., "You seem so proud that you were able to get that puzzle finished." or "I can see from your jumping body that you are excited about going to school today!") Instead, parents may be more likely to respond to children's upset or dysregulated feeling states. Parents are encouraged to try to label 3-4 positive emotions for every negative or uncomfortable one.

Parents are encouraged to try to label 3-4 positive emotions for every negative or uncomfortable one.

Parents also learn to be thoughtful about the way that they label uncomfortable or upset emotions. They learn to pair the labeling of negative feelings with a coping statement. This validates the feeling and helps the child understand and identify her emotions while also providing her with a way for her to manage the feeling. For example, the parent might say, "You look frustrated with that math problem, but you are staying calm and you keep trying hard. I think you are going to figure it out." In other words, the parent labels the feeling without letting it paralyze the child's efforts and predicts that the child will be able to manage the frustration, continue working hard, and eventually be successful. If the parent said, "you look really frustrated," the child might be more likely to remain stuck in the frustrated state and give up. This approach helps children to recognize and talk about uncomfortable emotions, while teaching them that they will be able to cope with and work through these difficult feelings.

At first, children will need considerable help as they learn to manage uncomfortable or unhappy emotions. Emotion coaching is one way to provide children with the support they need when they are upset. It is important for the group to also talk about how to recognize when a child is too upset to be able to benefit from coaching (for example, a child who is in the midst of a temper tantrum). At these times, parents may need to give a child time and space to calm down before providing coaching and support.

I need help knowing how to coach my child with ADHD.

"My child has ADHD and is very active and impulsive. He is inattentive and doesn't listen to what I say anyway. What kind of coaching should I use with him?"

Coaching a child with ADHD is difficult because such children are constantly on the move, don't seem to listen, and rarely respond to the parent speaking. Research suggests that children with ADHD are delayed socially and emotionally. While these children may be intellectually bright, their social-emotional development is often delayed by about 1/3 of their chronological age: in other words, a 6-year-old may be more like a 4-year-old socially. Persistence and social coaching will be very helpful for these children because it will help them stick longer with an activity and learn some of the social skills that seem to come more easily for the typical child (for example, sharing, waiting, listening to others). Additionally, children with ADHD often love this type of coaching and parental attention because it does not require them to respond to questions or commands. This coaching approach helps strengthen the parent-child relationship because the child feels that the parent is following everything he is doing.

During the parent group, it is useful to have a discussion about the variety of ways that children will absorb and respond to descriptive commenting. Many children with social emotional delays, particularly those with attention problems, may appear to ignore or fail to notice their parent's comments. These children may not look at their parents during play, or give any indication that they have heard the comments. Therapists can reassure parents that children are hearing much of what they say, even if they don't show it. These children may simply find concurrent visual and verbal contact to be too much stimulation at once.

Couldn't imaginative play result in crazy behavior?

"I see my child talking to make-believe friends and making up all kinds of things that aren't true. Isn't that a sign of emotional disturbance? Isn't it a form of lying?"

Some adults are reluctant to engage in imaginative play: to crawl on the floor making train noises or to act out fairy tales or to use puppets. They may feel silly and embarrassed. Fathers, in particular, seem to feel uncomfortable playing house or dress up games with their children. Some parents have told us that they consider make-believe to be a sign of emotional disturbance. This is far from the truth. When children engage in make-believe play, they are learning to manipulate representations of things rather than the concrete objects themselves. Most healthy youngsters are beginning to do this by the age of 3, and some as early as 18 months. Imaginary companions are common among 4-year-olds. Play that involves fantasy steadily increases into middle childhood (about age 8) and then begins to disappear.

It is important for parents to encourage this kind of play because it helps children to develop a variety of cognitive, emotional, and social skills. Parents should be encouraged to allow boxes to become palaces, and action figures to turn into relatives, friends, or favorite cartoon characters. Fantasy helps children to think symbolically and gives them a better idea of what is real and what isn't. Puppet play helps children to experience the feelings or perspectives of someone else, which supports their understanding and sensitivity of others.

Therapists help parents understand the importance of imaginary play in promoting children's understanding of others' perspectives and empathy.

TEACHING PARENTS ABOUT PRAISE

Parents of children with behavior problems often find it hard to praise their children. Some parents believe that children should behave appropriately without adult intervention or that praise should be reserved for outstanding performance. These parents would never think of praising their children for playing quietly or for doing their chores without complaining. Other parents simply do not know how or when to give praise and encouragement. These parents may have received little praise from their own parents and because they are unaccustomed to hearing praise, the words may seem awkward or artificial. Or perhaps these parents are so stressed that they cannot see praiseworthy child behaviors when they do occur. It is the therapist's role to help these parents to look for positive behaviors and to praise them.

Sometimes parents will say that their child is so defiant and oppositional that they can find nothing to praise. Sometimes these are depressed parents who are seeing their child through their own negative lens. Other times, children may be exhibiting such high levels of intense negative behaviors that it is very hard for parents to see past this to the more subtle positive behaviors that are occurring. The goal is to help parents see that all children exhibit positive behavior some of the time, and that it is particularly important to notice and reinforce this behavior in children who also engage in high levels of negative behavior.

The role of the therapist is to teach parents to identify small positive behaviors and to praise them. Therapists first use the program vignettes to help parents learn to identify positive prosocial behaviors in a child other than their own. Therapists then encourage parents to look for any small positive behavior in their own child. Once parents have brainstormed concrete positive behaviors that could be praised (e.g., coming into the kitchen when called, putting on socks independently, hanging up backpack when reminded, putting dishes in the sink), they script statements to praise these behaviors. Next parents role-play using these specific praise statements (e.g., "Thank you for coming in here the first time I called you!" "I really appreciate the way that you followed directions." "You got your socks on all by yourself. I'm impressed!") It is important that each parent leave the session with an idea about a specific behavior that they will praise and with specific language examples for how to give this praise.

If parents are bringing children to childcare during the parenting session, therapists may model praising the child in front of the parent during pick-up and drop-offs. Later the therapist and parent can talk about the behaviors that the therapist noticed. Seeing the child through the positive lens of another person may help the parent to think differently about the child.

Regardless of whether the reinforcing act is attention, a hug, a smile, or verbal praise, the task of teaching a child a new behavior is long and difficult, and often very slow. It involves trying to praise the positive behavior every time it occurs. If there are two adults in the family, they should discuss which positive behavior they want to improve and how they will try to praise that behavior. With both parents participating, things should go more quickly. In addition, adults can double the impact of praise by praising children in front of other adults and by modeling self-praise.

Questions parents ask about praise

Don't children *know* how to behave?

"My child should know how to behave. Surely I don't need to praise her for everyday things like doing chores or sharing toys."

Rules or instructions about expected behavior are not sufficient to motivate behavior. Children learn to engage in particular behaviors when those behaviors receive attention and praise. Behaviors that parents notice and comment on positively are more likely to occur again. Behaviors that are ignored are less likely to be repeated. Expecting a child to behave well without some positive feedback is unrealistic. No good behavior should be taken for granted or it will soon disappear.

Doesn't praise spoil children?

"Isn't there a danger of spoiling my child with praise? Won't she learn to cooperate only for the sake of some external reward or adult approval?"

If there are any examples of children who have developed behavior problems as a result of receiving too much praise, I have not heard of them. Praise does not spoil children as long as the praise is genuine and thoughtful. Neither does praise train children to work only for external approval or rewards. In fact, I have observed the opposite to be true: children who are motivated only by external approval and attention tend to be those who have received little praise or reinforcement from adults.

The self-esteem of these children is so low that they are always seeking others' approval, or demanding a reward before complying with requests. On the other hand, children who are frequently and genuinely praised for their appropriate behaviors develop increased confidence in their abilities. This positive self-esteem eventually makes them less dependent on approval from adults and external rewards; they become increasingly capable of providing themselves with positive self-evaluation.

The principle that operates here is "you get what you give."

Children who receive positive messages from their parents are also more likely to praise others. This can have far-reaching effects. The principle that operates here is "you get what you give." Research indicates that children who give many positive statements to others are popular in school and receive many positive statements from others in return, which in turn bolsters their self-esteem. Because children imitate what they see and hear, if they frequently receive positive messages from their parents, they are more likely to internalize this form of thinking. Children in turn, use this positive "self-talk" to motivate themselves and communicate positively with the people around them. Of course, if parents are negative and critical, the opposite effect is possible. Children are likely to imitate this negative behavior and mirror it in their "negative self-talk" and critical communication with others.

Although I can firmly say that praise will not hurt children, there are ways of praising that are more or less effective. During the praise unit, therapists will help parents to develop a list of principles of effective praise, giving parents an understanding of how to give praise that will most benefit the child their behavior goals.

Isn't there a difference between encouragement and praise?
"I make a point of encouraging my child. Isn't that enough?"

Some parents believe that they should encourage their children but not praise them. Often these are the same parents who worry about spoiling or ending up with children who work only for external rewards. They make supportive comments, but try to avoid any statements that sound like praise. Out of concern that their encouragement might really be praise, they continually edit what they say. This creates an unnecessary complication, since children aren't likely to notice the difference. Parents should not worry about the form of their positive statements but simply give specific encouragement/praise whenever they notice a positive behavior.

Shouldn't praise be saved for really outstanding achievements?

"I prefer to save my praise for something that's really worth praising; an A in math, a perfectly made bed, or a really good drawing. Doesn't this help a child reach for the top?"

The problem with this attitude is that no person, child or adult, achieves perfection without much imperfection and many mistakes along the way. A goal is eventually attained by completing many small steps, and the process involves attempts, failures, and frustrations as well as achievements. A parent's focus should be on the process of drawing, *trying* to make the bed, or attempting to complete the math problems, rather than the end product. If parents do not offer praise for the process, the opportunity to praise may never come; the child of a parents who reserves their praise for perfection usually gives up trying before they have attained it. If parents can focus on the fact that their child is trying to make the bed, or do the dishes, or solve the problem, they will gradually shape his behavior in the desired direction. In other words, praise should reward the effort to achieve, not just the achievement.

Praise should reward the effort to achieve, not just the achievement.

In addition to praising children's attempts at doing something positive, therapists help parents praise their children's everyday mundane positive behaviors such as: talking with a quiet voice, going to bed when asked, complying to a request, saying "please," sharing a toy with a friend, reading a book, and helping pick up the bedroom. Therapists caution parents to avoid hoarding praises or saving them for outstanding achievements, lest the positive everyday behaviors disappear. No positive behavior should be taken for granted!

Avoid Combining Praise with Commands, Criticisms or Put-Downs.
"I tease my kids quite a bit when they do something well; is there a problem with this?"

Some people give praise and, without realizing it, undermine the praise by being sarcastic or combining it with a punishing word. This is one of the most disruptive things a parent can do in the reinforcement process. Some parents may be tempted to give a sarcastic or critical remark when their child tries to do something they haven't done before. For example, a parent might give one of the following praises: "Tony and Angie, you both came to the table the first time I asked you. That's great. But next time how about washing your face and hands first;" "Lee, I'm glad you're trying to make your bed, but you are doing it all wrong. Look how bumpy it is. Start with the sheets first, then straighten them, then put the pillow on..." or "I can't believe you finally managed to get your homework done."

In these examples, the parents may feel they have praised their children's efforts, but they have undermined their praise by adding commands and criticisms. Perhaps they think that giving praise allows them to "slip in" some criticism or instructions. In any case, the child will tend to hear the parents' comments as criticisms, not praise. Because children they will hear these comments as an indication that they didn't do a good enough job, they may react with discouragement and stop trying in the future. It is important that when parents give praise, it should be clear and unequivocal, without reminders of prior failures, observations about a less-than-perfect performance, or commands regarding future performance.

Can praise be used with children who consistently misbehave?
"My child has been consistently naughty. She is nothing but trouble. I can't start to praise her until she changes her ways."

When parents feel this way about their children, there is a stalemate situation. For example, consider father and son pair Sam and Steve. Sam is constantly irritated by the fact that his 8-year-old son, Steve, is defiant and uses smart talk when he asks him to do something. Moreover, Steve's teachers have reported their concern about his inattentiveness, aggressive behaviors with his peer group, and poor reading skills. As a result, Sam is never in a mood to notice that Steve regularly sets the table and completes his chores. If this were pointed out to him, Sam would likely say "So what?" because he has become totally focused on Steve as a disobedient and "difficult" child. With attitudes like these, a parent is unlikely to praise or reward the child, and it is unlikely that the child is going to be able to initiate a behavior change on their own. To end the stalemate, the parent must put an end to these negative interactions. Coaching and praise is the best tool at a parent's disposal.

Even a child who misbehaves 90% of the time is doing some things right. The 10% of his behavior that is positive or appropriate provides an opportunity for using coaching and praise to build his self-esteem and to break the negative cycles. If parents learn to spot their child's positive behaviors and coach and praise them for their efforts, their child will likely repeat and expand these positive behaviors.

It is the therapist's task to help parents understand that the only way to achieve positive changes in the relationship is for the adult to take responsibility for changing first—for ending the stalemate. This same principle is true of any relationship. Whether it be a relationship with a spouse, older child, or colleague, if one person becomes obstinate and refuses to forgive and make a positive change in their behavior, the status quo is maintained and the relationship is unlikely to improve.

What if praise feels unnatural and phony or is not part of my culture?

"It's not that I have any real objection to praising my child, it just isn't something that comes naturally to me. If I make a conscious effort to praise him, I just end up feeling phony."

"In my culture, we don't praise. We feel that it is important not to put one person's accomplishments on the spotlight. If I go against this and praise my child, I will be going against what my culture believes."

As we learned earlier, any new behavior feels awkward in the beginning. This is a natural reaction and is to be expected. However, the more parents use praise, the more natural it will feel. If parents are worried that praise is not part of their culture or personality, the therapist might help the parents to develop encouraging language that seems more natural for them. The precise language of praise is not as important as the warm, positive parental attention that is given to the child when they are exhibiting the prosocial behavior.

Therapists explore ways of giving praise and encouragement that fit within a parent's culture or personal style.

Therapists can also explore ways of giving praise and encouragement that fit within a parent's culture or personal style. There are many effective ways of acknowledging that a child has done something well. Some parents may be comfortable with an exuberant: "Wow! You are so good at building. You've made a whole city!" Other parents may give more understated praise: "I appreciate that you are listening to me." One parent may give an enthusiastic hug along with the praise while another might smile and touch the child's shoulder gently. As long as the parent means these statements and gives the praise in a way that the child can understand, the praise will be effective. In the group, therapists can help parents practice ways of giving praise or approval that fit their personality and culture.

When parents are having difficulty with the idea of praising, it is often helpful to return to the goals they identified for their child and for themselves during the first parent session. These goals will be varied between parents in the group—some parents may want to encourage their children to be more independent, others will want to increase compliance or respect, and others will want to work on the child's social interactions with peers or siblings—however once they are identified, the group can have a discussion about how praise and encouragement will help to foster these goals. The therapist might also suggest that the parents try out an experiment to see if praise or encouragement improves their child's behaviors. Parents who see that the praise is successful will be more likely to continue to use the strategy.

Parents who find praise "unnatural" are often people who received little praise as children and who rarely praise themselves. Far from praising themselves, these parents are often self-critical about their mistakes, conflicts, and difficulties. Although these parents may tell their children about problems they have, they rarely mention their successes, aspects of themselves they feel good about, or achievements they are proud of. These parents are not modeling self-praise. However, it is very important for children to see their parents modeling self-praise statements. By modeling self-praise for our children, we teach them how to internalize positive self-talk. A mother might say aloud to herself, "I did a good job on my assignment at work," or "That was a tough situation but I think we handled it well," or "That casserole I made tonight tasted good." In the group, therapists should have parents practice giving praise to themselves, their partners, and other parents. Although this is often awkward at first, many parents are surprised at how much they value receiving this praise. Lastly, throughout the program, therapists model how to give praise by praising the parents in the group.

Isn't praise manipulative?

"Isn't it rather manipulative to use praise to bring about a particular behavior in my child?"

The word *manipulative* implies that a parent is contriving secretly to bring about some desired behavior against the child's wishes. In fact, the purpose of praise is to enhance and increase positive behavior with the child's knowledge. Praise which is clearly described brings out the best behavior in children because they know what is expected of them.

What if a parent forgets to praise?

"Sometimes I forget to praise and do it later. Is there a problem with this?"

Although it may seem nice for a mother to mention that she appreciated her daughter cleaning up the kitchen a week after it happened, unfortunately, praise loses its reinforcing value over time. Furthermore, when praise comes long after the behavior occurred, it tends to sound more artificial. While delayed praise is better than no praise at all, the most effective praise for young children is given *within five seconds of the positive behavior*. This means that if a parent is trying to encourage a new behavior, she should watch for every occasion when the child attempts the behavior. Therapists encourage parents to praise their children as soon as they begin to perform the desired behavior, rather than waiting for the clothes to be put on perfectly or the toys all put away before praising. The praise should be frequent and consistent in the beginning, and then gradually it can be replaced by more intermittent praise.

What about when the praise seems to disrupt the play?
"When I go in and tell him he is playing well with his sister, they stop playing. I feel I should have just left them alone. They were doing so well, and the praise actually ruined the moment."

While we recommend that parents use child-directed play daily with their children and use praise during those play sessions, times when children are playing by themselves provide a different opportunity to praise. After all, quiet, cooperative, and self-motivated play is an extremely desirable behavior that deserves positive attention! However, going into a room to praise children for their quiet, cooperative play may have the unwanted consequence of disrupting the play. Sometimes the children will stop playing and ask the parent to stay and play. Other times, the praise may seem to trigger sibling disagreements and arguments! When parents first start praising their children for playing quietly, they can expect this reaction. The parents' behavior may be new for the child, and parents' positive enthusiasm can make children want to spend more time playing with their parents. Nonetheless, as children get used to parents peeking in their rooms to notice how they are playing, the praise will seem less disruptive and the children will know their parents feel good about their cooperative play. A parent might ask, "Why praise children when they are playing quietly? If observing them and commenting is disruptive, why not leave them alone?" Unfortunately, if children's independent and cooperative play goes unnoticed by parents, the behavior will likely decrease only to be replaced by arguments and fights; which will be guaranteed to receive parent's attention!

What about when a child rejects praise?
"Whenever I try to praise my child, he throws it back in my face. He never seems to believe what I say. It's almost as if he doesn't want me to praise him."

Temperamentally difficult and aggressive children can be hard to praise. Their behavior often makes parents angry and undermines their desire to be positive. To make matters more difficult, these children may reject praise when it is given to them. It seems that such children internalize a negative self-concept because of the constant criticisms they have experienced from parents and teachers as well as the rejection and ridicule from their peer group. When parents present them with an alternative, positive view of themselves, the children find this image difficult to accept, preferring to cling to their familiar, negative self-image. Oppositional children may also reject praise because they have found that they can get more of an emotional response from parents when they are defiant than when they are compliant.

Therapists may spend extra time helping parents become comfortable with coaching methods before moving on to the praise.

While "difficult" children are hard to praise and reward, they need this positive acknowledgement *even more* than other children. Therapists must help parents to understand the importance of constantly looking for positive behaviors that they can praise, while ignoring the resulting argument or eye rolling that may happen at first. Once the child begins internalize a more positive self-concept, they will no longer have a need to reject praise in order to maintain their poor self-image. However, this is easier said than done. It can be incredibly difficult for parents to continue to be positive with a defiant child who rejects their praise and efforts to break a stalemate. The therapist will need to support such parents while they go through this difficult process.

What is the difference between coaching and praise?

"I am more comfortable with praise, and I find descriptive coaching much harder. Can I just do the praising and not worry about coaching?"

Without coaching language parental praise will be less effective. Coaching language is necessary in order to clearly describe the child behavior that the parent is trying to encourage. The therapist should spend extra time helping parents become comfortable with coaching methods before moving on to the praise. Once parents have mastered coaching, adding praise should be easy because it simply adds a parent evaluation component to the statement. Consider a persistence coaching statement such as, "You are working so hard on that project. You are staying focused and keep trying again and again to work it out. It looks like you are getting close to figuring it out." If the parent wanted to make this a praise statement, she would add, "I am so proud of you for that, you did a good job." If the parent had only given the praise statement the child would not have known precisely what his parent was proud of.

INCENTIVE PROGRAMS

In general, there are two methods for using incentives to reinforce good behavior. The first is for the parent to spontaneously give the child a surprise reward when the child displays a desired behavior, such as sharing, sitting still in the car, or helping a friend. This approach works if the child already exhibits the appropriate behavior fairly regularly and the parent wishes to increase the frequency with which it occurs. The second approach is for the parent to plan in advance with the child or create a contract of the reward that will follow from a certain behavior. This type of program is recommended when parents wish to increase an infrequent behavior. Therapists will need to work with parents to pick attainable, clearly defined behaviors and developmentally appropriate incentives for these behaviors. Preschool children (ages 3- to 5-years) will be rewarded by a special sticker or hand stamp without needing a back-up reinforcer. For example, a parent of a 3-year-old might give his son a sticker each time he uses the toilet or cooperates with teeth-brushing. Beginning in elementary school, most children can be engaged in a program in which they earn a number of stickers or points and trade them in for a reward. 5- to 6- year-olds will likely need to trade in their stickers for a small daily reward, whereas children who are 7 or older may prefer to wait several days to earn a slightly bigger reward. For example, a parent of a 6- and 8-year-old who fight frequently might set up a system in which the children receive a sticker for each half hour that they share and play quietly. Together the parent and children could make a list of possible rewards to choose from once they receive a certain number of stickers. Possible rewards might include reading an extra story at bedtime, going to the park with Dad, choosing their favorite cereal at the grocery store, or picking something from a surprise grab bag. It is a good idea to make the reward menu varied with small, inexpensive items. This list can be added to as children come up with new suggestions. While incentive programs may seem simple, there are, in fact, many pitfalls to be avoided if they are to be effective. The therapist will need to spend time reviewing reward charts and trouble-shooting issues which arise as parents begin these programs.

Questions Parents Ask About Tangible Rewards

Aren't you bribing children?

"When you give stickers or points or prizes, aren't you bribing children?"

What is the difference between a bribe and a reward? A bribe is an attempt to produce the desired behavior and is often offered in desperation when the child is already misbehaving. Consider a father whose daughter is having a tantrum while they are in line at the bank, "Eliza, here is a piece of chocolate. Now stop screaming." Or a father whose child has been getting out of bed at night who says, "Sunjay, I'll give you this snack if you go back to bed afterwards." In these examples, the chocolate bar and the snack are bribes because they are given before the desired behavior has occurred. They are not contingent on the positive behavior, regardless of what the parent intended. In fact, bribes reinforce inappropriate behavior, since the "reward" (that is, the bribe) followed the inappropriate behavior. Ironically, parents in this scenario are teaching their children that if they behave badly, they will be rewarded.

Rewards are given for positive behaviors after they have occurred. It is helpful for therapists to remind parents of the "first-then" principle. First the child must behave appropriately or comply, and then s/he gets the reward. In the bank example, Eliza's father could have said before going to the bank, "Eliza, if you stay by my side quietly in the bank,

I will give you a piece of chocolate when we are finished." Sunjay's father could have said, "If you stay in your bed all night without getting up, you can have pancakes for breakfast." The parent gives the reward only after seeing the desired behavior, and the child understands what behavior he has to exhibit in order to get the reward.

Won't children become dependent on tangible rewards?

"I worry that my children may become dependent on such rewards to motivate them—and life doesn't always reward hard work with success at work. What happens when I want to get them off the reward system?"

Parents often worry about using or overusing tangible rewards. They are concerned that instead of developing internal controls, their children will learn to behave correctly only for a "payoff." This is a legitimate concern and could occur in two kinds of situations. The first involves a parent who is "sticker dependent," giving stickers or points for desirable behavior, but never providing social approval (attention and praise). In essence, this parent is teaching the child to perform for payoffs rather than for the pleasure both parent and child feel when they accomplish something. The use of tangible rewards should be seen as a temporary measure to help motivate children to learn a behavior that is difficult for them. Furthermore, tangible rewards must be accompanied by social rewards.

Therapists help parents know how and when to phase out rewards gradually.

The second situation arises when a parent does not plan to phase out the tangible rewards by maintaining the behaviors with social approval. In other words, the parents do not give their child the message that they expect them to eventually be able to behave on their own without tangible rewards. For example, a parent of a child who has been earning stickers for making his bed in the morning might say, "You have been earning stickers every day for making your bed and that's great. Now you're ready for a new challenge. In order to get a sticker you have to make your bed and put your pajamas away each morning. I think you can do it!" Once parents have taught the new behaviors, they can gradually phase out the tangible rewards and maintain them with social reinforcers. For instance, a parent might say, "Now that you are going pee in the toilet almost all the time, and earning lots of stickers, let's make the game more fun. Now you have to have dry pants for two days before earning a sticker." Once the child is successful on a regular basis for two days, the interval can be extended to four days, and so forth, until stickers are no longer necessary. At that point, the mother may want to use stickers with a different behavior. She could say, "You remember how well you did learning to go pee with the sticker game we played? Well, let's help you learn to get dressed faster in the mornings using stickers." Thus, reward programs can be phased out and begun again for different behaviors. Parents will often find that as children master a particular behavior, the reward system fades out on its own. As the new behavior becomes a habit, the child is motivated by a sense of accomplishment, and moves past the need for a reward. When this happens, the behavior has become internalized!

Therapists help parents learn how to strengthen their child's internal motivation rather than rely on external rewards.

An important aspect of a reward program is the message that accompanies the reward. Parents must clearly communicate both that they approve of their child's success, and also that they recognize that their child's effort, not the payoff, per se, is responsible for the success. In this way, parents help strengthen the child's internal motivation and sense of competence. For example, a parent may say, "Wow you have had dry pants all week and earned 3 stickers. You must be really proud of that, I think you are really growing up."

Rewards that can bankrupt parents or are earned too easily.
"I can't afford these programs. I don't have the money to buy rewards."

Believe it or not, I have seen reward programs that almost bankrupted their planners. All children will want to include expensive items such as a bicycle or a trip to Disneyland on their reward menu. Some parents may give in and place such items on the list, either because they think their children will never earn enough points to get them or because they feel guilty and would like to be able to give them these things. Other parents may include expensive items because they have trouble setting limits with their children.

Even if the motives are good, it is important that therapists help parents understand that inclusion of unrealistic rewards is destructive to their program. All too often children do earn the required number of stickers or points. Parents then find themselves in the awkward position of either being unable to afford the reward, or of giving their children the reward but resenting it. In this case, children receive a mixed message about their parents' pleasure in the achievement of their goal. This defeats the purpose of a reward program and undermines the parents' credibility for promoting positive behaviors in the future. Even when families can afford more expensive rewards, exclusive use of such rewards teaches children to expect big rewards for their successes. The emphasis is placed on the magnitude of the reward, rather than the satisfaction and pride felt by both parent and child at the child's success.

Generally, it is a good idea for parents to set a limit on the expense of any one item on a list, such as two dollars or less, depending on what the family can afford. Children can be told this at the beginning. Although they will ask for expensive items and test the rules around this, in general inexpensive (or non-material) things are more powerful reinforcers. Young children often like to earn time with parents, such as extra story time or a trip to the park. Small food items such as raisins, goldfish crackers, a favorite cereal, or special dessert can also work well. Older children like to earn money and special privileges such as extra television, having a friend overnight, using the telephone, or a family movie night.

Tangible reward programs don't work with my child.
"My child is uninterested in tangible reward programs. I've made up charts for her before and she doesn't seem to be motivated by the program. Aren't some children just not motivated by such things?"

It is a rare child who is uninterested in rewards. Chances are that it is some other aspect of the program that is not working—most likely the behavioral expectations. Programs sometimes fail because too many negative behaviors are tackled at once or too many behavioral goals have been set. I have seen highly motivated parents start reward programs that included compliance to parental requests, not teasing siblings and peers, going to bed without an argument, and getting dressed on time in the mornings. Such programs are too complex. The pressure to succeed in many different areas of life may be so overwhelming that children give up before starting. Rather than "not motivated," the child may be too discouraged.

Another drawback of specifying a multitude of behaviors is that the child's behaviors require constant parental monitoring. For example, consider only the first goal in the list above, compliance to parental requests. For a parent to monitor compliance and noncompliance throughout the day would require a tremendous amount of effort, since these situations occur so frequently. Remember, if parents cannot realistically monitor their child's behavior and follow through with consequences, even the best-designed program is bound to fail.

There are three main things therapists should consider when helping parents decide which behaviors to teach at once: the frequency with which each behavior occurs; the child's developmental stage; and the parent's ability to carry out the program. With regard to frequency, behaviors such as compliance or noncompliance, polite voice vs. whining, teasing or arguing occur often and therefore would require a great deal of parental supervision. Realistically, parents will not be able to focus on more than one of these behaviors at a time. On the other hand, behaviors such as dressing, brushing teeth, or wearing a seat belt in the car occur relatively infrequently and three or four of these could be included on a chart at the same time.

The second important point to consider is the developmental stage of the child. Young children require easily understandable programs that focus on one or two simple behaviors. Learning to be compliant to parental requests or staying in bed at night are major developmental tasks for a young child. Each will require many repeated learning trials over time and much patience on the part of the parents. However, for older children (school-age and adolescent), tangible reward programs can become somewhat more complex because children can understand

and remember them better. Furthermore, the problem behaviors usually occur less frequently at this stage and are easier to monitor. Therefore, it would not be unrealistic to establish a program for a school-age child that included points for completing various chores by a well-defined time, finishing homework without a reminder, and being dressed and ready for school in the mornings.

Therapists make every effort to ensure that parents are setting up programs that are realistic for them as well as their children.

Evaluation of how much monitoring parents can realistically expect of themselves is the third factor in deciding which child behaviors to focus on. Even if a parent does not have an outside job, they are unlikely to be able to monitor child compliance throughout the whole day. Therefore, the parent may want to choose a period during the day when he can focus on problem behaviors. For instance, he might decide to limit the reward system monitoring to the hour when the baby naps, in the morning when the older child is in school, or during the afterschool period. During this time, the parent will be vigilant about reinforcing every instance of the desired behavior. At other times during the day, she will look for spontaneous opportunities to catch her child being good, but will not "catch" and reinforce every positive behavior. On the other hand, a mother who is rushed to get ready for work in the morning and exhausted by evening may only have the energy to monitor problem behaviors every morning for half an hour. The therapist must make every effort ensure that parents are setting up programs that are realistic for them so that they may be most successful in their first efforts at behavior change.

Another possible reason that programs fail is that they focus exclusively on negative behaviors. Parents may clearly identify a negative behavior they want to eliminate, such as fighting. Their program outlines the rewards that their children will receive for going an hour without fighting. So far, so good; but the program hasn't gone far enough. While it tells children clearly what they should not do, it neither describes nor rewards the appropriate positive opposite replacement behavior. Thus, in this example, the inappropriate behavior is receiving more parental attention than the appropriate behavior. Consequently, the behavior will likely worsen.

It is important to help parents identify the positive opposite behavior of the negative behaviors they wish to eliminate. Children should be rewarded for sharing and playing quietly together, as well as for going 60 minutes without getting into an argument with brothers and sisters. It is critical that the positive behaviors be spelled out at least as clearly as the behaviors that parents wish to eliminate.

Therapists continue to help parents focus on the positive opposite behaviors of the negative ones they wish to eliminate.

Another reason an incentive system may fail is because the chosen reward is not motivating for a particular child. It is important to remember that one size doesn't fit all when it comes to incentives! If a parent has organized a well-defined system with achievable behaviors and yet the child is not interested, the therapist can help the parent to look at alternative rewards. This is a good time to consult the child about what he or she might want to work for.

Unrealistic Goals.

"We set up a system to reward our son for each day that he came home with a perfect daily report, but that was totally unsuccessful."

One reason many reward programs fail is that parents set their behavioral expectations too high. When the conditions for earning a reward are so difficult that the child feels that it is impossible, they may give up altogether. A good incentive program incorporates small steps towards achieving the goal. Therapists should first ask parents to observe how often the misbehaviors occur over several days. This baseline will be the key to establishing the right steps for their child. For example, if the child in the example above is struggling all day in school, expecting a perfect day is unrealistic. For this system to be successful, the parent will need to work with the teacher to define small, positive behaviors that are attainable. Perhaps this means breaking work time into 15-minute blocks and providing a reward if the child was focused for 3 out of 5 work blocks during the day. With this approach, the child has a good chance of being successful and will gradually feel confident in her ability as a focused and able learner. The idea is to help parents gradually make progress by carefully defining the small steps necessary to achieve the desired goal.

Saving tangible rewards for special achievements.
"I save big rewards for something really special—like getting all his math questions right. The problem is he hasn't earned anything yet."

Some parents save tangible rewards for their children's special achievements such as getting A's on a report card, cleaning up the entire house or being quiet during a two-day car trip. These are instances of setting a goal too high or making the steps too big. Not only are these parents waiting too long to give the rewards, but they also reserving rewards for perfection. As mentioned before, if parents expect perfection in order to reward their child, it is unlikely that he will ever earn a reward. This gives their children the message that everyday behaviors and everyday efforts don't really count.

Therapists can help parents to think about giving small, frequent rewards. For example, parents who want a quieter car trip might prepare a surprise bag (crayons, books, puzzles, games) to be opened every 80 to 100 miles if their children have been quiet and cooperative. Such rewards can also help satisfy the children's need for stimulation during a long car ride. Certainly parents can plan rewards for special achievements, but they should also use them for smaller steps along the way, such as doing math homework, putting away toys, sharing, sleeping all night, and going to the bathroom. Only by rewarding the smaller steps can the larger goals of good grades, consistent compliance, good relationships with friends, or toilet training be accomplished.

Rewards seem to cause more misbehavior.
"This reward system has caused a lot more problems in my house. Now my son demands rewards to do something or comes to me arguing that he has earned a sticker. And when his sister earned a prize for her sticker chart, he ripped his chart off the wall and threw a giant fit."

It is not unusual for parents of children with conduct problems to develop power struggles with their children around their sticker charts; these children are experts at being oppositional and parents often have difficulties with limit setting. If rewards are resulting in more misbehavior and arguing, the parent has lost control of their reward program. Something is undermining the reinforcing effect of the reward.

There are several ways parents can lose control of their reward program. The first is by rewarding "almost performance": giving rewards to children when they haven't actually done the required behavior or earned the required number of points. This usually happens because children argue for the reward, claiming they've done everything required. Unfortunately, providing a reward in this instance undermines the rules of the contract as well as parents' authority. Rewarding for "almost performance" is also likely to result in escalated begging and debating over the attainment of points in the future. Instead of solving a behavior problem, a new one—excessive arguing—is created. A second difficulty occurs if parents leave the stickers and/or rewards around the house so the children have access to them. Why work for the reward if you can get your hands on it directly? Lack of follow-through can be a third problem. This happens when the children have followed the program but parents fail to notice the positive behaviors or forget to give them the stickers. When rewards do not follow promptly on the heels of the positive behavior, their reinforcing value is minimal. The same is true when parents are inconsistent about rewarding desired behavior. Tangible reward programs require a lot of work on the part of parents in order to be effective!

Parents need to control access to the rewards and when they are given.

Only if parents have observed the behavior or know with certainty that it was done should parents give stickers to children who claim they performed a specified behavior (such as sharing). If parents and children are working on high frequency problems such as noncompliance to requests, no teasing, or going without whining for 15 minutes, then a great deal of vigilance will be required. Rewards are most effective if they are given immediately after the desired behavior is performed. Also, in order for these programs to work, parents must hold firm on their expectations. All children will test the limits and try to see if they can get rewards for less work. This is natural, but therapists must help parents prepare for this testing, by staying committed to the plan or "contract" and readying themselves to ignore any arguments or pleading when their children have not earned enough points. Finally, parents need to control access to the rewards. Prizes and stickers should be hidden and the awarding of points and stickers determined by parents, not their children.

Handling Disappointment.
"Some days when my child hasn't been able to earn anything, he gets very upset. I sometimes just give him a point so he will feel better. Is that a problem?"
"I feel so annoyed with my son. He agreed to our sticker system and then he didn't even try to earn his points today!"

What happens when parents put a lot of effort into setting up a reward program but their children fail to earn points? The two parent comments above reflect sticker chart "traps" that parents can fall into. When a child is upset because he hasn't earned his reward, it may be tempting for the parent to give in and reward the child anyway. Perhaps the parent is feeling sorry for the child or is worried that the child's upsetting response will escalate. While this leniency may temporarily make the parent and child feel better, in the long run it will undermine the system and will give the child the message that his parent doesn't really believe that he is capable of being successful. At other times the parent may be tempted to respond to the child with criticism or lectures on trying harder. Unfortunately, this not only gives children a discouraging message about their ability (which could become a self-fulfilling prophesy), but the negative attention and ensuing power struggle could also inadvertently reinforce misbehavior or noncompliance with the program. A system where the child gets more payoffs for not doing the program than for doing it will not be successful.

If a child fails to earn points or stickers, it is best for the parent to calmly say, "You didn't get one this time, but I'm sure you'll earn some next time." In this case the parent is predicting their positive expectations for the future. If the child continues to have difficulties earning points, parents should make sure that they have not made the steps too big or unrealistic.

Using loss of rewards as a punishment for children.
"If my child is bad I take away his points; the only problem is now he in point debt and needs to earn 5 points to get back to zero."
"Well, I give green tokens for good behaviors and red tokens for bad behaviors."

Some parents create tangible reward programs and then mix in punishment. For example, a parent might reward their child with stickers for sharing and then take them away for fighting. In this example, the stickers take on negative rather than positive associations. This approach can be even more problematic if the child is left with a negative balance. If the most that a child can hope for from good behavior is to get out of "debt," all positive incentive for good behavior disappears. The natural outcome of this approach is for the child to become discouraged and abandon all efforts to change.

The therapist helps parents understand the importance of keeping their reward program separate from their discipline program. Parents should not remove earned points or rewards as a punishment. This system will defeat the purpose of the program, which is to give attention to appropriate behaviors. The parent who awards green tokens for good behavior and red tokens for bad behavior is giving attention and reinforcement to both good and bad behaviors. Instead, parents are encouraged to strive to give positive behaviors positive responses and to ignore negative behaviors or discipline them with logical consequences. If parents want to use privilege removal as a discipline technique, they should keep those particular privileges off of the reward menu (e.g., TV time, use of bicycle).

SUMMARY

In the first half of the parenting program (usually the first 8-9 sessions), the group leader will help parents apply the positive foundational skills from the bottom half of the pyramid to their individual parenting and

Therapists helping parents understand the first half of the pyramid is the bedrock of the treatment program.

child behavior goals. By the program's midpoint most parents will already have seen behavioral improvements in their children's social, emotional and academic behaviors and will be experiencing more confidence as parents, and will report a more positive and secure relationship with their child. Parents will also be developing a support team with the other parents and with the therapist. The bottom of the pyramid is the bedrock of the treatment program and can be challenging for some parents, depending on their child's level of aggression and noncompliance and their family stress level. During the second half of the program the therapist will help parents move up the parenting pyramid and begin to decrease negative behaviors and use proactive discipline when needed. Chapter Eight will further explore some of the therapy processes and methods used for maximizing family engagement and minimizing children's resistance and problem solving when things don't go according to plan. The therapist needs to think things through flexibly from these first foundational principles.

Content of the Incredible Years® Parenting Pyramid™~Discipline: Reducing Children's Conduct Problems

In the first half of the Incredible Years BASIC program parents build positive attachment with their children and gain an understanding of the tools used to promote children's social skills, emotional literacy, and academic readiness. It is during this portion of the program that parents learn to scaffold the positive opposite behaviors, cognitions, and emotions that are necessary to replace the negative behaviors, thoughts, and feelings. It is likely that behavior problems will have already improved at this point in the therapy as well as the parents' relationship with their child.

THE INCREDIBLE YEARS BASIC PARENTING PYRAMID - DISCIPLINE

Rules, Routines and Predictable Schedules Programs

The therapist begins the second half of the program by asking parents to brainstorm the benefits of predictable schedules and share their existing routines. In the Baby Program parents learn about when it is developmentally appropriate (around 5-6 months) to begin establishing routines for feeding, sleep, baths, and playtimes. Therapists help parents think about the benefits of routines for promoting their baby's feelings of security and safety. The Basic programs for toddlers, preschoolers, and school age children continue to emphasize the importance of routines at each developmental level. In the Toddler and Preschool Programs emphasis is placed on routines for parent separations and reunions at daycare or school. Routines for such daily transitions as getting ready for the day, meal times, and getting ready for bed are discussed and planned. The School Age Program builds on these established routines by introducing after school routines and monitoring, homework, reading schedules, and family chores. Therapists help parents understand that even for adolescents who are developmentally driven to be independent and seem not to acknowledge parental input, this ongoing monitoring of their daily activities serves to strengthen their attachment, supportive parent-child relationships, and sense of family responsibility. Therapists will find that some families have no predictable routines or rules for monitoring older children's whereabouts. Therapists can help these families discuss the benefits of setting up routines as well as methods for overcoming barriers to doing so. Therapists should also explain that once predictable routines have been well established, parents will be able to reduce their commands, corrections, and saying "no," because children will have learned what to expect in day-to-day

Ongoing monitoring of adolescents' after school activities strengthens their attachment and sense of family responsibility.

activities. In the early years, routines can help to prevent tantrums, misbehavior, and distress. Having routines, especially during transitions or times when parents need cooperation from their child (such as bedtime or getting ready for preschool), helps parents and children get through the day smoothly. As children reach school age, routines help children to understand and follow household rules and limits and encourage their independence and self-care.

Positive Discipline – Effective Limit Setting Programs

In the Toddler and Preschool Programs, the therapist helps parents learn to use positive discipline tools such as distractions, redirections, warnings, clear and respectful limits, and ignoring. Therapists should explain to parents that it is the toddler's developmental job to explore and discover, to develop a sense of self, and to test limits, so tantrums, pushing, biting, and saying "no" will most likely be frequent occurrences. Since this common type of toddler behavior can be very challenging to parents, much of this component of the program is focused on helping parents understand and empathize with toddlers' developmental needs, while learning strategies to minimize the intensity of their child's tantrums and keeping them safe. Therapists should continue to remind parents to consider the "attention principle" in this unit: "*behaviors that receive parental attention will increase, while behaviors that get no attention will decrease.*" Therapists should help parents consider what this means in terms of their response to misbehavior. They should explain that big reactions like yelling, scolding, or lectures will actually increase negative behaviors while ignoring, redirection, and calm consequences will decrease the behaviors over time.

It is the toddler's developmental job to explore, discover, test limits and develop a sense of self and the parents' job to keep them safe.

School age children also test their parents' rules and standards by arguing and defending their viewpoint. In fact, typically developing children disobey or test their parents' commands about 1/3 of the time. Parents should be helped to see that these are not personal attacks, but

Typically children disobey or test their parents commands about 1/3 of the time.

learning experiences for their children; their children are exploring the limits of their environment and learning which behaviors are appropriate and which are inappropriate. Consistent limit-setting and predictable responses from parents help give children a sense of stability and security about their relationships and the rules in their environment. All children test parents' rules to assert their autonomy, see whether their parents will be consistent and determine whether it is actually a rule or just a one-time command. Therapists must explain that only consistent consequences will teach a child what is expected. If parents' rules have been inconsistent or unreliably enforced in the past a child may have learned that long and hard protesting can get their parents to back down. These children will escalate their noncompliance accordingly. The therapist should reassure parents that children who feel a sense of security and predictability regarding the limits of their environment have less need to test it.

Children who are diagnosed with ODD and ADHD or who have conduct disorders show more extreme levels of noncompliance. They usually disobey more than 2/3rds of their parents' commands. These parents are engaged in power struggles with their child the majority of the time, making it very difficult for them to adequately socialize their child. For these parents of these children, the therapist will focus more on teaching the importance of limiting commands to the most important ones and then consistently following through with predictable consequences for these requests. In this way parents are able to reduce the overall level of conflict in the family, while helping their child learn that their rules consistently apply. Once the parents are able to achieve more compliance from their child, therapists will begin to teach other social skills. All of this progresses more quickly when the parents have worked on the parenting pyramid relationship skills first!

While family stressors (such as marital discord, single parenting, poverty, unemployment, depression) make it difficult for parents to be consistent, a strengthened commitment to respectful limit-setting (as well as positive playtime and coaching) can help buffer the disruptive effects of these stressors on parenting. One of the ways the therapists may elicit this commitment is to engage the parents in an exercise of listing the advantages as well as the possible barriers to limit setting. The subsequent problem solving discussion in the parent group helps parents overcome some of the obstacles they face regarding consistent limit setting. This exercise is also helpful for grasping the importance of limit setting for their children's social and emotional adjustment and their parent-child relationship.

Positive Discipline – Handling Misbehavior Programs

All young children engage in negative behaviors such as whining, biting, refusing to follow directions, teasing, arguing, swearing, tantrums and hitting. The frequency of aggressive and noncompliant behavior peaks between 2 and 3 years of age and in most children will begin to decrease between 4 and 5 years of age. Some children misbehave with higher intensity and frequency and for a longer period of time than others. This can be due to their language and developmental difficulties, temperament, the emotional climate and amount of stress at home, and/or the amount of attention these behaviors receive from parents. These defiant and aggressive behaviors frequently lead to parental negative attention and anger as well as peer rejection, isolation and emotional dysregulation. The therapist helps parents feel confident that they can socialize young children out of their immature, disruptive and aggressive behaviors and teach them to use more productive social and emotional regulation responses. Therapists teach parents to sort children's misbehaviors into two categories: those that are merely annoying or disruptive (but safe) and those that are unsafe. Behaviors in the first category are usually responsive to ignoring, distraction, or redirection. The therapist helps parents understand why it is important to begin by choosing less intrusive discipline tools from the middle of the pyramid first before using those more intrusive discipline tools at the top of pyramid. Parents often choose the more intrusive tools too quickly in response to child

For toddlers the first four steps in the discipline hierarchy will be sufficient.

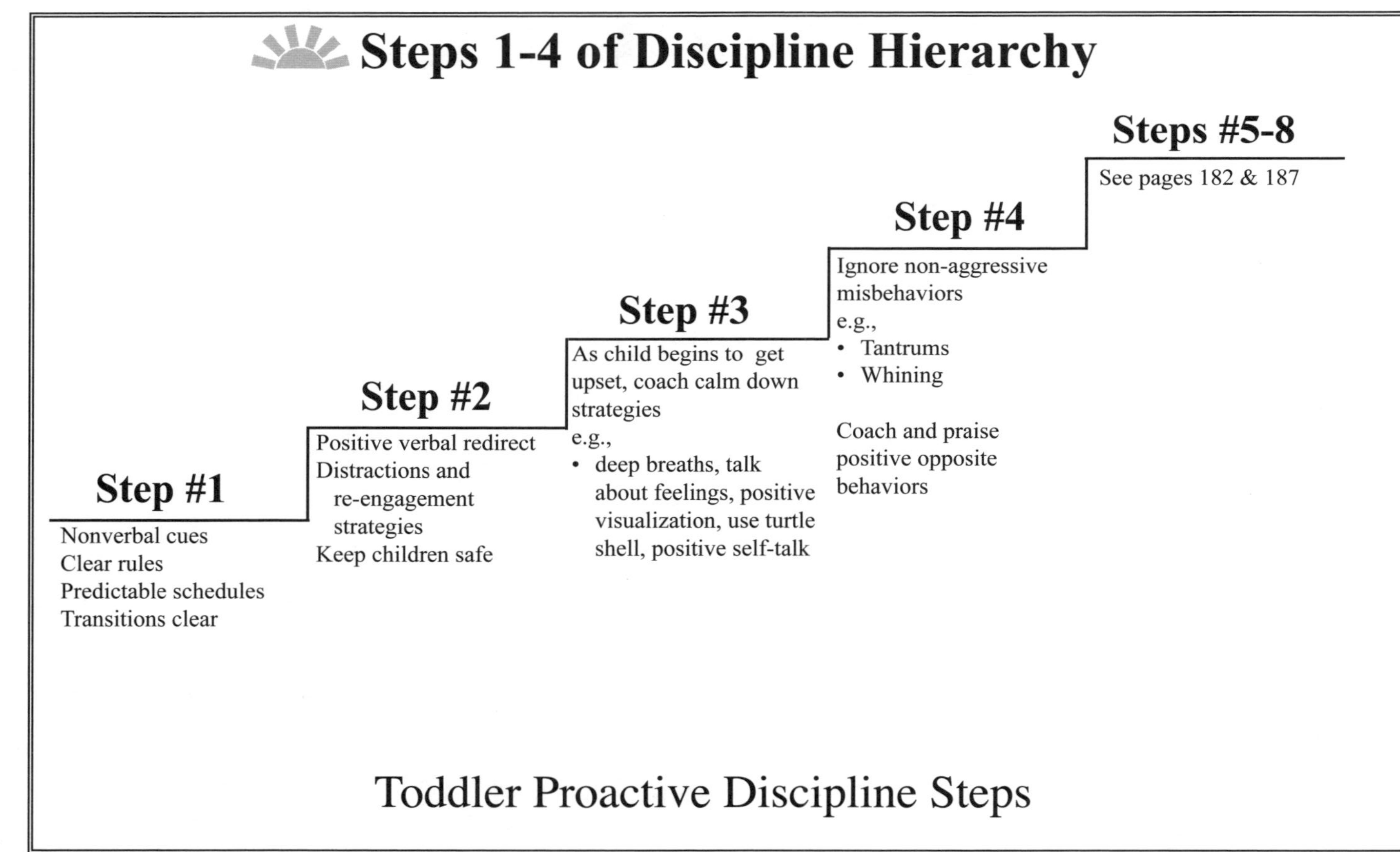
Steps 1-4 of Discipline Hierarchy
Step #1
Nonverbal cues
Clear rules
Predictable schedules
Transitions clear
Step #2
Positive verbal redirect
Distractions and re-engagement strategies
Keep children safe
Step #3
As child begins to get upset, coach calm down strategies
e.g.,
• deep breaths, talk about feelings, positive visualization, use turtle shell, positive self-talk
Step #4
Ignore non-aggressive misbehaviors
e.g.,
• Tantrums
• Whining
Coach and praise positive opposite behaviors
Steps #5-8
See pages 182 & 187
Toddler Proactive Discipline Steps

misbehavior. For toddlers the four steps in the discipline hierarchy shown in the next figure will be sufficient discipline.

Ignoring. Ignoring (Step #4) is one of the most difficult approaches for therapists to get parents to practice. Many parents argue that ignoring is not discipline at all and by ignoring disrespectful or annoying misbehavior, they feel they are not both allowing and teaching their children to be disrespectful. It is particularly important for the therapist to explain the rationale for this approach. The rationale for ignoring is straightforward: children's behavior is maintained by the attention it receives. Even negative parental attention, such as nagging, yelling, and criticizing, provides children with powerful parental attention. On the other hand, when parents ignore misbehavior, children receive no payoff and will eventually stop the behavior if the ignoring is maintained. If, at the same time, children receive consistent approval, attention, coaching, praise, incentives, and respect for appropriate, positive opposite social behaviors and emotional responses, they learn that it is more beneficial to behave appropriately and calmly than inappropriately.

In addition to ignoring disruptive misbehavior, therapists also help parents learn to use other discipline strategies such as giving controlled choices, warnings, redirection, and distractions. Parents are

Steps 5-6 of Discipline Hierarchy

Step #5

Use small natural and logical consequences e.g.,

- No computer time
- Activity removed for few minutes
- Loss of privilege
- No bike riding for afternoon
- Loss of 15 min of screen time

Step #6

For agressive, destructive behavior

- 3-5 minutes time away or Time Out to Calm Down
- Work Chore

For noncompliance

- Time out followed by command repeated

Early School Age Discipline Steps

"Always choose the lowest, least intrusive steps first."

simultaneously reminded to focus on teaching positive replacement behaviors by coaching children to use self-regulation strategies when they are becoming frustrated.

Structured Ignore. Some behaviors are unsafe and, thus, cannot be ignored. Hitting, biting, kicking, stealing and extremely destructive behaviors fall into this category. In particular, toddlers display aggressive behaviors at a high rate. This is developmentally normal, but does require some parent intervention. Parents of toddlers who bite others learn to respond with a calm, but firm, command ("no biting") coupled with a quick temporary separation of the children so the biter doesn't continue to hurt the other child. The child who has been hit or bitten may be coached with words to tell her friend, "I don't like that." After a brief separation (1-2 minutes) during which the biter is ignored, he is then redirected to a new activity. In essence this structured ignore procedure gives the child a chance to calm down, avoids giving attention for the misbehavior, and keeps the other child safe from being hurt.

Natural and Logical Consequences. In the Preschool and School Age BASIC program parents learn Step #5 in the discipline hierarchy: how to use natural and logical consequences in addition to ignoring, redirection, distractions, and occasional Time Outs to calm down. More than Time Out or ignoring, natural and logical consequences teach children to take responsibility for their own behavior (see figure page 182).

A natural consequence is whatever would result from a child's action or inaction in the absence of adult intervention. For instance, if 6-year-old Ryan refused to eat dinner, the natural consequence might be his waiting until the next meal for more food. Or, if Caitlin did not want to wear her boots on a rainy day, then her feet would get wet. In these examples, the children experience the direct consequences of their own decisions; they are not protected from the possibility of an undesirable outcome of their behavior by their parents' commands. Experiencing a natural consequence can be a powerful learning tool, in some circumstances. Many times it is not advisable or safe to use a natural consequence, especially for toddlers or preschoolers. For example, while letting a child touch a hot stove would produce a logical consequence, it is not a safe or reasonable response to a child who starts to disobey the command "hands away from the hot stove." Instead, the parent should remove the child from the stove and keep her from hurting herself.

Understanding the developmental stage of the child is important in determining appropriate logical or natural consequences.

A logical consequence, on the other hand, is set up by parents specifically to hold children accountable for their behavior. Because parents pick the consequence, the therapist can help them to ensure that the consequence is developmentally appropriate. A logical consequence for a preschooler who colors on the dinner table might be to have the child help clean the mess and remove the crayons for a few hours. A logical consequence for a school-age child who broke a neighbor's window might do chores in order to make up some of the cost of the replacement. A logical consequence for an 8-year-old who steals something from the store would be to take the object back to the store, apologize to the owner, do an extra chore, or lose a privilege. Understanding the age of the child and their development level is important in determining logical or natural consequences. For example, young children who vacillate between fantasy and reality do not understand that taking something from a store is wrong, whereas a typical 8-year-old is capable of understanding that this action is wrong. A 12-year-old who misses the bus might be asked to walk to school (assuming this was safe), whereas this would not be a safe consequence for a preschool child.

Natural and logical consequences are most effective for recurring behaviors where parents are able to decide ahead of time how they will follow through if the misbehavior recurs. For example, the parent who says to a school-age child, "If you spend all your allowance on candy, you'll have no money for that movie you want to rent," is allowing the child to think ahead to the consequences of different behavior. In effect, the child has a choice and is responsible for the outcome. In the case of a misbehavior, the parent might give a warning like this: "If you do not finish your chores by dinner time, then you will not be allowed to watch TV after dinner." On the other hand, the parent who does not specify the consequence ahead of time is not helping the child see the connection between the behavior and the negative outcome. All too often consequences are too long, too severe and developmentally inappropriate. For example, taking away the 6-year-old child's bike for a week because he forgot to put it away doesn't give him a new learning trial soon enough to experience the opportunity to be successful. The most important aspect about effective use of consequences is they are immediate, quick and the child is given a new learning trial as soon as possible.

Time Out to Calm Down. In the Preschool Program for children ages 3-5 years and the School Age Programs for children ages 6-12 years, therapists teach parents how to use the Time Out to calm down strategy for high-intensity child problems, such as fighting, hitting, and destructive behavior. This strategy is used sparingly and only when the parent has learned the value of the earlier less intrusive discipline strategies outlined in Steps 1-4.

Time Out is step #6 in the discipline hierarchy, and is not taught until children are at least 3 years old and are developmentally and cognitively capable of following instructions and able to sit still quietly in a specific spot for a brief period of time. The therapist explains to parents that Time Out is actually a structured form of parental ignoring in which children are removed for a brief period from all sources of positive reinforcement, especially parental attention. Time Out assures that the child's misbehavior is not being reinforced by parental attention, and models for children the parent's use of self-control and a nonviolent, calm response to a conflict situation. Time Out gives the child (and the parents) time to cool down, self-regulate, get control over misbehavior, and reflect on what has happened. Because Time Out forces children to reflect and calm down, they are more likely to develop appropriate guilt, and an internal sense of responsibility or conscience over time. The therapist should also help parents understand that Time Out is a discipline approach that fosters a warm, respectful relationship rather than a fearful, power-based relationship (i.e., based on fear of being hit

Effective consequences are immediate, quick and child is given a new learning opportunity as soon as possible.

Be prepared to ignore the child who tries to "huff and puff and blow the door down."

by parent). Time Out is a discipline strategy that contributes to open communication rather than devious sneaky behavior on the part of the child who wants to avoid punishment. Parents should explain Time Out to their child when they are both calm. Parents should also be encouraged to practice calm down techniques with their child that they can use during Time Out. Examples of calm down strategies include, taking deep breaths, using positive imagery and encouraging oneself, "I can calm down, I can do it."

Parents are often quite resistant to use Time Outs, for various reasons. First, it is inconvenient; it requires advance planning in terms of the procedure and the location. Second, it can be time-consuming and requires that parents keep themselves under control for a long period of time. Third, Time Out can be frustrating for parents because the child's misbehavior may escalate during the first several Time Outs, with children screaming, banging on the walls, or breaking something. Some parents resist Time Out because they don't think it produces enough remorse or retribution in children, things they believe to be necessary for punishment to work effectively (some children even indicate they like Time Out!). Other parents may resist Time Out because they feel it communicates rejection to the child.

Steps 7-8 of Discipline Hierarchy

Step #1-6

See pages 180 & 182

Step #7

Review BehaviorPlan

- Check frequency of positive attention for prosocial behavior
- Check incentive program is motivating child
- Check that no attention is given during Time Out

Step #8

Give Repeated Opportunities for New Learning Trials

- Model, coach & practice alternative desired behaviors
- Praise replacement behaviors
- Practice problem solving with stories and puppets

"Always choose the lowest, least intrusive lower steps first and set up a new learning trial as soon as possible"

Conversely some parents prefer spanking or hitting or yelling as a discipline strategy because it is efficient and immediate, and most likely will stop the inappropriate behavior in the short term. It can even feel good to some parents because it "evens the score." Parents may even feel that they have obtained revenge for their child's misbehavior by inflicting pain as punishment. For some parents, the use of spanking is important because it allows them to feel dominant and maintain control of the situation. However, research has shown that spanking, lecturing, criticism, and expressions of disapproval are ineffective methods of discipline. Furthermore, parents who use these types of discipline often find themselves spiraling into increasingly uncontrolled spanking and yelling in order to get their children to respond. Therapists teach parents that nagging, criticizing, hitting, shouting, or even reasoning with children while they misbehave reinforces the particular misbehavior. Rather than improving behavior these approaches result in children learning to nag, criticize, hit, shout, or argue in response to their parents because of the observational modeling. Spanking and yelling teach children that it is all right for someone who loves you to hit you when displeased with your behavior. Moreover, the violence of spanking increases children's resistance, resentment, and anger toward the parent and erodes the parent-child relationship and attachment. Consequently, rather than the child reflecting on his mistake and feeling guilt and remorse for what he has done, the child externalizes the event with resentment and blame directed toward the parent for hitting him.

Steps 7 and 8 in the hierarchy involve reviewing the behavior plan and giving children new learning opportunities and teaching in problem solving through puppets and stories.

Teaching Children to Problem Solve through Games, Puppets and Books Programs

This program is offered as part of the Preschool BASIC Program Series and a more complex version of this is offered in the ADVANCE Parent Program Series, for after parents have participated in the School Age BASIC Program. Offering the problem solving program content after they have completed the routines, limit setting and discipline strategies, brings parents back to their early learning of child-directed play, coaching, and praise focusing on positive social and emotional solutions. Therapists help parents learn how to use social and emotional coaching plus problem solving vocabulary with their children at times when the child is calm and relaxed. Through peer coaching, role-plays with puppets, and the exploration of book characters' problems, feelings, and solutions, parents help their children learn a series of steps to effectively solve problems. Parents use *Wally's Detective Book for Solving Problems at Home* and *Wally's Detective Book for Solving Problems at School* to practice solving common problems with their children, such as being rejected, a peer not sharing, feeling disappointed or angry or afraid, losing at a game, being bullied or teased or hit, making a mistake, or having trouble learning something. In the ADVANCE program parents learn how to extend these problem-solving steps into weekly family meetings.

Academic Skills and School Readiness Training

As noted in Chapter One a number of studies have indicated that children with conduct problems also have difficulties with learning disabilities, language and reading delays, and problems with attention deficit disorder and hyperactivity. Parents of school-age children with academic difficulties and social and emotional difficulties will need to support their children's academic skills as well as their social emotional skills. The IY SCHOOL Program (for school aged children) focuses on ways for parents to promote and foster children's academic competence, self-confidence and good learning habits as well as how to support a child who feels discouraged with learning, have successful meetings/conferences with teachers, provide homework and reading support, and promote literacy skills. This program should be offered to families whose children have learning and academic difficulties and/or reading delays in addition to social and emotional problems.

Parents of preschool children may also complete an optional SCHOOL READINESS program that fosters children's expected classroom behaviors, peer relationship and interactive reading skills.

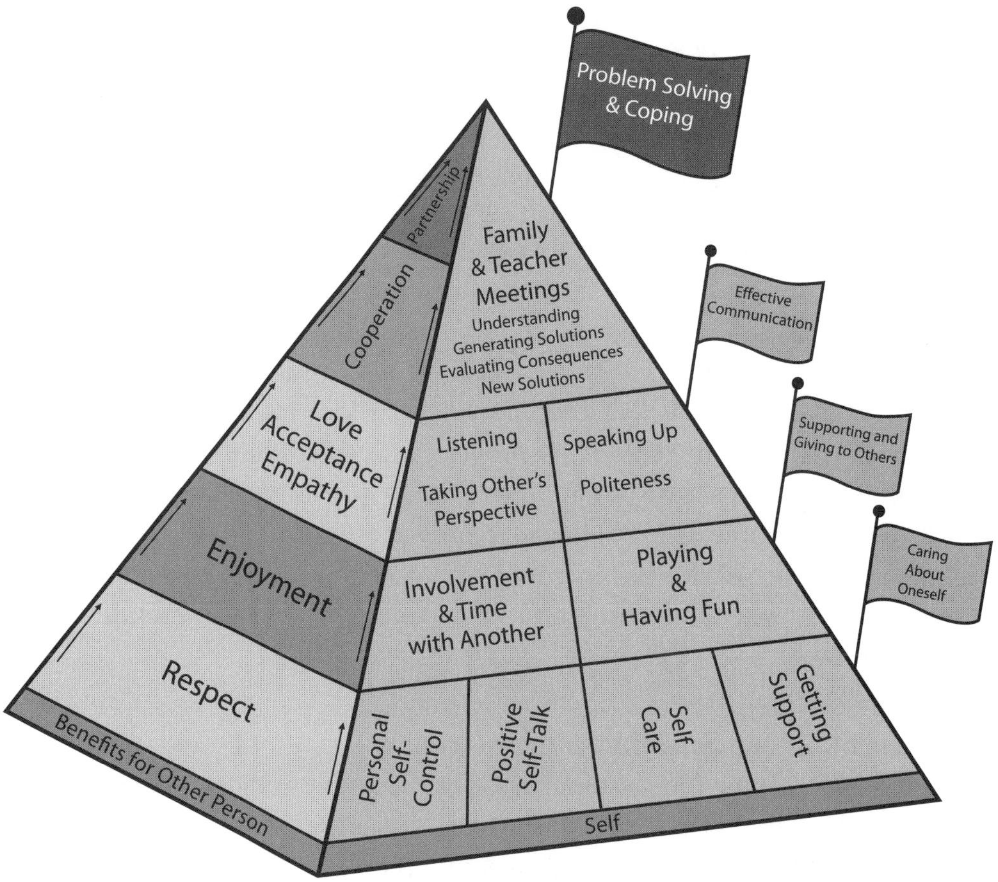

Pyramid for Building Relationships™

THE INCREDIBLE YEARS ADVANCE PARENTING PROGRAM SERIES CONTENT

The ADVANCE parent program series was developed in response to the research outlined in Chapter One indicating that a family's ability to benefit from parent training is influenced by risk factors such as maternal and paternal depression, marital conflict and hostility, isolation, negative life stressors and socioeconomic status. While therapy cannot alter a family's life stressors and economic situation, it can help parents and children cope more effectively in the face of stressful situations.

Including broader interpersonal and problem solving training for parents enhances outcomes.

The ADVANCE parent program series consists of three programs. The first program, How to Communicate Effectively with Adults and Children, consists of three parts: active listening and speaking up; communicating more positively to oneself and to others; and giving and getting support. The second program, Problem Solving for Parents, also consists of three parts: problem solving about children's problems; problem-solving about interpersonal issues; and problem solving with teachers. The third program, Problem Solving with Children, consists of two parts: teaching children to problem solve in the midst of conflict, and family problem solving meetings. In this program parents learn that children are constantly absorbing information by observing their parents' interactions with each other and with others in their community, including teachers and neighbors. See goals and objectives on web site.

www.incredibleyears.com/program/objectives.asp

This ADVANCE parenting program is recommended for the treatment protocol for parents with children with ODD/CD and ADHD or high risk families who are experiencing a high degree of marital stress, family stress, depression, anger and conflict regarding child rearing strategies as well as for child protective service referred families for abuse or neglect. Like the BASIC programs, the therapist needs to pace the length of this program according to the needs of the parents. This program should only be offered after the BASIC program has been completed. It takes approximately 22-26 sessions to complete either the Preschool or School Age programs plus the ADVANCE program (outlines of weekly sessions for both programs are available on Incredible Years web site). **www.incredibleyears.com/Resources/PP.asp**

Group therapists may want to offer these programs as Part 1 BASIC and Part 2 ADVANCED series and require completion of one curriculum before starting the next curriculum. Ideally the same parents should complete both programs together due to the considerable trust and intimacy they will have achieved by the end of the BASIC program. This intimacy allows them to more readily to talk about these more personal issues in a group.

Research has indicated that families who received this broader program of training in personal and interpersonal skills showed additional significant improvements in parental communication skills, problem-solving skills, and consumer satisfaction, as well as children's increased knowledge of prosocial solutions to problem situations (Webster-Stratton, 1994). These data suggest that interventions such as these may strengthen the family's "protective factors," thereby mediating the effects of other, more intractable risk factors such as socioeconomic disadvantage and negative life stressors.

Communication Program

Many parents—whether or not their children have conduct problems—find themselves in disagreement over how to discipline their child. This is to be expected, given that parents have each experienced different parenting styles during childhood. These different perspectives often result in anger and even open conflict between couples over how to raise their children. In the case of conduct problems, this parental conflict only aggravates the problem. Frequent marital conflict and negative affect can lead to ineffective parenting, contributing to child conduct problems which, in turn, contribute to further marital distress and depression. Moreover, children become increasingly aggressive and emotionally dysregulated when they frequently observe negative interactions between their parents. A similar pattern can occur for the single parent, the only difference being that s/he may be angry with an ex-partner, teacher, family member or someone in the community, either for their lack of support or inability to understand the difficulties of raising a child single-handedly. In teaching communication skills, the goal is to enable parents to resolve current problems and avert future ones, and to model these proactive communication skills for their children. In Part 1 of the Communication program parents learn the communications skills of listening, speaking up, using feeling language, avoiding mixed messages, and making requests. In all units in the ADVANCE program, parents are encouraged to think about how the concepts apply to all their relationships including parent-child relationships and all types of adult-adult relationships.

Effective Listening. The first skills parents learn is effective listening; that is listening without interrupting, giving advice, criticizing or arguing. The listener is asked to put herself in the shoes of the other person who is speaking. As part of this exercise, therapists sometimes use props to help parents remember if they are in the listening mode (perhaps holding the speaker's shoe or a card with a picture of an ear) or the speaking mode. Parents learn to be effective listeners through the use of skills such as paraphrasing, summarizing, reflecting and validating statements made by the other person. In many ways this is a more sophisticated form of the literal descriptive commenting used in communication with young children.

Speaking Up. Among a group of parents who want assistance with their children's conduct problems are a subgroup of "conflict avoiders" who, because they dislike arguments, store up grievances and resentments until they finally explode in anger. The therapist helps parents learn how to bring up difficult issues and feelings about parenting and child behavior problems in parent groups in a respectful and non-blaming way. In order to highlight the speaker's role, the speaker is given "the floor" and for humor, we quite literally give them a piece of floor tile to hold (remember that the listener might be holding the speaker's shoe!). By parents hearing each other discuss problems, they often realize others have similar problems and feelings and this helps them become more comfortable with talking about conflict. This is, of course, a long-term process that already began when parents learned about praise, encouragement, and coaching communication at the bottom of the parenting pyramid.

During parent sessions, parents practice in pairs how to bring up a problem as the speaker and to be the listener. Some of the ground rules for the speaking up and listening practice exercise include:

Politeness. Therapists help parents learn about the politeness and respect rule and how important this is in order to bring about an effective resolution of a situation regardless of how their child or partner is acting. Just because someone else is rude and childish does not make it acceptable to behave similarly. This means parents must do a bit of editing before they speak up. It is amazing but true that families are much more likely to say mean or insulting things to the people they

know and love than to strangers. Family members frequently interrupt each other, put one another down, and hurt each other's feelings. Put-downs evoke anger, resentment, defensiveness and guilt or depression, and they undermine effective communication and problem-solving.

Permission to Stop (Truce). Therapists help parents know when to call a "stop" or "truce," and to halt all discussion when they find themselves becoming increasingly critical or angry. The parents are asked to decide in advance exactly how they are going to signal verbally or nonverbally of the need for a "stop" or "truce." They might simply say, "I need to stop talking about this right now," or "I'm getting anxious. Could we talk about this later when I calm down?" (Note the use of "I" messages and feeling language.) Everyone in the family needs to agree that even if only one person gives the signal, the discussion will end temporarily. However, the person who calls the truce is then responsible for setting another time for resuming the discussion. Cooling-off periods should be no longer than 24 hours or the parents may avoid resolving the problem altogether.

Avoiding mixed messages. Avoiding "mixed messages" has already been covered in basic parenting training program and parents have learned that this type of communication, when habitual, can have such devastating psychological effects on children; even when it occurs only infrequently, it undermines the parent-child relationship. Parents think about the impact of mixed messages on their children and on their partners and loved ones. When one aspect of a person's communication conveys approval while another conveys criticism, the listener is confused and his or her self-esteem suffers. When a person's words say one thing and his or her behavior another, the listener does not know what to believe, what to trust, and loses confidence in his or her own perceptions. So speakers undermine themselves when they deliver mixed messages. Therapists emphasize the importance of being clear and consistent, so that the content and feeling of their communication match, as should the verbal and nonverbal messages. Research indicates that when there is a discrepancy, the listener tends to weight the nonverbal or feeling messages as truer. Thus even if the words are positive, when the affect is negative the child or partner will hear the message as negative.

Making requests. Probably the most difficult of communication transactions between partners, and the most common between parent and child, is that of asking someone to do something: requests and commands. In relationships where an ongoing conflict exists, these can be particularly troublesome. A direct request for a specific behavior may be perceived as authoritarian and compliance might then be felt as an acceptance of the hierarchy rather than simple cooperation. People in such relationships find themselves arguing over the specific request when the real issue is the power struggle: who is in control? Therapists help parents learn about the importance of being able to make requests in a polite way and the necessity of complying to requests in any relationship; reciprocity in the relationship is emphasized as the goal as opposed to one dominating the other. Therapists explain that accepting the influence of one's partner or one's child and complying to their requests is making a positive love deposit to their joint emotional bank account.

Repair and Support Statements. Just as parents are taught to praise their children, they are also taught to praise their partners and show appreciation for each other's efforts. For single parents we emphasize the importance of praising teachers or other family members who are

If you are begining to "see red," take a cooling off period.

assisting them with their children. These supportive and positive comments are practiced first within the group as parents applaud each other's efforts and successes, acknowledge each other's ideas, and provide support. Of course all relationships have moments of disagreement, negativity, and criticisms. These will be successfully buffered if the parents have worked at building up their positive bank account with that person. The therapist teaches parents the importance of repairing these stressful interactions with repair feedback such as, "I'm sorry, I apologize," or "How can I make things better?" or "You may be right. I never thought of that" or "I lost it. I was feeling defensive." Forgiveness is one of the tools in the parenting tool kit whose use is encouraged along with being respectful, caring, calm, loving and a good listener.

Managing Upsetting Thoughts Program

In Part 2 of the Communication Program, parents learn more about managing their upsetting thoughts. While this has been briefly discussed in the basic program, it is focused on in more depth here and is especially important for parents who have difficulty with depression, anger, and emotional self-regulation. Indeed it is difficult to speak up effectively about a problem or to listen if one cannot manage one's emotional responses. All parents have their moments of anger, stress, depression, frustration, and guilt (sometimes all at the same time) when dealing with their children's misbehaviors. Upsetting feelings are not only to be expected, but are beneficial in that they signal the need for change and provide motivation. Danger arises, however, when these feelings so overwhelm parents that they are immobilized or lose control. The aim for therapists is to help parents learn how to cope with their emotional responses to parenting in a manner that preserves their feelings of efficacy and self-control. Parents learn how to defuse negative thoughts in some of the following ways:

- Identify, stop and interrupt negative thoughts.
- Challenge and modify negative self-talk thoughts and replace them with positive coping thoughts and self-praise.
- Reschedule worries and anger for defined period of time.
- Forecast positive and realistic changes and use positive imagery.
- Objectify the situation and normalize it.
- Take personal Time Outs to calm down or refuel, and engage in self-care.

(See *Incredible Years* parent book Chapters Eleven and Twelve for specific examples or *Incredible Toddlers* book Chapter Seven.)

Therapists help parents identify negative labels they may carry regarding their children's or partner's personalities (e.g., he's totally irresponsible) or life circumstances and then help them to refute the negative attribution and refocus on specific positive behaviors they want to encourage or their goals. Therapists encourage parents to dispute their negative thinking by asking, "*Is that always true?*" or "*Is that totally accurate?*" Most likely the behavior is only true for the moment. When parents move from behavior in general to the specific behavior that is annoying them, they may be able to come up with a coping statement. For instance, Robbie's dad might say to himself, "I seem to be getting angry at Robbie for things he can't do because he doesn't have the developmental ability to articulate his needs and feelings yet. When he has more language and social skills he will eventually be able to play successfully with other children. He's already making some progress." Or, Melinda's mother might say, "She is upset because of our separation and is an emotional girl (like I am). She is testing the security of her relationship. I need to focus on helping her feel loved and in a predicable routine with clear consequences. I can help her learn to be more compliant." The therapist reminds these parents that their children's wiring and temperament means they may throw more tantrums, disobey, act impulsively, fail to listen and behave aggressively from time to time because they are delayed in their emotional, social and attentional development. However,

Parents' Viewpoint

SELF-TALK IN PROBLEM SITUATION

Identify a problem situation and the upsetting thoughts you have at the time. Write down some alternative calming thoughts that you might use to redefine the situation. Next time you find yourself using negative self-talk, give yourself some time to think positively and consider the alternative thoughts available to you when thinking about the situation.

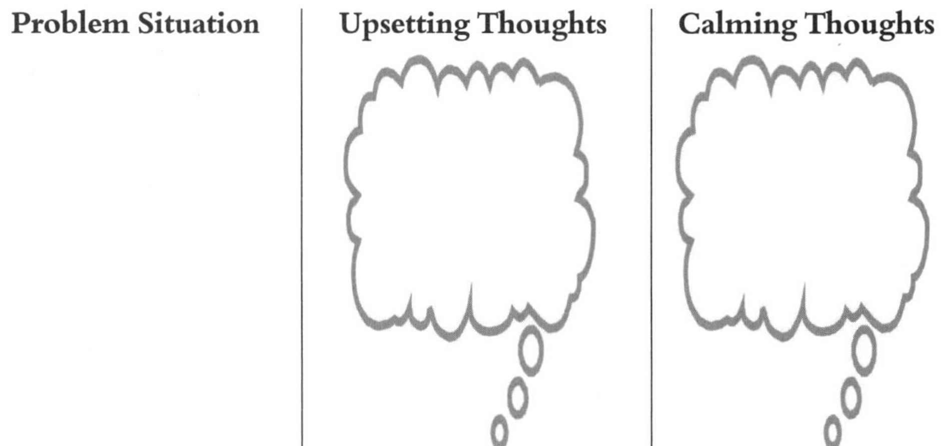

Positive Actions

with their parents' coaching, patience and loving parenting they will be able to help them learn these skills. The therapist helps parents cognitively focus on the behaviors they want to improve and to avoid speculating about motives. Instead of the mother thinking, "Melinda is doing it on purpose to make me mad," she might say to herself, "I don't know what has upset her today. I can help her learn to calm down." The mother has chosen to see herself as a facilitator of change rather than a victim of her family situation.

As parents learn to use coping, calming thoughts, and self-praise when confronted with a problem, therapists encourage them to model them for their children. While a family is seated at the dinner table, Robbie's mother might say to Dad, "Peter, we all worked hard to make today a good day. Robbie and Sam (his brother) played together this morning while I was getting Erin (the baby) dressed. I appreciated that they were cooperative, and that gave me time to get us ready to go out. We had a good time walking to the playground, and Robbie helped by holding Sam's hand on the sidewalk. Erin was fussy when we were coming home because she was tired, but Robbie and Sam and I sang to her and tried really hard to stay calm. She finally fell asleep and we all smiled! I'm proud of all of us for working as a team." Here Robbie's mother is highlighting self-control strategies that she and the children used, she is modeling self-praise and praise for her children, and is bringing the older children in as her allies and helpers with the baby. Parents modeling self-praise and pride at their own and their children's achievements are teaching their children how to praise themselves.

Therapists help parents see themselves as facilitators of change rather than victims.

The therapist helps parents script the calming and coping thoughts and self-praise statements by having them write them down with their buddy and then share in the larger group. Parents are then given an assignment to choose one or two of their favorite coping thoughts to practice during the week whenever they feel their stress is increasing.

Time Out for a breather.

Personal Time Outs To Calm Down

Modifying negative self-talk and developing a repertoire of coping thoughts helps parents lower their levels of stress. The therapist also encourages parents to develop the habit of taking personal "Time Outs" from stress that can provide an opportunity for physical, mental, and emotional relaxation and recuperation. In most sports there is provision for Time Out. These breaks give the coach and team a chance to catch their breath, strategize, and then re-enter the game with renewed energy. In our daily lives, however, there are very few Time Outs. Even coffee breaks are usually filled with stimulation rather than relaxation. Certainly there are very few opportunities for recuperation in the average parent's day, especially for at-home parents of young children. And yet it is the at-home parent who is particularly in need of opportunities to catch their breath, strategize, and re-enter the "game" of parenting with renewed energy.

The essence of parental Time Out is for parents to step back from the stress of interacting with their child and refocus on what is essential. Once parents have gained perspective on the situation and calmed their physiological reactions such as racing heart or muscle tension, they have robbed it of the power to overwhelm them. Parental personal Time Outs may last a minute or they may last an hour—whatever is possible given the circumstances. One to two parent group sessions are devoted to this topic, although aspects of these themes are interwoven throughout every session. Here are some variations on parental Time Out:

- **Time Out for a Breather.** This involves breathing deeply and slowly, ideally in a quiet place. If possible, the parent also practices deep relaxation. Actually, the mere act of deep breathing will result in some degree of muscle relaxation.
- **Time Out on the Go.** This technique can be used anywhere, while grocery shopping, doing the dishes or watching your child play. Parents are taught to systematically tense and relax certain muscle groups and to visualize their muscles relaxing and releasing tension. For example, breathe in, tensing one arm and fist as tightly as possible. Hold for a count of four, then relax fully while breathing out. Repeat for other parts of the body.
- **Time Out for Visualizing.** A third use of Time Out is to visualize or imagine a calm scene or positive future. Parents choose their own personal visualization—a cloudless sky, an expanse of ocean, a cozy beach, a quiet library, or an intimate moment they have had reading or holding their child etc. These are memories of happy, relaxed moments they have had at some time. They can also be visualizations of times when things will be better such as a time when the child doesn't need constant diaper changing or is sleeping through the night, or a time when a

parent's demanding school or work project is completed successfully. Once therapists help parents to select this image, parents can use this visualization whenever they find themselves becoming tense.

- **Time Out to Control Anger.** While some parents believe that "blowing off steam" by shouting and swearing will drain off violent energy and reduce aggression, outbursts of anger inflame aggression and violence rather than having a cathartic or beneficial effect. Studies have shown that couples who yell at each other do not feel less angry afterwards; they feel more angry. Angry outbursts are self-reinforcing because they give people a false sense of power. They often feel that their anger forces others to take them seriously or results in others' compliance. Therapists help parents to look at the long-term negative effects of anger on themselves, their relationships and on their children. When parents are taking a Time Out to control anger, therapists coach them to practice their deep breathing and visualization exercises and focus on coping self-statements.
- **Time Out for Self-Talk about Stress.** Parents are taught to use their self-talk as ways to manage stress—i.e., stopping stressful thoughts by refuting or disputing them, or putting the stress in perspective. For example, thinking, "This is normal. Stress is a reasonable and normal response to what I'm dealing with today. This is the way I usually feel when he yells at me." Parents learn to use these feelings of tension as allies in coping with the situation. They serve as a signal for parents to say to themselves, "Relax, take a slow breath. Take it easy." Therapists help parents realize their stress will rise at times and to remember that the objective is not to eliminate it totally but to keep it manageable. The idea is for parents to normalize stress and recognize it as a part of family life. Therapists help them think about it as temporary rather than ongoing, to focus on what is controllable instead of what is uncontrollable, to focus on coping rather than on feelings of being overwhelmed, and to define steps they can take to solve the problem rather than blaming others.

- **Time Out for Fun.** Therapists will need to work hard with some parents to encourage them to use Time Out for doing something pleasurable such as reading, going for a walk, taking a bath, having coffee with a friend etc. The focus is on pleasures involving little or no expense and on those that are nurturing rather than destructive to one's health.

All the above uses of parental Time Out can help parents release tension and anger, regain a calmer physiologic state, and gain a greater sense of control over their own emotional state and their own behavior—thereby helping them be calmer and more effective parents. All might be termed "self-care."

Self-Care to Refuel

Research has shown that the notion of parental self-care is a foreign concept, specially with low-income families, who are typically so overwhelmed with daily tasks and depressed about their life circumstances that they feel unable to focus on self-care. For instance, talk about Time Outs for personal or no-cost or inexpensive pleasures, is often met with resistance: "I can't take care of myself. I can't afford a sitter, and I can't leave my children alone to take a walk," or "I can't go to a movie. I don't have a car or any money!" or "You've got to be kidding. I've got enough to do!" The first homework assignment on this topic is, therefore, for parents to make a list of low cost things they could do to give themselves a pleasurable break from parenting. Another homework assignment is to list typical daily stressors and come up with a positive strategy for handling the stress. Discussion on this topic includes an exercise where parents list all possible obstacles to following through with their plan to reduce stress and think about ways to counteract some of these obstacles. As groups hear themselves talk in terms of devaluing themselves and their needs and feeling trapped, they begin to brainstorm ways they could help each other to accomplish this goal. Therapists teach parents several ways to take a personal Time Out in order to learn how to release tension and anger, and gain more self-control.

Problem Solving for Parents

Although many people might like to think that the ideal family or a couple has an absence of conflict, we know otherwise. Conflicts and disagreements are inevitable in families and couples because of competing needs, differences in individual viewpoints, and developmental changes. What marks a resilient family or couple is not the absence of disagreements and conflict, but the ability to resolve them to everyone's satisfaction (more or less). Families and couples that can successfully negotiate their differences and can accept compromise, resolving problems collaboratively so that everyone has input into the shared resolution will be better able to maintain satisfying relationships in the face of inevitable difficult periods; whereas families and couples who cannot do so will break apart under the strain.

The second program in the ADVANCE curriculum, Problem Solving for Parents also consists of three parts: problem solving about children's problems; problem-solving about interpersonal issues; and problem solving with teachers. The therapist explains that problem solving is not like other types of discussion. It is neither spontaneous nor natural; it is highly structured. Problem solving involves a specific set of

Brainstorming—use humor and creativity.

methods designed to enhance one's ability to think effectively about issues and to work towards resolution of the conflict. However, the fact that it is structured does not mean that it must be dull. On the contrary, many families report the fact that it is structured to be an interesting process that brings them together by encouraging flexibility and collaboration.

Problem-solving skills incorporate the communication and cognitive skills learned in the prior sessions. It is important that these be taught first, before the problem solving content. Anger can cause a narrowing of vision that blocks the ability to define issues and perceive options. It may also fuel the belief that other people have deliberately caused a problem and an attitude that action must be taken immediately, without time for deliberation. Depression can cause withdrawal from the process or a passive attitude towards problems. Parents must have some control over feelings of intense anger or depression before effective problem solving can begin.

Parents are taught six steps to effective problem solving be it with a partner, friend or a teacher:

Parents' Problem-Solving Steps

Step #1 Set aside a time and place to discuss a problem and decide on agenda.
Step #2 Define and describe the problem.
Step #3 Determine goals and expectations.
Step #4 Brainstorm solutions.
Step #5 Choose the best solutions and make a plan.
Step #6 Follow up with an evaluation of the plan.

In the first part of this program, parents practice problem solving about specific behavior problems they want solve. This process is similar to what teachers do when they develop behavior plans for students. First step is for the therapist to help the parents establish a time and relaxed place they can have this discussion with their partner, friend or teacher. Secondly, they need to learn how to define one behavior problem (not five!) they want to reduce and its positive opposite behavior. So for parents who are trying to help a child who is anxious, fearful, and withdrawn their goals might be to help her to be brave and initiate play with another child. Or, for the hyperactive and impulsive child, it may be helping him to be able to wait for a turn or use his words rather than grab something away. Therapists help ensure that parents are addressing positive prosocial behaviors that are developmentally appropriate for their particular child. For example, there would be many steps needed before an impulsive child could achieve the goal of playing independently with another child. First he needs to learn some social and self-regulation skills.

Once the goals have been established, then the fourth step is to brainstorm a variety of solutions or strategies that can be used to achieve that goal. Here the therapist helps the parents pick parenting strategies from the bottom of the pyramid as well as appropriate discipline strategies. Once parents have a list of possible strategies then they decide which ones are realistic and can be achieved. Finally they make a plan to try them out and to meet again to review their success.

In the group, therapists ask parents to practice the problem-solving steps with their partner or friend/buddy. First parents pick a specific child behavior problem to work on. Since at this point parents have learned a lot of parenting strategies, they may be surprised at how good they are at coming up with plans for solving these problems. Next parents learn how to use this problem solving process with teachers. Parents set up times with teachers to discuss their child's problem and goals and possible solutions or approaches that might be used both at home and at school. This collaborative approach is not only beneficial for the children but also usually results in parents and teachers who feel they are on the same team and supporting one another. The final section of this process is used for parents who have other interpersonal problems they want to try to solve such as who does particular household chores, vacation planning, financial problems, differing parenting styles, or support needs.

TEACHING CHILDREN TO PROBLEM SOLVE PROGRAM

Once parents have learned to problem solve in their own lives as adults, it then becomes easier for them to teach children how to problem solve. First and foremost, parents will already be teaching these skills by modeling their use. It is a rich learning experience for children to watch parents discussing problems with other adults, negotiating and resolving conflict, and evaluating the outcome of their solutions in an appropriate, non-hostile manner. While parents may not want their children to observe all their problem-solving meetings, many daily decisions they make provide good opportunities for them to learn. For instance, children learn from noticing how their parents say "no" to a friend's request. They watch with interest as Dad receives Mom's suggestion to wear something different. Is Mom sarcastic, angry, or matter-of-fact in her request? Does Dad pout, get angry, cooperate, or ask for more information? Watching parents decide which movie to see on Saturday night can teach children much about compromise and negotiation. Watching them discuss financial problems teaches children how to carry on a problem-solving discussion in the face of stress and worry.

Problem Solving Readiness Training. Besides parents modeling problem-solving skills, therapists can help parents learn how to teach these steps to their children directly. In the IY Preschool BASIC program the therapist helps parents learn to teach their children problem solving vocabulary through the use of books and puppets. In this case, the children are not engaged in a real-life emotional conflict but are talking about imaginary hypothetical problem situations and feelings raised by the puppets or characters in the stories. They learn to brainstorm many solutions by being "problem solving detectives." The therapist gives parents a list of possible "suppose games" they can play with their children at home for problem-solving practice. For example: Suppose a child much younger than you started hitting you. What would you do? Suppose a boy had been playing for a long, long time with a toy, and you wanted to play with it. What would you do? The objective for parents is to make these problem-solving discussions fun by using

Parents teach children how to problem solve.

cartoons, stories or puppets. They might even suggest that they write a story together. Parents are cautioned to avoid criticizing or ridiculing any of their children's ideas, no matter how silly they are. Instead, they are urged to encourage creative thinking and try to model creative solutions themselves. For younger children, 3-5 years old, most of the focus of problem solving is on generating many different solutions and practicing what those solutions look like (asking, sharing, taking turns, helping, waiting). For example, in the case of a 4-year-old child whose favorite toy is trains, a parent might set up an imaginary situation such as the following. A puppet in role as train conductor (played by the parent) says to the boy, "I have a problem because there is another train on the track and I want to start my engine. What should I do?" The boy responds, "Wait till the other engine moves." The conductor replies, "That is a good solution. I will be patient and will wait to start my engine. I'll practice blowing out my steam while I wait." In this way the parents began to introduce the problem solving and feeling language to prepare him for eventual problem solving on his own.

Children in the 5- to 7-year-old age range can start to look beyond their solutions to think about possible consequences. In other words, "what might happen if I use that solution?" Often, children are surprised or upset when things don't go as envisioned. This reaction can be partially avoided if they stop and predict several outcomes that might result from their behavior. For instance, a child might say that tricking or hitting a friend to get a toy is a solution. The parent would then help the child to consider the possible outcomes, such as losing a friend, getting into trouble, or getting the toy. The consequences of asking the friend for the toy might include being turned down or ignored—or it might get them the toy. After reviewing possible outcomes, parents help their children decide which one or two solutions might be the best. For an 8-year-old girl with attention and impulsivity problems, the mother still focuses on hypothetical situations and uses emotion language and non-aggressive solutions. For example, when playing with modeling clay, the mother in role as a doll character says, "I have a problem because I don't have any blue clay, but you have some, can I have it?" If the girl chooses to share, her character says, "Thanks for sharing that with me, I am happy." In mother role, she praises her by saying, "That was a good solution and makes your friend feel better." If the child does not share, the character replies, "Well I guess you aren't done, but I can be strong and wait." These problem-solving sessions and practices should be used for a few weeks before the parent uses them in real conflict situations. For example, when the same girl was beginning to escalate because she couldn't have something she wanted, her mother replied, "You seem disappointed about that and that is a problem. Do you think you have a solution that can help you feel better?" She helped redirect her to think about a way she could solve her problem and then praised her for staying calm.

There are two Incredible Years books, *Wally's Detective Book for Solving Problems at School* and *Wally's Detective Book for Solving Problems at Home* that present common problem situations for the children to try to solve. The parents explore possible solutions to the problem with the children and act them out with puppets. Either before or after these practices they look to the back of the book to see what solutions Wally has come up with. Parents praise children for their good solutions or ideas to solve the problem.

School-Age Problem Solving Training. Many parents confuse telling their children what to do when a real life conflict situation occurs with helping them learn to problem solve. There are many obvious problems with this approach, for example, parents may tell their children what to do before they have found out what the actual problem is—that is, from the child's viewpoint. Thus, one of the first tasks for parents when their children are engaged in conflict is to try to listen and understand the problem from their child's point of view. Parents need to learn to ask questions such

Parents learn to gauge a child's emotional readiness to engage in problem solving.

as, "What happened?" "What's the matter?" Or "Can you tell me about it?" and to deliver them in a non-accusatory tone and patiently listen so that the child will be more likely to talk openly about it. This questioning and listening not only helps the child to clarify the problem in his or her own mind, but also ensures that the parent won't jump to the wrong conclusion about what's going on. Any solution must be relevant to the child's perception of the situation, and when children believe that their parents understand their point of view, they are more likely to be willing to deal with the problem cooperatively. Rather than being told what to think and having a solution imposed upon them, children are encouraged to learn how to think. It is also important for parents to gauge a child's emotional state before trying to engage in problem solving. A child who is too upset will not be able to explain the problem or generate solutions until he or she has had time to cool off. Therapists can help parents to understand that learning to problem solve is a long process. Children of all ages will need to spend quite a bit of time with hypothetical problems and solutions at times when they are calm. It takes a great deal of self control from children to be able to problem solve in the midst of a real conflict.

The therapist teaches parents to identify times when their children are emotionally ready to problem solve and then to follow six problem solving steps when a real problem occurs. These are similar to those that parents used in their adult problem solving sessions:

School Age Children's Problem-Solving Steps

Step #1 What is my problem and how do I feel?
Step #2 What are some plans? (brainstorm solutions)
Step #3 What are the consequences? (Is it safe, fair, good feeling?
Step #4 What is the best plan or choice? (evaluate consequences)
Step #5 Am I using my plan? (implementation)
Step #6 How did I do? (evaluating outcome)

For children in the preschool age group the therapist will help parents focus on hypothetical problems and steps 1 and 2. Then the solutions will be practiced. For early school age children, the parents can begin to help them evaluate solutions; that is, whether the solution is safe, fair, and leads to good feelings. Here the children have to have the cognitive skills to be able to think ahead to future consequences or outcomes of specific solutions. Younger children with limited language skills or children with ADHD will be more likely to be "in the moment" and want to act immediately than to think and plan ahead. The focus with these children will be learning strategies such as using their words, asking, waiting, sharing and taking turns rather than grabbing or hitting or tantruming. Throughout the process, the therapist helps parents to encourage their children to talk aloud as they think and praise their ideas and attempts at solutions. In this way, parents reinforce the development of a style of thinking that will help them to deal with all kinds of problems.

The fourth and fifth steps are for parents to help children actually implement a solution (if the problem is a real-life problem). Real-life problem solving, is, of course, much harder than problem solving in a hypothetical or neutral situation. In conflict situations, children may be so angry and upset that they cannot think clearly. Parents will need to help them calm down, so they can come up with some solutions. Sometimes children may be so emotional that they need to go for a brief Time Out until they cool off. Occasionally a problem is so distressing that it is best discussed later when both parents and their children have had time to calm down and gain some perspective.

Therapists encourage parents to guide their children into thinking about what may have caused the problem in the first place and invite them to come up with a possible solution. If parents want to help their children develop a habit of solving their own problems, children need to be encouraged to think for themselves. Parents can teach their children how to think about a problem but should not teach them what to think about it. The only time parents need to offer solutions is if their children don't have any ideas. When parents do offer solutions, they should be careful to present them in the form of suggestions, that children can accept or reject, rather than as mandates for how the child must solve the problem.

Sometimes parents think they are helping their children learn problem solving by telling them to work it out for themselves. This presumes that their children already have good problem-solving skills; but, for most young children, this approach will not work. For instance, if two children are in conflict over a toy, parental ignoring will probably result in continued arguing and the more aggressive child getting the toy. The more aggressive child will be reinforced for his inappropriate behavior (because he got what he wanted), and the other child is reinforced for giving in (because the fighting ceased when he backed down). The children learn from this situation, but it is not a lesson we want them to learn.

SUMMARY

By the time a group of parents has participated in the 22-26 weeks of the BASIC plus the ADVANCE parenting program, they have used all the tools on the parenting pyramid, moving from the bottom of the pyramid, to the top, and back down to the bottom. The goal is to help parents think of themselves as effective problem-solvers for any issues that come up with their children. Rather than teaching parents a specific tool to cover each and every possible child behavior that might occur, parents learn to think about why a behavior might be happening and then to go through the pyramid systematically to pick the most appropriate tools to respond. They are encouraged always to start with the bottom of the pyramid by checking in about their current relationship with their child, then to move up to think about how they are coaching, praising and rewarding the positive opposite behaviors, and finally to think about whether a consequence is necessary. All the while, they are encouraged to monitor their own emotional reactions to the issue, and to work with other adults in the child's life to get support and consistency for their plans. A good outcome from a parenting group is for a parent to report:

> *"There are still a lot of issues that come up with my child, but I feel like I have the tools to handle these problems. I feel more competent as a parent, and I also enjoy being with my child again."*

Content of the Incredible Years® Parenting Pyramid™ ~ Discipline: Typical Questions

This chapter presents a number of questions and objections that parents frequently raise when discussing the discipline content in the program, covered in Chapter Six. This content is one of the trickiest areas for therapists to discuss with parents because of parents' feelings of guilt, shame, anger, sadness, ambivalence and loss of control. Their emotional state and prior experiences being disciplined as children in their own families will influence their receptiveness or resistance to this content and their openness or motivation for change. The therapist unconditionally accepts the parents' view of the problem, listens reflectively, and skillfully explores through open-ended questions some incongruities among their experiences and values. Through the collaborative process, the therapist teaches and reinforces change in parents' thoughts and self-talk as it relates to their personal goals for themselves and their children. Through values benefits and barriers exercises discussed in more detail in Chapter Nine, parents are helped to recognize the value of change and recognize that they have a support team who is on their side.

RULES, ROUTINES AND PREDICTABLE SCHEDULES

The topic of rules, routines, and schedules can be challenging for families of children with conduct problems because boundaries between the parents and child (and often the extended family) have often become unclear and may be beset with relationship problems and conflict regarding rules. Below are some of the commonly asked questions and barriers that parents encounter in this unit.

My partner doesn't have rules or schedules so what benefit is there in my trying to have them?

"I share custody with my ex, and when my son goes to his dad's house he can do whatever he wants. He goes to bed late, eats anytime, and has no rules. When I try to establish a bedtime my son argues that his dad lets him do what he wants. Is it worth it to try to have rules or a schedule when it changes at his dad's house?"

While it is true that consistency between parents is ideal, perfect consistency is never possible, and circumstances like those described by the parent above are common. It is important that parents know that their own internal consistency in their own home is very important, and that children will eventually learn to adjust to different parenting styles. Just as children learn there are different rules for church, the classroom, afterschool, and a friend's house, they learn what is expected at one parent's home versus the other. While it would be nice for children to have consistent bedtime and homework routines from one home to the other, it is still possible for children to learn and respect the different rules at each house. What is important here is that the parent is clear and consistent in her own relationship with her children. Although it is natural for children to push the limits and to complain about rules, in the long run, children are more securely attached to parents who are warm and responsive but enforce rules and provide consistent limits and healthy parent-child boundaries. In other words, it is absolutely worth having predictable rules, schedules, and expectations at one house, even if these are different from those in another setting. In fact, if a child is exposed to one setting that is chaotic and unpredictable, it is all the more important for the other parent to strive for a predictable and supportive environment in the other setting.

Children are more securely attached to parents who are warm and responsive but enforce rules and provide consistent limits.

Schedules are impossible in my house due to my work hours.

"I work flexible hours and sometimes I come home late and some days I have my mother taking care of the children and some days someone else. Things are constantly changing and it would be impossible to have a predictable routine."

The therapist can help parents think about what aspects of their day can be routine even if the children are taken care of by someone else. For example, help them develop and post a schedule that tells caregivers when children have meals, snacks, naps, and go to bed. Important household rules could also be posted letting caregivers know how much TV or computer time is allowed, if older children can use the phone, and the expectations for cleaning up. School age children, who may have more independence during the after school hours, should still have set expectations for homework, snack, and approved activities. Adult monitoring by means of scheduled telephone calls, or neighbor check-ins will give children the message that rules are being enforced and that their well-being is important even when parents aren't home. This will clarify the rules to everyone and avoid confusion. This consistency will help in terms of more positive child behavior and will provide security for the child and a positive relationship, regardless of their age.

I can't just drop my preschool child off at school, he yells, screams, and tantrums. He won't let me leave.
"I don't have a routine for dropping him at school. Usually I sneak away when he is not looking because I don't want to have to handle his tantrums when I tell him I have to go to work."

While understanding how difficult it is to leave a young child, the therapist can compassionately explore with this parent the child's point of view and feelings that result when a parent does not say good-bye. The group might think about the following questions: "How do you think your child will feel when he realizes you have gone without saying good bye? Might this create anxiety in the future? What do you want your child to feel about being left at school? If you had a predictable routine for saying good-bye, might this help your child feel more secure eventually? " Here the therapist is trying to get the parents to understand that while it is easier to sneak away in the short term, in the long term this may create anxiety and insecurity in the child. Then the therapist can help the group explore the value of learning to manage distressed or tantruming responses by asking, "What does it mean when a child tantrums when a parent leaves?" She helps parents see this as normal behavior and a sign that their child is very attached and will miss them. By gently and consistently saying goodbye, and then leaving, even if the child cries, parents are actually helping their children learn that although good-byes are hard, parents do predictably come back. As children understand this, it becomes easier for them to regulate their emotional responses.

I ***can't follow through with rules and schedules for my 11-year-old after school because I am not home from work yet.***
"My daughter gets home from school at 3 pm but I don't get there until 6 pm. I can't see how I can get her to follow the schedule of doing her homework and her chores."

Here the task is for the therapist to help this parent articulate exactly what routine she wants for her daughter after school and to set realistic expectations for what will be completed during that time. It is also important for the therapist and group to discuss the importance of monitoring middle school children after school. The group can discuss questions such as "How can you ensure that your child is at home during this time?" "What expectations do you have for your child about screen time and phone time during this time?" "How can you monitor these activities in a way that allows your preteen some independence but still make sure that he or she is making safe choices?" Next the group can brainstorm specific ways to monitor such as checking in by phone, having another parent or neighborhood teen drop in, reviewing homework together, and following through with chore expectations. At this age, it will also be important for the parent to work together with the child on this plan. The parent and child might set up a contract together, with an incentive if the child completes the agreed upon homework and chores.

Therapists help parents plan predictable routines and understand the importance of monitoring.

POSITIVE DISCIPLINE ~ EFFECTIVE LIMIT-SETTING

Children test parents' rules to express their individuality, and to see whether their parents are going to be consistent. It is only by breaking a rule that children can determine whether it is actually a rule or just a one-time command. The therapist helps parents expect and be prepared for this testing. Of course, the therapist needs to be sensitive to the fact that negative life stressors, such as marital discord, single parenting, poverty, unemployment, depression, and lack of support may make it difficult for parents to be consistent. However, strengthening parents' sense of competence regarding the way they limit-set and respond to children's protests can help buffer the disruptive effects of these stressors on parenting skills.

Should the parent always be in charge?

"Isn't it better for children to be free to do their own problem-solving and learn from their mistakes rather than to impose a lot of rules and limits on children? Won't this approach help children to develop their own internal controls, and won't adult-imposed limits create children who rely on adults to come up with the limits?"

Sometimes parents perceive limit-setting as an interference with children's right to self-determination or their need to learn to work out problems for themselves. Helping parents think through the possible outcomes of this can be helpful. To take a concrete example, if two children are fighting over a book and the parent does not step in to set limits on the fighting, the arguing will probably continue and result in the more aggressive child getting the book. Therefore the aggressive child will be reinforced for his inappropriate behavior, after all, he got what he wanted, and the other child will be reinforced for giving in because the fighting ceased when he backed down. In another example, if a parent of a school aged child lets the child decide how much television to watch, it is possible that the child will choose to watch many hours each day, and will miss out on other important life activities. In situations like this one, the parental role is to set clear limits, to protect children from hurting each other and to help them make healthy decisions. Limits around safety issues should be stated in a positive, firm, and polite manner, but should be non-negotiable. In the case of seat belts, hitting, not taking bicycles out onto the street, it should be obvious that parents need to exert firm control over their children. Parents should also be in charge of areas such as television watching, video games, computer use, phone use, and after school activities since, left on their own, children are unlikely to moderate their own behavior in these areas.

It is important for children to make their own decisions, however, and therapists can help parents think about times when children can make their own choices. Why not allow children to have control over decisions such as what clothes to wear, whether or not to eat all the food on their plates, what stories to read before bed? Allowing children to be "in charge" of these decisions helps them develop a sense of autonomy and allows them to learn from experiencing the consequences of their own choices. Under still other circumstances, parents can share control with their children by involving them in problem-solving. Here the parent's role is to help children understand different perspectives and to encourage them to come up with alternative solutions. While this problem-solving approach will be a slow process, and becomes effective only when children are older, introducing negotiation and discussion with children as young as four or five can provide excellent early training. For instance, there are times when parents can involve their children in the decision regarding a rule. Consider two preschool children who are fighting because they both want to play with the bubbles and there is only one bubble blower. Their father might respond by giving a command: "First, Doug, you will use it. Then, Susie, it will be your turn." But an alternative approach, one that involves sharing control, would be for the father to involve both children in deciding how to handle the problem. He might say, "There is only one bubble blower and two of you. What should we do? Do you have any ideas?" If Doug and Susie come up with some solutions, then Dad can reinforce their problem-solving ability. By avoiding the authoritarian approach, he can encourage his children to find their own solutions to a problem and help them learn to think through different solutions. As children get older and have more self-control, parents will gradually begin to modify the limits so that children have more independence and input, but still with parental control over the end outcome. Certainly the goal is that by the time children are in their late teenage years, they are ready to make their own decisions. An authoritative approach, where the parent is in charge, but is respectful of the child, gives the child power in some decisions, and shares power at other times will help children develop good decision-making judgment.

Therapists help parents think about times when children can make their own choices.

Can a parent do too much limit-setting?

"I feel that I am limit-setting, or rather yelling and telling the kids what not to do, all day long. My problem is not in failing to limit-set. Could I be doing too much limit-setting?"

Few parents are aware of the actual number of commands they give their children. Would it surprise you to hear that the average parent gives 17 commands in half an hour? And in families where children have behavior problems, the number rises to an average of 40 commands in half an hour! Moreover, research has shown that the children of parents who give an excessive number of commands develop more behavior problems. Frequent commands, then, do not improve a child's behavior. For one thing, if parents are giving 20 to 40 commands in half an hour, it is impossible for them to follow through with each command. The result is that confusing messages are given to children about the importance of commands: sometimes the commands are important and need to be followed, and other times they are dropped by the parents. How is the child to know which are the important commands to follow? Another reason frequent commands are not helpful is that usually the rapid commands are being given at the time when the child is being oppositional and noncompliant. This parental attention (in the form of repeated commands) actually reinforces the child's noncompliance. Therefore, it is essential for therapists to help parents self-reflect both on the number and type of commands they give their children and to reduce them until they are giving only necessary commands, commands they are willing to follow through on with consequences for noncompliance.

Therapists help parents self-reflect both on the number and type of commands they give their children and how to reduce unnecessary commands.

Some parents tend to give a command when the child is already engaged in the action or to repeat a command even when the child has begun complying. For example, the parent tells the child to get her shoes on when she is already in the process of putting on her shoes. This tends to sound like criticism to the child; it implies that she is not complying when in fact she is complying. Thus it undermines her efforts to be compliant. Other parents give commands about issues that are not actually important to them. They might say, "Color that frog green," "Wear your blue shirt," or "Finish your dessert." Does the parent really care about these things? If the issue is not an important one, then children should be allowed to decide for themselves rather than become involved in a battle of wills with their parents. The key idea here is that parents should reserve their commands for the important issues.

Before giving a command, parents should think about whether the issue is really an important one, and whether they are willing to follow through with the consequences if their child doesn't comply. One exercise that can be helpful is to ask parents to write down the important rules for their family. Parents will probably find that they have between five and ten that are "unbreakable." These should be posted on the fridge or in some other place where all the family can see them. In this way, everyone, including baby sitters, will know what the rules are. Such a list might include:

- Seat belts must be worn in the car at all times
- Gentle hands and bodies with others (no hitting or hurting)
- Ball play and roughhousing are for outside
- Homework must be finished before TV time
- 30 minutes of screen time allowed on weekdays, 60 minutes on weekend days
- Food must stay in the kitchen

Parents will find that clarifying their household rules helps them be more precise when stating the rules and the commands that enforce the rules. They will also be able to reduce the number of unnecessary commands given. With fewer and more precise commands, it will be easier to follow through with consequences when necessary. The result is that children will learn that parental commands are important and that compliance is expected.

Isn't it better to "disguise" or "soften" commands?

"My child is more compliant when I disguise my commands. If I give an order, he fights back. So I say, "Oh my goodness, your coat is on the floor. I wonder why it is there?" Sometimes I get him to do what I want by demanding the opposite, for example, " You're not going to put away your coat."

While some parents of children with behavior problems are authoritarian and have too many rules and commands, others avoid giving direct commands. They may do this because they are too tired or overwhelmed to face a negative reaction from their child. Past experience has taught them that their child will tantrum, talk back, or refuse to comply, so they bypass the command altogether or soften it in the hopes that their child won't object. Other times parents feel guilty when they tell their children to do something that their children might object to. Parental guilt can occur for many reasons: because of divorce or a distressed marriage, because the parent works full time and has precious little time with the child, because the child has a chronic disease or developmental delay, or because the child was adopted or had a parent that died. In these cases, guilt over the particular family problem can make the parent somewhat overprotective and wanting to prevent the child from experiencing any further pain or distress. In the above situations parents may disguise their commands with vague and indirect language. Some typical examples of indirect commands are phrased in such ways as, "Don't you think you should. . ." or "It would be nice if you . . . " or "Why don't we . . .?" or "How about. . .?" This form of command can confuse a child because it is unclear whether the behavior is optional or expected.

Another type of "disguised" command is the one that a parent states as a descriptive comment. For instance, Delia says to her daughter, "Oh Denise, you're spilling your milk." Or Derek's father looks out the window and says, "Derek, your bike is still in the yard!" In addition to lacking clarity, these statements contain an implied criticism. Not only is it difficult to get a child to comply to statements, as opposed to direct commands ("Hold the glass with both hands." "Please put your bike away."), but the critical aspect of such statements is likely to breed resentment.

"Let's" commands are another problematic command. In an attempt to soften the request the parent may say: "Let's wash the dishes," "Let's get ready for bed." This kind of command can be confusing for young children if their parents have no intention of becoming involved. For instance, a mother who has been playing with her two sons in the kitchen now wants them to put away the toys. She says, "Let's put the toys away." If she isn't willing to help them, they probably won't cooperate and she will become cross with them; but the fault lies with her command, which does not clearly convey her expectations. If on the other hand, she really intends to help with clean up, then a "let's" command is a good way to convey her willingness to cooperate with them.

Other examples of vague and unclear commands are: "Watch out," "Be careful," "Be nice," "Be good," "Knock it off," and "Just a minute." These statements can be confusing to a child, because they do not specify the expected behavior. It is important for parents to be specific about the behavior they want from their child when they give a command. If Kim asks her mother to play with her, instead of the mother saying "Just a minute," she might say, "Wait 5 minutes, then I'll play with you." Instead of telling Robbie to "Be careful" when he is spilling juice, the parent might say, "Use both hands to pour the juice into your glass." Instead of saying "Be nice," the parent could say, "Please let your brother use that when you are done."

Paradoxical commands such as, "Don't eat those peas" (when the parent in fact wants the child to eat the peas), may work in the short run because they provide some humor. However, such mixed message commands have the potential of backfiring. If these paradoxical commands work, then the child is getting reinforced for noncompliance. There may be situations in the future where the parent truly doesn't want the child to do something and the child doesn't believe him/her. (This is the parental version of the "Boy Who Cried Wolf" situation.)

It is useful to have a conversation about the fact that clear consistent commands are particularly important for children who are noncompliant much of the time. With children who have difficulty following directions, parents will want to be as clear as they can be in order to avoid any confusion. These are children who notice inconsistencies in parenting and will test any perceived "weakness" in the system. Parents of easy going children are likely to be able to get away with occasional "sloppy" or humorous commands because their children's temperaments are more forgiving.

"Chain" Commands and "Repeat" Commands

"I have to ask my child at least 10 times to get him to go to bed or to get dressed in the mornings. I feel like such a nag, but he doesn't seem to hear me when I make requests."

Sometimes parents string commands together in a chain, without giving their child time to comply with the first command before going on to the next. For young children, this can result in information overload. For example, Eva tells her 4-year-old, "It's time for bed. I want you to put your markers away, pick up your papers, go upstairs and get your pajamas on, go the bathroom and then brush your teeth." A series of commands such as this is difficult for children to remember, especially active children with a short attention span. Most can retain only one or two things at a time. Another problem with rapid commands is that the parent is not able to praise the child for complying with any of the individual commands, so that the child is not reinforced. Eventually, this results in more noncompliant behavior partly because the child simply can't comply with everything, partly because there is no reinforcement for compliance.

Child in a command storm

A related type of communication problem involves the parent repeating the same command over and over again as if the child has not heard it. Many parents repeat the same request four or five times, and their children quickly learn that there is no real need to comply until the fifth time, when the parent sounds angry. Moreover, chain commands reinforce noncompliant behavior because of the amount of attention the child receives. The therapist helps the parent learn to state the command once, clearly and respectfully, and then wait to see whether the child will comply. Parents can be coached to count slowly to 5 while they wait to see how their child will respond. This will help parents resist the impulse to nag. If the child complies, parents can praise the response and if not, they can enforce a consequence.

Therapists help the parents learn to state the command once, clearly and respectfully, and then wait for compliance.

Aren't angry commands and threats useful at times?

"It's not until I get really angry or threaten to take away something that my child will finally does what I want."

When parents are angry, their commands may take on an angry, hostile affect, critical or demeaning tone. This is understandable; all parents feel frustrated with their children at times, and all occasionally lose their cool. For example, Billy's dad might say, "Billy, why won't you sit still for once in your life!" Or he might tell Billy to sit still in a sarcastic tone of voice, "Can't you do any better than that? What a baby!" Or," I'm sick of this mess. You're a slob! Clean this up."

A major theme in the second half of the program is to help parents think about the impact of their own emotional state on the effectiveness of their discipline. Parents discuss the reasons why parental anger and frustration detract from the effectiveness of their discipline. For example, negative commands cause children to feel incompetent and discounted. They may react by becoming defensive and less inclined to comply. Negative or angry commands also are a signal to the child that

Exercises in positive self-talk, calm-down strategies, coping thoughts and seeking support are woven throughout the discipline sessions.

the parent is losing his or her cool. For many children this is a very reinforcing and powerful position to be in, and they may continue the noncompliance to see how much control they have over the situation. Both of these are good reasons for parents to work to control their emotions; negative and critical commands are not good for the child's sense of self worth, they damage the parent-child relationship, and they are not likely to be effective! Commands should be stated positively, politely, and with respect. Otherwise, the child may choose not to comply as a way of retaliating for a parent's criticism, and as a way of defending their own self-worth.

For the therapist, the issue of parent anger involves a two-step challenge. First parents must be convinced, through the collaborative, self-reflective process, role play practices, and vignette discussion, that anger and frustration are not healthy or effective ways of disciplining. Next, therapists must find ways to help parents manage these emotions. Exercises in positive self-talk, calm-down strategies, coping thoughts and seeking support are woven throughout the program, particularly in the discipline units.

"Stop" Commands and Prohibitions versus Positive Commands and Permissions

"Why should commands always be stated positively? Isn't it better to give a clear message about the problem or the misbehavior?"

Another type of negative command is a "stop" command. A "stop" command is a type of negative statement that tells a child what not to do. "Stop shouting," "Don't do that," "Quit it," "Shut up," "Cut it out," and "Enough of that" are all stop commands. These commands contain a criticism of the child's behavior and focus on the misbehavior instead of telling the child how to behave correctly.

Sports psychologists have found that if the coach tells the pitcher, "Don't throw a fast ball," a fast ball is just what the pitcher is likeliest to throw; not out of defiance, but simply because that is what the coach's words have made him visualize. It's worth making every effort, therefore, for parents to give positive commands that specify the behavior they want from their child. Instead of saying, "Stop yelling," or "Stop splashing," the parent should say, "Please speak quietly," or "Keep the water inside the tub." Whenever a child does something the parent doesn't like, the parent should try to think of what alternative behavior s/he wants and then phrase the command to focus on that positive behavior. One exercise in this unit is to have parents think of behaviors that they want to see less of. Then the group brainstorms the "positive opposite" behavior and the positive command that they could use. The goal is for parents to leave the session with a repertoire of clear, positive commands that are specific to behaviors they are working on at home.

A related issue is that of prohibitions versus permission. Many times parents' commands prohibit their children from doing something they want to do, such as playing with friends or watching more television. In such instances parents tell their children what they cannot do, but forget to tell them what they can do instead. When children feel rigidly restricted and prohibited from fun activities, they may react with protests and noncompliance. Commands that prohibit a child from doing something should include permission or suggestions for alternative activities. A parent might say, "You may not watch TV now, but you can play with this puzzle with me," or "You can't play with Daddy's tools, but you can build a fort in the basement." Giving an alternative to the prohibited behavior can help reduce power struggles because, instead of staying with arguing the issue under dispute, the parent is turning the child's attention towards another activity, a positive one which the child is free to engage in.

Decreasing Resistance Through Warnings

"My child hates being interrupted when she is working on something. How can I deal with her resistance to limit-setting?"

Sometimes children react adversely to parent commands when they are given abruptly, without any warning. Picture this scene: Jenny is totally absorbed in building a castle with her blocks. Suddenly her father walks into the room and tells her to go to bed. What happens next? Probably much protest and resistance from an unhappy Jenny.

Whenever feasible, it is helpful to give a reminder or warning prior to a command, in order to prepare for the transition. If Jenny's dad had noticed that she was engrossed in playing with her blocks and said, "In two more minutes, it will be time to put your blocks away," Jenny might have still objected to stopping, but she would have had time to wind down her play. Over time, children who are giving ample transition warnings learn to regulate their behavior during transitions.

Therapists help parents learn to give transition warnings.

There are many ways to give warnings. For young children who don't understand the concept of time, a timer can be helpful. Then parents can say, "When the timer goes off, it will be time to put these blocks away." Or the warning can be tied to completion of a specific task. "When you finish putting those three blocks on the tower, it will be time to stop" or "We have time for one more story and then we will turn out the light." For older children, parents can refer to a clock.

Children's requests and preferences should be considered, as well. For instance, if an 8-year-old is busy reading a book, the parent might ask, "How many more pages are there before the end of your chapter?" If the child replies, "One more page," the parent could say, "Okay, when you finish that page, I want you to set the table." When parents are responsive to their children's wishes and give them some lead time, they are more likely to obtain compliance. Similarly, there are times when a parent might let a child negotiate the transition. For a young child this might sound like: "We need to go soon. Would you like to clean up now or in 5 minutes." For an older child, a parent might say: "We have an hour before dinner and I need you to mow the lawn before we eat." The child could have the option of choosing when to mow the lawn, as long as it was finished by dinner time. When children feel they have some control over situations, they are more likely to be cooperative. Of course, in these cases, the parent still has ultimate control and if, at the end of 5 minutes, the child tries to negotiate for more time, then the parent follows through with the clean up command.

How important is consistency?

"How important is it to be consistent with limit-setting? I mean, if you say bedtime is 8 p.m., how harmful is it to then let a child stay up until 9 p.m. one night?"

Effective limit-setting does not require parents to be authoritarian or to rigidly enforce the rules regardless of circumstances. Rather, the emphasis is on parents thinking carefully before giving a command to be sure that it's necessary, and that they're prepared to follow through with the consequences. When thinking about commands or household rules, it is important to strike a balance between a child's choices and adult rules. Once a parent has decided a command or household rule is important, then s/he should be consistent in following through with its enforcement. If parents are consistent with their commands, then children will learn to accept them and their initial protests will subside. If parents are chronically inconsistent about the importance of their rules and fail to follow through, children will learn to protest and test the limits more and more often.

Consistency is a virtue, but not when it becomes an inflexible policy. For instance, if the parent's household rule is an 8 p.m. bedtime, and one night the parent's usually reserved child begins to talk about a challenging school situation 5 minutes before bedtime, a competent parent will realize this is a good time to make an exception to the rule and let the child stay up later to talk. Inconsistency, in this case, is justified by the parent's sensitivity to the unique needs of her child at that moment. On the other hand, if the parent found that delaying bedtime with conversations was becoming a pattern every night, then the parent would need to re-enforce the rule regarding bedtime. If parents have allowed some inconsistency about a rule (for whatever reason), children will often protest when the parent begins to be consistent again. This is to be expected and after a few days, the child will accept the limit again with less fuss. If parents are aware that they are being inconsistent or making an exception to the usual rule, it can help to explain this to the children so that they are prepared ahead of time for things to resume to normal on subsequent days. For example: "Tonight we are going to all watch a movie together, so you will get to stay up an hour past your usual bedtime! This is a special treat, and tomorrow we'll go back to your regular bedtime." Such an approach can help minimize some of the costs of inconsistency.

TEACHING PARENTS ABOUT IGNORE SKILLS

Most children will occasionally exhibit high rates of irritating behaviors such as whining, teasing, arguing, swearing, and tantrums, especially when they are denied something or can't do what they want. Testing the limits in this way is usually not dangerous to children or other people, but if parents are not able to systematically ignore the arguments or defiant attitude these protests will usually increase. The therapist will find that ignoring is one of the most difficult approaches for parents to use. Many parents will argue that ignoring is not discipline. Thus, the therapist needs to help parents understand why this discipline approach works and the principle behind its effectiveness. Below are some of the many questions that arise during the ignoring unit.

Isn't ignoring children's misbehavior unrealistic and irresponsible?

"I just can't see ignoring a child when he or she is smart-talking; being defiant is disrespectful. Why let a child verbally abuse you? These behaviors need discipline! Ignoring this is teaching your child he can be disrespectful."

Frequently parents of children with behavior problems don't feel that ignoring is sufficient discipline. However, ignoring is an effective discipline approach because it maintains a positive parent-child relationship based on respect rather than fear. Ignoring teaches children that there is no payoff (such as parental attention in the form of facial expressions, talking, or body language) for inappropriate behaviors. When parents do not visibly react to these misbehaviors, their children lose their motive for continuing to use them. Ignoring also reduces power struggles because by ignoring, a parent is dropping the rope and refusing to be drawn into arguments, pleading, or negative exchanges. When children come to realize that swearing and talking back don't get a reaction or result from their parents, whereas asking nicely results in approval and positive attention, they will begin to substitute positive behaviors for negative ones. Moreover, when a parent ignores swearing or screaming instead of yelling at or criticizing the child, the parent is showing the child that s/he can maintain self-control in the face of conflict and anger; it is effective modeling. Therapists must work hard to help parents understand the "attention principle" and the rationale for ignoring through explanations, video modeling, and practices discussed in more detail in Chapters Eight and Nine.

Therapists must work hard to help parents understand the "attention principle" and the rationale for ignoring.

How long should you ignore?

"I can do the ignoring approach for only so long; then I explode and yell at him."

Sometimes well-intentioned parents start to ignore misbehavior such as tantrums or arguments without being prepared for their child's response. Most children, when ignored, will initially react with an increase in negative and oppositional behaviors. They're attempting to see if they can get their parents to back down. For instance, 5-year-old Megan wants to go outside. She argues with her mother about this for several minutes. Finally her mother tells her she may not go outside and proceeds to ignore any protests. Megan escalates her demands to see if she can get what she wants. This goes on for ten more minutes until her mother, exasperated and worn down by the arguments, says, "All right, go outside!" By giving in for the short-term benefit of making life more peaceful, the mother has created a long-term problem: Megan has learned that if she argues long and hard enough, she will get what she wants. Thus, her inappropriate behavior has been reinforced and next time her mother sets a limit, Megan will be prepared to protest for at least 10 minutes!

The therapist can help parents understand that when they first start ignoring a misbehavior, it will usually get worse. If they are going to use this powerfully effective approach, they must be prepared to wait out this period if the behavior is to improve. If they give in, their children will learn that persisting in the misbehavior is an effective way to get what they want.

Choosing to ignore misbehavior doesn't mean that there is nothing positive a parent can do to improve the situation. In fact, failure to provide distractions or suggestions for alternative, more appropriate behavior can lock parents and children into a power struggle and cause the children to prolong the misbehaviors. Consider this scenario: Tony, a 4-year-old, asks his father to buy him a toy while they're out shopping. His father refuses and Tony starts yelling and screaming. His father effectively ignores this by walking away, and in a couple of minutes the screaming subsides. Tony's father continues shopping without paying any particular attention to Tony. Tony, feeling ignored, begins to scream again in an attempt to gain his father's attention.

Instead Tony's father could be coached to return his positive attention back to Tony as soon as the tantrum subsides. He might try to distract him by having him help find items to put into the cart, talk about what they will do after they shop, or begin telling silly jokes. Distractions are particularly useful with young children, who often exhibit a high rate of tantruming behavior, but they also work with older children. It is vitally important that children learn that there is more payoff (in the form of attention) for calm, cooperative behavior than there is for negative behavior. The principle is to ignore the child's negative behavior, and then distract him as soon as he starts behaving more appropriately. Of course, if the child misbehaves again in response to the distraction, the parent would need to resume ignoring.

What if you can't ignore the misbehavior?

"I can't ignore foul language. He verbally abuses me, and I don't think it's right to let him do that to me. It fills me with such rage that after ignoring it a couple of times, I just lose it and yell at him."

Sometimes parents try to ignore a misbehavior that really bothers them. Then as the misbehavior escalates, they suddenly feel they can't stand another minute of it and they explode with anger. There are several problems here. First, these parents wait until they are boiling with anger and about to lose control. Second, they give the child no warning. Third, this approach does not teach children anything except an explosive response to frustration.

Parents may not even be aware of the mounting anger that certain inappropriate behaviors trigger in them until they explode. The therapist can help parents learn to monitor their reactions to particular misbehaviors. Then, if parents find that swearing or whining (or any other behavior) triggers a strong emotional response, they may decide that it isn't possible to ignore this behavior for very long. If this is the case, then the therapist should suggest the "Three Strikes and You're Out" Rule: parents tell their children that interrupting (or swearing) three times will result in a Time Out. The first time a child interrupts, the parent might say, "That was your first interruption." Then "That was the second interruption," and finally "That was your third interruption. Go to Time Out to calm down." This approach

Three strikes and you're out!

warns the child that the behavior is inappropriate and alerts the parent to his/her mounting annoyance level. With this approach, the parent is clear about exactly what type of behavior will result in Time Out and models an effective, calm and rational approach to a problem behavior. At the same time, the parent should be coaching, praising, and perhaps setting up an incentive system for waiting for a turn to talk. Since Time Out comes after ignoring in the program's sequence, it is important not to jump too quickly to the Time Out step. During the ignoring unit, it is important that all parents choose some behavior to ignore and learn how to ignore effectively. As in every other unit, parents set their own individual goals, so the parent who knows that she can't ignore swearing would be encouraged to pick a different behavior, perhaps whining or nagging, to ignore. Sometimes when parents have success ignoring lower level behaviors first, they are convinced of the power of this strategy and they find that they are willing to attempt ignoring with higher level behaviors.

What if I am ignoring my child but others are not?
"I tried ignoring his tantrums, but all the other children in the classroom laugh at him and at home my husband refuses to ignore such misbehavior; so what good does it do for me to ignore?"

This is an important point. If the child's misbehavior is being reinforced or given attention by other children or adults in the room, then the parents' ignoring is probably going to be ineffective. In such a case, the parent needs to remove the child to another place where the child can be ignored effectively (as in a Time Out). Otherwise, another strategy should be used, such as telling the child s/he will lose a privilege or have to do a chore. Meanwhile, the parent should work to minimize the amount of attention the child is getting. Parents may also want to consider informing relatives, babysitters, neighbors, and teachers about the ignoring strategy and the targeted misbehaviors. If parents can get the cooperation of relatives and teachers in their ignoring efforts, they will likely see fast improvement.

It is worth revisiting the issue that within parent consistency is also important and that any successful ignore sequences will make a difference. If a mother is ignoring whining consistently at her house (at times when no other adults are around), but the whining gets attention at grandmother's house, the child will eventually learn that whining doesn't work with his mother.

How can you ignore a child who clings onto you?

"I find that when I ignore his tantrums and yelling, he gets worse and starts to pull on my body and follow me around screaming. Sometimes he even ends up breaking something. It drives me crazy and I explode."

When ignoring a clinging child, it may help for the parent to physically move away, to stand up and walk to another part of the room. If the child follows the parent, holding on to her legs or arms, the parent must evaluate whether he or she can continue to ignore. For example, it might be possible to ignore a 2- to 4-year-old child who is pulling on the parent's legs and crying. Possibly the parent could move to the kitchen and wash dishes, chop food for dinner, or otherwise look engaged, while standing up. If the parent appears not to notice the clinging, the child will eventually realize that the tantrum isn't working, and the ignore will have been successful.

Therapists should not jump to Time Out until parents have mastered a structured ignore and learned some calm down strategies.

Sometimes parents ignore their child's misbehavior by walking out of the room when their child is clinging and physically demanding attention from them. However, the difficulty with leaving the room is that the parent won't be able to give back attention to and reinforce appropriate child behavior as soon as it occurs. In addition, young children may follow the parent or escalate further and it is not wise to leave a young and highly dysregulated child alone for any length of time.

Therapists will also need to have a discussion about what to do if the child's behavior escalates to a point where the parent really can't continue to ignore. For instance, what should happen if a child begins to hit the parent hard, throw things in a way that seems dangerous, or is otherwise engaging in behavior that is unsafe or hurtful. At this point, parents will be coached to switch from an ignore to a Time Out, which is really a structured ignore. In this way the hard work of the ignore is not lost, but the parent has more control over the placement of the distressed child. Again, therapists should not jump to this step in the discipline hierarchy until the parents have mastered ignoring, and have learned the proper Time Out sequence.

Threatening the ultimate ignore?

"Okay, well, if ignoring works, then I decided to use the ultimate ignore. He wouldn't get dressed and I asked him a hundred times so I finally said, 'If you don't get your shoes on I will leave without you.' Well, he wasn't ready so I got in the car and drove down the street. When I came back he was dressed and standing crying on the street, so it worked."

Parents who take ignoring to an extreme and threaten to leave, or actually leave, their children believe that the fear caused by their leaving will mobilize the children into being more compliant. While such threats may get the child out the door, they have several long-term disadvantages. Parents have resorted to a fear approach rather than a respectful approach. In order to continue to be effective with this approach, all threats need to be backed up with the threatened consequence. Once a child realizes the parent is only pretending to leave, she may respond by taunting: "Go ahead and leave me. See if I care!" The parent is then left in a powerless position because the child has called her bluff. To not leave is to fail to follow through. Yet leaving isn't really an option, since a young child is not safe alone at home. The emotional hazard is also great, as threats to abandon children make them feel insecure and lead to poor self-esteem. Furthermore, parents are providing a powerful negative model, namely, avoiding conflict by running away from it. We have seen children treated with this approach begin to threaten to run away or even leave home to test the power of this tactic for getting what they want.

Parents should be cautioned never to threaten to leave or abandon their children, no matter how great the temptation. There are more effective strategies for inducing compliance. If parents can muster the self-control to ignore the behavior that makes them feel so angry, their child will begin to behave more appropriately, and the parent's frustration will decrease. If parents can't use ignoring, they may need to try another discipline technique such as Time Out, chores, or loss of privileges. While these strategies will take more of parents' time in the short run, unlike leaving, they teach children that the parent-child relationship is secure, regardless of conflict. These strategies are far preferable because they are based on respect, rather than on fear of abandonment.

There are times when a parent might decide that he or she needs a break from a tantruming child in order to self-regulate. When there are two parents or other caregivers working together, parents can be encouraged to tag team, if necessary. This is different than abandoning the child because it is planned and supervised. In addition, the parent does not make a threat to leave, but merely takes a break while another caregiver takes over monitoring. In these cases, it is important for parents to have a way to signal the need for a switch off to the other parent/caregiver. The other parent then takes over the ignore, including looking for a chance to give positive attention back to the child when the tantrum is over. For the single parent, back up plans can be made to call her buddy or therapist for support when a break is needed. Often times just talking on the phone distracts the parent as well as taking the parental attention away from the child, resulting in the tantrum subsiding. Parents and their buddy can plan these telephone discussions and can support each other to use coping thoughts or self-talk to calm down. Therapists who are working with parents with anger control problems will particularly want to discuss these options with parents.

TEACHING PARENTS ABOUT EFFECTIVE "TIME OUT" SKILLS

In the initial weeks of intervention, the therapists' main focus is to teach the parents the importance of providing the problem child with ongoing and regular communication and expression of parental love, support, coaching, praise and understanding and incentives. This provides the foundation for the child's ongoing emotional and social development. Next the therapists teach parents how to provide predictable routines

Therapists help parents understand how Time Out to Calm Down has more long-term advantages that make it worth the extra effort in the short term.

and rules, clear limits and consequences for their children's misbehavior. At the top of the pyramid, parents learn to use Time Out for aggressive, unsafe, or highly oppositional behaviors.

Like ignoring, the Time Out content is often met with parental resistance by parents who have used spanking as their primary discipline strategy or with difficulties in implementing the procedures when children's behavior is extreme. The therapist's job will be to help parents understand how Time Out to calm down has more long-term advantages and is worth the extra effort in the short run. Therapists will also work with parents to refine Time Out procedures and trouble shoot barriers. Below are some of the questions that parents often ask about Time Out.

Isn't spanking or smacking preferable to Time Out?

"I think spanking is better than Time Out because it works to get my child to obey; it's quick and lets the child know I am in control. After all, I was spanked as a child and I turned out okay."

Spanking or smacking is commonly used by parents because it is quick and usually stops the misbehavior in the short term. The problem with spanking is that it has long-term disadvantages. The first is that when a parent spanks a child, s/he models an aggressive response to misbehavior; children who are spanked frequently learn to resort to aggressive responses when they are frustrated. Even worse, when parents spank, they are often out of control or feel out of control. Besides being a frightening and potentially harmful experience for their children, this loss of control creates feelings of guilt in the parents once they calm down. They may then respond by overcompensating with gifts (sometimes causing a child to endure spankings for the sake of the rewards) or by avoiding any use of discipline in the future. Another difficulty with spanking is that it tends to "wipe the slate clean" for children, leaving them with no ongoing sense of remorse for misbehavior. Frequently, the result is children who are compliant and conforming in the parents' presence but who are likely to behave inappropriately elsewhere. Yet another result of spanking is that children learn to hide or lie about problems in order to avoid being hit. In fact, the more hurtful the discipline, whether it be degrading criticisms or physical punishment, the more devious and resistant children become.

The task for the therapist is to teach parents a nonviolent and respectful approach to discipline that simultaneously lets children know which behaviors are inappropriate, gives children the positive expectation that they will be able to do better next time, and conveys the message that they are deeply loved. Methods such as ignoring, logical consequences, loss of privileges, problem solving, and Time Out are effective discipline approaches that meet these criteria. Besides its ethical advantages, Time Out offers several practical advantages over spanking. It models a nonviolent response to conflict, stops the conflict and frustration, provides a cooling-off or calm-down period for both children and parents, and maintains a respectful, trusting relationship in which children feel they can be honest with their parents about their problems and mistakes. Unlike spanking, Time Out teaches children to calm themselves down and think of a better solution than hitting, and fosters an internal sense of responsibility or conscience.

Therapists deal with parents' resistance by means of a values clarification.

One of the ways therapists deal with parents' resistance is by means of a values clarification exercise. The parent group leader brainstorms with the parents a list of the advantages of spanking versus Time Out. Next they list and discuss the disadvantages of spanking versus Time Out. Through this process parents come to realize that spanking has short-term advantages for the parent (not the child) and long-term disadvantages for both. On the other hand, Time Out has short-term disadvantages for the parent and long-term advantages for both the child and the parent. Parents' understanding that they are working towards a long-term solution rather than a short-term "quick fix" helps create a willingness to try alternative approaches.

Isn't Time Out psychologically harmful?

"I disagree with Time Out. It is harmful to children because parents are withdrawing their love, which is devastating for children."

Some parents avoid using Time Out because they want their relationships with their children, including discipline, to be democratic and equal. They believe that parents should never impose their authority or exercise their power over their children, and that reasoning with youngsters about their problems is preferable to putting them in Time Out. They may feel that Time Out is disrespectful to children and even a form of rejection, because it represents withdrawal of love.

First of all, it is important not to equate Time Out with a general style of child rearing. Some parents are autocratic and expect complete obedience from their children. Such people may use Time Out to crush children's independence, creativity, problem-solving, and questioning of values. For example, they may use Time Out frequently throughout the day and for minor offenses. Such parents might say in a critical tone of voice, "What is wrong with you? You never remember to pick up your things. You are driving me crazy! Go to Time Out." This approach doesn't help kids believe in themselves and inspires hostility from the child.

When Time Out is used in the context of a loving and respectful parent-child relationship, it can be a very effective positive discipline approach. In this case Time Out is used, not as punishment, but to teach children that there are consequences for misbehaving and how they can calm themselves down before handling a conflict situation. For example, such a parent would say to his 5-year-old child who has just hit his brother, "I can see you are angry about your brother using your toy, but hitting is not okay; you need to use your words. Please go to Time Out for 5 minutes." Remind parents that an authoritative child-rearing does not mean unlimited freedom with no rules, but rather guided freedom within limits. These limits have

Therapists help parents understand that Time Out teaches children how to calm down.

to be set and imposed, and within most families they usually include not hurting people or destroying things and cooperating in a respectful way with each other.

Secondly, Time Out should not be perceived as a substitute for reasoning with children and teaching them. It is only one tool to be used briefly when a child's anger or frustration level is high and to help the child learn how to calm down through deep breathing, positive imagery, and positive self-talk. Later, when things calm down and the child is behaving appropriately, parents can model, teach, and talk about other more appropriate problem-solving behaviors. Time Out is only one type of discipline strategy, and discipline strategies (including Time Out, logical consequences, loss of privileges, and ignoring) are only one aspect of managing behavior used after many other steps on the discipline hierarchy have been tried. Parents must capitalize on the many opportunities to teach their children appropriate behaviors; through child-directed play, coaching skills, praising, encouraging, and building self-esteem whenever their children do something positive. Moreover, the parents' ability to model effective communication, conflict resolution, problem solving, positive self-talk, playfulness, and empathy for another's feelings is integral to children's social and moral development. In a sense, what parents do is build up their family "bank account" with deposits of love, support, and understanding. Every now and again it will be necessary for a parent to temporarily make a "withdrawal" from the bank account and use Time Out. Therefore, it is important to constantly keep the account growing.

Therapists continue helping parents keep their family bank account of love, support, and understanding growing.

Isn't Time Out ineffective for some types of children?

"I've tried Time Out and it doesn't work. He just gets angrier and more destructive and misbehavior occurs again the next day. When he's in Time Out, he has broken shelves and thrown things against the walls, leaving holes in the wall. I don't think this is right."

Be sure to prepare parents for the possibility that when they first start using Time Out, the inappropriate behavior may get worse before it gets better. In fact, when some children are put in a Time Out room, they react violently by throwing things, breaking things, even banging holes in the door. Some parents react by opening the door and spanking the child. Others refuse to use Time Out again for fear of getting the same response.

The therapist should explain that it is not uncommon for children to react strongly to Time Out, especially in the beginning, and especially for children who are oppositional or easily dysregulated. After all, if they can yell long and hard enough, they may be able to get what they want. If violent behavior has worked in the past to get a parent to back down, they will try long and hard enough until they are convinced that no matter what they do, such misbehavior results in no payoff. On the other hand, if parents are persistent, children will discover that calming down quietly gets them out of Time Out sooner.

The therapist can help parents plan for possible difficulties with Time Out. If the child damages things in a room during a Time Out, parents can respond in several ways. First, the original command (if this is a Time Out for noncompliance) must be repeated. For example, if the child was in Time Out for not putting his bike away, then s/he will first have to put it away after the Time Out period is completed. Afterwards, he should be asked to clean up the Time Out room. If he has broken something, then *he should be held responsible* for paying for it out of his allowance (if he is school age) or have some privilege removed for that day. If messes in Time Out are a frequent problem, then the parent may need to find a bare room (as bare as possible) or hallway that will be less interesting or reinforcing because it will provide a minimum of opportunities for making messes or breaking things.

Isn't Time Out too noisy to be used?

"I don't see how I could do Time Out: I live in an apartment with thin walls and if I put my son in Time Out he would scream so loudly that my neighbors would complain. They might even refer me to Child Protective Services. Already they complained to the landlord about the noise my son makes while he is playing."

A child yelling, screaming, swearing, and banging on the door during Time Out can be an exhausting experience for parents. It's difficult to listen to children misbehaving without feeling anxious, depressed or angry, and wondering "Will she ever stop this?" or "What did I do wrong?" or "It can't be good for him to get so upset." It is also disconcerting for neighbors to listen a child screaming in an apartment when they don't know what the parent is doing to evoke such a reaction. Their criticism of parents is often based on the fear that something abusive might be happening to the child. Thus not only the child's reactions, but also the fear of neighbor complaints can make it hard for parents to continue Time Out for the period of time it takes for a child to calm down. After a noisy Time Out, parents may suffer a "hangover" from trying to use Time Out and may decide not to use it in the future. If this happens, the child has "won": he has been successful in getting the parents to back down and stop using this technique.

Therapists help parents learn how to remain consistent, calm, and cope with stress.

It is important for the therapist to explain to parents that Time Out will be difficult at times because all children will test the limits of discipline. This means that if parents use Time Out for hitting, their children will hit again several times in order to determine whether Time Out will follow predictably and consistently. If they don't experience a consistent response from their parents, children will continue to use hitting as a method of handling conflict. The therapist needs to help the parent problem solve how to remain consistent and calm, how to cope with the stress of enforcing a noisy Time Out, and how to handle complaints from others who witness or overhear the Time Out. Some possible strategies for the parents to cope with Time Out reactions are to try distractions such as calling a supportive friend, turning up the volume of the TV, listening to some calming music on headphones, or doing some deep-breathing exercises. Parents can be urged to try to plan their first attempts at Time Out during times when neighbors are at work, so that they will not be overheard. Parents can also explain the program to their neighbors so that neighbors understand what the parent is doing and why this approach is being used. Neighbors can be told that within several weeks there will be less and less use of Time Out and that the overall noise level will be considerably reduced if initially the child is forced to stay in Time Out until he is able to be quiet.

Where can I do Time Out?

"I don't see how I can do Time Out because I have no space. I live in a small trailer which has one bedroom, a bathroom, and a living room. It's packed with things. There is no place to do Time Out."

The therapist needs to help parents carefully consider where they will have Time Out for their children. Once children have learned to take a calm Time Out, any safe and slightly removed area in the regular family living space will work (hall way, corner of the living room, bottom step of staircase). In fact, it is preferable for the child to be in the same room as the parent during Time Out, so that the parent can monitor the child's behavior and can end the Time Out when the child is calm and regulated. However, for children who are highly oppositional and dysregulated, parents will likely need a backup room when they are first implementing Time Out because the child will probably test the limits by getting out of the Time Out spot and may be destructive or disruptive. Part of the Time Out procedure is to let the child know that if she cannot take a calm and quiet Time Out in the common living space, then she will need to take her Time Out in another room. Ideally this back up room should be dull, boring, and safe for a child to be alone in. Some families who have little space will need to use a bedroom for Time Out. This works for some children, but may not for others. The problem with the bedroom is that it usually contains items the child finds interesting. (The same can be true of any room.) Thus the lack of the parents' attention will be partially compensated for by the interesting features of the room, and the Time Out will lose its effect. However, if the parent has worked hard to build a strong relationship with their child, the child will find it preferable to get their attention back more than anything else in the room.

There is also the issue of safety; both of the child and of property. Some children cannot be safely left alone in a bathroom. For the highly aggressive child, any breakable items will need to be removed. If this is impossible (i.e., if the child is liable to damage a door or furniture) some other place must be found, such as a hallway.

How long should I do Time Out?

"He deliberately threw a rock and broke a neighbor's window. I was so mad I sent him to his room for a day-long Time Out. I don't think 5 minutes is long enough for something as bad as breaking a window. That misbehavior needs a more serious consequence."

A general rule of thumb is 3 minutes for 3-year-olds, 4 minutes for 4-year-olds and 5 minutes for children 5 and older. Time Outs longer than 5 minutes are not more effective. However, children should not be let out of Time Out until there have been two minutes of quiet time, signaling that they have calmed down. This means that when you first use Time Out it may last longer (30 to 40 minutes) if children continue to scream. Once children learn that screaming does not get them out and that being quiet does, the Time Out will gradually become shorter (five minutes or so). The main idea is to make it as brief as possible and then to immediately give them an opportunity to try again and be successful. Therapists remind parents that the most effective discipline is IMMEDIATE, BRIEF, and followed by a NEW LEARNING TRIAL.

It's easy for parents to believe that Time Out is more effective if they make it longer, especially if their children have done something really bad like breaking a window or stealing. Some parents add time on whenever their children yell or misbehave in the Time Out room. This is especially problematic if parents are also yelling through the door, "That is one more minute for that scream," since this attention will actually increase the misbehavior. Instead, the parent can remember that the Time Out will not end until the child is calm and quiet, so there is no need to impose additional time for each disruptive behavior during Time Out. Overly long Time Outs tend to breed resentment in children, and the isolation keeps them from making new efforts to behave appropriately, thereby learning and experiencing success.

The most effective Time Out need only be 5 minutes, provided there has been 2 minutes of quiet at the end. Adding time on for misbehaving doesn't make it more effective or eliminate the problems and in fact, may do just the opposite. Remember, with children, there's no need for the punishment to fit the crime. Time Out is not meant to be like a jail sentence for adults. Its purpose is to provide a cooling-off period to calm down and a clear, unrewarding consequence for misbehavior. The objective is for parents to get their children out of Time Out either in 5 minutes or as soon as they are quiet, so as to give them another chance to try again and be successful.

What should you say to the child while he is in Time Out?
"When a child misbehaves, what should you tell the child about Time Out? I usually remind him several times while he is in Time Out that he needs to be quiet before he can come out. Sometimes this makes him scream longer, but I'm not sure he remembers what he needs to do to get out of Time Out."

Some parents inadvertently give attention to their children while they are in Time Out. For instance, Timmy yells in the Time Out room, and Timmy's dad responds to each yell with "You must be quiet before you can come out." Other parents respond to their children each time they ask, "How many more minutes?" Still others go in and out of the Time Out room, either to check on their children or to return them when they come out. All these actions defeat the purpose of Time Out and are very reinforcing for children's misbehavior.

There should be no communication with children when they are in Time Out. No matter how many times a parent explains to a child that she must be quiet to get out of Time Out, the child will not really understand the rules of Time Out until she has experienced them. For example, once children have experienced no response from their parents for yelling profanities, but have experienced that their quiet behavior gets them out of Time Out, they will begin to really understand the concept. If a parent is likely to feel compelled to enter a Time Out room for fear that his daughter will break something, any items she could break should be removed from the room or a new location found. If a child keeps coming out of the room, it may be necessary to put a temporary latch on the door handle for a short while until she learns she can't come out until she is quiet. The therapist will only recommend this in the case of a child with ODD/CD who runs away and is unlikely to be needed if the parent has built a strong relationship foundation and the parent has practice implementing Time Out in the parent group using all the appropriate steps for managing resistance. If the parent uses a Time Out chair and the child manages to attract the attention of the dog, siblings or other adults, it may be necessary to move the chair to a duller location, away from the rest of the family.

Once Time Out is over, shouldn't you remind your child of why he was put there?

"I always discuss the problem with my son again after Time Out is over. I want to be sure he understands why he went into Time Out in the first place. I don't want him to be making the same mistake again."

Sometimes parents feel they have to remind their children why they had to go to Time Out: "You were put in Time Out because you hit. Remember not to hit. You hurt your friend and he won't want to play with you. It makes me really angry." This is rubbing the child's nose in the mistake and reviving the child's image of himself misbehaving. The reminder of past misbehavior becomes, for the child, a prediction of future misbehaviors. It's better to say, "Now let's try again. I know you can be friendly." Once Time Out is over, the parents should view this as a clean slate or a new learning trial, a chance to try again and be successful. They should predict success, not remind children or "lecture" them on what they did wrong. Then they need to be ready to praise the first positive social behavior they exhibit.

What should you do if your child runs away?

"My child runs away when I ask him to go to Time Out. I end up chasing him and dragging him to Time Out. Sometimes I have to spank him to get him to go to Time Out. Then when I finally get him in Time Out, he won't stay there and keeps coming out."

When parents resort to spanking or physical restraint to get their children to go to or stay in Time Out, they may justify their use of these violent techniques by saying that they were used as a last resort. Or they may believe that since the spanking or restraint resulted in Time Out, their use was justified. The problem with this "the-end-justifies-the-means" analysis is that violent forms of discipline defeat the purposes of Time Out and focus only on the short-term goals of getting children to comply and maintaining control. Unfortunately, the short-term benefits are outweighed by the long-term disadvantages, as discussed above: increasing children's aggression and providing a model for violent approaches to conflict situations and result in a more fearful relationship. Such situations are much better handled by combining Time Out with a loss of privileges. This technique models a nonviolent approach that maintains good relationships with children.

The therapist can suggest alternative strategies. For younger children who refuse to go to Time Out, the parent can calmly but firmly take their hand and bring them to Time Out. This strategy should be done with a minimum of attention, and may also be used if the child leaves the Time Out chair. Children of any age who repeatedly leave the Time Out chair may need to take their Time Outs in a back-up room (boring place, like a guest room). In most instances the parent will only need to use the back-up room a few times before the child learns that he would rather stay on the Time Out chair in the living room than away from everything in another room. When the child is in the back-up room, at first the door is left open, but if the child comes out then the parent says, "if you come out again, I will have to close the door."

For children older than 6 or 7 parents should first try the above strategies. If children respond to a gentle physical prompt (walking the child to Time Out) or the use of the back-up room, this is the least intrusive and most immediate way to implement a Time Out. However, many children 6 and older begin to test the limits in ways that make physical guidance ineffective and unsafe. These children may be too big or too dysregulated for the parent to move them to Time Out. In these cases parents can try a different approach when children refuse to go to or stay in Time Out. If the child leaves the chair or room, the parent gives a warning about a privilege loss. For example, "If you don't go back into Time Out now, you'll have your bike locked up for 24 hours," "There'll be no bedtime story tonight" or "No soccer game after dinner" or "No TV." If the child refuses to stay in Time Out, then the parent must enforce the loss of the privilege and the Time Out is dropped. Loss of privileges are not as effective with young preschool children because they cognitively have a difficult time seeing the connection between the misbehavior and the consequence enforced at a later time.

If the children are old enough to understand the concept of time (6 years and above) and they refuse to go into Time Out in the first place, parents can add an extra minute to Time Out each time the child refuses to go or comes out of the Time Out chair. For example, "If you don't go to Time Out, you will have 6 minutes." Parents are told only to add time up to 10 minutes (one minute at a time). At that point the parent gives one warning about a loss of a privilege: "If you don't go to Time Out now, you will not be allowed to watch television tonight." If the child still refuses to go to Time Out, the parent institutes the privilege loss, but drops the Time Out. For example, "Okay, you will not be able to watch television tonight." At this point, the parent should walk away from the child's protests and wait for an opportunity to re-engage the child in some other activity. Of course, it is very important for the parent to follow through with the consequence later in the day.

Time Out won't work if it's not painful to the child.

"My child just goes to Time Out and doesn't cry or anything. He used to scream and yell when I sent him there, but now he shows no remorse or guilt or pain. So I don't think Time Out is working anymore because he doesn't show any discomfort and he doesn't cry."

Some parents believe that in order for Time Out to be an effective form of discipline, it must result in a child expressing pain or remorse over the misbehavior. If this doesn't happen, they mistakenly think it isn't working and stop using it. They may consider spanking more effective because it is more likely to result in tears and expressions of remorse. However, as we have seen, physical punishment, even when it eliminates undesirable behavior in the short run, tends to cause more problems because it teaches children a violent approach to conflict and doesn't help them learn how to problem-solve or cool down so that they can cope with a problem. Tears may satisfy a parent's need for "just desserts," but they don't necessarily reflect effective discipline.

Therapists help parents understand the purpose of Time Out is not revenge, rather to withdraw the reinforcing effects of negative attention for misbehavior and teach self-control.

Time Out doesn't need to result in tantrums, crying or expressions of guilt in order to be effective. In the beginning, young children may react violently when Time Out is used, but if it is used consistently and frequently, most will eventually take it without much anger. This is good because children are learning to self-regulate more quickly. We have even found that some children put themselves in Time Out when they feel they are losing control. Thus, Time Out helps children learn *self-control*.

Therapists should warn parents that some children will tell them that Time Out doesn't bother them, but they shouldn't be fooled by this approach. Their children may be only bluffing. Besides, Time Out can achieve its purpose even if the child is not bothered by it. Remember, the purpose of Time Out is not to get revenge or make children experience pain, but rather to stop the conflict and withdraw the reinforcing effects of negative attention for a misbehavior. It gives children a cooling off period and a chance to calm down and think about what they have done.

What about the child who refuses to come out of Time Out?
"I put my child in Time Out for refusing to do her homework and she just stayed there. She wouldn't come out and eventually she fell asleep. What should I have done?"

Time Out can result in at least two types of standoffs instigated by children or by parents. The first involves those children who refuse to come out of Time Out once it's over. Some parents respond by letting their children stay in the Time Out room as long as they wish. This is inappropriate in the instance where Time Out is used as a consequence for noncompliance to a command. In such cases, parents are not following through with the original command; their children learn that they can get out of doing something by staying in the Time Out room.

If a child refuses to come out of Time Out to take out the garbage, the parent should close the door and add two minutes to the Time Out. This can be continued for up to 10 minutes and then a privilege can be withdrawn. If the child is in Time Out for hitting, the door can be opened and the parent can say, "Your time is up. You can come out now." It is all right in this instance if the child refuses to come out, because there is nothing that the parent has asked her to do. The parent can simply respond, "Come out whenever you are ready," and ignore any refusal.

Another type of standoff happens when a parent refuses to talk to a child when the Time Out is over: for an hour or even a whole day. This, in a sense, becomes an extended Time Out. As mentioned earlier, this does not teach children how to deal with conflict in an appropriate fashion; rather, it teaches them to withdraw from conflict. Refusing to speak to children for long periods after misbehavior only escalates tension and anger. As discussed above, overly long Time Outs breed resentment and, in this case, defeat communication. In this situation, the parent should think about what is bothering him or her, what behavior is expected and then state it clearly. For instance, "I'm angry that you broke my vase. You will have to clean up the mess now and pay for it out of your allowance. I'll help you pick up the pieces."

How do you do Time Out in Public?

"The reason I like spanking is because it is portable. I can use that strategy at the grocery store or park when he misbehaves. I don't see how you could use Time Out in situations like that."

When children misbehave in public places such as restaurants, movie theaters, and grocery stores, parents are often reluctant to use their usual forms of discipline. Some worry about how other people will react if they use Time Out with their children in public. Others are afraid their children will escalate their misbehavior into a full-blown tantrum, so they avoid discipline. Still others do not see how Time Out can be used anywhere but at home, and resort instead to threats and spankings. As a result, many children have learned that grocery stores and restaurants are places they can get their own way because their parents will give in to avoid a scene.

Once parents have established Time Out as a consistent consequence for certain misbehaviors at home, it's important to impose the same consequence when these misbehaviors occur in public places as well. This may mean leaving the grocery store to do a modified 5-minute Time Out in the car or next to a tree in a park. If there is no place for a Time Out, the parent can say, "If you don't stop yelling (or whining or leaving the Time Out spot), then you'll have a Time Out when we get home." Once parents have followed through once or twice, their children will learn that the rules apply regardless of where they are, and they'll stop testing and learn to behave more appropriately.

Can you use Time Out too much?

"It seems like I have him in Time Out most of the time he is home. Sometimes he is in there 20 times a day. Is there a problem with this?"

Time Out is frequently used by parents for all kinds of things, from whining, yelling and screaming to throwing, hitting and lying. Some parents report using it 20 to 30 times a day! This overuse deprives misbehaving children of opportunities to learn or demonstrate good behavior. It doesn't teach them any new and more appropriate ways to behave. While it keeps them out of parents' hair in the short run, in the long run it can cause bitterness and make children feel that they can't do anything right.

Therapists help parents reserve Time Out for aggressive behavior or severe noncompliance.

If any parents have become "Time Out junkies," the therapist needs to help them to focus on one or two misbehaviors that will result in Time Out. In fact, we recommend reserving Time Out only for aggressive behavior or for severe noncompliance problems. After three or four weeks, when these behaviors are eliminated, another one can be identified. More importantly, the therapist must help the parents ensure that they are spending more time supporting, teaching, coaching and encouraging appropriate social behaviors than they are focusing on negative ones. Sometimes parents are clear with their children about the consequences for misbehaving but do not provide attention, coaching and encouragement for appropriate behaviors. In other words, much emphasis is placed on what children should not do, and there is considerably less emphasis on what to do instead. Time Out will only work when parental attention, coaching and positive consequences for appropriate behaviors are frequent.

Won't Time Out turn my child into a compliant "little robot"?
"I don't want my child to be compliant all the time. I want her to be assertive, to question authority, and not to be a little robot. Isn't timing out for noncompliance going to make my child into a little marine recruit? For instance, I certainly want her to say 'no' to strangers."

This question is related to the preceding question because it refers to the misuse or abuse of Time Out. Just as it is possible to use Time Out too much, it is also possible to abuse it by using it as the sole discipline technique. Rather, the therapist should help the parents determine which misbehaviors (e.g., hitting, destructive acts) would be appropriate for a Time Out consequence, which misbehaviors will be handled through problem solving, logical consequences, loss of privileges, and praising alternative positive responses. However, this parent may be raising a larger question than the use of Time Out per se; that is, how much to discipline children's misbehavior or enforce compliance. As we discussed in the Limit-Setting questions section, the first task for parents is to decide on their important household rules and to limit their rules and commands to those that are important enough to follow through on. Thus the parent allows the child to make his/her own choices when possible, fosters independence and self-assertion, but sets clear and consistent limits when children are breaking important rules or hurting others. Moreover, it is also important for parents to understand that Time Out for noncompliance is reserved for children who are noncompliant 75-100% of the time a parent gives a command. It is normal for children to object 1/3 of the time, for children who fall into this range of noncompliance, then restating the command, ignoring the protests, using "if-then" statements, and focusing on the compliance even if there is a sassy attitude will usually do the trick.

The other issue raised by this parent is one of whether forcing children to be compliant could lead them into potentially dangerous situations because they do not know how to say "no" to strangers or to people who ask them to do inappropriate things. The key point here is for parents to teach their children how to respond to adults (or children) who are asking them to do something that is unsafe or dangerous; in this case, the child needs to learn how and when to be assertive.

Time Out doesn't work

"I've tried Time Out and it doesn't work for my child."

Some parents claim that Time Out doesn't work for them. The reason may be any of those we have discussed, or it may simply be that they have tried it a few times and then given up. It's a mistake, however, to try Time Out four or five times and expect the problem behavior to be eliminated.

Therapists remind parents that behavior changes slowly.

Time Out is not magic. Children need repeated learning trials. They need many opportunities to make mistakes and misbehave, and then to learn from the consequences of their misbehaviors. Just as it takes hundreds of trials for a baby to learn to walk, so it takes children hundreds of trials to learn appropriate social behaviors. The therapist's job is to remind parents that even when Time Out is used effectively, behavior changes slowly. Parents need support from therapists to be patient and persistent. Remind parents that it takes many years to learn all the mature adult behaviors their parents would like to see them demonstrate.

What do you do when you know you are so angry you won't be able to do a Time Out?

"Sometimes I feel so angry I just don't have the patience to do Time Out. I just want to hit him and make him suffer."

Parents sometimes overreact to their children's misbehaviors because they are exhausted, angry, or depressed about some other events in their life. A father who gets angry at his daughter may really be angry at his wife for ignoring his efforts with the children. Or, a mother who has had an exhausting day at work and had a conflict with her secretarial staff may become cross with her children for making noise and not letting her relax. Depending on the mood and the energy level of the parent, the same behavior from a child can seem cute one day and obnoxious the next.

Even the kindest, most well-intentioned parents get frustrated and angry with their children. No one is perfect. But the important task is for parents to recognize the "filters" they bring to their perceptions of their children at any particular time, and to learn to cope with their anger or frustration. Sometimes it is the parent who needs a Time Out. If a parent is depressed because of work problems, it may be a good idea take a Time Out away from the children in order to relax and gain perspective. If a parent is angry with his/her spouse, s/he may need Time Out to problem solve. In helping children become less aggressive and more able to problem solve and handle conflict constructively, it is vital that parents use personal Time Out when they feel anger building, and to model ways to resolve conflict and ways to support one another. The therapist will help parents build their support team and think about ways to use some self-care to give themselves some fun times.

Therapists help parents build their support team.

Is Time Out appropriate for children who have experienced abuse and neglect?

"My foster daughter was abandoned by her mother when she was three. I'm worried that if I give her a Time Out, she will experience that feeling of abandonment

all over again. There are times when her behavior is so out of control that I don't know what to do, but I don't want to contribute to her attachment problems."

When working with children who have been abused and neglected, the issue of attachment and abandonment frequently comes up in reference to the topics of ignoring and Time Out. The most important thing for parents and caregivers to understand is the point that was emphasized at the beginning of this section: Time Out is used as a brief and infrequent strategy for severe and unsafe behaviors. More importantly, it is effective when used in the midst of a loving and caring environment. If children who have been abused in the past are now living in a stable and positive environment with caregivers who are providing consistent play times, coaching and praise, Time Out can be used by these caregivers as a way to help the child learn how to calm down. Remember, in most cases, Time Out is brief, is done in the same room as the parent, and attention is given back to the child as soon as he or she is calm. This is a very different context than being abandoned by a caregiver.

Therapists who are working with parents who have been abusive to their children will use caution when recommending the use of strategies such as ignoring and Time Out. In these instances, parents will need to work hard to re-establish a positive and caring and secure attachment with their child first before using strategies that withdraw attention. Therapists will also work with parents to help them understand that these strategies are brief and require the parent to remain calm and respectful and monitor and return their attention when the child is calm. Before such parents implement the Time Out strategy at home, the therapist will have practiced anger management techniques, positive coping thoughts and practiced the Time Out scenario in group. Moreover, the therapist will be on-call and be available to provide support when needed during the first weeks that this is started. However, if the foundational work has been done regarding strengthening their attachment first, the Time Out procedure is likely to work well. In the end, if parents who have been abusive can learn to use ignoring and Time Out appropriately, they will have a nonviolent and effective way to manage high intensity behavior. For more suggestions about how to adapt the program for parents involved with Child Protective Services see Chapter Thirteen.

TEACHING PARENTS ABOUT NATURAL AND LOGICAL CONSEQUENCES

One of the most important and difficult tasks for parents of children with ODD/CD is to help their children become more independent and responsible. The therapist can help parents learn to foster their children's decision making, sense of responsibility, and ability to learn from mistakes through the use of age-appropriate natural and logical consequences. In other words, when parents use this technique, they hold children accountable for their mistakes, by experiencing the consequences of their choices. These strategies are most effective for recurring problems where parents are able to decide ahead of time how they will follow through in the event that the misbehavior recurs. Consequences, which occur in Step #5 on the discipline hierarchy (see Chapter Six), will be the first response to many problem behaviors, and will usually be used before Time Out. However, as detailed above, in cases where children are very resistant to Time Out, consequences may be combined with Time Out. Most parents understand and accept the logic and potential effectiveness of using consequences for misbehavior; however there are a number of common stumbling blocks around implementing consequences: for example, choosing developmentally appropriate consequences, deciding on the duration of consequences, and what to do if children seem impervious to consequences or if parents have taken away all possible consequences and the misbehavior still occurs.

What kinds of misbehaviors would I use a natural or logical consequence for?

"I get confused about when I should ignore a misbehavior, use Time Out, or use logical consequences. How do I decide which approach is correct?"

Natural and logical consequences are most effective for recurring problems where the parents can decide ahead of time with the child what will happen if the child continues the behavior. For example, a parent might warn a child, "If you can't keep the gum in your mouth, it will be taken away" or "If you don't eat at meals, there will be no food until the next meal." This approach can help children to learn to make decisions, be responsible for their own behavior, and learn from their mistakes. The therapist should help parents reserve Time Out for more serious problems when the child is hurting someone or breaking something. For these aggressive acts, it is not appropriate to give the child a warning; a warning only conveys a message that they have another chance to be aggressive again. Ignoring, on the other hand, can be used for minor annoying behaviors which are not hurting anyone, such as whining, messy eating, tantrums, and protests.

What kinds of consequences are developmentally appropriate for children?

"I tried making my 3-year-old child clean up his poopy pants as a way of discouraging him from messing in his pants, but that just made an incredible mess in the bathroom and I ended up yelling at him."

"When I found my teenager smoking, I told her that if she got an asthma attack (which she gets) that she would have to earn the money to pay for her asthma medicine. Was that logical?"

"I let my 4-year-old child walk to the bus stop in bare feet in the middle of winter as way of teaching him to get his shoes on in the morning. Isn't that a natural consequence?"

When thinking through the use of logical and natural consequences as a means of reducing children's inappropriate behaviors, it's important to be sure that parents' expectations are appropriate and safe for the child's age and development. Because of the cognitive skills and patience involved, in general natural consequences will work better for school-age children than for preschoolers. For example, young children will not often see the connection between not eating dinner and being hungry two hours later, or may not be able to think ahead to being miserably cold if they don't wear their shoes outside. On the other hand, rather than struggle to make a child put on his jacket, a parent might use a brief logical consequence. "If you don't put your jacket on, you will be cold." For a young child, the parent would then bring the jacket outside and offer it again when the child seemed cold. Logical consequences that are appropriate for young children might be "if—then" statements that have an immediate consequence. For instance, "If you don't keep your gum in your mouth, I will have to take it away." Or for a child who points scissors at someone, "If you can't use the scissors carefully, then I will remove them." In these examples, the logical consequence of not using something appropriately and/or safely is having it removed right away. In these cases, the child will learn the most from the consequence if there is a chance to try again soon. For example, after 5 minutes the parent might say, "Here are the scissors. Show me that you can use them to cut the paper."

In the other examples above parents have mismatched their consequences to their children's developmental levels. For instance, if Alexandra is not developmentally ready to be toilet trained, but she is made to clean her underpants or change her bed, she is being unjustly punished; the consequence is inappropriate for her abilities. Whether it is appropriate to expect a teenager to pay for her asthma medicine when she chooses to smoke depends upon the cost of the medicine and her ability to earn that amount of money. But few parents would likely be prepared to follow through with this threat if the child had an asthma attack. Additionally, most teenagers are not deterred by this kind of future threat; they feel invincible and don't believe that these kinds of bad things will really happen to them. Other consequences or loss of privileges would be more appropriate for the teenager who smokes.

Parents must understand their child's developmental abilities to use consequences appropriately.

Of course, natural consequences should not be used if children may be physically hurt by them. For example, a preschooler should not be allowed to experience the natural consequences of sticking a finger into an electrical outlet, touching the stove, running in the road, or going barefoot in freezing weather. Effective use of logical and natural consequences requires parents to really understand children's developmental milestones and individual children's cognitive abilities.

What about consequences that are neither natural nor logical?
"When he swore at me, I washed his dirty mouth out with soap. He doesn't swear at me anymore! Wasn't that logical?"

Occasionally parents come up with consequences that are not naturally or logically related to an activity. Consider the mother who washes her son's mouth out with soap because he swore at her. While she might argue that it is logical to clean out the mouth of a youngster who has been swearing, the "logic" is based only on a figure of speech (swearing = "dirty" talk). Her action is likely to make her son feel degraded and angry. Other parents create consequences that are too punitive. "Since you wet your bed last night, you can't have anything to drink after noon today," or "Because you didn't eat your dinner, you will have to eat it for breakfast," or "Since you bit me, I'm going to bite you." Children will feel resentful and may even retaliate against such consequences. They will be more likely to focus on the cruelty of their parents than on the consequences of their own behavior.

A calm, matter-of-fact, attitude on the part of parents is essential for deciding upon and carrying out consequences. The natural consequence of not wearing a coat when it's cold outside is to become chilled. The logical consequence of not doing homework might be to miss a favorite television program. The natural consequence of not putting clothes in the hamper is that the clothes don't get washed. These consequences are not degrading, nor do they cause physical pain. Instead, they help children to learn to make choices and to be more responsible.

Are some consequences too remote to be effective?
"I let him watch TV instead of doing his homework so that he could experience poor grades on his spelling test. Indeed he came home with many corrections, but he just seemed more helpless and I'm not sure the natural consequences approach worked."

The natural and logical consequences approach doesn't work when the consequences of misbehaviors are too remote in time. The natural consequences of not brushing teeth would be to have cavities and to have to submit to painful dental work. But this would never be effective as a motivator; the cavities would not show up for months or years! Similarly, overeating or eating unhealthy foods may have long-term health consequences, but these are too distant to affect children's behavior in the short-term. Permitting youngsters not to do homework and to watch television every night until the end-of-the-year report card shows they have failed is another consequence that is too delayed to have any influence on their daily study habits. Such long-term punishers may instead lead children to feel hopeless about their abilities.

For preschool and school-age children it's important that the consequences closely follow the inappropriate behavior. If 7-year-old Dan damages another child's toy, then the toy should be replaced as quickly as possible and he should have to help pay for it through chores or from his allowance. However it is the act of making some retribution that is most important. If the broken toy is unreasonably expensive, Dan might be asked to contribute a portion of the amount. For a school aged child, a consequence that stretches out too long will become ineffective. The same behavior would be treated differently in 3-year-old Lisa. She would need a brief and immediate consequence; for example, a brief break from playing with the desired toy, guidance to "fix" the broken toy or apologize to its owner. In this way, Lisa and Dan will learn from their inappropriate behavior and will probably behave more appropriately the next time.

I have trouble following through when I give a consequence. I feel mean.

"I am good at staying calm when I announce the consequence, but then I feel horrible later. Last night I told my son that he would lose his bedtime story if he didn't brush his teeth. He was defiant so I took away the story. At bedtime he sobbed and sobbed for a story, and I broke down and read him one. I just felt so awful for him and he seemed sorry."

When attempting to carry out natural and logical consequences, some parents find it difficult to allow their children to experience the outcomes of their actions. They are so empathetic towards their children, or they feel so guilty for not coming to their aid, that they intervene before the consequence occurs. For instance, Carol tells her daughter Angie that the natural consequence of dawdling in the morning and not being ready for day care on time will be to go in her pajamas. When

Remind parents that the consequences approach takes time, planning, patience, and repetition.

the time comes to enforce this, she can't bring herself to let Angie go in her pajamas and dresses her instead. Such over-protectiveness can handicap children by not allowing them to develop their own coping strategies, rendering them incapable of handling problems or mistakes.

When using consequences it's important for parents to think about the pros and cons of applying this technique to particular misbehaviors. The therapist can advise parents that they must be certain that they can live with the consequences and are not giving idle threats. Perhaps the mother above might decide that she does not want to use the removal of a bedtime story as a consequence because it is too unpleasant to end the evening this way. In that case, she might pick a different consequence. Once she has taken away the story, however, her failure to follow through will make it less likely that her son will brush his teeth. In the other example, Carol should have first considered whether or not she would be willing to follow through and take Angie to day care in her pajamas if she continued to dawdle. Failing to follow through with an agreed-upon consequence will dilute parents' authority and deprive their children of opportunities to learn from their mistakes. For both of these parents, reverting back to the praise and incentive tools might have been more effective than the consequence approach. Earning a sticker for getting dressed or brushing teeth may be more motivating and effective than threatening a consequence that the parent is not prepared to follow through on.

Can some logical consequences be too long?
My child kept forgetting to put his bike away and left it in the driveway, so I locked it up for a month. Do you think this was too long?

Sometimes parents come up with a consequence that lasts too long and constitutes undue punishment. Say that 7-year-old Ben rides his bicycle in the road after being told to stay on the driveway. The logical consequence would be for the parents to lock it up. Locking it up for a month, however, would be excessive; it would certainly make Ben feel resentful at the injustice. Moreover, he would be deprived of any new opportunities to handle his bicycle more responsibly. Although some people believe that the stronger (and longer) the punishment, the more effective it will be, the opposite is true. Brief consequences allows an earlier opportunity for behaving appropriately.

A more appropriate consequence in Ben's case would have been to lock up his bike for 24 hours and then allow him the chance to ride it according to the rules. If 4-year-old Kathy is using crayons and starts coloring on the kitchen table, a logical consequence to present her with might be, "If you can't keep the crayons on the paper, then I will have to take them away." If she continues to color on the table, then the crayons would have to be removed. However, they should be returned within half an hour to give her another opportunity to use them appropriately. The principle is to make the consequences immediate, short, to the point, and then to quickly offer the child another chance to try again and be successful.

Remind parents that the consequences approach, like any other parenting technique, takes time, planning, patience, and repetition. Most of all it requires a calm, respectful attitude.

TEACHING PARENTS TO TEACH THEIR CHILDREN TO PROBLEM SOLVE

The purpose of the child problem solving component of the program is for the therapist to help parents use all the parenting tools they have learned in the parenting pyramid to encourage their children's use of appropriate problem-solving skills. Of course, as was the case for all the other parenting tools used, parents modeling the use of effective problem solving in their own adult relationships is an important part of children's learning. If parents themselves do not routinely problem-solve, then the therapist may need to teach them these skills first using the Incredible Years ADVANCE parent program before teaching them how to help their children learn to problem solve. Below are some of the commonly asked questions for this topic.

Questions Parents Ask about Problem Solving

Shouldn't you tell children the correct solutions?

" I feel I need to tell my children how to solve the problem because they don't come up with the right answer on their own. In fact, some of their own solutions are really bad!"

Many parents believe that telling their children how to solve a problem helps them learn to problem solve. For example, two children may have trouble sharing a bicycle. The parent responds to the child who has grabbed the bicycle from the other child (who has refused to share the bike) by saying, "You should either play together or take turns. Grabbing is not nice. You can't go around grabbing things. Would you like that if he did it to you?" The problem with this approach is that the parents are telling the children what to do before they have found out what the problem is from the children's viewpoint. It is possible that the parent has misdiagnosed the problem. For example, in this case both children may have played a role in the problem. Perhaps one child had been using the bike for a long time and wouldn't share even when asked nicely. The child who grabbed did so because her prosocial solution wasn't working. Since the parent does not have this information, the child who grabbed is likely to feel misunderstood and will not be responsive to the parent's solution. Moreover, the parent's approach in this example does not help the children to think about their problem and how to solve it. Rather than being encouraged to learn *how to think*, they are told what to think and the solution is imposed upon them.

It is more effective for parents to learn to guide their children into thinking about what may have caused the problem in the first place, rather than to tell them the solution. Parents can invite their children to come up with possible solutions. If parents want their children to develop a habit of solving their own problems, they need to be supported to think for themselves. They should be urged to express their feelings about the situation, talk about ideas for solving the problem, and talk about what might happen if they carried out various solutions. The only time parents need to offer solutions is if their children need a few ideas to get them started. However, at first, young children may have very few appropriate prosocial solutions in their repertoires, so parents will be suggesting and practicing solutions with them.

Is there such a thing as too little guidance?

"Well, I just tell my children to work it out on their own. I think that's the only way children will learn to problem solve. Don't you agree?"

The parents' role is to teach their children to work it out on their own by guiding them. Parents can encourage their children to talk aloud as they think and then can praise their ideas and attempts at solutions. In this way, the parents are reinforcing the development of a style of thinking that will help them to deal with all kinds of problems throughout their lives. Parents need to encourage their children to first come up with many possible solutions. Then they can help them to shift their focus to the possible consequences of each solution. The final step in problem solving is to help children evaluate their possible solutions. For children ages three to eight, the second step, generating solutions, is the key skill to learn. While older children are more easily involved in anticipating consequences and evaluating them, youngsters need to be helped to generate possible solutions and to understand that some solutions are better than others. They are encouraged to think about if their solution is safe, fair and leads to good feelings.

Feelings don't have much to do with problem solving, do they?

"I don't talk much about feelings with my children. What value is there in this?"

When some parents problem solve, they avoid discussing feelings. They focus exclusively on the thinking style, the nature of the problem, the solution and the consequences. They forget to ask their children how they feel about the problem or how the other person in the situation may have felt. Yet these are important aspects of defining the problem. In fact recognizing a difficult feeling is the first step to knowing there is a problem to solve. It is also important for parents to be aware of their own feelings. Hearing a daughter report that she has been sent home from Julie's house for hitting may provoke feelings in the parent such as anger, frustration, or even depression. The therapist helps parents gain control of these emotions before trying to help her child with her feelings about the situation.

Parents need to encourage their children to think about their own feelings in a problem situation or in response to a possible solution, and parents can help their children consider the other person's point of view in the situation. For instance, a parent might ask, "How do you think Julie felt when you did that? How did you feel when she did that?" Parents can talk with children about how they might discover what someone else feels or thinks. "How can you find out if she likes your idea? How can you tell if she is sad or happy?" This will help parents encourage their children to be more empathetic and, because they try to understand other people's feelings and viewpoints, will result in more willingness to problem solve, compromise and cooperate. When parents discuss children's feelings, it also helps children to realize that their feelings are important and that their parents empathize with them.

ADULT COMMUNICATION AND PROBLEM SOLVING

As we noted in Chapter One, researchers have convincingly demonstrated that parental personal and interpersonal factors (depression, marital discord, etc.) and contextual factors (lack of support, increased environmental stressors, etc.) result in negative cognitions, disrupt parenting behavior and contribute to parent training treatment relapses (e.g., Webster-Stratton, 1990b, 1990c). The ADVANCE program helps parents to address some of these personal and interpersonal issues that can be barriers to effective parenting. As with each other unit, therapists need to be prepared to address some common barriers and questions.

"I'm a single parent. How does this apply to me?"

"I'm basically in this alone. I share custody with my child's father, but we are barely civil to each other. It is really painful to hear about the importance of good communication between parents when that's something I can't have. I have a hard time participating in these problem-solving role plays where the couples in the group are working out all their problems. I think I should skip this unit."

Therapists may find initial resistance to the communication and problem solving units of the program when working with single parents or with parents who are attending the group without a partner. Especially in groups where many parents are attending as couples, single parents may feel left out, and may not see how the communication and problem-solving exercises apply to their lives. It is important for the therapist to help the group extend the ideas of communication and problem solving to relationships beyond couple relationships. These are skills that are important for work with new relationships, friendships, extended family, ex-partners and work situations.

Although the relationship between two parents living in the same household will likely surface as one of the very important places that group members will work on their communication and problem-solving skills, it is important for the therapist to help extend this thinking. The therapist must help the group brainstorm the broad range of important adult relationships that influence their children's lives (parent-parent, parent-teacher, parent-grandparent, parent-neighbor, parent-ex-partner, parent-boss).

Therapists help the group extend the ideas of communication and problem solving to relationships beyond the child.

Most groups will contain a mixture of married and single parents with a variety of different types of relationships. When structuring role plays, the therapists should vary the pairings. For some role plays, coupled parents might work together with their partners while single parents are paired with other single parents. However, at other times, the therapist might pair two fathers together or a single mother with a married mother, or have random pairings where parents count off in pairs to practice a communication exercise. If single parents are always paired together, just as a result of their single-status, it will be easy for them to feel discounted or "left-over."

In addition to varying the pairings for role plays, it is important for therapists to vary the types of problems and scenarios that parents use for their problem-solving and communication issues. If all exercises involve communicating about household issues and problems, single parents who don't have another adult in the household will begin to feel irrelevant. If, on the other hand, some role plays are structured to practice parent-teacher communication, or problem solving with a babysitter or caregiver, or ex-partner or new boyfriend, single parents will be able to participate fully and will feel that the material is relevant to their situations. At times, of course, some roles plays will revolve more around interparental communication because this is an important skill for couples to practice. In these circumstances, single parents work to apply these skills to how to communicate with an ex-partner or new boyfriend, or other caregiver in the child's life.

Below is an example of how this material was adapted to work with Beatrice, a single mother who shared custody of her 5-year-old daughter Melinda.

BEATRICE

Beatrice initially felt quite challenged by this portion of the program. As a single mother who was sharing custody of Melinda, she was frustrated by her parenting interactions with Melinda's father, but felt powerless to change anything since he was not attending the parenting classes. She reported that their typical pattern was to talk when they were dropping off or picking up Melinda. She stated that during these times she was often angry and frustrated, trying to convey to Melinda's father that he needed to be more consistent or more strict with Melinda. Melinda's father would minimize her concerns, which made her furious. Melinda would watch these interactions with an uncomfortable interest, and would later make comments to her mother like, "Daddy doesn't mind when I don't pick up my clothes. He thinks you are too picky, and so do I! Daddy doesn't have so many rules."

As Melinda's mother worked on the material in this unit, she realized that this was not a good setting for these discussions and was also able to see that her emotional presentation of the problems were likely contributing to Melinda's father's tendency to minimize her concerns. First she practiced stating some of her concerns calmly, using "I" rather than "you" statements with a buddy in the group. She asked for feedback from the group about which concerns she should share with Melinda's father, and which she might keep to herself. After picking a few key concerns that she wanted to share with him (such as sharing her bedtime routine), she asked if they might meet together, on neutral territory (she chose a restaurant between their houses) and talk about how they could make the pick-up and drop-off times smoother. During this meeting, she worked hard to stay calm, state her concerns in a neutral and non-blaming way, and to invite Melinda's father to share his viewpoint. She reported at group that this was a hard task for her, especially since Melinda's father had not been a part of the parent group. However, she was pleasantly surprised by his response to the way that she presented the plan, and she was even more proud of herself for maintaining control of her own behavior. Although the conversation did not solve any of her long-standing big concerns or issues, they did agree that during pick-up and drop-off times, they would both try to remain polite and positive so that Melinda was not exposed to their conflict. They also agreed to meet monthly to discuss concerns and share their parenting strategies.

Although Beatrice felt relatively successful with this basic communication change with her ex-husband, she was not ready to work on more complicated problem solving, feeling that they had too much resentment to be able to calmly address anything other than the most basic co-parenting issues. Instead, she practiced the more advanced problem-solving exercises with a parent buddy from her group and her buddy did the same with her. Since she wanted to pick a problem that she had complete control over, she problem solved strategies for staying calm herself when her daughter was upset. Then she made a plan to help teach Melinda some self-regulation strategies. Beatrice and her buddy from the group (another single mother) set up several times to talk about their plans, and to report back about their successes and struggles. In subsequent sessions, Beatrice made a plan to use the strategies with Melinda's teacher who had been sending home some negative notes about her behavior at school. Finally, she made a plan to use the strategies in one of her meetings with Melinda's father. She asked him if he would mind problem solving with her about how to handle Melinda's noncompliance around getting ready for school in the morning. Although this session did not go perfectly, Melinda's mother felt good about her attempts to stay calm during this discussion and about the fact that she asked Melinda's father for his ideas. In prior problem-discussion with him, she realized that she had spent much of the time complaining about Melinda's behavior and blaming her father for the problems. This time, she managed to edit the criticism and found that he was more able to discuss the problem with her, and admit that he, too, had some difficulties with the morning routine.

Working with Parents of Children with Conduct Problems: The Collaborative Process Using Theory Driven Clinical Principles

There is a large body of literature describing the *content* of parent training programs as described in Chapter Four and Six. Strategies such as praise, differential attention, incentives, commands, Time Out, response cost, and logical and natural consequences, along with the social learning principles that underlie them, have been carefully outlined in detail and researched by many investigators (Snyder & Stoolmiller, 2002). But descriptions of the content of parent training programs do not elucidate the actual mechanisms of parent training; that is, the clinical methods, processes, and principles that therapists use to try to change or modify parents' attitudes, emotions, and parenting behaviors. While research indicates that highly skilled therapists who deliver evidence-based programs (EBPs) with high program fidelity or quality delivery produce superior outcomes compared with poor quality

Highly skilled therapists who deliver evidence-based programs (EBPs) with high program fidelity produce superior outcomes.

delivery (Eames et al., 2010; Henggeler, Schoenwald, Liao, Letourneau, & Edwards, 2002; Scott, Carby, & Rendu, 2008), there is less written about the actual clinical processes, theories, or behavior change methods recommended by developers to ensure quality delivery. Considering the documented effectiveness of various types of parent training programs, this is puzzling, for there are many questions to be answered concerning the therapist's role and strategies used in parent training. How do therapists handle parents' resistance to new concepts or failure to make change? What key principles guide their clinical approach with difficult and complex families? How do they ensure that homework is carried out? What are the preferred clinical methods and strategies? How collaborative or prescriptive should their teaching style be? When should confrontation be used? How do therapists ensure that the training is culturally sensitive? In group therapies, how do therapists balance specific family's needs with the overall group process and learning? What adaptations do therapists make to the program for less educated parents, or parents from different cultural backgrounds or for children with developmental isues? How do therapists promote self-confidence and self-efficacy in parents from socioeconomically disadvantaged environments? How much attention is given to changing parents' thoughts and emotions versus behaviors? Should therapists focus on cognitive understanding or behavioral practice to best prepare parents to use the parenting strategies at home?

Patterson and Forgatch (1985) first conducted research analyzing therapist-client interchanges in the parent training literature. They showed that directive therapist behaviors such as "teach" and "confront" increased the likelihood of parental resistance and lack of cooperation, while nondirective therapist behaviors such as "facilitate" and "support" led to reliable decreases in client noncompliance. Patterson and Chamberlain (1988) proposed a therapy model that postulates that therapist behaviors play a secondary role to extrafamilial, interpersonal, and child factors in predicting parent response during the early stages of treatment, but play a primary role in predicting client noncompliance in the later stages of therapy. In an earlier study, Alexander, Barton, Schiavo, and Parsons (1976) examined the role of therapist characteristics in predicting outcome (as defined by completion of treatment and recidivism rate) for families that participated in Functional Family Therapy (FFT). They found that therapist "relationship" characteristics (affect, warmth, humor) accounted for 45% of the variance in outcome, whereas "structuring" characteristics (directiveness and self-confidence) accounted for only 15%.

Therapists' group leader clinical methods and processes are key to parent behavior and emotion change.

These studies are important; however, beyond the understanding that therapist knowledge competence and therapeutic alliance or relationship support factors are important in assuring quality program delivery. It is not clear how different programs utilize various clinical methods or processes such as collaborative versus didactic teaching approaches, video versus live modeling techniques, or discussion versus practice exercises to change parents' thoughts or feelings or behavioral patterns. The purpose of this chapter, therefore, is to provide a qualitative description of the clinical methods and processes thought to be important elements or key principles underlying fidelity delivery of the Incredible Years Programs (Webster-Stratton, Reid, Hurlburt, & Marsenich, 2011).

THERAPY MODELS

There are many competing therapeutic models or intervention theories, each with different sets of assumptions about the therapist's role, the cause of family problems, the nature of the relationship between the therapist and the parent, and the level of responsibility assumed by the parent or therapist for resolving problems. For purposes of discussion, let us pose four hypothetical therapeutic models, each an extreme: Models A, B, C and D. In Model A, the therapist does not hold parents responsible for their problems; the responsibility lies with past experiences or the demands of society. Neither does the therapist hold parents responsible for arriving at their own solutions to the problems that brought them into therapy or that emerge during therapy. In such a model, the therapist, who is the expert in the relationship, has the responsibility for gradually uncovering the problems hidden in the client's subconscious, in past experiences, and/or in the family dynamics, and interpreting them to the individual client, or to the entire family. In such a model the client is seen as a relatively passive recipient of the therapist's analysis, interpretations, advice, and prescriptions. The advantage of Model A therapy is that it allows parents to seek and accept help for their own or their child's problems without feeling that they are to blame for the problems. However, this model brings with it the disadvantages of dependency on the therapist, usually over a long period of time, and in some cases isolates parents from the child's therapy process. For example, the child may be in play therapy with a therapist to work through some prior traumatic experience, while the parent is left out of the process and unaware of how s/he can help the child.

Model B therapies place the responsibility for the child and family problems on the parents and their inability to control certain aspects of their lives. For example, how often are cases of child abuse explained in terms of the parent's attachment to the child, either absence of attachment or distorted attachment? Emotional and physical abuse have been linked causally with a failure on the part of the mother to become "bonded" to her child (Belsky & Fearson, 2002; Lynch & Roberts, 1977; Valman, 1980; Van Izendoorn, 1995; Zeanah, 1996). Attachment theorists acknowledge the importance of parents providing the child with emotional security and being responsive and sensitive to children's needs (Cicchetti, Rogosch, & Toth, 2006; Grossmann, Grossmann, & Waters, 2005). Without this, maladaptive child behavior patterns towards the parents may ensue at times of stress, including avoidance, anxious-ambivalent and disorganized behavior. One possible disadvantage of such assumptions is that it leads to a therapeutic process that creates or reinforces a negative self-image in parents, a mistrust of self and a feeling that poor attachment is fixed or deterministic.

In hypothetical Model C, the therapist is not primarily concerned with the client's past, but rather focuses on the problem at hand. The therapist's job, according to this model, is to teach specific skills so that clients can feel more confident and assume the responsibility for solving their own or their family's problems. This theoretical assumption leads to relatively time-limited programs. Many parent training programs fall within this social learning theory model because, in them, parents learn new behavior management strategies to use with their children (e.g., Patterson & Capaldi, 1991) and may also learn some other specific cognitive strategies such as altering maladaptive or negative thoughts and reducing unrealistic expectations (Abramson, Seligman, & Teasdale, 1978). After treatment, families are expected to feel less helpless and be self-sufficient. Working from an assumption that behavior is intrinsically rather than extrinsically determined, such therapies allow parents to direct their energies toward solving their own problems and learning new skills. These newly acquired skills lead to an increase in parents' perceived self-efficacy (Bandura, 1989; Gross et al., 2003). Parents are given credit for their improvements; as a result, they come to feel more competent. Yet this therapeutic model has several possible disadvantages. First, it may suggest there are "quick fixes" for children's problems, when in reality many parents are living in highly stressful home situations and have other interpersonal problems or disadvantaged upbringings. Second, Model C may create feelings of failure or self-blame because of the raised expectations brought about by high levels of initial success, and the dashed expectations brought about by subsequent reversals of gains. Third, this type of therapy may be delivered in a directive or prescriptive fashion which, like Model A, will foster parents' dependency and lack of self-reliance, and may also leave parents feeling blamed for their childrens' problems.

In contrast to Models A, B and C, each of which assumes a deficit motivation, therapies based on hypothetical Model D assume the client has it within him/herself to find solutions and change. For example,

Rogerian theory (Rogers, 1983), which epitomizes the humanistic approach, is client-centered, non-directive, nonintrusive, and supportive. The Rogerian therapist's "unconditional positive regard" for clients helps them to help themselves by searching for their own answers, moving towards self-actualization and maturity. The advantage of this therapeutic approach is that it promotes the client's positive self-esteem and self-direction; on the other hand, this type of therapy can be a lengthy process and may not be appropriate for clients who do not have solid communication and problem-solving skills or who have inaccurate cognitions or developmentally inappropriate parenting strategies because of lack of knowledge or prior abusive experiences themselves as children.

The Incredible Years theoretical approach for working with parents integrates elements from several of the above models. While its theoretical underpinnings fall within the cognitive social learning theories of Model C, the therapy process draws heavily on the client empowerment focus from Model D as well as elements of promoting nurturing parenting and attachment in Model B (Ainsworth, 1974; Cicchetti et al., 2006). Additionally, there is a recurrent emphasis on helping parents to use parenting approaches that match their children's cognitive developmental stage (Piaget & Inhelder, 1962) and to recognizing the role of the wider systems or context that can impinge on a child, including for example the marital relationship problems, family economic stressors, or school neighborhood (Cottrell & Boston, 2002). Perhaps this might be called the collaborative, integrative Model E. It uses a set of principle-driven, dynamic theories and approaches that are flexibly adapted to each family's context, adjusting for individual families' culture and children's developmental abilities. Adjustments are made throughout the program to tailor the parenting strategies based on ongoing dialogue and collaboration between participants and therapists (see Webster-Stratton & Reid, 2010; Webster-Stratton, 2009; Webster-Stratton & Reid, 2008). The key cognitive social learning principles, video-based modeling vignettes, content sequence and participant books (Webster-Stratton, 1999) give structure to the programs, but flexible therapist implementation that promotes parent self-reflection, self-monitoring, and goal setting give voice to the parents and helps ensure that the content fits the context of their lives.

THE COLLABORATIVE MODEL IS ESSENTIAL TO PARENT LEARNING

We are reluctant to call our approach "parent training" because this term implies (as in Model C) a hierarchical relationship between the therapist and parent wherein the expert therapist is fixing some "deficit" within the parent. A term such as "parent coaching" is perhaps preferable. Terminology aside, the core underlying big principles we advocate for working with families are active or experiential, self-reflective, and collaborative. In a collaborative relationship, the therapist does not set him/herself up as an "expert" dispensing advice to parents about how they should parent more effectively. With a root meaning of "to labor together," collaboration implies a reciprocal relationship based on utilizing equally the therapist's knowledge and the parents' knowledge, strengths, and perspectives. Collaboration implies respect for each person's contribution and is a non-blaming, non-hierarchical relationship built on trust and open communication.

As professionals, therapists have considerable expertise in their fields. Does the collaborative therapist have to renounce this expertise? Not at all. Yet the collaborative training or coaching model acknowledges that expertise is not the sole property of the therapist: parents function as experts concerning their child, their particular family and culture, their community and their goals, and the therapist functions as an expert concerning child development, family dynamics in general, and cognitive, emotional and behavior management principles. The collaborative therapist also realizes that human behavior is not dictated solely, or even mostly, by knowing the "right" answers. The expert model of simply telling a parent how he or she should respond to a child's behavioral issues is very unlikely to meet with a successful outcome. Rather, human interactions are complex mixtures of knowledge, feelings, life circumstances, past

Collaboration implies respect and is a non-blaming, non-hierarchical relationship.

experience, personality, and many other factors. The collaborative therapist tries to understand and incorporate these factors by actively soliciting parents' ideas and feelings, understanding their cultural context, and involving them in the self-reflective learning process by inviting them to share their experiences, discuss their ideas, and engage in problem-solving. Collaboration implies that parents actively participate in the setting of goals for themselves and their children and self-monitoring their home activities and achievements. Collaboration implies that parents evaluate each session, and the therapist is responsible for adapting the intervention in response to their evaluations. A detailed description of the stages parents go through while engaged in this program can be found in Chapter Ten.

Collaboration Allows for Tailoring

Another aspect of the collaborative therapist's labor is working with parents to adapt concepts and skills to the particular circumstances of their family situations as well as the temperament and developmental stage of their child. The therapist recognizes and values cultural differences and diversity of parents' backgrounds. For example, a parent who lives in a one-room trailer is unlikely to have an empty room for Time Out and will even have difficulty finding a suitable spot to put a Time Out chair. A parent living in an apartment, where walls are not soundproofed, will be acutely sensitive to the possible reactions of neighbors when s/he tries to ignore the screaming child; with good reason, that parent may resist using the ignore technique. These parents may raise objections to the use of Time Out or ignoring. In traditional (hierarchical) therapy, these would be seen as instances of resistance, and the therapist would work to overcome the parents' resistance. In contrast, the collaborative therapist would operate from the assumption that the parent had legitimate grounds for resisting this aspect of the training, would attempt to understand the living situation and other circumstances of each family or their prior experiences and involve the parents in problem solving to adapt the behavior management principles to their particular situation. To take other examples, a highly active, impulsive child with ADHD may not be able to sit quietly and play attentively with his parents for more than 5 minutes. Such children will also have more difficulty sitting in Time Out than less active children. Other children are not particularly responsive to tangible reward programs. The therapist needs to be sensitive to these differences in child temperament, motivation, and developmental abilities so that s/he can begin to collaborate with parents in defining the approaches that will work for them and their particular child. Several articles about adapting the program with fidelity according to family interpersonal issues and child developmental factors can be found on the web site (Webster-Stratton, 1998a, 2007; Webster-Stratton & Reid, 2008a, 2010a).

www.incredibleyears.com/Library/default.asp

A non-collaborative approach is didactic and non-participative, the content is fixed—the therapist lectures, the parents listen. The non-collaborative therapist presents principles and skills to parents in terms of "prescriptions" for successful ways of dealing with their children. Homework assignments are rigid, given without regard for the particular circumstances or goals of an individual family. This approach has been rejected because, for one thing, it is unsuccessful (Fixen, Blase, Friedman, & Wallace, 2005). It is actually likely to lead to higher attrition rates and poor long-term maintenance. Furthermore, it is ethically dubious to impose goals that may not be congruent with parent goals, values, and lifestyles and that may not suit the temperament of the child. This is particularly important when there are cultural or socio-economical differences between the therapist and the parents, where assumptions arising from the therapist's own background or training may simply not apply. The collaborative model implies that, insofar as possible, the therapist will encourage the parents to generate solutions based on their experience with their child, and on their family's cultural, class, and individual background. When parents come up with solutions they view as appropriate, the therapist can then reinforce and expand on these ideas.

A collaborative therapist style is demonstrated by open communication patterns within the group and the therapist's attitude of acceptance toward all the families in the program. By building a relationship based not on authority but on rapport with the group, the therapist creates a climate of trust, making the group a safe place for parents to reveal their problems and darkest thoughts and feelings, to risk new approaches, and get support. The collaborative therapist is a careful listener. S/he uses open-ended questions when exploring issues, for they are more likely to generate discussion and collaboration, and s/he encourages debate and alternative viewpoints, treating all viewpoints with respect. The therapist's empathic understanding is conveyed by the extent to which s/he actively reaches out to the parents, elicits their ideas, listens reflectively, affirms positive steps taken and attempts to understand rather than analyze.

Collaboration leads to Empowerment

The partnership between parents and therapist has the effect of giving back dignity, respect, and self-control to parents who, because of their particular situations, may be in a vulnerable time of low self-confidence and intense feelings of guilt and self-blame (Spitzer, Webster-Stratton, & Hollinsworth, 1991). It is our hypothesis that a collaborative approach is more likely to increase parents' confidence and perceived self-efficacy than other therapeutic approaches. Bandura (1977, 1982, 1989) has called this strategy strengthening the client's "efficacy expectations"; that is, parents' conviction that they can successfully change their own and their child's behaviors. Bandura has suggested that self-efficacy is the mediating variable between knowledge and behavior. Therefore, parents with high "self-efficacy" will tend to persist at tasks until they succeed. The literature also indicates that people who have determined their own priorities and goals are more likely to persist in the face of difficulties and less likely to show debilitating effects of stress (Seligman, 1975).

The collaborative model is likely to increase parents' engagement in the intervention.

Moreover, this model is likely to increase parents' engagement in the intervention. Research suggests that the collaborative process has the multiple advantages of reducing attrition rates, increasing motivation and commitment to change, reducing resistance, increasing temporal and situational generalization, and giving parents and the therapist a joint stake in the outcome of the intervention (Meichenbaum & Turk, 1987). Some have called this approach "motivational interviewing" (Miller & Rollnick, 2002). On the other hand, controlling or hierarchical modes of therapy, in which the therapist analyzes, interprets, and makes decisions *for* parents without incorporating their input, may result in a low level of commitment, dependency, low self-efficacy, and increased resistance, as well as resentment of professionals (Patterson & Forgatch, 1995). In fact, if parents are not given appropriate ways to participate, or feel understood or see how the approach addresses their goals, they may see no alternative but to drop out or resist the intervention as a means of asserting their control over the therapeutic process.

In short, the net result of a collaborative model for working with parents is to empower parents by strengthening their knowledge and skill base, their self-confidence, and their autonomy, instead of creating dependence on the therapist and inadvertently perpetuating a sense of inadequacy or helplessness. There is a further reason for this model: since a goal of the program is for parents to adopt a participative, collaborative, empowering approach with their own children, it is important to use this approach with them in the parent program. In other words the therapist-parent relationship models the relationship style that parents are encouraged use with their children and other family members. Directly experiencing this form of collaborative learning has been shown to lead to greater internalization of learning in children, and very likely in adults as well.

Setting the Stage for Collaboration

The Setting. There are four main settings in which parenting intervention programs can take place: the home, school, a mental health clinic, or community center. Typical behavioral therapy, based on the one-to-one (dyadic) or behavioral family therapy (systemic) model, tends to take place in a clinic or home setting. Parent interventions based on the triadic or behavioral consultation model (using significant caregivers or teachers as mediators of change) may be located in the school. When parent training involves group work, the clinic or a community-based center is usually the preferred setting, but the school is certainly an option.

It is debatable whether there are clearly differentiated criteria for choosing the home as opposed to the clinic or school as the setting for parent interventions, or the related issue of choosing a group, as opposed to an individual (family) modality. The issue of group work being more economical, and, indeed as or more effective than individual casework, has been investigated. Webster-Stratton and others (Cunningham, Bremner, & Boyle, 1995; Webster-Stratton, 1984; Webster-Stratton & Herbert, 1993; Webster-Stratton, Kolpacoff, & Hollinsworth, 1988) have demonstrated clear advantages for the kind of group-based work that utilizes video modeling and the active, self-reflective, collaborative process of discussion and problem solving. Moreover, groups offered in schools have been shown to be less stigmatizing than clinic settings and more attractive to minority groups (Cunningham et al., 2000). Are there occasions, however, when there is a case for choosing an individual family approach to treatment? Are there particular clients who require something other than, or in addition to, the clearly effective group-based method? There appears to be a category of parents who may respond more favorably to, and welcome, interventions in their own homes (Webster-Stratton & Herbert, 1993; Webster-Stratton & Reid, 2010). They and/or their children find clinic and group settings somewhat daunting, for a variety of reasons. For example:

- They tend not to be very articulate and to suffer from very low self-esteem; they find the social/verbal ethos of the group difficult to cope with.
- They do not share consensus values about life and child rearing, and sense themselves as "outsiders."
- Family life is disorganized, if not chaotic. To come out to regular appointments (the organization required, and the mobility demanded) may be beyond them.
- They are particularly private about their personal/familial disadvantages, tragedies, and "failings" and cannot envisage public discussion of personal issues, whatever the preliminary briefing and reassurance given.
- Child/spouse abuse in the family makes them wary of a public commitment to therapy.
- They (and this often means the child) feel safer/more comfortable working from home.
- They believe the therapist cannot really understand their reality unless s/he sees what actually happens in the home.

- There is a potentially subversive partner (this usually is the father) who refuses to attend a clinic; the only way to access him may be to work with all the family in the home.
- Both parents are poorly motivated for therapy. The only way to "engage" them in a change process is a relatively long process of "joining" the family over many home visits and building a supportive relationship with them.

The group versus individual home-based coaching IY intervention is not necessarily an either-or choice. They may take place in parallel or sequentially.

These observations are based upon statements gathered from parents at intake evaluation sessions. None of these factors need exclude a group approach and in fact, for some parents with low self-esteem who feel like outsiders, being part of a group may actually be the best thing for them in terms of promoting their sense of connection to others; but when several factors converge in one family, it may be difficult for the therapist to engage the family in a commitment to clinic-based group meetings to which they have to make a regular self-directed journey. At times the group versus individual intervention is not necessarily an either-or choice. They may take place in parallel or sequentially if both modalities are thought to be required. A home-based coaching version of both the IY preschool and school age parent programs are available with a therapist manual, protocols, and parent self-study manuals (Webster-Stratton, 2008). The home-based version may be used in its entirety for those parents whose schedules or other mental health difficulties don't make it possible for them to attend groups. The home version can also be used to supplement the group program for parents who need extra home practice in a particularly difficult content area or who miss a group session.

If the therapy is to take place in the clinic or a room in a community setting (e.g., church or school) it is important to try to find a setting for services that is informal, friendly, and accessible. For example, it is necessary to provide an adequate size group room with comfortable chairs and a television and DVD or projector for watching the program vignettes. It is also important to have access to a kitchen for preparing snacks and making coffee or tea as well as a room for day care for children while the parents are in their groups. When such living room-like settings are available, parents will often come to group sessions early just to have coffee and cookies and chat informally with other parents before the group session starts. Initially, therapists provide snacks for the mid-group break, but it is often the case that parents will begin to offer to bring in snacks for the group. This informality helps to decrease the distance not only from the therapist but also from the other parents and promotes a comfortable, safe and secure home-like environment.

The Intake Interview. A collaborative approach begins at the very first encounter with the parents: the initial intake interview. During this interview, the therapist tries to enter into the parents' experience and feelings; a typical question is, "*Tell me what life is like at home with your child.*" Parents are asked to explain the disciplinary approaches and coping strategies they have tried, those that have worked and those that have not, as well as their theories regarding possible causes of the child's problems. Through questioning and careful listening, the therapist elicits the parents' explanatory model and cognitive attributions for the child's problems. Some parents may feel their child is genetically a "bad egg" and perhaps fear they are like another family member who is in jail, antisocial, or managing some mental illness. Other parents may blame themselves or their partner for the cause of their child's problems, feeling they were too harsh or too absent. The therapist listens in a nonjudgmental way to these fears and thoughts, for it will make a difference in terms of the approaches they will take in discussing parenting strategies with them. They ask the parents to list their child's problems and to prioritize them from their own perspective. They are also asked about their child's strengths so that a well balanced view of the child's strengths and difficulties are outlined. Ideally, parents come to feel that the therapist is making a genuine effort to understand their internal reality, thoughts, and feelings as well as their goals.

Next the therapist tries to elicit the parents' hopes and goals for the parent program by asking questions such as, "*What is your greatest hope for what will happen as a result of participating in this program?*" Hearing the parents define their goals at the outset enables the therapist to correct any unrealistic expectations on their part. A secondary effect of goal definition is that, at a time when parents may be feeling depressed and vulnerable, it helps them focus on a more positive future. During the intake interview, the therapist listens carefully to the text and to the subtext of what the parents are saying; s/he listens with a "third ear" to discover not only what the child's problem are, but what those problems have meant to the family. Throughout the interview, the therapist tries to follow the parents' agenda, beginning where the parents want to begin and covering their points of concern. Thus, during the first interview the therapist has already begun to demonstrate empathic understanding and to involve parents immediately in therapy as a collaborative enterprise.

After discussing the parents' perceptions of their child's problems, their experiences attempting to deal with those problems, their explanatory model, and their goals and hopes for therapy, the therapist then shares with them the goals of the Incredible Years program, emphasizing its collaborative nature. For example:

> ***Therapist:*** *Our job now is to work together, to support you, and to consult with you so that the interactions between you and your child are more positive and so that you can achieve your goals. The way our program works is that we meet each week with a group of parents (whose children are similar to yours) in order to discuss and study together some strategies for managing child behaviors like the ones you've shared with me. We work together as a team and we expect you to be our "co-therapist" in this process. The group will work together in a variety of different ways. Each week we will watch some DVDs showing common parent-child interactions and then together we'll analyze the video vignettes and decide what we think is effective about the interactions. We'll also practice new strategies during the session to see how they might work with your own children, and then you'll decide which of the parenting strategies are most appropriate for you to try out at home with your child. You will be the experts on what works or doesn't work with your child. When things don't work, you bring this information back to us and we put our heads together to come up with a revised strategy for the problem. You see,*

we each have a contribution: What we can offer is more alternatives, information about child development and resources, and what you can offer is help deciding and implementing the best strategy for your situation and for your particular child. How does that sound to you?

Therapists sometimes find that parents have a pre-existing cognitive "set" regarding therapy which may be quite different from this collaborative approach. For example, they may expect the therapist to "fix" their child through child therapy, or to alter the child's temperament with medication. Or, because this approach places such a strong emphasis on parental involvement, they may incorrectly assume that parents are blamed for the problems they are experiencing with their child. While self-blame and guilt are recurring themes throughout the process of therapy, it is important for parents to hear from the onset that this program takes a nonblaming, nonjudgmental stance towards the causes of the child behavior problems and that they experience this attitude reflected consistently in therapist interactions with them. Therapists help parents understand that they will be supported to improve their situation rather than determining who is at fault, and that the orientation is toward the malleable present and future, not the unalterable past. The therapist might say:

***Therapist**: We appreciate hearing your own theories regarding the reasons for your child's problems. Our own approach when we see children misbehaving is not to assume either that the child is at fault (a "bad egg") or that the parent is inept. Rather we feel that, for whatever reason, the interaction between the parent and child has gone askew and is "out of synch." This problem may have occurred because the child has a more difficult biological temperament, some developmental delays, or is reacting to a traumatic experience. Or, perhaps the stresses on the family make it particularly hard to keep up the difficult work of parenting such a child with consistent responses. Or, in many cases, it is some combination of these factors.*

The concepts of partnership, co-therapy, group support, education, experiential practice learning, self-reflection, and group problem solving are brought up repeatedly throughout the initial sessions to emphasize the collaborative nature of the program and to help parents understand the importance of these elements to successful achievement of their goals.

Initial Group Meeting

Identifying Group Rules. One of the most important aspects of the therapist's role is to assure group participants feel safe, comfortable, and accepted. Assuring a noncritical setting for parenting discussions where there is respect for different viewpoints and different cultural backgrounds is essential because if a parent feels criticized or isolated by other members, drop out is a certainty. Consequently, during the first meeting, the therapist must take enough time so the group members can discuss and come to a collaborative agreement on the rules that will help them feel safe and assure their privacy regarding their discussions. These rules are written down using the parents' terminology and are kept posted on the wall to be added to or referred to if necessary during weekly sessions. Examples of rules many groups come up with include: (a) everyone's ideas are respected; (b) there are no dumb questions or ideas; (c) anyone has a right to pass; (d) no "put downs" are allowed;

(e) what is said in the group is not shared outside the group; (f) cell phones turned off or on vibrate; (g) no texting allowed; (h) no alcohol permitted and (i) start and end meetings on time. As the group agrees on each rule, the therapist and group members discuss why they think these rules are important for them.

For groups that are very verbal and tend to get sidetracked or to digress, it is helpful to select a parent to act as a timekeeper for each session. The job of this parent-timekeeper is to help when a conversation is sidetracking, refer to the agenda that has been posted, and to keep the group focused on the group rules and main topics for the session. Evaluations indicate that parents become frustrated and disengaged if the discussion wanders, and they appreciate having enough structure imposed to allow everyone to talk and keep the discussions, vignettes, and practices moving along. By rotating the job of timekeeper, the task of monitoring the group discussion becomes everyone's responsibility; everyone is committed to the group functioning well.

In addition to keeping the group discussions on track, the therapist enforces the time schedule. Meetings have a tendency to start later and later unless a definite starting time is established. Meetings should begin on time even if only two people are present. After the coffee break, therapists may need a signal, such as a bell, to indicate to parents that the group is going to start again. While it's a good sign if parents are enjoying visiting with each other during breaks, many minutes of precious group time can be lost if the therapist does not restart the group in a timely manner. Similarly, the therapist needs to end the meetings on time. This may be difficult when groups are in the middle of an enthusiastic discussion; however, this is actually a good time to end a meeting, since everyone will leave feeling stimulated and excited about their involvement in the program.

Participants Set Personal Goals. Collaboration implies that parents actively participate in setting goals. At the initial parent group, the therapist asks each parent to share some of their long-term goals for what they want to accomplish in the program. Sometimes it is helpful for therapists to ask parents to share one goal about what they want from the program for themselves and one goal for their child. These goals are posted on a flip chart on the wall so that they can be referred to or added to throughout the program. This initial discussion often produces immediate group rapport as parents realize they have shared difficulties and are working toward similar goals. These initial long-term goals support the development of short-term goals between sessions. Following every parent group session, parents are also asked to delineate their short-term goals for the week regarding the home activities they will try to accomplish. These are related to the weekly content such as which specific positive child behaviors they will praise, the days or times they will engage in child-directed play times, or amount of reading they will complete. Several times during the program, the therapist draws up a composite list of those goals for specific behaviors that parents are working on so that group members can see the similarities in some of the challenges they face. This promotes ongoing group cohesion, as well as attention to individual goals, thereby making the program relevant to each parent and increasing parents' commitment to the program.

Collaboration implies that parents actively participate in setting goals.

During this initial session (as well as later on), the therapist uses open-ended questions when exploring goals, for open-ended questions are more likely to generate lively discussion and reflection, whereas "yes-no" questions tend to produce very little exchange of ideas. Open-ended questions include questions designed to elucidate factual information (cognitive questions) as well as feeling information (affect questions) about goals. For example, useful open-ended questions for a parent who says her goal is for her child to be less disruptive might be, "*What specific positive behaviors do you want to see more of?*" (delineate positive goal) or, "*Why do you think your son gets so frustrated?*" (determine parent's attributions regarding cause of the misbehavior) or, "*How do you feel when this is happening to you?*" (understand parent's feelings) or, "*What kinds of thoughts do you have in this situation?*" (determine parent's cognitions). Alternative perspectives are encouraged so that the therapist and parent groups can begin to understand each other. All viewpoints are respected; when possible, parents are encouraged to draw their own connections and develop their own insights.

The therapist's empathic understanding will be conveyed by the extent to which s/he actively reaches out to the parents, attempts to understand (rather than analyze) their perspectives and goals, listens reflectively and elicits their ideas about why the problem is occurring.

Therapists Work Together Collaboratively. Although the group can be run with one therapist, we recommend having two therapists per group. These therapists work together to plan their group each week and to decide upon leader roles. For example, therapists should decide who will take primary responsibility for leading the discussion of particular vignettes and who will be looking for "principles" from parent comments, handing out prizes, and writing down key ideas on the flip chart. It is very helpful for parents to see the leaders collaborating and working together to lead the groups. When breaking out for small group practices each therapist can coach a different dyad or triad and give individual feedback. Leaders should also respect each other and praise each other's ideas.

It is generally a good idea for therapists to take turns being the designated "content leader" and "process leader." Halfway through the session, after the break, therapists usually switch roles. The content leader takes responsibility for the new content being presented by leading the home work discussion, showing vignettes, and guiding the

USE VIDEO IN A COLLABORATIVE WAY
TO ENHANCE TEACHING

discussion. The process leader watches group dynamics and identifies parents who want to speak, praising their ideas and giving special rewards for goals achieved or big ideas, pulling out principles, writing key points on the flip chart, and summarizing new concepts. The process therapist can expand on a point that a leader is making, but in general is following the lead of the primary leader in terms of content being learned. If an experienced therapist is working with a new group leader of the program, then they can decide when the new leader feels ready to try out leading some vignettes. It is not uncommon for new group leaders to start by observing groups, helping with writing down key points, and supporting the therapist during practice sessions.

METHODS TO SUPPORT THE COLLABORATIVE PROCESS

Video Modeling and Mediation of Vignettes. The Incredible Years Series relies heavily on social learning, modeling, and self-efficacy theory (Bandura, 1977, 1982, 1989) which contends that observation of a model can support the learning of new skills. As applied to parent training, the modeling theory of learning suggests that parents can improve their parenting skills by watching video examples of other parents interacting with their children in ways that promote children's prosocial behaviors and decrease their inappropriate behaviors. The therapist selects from over 300 video vignettes showing parents and children of different sexes, ages, cultures, socioeconomic backgrounds, and child temperament styles and developmental abilities. These vignettes include older vignettes from the original IY parenting program that tend to be brief examples of a particular point as well as recently updated, longer, and somewhat more complex vignettes. All vignettes show parents interacting with their children in natural, unrehearsed situations, such as during mealtime, getting dressed, toilet training, taking a bath, going to the grocery store, doing a chore, handling disobedience, resisting going to bed, or doing homework. Children are shown responding in a variety of ways; some are engaged and compliant and some are defiant and aggressive. Children also represent a range of ages,

In order to make the training personally relevant, therapists help parents discuss how the concepts illustrated in the video vignettes apply or don't apply to their own unique situations.

temperaments, and developmental levels. The parents in the vignettes are culturally diverse and are using a variety of parenting strategies: some more effective and some less effective. The intent in showing less effective as well as more effective examples is to demystify the notion of "perfect parenting" and to illustrate how parents can learn from their mistakes. When delivered in groups, video-based modeling has the added benefit of triggering group discussion, self-reflective learning and practices to re-enact vignettes. When a vignette is shown, it is mediated by the therapist to define words, ensure that the discussion addresses the intended topic, is understood by the parents and used to help parents reflect on their next steps. In order to make the training personally relevant and bridge the gap between the specific structure and content of the vignettes and the varied backgrounds represented by the participating parents, therapists help parents discuss how the concepts illustrated in the vignettes apply or don't apply to their own unique situations. When they don't apply, the therapist sets up practices where the parents "act out" what would happen at home and the group problem solves how to respond.

Our research has indicated that therapist-led group discussion utilizing video modeling is superior to therapist-led group discussion without videos, as well as to video alone self-study (Webster-Stratton, 1990b; Webster-Stratton et al., 1989; Webster-Stratton, Kolpacoff, & Hollinsworth, 1988). Moreover, this method of training is thought to be more effective than other methods (e.g., didactic instruction, lectures, written handouts), especially for less verbally oriented parents, in promoting better generalization (and therefore long-term maintenance) by portraying a wide variety of models in a wide variety of situations and different contexts.

The therapist will show approximately 8-10 vignettes for discussion during one 2-hour session. Core vignettes are recommended for each session that provide a mix of vignettes selected to cover key points. Other vignettes may be selected to represent the particular culture of the families in a parent group, or the specific difficulties and development of their children. For parents who find the material new, unfamiliar, or confusing, the therapist will want to show more vignettes to help them understand key concepts. Therapists will also match specific vignettes such as those related to toilet training, coping with grocery store routines, talking on the phone, getting children to bed, or doing homework to particular parent goals and will show these vignettes even if they are not listed as core. The therapists need to study all the vignettes in the program in order to make good choices about the vignettes most applicable to a particular group.

Therapists match specific vignettes to particular parent goals.

Before the therapist shows a vignette, s/he begins by helping the parents understand what they are to focus on when they watch the vignette. For example, the therapist says, *"In the next vignette, see if you can determine why this parent is effective, or what she does to prompt a positive behavior."* Then when the therapist shows the vignette, s/he pauses the vignette at various points to give parents a chance to discuss and react to what they have observed. The newer, longer vignettes are sometimes paused 2-3 times to get parents to reflect on what they would do next. Sometimes group members are uncertain about whether the kinds of parenting interactions they have just observed are appropriate or not. Thus, the therapist asks open-ended questions such as, *"Do you think there was a better way to handle that situation?"* or, *"How would you feel if your child did that?"* (suggested questions and discussion topics are included in therapist manual). If participants are unclear about specific aspects of the parent/child interaction, or if they have missed a critical feature of the vignette, the therapist shows the group the vignette again. The goal is not only to have parents grasp the intended concept, but also to ensure parents become actively involved in reflecting on the interactions, problem-solving, and sharing ideas about parenting strategies. The therapist can promote integration and relevance of the concepts or behavioral principles by asking how the concepts illustrated in the vignettes apply or don't apply to parents' own situations. For example, a mother makes the following comment after watching a few of the play vignettes:

Mother: *I don't have any toys at home. I can't afford toys like those shown on the DVD. I'm living on a welfare check.*

Therapist: *You know, even if you had the money it is not important to have fancy toys. In fact, some of the best toys for children are things like pots and pans, empty cereal boxes, dry macaroni and string, water and cooking utensils—why don't we brainstorm some ideas for inexpensive things you could use to play with your child at home?*

This interaction between the therapist and mother illustrates the importance of collaborating with parents in order to be sure the concepts shown on the video vignettes are relevant for their particular cultural and socioeconomic situation.

Key Points for Using DVD Video Vignettes

- Introduce the vignette and help the parent focus on what they are to watch for.
- Show "core" vignettes recommended and choose other vignettes according to culture of population being addressed or development of children.
- For families whose English is not fluent, or for families who find the content unfamiliar, begin with the older, shorter, simpler vignettes.
- Pace parents' learning by integrating the presentation of vignettes throughout the entire session. Avoid waiting until the last half of the session to show the majority of vignettes.
- Allow for discussion with every vignette. Do not run vignettes together without mediation and problem solving discussions.
- Allow for parents' first impressions (insights) to be expressed before therapist offers analysis and interpretation.
- If parents' reactions are critical of the behavior shown in a vignette, balance their perspective by noting some positive features of the parents' behaviors. (If you allow a group to become too negative, parents may feel you could be just as critical of their mistakes.)
- Remember to model a realistic perspective of parenting.
- Pause introductions to vignettes as well as vignettes themselves to clarify terminology, to allow for questions, to predict next steps

and to be sure parents are understanding and have time to digest the essential content in the narration.

- Ask open-ended questions when showing vignettes that focus on parents' or children's feelings and thoughts as well as their behaviors.
- Pull out key learning principles from parents' reflections and ideas, and using their own words, write these principles down next to their names.
- Be sure to see if principles learned from vignettes can be applied to parents' individual situations at home and their targeted goals.
- Use video vignettes to trigger replays or practices of parenting strategies shown in vignettes.

It is important to emphasize that the DVD vignettes are used in a collaborative way, as a catalyst to stimulate group discussion and problem-solving, not as a device that renders the parents passive observers. Parents' reactions to the vignettes and the ways in which they process what they saw are more important than what is actually shown in the vignette. The vignettes have been designed to illustrate specific concepts, it is up to the therapist to ask questions that permit the parents to self-reflect and discover the key behavior management or communication principles. It would be inappropriate (and non-collaborative) to show the vignettes without pausing or inviting extensive discussion and to explore how the principle discovered can be applied to parents' goals for themselves or their children.

Role Play, Practice, and Experiential Learning. Role playing, rehearsal, or practice of unfamiliar or newly-acquired behaviors and cognitions is one of the most important components of the parents' learning process and has been shown to be quite effective in producing behavioral changes. A therapist might think from the discussion of the vignette that parents understand the principle or content, but until the parent is seen "in action," it will not be clear whether he can put the ideas into real-life behaviors. There can be a discrepancy between parents' cognitions and beliefs about how they would ideally like to behave and how they actually behave with their child. It can be very difficult to think of the right words to use with children, manage angry thoughts and stressful feelings when children argue or disagree, or to follow through with consistent

USE ROLE PLAY TO ENHANCE PARENT LEARNING

responses. Role play or experiential learning is effective because it helps parents anticipate situations more clearly, dramatizing possible sequences of behaviors, feelings, and thoughts. It helps them rehearse behaviors, practice staying calm, use positive self-talk, and get feedback from the group and therapist about their skills. It is recommended that therapists set up *at least three to four* brief practices during each group session.

Large Group Planned Practices. Therapists begin the first role play/practices in the large group by selecting parents they think understand the concepts and will be comfortable demonstrating them. They invite parents' involvement in these practices by saying, "*Susan, you had some great ideas with that vignette, will you help me show others how coaching works with children?*" Or, "*John, can you show me what your child is doing to upset you so we can understand it better and plan a response you will feel better about?*" The therapist reduces parents' self-consciousness and anxiety about role play/practices by reviewing key ideas written on a flip chart that were developed from parent discussions, addressing their personal goals, scaffolding practices carefully with scripts, and supportive coaching of the role of the child and parent. It also helps to make the role play practices humorous through exaggeration. For example, one parent may be asked to go out of the room and shout from a distance (e.g., kitchen) for the child (role-played by parent) to put away the toys. This usually raises chuckles of recognition, for there is no way for the parent to know whether the child is complying or not, or whether the child has even registered the command. Sometimes if a parent is at a loss for what to say in a practice scenario, the therapist can "freeze" the practice scene and ask the group to brainstorm some ideas, "*What is the child trying to communicate or achieve by behaving like that?*" or, "*Now what should this parent do?*" Then the therapist rewinds the scenario for the practice experience to continue using some of the group's suggested ideas. This process of pausing the live practice to give praise to those acting, to explore further ideas, or work on some positive self-talk cognitions is utilized in just the same way that a video vignette is paused and reflected upon.

After the therapist large group role plays have been demonstrated, the therapist debriefs the demonstration by asking the parent in role as child how she felt and the parent in role as parent how the experience was for him. The group then gives the parent positive feedback for the skills he used in the practice. Parents who do these practices are praised and their contribution to everyone's learning is recognized by a reward from the therapist such as candy, a special sticker, or a prize from a treasure box.

Small Group Practices. Once the large group practice has been demonstrated by the two parents, the parent group is divided into triads so that everyone can practice the particular skills being covered in the session such as persistence, social or emotion coaching, explaining family rules, or problem solving. During these practices one person is child, another person is parent and the third is observer who watches the interaction with a handout, and offers suggestions and support if needed. At the end the observer gives positive feedback to the parent for the skills she observed. Then the triads exchange positions. At the end of these small group practices, the triads report back to the larger group the key idea they learned from this experience.

Spontaneous Practices. Because the video vignettes tend to focus on more positive interactions than negative ones, parents of children with conduct problems often react with, "My child wouldn't be that compliant" or "My child would never..." or, "Parents in our culture don't praise like that…" This is the strategic moment for the therapist to immediately do a *spontaneous role play or practice* and ask the parent to take the part of their child, "*Show me what he usually does, and then we'll try out some different responses.*" It is better to have the parent demonstrate the negative behavior their child exhibits with a scaffolded response than to show a highly negative interaction on the video. Videos with high levels of negative child affect cause parents considerable distress, and those negative vignettes tend to be remembered more than the positive ones that contain the images that we want them to retain and model. Another reason for showing vignettes with milder levels of child behavior is that it is important for parents to focus on the parent behavior and the skills that the parents in the vignettes are using. It is much harder to practice a new skill when a child is highly dysregulated or noncompliant. At first, therapists will structure role plays with mild child behaviors so that parents can practice the new skills with success. Once they have mastered the skill, then they will be ready to practice responding to higher levels of misbehavior. Moreover, when parents put themselves in the role of their children, they perceive the world from their child's point of view. This provides them with an important perspective about what it feels like when a parent doesn't engage in the power struggle or doesn't respond to their efforts to get attention. It helps them experience the power of differential attention and how it works.

Carefully scaffolded parent practices using clearly defined scripts are immensely useful.

Another place for effective use of spontaneous role plays or practice is during the home activities review discussion. Parents who report successes with a particular strategy can be asked to show the group how they did this parenting and parents who felt their child wasn't responding to their strategy can be in role as child with other parents trying various approaches. Weekly evaluations indicate that over time parents find the role plays extremely useful to their learning and often request to act things out. Usually it is the therapist who is most resistant to the idea of doing these practices, for effective role playing requires that the therapist allow him or herself to take risks, to be playful, to be vulnerable, and to relinquish control. However, carefully scaffolded practices, with the therapist as director, using clearly defined scripts, starting by practicing simple skills and scenarios and gradually adding more complexity as parents learn more strategies, are immensely useful.

Tips for Setting Up Role Play/Practices in Groups

- The therapist is director of the role play/practice and chooses the actors, sets the stage, and determines the script and roles.
- Be sure to cover essential content or key points prior to doing the role play practice.
- Start with a simple role play and remember the goal for the skill the parent is learning.
- Select parents for large group role play who seem to understand the concept.
- Be sure to provide structure and "scripts" for both the parent and child in the role plays; the child in role should know his age, temperament, developmental level, and whether or not he is to misbehave. The parent should know what child behavior to expect and should have a plan for how to respond.
- Start with role plays where the child is cooperative or only mildly disruptive. Before moving to more disruptive behavior think about whether parents have learned the skills to manage the behaviors.
- Get parent group ideas for how to respond to the scenario being set up ahead of time; using their suggestions walk through the parent's part in the practice.
- Provide parent in role as parent with plenty of scaffolding to be successful.
- Freeze scenario at any time to give parent feedback for effective skills, or to redirect or clarify something.
- Debrief at end of practice to find out how parent and child each felt.
- Rerun role play with a different response, using appropriate ideas of a different parent or replay with different parent as child.
- Use spontaneous role plays that emerge out of a discussion of a difficulty a particular parent is having at home or from an idea that emerges from discussion of a vignette.
- One therapist should coach parent in role as parent and one coach the child; therapists can whisper ideas to parent or child regarding behaviors to try.
- Praise and reward all parents who participated in the role play.

Buddy Buzzes. In order to keep all parents actively involved in self-reflective experiential learning during the group sessions, the therapists frequently do buddy "buzz" exercises. Buzzes are when parents are paired up with a buddy to work on a specific exercise such as writing praise statements for their targeted positive opposite behavior, sharing calming strategies, establishing a bedtime routine, rewriting negative commands or negative thoughts into positive statements or coping thoughts, or making a reward menu. The benefit of doing a paired buzz instead of a group brainstorm is that every parent is immediately engaged in a task and involved in coming up with solutions. In large group brainstorms, perhaps only half the group contributes ideas and the other half is disengaged, quiet, or distracted. After these buzzes (3-5 minutes), each buddy can report to the group on their buddy's ideas and these are recorded by the therapist on a flip chart. Buzz handouts are included in the therapist manual for use in these exercises. When setting up these buzzes, the therapists should plan parent pairs ahead of time, placing matching stickers on each buddy pair's name tags. Parents can change chairs during the session to have these buzz discussions. Give parents a warning or ring a bell to warn them when the buzz time is coming to an end.

Setting up Live Home Practice Experiences for Parents and Children. Parents practice the parenting strategies they are learning first in the group with other parents and subsequently at home with their children in their weekly home activities. They report back to the group on these experiences each week and the therapist helps fine tune their approaches with further role plays as needed. For the majority of parents this will be sufficient, but for some families who are having difficulty using these approaches it can be helpful to set up some additional parent coached sessions with their children. Therapists may do this by encouraging parents to sign up for times to come early before the group with their child to do a practice of their child-directed coaching interactions. Or, therapists may make home visits to support and coach parents using these strategies with their children.

When coaching live parent-child play interactions, the therapist sits next to the parent as s/he plays with her child. She praises the parent's approaches, models some coaching language occasionally, and whispers some ideas for the parent to try with the child. For parents who are struggling to find the right coaching language, the therapist can tell the parent just to copy her language at first, and just to repeat everything that she says. After the play practice is completed, the therapist gives the parent feedback on his/her strengths and together they determine goals and write down any key scripts for future interactions at home. A home-based coaching manual for each of the four major sections of the IY program is available for the therapist/coach and for the parents.

In summary, the therapist uses a variety of methods to collaboratively support the parents' therapy goals and make the material relevant to each family's needs and circumstances. The next chapter will discuss the different roles that therapists take in order to work collaboratively and effectively with families.

Therapist Roles in Facilitating the Collaborative Learning Process

While the collaborative learning process is the underlying structure for the Incredible Years process of intervention, within this relationship the therapist assumes a number of different roles. These include: building a positive relationship with parents; empowering parents; building family and group support systems; and using evidence-based teaching methods such as video mediation, experiential practice, self-reflective learning, coaching, leading and predicting change. Each of these roles is one specific expression of a collaborative relationship. In the next figure I have depicted the collaborative process as a jigsaw. The therapist's job is to creatively and flexibly determine where and when to use each of the pieces of the puzzle; only when all the pieces are integrated will the collaborative learning process be complete and will the parents' and children's cognitive, emotional and social learning take place.

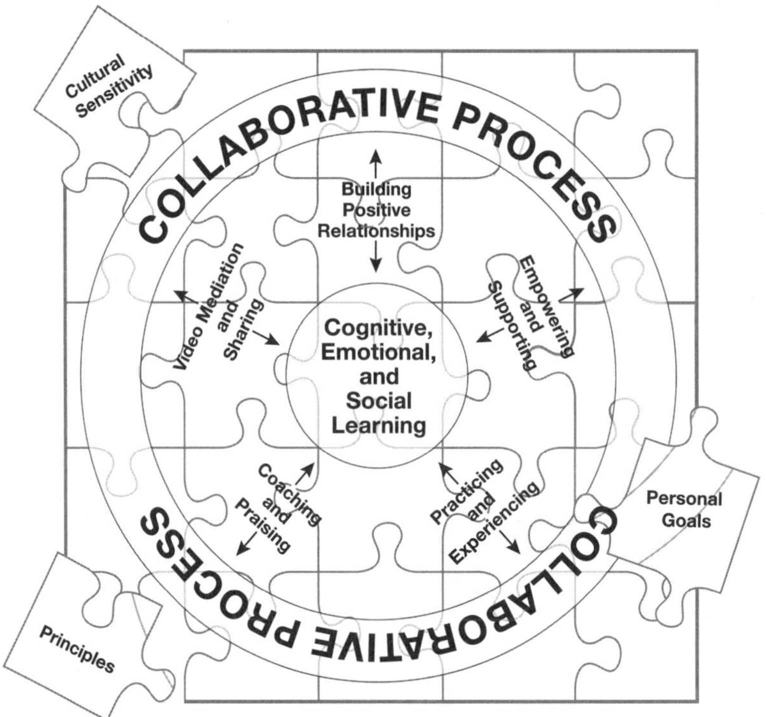

The Collaborative Learning Process

Therapist Role #1: Building Positive Relationships

As mentioned above, a collaborative approach requires that the therapist be empathic and use effective communication skills. This chapter will not review these counseling skills, as there is an extensive literature describing the therapeutic skills needed for effective relationship enhancement. Suffice it to say that empathy involves recognizing the feelings and perceptions (conscious and unconscious) that the parent has communicated. Empathy is conveyed unambiguously through reflective listening, the use of summaries of the parents' statements as well as supportive statements. In our therapy, we emphasize several relationship-building strategies in particular.

Use of self-disclosure. As discussed earlier, the collaborative therapist does not present her/himself as an "expert" who has worked out all the answers to the parents' problems, an expert who stands apart from the families' problems. Instead, the therapist is not only empathic and caring, respectful and kind, but "genuine." These core conditions (as described by Carl Rogers, 1951) are necessary underpinnings for the cognitive-social learning methodology. One way to be "genuine" is for the therapist to be willing to be known; to share personal experiences, feelings and problems of his/her own. Therapists always have a rich array of stories, either from their own families or from work with other families, that they can draw upon at will. I once shared with a parent group my intense anger and frustration when my 4-year-old child would not go to bed during the months following the birth of my second child. Afterwards, a father who had been very quiet throughout the first sessions came up to me and said with an incredulous expression, "You mean you have problems too?" This led to an important discussion between the two of us and much more active participation on his part in subsequent sessions, which in turn laid the basis for a stronger therapeutic relationship.

This use of self-disclosure concerning one's personal issues should, however, be planned strategically. It cannot be overemphasized that the purpose of this strategy is not for families to learn about the therapist's feelings and problems; rather, the purpose of such examples is to help parents learn about themselves. By sharing some personal experiences, the therapist can help families understand that the process of parenting for everyone involves learning to cope and profit from mistakes; it is not a process of achieving "perfection." Thus the therapist's personal example in this case was intended to demystify the therapist and to discredit the notion that there are perfect parents. It served to normalize the parents' reactions and to give them permission to make mistakes and to talk about their feelings. The therapist's intended message was something like this: "*Even the therapist, in her 25 years of studying children, doesn't know what to do at times. She makes mistakes and gets angry too. I guess I'm not such a bad parent after all.*" It can be helpful when a therapist shares a personal example to

This use of therapist self-disclosure should be planned strategically.

also share what she learned from the experience and how she coped with it successfully. A coping model, in which the therapist puts herself on the same level as the parents and models her own learning is more effective than a mastery model, which would simply demoralize parents further because of the perceived discrepancy between their skills and the therapists'. Moreover, this genuineness on the part of the therapist serves to enhance the therapist's relationship with the group members, introducing intimacy, affection, and closeness. Such a relationship, combined with the respect parents feel for the therapist, fuels the collaborative process.

Use of Humor. IY therapists make deliberate use of humor to help parents relax and to reduce anger, anxiety, and cynicism. Parents need to be able to laugh at their mistakes; this is part of the process of self-acceptance. Humor helps them gain some perspective on their stressful situation, which otherwise can become debilitating. Some of the DVD video scenes in our program were actually chosen more for their humor value than for their content value. Therapists can also use humorous personal examples to interject a comic note to the discussion. Humorous cartoons of parents and children, which are found in abundance in newspapers and magazines, are also helpful; parents can take them home to put on their refrigerator to laugh about. Another strategy is to rehearse or role-play a situation doing everything "wrong;" i.e., with lots of criticisms, anger and negative self-talk. This exaggeration inevitably evokes lots of laughter and helps build group spirit. Furthermore, when the parents find themselves engaging in some of this behavior at a future date, they may be able to stand back and laugh at themselves.

Optimism & Encouragement. Another form of support is for the therapist to establish positive expectations for change. Parents are often skeptical about their ability to change, especially if they see in their behavior a family pattern, for patterns often seem fixed and irreversible. For example, one parent said, "My mother beat me, now I beat my children." In such a case, the therapist must express his/her confidence in the parent's ability to break the family cycle. The therapist can point out and praise each small step toward change, even the step of coming to therapy in the first place, as evidence that the problem is not fixed or irreversible. Parents need to be reinforced through positive feedback for each success, however small, and for each change in their behavior or thought pattern, whether or not it results in improvement in their child's behavior. It can be helpful to cite examples of other parents in similar situations who have been successful in teaching their children to behave more appropriately.

> ***Therapist:*** *It is good that you are working with your child now while he is still young and his brain is still under construction. You are helping him stop his negative behaviors before they become permanent patterns. You are helping him build positive relationship neuron connections.*

Most importantly the therapist should frequently praise parents' reflections and efforts to change. Sometimes therapists are so preoccupied with the vignettes, schedule, and process methods that they forget to praise parents for their input. It is important to listen carefully to what parents are thinking and what they have tried at home and praise their small steps towards change. Therapists might challenge themselves to give out a certain number of praises at every session. Often the co-leader therapist can focus on praising parents' ideas, principles, and insights, and passing out special stickers or "gem awards" and rewards when she notices parents sharing or completing home activities. Indeed therapists are modeling the very skills they want parents to use with their children. When parents experience the therapist's enthusiasm, praise, and recognition for their insights, they begin to understand how it can help their children learn.

Therapists listen carefully to what parents are thinking and what they have tried at home and praise their small steps towards change.

Advocating for Parents. Each of the therapist approaches discussed above, self-disclosure, humor, optimism, and positive reinforcement, serves the overall purpose of building a positive and supportive relationship. The therapist can also actively support parents by acting as an advocate for them, particularly in situations where communication with other professionals may have become difficult. In the role of advocate, the therapist can bring relevant persons, programs, and resources to the family, or bring the family to them. For example, the therapist can organize and attend meetings between parents and teachers so as to help the parents clarify the child's problems, agree upon goals, and set up behavior management programs that are consistent from the clinic to home to school.

The ultimate goal of this advocacy role is to strengthen the parents' ability to advocate for themselves and for their children.

It must be emphasized that the ultimate goal of this advocacy role is to strengthen the parents' ability to advocate for themselves and for their children. The danger of advocacy is that it can become a "rescue" or an "expert" role, resulting in the parents feeling dependent or being uncommitted. An example of this might be the therapist who makes recommendations to a child's teacher, without the parent being involved. On the other hand, the collaborative advocacy approach in this situation would be to say to the parent, "*It would be helpful for you to share with the teacher the strategies that are working for you at home in order to see whether s/he might consider setting up a similar program at school. You have learned a lot about what works with your son.*" The therapist accompanies the parent and provides support, but encourages the parents to communicate directly with the teachers. By giving parents responsibility for their own advocacy, sharing their own solutions, and advocating with (rather than for) parents, therapists again emphasize the collaborative process.

Making Personal Connections through Weekly Phone Calls. The therapist does a personal telephone "check-in" with every parent each week to ask how things are going and find out whether parents are having any difficulty with the assigned home activities. These calls allow the therapist and parents to get to know one another outside the group, and are particularly useful in the case of the quiet parent who is reluctant to bring up some private matter in the group. These calls promote engagement with the program, the relationship with the therapist, as well as revealing how well parents are assimilating the material presented in group. The therapist reviews the parents' session evaluations before making the call and can use this call as an opportunity to address neutral or negative weekly evaluations to see if s/he can address the parents' learning needs more effectively. While these calls are an opportunity to address individual concerns, it is the goal of the call to supplement and enhance the group's effectiveness, not to provide individual therapy. Occasionally, the calls may seem to be discouraging a parent from sharing in the group; the parent may feel that the one-on-one dialogue with the therapist is more important than the group support and process. If this is happening, the therapist should work to encourage the parent to share their success, struggles, or thoughts with the group. The therapist can emphasize the value of this for the whole group's learning and for what the parent might learn from the group. Sometimes the therapist might ask for permission to share something the parent has said: "*Would you mind if I shared this story next week, or would you tell it yourself? I think that there are other parents in the group who are feeling this same way, and I know they would appreciate hearing how you are coping with this.*"

When a parent misses a session, the therapist calls right away to let the parent know they were missed and that absences are taken seriously. It also gives the therapist an opportunity to help the parent schedule a make up session and do the assigned home activities before the next session. These individual calls are rated very highly by most parents because they feel their individual goals and concerns are being cared about. If phone calls are difficult for parents, the therapist can also do a check-in via email or texting.

Individual therapist calls are rated very highly by most parents.

Therapist Role #2: Empowering Parents

The essential goal of our collaborative therapy is to "empower" parents by building on their strengths and experience so that they feel confident about their parenting skills and ability to respond to new situations that may arise when the therapist is not there to help them. Bandura (1977) has called this strategy strengthening the client's "efficacy expectations"; that is, parents' conviction that they can successfully change their behaviors. There are several strategies that can help to empower parents.

EMPOWERING PARENTS

Praising and validating parents' insights. Through the use of open-ended questions, therapists encourage parents to reflect on their prior experiences, to assess their child's developmental readiness for the behavior targeted, and to share ideas and problem solve with each other. Parents are helped to explore different solutions to a problem situation, rather than settling for "quick fixes" or the first solution that comes to mind. The therapist studiously avoids giving any pat answers, keeping the focus of the discussion on the parents' insights, reflective learning, and long-term goals.

When therapists notice and praise a parent's problem-solving skills, parents feel validated. This affirming process helps parents to have self-efficacy, confidence in their own insights, and in their ability to sort out problems and to learn from their mistakes (Brown & Harris, 1978). For instance:

> **Father:** *I was just so frustrated with him! He wouldn't get dressed and was dawdling. I was going to be late for work. I got angrier and angrier. Finally, I went into his bedroom and shook him by the shoulders and yelled, "You want negative attention? You're going to get negative attention!" Then suddenly I thought, "What am I doing? Where is this getting me? This won't help him learn" and I walked out of the room.*

> **Therapist:** *Wow—that is awesome! You were able to stop yourself in the middle of an angry tantrum before you lost it. Good for you! That's remarkable. It sounds like your ability to stand back from the situation, to be objective and think about your goals, really helped you stop what you were doing. Is that true? What do you usually find helps you keep control of your anger? Would you do anything differently now? How would you replay the situation when it happens again?*

In this example, the therapist's role is to praise the father's insight and self-reflection and to draw attention to the coping skills he used during the frustrating situation. The therapist also helps the father to learn from the experience by rehearsing and planning how to respond in the future.

Because in most groups there are varying levels of educational background and communication skills, it is important that the therapist encourage and praise every parent for sharing his/her ideas so that every member gradually feels comfortable participating in the discussions. As part of this process, the therapist has to clarify for the group any parent comments that are unfocused or confusing statements so that they are not ridiculed, ignored, or criticized because of something they have said. We call this "finding the kernel of truth" in what a parent has said: underscoring its value by showing how it contributes to the understanding of the topic under discussion. One approach is for the therapist to keep a flip chart on which parents' useful ideas are recorded such as, "*Sally's meal time principle of letting her child decide how much to eat*" or "*John's principle of walking away to calm down when frustration is building*." Some literature suggests that mothers who have confidence in their child-rearing, and who feel they have broad community support for what they do, actually do better at parenting (Behrens, 1954; Herbert, 1980).

Modifying Powerless Thoughts. When parents seek professional help for their problems, they usually have experienced or are experiencing feelings of powerlessness and mounting frustration with their children due to a history of unsuccessful attempts to discipline them. This powerlessness is often expressed in terms of feeling victimized by their children: "Why me?" The feeling of helplessness typically is accompanied by intense anger and a fear of losing control of themselves when trying to discipline their children.

> **Father:** *My wife's been at work and comes home and asks, "How did things go tonight?" I say, "Do the words 'living hell' mean anything to you?" That's our sort of little joke. I'm labeling the kids in my mind as never doing what I say and I'm very angry at them.*

Because none of us feel good about ourselves when we become angry at our children, parents' anger towards their children is likely to cause them to blame themselves and to then feel depressed in reaction to their guilt. Furthermore, they feel depressed about their interactions with their children, seeing themselves as a causal factor in their child's problems.

Therefore, a powerful and necessary aspect of empowering parents is to help them learn to stop the spiraling negative self-talk and, more generally, to modify their negative thoughts. For example, a parent may say, "It's all my fault. I'm a terrible parent. This is more than I can cope with. Everything's out of control." The therapist then helps the parent learn how to stop this kind of powerless, self-defeating, blaming train of thought and to challenge it by substituting calmer, coping self-statements such as, "Stop worrying. These thoughts are not helping me. I'm doing the best I can. He's just testing my limits. All parents get discouraged at times, I'm going to be able to cope with this. I can manage. Things will get better." Parents are asked to keep records of their thoughts in response to extremely stressful situations with their children and are then invited to share some of this record with the group. As the group shares these thoughts, unrealistic expectations and irrational beliefs are challenged and become modified through discussion and by rewriting coping thoughts in their journals. This strategy is in accordance with the cognitive restructuring strategies described by Beck and his colleague (Beck, 1979; Beck, 2005) and Seligman's "learned optimism" (Seligman, 1990). The process of recognizing angry, helpless, self-critical, blaming, catastrophizing thoughts, and learning to substitute more adaptive and positive coping thoughts empowers parents by showing them they can cope with their thought patterns. This, in turn, changes their emotional responses as well as their behaviors.

Mother: *I just can't get the hang of it. I know I should be less critical, yell less, and be more positive, but I just blew it when he wouldn't get dressed this morning.*

Therapist: *Hey, but that's the first step in behavior change. You are now aware of what you are thinking and doing. Recognizing something after you've done it is a good place to start. Reflecting and analyzing that situation and thinking about what you want to do differently will help you the next time it occurs. When you do this reflection, next time you might catch yourself in the middle or even before you start to yell because you have planned how you will respond. But let's back up a bit and tell me what your thoughts are when your son won't get dressed in the morning. Then let's see if we can re-script them.*

It is often necessary to counter the myths and attributions that get in the way of therapeutic change. Below are some typical examples of some myths and unhelpful attributions that need to be rewritten.

Sole Ownership

- It's my child's problem; s/he's the one who has to change.
- It's me who's to blame because I am a single parent.

If it Doesn't Hurt it Doesn't Work

- A good belting is all he needs.
- Kindness doesn't work with him/her! All s/he understands is a good hiding.

Narrow Limit-Setting

- Give her/him an inch and s/he takes a mile.

Broad Limits

- S/he won't love me if I set a limit.
- I feel so guilty if I say no.

Gender Issues

- Only fathers can set firm limits.
- It's a mother's job: the discipline side of things.

Scapegoating

- It's his father's bad blood coming out in her/him.

Attributions

- There's a demon in her/him.
- He's adopted and didn't attach to me; nothing I do can help him.

Catastrophizing

- I'm a complete failure as a parent.
- I can't forgive myself for the mistakes I've made.

Intergenerational Ideas

- The whippings I had from my father did me no harm, so they won't do her/him any harm.

Unrealistic Assumptions

- Other parents all seem to cope.
- Children should change overnight.
- Why should s/he be praised for doing what s/he should be doing anyway?

Discussing distressing thoughts in a parent group is also very reassuring for parents because it helps to "normalize" thoughts that they may previously have considered abnormal or crazy. As parents discover that other parents have the same kinds of "crazy" thoughts and feelings, they stop blaming themselves. For example, a parent who is feeling overwhelmed might have the thought, "I wish he had never been born" or "I can't parent this child," and then might experience tremendous guilt about these feelings. Admitting these thoughts to the group and hearing that there are times that all parents are overwhelmed and frustrated may help the parent move past guilt and frustration so that he/she can use coping strategies to get needed support. It also helps if the therapist can share some examples from his or her own experience in which negative cognitions led her/him to respond inappropriately. The therapist can then provide a coping model of how trying to change these thoughts helped him/her to respond more appropriately.

PROMOTING PARENT SELF-EMPOWERMENT

In addition to worrying that their own reactions are abnormal, parents often see their child's behavior as abnormal or pathological. For example, the parent described above felt that other 4-year-old children got dressed easily in the morning, and when she shared this with the group she felt relieved that many other parents had the same difficulty. The therapist may also normalize this behavior by saying, "*Indeed, things don't sound happy, and I know you are feeling awful, but all children have behavior problems from time to time and all parents 'lose it' with their kids. No one is perfect.*" Thus the therapist helps the parents reexamine their expectations for themselves and their child, with the result of reducing their self-blame and anger. As these perceptions are altered, the parent feels less abnormal and more empowered.

Promoting Self-Empowerment. Another element in working with parents is self-empowerment. The therapist helps them learn how to give themselves a psychological "pat on the back" by looking at their successes and thinking about how effectively they handled a particularly difficult situation. Therapists ask parents to express their positive feelings about their relationship with their child and to remember good times before this stressful period. Parents learn how to actively formulate positive statements about themselves such as, "I had a good day today with Billy, I handled that situation well," or "I was able to stay in control. That was good." Parents, too, need tangible rewards for their efforts, such as dinner out with a spouse or a friend, a long hot bath, or a good book; and therapists can help them learn to set up these rewards for themselves.

Respecting and Valuing Cultural Diversity. The collaborative nature of the groups and allowing parents to set their own goals based on their backgrounds and experiences with their children allows the program to be tailored for implementation with parents from a variety of cultural backgrounds. The therapists acknowledge, respect, and affirm cultural differences using the collaborative approach to learn about the parents, their culture, values, parenting practices, attitudes, and goals. By asking parents to share their goals in the very first session, the therapists can begin to get a sense of what is important for individual parents and support them in learning the principles that will help them achieve their goals. In this way, generic content can be individualized to fit with the specific experiences and backgrounds for group members, without the need for different curricula for different cultural groups. Another way to bring more cultural diversity and sensitivity is to show more vignettes that represent the culture and backgrounds of the people in the group. If there are no vignettes of a particular culture, then these parents can be encouraged to demonstrate and share their approach for others.

Even more important than surface level cultural adaptations are the deeper structural delivery principles than ensure cultural sensitivity and relevance. This includes the therapist's ability to be culturally responsive and receptive to new ideas. Any possible cultural barriers can be openly discussed and efforts made to reframe the content or adjust for cultural and attitudinal barriers to help parents see how the particular approach might be potentially relevant for achieving their goals. For example, we use the piggy bank metaphor to encourage parents to build up their bank account with their children. This is not used with people of the Muslim faith because of their belief that the pig is unclean. In other cases, parents' cultural beliefs may seem contrary to a particular recommendation of the program; for instance the first units that encourage parents to play with their children. In cultures where parenting is done from a distance in a "hands off" model, or where parenting is more hierarchical and parents are only disciplinarians, the assignment to play will be very hard for them to implement. Therapists will explore these ideas with parents and will discuss their thoughts about the potential benefits of play with respect to their particular goals for their children. The group will also discuss how the concept of play might be woven into the parent's life in a way that remains consistent with their culture and beliefs. In all cases, parents are allowed to make the ultimate decision about how they implement the different aspects of the program, although it is the therapist's job to work with parents to implement in a way that is most likely to help the parent achieve his or her goals. More information on ways to promote more cultural diversity can be found in Chapter Eleven.

Therapist Role #3: Building the Parents' Support Team

Group Support. Parents struggling with day to day management of children with conduct problems experience a sense of being stigmatized and socially isolated from other parents; those with "typical" children. They don't feel they can share the burden of the many decisions they make each day and fear that if they are honest with their friends about their difficulties with their children, they will be met with misunderstanding, indifference, or outright rejection. The therapist's role, then, is to facilitate the parent group so that it serves as a powerful source of support, an empowering environment.

During group discussions, the therapist can help parents to problem-solve ways to obtain greater support when they are feeling isolated and overwhelmed. Parents also learn to collaborate with each other in problem solving, to express their appreciation for each other, and learn to cheer each other's successes in tackling difficult problems. The other side of the coin is that the therapist can encourage parents to share their feelings of guilt, anger and depression, confusion about a new culture or school's expectations, as well as experiences that involve their own mistakes or relapses in their child's progress.

The therapist's role is to facilitate the parent group so that it serves as a powerful source of support, an empowering environment.

This sense of group support and kinship increases parents' engagement with the program.

(However, swapping "horror stories" must not go on too long or they will engender a mood of pessimism.) These discussions serve as a powerful source of support. Through this sharing of feelings and experiences, commonality is discovered. Feelings of isolation decrease and parents are empowered by the knowledge that they are not alone and that many of their problems are normal. This sense of group support and kinship increases parents' engagement with the program. For instance, the following comments were made in one group:

Father: *You know when this program is finished, I will always think about this group in spirit.*

Mother: *This group is all sharing. It's people that aren't judging me, that are also taking risks and saying, "Have you tried this? Or have you considered you are off track?"*

Parent Buddy Calls. One of the ways the therapist helps parents become support systems for each other is by assigning everyone a parent "buddy" in the second or third session. Throughout the program parents are asked to call or contact their buddy each week (buddy pairs are switched several times) to share a specific parenting experience from the week (coaching experiences, favorite play activity, praise statements, or behaviors ignored). Parents can make these weekly contacts in a variety of ways: texting, e-mail, web groups, phone calls, or meeting in person. Initially parents are often hesitant about making these contacts, but as they experience the sense of support they receive from other parents, they usually express a desire to continue calling their buddy even after their assigned buddy has been changed. Many fathers voice that this was the first time they had ever talked to another father about parenting matters. When a parent misses a session, his/her buddy is encouraged to call and share information from the session and convey the message that they were missed.

Family Support. In addition to building the support system within the group, the therapist can also build support within the family. Parents often report frequent conflicts with partners, grandparents, and teachers over how to handle their child's problems, resulting in stressed relationships and stressed individuals. Therefore, in addition to building the support system with the parent group, the therapist emphasizes building support within the family and home life. Every parent is encouraged to have a spouse, partner, close friend, or family member (such as grandparent) participate in the program with them to provide mutual support. Program follow-up studies have indicated that the greatest likelihood of relapse occurs in families in which only one person was involved in the program (Webster-Stratton, 1985). During parent groups, the therapist helps partners define ways they can support each other when one was feeling discouraged, tired or unable to cope.

Frequently, the energy required to care for the children, coupled with financial constraints, leaves parents feeling exhausted and too tired to make plans to spend time with each other or with adult friends, let alone interact with them. Yet, time away from the child with a partner or a friend can help parents feel supported and energized. It helps them gain perspective so they are better able to cope with parenting. Wahler's (1980) research has indicated that single mothers who had contact with other people outside the home fare much better in their parenting than mothers without such contacts, while maternal insularity or social isolation results in the probability of intervention failure (Dumas & Wahler, 1983; Wahler & Barnes, 1988; Wahler, Cartor, Fleischman, & Lambert, 1993). In the groups, parents at times seemed to have almost forgotten their identity as individuals rather than as parents. Thus, several of the home assignments have to do with doing some self-care activity in which parents do something pleasurable for themselves. Paradoxically, the result of spending some time away in "self-care" activities was often a feeling of support and understanding for the partner or the other adult who made it possible.

During therapy sessions, the therapist helps the parents (or the parent and partner) define ways they can support each other when feeling discouraged, tired, or unable to cope with a problem. This feeling of support and understanding from another family member or friend contributes to a sense of empowerment.

Therapist Role #4: Using Evidence-Based Teaching And Learning Methods

What about the therapist's role as teacher? Since a knowledgeable therapist might also be called an "expert" in his/her field, there may be some question about whether the collaborative approach allows the therapist to function in a teaching capacity. Is there a contradiction between being a "collaborator" and having "expertise"? Does the collaborative therapist have to renounce her expertise?

It is my contention that a therapist's teaching expertise and use of evidence-based teaching methods is not only compatible with but essential to a collaborative learning process. In other words, therapist expertise is necessary but not sufficient without the collaborative process. Just as the parents function as experts concerning their child and have the ultimate responsibility for judging what will be workable in their particular family, culture and community, the therapist functions as expert concerning children's developmental needs, behavior management principles, and communication skills. (The specific content of parent programs is discussed in Chapters Four and Six.)

The therapist in her role as teacher uses effective teaching methods to enhance parents' learning including: explanation and persuasion; generalizing and contextualizing the learning process; tailoring the teaching; reviewing and summarizing learning; giving weekly home practice assignments; self-monitoring and reflection; and learning from evaluations.

Therapist knowledge and expertise is necessary but not sufficient without the collaborative process.

Explanation and Persuasion. Therapeutic change depends on therapist explanations and persuasion skills in order to bring about parents' full understanding. This implies that parents must be given the rationale for each component of the program. It is important for the therapist to be knowledgeable about the theoretical underpinnings of the program as well as the research that supports the use of each theory. This means a familiarity with the developmental literature and cognitive social learning theory, as well as attachment and family systems theories. Therapists will avoid using psychological jargon with parents, but will be able to clearly articulate research supported rationales for the parenting practices and processes used in the groups. The parenting program principles, objectives, and learning methods should not be shrouded in mystery. Research has indicated that parents' understanding of the social learning and relationship principles underlying the parent training program leads to enhanced generalization or maintenance of program effects over time (McMahon & Forehand, 1984).

However, it is also important that these rationales and theories be presented in such a way that the parent can see the connection to his/her stated goals. Rationales should be given not as absolutes or commands, but rather in the context of thoughtful discussion. When a therapist introduces a new parenting principle or component of the program, she connects it to topics previously discussed as well as parents' goals. For example, when providing the rationale for the child-directed play and coaching methods, the therapist explains how this approach fosters the child's language development, emotional and social competence, attachment to parents, commitment to family responsibilities and eventual success at school, while at the same time decreasing the child's need to obtain control over parents with negative behaviors. In this example, supplying the rationale is important because parents may not immediately see the connection between learning child-directed coaching methods and helping their child be less aggressive; their primary reason for seeking help (e.g., reducing their child's defiance). If they do not understand the rationale for the parenting approach and how it helps them achieve their goals, they may not be motivated to do this at home.

In the example below, a therapist provides a father with some developmental information about the expression of empathy;

> **Father** (*of 4-year-old Charlie*)**:** *Charlie hit his little sister and hurt her. I have talked to him over and over about how he's making other children feel bad. I get so frustrated with him. He doesn't seem to understand his impact on other children's feelings or have any guilt when he hits or hurts them.*

Therapist: *Yes, that is frustrating. But it looks like you're doing a nice of job of beginning to help Charlie understand the perspective of others by explaining to him how his sister felt. You know, the development of empathy in children, that is, the ability of a child to understand another person's point of view, takes years. Not until adulthood is this aspect of brain development fully matured. Young children's brains are still maturing and developing and are at the very beginning steps of gaining this ability. The paradox of this is that one of the best ways you can help your son learn to be sensitive to the feelings of others is for you to model your understanding of him as well as others. Children need to feel understood and valued by their parents before they can value others. You can also do some of this work during your coaching play sessions. Let's talk about what to do when he hits, we want to be sure the attention you give him at this time doesn't reinforce that behavior.*

In this example, the therapist identifies the parent's frustration with his son's disruptive behaviors, empathizes with it, reinforces his efforts to promote empathy in his child and then explains some child development principles. In doing so, the therapist is collaborating with the parent's goal of promoting empathy in his son as well as reducing his aggression and helping the parent gain a new perspective on how he can help him achieve this goal. The therapist also helps him develop an age appropriate understanding of children's ability to develop empathy. This sets the stage for her to then explore the concepts of ignoring and Time Out with the parent and the group as a whole. If she had moved straight to instructing the father to use Time Out for hitting, she would not have addressed his concerns about this son's lack of empathy. Moreover, she reminds him of the importance of the foundational coaching methods in order to achieve his ultimate goal.

Generalizing and Contextualizing the Learning Process. Generalization means teaching parents how to apply the specific skills being taught to their own unique situations. It also means being able to extrapolate from current learning to other settings or to new types of misbehavior that may occur in the future. For example, some parents learn how to manage their children effectively at home, but have diffi-

Generalization means teaching parents how to apply the specific parenting skills they are learning to their own unique situations.

culty knowing how to handle misbehavior when it occurs in public. They have difficulties seeing how principles such as ignore, time out or consequences can be applied in the grocery store, cinema, or school. Other parents have difficulty knowing how to use the approaches with siblings who are exhibiting somewhat different behaviors. To counter this inability to generalize, the therapist can periodically interject a few different types of problems and situations (not raised by the group) and ask the group to problem solve strategies to deal with them. After working on a problem area the therapist asks regularly, *"For what other child problems could you apply this strategy?"* or, *"Are there situations where this strategy wouldn't work?"* Solving future parenting challenges is enhanced when parents are exposed in the group to a variety of other family life situations and approaches to solving problems and by group problem solving. The therapist also works to increase generalization of skills by choosing a variety of vignettes of families with different aged children and using probing questions that are especially relevant for parents in the group. For example, the therapist asks a foster parent of a child who has been neglected *"Why is daily child-directed play and emotion coaching particularly important with a child who has been neglected in the past?"* Or, *"Why might your foster child distrust you and be suspicious of your praise?"*

Finally group problem solving and discussion also supports this generalization process. For instance, the therapist compiles a list of child behaviors that parents want to encourage or discourage and asks the group to come up with as many ideas or parenting tools as possible for dealing with those behaviors. Generalization is also enhanced by what is called *"principles training"*; pointing out or having a group member state the underlying principle that can be applied across multiple situations. These principles are listed on a poster and brought to each session to facilitate continued applications of the principle to different problem situations. Each principle is identified by the group member's name who first stated that principle and recorded in the parents' words; for example,

Tim's attention principle: Behaviors that receive parent attention occur more often. Or, Sarah's fun principle: Children want to learn when the experience is fun. Or Judy's respect principle: Children who are treated with respect become more respectful.

Contextualizing the information presented by parents can also support generalization and use of skills in a variety of situations. For example, parents are asked to identify the particular circumstances in which they find it difficult or impossible to apply what they have been learning in the training. Often parents will identify high stress times of the day, such as the first 30 minutes after they get home at night from work, times when they are late for an appointment, have relatives visiting, or when children must be ready on time for a bus schedule. Parents are encouraged to identify these vulnerable periods and to strategically plan ways to deal with them. When parents have been successful in maintaining control during a stressful situation, they are encouraged to reflect on this and to share their strategies by asking such questions as, "*What made it possible for you to maintain control in such a stressful situation? What were you thinking to yourself at the time? How did you do that?*" Here the therapist aims to help the parents recognize their positive coping skills.

Therapist: *So you have had a really stressful day at work and are upset about your boss's response. You are coming home from work and are thinking about all you have to do to get dinner ready and do homework with your kids. You know this is a time when you usually yell at your kids and things are chaotic. What can you do to help yourself stay calm and plan for this before you even enter the house? What has helped you be successful with this transition in the past?*

Parent: *Try to think about being positive when I greet my child.*

Therapist: *That is a great strategy because if you look stressed or upset the child might think he is the cause of this stress. He won't understand you have had a bad day. How can you stay calm during this time?*

Tailoring the Teaching Process. In addition to persuading, explaining, reframing, generalizing, and contextualizing the learning process, collaborative teaching involves working with parents to tailor concepts and skills to their particular circumstances, family, cultural and educational backgrounds, and their child's temperament. For example parents who live with other family members may need support and planning to cope with feedback that contradicts what they are learning in the group (e.g., perhaps the grandmother believes that she should comfort her tantrumming grandson or perhaps the child's aunt criticizes the child's mother for ignoring backtalk, believing that disrespectful talk should result in a spanking). Without group problem solving and support, it will be extremely hard for parents to make changes at home in these circumstances. A collaborative approach means that the therapist attempts to understand the living circumstances of each family and involves the families in problem solving to adapt the behavior management concepts to their particular situation. To take another example, in a group where children range from 6-8 years of age, many families will be implementing sticker charts in which children are saving up stickers for a larger reward, perhaps given at the end of the day, or even at the end of several days. However, if some of these children have ADHD or are very impulsive, this type of incentive program may not be appropriate. Therapists will help parents understand that a child's developmental readiness is different than his or her chronological age and will guide the parents to set up a system with smaller behavioral goals and immediate reinforcement. The therapist needs to be sensitive to these individual differences in child temperament and development so that s/he can begin the collaborative process of defining with parents which approach will be best for a particular child.

Some parents will come to the group with limited knowledge of child development, cognitive delays, extraordinary life stressors, or past experiences of abuse. These parents will need much higher levels of support and the therapist will need to make adjustments to the pacing

The therapist must monitor the understanding of parents in the group and utilize additional vignettes and practice activities as needed.

and delivery of the material. For example, for high risk populations or those with children with diagnoses, lengthening the number of sessions to allow for slower pacing, and additional time for extra program content, more practices, and more discussions will be immensely helpful. The therapist must monitor the understanding of parents in the group and utilize additional vignettes and practice activities as needed before moving on to a new topic. The therapist works with the parents to create realistic goals to enable parent success and to support their self-efficacy and confidence. With very high-risk groups, the therapist must become more directive in some ways (since parents may not be able to generate some of the key ideas without clear help), but will also need to be even more collaborative (since these may be parents who are distrustful of authority and may be at higher-risk of dropping out of the process).

Reviewing and Summarizing. Another aspect of the teaching process is reviewing and summarizing for the benefit of all. The therapist can end each session with a summary of the major points of discussion from that session and a review of the handouts and assignments for the next week. Parents are given notebooks where they can put handouts that review each session's content, as well as take notes and record their weekly assignments. Along with ensuring that everyone understands the assignment for the next week, the therapist needs to express confidence in the parents' ability to carry out the assignment. Parents may also be provided with current articles that either reinforce concepts or stimulate group discussion. These, of course, will only be useful for parents with reading skills. For illiterate parents, we use "cues" such as cartoons, pictures and stickers to help remind them of essential concepts at home. For example, using red sticker dots to remind parents to decrease their negative self-talk, and green dots to increase positive self-talk. It is suggested that parents put these cartoons and stickers on the refrigerator or a place where they will see them often and be reminded of the concept.

Individual Behavior Support Planning. To further individualize the parent program content to the specific challenges faced by the parents, the therapists and parents develop behavior plans for their children. During the sessions, the parents break out in small groups to work together to identify their goals regarding the specific child behaviors they want to see less of and those positive opposite child behaviors they want to see more of. Then they list possible parenting strategies or tools they can use to achieve these goals. The therapist encourages parents to share these plans with teachers and other child care providers.

Weekly Home Activity Practice Assignments. Home practices are assigned each week and are an integral part of the parents' learning process because they help transfer what is talked about in the group to the home situation. Learning about a parenting skill in a group session is quite different from implementing it with one's own difficult child at home! For example, one home activity assignment asks parents to use child-directed play and coaching strategies one-on-one with their child each day for 15 minutes; another assignment is to record how often they praise between 5 and 6 p.m. for 2 days, and then to double their base rate for the remainder of the week. A third example of an assignment is for parents to keep track of their thoughts in response to a conflict situation with their child on three occasions and to rewrite their negative thoughts into more positive coping thoughts.

Parents need to understand the purpose of the weekly home activity assignments and their value as an integral part of the learning process.

> **Therapist:** *You can't learn to drive a car, play the piano, or swim without practicing, and this is also the case with the parenting skills you are learning here. The more effort you put into the home activity assignments, the more success you will have with the program.*

For a 2-hour session, therapists will spend the first 20-30 minutes for a home activities review. Parents are more likely to take the home assignments seriously if they know the therapist is going to begin each session by asking them to comment on their experiences during the past week. Therapists explore with parents what they have learned from their experiences, problem solve barriers that parents report, and help parents to develop realistic goals for the subsequent week. Therapists also give out surprise rewards to the parents for completing their home activities and achieving their goals for each week. Sometimes group celebrations occur when everyone in the group completes their home activity or reading for the week.

When a parent questions the usefulness or feasibility of a home assignment, this should receive immediate attention, though not the kind of attention it might receive from a "hierarchical" teacher. Rather, the problem should be explored in a collaborative fashion. For example, a single parent with four young children says she is unable to do 15 minutes of play time each day with an individual child. The therapist responds:

> **Therapist:** *I imagine you barely have 2 minutes to yourself all day, let alone 15 minutes with an individual child. Let's talk about ways to practice the play skills with several children at the same time. Or, would it be possible to play in brief bursts of 2-3 minutes throughout the day? I wonder if other parents in the group have suggestions about how to handle this? Let's find a plan for a realistic goal for you.*

Parent goals should be manageable and realistic, optimizing the chance of success.

When a parent fails to complete a practice assignment from the previous session, the reasons for this should be explored in a collaborative fashion. For example, the therapist can ask questions such as: *"What made it hard for you to do the assignment?" "How have you overcome this problem in the past?" "What advice would you give to someone else who has this problem?" "Do you think it is just as hard for your child to learn to change as it is for you to change?" "What can you do to make it easier for you to complete the assignment this week?" "Do you think there is another assignment that might be more useful for you?"* These questions could be explored as a group discussion topic. Frequently other parents will have good ideas for how to help a particular parent overcome a barrier. Other times a parent who has had difficulty completing homework activities may be inspired by the success that other parents are having. It is important to explore reasons why some parents might be having difficulty doing their home assignments; otherwise, parents may conclude that the therapist is not really committed to the assignments, or does not really want to understand their particular situation. Parents are asked to set their own goals for assignments for the following week. These goals should be manageable and realistic, optimizing the chance of success. Therapists can give parents personal mottos to use when trying to accomplish a goal:

> *Challenge but don't overwhelm yourself.* For instance, if you were learning to drive, you wouldn't immediately venture out into the freeway.
>
> *Gets worse before you feel better.* Engaging in difficult homework tasks may make you feel worse at first; but you are learning to cope better. This is true of recovery from various conditions such as a broken limb or an operation.

Parents bring their homework successes and challenges to the next week's session. Thus, these practice assignments serve as powerful experiential learning opportunities and stimulus for discussion, review and refinement of strategies and additional role plays in subsequent sessions. At each session, the therapist begins by asking parents about their specific home practice experiences and then helps to fine tune any issues that arise.

> **Therapist:** *You can't learn to swim without practicing, and this is also the case with the parenting skills you are learning here. The more effort you put into the home practice assignments, the more success you will have with your child. As your coach, I am here to help you stay afloat, give you a kick board if needed, and then help you learn all sorts of swimming skills so that you can become self-confident and independent in the water.*

Moreover, home assignments convey the critical message that sitting passively in the group is not "magic moon dust;" parents must collaborate with the therapist by working at home to make the changes they have targeted with their goals.

Weekly Reading Assignments. The *Incredible Babies* (2011), *Incredible Toddlers* (2011), and *The Incredible Years—a Troubleshooting Guide for Parents of Children Aged 2-8 Years* (2005) books are provided to the parents who are participating in the groups. Each week they are asked to read a chapter to prepare for the subsequent session. For those parents who cannot read, CDs of the basic book are available. Along with the reading assignment, home activities also involve asking parents to observe and record or journal their own behavior or thoughts as they practice a particular parenting strategy. During the homework review, parents are also asked to share their reflections on the reading assignments.

Self-Monitoring Checklists ~ Personal Folders. Each week parents complete self-monitoring checklists, setting individual goals for themselves for the following week. Even though parents are given standard home practice assignments, they are asked to personally commit to what aspect of the home activities they will try to achieve that week. Each week the therapist reviews these goals and gives parents personal written feedback as well as placing surprise stickers, chocolate, cartoons, or cards in their personal folders to applaud a particular achievement. These personal folders become a private communication between the therapist and each parent. Parents place completed home activities and journals in the folders each week, record progress on their personal goals, and pick up the therapist's comments from the prior assignment. The individual attention to the home assignments encourages parents to self-monitor their own progress; therapists frequently find parents asking them if they can still get credit for the home activity or reading assignment if they do it the following week!

Weekly Evaluations. Parents complete a brief weekly session evaluation form after every group. This provides the therapist with immediate feedback about how each parent is responding to the therapist's style, the group discussions, the content, and vignettes presented in the session. The evaluations bring problems to light: the parent who is dissatisfied with the group, the parent who is resisting a concept, the parent who doesn't see the relevance of a particular concept to his/her own situation, or the parent who wants more group discussion. The therapist may want to call or meet with parents individually to resolve these issues. If several participants are having difficulty understanding a particular concept, the therapist will want to bring it up in a subsequent session with the whole group. This ongoing process where the therapist responds to parents' evaluations by taking action emphasizes the collaborative nature of the therapy process. At the end of the program, the entire treatment program should be evaluated. This information is useful not only in planning future parent groups, but also in identifying parents who may need further help.

Effective Time Management. Therapists must use effective time management skills and manage the group time with a predictable schedule and routine. This will assure they will cover the content adequately, and will also be reassuring for parents and help them feel safe in the group. If too much time is spent exploring one person's personal problems in depth, other parents lose interest, become disengaged, and feel they are being ignored and are not as valued. It is best if therapists are specific about what they want parents to report on in regard to home activities review. For example, they might ask parents to report on one success they have had being child-directed or staying calm. It is not necessary for every parent to report each week in depth or it will not be possible to cover the new material. The therapist has the weekly telephone calls to check in with parents as well. It is important to balance who shares home activities so that over the course of few sessions, every parent had reported in and has had a chance to contribute ideas or concerns. The following schedule is suggested for each session:

Therapists must use effective time management skills with a predictable schedule and routine.

AGENDA

30 min: welcome and review of home activities with spontaneous practices; 3-4 different parents may be selected each week to discuss their experience in more depth. Other parents might share 1-2 highlights.

30 min: introduce new topic and show 3-4 vignettes for discussion with practices.

10 min: coffee break

30 min: continue new topic and complete another 3-4 vignettes with practices.

15 min: summarize most important learning principles; review refrigerator notes; and new home activities for week.

5 min: parents complete self-monitoring form, set weekly goal and session evaluation.

Therapist Role #5: Interpreting & Changing Parents' Cognitions

The therapist role of teacher is closely allied to another role; that of interpreter. As an interpreter, the therapist "translates" the language of cognitive, emotional, behavioral, and developmental concepts into words and behaviors that the parents can understand and apply. But the interpreter role is more than this: The therapist must also interpret the language and culture of the family in order to help that family. The latter can occur only if there is collaboration. It is here that therapy shows itself as a craft, an amalgam of applied science and art. No matter how good the science (the theoretical framework and empirical findings), without the creative element of translating abstract and complex ideas into concrete, interesting applications that are relevant to the family's circumstances, the science is not likely to achieve much.

Use of Analogies and Metaphors. The therapist can be a more effective interpreter by using images and analogies to explain theories and concepts. S/he needs to be creative in thinking up vivid mental pictures to convey important concepts. Ideally, these analogies should be developed out of themes that are meaningful to a particular community or cultural group. Here are a few that we have either invented or borrowed from discussions with other therapists.

> *Hard wax/seal analogy:* Socrates used to send out letters to his friends and seal the letters with wax and his seal. His friends would complain when they received the letter that they couldn't make out the imprint of the seal and would ask him, "Why don't you get a new seal?" Socrates commented, "No one ever asked me if the problem was that the wax was too hard to receive the seal."
> *Therapist's Interpretation:* We can't change the nature of our children's "wax," but we can work hard to get the best imprint possible.

This analogy depicts the concept that socialization takes longer with some children; children with conduct problems or ADHD or developmental delays don't "take the imprint" easily. By pointing to the wax rather than the seal, or the person who tries to use it, as the source of the difficulty, this analogy shifts the blame away from the parents. Further, it helps them to make allowances for their child's temperament.

> *Diamond Analogy:* These children are like diamonds. Parents need to carefully chip away the hard edges of the diamonds to see their beauty. Of course, hard diamonds are very valuable.

This analogy is used to reframe the parents' negative perceptions of their child's temperament. Thinking of these difficult children as hard diamonds waiting to be made beautiful emphasizes not only their innate value, but also the parents' socialization role.

> *Flossing analogy:* Teaching children is like flossing your teeth: You have to keep doing it over and over to get long-term results.

With this analogy we hope to convey the notion that daily repetition and constant monitoring can achieve long-term results, even though it seems that not much is accomplished day by day.

> *Bank account analogy:* Think of praising and playing with children as building up your bank account. You have to keep putting something in all the time. Only then will you have something to draw on when you need it. Time-Out and other forms of discipline will not work unless there is a "bank account" of positive resources to draw from. In fact, Time-Out from an aversive relationship may actually be reinforcing.

With this analogy we are emphasizing the need for positive interaction with the child as a foundation for discipline.

> *Loaf of bread analogy:* Imagine you buy the same loaf of bread from the same supermarket each week. For 51 weeks the bread is fresh and you use it daily without any thought. But on the 52nd week of the year you find it is moldy and stale. You can't wait to tell everyone how awful the bread is and that you are not going to buy bread there again. Remember, for 51 weeks the bread was fine! But not once did you comment or tell your friends what a delicious piece of bread you had for breakfast; not once did you recommend that bread because it was so fresh. This is just like the child who behaves appropriately for 59 minutes of an hour but who is not noticed, only to be criticized or shouted at for the one minute in the hour he misbehaved. It is easy to miss the opportunity to praise and reinforce the desired behavior. It is useful to imagine yourself wearing a special pair of glasses designed to catch your child behaving appropriately.

This analogy is used to encourage parents to focus more on their children when they are behaving appropriately than when they are misbehaving. This the first step toward labeled praise.

> *Priming the pump analogy:* You know the old farm pumps that had to be pumped a dozen times before water would come out? Parents have to "prime the pump" with lots of supportive input to build children's self esteem. You also have to "prime your own

pumps" so that you can keep on functioning as an effective parent. That is, you need to fill yourself with positive thoughts and take time to refuel your own energy.

With this analogy we are explaining the idea that parents need to keep "pumping in" positive messages to themselves and their children before they will receive positive behavior in return.

Gas on the Flames Analogy: Arguing and reasoning with a child when he is noncompliant and angry is like throwing gas on the flame.

This analogy is used when trying to help parents learn to ignore children's misbehavior rather than yell and scold. It is important they understand that such an approach actually fuels the problem rather than dampening it.

Megaphone Analogy: Think about yourself using a megaphone when you praise your child. That is, do it more strongly and enthusiastically than you might otherwise be likely to do. Sometimes these children seem deaf, as if hidden in a suit of armor and a helmet. There is so much armor that it takes quite a lot of repetition to penetrate. Sometimes these children even deflect the praise because they have a hard time accepting a new, positive, image of themselves and are more comfortable with the old image.

This analogy is used to encourage parents to praise their children more frequently and more often than they otherwise would. It also helps prepare them for the occasions where children reject praise and suggests why this may happen.

Vending Machine Analogy: Remember, when you first ignore a child's misbehavior, it will escalate before the behavior improves. For the child, the experience of being ignored is a little like the experience that sometimes happens with vending machines. Let's say you put in a dollar but no cola comes out. You press

> the lever a few times; still no cola. Then you start banging the machine because the machine is ignoring you. But what would happen if a Coke happened to come out as you were banging? Next time you lost a dollar and needed a drink you would start out banging!

This analogy is helpful to parents in preparing them not only for the tantrums and misbehavior that will be the child's response to Ignore and Time Out procedures, but also as a warning to parents of what will happen if they give in to this misbehavior.

> *Choose Your Battles Analogy:* Your resources are not unlimited. Think about choosing those battles that are really important to you and save your energy for those. For example, wearing seatbelts, not hitting, and getting to bed on time may be more important than clean plates, wearing a different shirt, or picking up toys. In that case, it's not worth expending your resources for those less important causes.

This analogy helps parents prioritize which household rules they are prepared to enforce and which ones they can let slide for the time being.

> *Radar Antenna Analogy:* Monitoring kids means keeping your radar antenna up at all times, so that you know where your child is, what he or she is doing and that he is safe. That way, you can spot potential problems before they develop. Antenna are important not only so that you can assure yourself that your child is not in trouble and is safe, but also so that you can spot positive behaviors that need to be reinforced.

Parents sometimes have false expectations that children can be left unattended. This analogy helps parents understand that constant monitoring on their part is required at all times. This analogy also encourages parents' understanding that effective parents anticipate problems and nip them in the bud (based on an early signal on their "radar") by distracting their child or by stopping the behavior early on.

Tug-of-War Analogy: Arguing with children is like parents and children playing "tug of war," both pulling the rope at opposite ends. The harder each party pulls, the bigger the struggle. When you find yourself in such a struggle, say to yourself that you're going to drop the rope. It's impossible to play tug-of-war with one person!

This analogy helps parents understand that constant arguing only perpetuates the struggle, whereas withdrawing from the tug-of-war ends it.

Children are wearing L plates: In England, when one is learning to drive, an L plate—for "Learner"—is put on the car. Imagine that your child also has an L plate on his or her back. This will remind you to be patient and tolerant when your child makes a mistake. Children are, after all, learners in life.

This analogy helps remind parents of children's developmental processes. They are still learning and, like the person who is learning to drive, will behave unpredictably and make mistakes.

Parenting Tool Box or Parenting Pyramid Architectural Plan: Parents are like builders and they have a lot of tools to use for different things. First parents build a strong and trusting relationship foundation with their children by using their attention, child-directed play, coaching, praise, monitoring and incentive tools quite liberally. Then parents support their child's learning with safe, secure scaffolding such as predictable rules, routines and respectful limit setting. Finally, parents have special tools which are used sparingly to reduce target negative behaviors such as ignoring, redirecting, and consequences.

The building or tool box metaphor is used with parents as they learn each parenting tool on the pyramid. They begin by learning the tools for building a strong foundation of positive behaviors and relationships with their children. Each family develops individual goals to scaffold their children's learning, motivation, and a realistic view of the necessary work it takes for children to learn something new. Next parents learn tools for reducing misbehavior, making corrections, and repairing mistakes. By the time that parents have completed the program, they will have learned how to choose different tools from their parenting tool box for different kinds of problems, according to their children's developmental abilities and needs. Certain tools are used more extensively than others at different developmental stages of children's cognitive, emotional, and social development.

> *Thoughts, feelings, behavior cycle:* You are coming back from work and it has been a bad day. Your boss was upset with you because you didn't get the project completed. Your colleague who you share an office with was upset because you left the office messy. You have heard that some people are going to lose their jobs because of the budget cuts in your agency. You get home, step out of your car and step into your dog's poo. You walk into the kitchen and your 4-year-old son has being playing in the kitchen sink and has water all over the floor. How do you feel at this time? (Identify emotions) What thoughts are running through your mind? What do you think your child has done? (Identify thoughts and reasons for the behavior such as, "he did it on purpose") Summarize feelings and thoughts and ask, "What is your parenting behavior likely to be in this situation?" (Identify specific actions such as shouting, smacking). Continue with the sequence of the cycle by considering how this parenting behavior makes the parent feel and think about himself ("I'm a bad parent").
>
> Contrast this with a day when the parent was praised at work for a good job on a project and got a salary raise plus reassurance that despite the economic situation her job was safe. This parent comes home to the exact same child scenario: water on the kitchen floor. The therapist explores her feelings, thoughts, and behaviors.

This example gives parents a framework for understanding how their prior experiences, thoughts, and feelings impact their parenting behavior. The story telling aspect makes the model accessible and adding humor to the situation can make it even more engaging. This awareness enables parents to stop and think before reacting to many difficult situations when dealing with their children's misbehaviors. It also helps them work on changing the way they think about children's behavior, which in turn affects their feelings and their own behavior.

Reframing Parents' Perspectives and Cognitions. As we have seen with the use of metaphors, therapeutic change depends on providing explanatory "stories," alternative explanations that help parents to reshape their perceptions of and their thoughts about the nature of their problems. A common barrier to effective implementation of new parenting practices is parents' own internal dialogue about themselves, their world, and their future. Quite often, parents are unaware of their self-dialogue. For example, the single parent who has worked hard with a child with ADHD without success may have developed very negative views of the child or herself. This, in turn, influences her parenting interactions. Frequently thoughts like, "he is hopeless" or "he is never

Challenge irrational thoughts

going to change" or "I can't handle this, I'm going to explode" make it likely the parent will have negative feelings, hostile interactions, and will be unmotivated to implement effective new strategies. Reframing or cognitive restructuring by the therapist is a powerful interpretive tool for helping parents challenge these self-defeating thoughts and for understanding their children's behaviors differently, thereby promoting change in their feelings, leading to change in their parenting responses. This involves altering the parent's cognitive and/or emotional viewpoint of an experience by placing the experience in another "frame" which fits the facts of the situation well, thereby altering its meaning. There are numerous exercises throughout the parent program that focus on changing negative self-talk, such learning to use positive self-praise, challenging negative thoughts with accurate knowledge about child development, and rewriting negative thoughts with positive coping and calming thoughts.

One type of reframing that is frequently used is to take a problem a parent is having with a child and reframe it in terms of normal child development stages. Reframing a difficult child's behavior in terms of a psychological or emotional drive such as a drive for exploration and discovery, testing the security of his limits or trust, reacting to the loss of an important parent, moving towards independence, or understanding the immaturity of empathy development in children, helps the parents see the behavior as appropriate or normal; in some cases even positive. Seen in this light, problematic behaviors are the expression of normal emotional and developmental stages. Viewing situations in this manner, parents can see that they are essential architects in a process of scaffolding and supporting their child's safe and healthy growth and development. This attitude enhances parents' coping responses and decreases their feelings of anger and helplessness. When understood in terms of children's needs to test the security of their environment, or to test the love of their parents, parent-child conflicts become less overwhelming and parents are better able to remain committed to the hard work of socializing a child. Remember the father who was worried about his son's lack of empathy? Notice how the therapist continues to reframe his understanding of Charlie's individual developmental task involving self-regulation.

Father: *Okay, I guess I get that Charlie may not be ready to understand his sister's feelings, but he's so impulsive that he really can't even be near his sister. One minute he's sitting and playing, and the next minute he's grabbing her toys or hitting her. Charlie goes from 0 to 100 in a split second. There's no in between. I can never predict what will set him off.*

Therapist: *Yes that is typical of all young children's immature brains, especially a child like Charlie who has ADHD. It will take further coaching and modeling by you and time for his brain to continue to develop and his neuron connections to be strengthened before he learns to use better solutions to his problems. But one of the advantages of Time Out for hitting is you are not reinforcing his aggression with your attention, and he is also learning some calm down strategies to help him self-regulate. By teaching him to take deep breaths in Time Out, to use positive self-talk and to think of his happy place, he is learning to calm himself down and then he can begin to reflect on a better solution.*

Here are some other examples of how therapists help parents understand the meaning of their child's misbehavior and their developmental task:

Father: *He's so defiant! He should be able to be toilet trained by now—he's 3-1/2 years old! He's doing it on purpose! He even tells us right after he has had a poop in his pants. I get so angry with him!*

Therapist: *Hey, but you know what? That's a great sign; the fact he's telling you after he poops means he's getting ready to be trained. Remember how we said we recognize something after we've done it and change it the next time. When children tell us something afterwards, that's their way of doing this! But with your support he will soon learn to recognize the sensations before he goes. You know, the fact he is telling you he has done it in his pants is also a very good sign; it's much harder when children fear their parents' anger and learn to hide their underpants in closets.*

Father: *But it feels so deliberate to me. He's so advanced in other areas of his development, such as his manipulation skills with my tools and his talking. He should be toilet trained by now.*

Therapist: *Ah, this is often the case with development: As one area is maturing and developing, another area may lag behind. Think about babies. When they are learning to walk, they often slow down in their language. And for others it is the reverse; while their language is developing, they are not walking. All these areas of development: verbal, intellectual, social, moral, physical, language develop at different rates, as does control of bowel movements.*

OR

Mother: *She yells and screams at bedtime and needs water, a cookie, a hug, and on and on. She is so needy and manipulative.*

Therapist: *Yes, those bedtime rituals get to be a drag. But you know they are so important, because if they are predictable, they will give the child a sense of security. And going to sleep is a time when children really need this predictability and routine, because going to sleep represents a separation from you; a loss of something pretty special. She may not be sure of where you go when she goes to sleep. As annoying as all her behavior is, she is showing you that she wants to be with you more than anything else. That doesn't mean you should give in to her behavior, but maybe it's nice to know that you mean so much to her.*

OR

Parent: *Now he just stands at the window screaming at other kids to come and play with him. He is so needy for friends, but his behavior alienates the other children. I don't understand why he has to do that.*

Therapist: *Well, you know, these aggressive kids have frequently been rejected by other kids, so they are pretty insecure about friendships. It will take time to teach him the positive social skills so that he* *learns how to approach other children more appropriately. But, you know, the fact he is so interested in making friends is really a good sign. He hasn't gotten to the point of rejecting other kids himself.*

OR

Parent: *My son has these incredibly long, angry outbursts when he is in Time Out. He's really out to make it difficult for me.*

Therapist: *Do you suppose he might be really testing the strength of your limit setting to see if he can get you to "lose it" or back down? By responding in predictable ways, he will eventually learn that tantruming doesn't get the attention that he wants. In past this has worked. Now he has to unlearn that and find out that his positive behavior is what will get your attention and praise.*

OR

Parent: *My child has gotten incredibly worse this week. She is impossible to handle and I've had to use Time Out a lot. She's wearing me down.*

Therapist: *You know, I think kids always regress to test the security of the limits in their environment before they take a major new step forward in their development.*

OR

Therapist: *Rather than thinking of your child as having a problem or being a problem, it may help to think of her/him as trying to solve a problem. That behavior you don't like may be her/his way of trying to deal with one of life's difficulties (not very successfully; but after all he/she's a learner). Let us try to see what s/he is trying to achieve; what are the developmental tasks s/he has to solve at this stage of her development? Could she be asserting her independence and autonomy now?*

Reframing parents' thoughts involves changing a negative label for a behavior into a positive one; it can be a tool of empowerment for parents.

In all of the examples above, the parents' thoughts involved seeing their child as manipulative, or deliberately uncooperative and trying to make their lives difficult on purpose. One parent was catastrophizing that her child was getting worse. Such negative thoughts on the part of parents increase their stress level, are exhausting, and contribute to escalating angry or depressive feelings. The therapists help parents to reframe their situations and to understand the developmental stage the child's behavior represents as well as the child's emotions in the situation. Helping parents perceive their child's misbehavior as testing the security of limits, or reacting to the loss of an important parent, or moving towards independence helps the parents to rewrite their thoughts and see the behavior as appropriate or normal; in some cases even positive. Seen in this light, the situations are part of the normal developmental process. Thinking more positive thoughts about the situation will lead parents to more positive feelings and calmer responses. Parents begin to realize that they are participating in ensuring a healthy process of growth for their child's development, rather than becoming angry or feeling helpless. This attitude enables them to cope more effectively. In essence, reframing parents' thoughts involves changing a negative label for a behavior into a positive one; as we mentioned earlier, it can be a tool of empowerment for parents because they respond in ways that lead to better outcomes for their children and themselves. It is recommended that parents use the buzz handouts or thought cards to record actual thought statements that they will use related to self-praise, calming thoughts, and managing stress. Changing cognitions is very challenging, almost like thinking in a new language, so parents will need these written prompts to use in their practice at home. In addition, each parent can be encouraged to choose one or two positive thoughts that are particularly meaningful (e.g., "I can do this." "I'm helping him by staying calm." "This will get better.") These thoughts can be used as a mantra when the parent starts to feel dysregulated or angry. Practicing one thought pattern over and over again will help to establish new more positive thought pattern. Also the therapist might laminate some of the key statements or thoughts on these thought cards so parents can keep them and place them in a prominent place at home as a visual reminder.

Making Connections. Another cognitive reframing strategy that the therapist can use to promote parents' empathy and bonding with their child is helping them see the connections between their own childhood experiences and/or temperament and those of their child.

> **Therapist:** *As you talk about your child's impatience, high energy level and difficulty conforming in the classroom, do you see any similarities to yourself or your experiences as a child?*
>
> *How do these similarities between you both affect your reactions to your child?*
>
> *Having been a high energy and independent child yourself, what do you think helped you the most? Or the least?*

One homework assignment is to have parents complete a temperament measure on their child as well as on themselves. Afterwards parents discuss similarities and differences between their personality and their child's.

In the case where the parent does acknowledge similarities between his/her personality and his/her child's, the therapists' role is to help the parent see how similar personalities may sometimes lead to parent-child conflict. For example, if both the parent and child are quick to become emotionally dysregulated, that may result in quickly escalating anger. Therapists can help parents see that temperamental similarities also makes the parent uniquely suited to judging what parenting strategies might be most useful with the child.

When parents report that their temperaments are different than their child's, the therapist explores the impact of this on the parent-child relationship. In this case the parent may need to work harder to put him or herself into the child's shoes since the child's experience and reactions may be very different than the parents. In these cases often parents report being baffled by their child's reactions. On the other hand, there are times when differences in temperament mean

PROPHESIZING SUCCESS

that parents and children have fewer clashes. A parent who is calm and deliberate may be able to de-escalate an active and excitable child more easily. See below for an example of how a therapist might approach this discussion with parents.

> **Therapist:** *So you are quiet, thoughtful and a somewhat anxious person who finds it hard to take risks, and your son is outgoing, hyperactive, impulsive and loud. You have different temperaments and that is part of your genetic biology and your uniqueness. Let's think about the possible advantages of this temperament for your child and how your thoughtful approach can support him in a positive way to bring out the best aspects of his personality.*

Reframing the Future. Parents are often skeptical about their ability to change their child's behavior and even their own responses, especially if they see in their behavior a family pattern, for patterns often seem fixed and irreversible. Thus, another function of the therapist is to counter that skepticism with positive expectations for change in the future. For example, one parent said, "Hot tempers run in my family. My grandfather and my mother are both yellers. Whenever anything went wrong, they always exploded. Screaming is just the way we deal with things in our family. I got that from them. I don't think I'm programmed to be able to stay calm." In response, the therapist expressed her confidence in the parent's ability to break the family intergenerational cycle. Each small step toward change, even the step of coming to a parent training program in the first place, can be pointed to as evidence that the problem is not fixed or irreversible.

Therapists work to strengthen parents' self-efficacy in order to bring about consistent parenting responses.

The therapist strives to convey optimism about the parents' ability to successfully carry out the strategies required to produce positive changes in the child's behaviors. According to Bandura (1989), all psychological procedures are mediated through a system of beliefs about the level of skill required to bring about an outcome and the likely end result of a course of action. Thus, successful change in the parent depends on the ability of the therapist to strengthen parents' expectations of personal efficacy ("I am able to do it").

In the next scenario, notice how the therapist works on building the parent's self-confidence and belief in her ability to change her typical response.

> **Mother:** *My mother was depressed a lot because we were so stressed by never having any money. She hit me a lot when I was a child. I never could please her, and now I am just like her.*

> **Therapist:** *Remember back then parents didn't know as much about parenting as we do now, and your mother didn't have the advantage of taking a parenting course to learn some different discipline strategies. You learned some parenting approaches from your mother that you are now seeing yourself use with your child. That is normal. But now you realize you don't want to repeat that approach, and you are learning some other parenting tools that have been shown to be more successful at helping you reach your goals. Unlike your mother, you now have a support team in the group. You can change your family pattern.*

In this example the therapist is not only reframing the mother's perspectives of her ability to change her parenting but also her view of her experiences as a child with her own mother. The therapist helps her see how her parenting reactions and responses have been based on her own experiences as a child (either imitating or reacting to the parenting she experienced). She helps her understand that while these prior experiences may create resistance to alternative parenting styles, she now has the knowledge and support to parent differently.

In the next example, the therapist responds to a father who is sharing how his experience with his own father colors how he responds to his son.

Father: *When my son gets angry and defiant like that, I think to myself, my father would never have put up with any of this crap! He would have smacked me hard.*

Therapist: *How do those thoughts about your father influence your ability to stay calm? What do you tell yourself when you hear your father's voice in your head? How do you counter those negative thoughts?*

Here the therapists' role is to help the parent see the connection between what the father learned from his own father regarding parenting, how this influences him (e.g. escalates his anger level toward his son), and what he would like to do differently or the same with his son.

There is therefore a place in the collaborative model for brief consideration of the parents' past histories. These stories are often negative, filled with pain, anger, self-deprecation, bitterness, and regret. It may be necessary for the therapist to help parents "lay the ghosts to rest" before they can apply themselves wholeheartedly and optimistically to different ways to address the problems in the here-and-now. See how the therapist below attempts to help parents do this.

Therapist: *You may be finding it difficult to put all your thought and energy into the present difficulty. Perhaps there are some 'ghosts'* *from the past that still haunt you. These might be childhood hurts or feelings of guilt and blame left over from the way your parents responded to you. Let us try to put them to rest by talking about them; then you may feel more confident about facing the future.*

It is one of the strengths of behavioral work that treatment and the choice of methods does not depend necessarily upon the discovery and understanding of the historical causes of behavior problems. The identification of the current problem and its contemporary antecedents and consequences is the main agenda in treatment. Very rarely can current problems be traced to specific past experiences with any degree of confidence. Nevertheless, many of the therapeutic methods in traditional psychotherapy are formulated as a response to an historical analysis of the parent's life. Such a retrospective look at past events is often of interest (and potentially of use), but an exclusive or predominant preoccupation in assessment with the past history has the effect of "distancing" the problem, keeping it vague because it remains at arm's length. It certainly tends to alienate parents who are struggling with current problems in the child. Nevertheless, there is a place in the collaborative model of treatment for a brief consideration of the child's and parents' past. The stories people tell themselves about themselves and their offspring (schema) are important because they influence their actions. The therapist's role is to help parents understand, talk about and begin to heal from these past experiences so that they can apply themselves whole-heartedly (i.e., without debilitating and regret guilt) to problems in the here-and-now.

The therapist's role is to help parents heal from these past experiences so that they can apply themselves whole-heartedly to problems in the here-and-now.

Therapist Role #6: Leading and Challenging

Are there times when the therapist must take control of the group, even confront parents? If so, how does this role fit into the collaborative model?

The most obvious reason for the therapist to lead the group is that otherwise the group will lack focus and organization. Our evaluations have indicated that parents become frustrated if the discussion is permitted to wander or if one person is allowed to monopolize the session. Parents appreciate having enough structure imposed to keep the discussion focused and moving along. Another reason the therapist must exercise leadership is to deal with the group process issues, such as arguments and resistance, which are an inevitable part of every group's therapy process.

But there is an apparent tension between this role and the collaborative model, since in collaborative therapy power is shared. There are several strategies which we use to preserve the collaborative spirit while allowing the therapist to function as leader. For one thing, the therapist shares with the parents the agenda for each group session and how the content addresses their goals. Parents also have a role in determining the agenda for each session by sharing their experiences using the new strategies with their children and asking questions about areas of difficulty.

> ***Therapist:*** *Today's agenda will be to learn how to do social coaching with children. This approach will help your children learn some of the friendship behaviors many of you included on your goals for your children. I also want you to have time to share and ask questions about your experiences at home this week using academic and persistence coaching so we will spend the first 20-30 minutes on that. Who would like to start to share your efforts to use the coaching methods this week?*

Parent group sessions always begin with parents and the therapist reviewing the agenda and goals for the session, debriefing the home activities assignment for the previous week, evaluating progress, and discussing how things currently are going at home. The therapist's job then is to connect parents' input, their questions, concerns, reactions to the assignments, and experiences at home, into the overall framework and new topics for that particular session. The trick is keeping a good balance between the parents' individual needs and the group's needs for leadership. The sessions always conclude with assigning the tasks to be completed before the next session. The following are some other strategies which the therapist will find helpful in leading the sessions.

Setting Limits. One of the most important aspects of the therapist's leadership role is to prevent the group process from becoming disrupted and off-task. The therapist must impose sufficient structure to facilitate the group process. As discussed earlier in this chapter, agreed upon group rules help to keep things running smoothly. Sometimes there is a parent in a group who is critical and verbally aggressive toward either their spouse or another parent in the group. In such instances the therapist intervenes quickly to stop the bullying pattern; otherwise, the other parent will withdraw. For example, the therapist may say in a supportive but firm manner, "*I need to interrupt you right there.*" The therapist then explains why s/he is cutting off the speaker. "*I can see that this is an emotional topic, and I hear your frustration. I'm worried that this conversation is going in a direction that doesn't feel safe and supportive of the group.*" Depending on the issue, there may be a way for the therapist to guide the discussion around to address the parent's concerns, but in a way that maintains a positive problem-solving approach. At other times, the therapist may choose to talk with the aggressor outside the group, to try to understand his or her anger, and problem solve ways that concerns can be addressed without bullying behavior.

The group process can also be disrupted by a participant who challenges the therapist's knowledge or advocates inappropriate child-rearing practices. It is important that the therapist not seem critical or frustrated with this person's comments, for this is the "coercion trap" many parents have experienced in the past. Instead, the therapist listens carefully, looks for the relevant points in what the person has said, and reinforces them for their contributions to the group. By conveying acceptance and warmth, even towards a parent who is obviously a difficult group member, the therapist models acceptance and helps group members see that the goal is to understand and respect everyone. At the same time, the therapist does provide guidance and information to the group so that the parent's ideas are respected, but not necessarily endorsed.

> ***Parent:*** *I'm really sick of listening to all this nicey-nicey bullcrap. When my son is disrespectful, he needs to learn a lesson, and the only lesson that works is a hard smack on the butt. I do it every time, and you can bet he thinks twice about using back talk around me. The stuff you're talking about in the group is going to turn him into a sissy, and it sure as hell isn't going to make him behave.*
>
> ***Therapist:*** *I hear that you are really worried about making sure your son understands that disrespectful behavior is unacceptable to you. I bet that many parents in this room have that same goal, and it's an important message for children to learn. It's also good that you realize the consistency is important. I'm sure that there are many people in this room who have also experienced that spanking is effective to stop their child's behavior. Over the next couple of classes, we're going to explore this issue in a lot of depth. We'll think about the advantages and disadvantages of spanking and some of these other methods, which you're not so convinced of. I'll be interested to hear what you think as we go through this process. It's really important to this process that you're willing to share your thoughts.*

Notice that the therapist has been respectful of the parent, has validated his worries and concerns, and has not responded to his anger and confrontational style. The therapist has also not tried to talk this parent out of his opinion, for that would likely make him more set in his ways. The therapist even validates that spanking is a commonly used method of dealing with child misbehavior. However, the therapist did not validate that spanking was an effective method of discipline and suggests that the group will be exploring alternatives to spanking. In this way, he has treated the father respectfully, but has also given a message to the group that spanking is not a strategy that the program advocates.

Pacing the Group. Another important aspect of leading a group is pacing. Some parents pick up the concepts easily, while others need more time. The therapist must pace the group so that everyone understands the concepts and is ready move on to the next component. This may mean that some group members become impatient, ready to move on. However, the skilled therapist will take advantage of the parents in the group who seem to have a good grasp of a particular concept by soliciting their help in explaining things to other members. For example, the therapist might ask one member of the group to summarize for the group the previous week's discussions, or ask another to come up with an application of a particular concept or to model its use in a practice demonstration. These strategies emphasize the collaborative process. Throughout each session the therapist's leadership skills will involve paraphrasing and summarizing parents' viewpoints. This process helps uncover misunderstandings; it also helps parents review the material. Further, it demonstrates the therapist is listening to their points of view.

Dealing with Resistance. Resistance is a necessary part of the therapy process and the therapist needs to be prepared for it. In fact, Patterson's (1985) research indicates that considerable resistance will peak midway through the treatment process. Resistance may occur in a variety of ways such as failure to do home activities, arriving late for group sessions, blaming the leader, blaming the child or life circumstances, negatively evaluating the sessions, or challenging the material presented.

Put aside any notion a parent's resistance is either a sign of failure or a sign that the parent is noncompliant or unmotivated.

Resistance may occur for many reasons, some having to do with the therapy change process (as Patterson's research suggests). For example, the resistance may be part of the parent's efforts to maintain self-efficacy and self-control in the face of family dynamics which are changing too quickly; in effect, the parent is "putting on the brakes." Perhaps the parent doesn't adequately understand the concept that the therapist has explained. Perhaps the parent is resisting because s/he feels his/her stressful life circumstances make it difficult to find the time to do the home assignments. Or perhaps parents have unrealistic expectations for behavioral change and are not prepared for the long hard work involved. The resistance may pertain more directly to some quality of the therapist. For example, the parent may not feel understood by the therapist; s/he may perceive the therapist as patronizing or think the therapist is presenting "pat" answers and solutions without really understanding his/her situation. On the other hand, resistance may stem from external factors. For example, perhaps the parent has had a previous learning experience that has given him/her a different explanatory model. Or perhaps the parent feels the child's behavior should change first, before any change in parental behavior.

Whatever the reason, the first task for the therapist is to put aside any notion that the parent's resistance is either a sign of failure on the part of the therapist, or a sign that the parent is noncompliant or unmotivated, a "difficult person." Instead, the therapist needs to recognize the resistance an important marker in the therapy process a developmental step for the parent.

> **Mother:** *I feel I just can't absorb it all and I'm getting behind at home. I just can't do all this play stuff, there isn't any time.*
>
> **Father:** *Yeah, I go out of this group charged up, but when I get home I lose it. I don't start thinking about applying all this stuff until right before our group is to meet again.*
>
> **Father:** *I'm sorry, but I don't buy this. You're telling me that I should ignore when my child talks back. I can't allow that kind of disrespect in my house. If my child is rude, he's going to hear from me that it is never acceptable to challenge his mother or me.*

When the therapist knows the parent is resisting a basic concept or doing something that it is counterproductive to the goals of the therapy program, should the therapist confront and challenge the parent regarding this, or just let it go in the interest of fostering collaboration and offering support? The therapist may be worried that confrontation will jeopardize the goals of collaboration. Some therapists may be tempted to avoid conflicts with parents. Yet this failure to address the issue really constitutes a kind of collusion with parents in regard to their parenting practices. Consequently, how this resistance is handled by the therapist is crucial to the therapeutic relationship.

Once the resistance is identified, it should not be directly confronted, for this is likely to increase the parent's defensiveness. Furthermore, it devalues the parent in front of the other group members. In fact, in one of the few studies to do a microanalytic analysis of therapist-client interactions, Patterson and Forgatch (1985) found that resistance met by direct confrontation or teaching on the part of the therapist actually *increased* parents' noncompliance. It is our contention that instead of confronting the issue raised by the resistant parent, the therapist needs to explore the resistance itself, gently, by asking about it in a non-defensive and non-confrontational manner. In other words, the therapist needs to collaborate with the parent in understanding the resistance.

> **Therapist:** *I hear frustration in your voice when you talk about your week and the play home assignment. I'd really like to know what's going on for you. Would you mind sharing more about your experience with this home activity?*
>
> **First Mother:** *I just don't have the time to play. There always seems to be so much to do.*
>
> **Therapist:** *What seems to get in the way of doing the play assignment?*
>
> **First Mother:** *I'm just so stressed out about everything in my life.*
>
> **Therapist:** *So am I right in understanding that doing the play assignment is pretty stressful?*
>
> **First Mother:** *Yeah, well, he's just so abusive to me—he's so violent. It's hard to keep the play positive.*
>
> **Therapist:** *Yeah, it's pretty hard to want to praise and play with a defiant child who has made your life so miserable. That seems like a logical reason for feeling resistance to doing the assignment.*
>
> **First Father:** *For me it's not so much that the child is stressful, but it's me that's so stressed out!*

Second Mother: *I find it hard because my older daughter keeps complaining she wants the play time too. So now I've got one more person making demands on me for time.*

Second Father: *Well, in our case we've got twins and each child had a major tantrum when I played with other child and then tantrummed again when I ended the play.*

Therapist: *You probably wonder if it's worth it! You can see from just this play exercise how families will resist change. Well, you know (to second father) one good sign in your situation is the fact the children didn't want the play with you to end. That's an important signal that the play was very reinforcing to them. Clearly time with you is really important to them!*

Third Father: *Well, you know in my situation, I didn't want to do the play assignment. I felt stressed out and the kids were really on my nerves but I made myself do it. And do you know, it really helped. I was so surprised that I was actually calmer afterwards!*

Therapist: *That's great. Many of you will find the same thing happens to you after a while. But how did you get yourself mobilized to do the play when you really didn't want to?*
Third Father: *I just told myself I had nothing to lose by trying it once.*

Therapist: *Good for you! Well, for those of you who didn't do the play this week let's put our heads together and brainstorm about some ways it might be possible to try it this week. . . .*

Other questions the therapist might ask to explore parents' resistance to the home assignments are, *"What thoughts come to mind when you think about this home activity?" "What makes it hard to do?" "Does this seem relevant to your life?" "How could we make this more helpful?" "Can anyone in the group think of a way that might help her try the assignment?"*

A common area of resistance is parents' reluctance to use Time Out as an alternative to spanking.

Father: *Well, all this Time Out stuff is well and good, but in the final analysis I think spanking is what you really need to do. Especially when something bad happens, like a broken window.*

Therapist: *So you really see spanking as the final "big gun"?*

Father: *I do. You know, I was spanked by my father and it didn't do me any psychological harm.*

Therapist: *Tell me how spanking works for you and when you would be most likely to use it.*

In a collaborative relationship the therapist deals with resistance by starting from the premise of respect for the legitimacy of the client's views; in this case, respecting the parent's preference for spanking as legitimate. She would then explore the viewpoint with nonjudgmental questions such as, "*Tell me how spanking works for you? How often do you use it? How do you feel afterwards? How does your child feel about it? How does it affect your relationship? Do you ever feel you lose control when you spank? What do you see as its advantages? Are there any disadvantages? How did it affect your relationship with your parent when you were spanked as a child?*" Similar questions might then be asked about the alternative approach, Time Out. "*Let's look at an alternative approach. What are the difficulties with Time Out? What don't you like about it? What are its disadvantages? Are there any advantages?*" Notice that the questions are in the form of "What do you mean?" or "How do you feel?" or "What do you think?" rather than "Why?" or "Why not?" These questions serve to clarify the parents' feelings, thoughts, and experiences surrounding the resistance and to facilitate problem-solving and collaboration.

In a parent group this kind of approach between the therapist and a resistant parent would quickly draw everyone into the discussion, which helps to present many different view points. A judgmental or authoritarian response from a therapist, on the other hand, would tend to result in group members becoming silent. When resistance to a concept occurs, we find it helpful to organize the discussion by listing the advantages and disadvantages, short-term and long-term consequences for the child and for the parent on a blackboard. At the end of this discussion, the therapist summarizes the ideas that have been generated, clarifies misperceptions and adds his/her own interpretations if they have not already been covered. This process of collaborative problem solving in the group serves to move people away from "absolutist" positions (i.e., seeing the situation in terms of right and wrong) and opens people up to new ideas that they may not have considered previously, thus reducing resistance. On the other hand a noncollaborative approach, where the therapist directly confronts the parents' ideas, creates a boxing match where the therapist and parent each have to defend their own position in order to protect their integrity.

Once the reasons for the resistance are understood by both the parents and the therapist and problem solving has occurred, the therapist then is ready to invite the parent to consider a short experimental period.

> ***Therapist:*** *I understand your viewpoint regarding Time Out and that you think children should be spanked for misbehaving. At the same time, Timmy seems to have been having more and more problems with being aggressive with his peers and at school and I know you are eager to help him with this problem. I'd like to suggest that we do an experiment. Would you be willing to give Time Out a try and act as if you believe it will work. I'd like you to try doing Time Out for a month and keep records, and then at the end of a month let's evaluate how it looks. You see, if it doesn't work, you can always go back to the way you have been doing things and won't have lost anything. What do you think about that?*

In the example above, the therapist does not attack the resistance by confronting it directly or repeating the rationale for why s/he thinks Time Out is right (and why the parent is wrong to use spanking). Rather, the therapist is engaged in a process of gentle persuasion. Although she does not confront the resistance directly, she confronts the difference of opinion with open, honest communication. This process of exploring the reasons for the resistance, followed by the exercise of looking at the advantages and disadvantages of spanking versus Time Out, is a kind of values clarification and problem-solving exercise which helps clarify feelings and experiences surrounding the issue. This strategy serves to join people rather than alienate them. It is more likely than direct confrontation to result in a gradual change in parents' perceptions and behaviors, especially if conducted in the context of a supportive relationship.

Reframing is also a helpful strategy when responding to resistance. Once the therapist has collaborated to understand the reason for the resistance, then s/he can then reframe the treatment objectives in such a way that parents can cooperate and carry out the experiment. For example, one parent said she could not put the child in a Time Out room because she felt it would create bad feelings about the child's room and, more importantly, the child would feel abandoned. Further exploration by the therapist uncovered the fact that this parent had been locked for hours in her bedroom by her own parents! As a result of this discussion, the therapist and parent set up a Time Out strategy based on a chair in the corner of the living room rather than the bedroom. Over future sessions, the therapist reframed the situation to help the parent understand that short Time Outs with the parent in control help children to feel more secure in their relationships with their parents, and that children whose behavior is not controlled by their parents actually may come to feel psychologically abandoned. By joining with the parent and then reframing the situation so that the parent perceived the objective as promoting security (rather than abandonment), the therapist enabled the parent to accept the strategy for herself and her child. This is the essence of collaborative therapy.

Reframing is also a helpful strategy when responding to resistance.

Often the group is useful when dealing with resistance. Resistant parents may be more willing to listen to another parent, whom they may perceive as more similar to themselves than the therapist. If the therapist can maintain the kind of respectful and open discussion and dialogue described above, other parents may be willing to share successes or perspectives. Hearing that another parent was skeptical, but tried a new strategy and saw results may push a reluctant group member to try something new. At strategic times, the therapist may choose to turn to other parents and invite their thoughts and experiences. This can be particularly helpful if the therapist feels that he is at an impasse with a particular parent.

Benefits and Barriers Values Exercise. The purpose of these exercises is to introduce a new parenting strategy and find out what parents in the group think about a particular topic in advance of showing the vignettes. In many cases, these exercises serve to defuse parent resistance before it arises because parents see that the therapist is interested in hearing differing points of view. In addition, since the barriers part of the exercise invites parents to state their difficulties with the new topic, they are assured that these will be considered and addressed.

Knowing the barriers ahead of time can help the therapist target discussion questions and possible practice role plays.

The therapist starts by asking the parents in either a buzz format with a buddy or in a large group brainstorm to list the benefits of using a particular parenting strategy such as emotion coaching, praise, incentives, predictable routines, limit setting, or ignoring. The therapist gives a brief introduction to the topic by referring to the pyramid and then asking the group to think of as many benefits as possible, for example, "*So far we've been talking about building your relationship foundation with your child through child-directed play and coaching tools. Today we're going to move up the pyramid to think of ways that you can give your child positive feedback. One of those ways is through praise. Let's take a few minutes to think of as many benefits to praise as we can.*" As parents reflect on this and suggest ideas, the therapist prompts them to think of benefits to both the child as well as to themselves. Then after the benefits list is complete, the therapist comments, "*We have a great list of positive things about praise, but sometimes there can be things that get in the way of giving praise, or there may be things about praise that make you uncomfortable. Let's brainstorm a list of possible barriers to giving praise.*" As group members bring up barriers, the therapist's job is to acknowledge that their idea is a barrier and write it down. This is not the place to try to convince parents that their barrier isn't a good one, or to try to make them see that praise is effective. At the end of the list, the therapist summarizes the benefits and barriers and helps the parents look at the short-term and long-term outcomes for using praise for the child or parent or their relationships. Frequently this exercise results in parents discovering that in the short term the praise strategy is hard for the parent to do because of barriers such as lack of familiarity with how to use it, or because it takes too much work and energy or because of their feelings about their child. However, in the long term they see the benefits for not only for their children's developmental growth but also for their relationship. After this summary the therapist introduces their learning together by watching the vignettes by saying, "*So, now we're going to watch some vignettes and I'd like us to think about and share what makes the praise these parents use so effective. We want to think of ways to praise that will lead to all of these benefits we have identified. We also want to talk about how to overcome some of the barriers to praise that are experienced by many of us.*"

A couple of caveats to the benefits/barriers exercises are worth noting. In the first parent group session on child-directed play, the therapist only does the benefits part of the exercise for discussing the value of play. The discussion of barriers to child-directed play is saved for the subsequent session after parents have tried to do the play homework activities. This results in the barriers discussion emerging from the actual difficulties they have experienced playing at home that week. Then the therapist can troubleshoot some possible ways to overcome those barriers with the group and help parents set realistic goals for this activity. For the praise, incentives, and limit setting sessions, the therapist will do both the benefits and barriers at the beginning before the vignettes are shown. This will help the therapist have an idea of what knowledge level the parents have about the strategy and what to focus on when showing the vignettes. Knowing the barriers ahead of time can help the therapist target discussion questions and possible practice role plays related to the parents' barriers. For the Time Out strategy, the therapist doesn't do the benefits/barriers exercise until after teaching parents the purpose of Time Out (to teach children to calm down and self regulate) and how to use it. This is because parents will come to the group with many different experiences and opinions about Time Out. Since Time Out has been used (and sometimes

PROPHESIZING SETBACKS

abused) in so many ways, it is important that the entire group understands the kind of Time Out that is being advocated in the IY program before considering the benefits and barriers. Therefore 1-2 sessions are used to teach Time Out and parents begin to practice using it at home. Then therapists lead parents through the benefits and barriers discussion. In this unit, the benefits and barriers discussion is usually combined with a discussion of the benefits and barriers to spanking and other physical discipline.

Therapist Role #7: Prophesizing

Children's behavior improves slowly; regression in their misbehavior is inevitable, despite parents' hard work. When some families encounter these setbacks, they react with disbelief, depression, and anger. They may even decide to drop out of the program at this point. As a "prophesizer," the therapist can help prepare families for future relapses not only in their children's behavior, but also in their own behavior. The therapist's role as prophesizer also includes predicting resistance to change as well as forecasting for improvement.

Anticipating Problems and Setbacks. One helpful strategy to prevent disillusionment for parents is for the therapist to predict setbacks in children's behavior, anticipating potential problems and regression and discussing these with parents before they occur. The therapist can engage in a hypothetical problem-solving discussion of how parents might handle particular problems should they occur in the future. For example, the therapist could prepare families for the negative behavior that is likely to occur when children encounter changed circumstances such as a prolonged illness, a return from a week's visit with relatives or the other parent, or the arrival of step-siblings who come to stay for summer vacation. Or, after an episode of particularly difficult behavior in public, the therapist collaborates with the parents to prepare a plan for dealing with the behavior more successfully next time. Similarly, the therapist could help parents develop a strategy for having a more successful visit with their in-laws. By mentally rehearsing how parents will handle the worst possible scenario, parents' anxiety is reduced because they feel prepared to cope effectively with conflict situations. Moreover, when the "worst" doesn't happen, they are pleased with themselves and their progress.

Prepare parents for the fact that there will be inevitable relapses in their own parenting behavior and these are a signal to use a different parenting tool.

Within the process of a 14- or 20-week parent group, there is a common pattern to parent and child responses. Parents often feel a combination of hopeful and skeptical for the first several weeks. Those who are doing the home practices will often experience immediate success and will sometimes feel that the program has been a miracle! This provides them with the enthusiasm to carry on for several more weeks, working hard, and seeing progress with their children. After several honeymoon weeks, there is a mid-program lull and parents begin to report that their children have relapsed. This can be devastating to parents, especially if they experienced so much initial success. The relapse may be because the newness of the positive strategies has worn off and parents are less consistent with them. It also could be that children are testing the limits of their parents' newfound positive responses. At this point in the program parents only have half a tool box of strategies, so they are at a disadvantage! As parents move to the second half of the program, they typically feel a new mastery over their own responses and their parenting. They see how their own responses influence their children's behavior, and they have learned a set of skills that they can generalize to all settings. Because of this, when they have a bad day or a bad week, it is less devastating. They know that they have the skills to regroup and respond to the behaviors. While not all families will experience this, it can be helpful for the therapist to remember this cycle, and to share parts of it with parents as a way to normalize what they are going through.

The therapist also needs to prepare parents for the fact that there will be inevitable relapses in their own parenting behavior after the program has ended. The therapist should reassure parents that relapses are normal parts of the learning process. Relapses should be construed as a "signal" that some strategy or parenting tools need to be implemented; parents can be encouraged to see regression as an opportunity to practice or coach a new positive opposite skill or go back to securing their foundation with special time with children, coaching and incentives for targeted behaviors. It is a good idea to rehearse with parents what they might do when a relapse occurs. For example, they might call their buddy or a friend for support, contact the therapist, practice program home activities again, review parenting strategies and read the parenting book, arrange for time away to "refuel," or focus on positive alternatives. Here is an example of how the therapist might start preparing parents for relapses by reframing the usual interpretation.

> ***Therapist:*** *Expect and be prepared for relapses. They are part of your own and your child's learning process. The child needs to relapse and test the security of his environment every now and again to see if the rules still hold. Then once he knows his base is secure, he can tackle a new challenge. You know, it's a bit like the old adage: "two steps forward, one step back."*

Predicting Parent Resistance to Change. It helps to predict in advance that parents will resist some strategies and assignments and to offer some reasons for this opposition. Otherwise, if the difficulty of making behavioral, cognitive, or emotional change is not acknowledged by the therapist, the parent may feel s/he is incapable of change. Some parents may even become angry at the therapist for asking them to do assignments that are so hard for them to do and "not part of their personality make-up." These feelings will lead to increased resistance. When parents are prepared in advance, they need not be surprised or anxious when these feelings occur; they can perceive these reactions as a necessary part of the behavioral and emotional change process.

> **Therapist:** *Be prepared to feel awkward when you do this kind of coaching. Be prepared for yourself to resist wanting to do it because it does feel awkward. And be prepared for your child not to like it at first. Whenever someone learns a new behavior, there is a natural tendency for family members to resist this new behavior and to revert back to the status quo. In fact, some family members might actually try to pressure you to return to the old way of doing things.*
>
> **OR**
>
> *Using more praise may feel awkward at first, especially if you haven't done much of this in the past. You may even feel your praise sounds phony. So don't wait for yourself to feel warmth towards your child in order to praise. Just get the words out, even if they are kind of flat. The feelings and genuineness will come later. The more you practice, the more natural it will become.*
>
> **OR**
>
> *Lots of parents don't like Time Out at first. Compared to spanking it's more time-consuming, it is harder to keep the self-control you need (especially if you want "revenge" on your child), and it feels awkward. But with practice it will become automatic and your child will learn exactly what to do. You will feel good because you are teaching your child a nonviolent approach to dealing with conflict and how to calm themselves down. There will be long term benefits but it takes patience for this to happen.*

OR

We all find it difficult to change; indeed it can be painful. We get used to the figurative 'goggles' or 'glasses' through which we look at the world in general, and our child in particular. To have to put on a different set of goggles can be quite confusing at first. We feel comfortable with what's familiar; so the new perspective is strange and rather scary. But that feeling soon wears off.

Therapist: *Changing our negative thoughts can be difficult; the first step is to recognize them and then write them down. Then we will work on rewriting them and practicing using positive coping thoughts. We will have reminder cards so we can rehearse this internal dialogue. It is a bit like learning a new language – remember when you tried to learn Spanish or some other language. First you had to say the word over and over, maybe only a few words at a time. Then you gradually added more words and eventually sentences. With time and repetition it gets better and becomes more automatic.*

In addition, it is important for therapists to tell parents to call in if they are having difficulties with any of the assignments, thereby indicating the therapist's willingness to listen to their resistance and help them to overcome their personal barriers in order to reach their goal.

Another strategy to use when discussing resistance to change is to help parents understand that change is not without cost. Here it can be helpful to ask the parents to list the pros and cons of adopting a certain approach. For example here is how we would list out the advantages and disadvantages of yelling and screaming.

Therapist: *You find it difficult to give up the anger and resentment you feel all the time for your youngster's aggressive responses and for making life difficult for you. Let's try to see why it is so hard to give up anger. We'll make two columns headed 'advantages' and 'disadvantages' of letting go of anger.*

Parent: *Advantages—I'd feel better; I'd be less tense; I'd be more rational; I'd avoid a CPS referral or hurting my child; I have better parenting responses for my child and better future relationship.*

Disadvantages—It would look as if I couldn't control his behavior or that his misbehavior was unimportant to me; I'd lose self-respect; people may think I don't care in my rearing of children; my child wouldn't understand how much he has hurt me if he doesn't feel pain.

Therapist: *You can see that there are some good reasons in your mind, to not give up your anger. So change is costly. What you need to think through are the relative costs of changing as opposed to not changing. Also let's look at some of the thoughts about letting go of anger to see if they are realistic. Does a child need to feel pain in order to learn? What actually does he learn when he is hit?*

Predicting Positive Change and Success. The therapist should build parents' expectations for positive change in behavior if they do persist with the home activities and implement the program. It is important for the therapist to express confidence and optimism in the parents' ability to successfully carry out the thought and behavior changes required to produce positive changes in their child's behaviors. According to Bandura (1977), all psychological procedures are mediated through a system of beliefs about the level of skill required to bring about an outcome and the likely end result of a course of action. Efficacy expectations are thought to be the most important component. Successful treatment will depend on the ability of the therapist to strengthen the parents' expectations of personal efficacy ('I am able to do it').

Therapist: *We have found that after parents do the daily play sessions for several weeks and increase their coaching and praise statements, their children's behavior improves substantially. We have also found that when parents give their children attention for positive behaviors, they actually have more time for themselves in the long run, because their children stop behaving inappropriately to get their attention.*

OR

We've worked with a large number of families now and, although we don't have perfect success, we've found at least two-thirds of parents are able to make impressive changes in their children's behaviors. And although some children are still quite challenging to manage at the end of the program, all parents who are practicing these new skills feel more confident in their ability to deal with whatever behaviors their children exhibit.

It is also important to predict that other family members can benefit from the program, even if they do not attend the sessions. For indeed, research (Patterson, 1982) has suggested that all members of the aggressive child's family are victims; they all experience the pain of the family interactions. If non-participating members of the family are not helped by the participating member to see some possibility of payoff for themselves, they may actively sabotage the participating members' efforts to change. The therapist should therefore work with the participating members to see how the program can be extended in a nonintrusive way to other family members. For example, the therapist can predict that the siblings who previously have been "good" children may regress in an effort to gain attention and to compete for play sessions or a sticker chart that has been started with the target child. This reaction should be presented as a positive outcome for all the children, although more demanding for the parent. Predictions should also be made about the nonparticipating fathers who may initially be suspicious of the program. However, if mothers continue to competently use coaching methods, praise, incentives, and Time Out and other consequences respectfully and consistently, they will soon find fathers following suit because they have become effective models.

The role of therapist as prophesier is consistent with a collaborative model because the therapist brings her expertise and knowledge of possible family reactions to bear on the parents' unique situations and experiences; the single parent who is co-parenting with an ex-spouse, the family with several children of differing ages, the mother with a noninvolved father, or the parent with backgrounds of alcohol or spouse abuse, and the parents bring their ideas and insights to bear on planning how to deal with those possible reactions. It should be obvious that the therapist can effectively prophesize only if s/he has collaborated with the parents to understand their situation. Moreover, by anticipating problems beyond the immediate child problems, the concept of "working together" is enriched.

Preparing for the Long Term. About 3 sessions before the end of the program, the therapist starts to keep a list on a flip chart of things parents will do to get support after the program ends. Many groups will also want to continue on their own as a group or keep in touch with their buddies. This is encouraged as one aspect of developing their support team. The following are some of the ideas our groups have discussed:

How to Continue to Feel Supported as a Parent

- Continue to meet as a group to support each other once a month. Study some of the other DVD learning modules together.
- Identify two parents from the group who are willing to act as "touch points," who check out a set of the DVDs from the therapist and provide a place to meet to discuss parenting issues that arise.
- Put program notes on the refrigerator, telephone, or bathroom mirror to remind oneself to use specific concepts such as coaching and praising positive opposite behaviors, using positive self talk, and ignoring inappropriate behavior.
- Review the program notes and handouts with a partner or a friend once every two weeks. Reread or listen to CD portions of the book.
- Reward oneself once a week for working on parenting skills by going out for coffee or to a movie with a partner or a friend.
- Plan discussions of parenting issues with a partner or friend once every two weeks.
- Tell yourself that you are doing a good job!
- Set aside some time to relax and refuel one's energy on a daily basis.
- Recognize that it is okay for parents and children to make mistakes and learn from them.
- Put parent toolbox poster on refrigerator and practice using 1-2 parent tools each week.

An ongoing theme reiterated by the therapist throughout the training program is that it is hard work to be a parent. It is a difficult challenge that very few of us are adequately prepared for. One of the most common mistakes that parents make in relating to children is to go for the short-term payoffs (for example, to give in to a child's tantrum to stop the unpleasant behavior) at the expense of the long-term consequences (the child learns to have tantrums to get what s/he wants). The therapist emphasizes that although the parenting skills presented in the program need to be repeated hundreds of times and take a lot of work, the long-term benefits make it worth the effort: helping a child to become a self-confident, creative, nonviolent, and happy individual. As one of our parents so aptly put it: "You mean there is no magic moon dust?" No, the program has no magic moon dust to sprinkle; rather, the objective is to encourage parents to be patient with themselves and to be committed to their growth as parents as well as their children's growth and development.

THE SCRIPT FOR PARENTS: LEARNING TO COPE MORE EFFECTIVELY

The therapeutic process that we have been describing is one in which the therapist collaborates with parents in multiple roles in order to help the parents gradually gain the knowledge, control, and competence they need to effectively cope with behavior problems and support their children's development. Parents gain an understanding of the developmental issues that occur for all children as they strive for independence and explore their environment, as well the added stresses of parenting a child with conduct problems, ADHD or some developmental and language delays. To put it differently, the "script" for the parents involves learning more effective coping strategies and parenting skills so that ultimately they strengthen their children's social and emotional competence and prevent or reduce their behavior problems. Several themes are constant throughout the therapy process as part of this coping model "script" for parents.

Theme #1: Parents Learning To Problem-Solve

By now it should be clear that problem solving and collaboration between the therapist and parent go hand in hand throughout the sessions. Often we find parents have initially come to us with the belief

PROMOTING PARENTS' PROBLEM-SOLVING AND EFFECTIVE COPING STRATEGIES

that there is a single cause for the child's misbehaviors and consequently a single solution for the problem. The goal is for parents to come to realize by the end of the program that there is no single magical solution or recipe for parenting. Rather, parents become confident in their own ability to reflect and think sequentially and to analyze parent-child interactions, to search for external causes of misbehavior (as opposed to attributing it to the child's "bad" nature) and to generate a rich smorgasbord of possible solutions. They acquire the problem-solving strategies necessary to evaluate possible solutions in terms of their desirability and relevance, to commit to trying them out, and to evaluate whether or not a particular solution is working. In essence, by the end of the therapy the parents have become their own therapists.

Theme #2: Parents "Coming To Terms"

The therapist gradually helps parents come to terms with the realistic facts concerning their child's temperament and biology. They must learn to manage the anger and grief related to the loss of their hoped-for "ideal" child and learn to accept their child's difficulties and strengths and extra needs for committed parenting. Because many of these children's problems are to some degree chronic; characterized by unpredictable relapses, constant vulnerability to changes in routine, and the emergence of new problems whenever the child faces new settings or schedules, parents must be helped to face the fact that they must invest a great deal of time and energy in the hard work of anticipating, monitoring, and problem solving for many years to come.

Therapists remind parents of their short-term successes and the small steps towards their longer term goals.

The therapist can prepare parents for this partly by helping them balance long-term and then short-term goals. Keeping focus on those long term goals, such as having a well-adjusted and well-regulated child can help a parent be consistent through a challenging short-term behavior, for example, a temper tantrum or melt down in response to setting a limit. While parents may be tempted to give in to these behaviors to obtain short-term peace, their focus on the long-term goals can remind them why they must persist. On the other hand, since long-term goals are often many years away, it's important for therapists to remind parents of their short-term successes and the small steps towards the longer term goals. Parents must be encouraged to celebrate small moments with their child, to take the time to play and enjoy each other, and to reflect on progress (however small). This "in the moment" appreciation of their child will provide fuel for getting through the more difficult moments.

> ***Therapist:*** *Your child needs to have hundreds of chances to try to learn from his mistakes. Learning more appropriate social skills and emotional regulation is just like when your child was a baby and was learning how to reach out, then turn over, crawl, finally walk. Do you remember how often your child tried to get up and fell down or how long she held on to something before she could take off on her own? Well, this is just the same. It takes lots of small steps and experiments for a child to learn appropriate social skills and to control their emotional responses ~ especially as they are biologically driven to explore. And just as you must constantly support the baby who is stumbling (so that she does not injure herself), so must you support the child who is developing her social and emotional skills.*

Moreover, the therapist may even depict the environment provided by parents for children with conduct problems, ADHD, or developmental delays as a sort of "prosthetic environment" or scaffolding of parent coaching, prompting, praise, incentives, positive attention, discipline, and monitoring. And, as with a child with a chronic medical problem, if parents withdraw the treatment, the child is likely to relapse. Words such as "repeated learning trials" and "opportunities to make mistakes" and "developmental struggles" help prepare parents for this long-term coping process.

Theme #3: Parents Gaining Empathy For The Child

Besides helping parents come to terms with the hard work of parenting, it is also important to help them understand, empathize with, and accept their child's unique personality and temperament. It is especially hard for parents of "difficult" and demanding children to remain patient, to constantly be "on guard" for monitoring, and to consistently limit set. Parents can do this more easily and can be more supportive if the therapist has helped them to understand that some of the child's oppositional behaviors are really needs for independence and autonomy or needs to test the security of their environment. Information about typical developmental milestones for toddlers, preschoolers and school age children can help parents build not only patience, but empathy. Parents can also learn to reduce some of their unnecessary commands and criticisms if they understand that children need the opportunity to learn from their own mistakes. Empathy for the child will foster a warm relationship, involving increased tolerance of mistakes and more appropriate discipline from the bottom of the discipline hierarchy, rather than the top.

Theme #4: Parents Aren't Perfect

Coping effectively implies parents coming to accept and understand not only their child's strengths and difficulties, but also their own imperfections as parents. The therapist helps parents learn to stop belittling and berating themselves for their angry or frustrated reactions and depressive or anxious thoughts. They come to understand that these reactions to their child are normal and to replace them with coping thoughts and positive forecasting.

Theme #5: Parents "Refueling" To Ensure Maintenance

In addition to becoming more confident and knowledgeable in their parenting skills and their ability to cope with the child's problems, parents need to recognize the importance of "refueling" themselves as individuals and couples. The therapist can assist this by asking parents such questions as, *"How are you going to keep going when the program is finished?" "How do you keep yourself reinforced for the work of parenting?"* The therapist can encourage the parent support groups to continue meeting after the formal program has ended, and can suggest that parents baby-sit for each other so they can get time away from their children. Monthly "booster shots" for the groups with the therapist can also be scheduled routinely so that there is a structure of ongoing support.

Theme #6: Parents Feeling Empowered

As we discussed earlier in this chapter, one of our primary goals in therapy is to help parents feel empowered so that they feel confident about themselves, their parenting skills, and their ability to cope with the new situations in which they and their children will find themselves over the course of time at home or at school. Empowerment is the antithesis of dependence on the therapist. It encompasses competence, but it is more; namely, the conviction of one's own competence, a sense of security about one's own abilities and capacities. A collaborative therapist empowers parents not only through building their skills, but through continual validation of them.

We empower parents through a three-pronged approach: first, by assuring they have an accurate knowledge base and cognitions concerning children's developmental needs, behavior management principles, and individual or temperamental differences and how these affect parent-child relationships; second, by helping them learn the important parenting skills involved in child-directed play, academic, persistence social and emotional coaching, problem-solving, self-reflective thinking, and enhancing their children's developmental milestones; third, (by building positive emitions and relationships), by accepting and respecting parents' values, culture and beliefs and trying to understand how these impact their family life, rules and relationships. The specific content, methods, and processes we use have been described earlier and are outlined in the Sources of Self-Empowerment table below.

SOURCES OF INCREASED SELF-EMPOWERMENT

Parent	IY Program Content	IY Therapist Process
Accurate Knowledge/ Cognitions	Developmental milestones and temperamental differences Appropriate expectations Cognitive social learning principles Proactive discipline Relationship building/responsiveness/attachment Resources (support, sources of assistance) Parent monitoring/home safety proofing Importance of social support Strategic thinking (working out goals) Challenge, rewrite, replace negative/irrational thoughts Tactical thinking (use of techniques/methods)	Collaborative and problem solving Practice (role play) challenging negative self-talk Culturally appropriate metaphors/analogies Home activity practice assignments Video modeling and mediation Promoting parent self-observation/self-reflection Developing positive cognitive scripts Teaching, persuading, providing rationale Adapting to each child's developmental stage Reading assignments/journaling or logs Encouraging long-term perspective
Appropriate Skills & Behaviors/Strategic Attention	Child-directed play (responsive, nurturing) Differential attention (ignore and attend) Academic, persistence, social and emotion coaching Predictable routines/rules Proactive discipline Social/relationship building skills Identifying goals and target behaviors Problem-solving strategies Effective communication Partnering with teachers	Short-term and long-term goal setting Reinforcement/celebrations for parent efforts Promoting parent self-praise and self-reflection Group practice exercises and live modeling Homework tasks and experiential learning Video modeling & vignette mediation Therapist relationship building Therapist use of humor/optimism Clarifying and explaining rationale for strategies Identifying behavior change principles Adapting for culture and goals Explaining behavior-change processes
Positive Emotions/ Relationship Building	Anger, stress and depression management strategies Importance of emotional self-regulation and positive focus Gaining empathy for child's perspective ("coming to terms") Self-care activities Solutions to emotional barriers Connections from past history to change in future goals Developing a support team	Benefits/barriers exercises Sharing and listening Respecting/accepting imperfection Demystifying/normalizing Reframing from child's point of view Reducing conflict Building support networks Refueling, empowering, and building self-efficacy Predicting success

SUMMARY: SUPPORT FOR THE THERAPIST

The therapist's conscious use of a variety of roles such as collaborator, empowerer, supporter, teacher, coach, interpreter, leader, and prophesier helps to change parents' cognitions, emotions, and behaviors, to alter their attributions about past and present behaviors, and most importantly to increase their perceived self-efficacy and their range of effective coping skills. In this sense, the therapist's role with parents is a model for exactly the kind of relationship we are encouraging parents to develop with their children; in both cases, a non-authoritarian, non-paternalistic relationship.

The therapist needs a support group and ongoing consultation and video feedback to be most effective.

Just as parents get tired of the hard work of parenting, the therapist may tire of the hard work of filling all these roles. The implementation of these roles with a group of parents, especially in the face of parent confrontations and resistance, can at times be a formidable task. Collaboration requires a considerable degree of clinical skill; more so than other models, such as that of lecturer, listener, or analyst. It is important that the therapist also have a support system in which s/he can show videos of her group, analyze a difficult situation or group problem with colleagues and plan the most effective treatment strategy. By discussing a parent's situation with other therapists, it is possible to brainstorm and problem-solve how to reframe it, interpret it, or explain it in a different way so it makes sense to the parent, as well as to decide which role the therapist should assume in this situation. The added support and objectivity of colleagues can help the therapist immensely, sustaining enthusiasm and the will to persist in the face of highly resistant families. See website for peer- and self-evaluation form that group leaders can use when reviewing DVDs with co-leaders and other colleagues.

www.incredibleyears.com/Resources/PP.asp

In sum, it is important for the therapist also to view herself in a coping model; capable of making mistakes with parents, learning from the mistakes, being realistic about treatment goals, not expecting magical solutions, and feeling refueled by each family's gradual successes. From the therapist's point of view, one important advantage of the collaborative group therapy model is that it creates a feeling of support for the therapist because of the joint ownership of solutions and outcomes. Besides reducing the dependency of families on the therapist, collaboration is reinforcing for the therapist in that it is gratifying to see parents coping independently and feeling confident. Lastly, the collaborative process constantly provides new learning for the therapist, keeping us challenged, stimulated, and growing in our professional lives.

Parents Undergoing Therapy: An Experience of Gaining Knowledge and Control

In Chapter Three we learned a great deal about what parents of children with conduct problems experience within their families and communities. What about their experience in therapy? Our quantitative research had shown that compared to waiting list controls, families in the IY parenting program showed significant decreases in parental anger, stress, and depressive symptoms immediately post treatment; only 20% of mothers and 10% of fathers still reported depression or stress in the abnormal range (i.e., about the 90th percentile). Moreover, home observations of parent-child interactions indicated a significant decrease in parental critical statements, an increase in coaching and praise statements, and a significant reduction in child conduct problems and over 70% of mothers and 75% of fathers perceived their children to be in the normal range as measured by the CBCL (Achenbach & Edelbrock, 1991). See Chapter Two for reviews of research, and the library on the IY website for individual articles.

www.incredibleyears.com/Library/default.asp

These results attest to the value of the intervention, in terms of parents' emotional states (anger, depression, stress) and behavior (criticisms, praise). But this is limited information about the impact of therapy, particularly about the therapeutic process. We wanted to know more than the statistical outcome of the intervention; we wanted to know what parents experienced during the intervention, the broad range of interwoven emotional, cognitive, and interpersonal effects not necessarily captured by our usual quantitative measures and not necessarily reflected in behavioral outcomes. In part, this need to know more about parents' subjective experiences of therapy was a matter of good practice; that is, we wanted to understand what difficulties parents experienced as they worked with the concepts presented in the program so that we might improve our intervention. But also, in light of what we presented in Chapter Three we wanted to know the extent to which their attempts to change their parenting thoughts, feelings and practices affected the family system and their relationships within and outside the family. And, knowing about the initial isolation, anger, guilt, despair, and helplessness experienced by these parents, we wanted to know from the parents' point of view how the process of undergoing our parenting intervention affected these feelings and perceptions. To put it a little differently, while the end-product of parent training has been well researched, the process has not; we know little about the actual process of change brought about by such programs. What happens when parents' behaviors, attitudes, thoughts, and practices are challenged and modified by a parent training program? What emotional, social, and cognitive changes accompany changes in parenting practices? What difficulties do parents undergo as they work with the concepts presented in the program? How do these changes affect the family system; that is, what kinds of impact does the program have on different family members and on their relationships and interactions?

This chapter attempts to shed some light on this unstudied area by presenting the results of a second qualitative research study (Spitzer, Webster-Stratton, & Hollinsworth, 1991) following parents as they participated in the 20-week IY parenting program. Through qualitative analysis of video-taped interviews and therapy sessions, we examined how the parents experienced therapy, how they reacted to the video-based parenting program, their questions and unique needs while participating in treatment, and what they felt was missing from the program. The scope of the data allowed us to describe the process of cognitive, social, and behavioral changes that parents underwent from the initial intake interview to the point where the program ended, approximately 1 year later.

PHASE I: ACKNOWLEDGING THE FAMILY'S PROBLEM

It is not easy for parents to admit that they have a child with behavior problems, a child who is different from other children. This difficult admission was the first phase in the process of change in parents' attitudes and feelings toward and interactions with their children. A major consequence of this admission, and perhaps the reason behind its difficulty, was that parents had to face their own conflicting attitudes and feelings concerning their child's problems. Some families began to acknowledge their child's problems during the initial intake. For other families this realization came more gradually during the first part of the therapy process. Four categories of acknowledging the problem were identified in the data: anger and fear of losing control, self-blame and depression, and isolation.

Anger and fear of losing control. During the intake appointments and initial therapy sessions, many parents talked about long months during which they waited for their child to get older and to mature with the expectation that things would become easier for them. When things did not improve with time, when instead their child became increasingly defiant and noncompliant, a terror at home and at school—they began to realize that their child was different from most other children.

> **Mother:** *I remember waiting for him to turn 3 in June, and just waiting for this magical thing to happen. It never did. It's been very, very difficult from the very beginning. We're on pins and needles.* (Intake interview)

As parents felt a growing sense of inadequacy about how to handle these misbehaviors, their frustration with their child mounted. Parents talked about how their frustration and anger as their children escalated when they tried to discipline their children without success.

Mother: *I say to myself, "I'm not going to put up with this s*** anymore." And I feel outraged, and it helps because I'm more willing to be the tough guy—but it leaves me a lot angrier.* (Intake interview)

Along with the angry thoughts and feelings about their child, parents also expressed their sense of being victimized by their children. This sense of being a victim further inflamed their anger. Throughout the program, parents would frequently ask, "Why me?"

Mother: *Why is my child so different from others? I feel I'm really in the minority, because of all the mothers I've talked to, and they have never been hit by their child. I can't imagine—I mean it's absolutely unimaginable not to be slapped or kicked by your child. Other mothers have never experienced this. I'm a very non-aggressive person. I can't tolerate loud, aggressive people and I just don't associate with them—and I'm living with one!* (Intake interview)

During therapy, parents began to reveal their angry feelings and were then able to discuss their fear of losing control of these feelings when trying to discipline their child.

Father: *It's intense—I think I've been able to control it and I start thinking I've got to control myself. You know, I can't! It's like something's boiling inside of me and it's pretty emotional, pretty scary.* (Session 6)

Mother: *I've never done it, but I've thought of it when I get really, really mad. I've thought of running and throwing him out the window. But that's just what my head thinks, I've never done that.* (Session 13)

Self-blame and depression. The parents' anger and loss of control caused them to blame themselves and to feel depressed about these feelings and about their interactions with their children. They tended to evaluate their parenting skills as poor and to see themselves as a causal factor in their child's problems.

> **Mother:** *I'm stuck here—it will never get any better, this child is going to be a delinquent, I know it. I'm going crazy and I need help.*

> **Mother:** *Maybe I should just give up because I'm going down in a sinking ship.* (Intake interview)

> **Mother:** *I tell myself it is more than I can cope with, you're a no-good mother, everything's out of control.* (Intake interview)

> **Mother:** *Sometimes it's just a real small thing that sets him off. And all I can do is either hold him or spank him. And if I spank him hard enough he will stop. I don't like pounding on him but don't know what else to do. But at the same time I feel like I'm a child abuser or something when I do this. Because sometimes I have blown it completely and really spanked him hard.*

Social isolation/stigma/rejection. Another common theme identified throughout various stages of the program was parents' sense of being stigmatized and isolated from other parents of similar-aged children.

> **Mother:** *I mean, other parents look at me like I just walked off another planet. So I feel very isolated. I feel like no one is like me—no one has my situation.* (Intake interview)

Parents felt a lack of connection with and support from parents of "normal" children.

The next excerpt is taken verbatim from one of the parent groups talking about what they think would happen if they told their friends what their children are really like.

> **First Father:** *You can't tell your friends how you feel about your child—you can't say, "My son is a bastard."*

First Mother: *There's always the fear that if you share with somebody what your child is like, somebody will assume it's your fault, and think you screwed up as a parent.*

Second Mother: *Or they'll reject you and say, "God, I don't want to hear about this!"*

Third Mother: *They may say, "Gosh, my child never does that"—which is such a put down!*

Second Father: *Here's another one I've heard. "Oh well, we all have problems." That's like saying, "Well, I'm sorry you're having problems, but it doesn't matter to me."*

First Father: *Yeah, it's the indifference that gets to me.*

Third Mother: *Well, that sort of comment implies you're supposed to keep a stiff upper lip.*

Third Father: *I didn't know it was this dangerous to have a child. I didn't know I had blanks when I went into this war.*

Fourth Father: *Well, you know it's hard for me to ask for support sometimes because I might feel like I'm imposing.*

Fourth Mother: *One thing I know is that if I tell someone about my problem—you know, talk about how bad my child is—I don't want them to think badly of her, so I'd rather not tell them.*

Parents of children with conduct problems felt isolated from other parents, not only because they felt they had not been effective in producing a "normal child," but also because they thought that if they were honest about their difficulties, they would experience rejection or indifference. Or, worse yet, they feared reprisals in terms of the impact this information could have on others' perceptions of and interactions with themselves or their child.

In addition to feeling isolated from friends and other parents, these parents also experienced rejection from teachers.

> **Mother:** *At 2 years of age he was terrorizing the other children at preschool and we were asked to leave the school with no notice. There I was, scrounging around to find something else and it's kind of been like that ever since.* (Intake interview)

> **Mother:** *I would hear all these horrible, horrible reports from the teachers who would say he's going to be in the office every other day when he's in kindergarten. The teacher is telling me now about what my child will be like 2 years from now and all the problems I'm going to have with him.* (Intake interview)

PHASE II: ALTERNATING DESPAIR AND HOPE

Reexamining the blame and guilt. As parents participated in the parent training program and learned new parenting strategies such as child-directed play and coaching skills, effective reinforcement, nonviolent discipline approaches and ways to problem solve, their guilt about their previous use of punitive approaches, their regret about their earlier lack of parenting knowledge, and their failure to use these new approaches more consistently with their children (unfortunately, new sources of guilt!) were recurring themes.

> **Mother:** *These sessions have helped me feel a whole lot better about having more control about what's going on. I guess my biggest problem is that I feel guilty when I am not doing the right things and when I am going back to my other habits. I know we're not handling those (behavior problems) right, especially when he starts piling a lot of them at once, I tend to lose it completely and just scream hysterically at him, and spank him, which I don't want to be doing.* (Session 6)

The focus of parents' attitudes gradually shifted from assigning blame to attempting to understand and manage the behavior problems.

The guilt arose, of course, from a desire to attribute blame. Initially, parents were preoccupied with identifying who should be blamed for the child's problems. While some externalized the child's problems and blamed the child's personality on an absent parent, teachers, or society in general, other parents internalized the child's problems and attributed them to their own personal inadequacies or lack of parenting skills. During treatment, as parents viewed the video vignette examples of other parents interacting in similar and different ways with children of different temperaments, and as they listened in group to other parents' accounts of their family's interactions, they began to reexamine the blame. Their guilt began to give way to a realization that children with difficult temperaments demand higher degrees of parental supervision. They began to reframe their parenting goal as successful socialization of the type of child they had been given. They began to understand and believe that children with conduct problems simply required different parenting skills. With this new mind-set, parents were able to think more constructively about their child, focusing on which parenting techniques would work best to bring out prosocial behaviors, emotional regulation, and personality strengths and which strategies would decrease aggression and noncompliance. Thus, the focus of the parents' attitudes gradually shifted from assigning blame for their child's problem (and feeling guilty) to attempting to understand and manage the behavior problems.

Finding "magic moon dust". While parents initially expressed guilt over their failure to control their child's misbehaviors, as they began to learn new parenting strategies they reported feelings of excitement, even exhilaration, over the prospect of improving their interactions with their children.

Mother: *He wouldn't go to bed quietly, and the sticker chart took care of that just like that (snapped fingers). The first day that I used the sticker chart and I started positively reinforcing him, his behavior* *changed so fast I could not believe it. I also felt the changes in myself and felt great about it.* (Session 4)

Father: *I have this weird feeling that after 3 weeks in this class, my son is instantly better. Through bad habits and exhaustion I was using too much power. So I backed off and we don't have the power struggles any more.* (Session 3)

Most parents, after completing the first four relationship-building programs (child-directed play, coaching, praise and tangible rewards), experienced a major shift in their feelings and perceptions of their children's behaviors. They began to notice and appreciate their child's positive behaviors and deemphasize the negative.

Mother: *By keeping track of praises I was able to be aware of all the positive things he does. It is so easy to get bent up and think, "He can't do anything right." All of a sudden you start listening to yourself saying, "You did a nice job there. Thank you!" Once I started to use more social coaching and be specific in my praises, I noticed how many areas he is really trying to do right. You start thinking, "He's capable. He's probably been doing this a lot longer than I was willing to listen or give him credit for."* (Session 6)

Parents did not comprehend the sheer amount of work that would be necessary to maintain these initial improvements.

Father: *Once it got into a more positive cycle and I had more patience because I wasn't getting all this negative stuff all the time, I found myself willing to put up with some shenanigans, not let him get away with it but also not go through the roof because I wasn't at the end of my rope after a day of many positives.* (Session 6)

On reflection, it became obvious to us that the parenting techniques that we were teaching were all too often perceived by parents as "magic moon dust" that could cure all their child's problems. The immediate relief that they experienced as their child made initial improvements led them to believe that their child's problems would be easily solved. Moreover, they sometimes seemed to believe that these changes in their children's behavior would alleviate other family problems. They anticipated a "total cure." In this phase, parents did not consider the possibility that their child's behavior might regress or that improvement might cease at some point. Moreover, parents did not comprehend the long-term commitment and the sheer amount of work that would be necessary to maintain these initial improvements.

PHASE III: TEMPERING THE DREAM

In the next phase, parents faced the fact that there are no magical solutions and realized that they would need to "temper the dream" by adjusting their hopes and expectations. Three categories were identified in the data as part of tempering the dream: "apparent setbacks," resistance, and "no quick fix."

Apparent setbacks. Soon after the parents started to apply what they were learning in the program, unexpected changes started to take place in the child's conduct problems, in the parents themselves, and in the family system. Some of these changes were in conflict with the parents' expectations for the program, resulting in anxiety and anger in some cases. Three common themes characterized these apparent setbacks: role reversal within sibling relationships, conflicted parenting, and child's regression despite parents' hard work.

Role Reversal. Role reversal was evident when parents reported that as the target child's behavior improved, the behavior of the sibling became more deviant.

> **Mother:** *Our younger child, who has always been the one that's hard to get ready for bed, is cooperative lately. Boom! He's the first one ready because he knows if there's extra time, I'll play Legos with him. Now the older child, who has always been easy to get into bed, is dragging his feet. Try dragging a chunky 8-year-old up the stairs to bed.* (Session 8)

As parents put new strategies into practice with the target child, they observed that the other children in the family began demanding the same degree of attention, thus further taxing these parents' already depleted resources and energy. Often, the other children's demands took the form of noncompliance and deviance, with the result that parents felt more discouraged because they had made headway on one child's conduct problems only to have them surge elsewhere.

Conflicting Parenting. Conflicting parenting occurred when one partner participated actively in the program while the other parent did not participate, was critical of the program, or was invested in maintaining the status quo. These differences in level of participation led to debate as to the best way to handle the child's misbehavior and conflicts with the couple's relationship. Thus, at this stage, the intervention seemed to some parents to increase marital stress. Conflicted parenting also operated in some cases in which a single parent had a former spouse, a boyfriend, or a grandparent involved in raising the child but not participating in the program.

> *Mother: Now, what's happening is he goes to his father's house for 1 or 2 nights a week and his father doesn't reinforce him at all. And I tried to explain to him the sticker charts are not to be used as punishment, and he just sort of says, "Yeah, yeah, yeah, I know this stuff."* (Session 8)

Regression. The third type of setback occurred when the child's behavior seemed to regress in spite of the parents' hard work. Parents, whose hopes had been raised by seemingly miraculous initial success, were particularly devastated when this success did not seem to last and children's improvements slowed or reversed.

> **Mother:** *In the last 2 weeks, we've had a 75-85% regression. Complete—well, almost complete—reversal to where she was before this class began. I'm not certain why. I was really sick; maybe that had something to do with it. All of the sudden, out of the blue, he's had some real bad episodes and last week it was every day. It's like we've never been in this class. And the time before that—up through Christmas—was wonderful. But on Saturday, I mean both of us had*

to hold him down to get him dressed, amidst screaming and kicking and spanking. (Session 9)

Mother: *I had some really good weeks, and was real impressed with Jessica and how she responded to everything, and then she had a couple of bad moments. It was a big surprise to me. Because I had gotten so used to her good behavior, and then she surprised me.* (Session 8)

Mother: *My daughter with bedtime: she's gotten real great as far as going to bed. Then all of a sudden she'll regress and we'll kind of forget about Time Out. And you think this problem is all gone and it's not coming back—and it comes back! (Session 13)*

Mother: *I really feel that I give a lot. I see myself giving a lot of praise, a lot of attention, a lot of the right things. I know a lot of the times that I'm doing the right things, but then I get so burned out. I feel like I'm doing so much that I know is good and I'm not getting enough back. Sometimes I get so burned out and totally worn out. I'm tired of doing all these right things. I'm just tired of parenting.* (Session 9)

These emotions arose from a perceived lack of congruence between the parent's hard work at implementing the program's strategies and the child's failure to improve—so much work, so little progress. In some cases, as shown in the next example, the parents felt the children actively resisted their efforts to change the family dynamics.

Mother: *This morning I told him, "Well, you just did a really great job on your homework, I'm just real pleased, you just got it done, and like now you don't have to run." And he goes, "Yeah, yeah, right mom, yeah, yeah, right." And I'm getting mad. Almost a sarcastic feedback, like well, I've heard it several times in the past couple of weeks. It's almost like he's hip to the fact that I am praising him, it's like he doesn't buy it.* (Session 6)

Father: *I feel like no matter what I do it backfires, and I'm not finding anything good to do here, and you feel punished for your efforts and ask, "Why me?"* (Session 16)

Resistance. In general, parents did not have realistic expectations concerning the demands the program would impose on them and on their family life. They wanted and expected the program to lighten their burden, to decrease the amount of effort involved in parenting a child with conduct problems; instead, it was putting more demands on them, adding to the burden they felt. This was only for the short term, of course, but understandably that was where their attention was focused. Along with anger at these setbacks, they expressed resistance when they discovered that favorable changes in their child's behavior could be brought about and maintained only to the extent that they were willing to continue investing time and energy in implementing the program; to some, this investment was excessive. Although most parents accepted the rationale of the program, during this phase many exhibited resistance to the level of effort required. Frequently, this resistance was manifested in parents' failure to complete the weekly homework assignment. When asked about the homework, parents would give excuses such as a lack of time to play with their child or to buy stickers, forgetting the assignment, too much stress at home and at work, procrastination, and difficulty being motivated.

Sometimes parents resisted homework assignments involving interactions with their children because they perceived their children as controlling. It was as though the parent did not want to do anything that would cede further control to the child. In cases in which the child was verbally abusive of the parent, parents were even less inclined to spend time with their child. There was no reinforcement for doing so.

> **Mother:** *I feel like I am being held hostage some of the times by the kids, with some of the things we've tried. When I was doing the play time, I began to feel abused in that I would always be the bad guy, and Laars would always be doing something to the bad guy. He loves this time, but he orders me around. He is using words, "Do what I tell you," "I am going to decide what we are gonna do today." "I hate you. You are stupid, Mommy, you are not nice." So far the videos said let the child lead the way, and he does not seem to want to do much more than have this real negative interaction. What it does to me is make me not want to do this playtime. For me there is no reward, no pleasure.*

The more I realize the right things to do, the more the wrong things loom huge to me. And I'm feeling really discouraged by that. (Session 5)

Parents gradually came to understand It was not a matter of a "flaw" in their child that could be "fixed" like a broken arm or faulty heart valve.

No quick fix. The combined effect of the setbacks and resistance was apparent in a deterioration of the "total cure" myth and a dissipation of the "magic moon dust" phase. Parents gradually came to understand that there was no quick fix or cure for their child's problems or for their family as a whole. It was not a matter of a "flaw" in their child that could be "fixed" like a broken arm or faulty heart valve.

Mother: *I think we've seen them improve but it'll vary. If things are going bad, they generally go bad all day. There are some days when nothing works and I can't say a single positive thing. But there are other days, and more of them when the kids are doing better. You can kind of tell when you wake him up. I'll go wake him up I'll rub his back a little bit, if he wakes up rolls over and hugs me, I know it's a good morning. And if he says, "Leave me alone," it's going to be tough.* (Session 13)

Parents realized that although their child's behavior would improve, as would their overall parent-child relationship, the child's temperament and associated problems were long-term. The chronic nature of the problems would continue to exact a heavy toll from parents, requiring them to monitor the child continuously. This acknowledgement of the duration of the child's problems constituted a change in parental perceptions, and it was necessary in order for them to make a long-term commitment both to the intervention and to the principles taught in the program.

Father: *I've had a couple of horrible weeks. I feel like I have to be "on" all the time. I think I have to be telling myself to just try and mellow out, and it's difficult.* (Session 8)

PHASE IV: "MAKING THE SHOE FIT"

In this phase of learning to cope more effectively with their children's problems, parents began a process of "making the shoe fit;" that is, tailoring the concepts and principles learned from the standardized video vignettes to their own family situations and parenting style. This phase was a critical determinant of parents' degree of success in implementing the program. Data indicated that failure to tailor the program resulted in diminished success because of parents' inappropriate expectations, either for themselves or for their children. Two categories of "making the shoe fit" were identified in the data: understanding parenting techniques and generalizing parenting techniques.

Understanding parenting techniques. The analysis indicated that, in general, parents acquired a good understanding of the rationale for the parenting principles and techniques presented in the video vignettes. However, some difficulties were apparent concerning their understanding how to implement specific approaches in a realistic and age-appropriate manner.

For example, reinforcement menus were developed by some parents with inappropriate expectations and without concern for the child's developmental stage or the frequency and type of misbehavior. More specifically, parents demonstrated difficulties around the timing of the reward (i.e., how long the child should wait before getting the reward), the type of behaviors to choose for reinforcement, and the cost for each behavior (e.g., 2 points = sharing, 5 points = extra reading time, 25 points = visit to the zoo).

Of even greater concern to some of these parents of children with conduct problems was the fact that some children began to use the reward system as a tool in their power struggle with their parents; as a result, parents felt the tangible reward system actually decreased their control. Children refused to do anything without a reward, or took control of the reward system by getting access to the stickers.

> **Mother:** *He's trying to tell me how to use the sticker chart. He'll say, 'Mom, I'm not going to listen to you unless you give me a sticker."*

> *He says this for things that aren't on the chart. I know I'm supposed to reward him for cooperating, so I sometimes give him the sticker. But now I worry that he's manipulating me. He's already earned $20 this week and that's more than I planned to spend.* (Session 6)

Another parenting technique that posed difficulties for many of these parents was reducing the number of commands and giving the child adequate opportunity to comply with a command. Having come to expect noncompliance, parents had compensated with frequent repetitions of their commands (chain commands). This had become a habit, almost a reflex, which they found difficult to stop.

> ***Father:*** *I am the kind of a person that is very directive. I direct my son in almost everything he does, and so I am having a hard time dropping down the number of commands.* (Session 7)

Issues of unrealistic expectations, failing to consider the child's developmental status or type of misbehavior, also arose with regard to implementation of Time Out. For example, some parents had a hard time finding an appropriate place for Time Out in their home and gave this as an excuse for not using Time Out with their children. Others overused Time Out for child misbehaviors that should have been ignored or for behaviors which were actually age-appropriate. Sometimes it was difficult for parents to know which parent strategy (Command, Time Out, Ignore, Consequences, Distraction) should be used in response to a particular misbehavior or in a new situation.

Generalizing parenting techniques. Data indicated that some parents, in the process of "making the shoe fit," had difficulties generalizing the particular parenting techniques shown in the video vignettes to other children, other problems, and other settings. They did not readily see how a given parenting strategy could be used with different behaviors across different age groups. For example, without help from the therapist, some parents could not take the concept of the ignore technique, which is demonstrated on the video vignette as a response to tantrums, and generalize its use to a response to whining and swearing.

Parents also expressed difficulties understanding how to use the techniques in different settings. They commonly struggled with the use of Time Out and ignoring in public settings, and with more than one child.

> **Mother:** *He usually is just fine, but it's the minute that you get him into a store. Like yesterday at the store, he was going up to people, poking his hand and stopping them from moving, or grabbing them like grabbing women's skirts from behind. And the hard thing in the store you can't take him out and put him in the car for Time Out.* (Session 10)

Interestingly parents had less difficulty generalizing the techniques when their training involved group discussions. Presumably, the parent group sharing and problem-solving provided a rich array of examples of parents applying the concepts in different situations, which helped enhance parents' ability to generalize the concepts—i.e., to learn the skills.

PHASE V: COPING EFFECTIVELY

In this last phase of treatment, parents began to exhibit effective cognitive and emotional coping strategies: They could express empathy for their children's problems, understand their children's developmental needs, experience their own vulnerability without feeling victimized, and laugh at their own responses. As they discovered that they could cope successfully with the daily hassles of having a child with conduct problems, they gained confidence in themselves and in their ability to cope with future problems. In this phase, parents expressed the conviction that they would survive their children's and their own relapses. Having framed their children's behavior problems in terms of temperament rather than malevolence or their own failure as parents, they became experts at managing and responding to their children's special needs, which allowed them to act as their children's advocates in the larger community. Four categories of coping effectively were identified in the data: coming to terms with the hard work, accepting and respecting their child and themselves, self-refueling, and feeling supported.

Parents came to terms with the reality that their children's problems are chronic, characterized by unpredictable relapses.

Coming to terms with the hard work of parenting. By this phase, parents had realized that they had "high maintenance," temperamentally difficult children with some developmental delays in social, emotional, or language development. They came to terms with the reality that their children's problems are chronic, characterized by the unpredictable relapses, constant vulnerabilities to changes in routine, and the emergence of new behavior problems whenever the children entered new settings such as school or new schedules. They faced the fact that these problems require parents to invest an exorbitant amount of time and energy into the hard work of constantly anticipating, monitoring, coaching, and problem solving, and this investment would be required of them for many years. During this phase, parents were able to manage their anger and grief related to their hoped-for "ideal" child, to accept their child's difficulties, to appreciate their strengths, and to invest themselves in committed parenting.

> **Mother:** *I'm continually watching at home: How can we avoid these problems? How can we avoid the activating event? How can I derail something before it explodes? Okay now, cool it down. They're getting excited. Let's break it up.* (Session 15)

> **Father:** *He still has these fits, but they are farther apart and less severe—not as violent as they used to be. He relapses, but they're still not like they used to be.* (Session 15)

Accepting and respecting their child and themselves. In this phase, parents indicated empathy, understanding and acceptance of their child's particular temperament and sensitivity to the child's developmental struggles. Part of gaining this empathy for the child was parents being able to see beyond their own frustration and anger, to understand the child's feelings and perspective.

> **Father:** *You know, something we haven't talked about specifically in this parenting class, although it is in everything you've talked about, is respecting children and their space in the world. You know they should be treated as equal human beings—it doesn't mean you don't set limits and all that stuff but it means you know that they're human beings and as deserving of respect as you are.* (Session 20)

Coping effectively meant that parents not only had come to understand and accept their child's temperament and difficulties, but also had to accept their own imperfections as parents. They no longer belittled and berated themselves for their anger and impatience, but saw their emotional responses as normal ones and understood their need to maintain personal self-control. In the next example, the father is able to stop his angry response, to see his daughter's viewpoint, and then to recognize her capacity to help him cope.

> **Father:** *I went into the bathroom to get Sara to finish brushing her teeth and there was a puddle of water on the floor and a roll of wet toilet paper and I was angry and ready to lose it and said, "This is it!" as I threw the toilet paper. You know what she said? "Dad, don't talk to me like that. You know you can scare me." Normally she would have cried, but now I think she was thinking of my point of view. I said, "You're right, and I'm sorry. I'm real tired and it's wet in here." I felt saved by her.* (Session 20)

Self-refueling. Along with becoming more knowledgeable and confident in their parenting skills and more accepting of and able to manage their own emotions, coping parents also realized the importance of caring for themselves as individuals and couples. As the blame, guilt, fear, and anger subsided and the child's behavior improved, parents were able to get babysitters so that they could spend time away from the children. Parents expressed the view that taking time for themselves and being with their partners was a "refueling" process that allowed them to gain a more positive perspective and to maintain the energy they needed for coping with their child's problems.

> **Mother:** *If I'm grading my kids for controlling their aggression and for compliance and good behavior, I need to ask myself, "How many times do I lose it?" "How am I doing in keeping my temper and my anger, and how well am I doing in re-routing my thinking when I'm short-circuiting?" I need to keep track of that and reward myself. Hey, it's okay to get an ice cream cone or treat yourself to a baby-sitter for an hour or buy a new blouse. Hey, it dawned on me that my behavior needs to be measured too, since that's what we're really all discussing, how we can change to effect change in our children. Well, I even mentioned that to the kids and David was really cute, and said, "Well, Mom, we can move our sticker charts over on the refrigerator and make room for you too."* (Session 13)

Gradually, parents also experienced some "refueling" through their children. As their efforts began to pay off, parents began to experience their children as reinforcing.

> **Mother:** *In the mornings, instead of rushing around and yelling at them to wake up because I had to go to work, I wake them both up by real gently giving them a back rub and they just love it. Now they come up to me and say, "Mom, we need positive strokes." About 2 weeks ago they came up when I was sitting and started rubbing my arm and said, "You need positive strokes, Mom." So they are reciprocating now, which I thought was real interesting.* (Session 14)

Parents no longer felt isolated and stigmatized because of their child's problems.

Getting support. During this phase, parents no longer felt isolated and stigmatized because of their child's problems and their own parenting, but rather had found support. The parents indicated that the parent group provided a safe place where they could be honest about their difficulties and allow themselves to be vulnerable. Often, to their surprise, they found that the other parents all had had similar experiences and felt similar emotions. Thus, the parent group provided a much-needed sense of connection with other parents.

Father: *Out of all the thousands of people you meet from day to day and you have dealings with them, I feel very fortunate to have this class and this group of people that has really enlightened and enriched my life. And, ah, it's going to make me a better person from knowing everyone here.* (Session 14)

Father: *Even when this program is finished, I will always think about this group in spirit.* (Session 24)

Mother: *Well, this class has really made such a huge difference in my life, you know to the point of, I would say, making it or breaking it. I don't know where the boys and I were headed. I was at the point of saying, "I can't deal with them" and telling my ex-husband, "You can have them." The class and the sharing—I'm just so thankful.* (Session 12)

Mother: *This group's all sharing—and it's people that aren't judging me, that are taking risks and saying, "Ellen, have you tried this? or considered you are off track?" You know we're all putting a lot into this and my feeling is the more we as individuals put into it, the more we get out of it. It's the turning point—every class has been building stronger and stronger. I know we're going to make it—I'm going to make it—the boys are going to make it. The three of us are going to live happily ever after—we're going to have our problems, but we'll be okay.* (Session 18)

SUMMARY: THE THERAPEUTIC CHANGE PROCESS

The process experienced by the parents who were enrolled in this video-based parent training program was one of gradually gaining knowledge and control to effectively cope with the stresses resulting from having a child with conduct problems. Initially, parents had to acknowledge that their child had behavior problems that they did not know how to handle. On their trajectory toward effective coping, parents went through considerable struggles and setbacks. Far from being a linear process, it

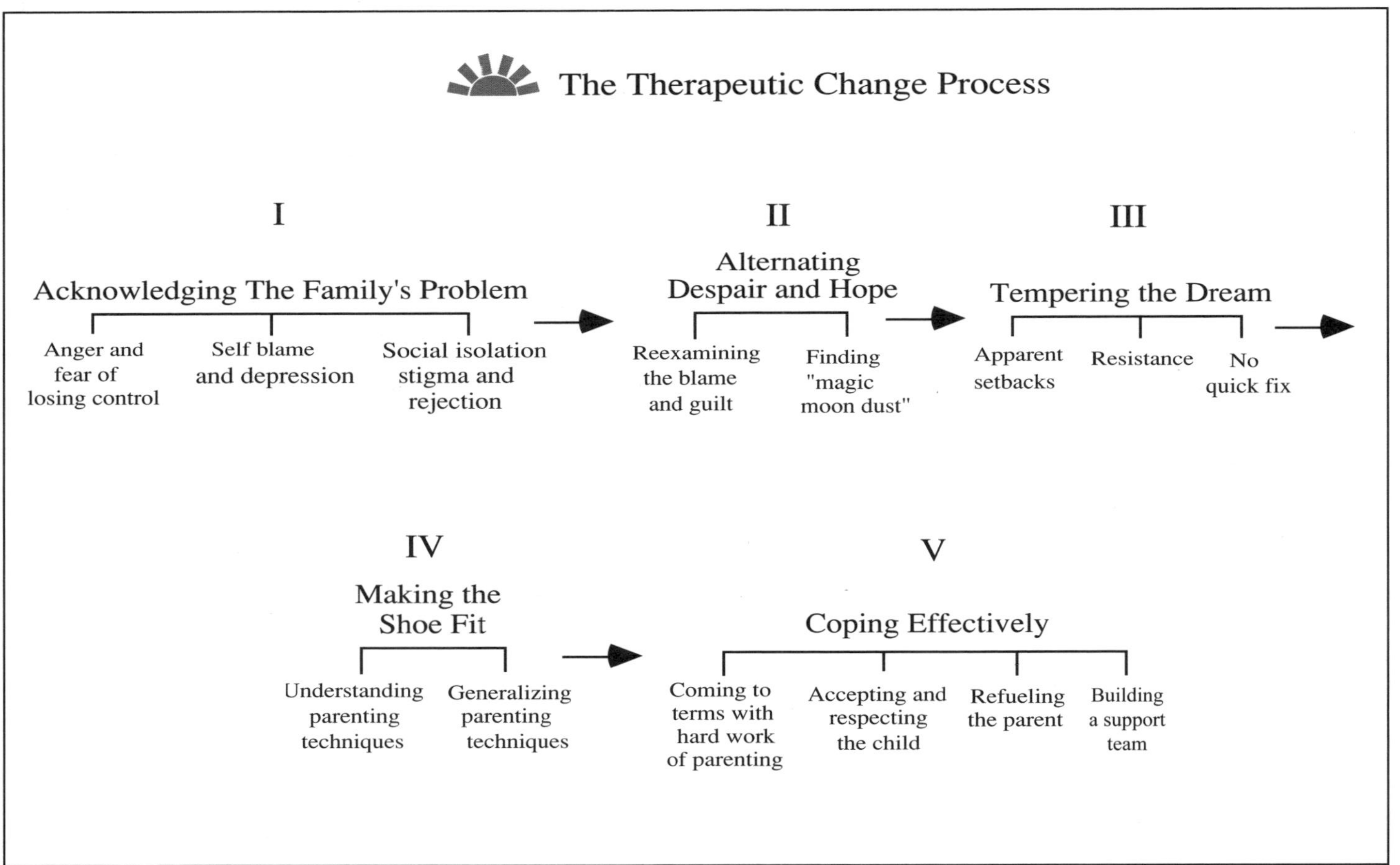
The Therapeutic Change Process
I
Acknowledging The Family's Problem
Anger and fear of losing control
Self blame and depression
Social isolation stigma and rejection
II
Alternating Despair and Hope
Reexamining the blame and guilt
Finding "magic moon dust"
III
Tempering the Dream
Apparent setbacks
Resistance
No quick fix
IV
Making the Shoe Fit
Understanding parenting techniques
Generalizing parenting techniques
V
Coping Effectively
Coming to terms with hard work of parenting
Accepting and respecting the child
Refueling the parent
Building a support team

involved many ups and downs, surges and reversals, and although the outcome was indeed positive, the same was not always true of the process at any given moment.

The process that parents undergo while in treatment involved radically different phases in the change process. See figure of the therapeutic change process next page. This understanding of the process is vital for clinicians delivering the intervention, for by anticipating these phases, clinicians can prepare themselves and the parents to deal with them. For example, clinicians can help temper their expectations, help them understand and cope with resistance, and provide them with strategies for countering their self-blame and discouraging thoughts when setbacks occur. Moreover, it is important to remember that from *within* the process, that is, from the standpoint of those who are undergoing therapy, a positive trajectory may not be evident. In fact, at many points, parents could see only that the behavior had not substantially changed and their own role was as difficult as ever. If anything, in light of the raised expectations that are the natural result of being in a treatment program, their situation seemed to them worse and they felt more discouraged at times.

These emotional and cognitive changes occurred in a certain sequence and were interwoven in complex ways, which suggests that they cannot be rushed.

I learned a great deal from the qualitative study about the particular emotional experiences and cognitive restructuring during treatment that are responsible for parents' new ability to cope by the end of the program. Experiencing new hope, having those hopes dashed by setbacks and regression, then experiencing anger at the child, at oneself, and at the therapists; experiencing empathy and support, moving from discouragement, even despair, to recommitment – these were key emotional steps in the process. Reframing the child's behavior problems as a matter of temperament and developmental phase; abandoning blame and guilt as a model and substituting the need for special parenting skills; incorporating the ideas of self-care and ongoing support as elements of one's own stability and well-being; arriving at a view of oneself as competent, though imperfect, rather than a victim or a failure – these are the cognitive shifts that are developed and discovered. In general, these emotional and cognitive changes occurred in a certain sequence and were interwoven in complex ways, which suggests that they cannot be rushed; for instance, parents were not ready to empathize with and respect their child until they had first gone through the "tempering the dream" phase; they were not motivated to generalize the techniques ("making the shoe fit") until they had first gone through the stages of unrealistic hopes and disillusionment.

In the last phase, parents expressed empathy with their child and acceptance of their child's problems. They affirmed their ongoing commitment to maintaining progress. While they still reverted to earlier phases and experienced some relapses and feelings of anger and self-blame from time to time, they had learned to expect these as normal reactions and as clues to the need for helping their child learn how to handle a problem. Once parents gained confidence in their knowledge and felt a sense of competence, they were able to cope more effectively by learning to utilize a support system and to "refuel" themselves. With greater personal resources and a sound support system, they reappraised the difficulties involved in having a child with conduct problems. This time, however, their positive reappraisal was the result not of unrealistic expectations, but of their own effective coping skills as parents and their recognition of conduct-problem children's long-term, ongoing needs for a social environment that acknowledges their ability to behave appropriately.

THREE-YEAR FOLLOW-UP: MOVING BEYOND THE INTERVENTION— "THE WORK CONTINUES"

I continued this work of understanding parents' experiences in the three years following completion of our parenting intervention. Quantitative data indicated sustained improvements in parenting behaviors and child behaviors (within normal limits) for two-thirds of the sample;

however, 25% of children were reported by their parents and teachers as continuing to have behavior problems that put them in the clinical range for aggressive behaviors. These numerical data did not help me understand what meaning these parents assigned to their own parenting efforts and their child's successes and failures. It did not tell me how families had coped with any child relapses that had occurred since completing the intervention, how they felt about their child's successes or problem behaviors and their progress in managing them, how they were coping with school-related difficulties. I wanted to know how they perceived their treatment experience in retrospect, and what it was like to end treatment. I was interested in the relationships within the family and the family's relationships with the community: Did the parents continue to experience a sense of isolation or stigma because of having a difficult child? Were the treatment efforts to teach cognitive restructuring and bring about emotional adjustment maintained?

Changed Relationships

"Cutting Loose". In our follow-up interviews, parents talked about their fears regarding the ending of the parent program three years earlier.

> **Mother:** *My immediate feeling was being cut loose. I felt very vulnerable. It was scary because it had been so wonderful to be with the other parents. Because that was the first time I had ever been around parents that had kids like mine. That was so reinforcing. I remember feeling terribly vulnerable when I left and being afraid that I wouldn't be able to continue. I wouldn't remember what to do. I was nervous. Over time I realized I had incorporated a lot of the basic stuff.*

Parents feared that once the program was over they would not be able to maintain their efforts or would not know what to do when a new behavior problem came up. Their feelings of vulnerability returned. They felt worried about relapses and were uncertain of their own skills. Parents who had not seen the dramatic changes in behavior that others had seen were worried that their child's behavior would not continue to improve without the help of the group sessions.

Mother: *I was afraid we couldn't maintain the changes without the support of the group and having to go in and report each week. I felt a sense of loss of the group because we had developed really good relationships and I knew that I would miss those people.*

The ending of the parenting groups represented a loss of support, not just from the therapists who had provided assistance in trouble-shooting behavior problems but also from the other parents who had provided so much moral support. How did these parents cope with the loss of support, the challenges posed by their children's behavior, the sense of vulnerability? The qualitative data gathered in these interviews revealed a number of common themes that fell into three categories: maintaining positive parenting attitudes and behavior, relationships with other parents, and parents' sense of self.

Maintaining Positive Parenting Attitudes and Behaviors

All the parents told stories of the successes and improvements that had been made in their children's social skills and emotional regulation over the subsequent years. In many cases, improvements were slow in coming.

Mother: *It took a long time for the principles in the program to really have an effect. The first year afterwards, things were still very hard—to travel, to go somewhere else, the level of aggression was still very high for her. It takes a long time to get results—like three years. Now you can see the results.*

Yet rather than feeling frustrated at the slow pace of change, these parents felt proud and confident of their own and their children's accomplishments. Their newfound pride has, it appears, two sources: First, they had learned to look for and celebrate the positive moments with their children.

Mother: *I have learned with these kids to take each moment by moment. I used to look at the day as a 24 hour unit—now I celebrate the wonderful moments with him when they come. And we have more wonderful moments all the time.*

Mother: *Someone gave me a journal, but I hate to write because I do so much of it at work. Instead I record the neat things that happen with my children and there are times I'll go and read it. For example, times when my kids are really insightful or funny or when they do something I feel good about, I record it. I've been doing that for three years now and it's wonderful.*

They noted the contrast between this perspective on their children and their perspective before treatment.

Mother: *I think what can happen is you could be so overwhelmed with the intensity of the difficult times that you don't see the good times. I know that was happening when I went to the Parenting Clinic.*

A second and more complex source of pride in their children's successes arose from their own newfound sensitivity to their children's temperament, emotional state, and developmental ability. The interviews reflected parents who had learned to read the cues in a situation and to decide what the optimal approach would be. To use a metaphor, over time they had become sensitive barometers to their children's reactions and had decided to adapt to the weather, rather than disregard the weather or act as though it were different.

Mother: *I don't make as many plans. I sort of wait and see how the day is going.*

Mother: *We really try to look at the right time for doing something. He's supposed to read to me every night but I can sense if it's not going to be successful and he needs to be doing something else. At one time I might have forced him—but now my motto is "seize the moment."*

Theme: Becoming a Strategist: Seeing the Big Picture

Related to their new determination and ability to adapt to their child's state-of-the-moment, these parents had maintained their grasp on the principles behind behavior management and had refined their sense of how to apply the skills within their family. In short, they had become "expert strategists."

> **Mother:** *It's the ability to first analyze, then internalize some of those parenting coping skills that make life easier.*

> **Mother:** *We're more skilled which helps a lot. I think skills with high maintenance kids are worth their weight in gold because it's still tough with skills. I can pull out things such as charts and I know ways of distancing the battle. Things are better in that respect.*

They were able to anticipate potential problems with their children and to head them off with preventive approaches; they had parental "radar" constantly on the alert. As one parent put it, they had become "constantly vigilant" so as to help their children stay out of trouble. They had learned how to structure each day so as to increase the likelihood that their children would behave positively and to decrease the potential for misbehavior.

This did not mean parents let their children do whatever they wanted, quite the contrary. Most parents found that they needed to structure their children's time, to establish clear expectations of what was expected, and provide clear descriptions of the consequences for not complying. Attending to their children's need for behavioral guidance required not only vigilance but also steadfastness and rigor.

> **Mother:** *He is such a volatile kid. I have found that I have to be incredibly structured. Everything is: " if you do this, then you can do this." You know, "when you follow the rules this week, then on Friday you get to rent a tape" which is a big reward for him. It's constant, "when you get your shoes on in the morning, then you can watch TV." It works. For example, to get him into bed at night I had to develop a set of structured steps and now he's incorporated them so it's not an issue.*

> **Mother:** *I have to be constantly vigilant, keep ahead of him because he acts before he thinks.*

Like the long-range planner, parents seemed to have developed a wide-angle view to be cognizant of the most effective parenting in accordance with a specific desired behavior, the larger goal, and the child's developmental ability.

> **Mother:** *I try to take more time for him now. My housekeeping suffers because I'm a single parent and I can't do everything. But in the big picture you know the messy house doesn't matter that much.*

This ability to be a strategist requires that parents see the big picture as well as be attuned to the moment-by-moment interactions. As one parent put it, she now had a blueprint for decision making that helped her feel in control, on track.

> **Mother:** *I can head off probably 80% of the problems with the parenting techniques I learned. I have a set of principles now that I work from—a blueprint.*

Coping with Relapses. All of the parents talked about times when their children had relapses in their behaviors. It was common for them to feel a sense of panic and even fear that all their prior efforts had been useless. Yet they described a variety of ways of coping with these relapses.

> **Mother:** *I remember this time my son got into this horrible cycle—worse than before we went to the Parenting Clinic. I was afraid all the gains we had made were lost—we were in a negative cycle and I was panicked. I was resentful because I had done so much for him like taking him to miniature golf and McDonald's and then when we got home he went crazy because there was something he didn't like. He was very destructive—throwing things everywhere because he couldn't get what he wanted. But then I realized he could only focus on the feeling of the moment. Later I also realized he had been good all day—that it was only one night.*

In this example the parent dealt with her reaction to her son's relapse by reflecting on his temperament and recognizing that he is an impulsive child who cannot focus on his earlier pleasure at the positive

Parents coped with relapses by reframing them as normal or natural and to be expected.

experiences with her. Once she reminded herself that her child can deal only with the feeling of the moment, in this instance anger, she was able to diffuse some of her feelings of anger towards him for his ungratefulness. Second, she placed the event in context and objectified the situation, realizing that for most of the day his behavior had been good. Many of the parents talked about their conscious cognitive work at deemphasizing the negative moments with their children and focusing on the positive times.

Third, parents coped with relapses by reframing them as normal or natural. By understanding that relapses were natural and to be expected, they were better able to prepare themselves to deal with them as well as to decrease their panic and fear. They also reframed the way they perceived these regressions by treating them as "learning experiences."

> **Mother:** *I remember that learning is a process of making mistakes and a little kid doesn't know everything you do as an adult—sometimes this is so obvious but when you live every day with a little character that's running around it is easy to forget.*

Yet another coping strategy was reframing the relapses as challenges that, with their newfound sense of competence as parents, they felt prepared to meet.

> **Mother:** *My life is more stressed now because of working full time and the step-kids moving in. But the way I feel about parenting is that I know what to do whereas before I'd be so frustrated and discouraged and think nothing would ever change.*

Having learned new skills and behavioral principles, they began to feel optimistic and competent with their parenting approaches, especially as they saw improvements in their children's behavior problems.

They felt confident that they had the skills to do what was necessary to help teach their child some new social behavior.

> **Mother:** *Now when he relapses I just assume there will be a way to problem solve it. And I have ideas instead of going around finding books everywhere. Like I'll go to the teacher and say, "okay we need to work out a plan" and I feel like it's manageable.*

Some parents turned to the Parenting Clinic for support when children relapsed. Paradoxically, this revived and strengthened their sense of competence, for they perceived it as a resource they knew how to utilize—one of their strategies for coping.

> **Mother:** *His behavior went downhill really fast when we separated. So I went to the Parenting Clinic as it felt like a place to go for resources and support and it's really worked. I've had to eat all my words about my fears—I guess we have more skills and my child has more skills now.*

Involvement in school activities was another skill that parents mentioned.

> **Mother:** *There is no doubt that my being active in PTFA helped our kid and you don't have to be working in the classroom, but if you're working outside the home it does behoove you to find a way to be active in school activities so that they recognize you're going to be there. I call up if he gets a demerit slip and his story isn't consistent with the writing on the slip. I call up and find out the teacher's perspective and I write a note. One time I wrote a note to principal that resulted in a meeting of the recess teachers. That in the long run supports my son and other kids. You need to know what is happening in school.*

Sometimes parents even talked about their own relapses and how they were able to get themselves back on the program.

> **Mother:** *My husband and I used to fight over how to handle our daughter. In the group we agreed on how to handle her behavior. I had to learn to stop interrupting and correcting my husband even if I disagreed. Well yesterday I didn't support him and he was really upset with me. So this goes deeper than parenting, more about loyalty and remembering to be supportive to the other.*

Other parents talked about how they had attempted to slow down the pace of life for themselves and build in restful times so that they are "refueled" and ready for the relapses when they happen.

> **Mother:** *I've been divorced for six years now and I used to think I had to be doing all these social things when I didn't have the kids. Now at least one night a week I come home, read the paper, do laundry and rest—I try to use that time so that when my kids are with me I have the energy for them and can give them attention.*
>
> *I wouldn't be able to be able to give them the attention they need if I didn't take time for myself. So that's one means of support for me.*

Relationships with Other Parents

Moving Forward: Building Networks and Finding Support. All of the parents we interviewed talked about the importance of their parent group and the tremendous support that the group had given them. Just knowing that other parents had children who were also challenging and difficult to manage helped to "normalize" their problems, to take away the stigma. Hearing those parents' week-by-week struggles with their children's behavior helped defuse their guilt, anger and frustration. Over the subsequent years, these memories of the other families in their group provided a kind of mental relationship that helped them to survive the tough moments of self-doubt and the isolation.

Because of this positive experience in the parent training group, all the parents we interviewed had attempted to get involved in or even set up other parent support groups in subsequent years. Several parents had become involved in Children and Adults with Attention-Deficit/Hyperactivity Disorder (CHADD); others had joined school parent organizations; one had started her own parent support group in her community;

another joined the adoptive parents support group; another had joined a Parents' Corps of Little League; several others continued to meet with parents from their group and to call them on the phone for support.

> **Mother:** *My husband talks about missing the group. More than me because I keep in touch with more people that give me feedback. But now that we are going to an ADD group that's nice for my husband.*

In general, parents seemed to derive the most support from other parents who openly acknowledged the difficulties of parenting and were nonjudgmental.

> **Mother:** *I've hooked up with other parents that have children like mine and it's been incredibly helpful. One friend of mine has kids just like mine and we have our club, "The Dark Side of Erma Bombeck" because you have to have humor in this. We have one rule that you can call any time. She and I have really gotten ourselves through this. And she's the one I talk to most often. But some other parents who have adopted kids, I talk to them too.*

In addition, many parents had kept up their connections with the therapists by periodically calling in about a concern. In some cases, this was only once or twice a year; for others it was more often. Regardless of the frequency of contact, knowing that the Parenting Clinic's support was available appeared to provide important psychological and emotional support.

> **Mother:** *I keep in touch with the therapist at the clinic by phone. So I'm not really feeling the loss. That's been positive. I feel like there's continuity and I still see it as a resource. I've stayed close to the people in the class.*

> **Mother:** *When I've been frustrated and not able to solve problems I call up the Parenting Clinic and I felt like there's this forever, underlying support there.*

Almost all the families requested follow-up sessions or a refresher course. They saw this supplementary training as a helpful way to trouble-shoot new issues as the children grew older.

> **Mother:** *I think for these types of kids and bumbling parents trying to deal with this it would be nice to have follow-ups or refresher classes. I think we hit the same issues as the children get older only at an upgraded level.*

Dealing with Isolation and Stigma. One of the few negative notes in these parents' accounts of the years since the intervention was the rejection they felt from parents of well-behaved children.

> **Mother:** *The hardest thing for me is the judgment of other people. I grew up being well-liked and now all these people are passing judgment on me as a bad person because of my kids' behavior.*

All had continued to experience the pain of other parents refusing to let their children play together. All still felt judged by other parents even though their children were behaving much better at home and at school.

> **Mother:** *Our neighbors won't let their kids play with my children because they think we're horrible people. One thing for me that has been particularly hard is the messages I've gotten from other parents at school, much more then neighbors and stuff. I mean the neighbors come over to my house and realize I'm an okay person that I'm not one of those dysfunctional single mothers. But at school those parents really don't want their children playing with my children.*

Even worse, these parents continued to experience alienation from their extended family members. They felt misunderstood and unsupported, which led to anger; at the same time, they felt embarrassed about their children's behaviors. These complex feelings led them to avoid contact with other family members.

Mother: *The messages I get today are that I am a bad parent because of the way my kids act. And I know deep down I'm not. But when you get these messages, I get them from my family, my extended family! I have given up going to family reunions because my kids are always the ones in trouble and it's not worth it. It's too hard.*

Their anger about their family's lack of support seemed to have lessened, however, as they realized it was a lack of understanding. They seemed to have moved beyond their anger, having learned not to position themselves in vulnerable situations and to look for their support elsewhere.

Mother: *I don't take my children to the office the way other parents do—it's too hard for me, but I still feel incredibly better about my parenting now.*

Mother: *I get no support from my family with this issue. They just don't get it. It's like if you haven't had cancer you don't know what it's really like. I'm convinced some of my closest friends think it's my fault —they could do better. I've wanted to say so many times, "You walk in my shoes and then make a judgment." I think the big thing is having friends who have kids like mine.*

Theme: Parents' Sense of Self

Maintaining and Building Self-Esteem. As they reflected on their experience in the parenting program, these parents talked about their experience as a kind of "crossroads" or watershed, a time when they moved on from feeling victimized and helpless to realizing that there were ways of coping more effectively with their child's problems.

Mother: *I look back on my experience with the Parenting Clinic as a crossroads. I have told people, "I shudder to think where we would be now without having gone through that." I felt such a profound sense of failure as a parent. I didn't know what to do. I was going to let him go and live with his dad forever. I couldn't handle it.*

> **Mother:** *In the beginning we didn't have the skills. And that isn't to say we aren't intelligent. We are both highly educated, hard-working people, it's just that we didn't have the skills and now we know how to use them.*

One of the themes from these interviews three years after treatment that was markedly different from our earlier interviews while the parents were still in the program was the parents' emphasis on conscious efforts to maintain and build their self-esteem. In the face of the feelings of blame and stigma from extended family and other parents, these parents had to work hard at reaffirming their own worth.

> **Mother:** *My friend and I who have children who are more challenging, we laugh at other parents who think they're such good parents when they're in fact the ones who have really easy kids. I think it's one of the biggest challenges when you have this kind of child, is to feel okay as a parent because you do not get those messages from other people. That's just the reality.*

For these mothers, a key strategy for maintaining a strong sense of self was periodically distancing themselves literally and figuratively from their child with conduct disorders.

> **Mother:** *I'm not a natural mother—so I needed help to learn the skills and it still is a lot of work. Getting some space and time for myself helps immensely. Talking to friends and getting away from the children helps me regroup.*

> **Mother:** *I think he needs other adults in his life besides me. I think he needs time away as much as I need time away.*

This theme is distinct from the "refueling" discussed earlier. Whereas the purpose of refueling was to renew one's resources as a parent (i.e., so as to be able to give more to the child), here the emphasis was on time apart as a means of maintaining and strengthening the parents' sense of identity as something other than a parent. These parents recognized the importance of having a strong sense of self apart from parenthood in order to function well as a parent.

> **Mother:** *I still feel ownership and get embarrassed by him. That's one place I'd like to work at. I need a little more separateness... Even though I know it isn't true, I still feel that if I was a better parent he would be better. I know that isn't true but my gut still says it is, so I wish I could have a little bit more gut distance from him so I could feel a little happier myself. If I got that distance I'd deal with him better and it would all work better, but I haven't been able to make that jump yet.*

> **Mother:** *I have to create my own reward system. I realized I have to establish an identity other than parenthood. I mean I very much identify myself as a single parent but I take great pride in my work. I go off with other women when I don't have the kids.*

This literal and figurative distancing, a form of establishing boundaries, allowed these mothers to de-personalize their child's behavior problems and to put them in a wider developmental context.

> **Mother:** *When he misbehaves, I am able to keep it in the context of a learning experience for him, a need for me to be consistent and to think. I ask myself, "What does this really mean? Is this something I should just let ride? How significant is it?" I don't blame myself now.*

Grieving, Accepting and Changing Expectations. Three years after treatment, while these children's behavior problems had improved (according to teacher and parent reports they were within normal range) on standardized measures, they were still very much a challenge to manage.

> **Mother:** *He's still volatile. He can escalate from zero to hundred in the snap of a finger and be that way for hours. He will throw furniture and take the room apart and totally wipe me out. Because I came from a mellow, laid-back family—and he's got a different temperament. He cannot wait one minute for dinner or anything.*

Parents still talked about what they had thought their parenting experiences would be like in comparison with the reality. As had been true in our earlier interviews, there was a sense of parents grieving over the hoped-for child, the harmonious home life, the easy road.

Mother: *You know you grow up thinking you are going to be a certain type of parent—and I had wonderful parents. Well you know I've had to learn that in our family we're not going to sit around the table and have wonderful discussions—they cannot sit still for more than five minutes.*

Mother: *Parenting is work. I wish it would be more fun and less work.*

Mother: *I still put a lot of time into parenting and probably a lot more than I have the energy for or a lot more than most people, but now I'm enjoying it a lot more, that's the difference. But it takes a lot of time.*

Mother: *I still want to be a sweet, nice mom—like Donna Reed. Why do I have to speak sharply– unless I go to him and say his name and get his attention he won't have heard me.*

With this acceptance of their child came greater acceptance of themselves as parents—self-respect and, at times, celebration of self.

As these examples reveal, grieving over the hoped-for child and hoped-for home life also implies the loss of a certain hoped-for sense of self as a parent. The child with conduct problems challenges a parent's sense of competence; these parents had to adjust their expectations of themselves as well as their child.

But balancing this theme of loss was a strong theme of acceptance. As mentioned earlier, parents had come to accept their children's temperament and therefore viewed their behavior differently.

Mother: *He used to be out of control all the time, almost daily with him, well now it happens maybe twice a year, or three times. Other*

> *people would come in and say he was totally outrageous, but I don't consider it totally outrageous. I have a different standard of what outrageous is than if I had my nieces and nephews as children.*

With this acceptance of their child came greater acceptance of themselves as parents – self-respect and, at times, celebration of self for having made the necessary accommodations.

> **Mother:** *I think I have had to do a lot of grieving about these children not being the kids I thought I would have. But I feel a bit better about me as a parent today. I don't feel great because, you know this culture measures parenting in terms of how your child behaves and my kids do not get high scores in that area. But it's so much better now.*

> **Mother:** *I have the handles I need to help him, but I think we're going to have a hard life along the road. I don't see it ever being easy. I don't think he is going to have an easy life. He just doesn't have the temperament to have an easy life. Yes, I wished for that and I still wish for that, and I wish there was a cure but I don't think there is. It is better now than it was.*

> **Mother:** *This indicates how far I've come. Last summer another woman and myself took eight kids camping and five of them were on Ritalin. That was so empowering for me. First of all, as women to be able to go camping. Second, that we were taking eight kids and five of them challenging kids and we did great. So I guess that's a real measure that I'm feeling a lot better about being a parent.*

In summary, our follow-up interviews indicated that generally parents are coping well, are maintaining their skills, and are feeling optimistic and in control of the situation. They had developed emotional and cognitive strategies to manage problem situations. Such coping strategies involved "seeing the big picture" and focusing on the long-range goals and overall positive improvements in the child rather than the moment-to-moment, specific negative behaviors; reading their children's behavioral cues and anticipating their reactions; reframing child behavior relapses as normal; organizing their daily routines so as to bring out the best in their child; building supportive parent networks; and promoting their own self-acceptance. This is in contrast to our interviews three years earlier, which were full of blame, loss of control, and helplessness. Parents no longer felt "under siege" by their children; they had taken charge. Nonetheless, the interviews indicated that children's behavior was still problematic, especially at school and that parents were having to devote a great deal of mental, physical and emotional energy providing an optimal environment for their temperamentally difficult children and in maintaining their self-esteem.

> **Mother:** *I hope that we one day can start operating from automatic and it doesn't take so much time and effort. I know parenting is always going to take a lot of effort but I wish it didn't have to be such focus. But I have an idea for what to do—that's probably a real important thing.*

Largely this work was being done without the support of extended family, parents of older children in their children's classrooms, or their teachers. This implies that the most powerful ways to help these parents is not to focus exclusively on child behavior improvements, but to focus as well on their ability to normalize their experience, to adjust their expectations, to self-refuel and to develop their support network.

SUMMARY

What have we learned from this qualitative study that we did not know from the quantitative research? We have seen the importance of understanding parents' subjective realities (e.g., feeling victimized or helpless) as well as understanding context (e.g., ripple effects involving teachers and community responses) in order to give enhanced meaning to parents' decisions and actions. First in Chapter Three, we grasped the gestalt of the child's conduct problems – namely, the child as tyrant, the sense of victimization experienced by parents, the isolation and stigmatization of the family. From this there emerged the theory of learned helplessness regarding parents with these children. Then we learned about the processes families experience during treatment as they gain knowledge and control, resist new ideas, cope with setbacks, experience a support network of parents, and arrive at a new view of themselves as competent. Here we found a conceptual framework of four phases that families will experience while engaged in treatment. Finally, we further refined this theory regarding parents' coping strategies as we learned how they maintain their sense of competence in face of relapses (in some cases, to pretreatment levels) and continuing stigmatization.

Parents need ongoing support and booster sessions to sustain their parenting efforts.

These findings enhance our understanding and also have important implications for treatment. They suggest the importance of treatment programs that enhance social support by involving fathers, partners, and teachers and that reduce stigmatization by creating new supportive networks of parents with similar children. Therapists can anticipate the phases that parents will be likely to experience during the parent training program, and prepare families for them. Finally, it seems apparent that broadening our interventions so that support to families extends beyond training parents in parenting skills; for example, by preparing families for what lies ahead with their children, by encouraging their effort to share the burden of responsibility through supportive groups and friendships, and by emphasizing aspects of the intervention that promote self-care, self-acceptance, and empowerment. Short-term efforts are clearly insufficient: We need to educate society at large in order to reduce the stigmatization and isolation that these families face in their day-to-day encounters.

> **Mother**: *The challenges keep changing and with different kids, but now I know ways to attack each one as it comes up. I don't think any more when old things come up again, "God! we failed or I thought we had taken care of that, it didn't work." I don't look at it that way, rather it's just going to be challenges all the way and we'll just keep applying what we have learned.*

The challenges certainly continue for them and for the therapeutic community.

A note: In a 10-15 year follow-up of 2/3 of these children post-treatment, results indicated that 75% were typically adjusted with minimal problems. Predictors of long-term outcomes were mother's post-treatment level of critical statements and father's use of praise. (Webster-Stratton et al., 2010).

PART THREE

Tailoring Incredible Years® Programs for Diverse Populations and Combining the IY Teacher and Child Programs

Affirming Diversity: Maintaining Program Fidelity while Achieving Cultural Sensitivity

Transporting Evidence-Based Programs to Diverse Cultures

The field of children's mental health is currently focused on the task of transporting evidence-based programs (EBPs) into "real world" settings with fidelity (Hoagwood, Burns, & Weisz, 2002; Schoenalkd & Hoagwood, 2001). Weisz and others (Weisz, Donenberg, Han, & Weiss, 1995) have reported that the effective implementation of EBPs in community settings will depend on such things as therapist adherence to the program content, methods, therapeutic processes and protocols as well as quality of therapist education, training, ongoing supervision and organizational support. At the same time, others have argued that the effectiveness of EBPs with increasingly culturally diverse populations have shown a mixed record of effectiveness (Reese, Vera, & Caldwell, 2006) and may be compromised because of a failure to address differing values, customs, child-rearing traditions and expectancies, language, and distinctive contextual stressors associated with different cultural groups (Weisz, Huey,

& Weersing, 1998) . These cultural factors may affect initial recruitment, ability to engage families in treatment, sporadic attendance, attrition, a reduced dose of the intervention, and ultimately, less effective outcomes (Haarachi, Catalano, & Hawkins, 1997; Weissberg, Kumpfer, & Seligman, 2003). Despite these warnings, response to treatment by ethnicity analysis is rarely reported in the literature. With families from minority groups representing approximately half of the clients served in community mental health settings (Center for Mental Health Services), there is a need to better understand how EBPs are being adapted to ensure cultural sensitivity and effectiveness with these populations.

While there are few logical objections to the importance of providing culturally sensitive EBPs that respect family values and traditions, there is a debate about how to accomplish this. There are those who advocate for adaptations to be made of each EBP for every cultural group. The caution regarding cultural adaptations is to guard against compromising the fidelity of the original EBP and thereby reducing the program's effectiveness. For example, core skill components of the EBPs have sometimes been left out and dosage reduced in order to accommodate adjunct culture-specific materials. Moreover, the proliferation of adapted variations of each EBP, for each clinical problem, every cultural group, or every country is costly and needs to be justified by superior clinical outcomes. The appeal of the more "generic," but *culturally sensitive*, EBP is that it is cost effective and allows for more flexibility in program delivery because it can be used with heterogeneous cultural groups rather than single culture groups. Multicultural groups can also foster greater understanding among parents of differing cultural backgrounds leading to more tolerant and respectful communities. The challenge of this approach is to train therapists to provide the EBP using culturally sensitive principles that are generalizeable across cultures.

Evidence-Based Parenting Programs

As we saw in Chapter Two, parent management training is one of the most well established EBPs for documenting effectiveness in promoting positive parenting skills and reducing child conduct problems (Brestan & Eyberg, 1998). There is, however, inconsistent evidence regarding the differential effects of EBPs with minority groups. Some researchers have suggested that minority parents have been less receptive to positive parenting strategies and have shown less improvement with discipline (Caughy, Miller, & Genevro, 2003) and in teacher-rated aggression (Conduct Problems Prevention Research Group, 2002). More often there have been concerns that it is more difficult to engage minority parents in the programs and that drop-out rates for minorities are higher than for Caucasians (Cunningham et al., 2000; Kazdin & Weisz, 2003). On the other hand, there is evidence that some EBPs have been effective with large, culturally diverse samples. For example, the effects of Parent-Child Interaction Therapy in reducing abusive parenting has been shown in Latinos and African Americans with no treatment by ethnicity interactions (Chaffin et al., 2004). The Incredible Years (IY) program has also shown effectiveness in several randomized control group trails (RCTs) in Head Start. For review of studies see (Webster-Stratton & Reid, 2010) with a number of different minority groups including Latino, African-American, and Asian-American populations (Gross et al., 2003; Reid, Webster-Stratton, & Beauchaine, 2001) as well as multicultural new immigrant populations (Kim, Choe, & Webster-Stratton, 2010; Lau, Fung, Ho, Liu, & Gudino, 2011; Reid et al., 2001).

It is noteworthy that in a RCT of 634 culturally diverse families with children enrolled in Head Start in the Seattle area (19% African American, 11% Latino, 12% Asian, 50% Caucasian), ethnicity analyses revealed few differences in intervention outcomes across ethnic groups according to observed parenting behavior at home. All groups made significant improvements in hypothesized directions. Consumer satisfaction indicated that all ethnic groups reported high levels of satisfaction with the program. Latino parents rated therapists more highly than Caucasian parents, and Asian families were more likely than the other groups to request future parent classes and had the highest levels of attendance. All minority groups had attendance similar or greater than the Caucasian group and rated the sessions on praise as the most helpful content area. In a second RCT where the IY program was offered in primary grade public schools (with 60% or more children receiving free lunch programs), culturally diverse families (52% minority), who had children exhibiting high rates of aggressive behavior were invited to participate in the IY parent program. Results again showed that mothers who received

The IY program is not a didactic, one-size-fits-all approach but rather is based on a collaborative model which respects cultural differences.

the program were significantly more positive in their parenting interactions than control families and their children had significantly less aggressive behavior (Reid, Webster-Stratton, & Hammond, 2007). In a third RCT with exclusively Korean families led by bilingual Korean group leaders, results showed that intervention mothers were significantly more positive and less harsh compared to control group mothers who relied more on authoritarian traditional discipline. Drop outs were minimal and consumer satisfaction was high (Kim, Cain, & Webster-Stratton, 2008; Kim et al., 2010). A fourth RCT was conducted with Chinese American families who referred from schools, community clinics or child protective services with concerns about parenting or child behavior problems. Retention and engagement was high and results revealed that treatment was efficacious in reducing negative discipline, increasing positive parenting and decreasing child externalizing and internalizing problems (Lau, 2011).

The Incredible Years program has also been evaluated with replicable results in other cultures and countries including Norway (Drugli & Larsson, 2006), United Kingdom (Scott, Spender, Doolan, Jacobs, & Aspland, 2001), Wales (Hutchings et al., 2007), New Zealand Maori population (Lees & Ronan, 2005) and American Indian communities (Dionne, Davis, Sheeber, & Madrigal, 2009). Several other randomized control group studies are ongoing in Holland, Portugal, Turkey, Portugal, and Russia. The program has been translated into Spanish, French, Norwegian, Danish, Dutch, Finnish, Russian, Turkish, Chinese, and Portuguese. These results provide support for the idea that rather than focusing on developing different interventions for every cultural group and country, it is possible to develop programs that are flexible enough to be used with diverse populations.

Incredible Years (IY) Program

Earlier chapters have outlined the content of the IY parent program (Chapters Four and Six) and the therapist/group leader methods and processes for the group-based program delivery (Chapters Eight and Nine).

As we have seen the program is not a didactic, one-size-fits-all approach but rather is based on a collaborative model including video modeling and self-reflective, experiential learning methods. Collaboration implies respect for each person's contributions, a non-blaming relationship built on trust and open communication, and self-management. Parents and children shown on the vignettes represent multiple cultural backgrounds. The leader's manuals provide recommended protocols for offering the baby, toddler, preschool, and school age parenting programs in 12 to 20, 2-hour sessions with groups of 10 to 14 parents. These protocols are considered the "minimum" number of core sessions, vignettes, and content to be covered in a particular basic parenting program in order to achieve results similar to those in the published literature. However, the length of the program, the number of vignettes shown, and the emphasis given to certain components of the programs are flexible and will be lengthened as needed according to the parents' cultural background experiences, education, knowledge of concepts, goals, and values.

Part of using the IY program model successfully is for the therapist to understand how to tailor the program according to each individual family's needs and each child's developmental, social, and emotional goals. Therapists (also called group leaders) can achieve flexible applications of the manual when there is understanding of the program on multiple levels, including the program model, content, methods, and clinical processes as well as the elements involved in tailoring the program to the individual needs of each family. Chapter Thirteen discusses how to tailor this program according to children's risk factors and developmental needs (Webster-Stratton, 2007). The purpose of this chapter is to describe the Incredible Years Parenting program "principles" that are built in to address attitudinal and cultural barriers to engagement and that are deeply embedded in the program delivery and the training of group leaders and interpreters. These principles promote and guide a culturally responsive structure for therapists delivering the program to diverse populations.

The length of the program, the number of vignettes shown, and the emphasis are flexible and will be lengthened according to group needs.

Becoming a therapist of multicultural groups is a dynamic process of learning more about families, their culture, their pespectives and experiences.

No therapist can claim to be aware of all the nuances of a culture that differs from his or her own, or be free of cultural biases. And, each therapist needs to examine his or her underlying prejudicial beliefs and attitudes and may need some training to do this effectively. Indeed, becoming a therapist or parent group leader of multicultural groups is an ongoing and dynamic process of learning more about families, their culture, and their perspectives and experiences. Affirming diversity means that cultural, linguistic, and other family differences are acknowledged, accepted, respected, and used as a basis for learning and teaching. Rather than ignoring diversity or viewing it as a burden, or even a barrier, it can be approached as integral to a successful learning process for parents. The following discussion provides a description of some of the principles that are considered important when therapists are working with multicultural parent groups.

A note: while this chapter focuses on cultural diversity, it is also important to recognize the heterogeneity that exists within any given culture. Even in a group that appears to be homogeneous in culture, parents will bring different experiences and beliefs. It is important that therapists strive to get to know each participant individually, rather than operating from preconceived notions based on their culture or family background. Thus, although the issues in this chapter are crucial for multicultural groups, they are also key strategies for working with any parenting group. In fact, each of the strategies illustrated in this chapter for working with culturally diverse families are core principles of the collaborative therapy process, and are part of the IY model for ALL parent groups. It is the goal of this chapter to show how these collaborative principles lend themselves to making the program culturally sensitive and effective with diverse families. Therapists who have read the earlier process Chapter Eight will recognize how the strategies from those chapters apply to cultural diversity.

Throughout this chapter excerpts are taken from transcripts of a training meeting between the program developer and interpreters representing parents from five different countries: Ethiopia (speaking Amharic, Arabic, Tigrinya, or Oromo), China, Vietnam, Somalia, and Mexico. These interpreters were first trained in the parenting program in order to prepare them for translating and coaching parents in upcoming IY parent groups and continued to have ongoing support from the group leaders as the groups continued.

Principle 1: Respecting and Affirming Cultural Differences

Therapist: *What concerns and goals do you think the new immigrant parents in this country have for their parenting? What help or support do you think they need to successfully navigate the American culture? What I'm asking you to do is to represent the point of view of the parents from your culture. We're going to brainstorm and write down our ideas to see how we can best support their parenting.*

Amharic/Tigrinya Translator: *These families think that because they are in America, they are free and their children are free, which means their children can do whatever they want. They are not comfortable with that idea because they feel powerless; especially fathers think children here have too much power.*

Arabic Interpreter: *Most of our parents come from very difficult circumstances. They've been deprived of freedom; so most of them are living their lives through their children. So there is no limit setting and love with no boundaries. They want to give their children everything.*

Education and orientation about being in groups. Many parents will have had little exposure to a parenting group before and will come to the first session with a variety of differing expectations for the group. Some parents may be expecting the traditional hierarchical teaching approach whereby the "professional" tells them what to do in a didactic fashion while they listen and remain passive. They may come from a culture where parents do not ask questions of professionals, who are viewed as authority figures and respected as such. In their culture they may not openly express disagreement with professionals, or they may believe that family matters are private and not to be shared outside the family. This will affect their willingness to share and participate in a group program. Other families may mistrust mental health programs or feel that participating in them is stigmatizing, or looked down upon by their community. On the other hand, some parents may come from a culture that tends to be more open and expressive and such parents may challenge group leaders to provide rationale and evidence for the approaches recommended. Nevertheless, none of the parents will know what to expect when they participate in their first IY parent group.

The therapist explains her own role as a supportive "coach" and facilitator of discussions and how s/he will share her knowledge and keep the group safe.

Therefore, the therapist will start the program by determining parents' goals and then providing an orientation to the IY program content and topic schedule (using the parenting pyramid) and give parents a chance to ask questions to determine if the program will address their needs. Therapists will also explain how and what parents will learn from the program and will encourage parents to ask questions and share ideas with each other, and to problem solve together as they watch video vignettes. The therapist explains the value of parents supporting and learning from each other and clarifies her own role as a supportive "coach" and facilitator of discussions and how s/he will share her knowledge regarding effective management principles and how to help their children be successful in school as they share with her their culture, values and goals. This program introduction is similar to that done with any IY parent group, but if this format seems uncomfortable or unfamiliar to parents in the group, the group leader will spend more time helping parents feel comfortable.

Group determining its own rules. Next, the group rules are negotiated and agreed upon. Group leaders carefully collaborate with each group about the particular group rules they want to adopt. Rules typically cover issues of confidentiality, right not to speak or to pass on a question, acceptance of all ideas and values, respect for others, and the opportunity for parents to ask any question that they want. For more details about setting the ground rules see the Group Process Chapter Eight.

The explanation by the leader of the group training process, the leader's role, and delineation of the rules is important because it helps parents who are reluctant to share to feel safe in the group and to take their time developing trust with other members. Indeed, there is evidence that non-Caucasian families rate programs that are short-term, somewhat structured, goal directed, and focused on the presenting problem and the future as more highly acceptable than long-term, unstructured, talk approaches focused on past experiences (Lee, 1988). There is also evidence that programs that are offered in non-stigmatizing locations, such as schools and churches, are more likely to attract multicultural groups than programs offered in mental health clinics (Cunningham, Bremner, & Boyle, 1995). Moreover, there is some suggestion that for cultures that emphasize cooperation and value the group above the individual, group approaches may be particularly suitable (Paster, 1986; Reese, Vera, & Hasbrouck, 2003).

Parents determining their own goals. Group leaders who have a multicultural perspective will be acknowledging, respecting, and affirming of cultural differences. This is accomplished through a collaborative process whereby group leaders learn about parents, their culture, values, child-rearing traditions, attitudes, and goals while at the same time parents also learn from group leaders about effective behavior management and principles of child development. One of the first ways group leaders start this collaboration with parents is by asking them what their goals are for their children and themselves. In the first session, parents share what they would like to accomplish in the parenting program. This information helps group leaders to understand family values and what role children play in their family. For example, do parents want their children to have a strong sense of respect and allegiance for their family, elders, community, and culture? Do they encourage their children to be obedient and dependent? Or, do they want their

Programs offered in non-stigmatizing locations, such as schools and churches, are more likely to attract multicultural groups.

children to be competitive and individualistic, even encourage them to challenge authority? Is it important that their children do well in school, and that they maintain their native language? How much value is placed on children being physically and verbally emotionally expressive? How important is nonverbal communication or open expression of feelings? How does socioeconomic disadvantage affect their ability to have time with their family? How is the extended family, such as grandmother involved in child rearing and discipline decisions? What role does the father play in parenting and discipline approaches?

> ***Arabic Interpreter:*** *It was interesting in our group last week to talk about the important rules in our different cultures. All of our four cultures in our group agreed that children's respect (politeness and no swearing) for the elders was an important rule and goal. The English-speaking American parents felt the same way. We were surprised. Everyone wanted their children to be obedient too.*

Certainly, parents' expectations and knowledge regarding children's development and behavior vary across cultures. Key attributes such as dependence, obedience, respect for authority, acquisition and expression of language, meaning of eye contact, self-control and social responsibility, and competitive or cooperative behaviors acquire different meanings in different cultures and in different families. However, it is also important to be careful not to make assumptions about entire cultures as if each culture produces a homogeneous set of values. Indeed, within each culture families come from a variety of backgrounds and parenting experiences which will affect their goals. By asking parents to share their goals in the first session, group leaders can begin to get a sense about what is important for individual families. Once this is understood, then group leaders can help them learn to use the parenting principles taught in the program to achieve their goals. In this way, generic content can be individualized to fit with specific experiences and backgrounds for group members, without the need for different curricula for different family backgrounds. Frequently this goal setting serves to begin parents' bonding with each other. As in the example above, parents are often surprised to find that their goals as very similar to those of other parents in the room.

Examples of Parent Goals:

- To decrease my child's disobedient behavior with authority figures
- To increase my child's respect for me
- To know how to help my child with homework
- To know how to talk to my child's teacher
- To learn how to encourage my child's social skills
- To meet other parents and make new friends
- To help my child be more respectful of his culture
- To manage my anger and hitting
- To know how to handle my child's angry outbursts
- To help my child be less fearful and separate from me more easily
- For my partner and I to be more consistent regarding parenting

Vietnamese Interpreter: *I want to say something about when a family is having difficulty disciplining children. It is also based on their experiences in their own countries. Each situation is different. There is one family in the group where the mother was a teacher in Vietnam, and the father an officer in the Vietnamese government. They are highly educated. So they understand that for children to be a success in life, you have to have support from parents. So when they come here and have children, they support their children. Both parents are working and the children go to school but they come home early and the father takes the children to the library. At dinner they are eating and talking about school, there is no TV.*

But another family I worked with was a broken family. The father was a farm boy in Vietnam, uneducated, and when he comes here—in his life, he only sees the importance of working: how to make money, how to bring food on the table, and he does not value education or children's success.

Therapist: *So you are saying the experiences they bring with them from their culture also determines their values. Within the same culture, the family values can be different. We should not assume the same values for everyone from a particular culture.*

Parents are encouraged to share family and cultural traditions.

Making culture visible and asking about cultural experiences. In addition to asking questions about parents' goals in the first session, throughout the program group leaders encourage parents to share their family and cultural traditions and experiences being parented as children. This approach shows respect for different cultures and parenting styles, and the sharing amongst the parents makes culture visible. Rather than culture being ignored and perhaps being perceived by parents as a source of shame or embarrassment, this interest on the part of group leaders will make sure it is a source of pride and empowerment.

Developing culturally relevant metaphors. The group leader can be more effective by using culturally relevant images and metaphors to explain developmental theories and concepts. Ideally these metaphors should be developed out of the themes that are unique to a particular community or cultural group and come from the parents themselves. For example the Incredible Years program provides an analogy called the "bank account" analogy. This analogy suggests to parents that they think of praising and playing with their children like building up their bank account with them. They must keep building their account by putting something positive in the bank all the time—so that they have something to draw on in the future when they might need to discipline. The point is made that discipline will not work unless there is a bank account of positive resources to draw from. One group leader who was working exclusively with American Indian tribes worked with the parents to develop an analogy that had more meaning for this population. Instead of a bank account she talked to the parents about the importance of planting the seeds of respect in their children. The idea was that these seeds would be watered daily with play, praise, and rewards so that they would grow. Then the analogy goes on to explain that once the tree has grown and is doing well, then it is important to trim and prune the tree. Watering alone is not sufficient for optimal development. The leader explains that pruning is the limit setting strategies like ignoring undesirable behavior, removing privileges, and Time Out. However, the leader cautions parents they want to be careful and not to do too much pruning or the tree will be whittled down to nothing (Dionne, personal communication, Spirit Project).

Another analogy that the IY program uses to describe the program components is the parenting pyramid. This is similar to the food pyramid where optimal physical growth comes from eating larger quantities at the bottom of the pyramid (grains and vegetables) and less from the top (fats and sweets). The base of the parenting pyramid shows the need to provide children with large doses of daily child-directed play, coaching, encouragement, joy, praise, and communication to encourage their social, emotional and language growth. The top of the parenting pyramid shows that discipline should come in much smaller quantities. A different analogy works more effectively for Native Americans. In this case the Incredible Years program is depicted as a Medicine Shield. The Medicine Shield is something the parents can use to protect their children. The outer circles hold the inner circles in place. Group leaders talk about how often people rush to the inner circles before strengthening the outer circles. If this happens, the inner circles will lose some of their medicine and become less effective. The outer circle is depicted as the parent-child relationship and the spirit of respect being strong in that relationship. In this circle there is play and spending time together. The next circle consists of honoring ceremonies and uses praise, rewards, and other incentives or celebrations to build good behavior. When these circles are strong then the relationship is peaceful between the parent and child and there is less need to use medicines from the inner circles. Still the first two circles are not enough. The center circles reflect limit setting designed to teach self-discipline.

Recently, when I was doing a consultation in New Zealand, we were talking about the Maori indigenous people. It was apparent that the bank account or pyramid analogies did not have as much meaning for them. We came up with the Maori basket of wisdom called a "kete." This basket traditionally was used for cooking—it would be filled with food and then lowered into hot mineral pools or a deep fire pit for cooking. There have been a lot of spiritual connections associated with the kete emanating from legends dating back to the first canoes arriving in New Zealand. There were four baskets of knowledge or wisdom, one spiritual wisdom, one with tikanga (customs and rituals of Maori way of doing things), and the other two were knowledge of ancestors and healing knowledge. We developed a metaphor where the parenting program was framed as filling their baskets with gifts of wisdom. When the parents completed the program their certificates were rolled up in small ketes. Moreover, when The Werry Centre, funded by the Ministry of Health, developed their brochure for the Maori population they aligned the tikanga Maori and IY core skills from the metaphor of weaving and harvesting all the parts of the flax (Harakeke) together. Both the Medicine Shield and the Basket of Wisdom or harvesting analogies are important because they connect to the spirituality and culture of the family and help them see a connection between what they are learning and their cultural beliefs.

Provide Modeling That Represents Diverse Cultures. "Surface structural cultural modifications" as defined by Resnicow, Solar, Braithwaite, Ahluwalia, & Butler (2000) include such things as cultural match between therapist and parents, translating video vignettes and written materials in the relevant languages, or showing vignettes of families that represent the same cultures of the families in the parent groups. Indeed, the importance of having group leaders who represent the culture of the parents they are working with cannot be underestimated, and there is a need to recruit parent group leaders who represent a variety of different cultural backgrounds. They can be powerful role models for the families they represent. However, this does not mean that only group leaders from the same cultural background can work with families from those cultures. Moreover, this is impractical since many parent groups are so culturally heterogeneous that it is not possible to have a group leader who represents every cultural group. What is required, however, is parent group leaders who are understanding, caring, and who affirm and respect each parent's culture.

Another way the Incredible Years program can bring in more cultural diversity and sensitivity is by showing parents video vignettes representing a variety of different cultures. Because group leaders have choices in the vignettes they can select from a particular DVD program component, they can choose vignettes representing the cultures of the parents participating in a particular group. Recently, the school age and preschool basic parenting programs were updated and a school readiness program was developed to provide more choice of video vignette examples including Vietnamese, Chinese, Ethiopian, Eritrean, Latino, African American, Japanese, and Caucasian parents and their children. Sometimes the parents on the DVDs speak in their own languages (with subtitles) and sometimes in English. Families are depicted during mealtimes, getting children ready for bed or getting them dressed for school in the morning, brushing teeth, doing homework, monitoring after school routines, reading with children, playing games, and going to the grocery store together. These vignettes can be selected by group leaders to provide more diverse models and examples of ways to interact successfully with children to promote their optimal social, emotional, and academic competence. When there are no video vignettes to represent the culture or language of a particular cultural group, the vignettes are still effective because parents are often surprised to find that parents of different cultures have similar concerns, questions and goals. The effect of showing culturally diverse models to all groups is that parents come to recognize the universality of parenting principles such as the importance of nurturing, communication, encouragement, respect, support, consistent rules, predictable rituals, balanced discipline, and supervision for optimal development in children, regardless of their culture. The group leaders can help translate the meaning of the vignettes to particular cultures by asking parents to demonstrate or role play how they would use that particular principle in their own unique way with their children.

Give Parents the Message That Linguistic Diversity is a Resource. There are multiple ways that group leaders can give parents the message that linguistic diversity is a valued resource. Here are some suggestions for group leaders:

- Start by learning to say parents' names correctly rather than changing them to English names.
- Check in with parents and interpreters to see if they understand the meaning of words such as ignoring, praising, and coaching or particular feeling words.
- Help parents practice using some of the newly learned coaching skills in their own language. This can be done by turning down

the volume on the video and asking parents to practice descriptive commenting, emotion or social coaching, or praising in their own languages.

- Help parents understand that the child-directed play homework can be just as effective or even more effective in their own languages and that it will not interfere in their children's learning to speak English; in fact, using native language in the home is not only an important means of maintaining culture and emotional attachment to family values, but has been proven crucial in children's development of literacy and preparation for school life.
- Avoid correcting parents' English.
- Ask parents to teach group leaders a few words or phrases from their own language; write them up on the flip chart; parents will be delighted that group leaders are showing a real interest in their language.
- Ask interpreters to translate notes from brainstorms and benefits exercises into their own language.
- Translate homework handouts, activities and key points into parents' languages.

Principle 2: Exploring, Understanding and Addressing Possible Cultural Barriers to Intervention Content—Key to Enhancing Parent Engagement

Even more important than surface level cultural adaptations are the "deeper structural" principles that guide the delivery of the program and ensure cultural sensitivity and relevance (Resnicow et al., 2000). Such principles include a group leader's cultural consciousness such his or her awareness of cultural history or amount of acculturation stress (e.g., first generation immigrant) experienced by families. Cultural consciousness also includes the group leader's sensitivity to cultural differences in child rearing, because there is wide variation in parenting practices and family values across cultural groups. This ability of the group leader to be collaborative and culturally responsive in the delivery of the program will make all the difference in terms of the parents' receptivity to new ideas and will promote greater program engagement and attendance. There are many possible cultural barriers to parents' understanding the content of what is presented in the parenting program. Noted below are a few examples of how we reframe the program content to adjust for cultural and attitudinal barriers and help parents see how a particular approach is potentially relevant for achieving their goals.

> **Chinese Interpreter:** *I see a problem that parents are so busy working 2-3 jobs that they don't have time for their kids. They think that bringing the money home is good enough for them. And they turn over their children to the school or to sources outside, friends or whoever, who can help their children learn. And sometimes if they don't speak the language they don't know what's going on in school because they can't read the papers sent home. Eventually they feel they lose control over their kids and their kids become interpreters for them. So they don't know what else to do and their children kind of slip out from their hands.*

Barriers to child-directed play. Child-directed play is the first concept discussed, and it seems foreign to many parents. In fact, parents from most minority groups frequently believe just the opposite—that their children need to be taught to be "parent directed," that is, to be obedient and respectful of them. They may believe that the way to achieve this obedience and respect from their children is by being very critical or physically punitive when their children are disobedient or disrespectful. Such parents will not respond positively to efforts on the part of group leaders to convince them that child-directed play encourages independence, creativity, self-confidence, or self-esteem. In fact, if they hold values emphasizing parental control and child obedience or respect, they will respond negatively to their child's bid for autonomy. Instead, group leaders will explore these feelings and attitudes and acknowledge them as important. They will remember the parents' goals for their children and show them how child-directed approaches can help them achieve their goals. For example group leaders will help them learn about the "modeling principle;" that is, what parents model with their children is what their children learn from them. Over time, leaders will help them understand that if they are too controlling or punitive, their children will become more disrespectful, however if they model respect, joy, and some compliance to their children's ideas, their children will become more respectful of them, more cooperative, and more fun to interact with. One of the most powerful motivators for parents taking the time out of very busy schedules to engage in daily child-directed play is realizing that when they do this they are helping their children become attached to them, their culture, and their family values. Within immigrant families, researchers have noted the adjustment difficulties as children acculturate more rapidly than their parents, resulting in attitudinal clashes, estrangement, and low family cohesion (Portes & Rumbaut, 2001). Once parents understand how this positive play time together can promote strong family relationships and cultural bonds, help their children retain their native language skills, and encourage their children's academic learning, they are committed participants taking the time to engage in this approach.

One of the barriers to play is that many parents were not played with as children by their parents and consequently are uncomfortable and uncertain about how to play. If this is the case, group leaders can set up fun play practice times for parents and children doing an art activity or playing with building blocks. During this practice the leaders coach and encourage parents for their efforts. As parents experience the joy and see their children's happy responses, this often provides the motivation for them to continue playing. Another activity is to ask parents to draw a favorite childhood place and include the activities they used to engage in there. Many parents end up drawing a stream, or tree, or small room and talk about how they used to "invent" their own entertainment as children. Group leaders help them realize this was imaginary play and prompt them to think about what it would have been like if their parents had participated. Parents who are helped to take the perspective of their children recognize that this is a positive and important relationship building time.

Amharic, Tigrinya Interpreter: *I can speak for myself. I was raised in a parent structured way. Parents are always right and children have to follow parents. Parents don't follow children. The idea in* *this program of following your child's lead in play was a big shift for me and for the families I was interpreting for. They didn't see it as a productive way of raising kids and at first they weren't comfortable with it. To be honest, I was worried they wouldn't come back. Knowing the families and knowing how I was raised, I didn't think they would understand it—I was nervous how the group would go. But that didn't happen—now they aren't perfect but they are conscious now, and they know they should follow their child's lead and understand why it is important. Most of the parents are now very, very comfortable with it and are telling me they are doing it at home and they feel that the play is changing something with their children. I was really surprised.*

Barriers to praise. A number of researchers have found substantial resistance to using praise for child compliance to parental instructions in a variety of cultural groups including African American families (Forehand & Kotchick, 2002) and Chinese families (Lieh-Mak, Lee, & Luk, 1984). Due to elements of shame culture, Chinese parents have found it difficult to praise because of the worry that if they praise, their children will feel they have done enough and will stop trying to do better. Parents from some cultures worry that if they praise their children, they will spoil them and their children won't work unless they get praise or a reward. Again therapists explore these attitudinal barriers and frame the strategies and goals in a culturally congruent manner. As noted in the interpreter discussion below, sometimes the problem with the concept is the use of the word "praise", which points to the importance of interpreters translating the underlying meaning of the words used rather than the literal translation. Sometimes therapists will ask parents to try an experiment to see what happens when they encourage and give attention to a particular behavior for a week. Once parents actually experience the change in their child's positive behavior, they no longer need convincing.

Chinese Interpreter: *One of the things someone from our group was talking about is they don't want to use the word praise. He said to him the word praise meant like praising God, and he wants to use the word encourage. So the leader tries to use the word encourage instead of praise.*

Spanish Interpreter: *There is also a distinction in Spanish between praising God and encouragement.*

Tigrinya Interpreter: *You cannot praise an individual—it is a religious type of word. Just use the word encouragement. So it is strange to talk about praising a child in our culture.*

Arabic Interpreter: *Traditionally praise is used to refer to God. Parents need to understand it is used to make a relationship with your child. You have to help them understand the concept—I explain to parents the difference.*

Barriers to ignoring. Many parents (from all cultures) find it difficult to ignore negative behavior especially in the presence of others. They are embarrassed by their children's inappropriate behavior and believe it is disrespectful to them. This disobedience can evoke stricter parental control and reliance on physical discipline. Parents find it difficult to understand why ignoring misbehavior can actually decrease a behavior rather than encourage it. As leaders help them understand how the attention principle works, they begin to see how their attention may be actually contributing to their children's misbehavior rather than decreasing it. They eventually learn how to use their attention contingently to encourage behaviors they want to see more of and to reduce the behaviors they want to see less of.

Understanding Cultural, Socioeconomic, and Other Barriers. Every Incredible Years group session protocol builds in methods to address attitudinal and cultural barriers to engagement. For example, for each new core component to be taught, the leader brainstorms possible benefits and barriers to using a particular parenting strategy. This exercise reveals reasons why parents might be resistant to using a particular parenting approach. For example, if parents think child-directed play will result in disrespectful or selfish children, then it is important for the leader to be aware of this so s/he can guide discussions and practices in ways that will illustrate how child-directed play can teach children to respect their parents. Often through the discussion of barriers, it is revealed that parents find a strategy difficult not necessarily because they do not understand its rationale or its importance but because their life is too stressful to be able to do it. Their priorities may be concerned with finding a job, or holding down two jobs to make ends meet, or working out how they will have enough money for their family's next meal. These basic life needs may overwhelm the goal of positive parenting or finding time to play with their children. In fact, this activity may seem very low on the list of their priorities. In economically disadvantaged families, often priorities are determined by meeting the most immediate basic need, such as getting food on the table, rather than thinking about long-term goals for their children and the implications and importance of building a positive relationship with their children. Parent group leaders must acknowledge these real and immediate life stressors and problem solve creative ways that parents can practice some of the new skills within their hectic life schedules. For instance, group leaders may help parents understand how they can do social coaching during bath times, meal times or when they are doing laundry, or incorporate some ideas when they pick their children up from school, or have some time off. Group leaders will make adjustments in home activities for parents to reflect these contextual factors that are disrupting their parenting skills.

In particular, the contextual stress associated with the challenges inherent in immigration, acculturation, and minority status need to be appreciated by group leaders and shared with other parents in their groups. Acculturation stress stems from problems including communication barriers, unfamiliar cultural norms, lack of extended family support, societal discrimination and change in social status, especially if their foreign training and education is devalued. Because stress disrupts parenting, these strains may lead to harsher, more controlling, or inconsistent parenting responses as well as difficulty in knowing how to advocate for their children's needs, particularly in schools. In a survey of 145 Chinese immigrant families (Lau, personal communication, October 5, 2007), cultural values were examined related to firm parental control, contextual stressors related to acculturation, and children's

Immigration, acculturation, and minority status need to be appreciated by group leaders and contextual stress shared with other parents.

problems in school. Lau's findings indicated children's school problems were associated with increased risk of physical discipline. Because in traditional Chinese culture, schooling is construed as the primary responsibility of parents, a child's success in school is perceived as an indicator of parental effectiveness defined as having strong values about the importance of parental control.

Even when we provide the program in the parents' own language and have parent handouts translated, another barrier exists for parents who are illiterate. Parents who have had little schooling or have had negative school experiences may find it difficult to relate to the program if it seems too "school like." They may feel embarrassed by their inability to read the chapters and a sense of failure if they do not do the homework. It is helpful to change the language of the group and talk about home practice rather than homework and to ask parents to let you know the way they learn best; either by practice, or viewing video vignettes, or discussion or reading or listening to books on tape.

> ***Vietnamese, Cambodian Interpreter (male):*** *Culturally, the mother is the one who takes care of the children. She has the responsibility to check on the children and what they are doing. But the father is going out to find work. He doesn't supervise the children because he believes his wife will take care of everything. So that is a big problem, because the father doesn't get involved with supervising the children's lives. He's working or away a lot, and he comes once in awhile and talks to them. But the father is not involved with the children much. He doesn't go to check on the school, what the children are doing, how the school is doing for the children, or what his children are learning at the school. He doesn't follow up. That is basically how it was in our country. But here it is different. Most of the fathers, even if they get involved, they have no control. And the father should be taught or in some way need to attend some classes to know what to do.*

> ***Somali Interpreter (female):*** *Yes, fathers need to participate more with the family's activity, especially for the children. The mother, she has to cook. She has to clean. She has to do the shopping. Everything*

is on her, and she cannot supervise the children. As you are saying, she doesn't have time. And there is the lack of male participation in the life of the children.

Arabic Interpreter: *Well, an additional problem that I see, too, for families that are trying to fit into this culture is that when families do start to make that shift into more Western ways, they don't get support from their own cultures. Women aren't supposed to work. The fathers aren't supposed to be in the kitchen and, you know, fathers aren't supposed to be sitting reading stories to their children. So when they do start to make that shift, not only is it all new to them, but they feel they are losing support or getting judged by the people in their cultural community.*

Therapist: *There's a sense that they're giving up or betraying some of their own cultural identity to do that?*

Arabic Interpreter: *Yes and some of the community support. I've heard some people say that, "When I have children, I'm just not going to have people from the community into my home because they're going to judge me. I'm doing things differently than we do back home. They'll be judging me as a parent and my children. So I just won't have anybody in, but it really isolates me."*

Helping Parents Think About the Possible Benefits of a Parenting Strategy. Before introducing any new parenting strategy such as child-directed play, coaching, praise, incentives, or limit setting, the group leaders brainstorm with parents about the possible benefits of a particular parenting strategy. These benefits are listed on a flip chart to refer to later. During this discussion, leaders ask questions about whether that particular skill (e.g., play, praise or ignoring) was part of their child rearing experience or culture. This is a helpful exercise because it reveals parents' values and prior understanding about the particular strategy before starting to present this approach. Once the leader understands whether this is a brand new concept or something parents are very familiar with, then s/he knows how much emphasis to give this concept and how to direct the discussions and questions.

Respond Flexibly and Lengthen Duration of Program. For many parents, these basic management principles are completely unfamiliar, foreign and, at first, difficult to grasp. When this is the case, it will take more time for leaders to present the program and for parents to understand, practice, and experience the results. Therefore, group leaders need to spend additional sessions on some topics, show more video examples than in the standard protocol, and provide many more opportunities for parents to practice and to receive feedback. In a recent focus group of a pilot study (Lau, 2007) of a Chinese translated version of Incredible Years Parent Program with monolingual first generation Chinese families, group leaders reported, *"monolingual first generation parents need more guidance, more support, and hands-on practice." In one group leader's words, "it's seems like we do not have sufficient time to walk them through the practice enough on those particular skills to be reinforced because we have to move on to the next topic."* Qualitative impressions from group leaders suggested that slower pacing and increased rehearsal of skills improved efficacy for immigrant families unfamiliar with basic parent management skills (Lau et al., 2011).

Do More Practice and Less Talking. Particularly for non-English speaking families, but also for families who find this material foreign, group leaders minimize the amount of talking, show more vignettes, and engage in a great deal of practice experiences. Whenever possible, after a vignette has been shown and discussed, leaders plan a short practice in families' native languages to model the new skill. Leaders use toys that families are used to and will have in their own homes, and show how the interaction is the same as the vignette regardless of whether it is Legos, pots and pans, sand and water, or empty cereal boxes and pasta that are the objects of play. Sometimes these video vignettes may be re-enacted by interpreters so that the parents have the opportunity to see the interactions modeled in their own language. Another strategy is to replay the video vignette with the volume turned off, and ask the parents to practice the coaching statements, encouragement, descriptive commenting, or emotion coaching in their own languages. Small break-out groups of 2 or 3 parents help every parent to get practice with the new skill and to receive positive feedback from the group leader and interpreters. When parents are practicing, the interpreters help by modeling the behavior and then by coaching and praising the efforts the parents make to try out the new ideas.

Principle 3: Helping Parents Apply Strategies to Their Goals

Parents are asked to make lists of child behaviors they want to see less of and behaviors they want to see more of. Group leaders help parents to understand how particular strategies can be used to achieve these goals. Role plays or practices are set up based on the child behaviors that parents have selected. At first some parents might find these practices intimidating, but after a few tries, most parents actually ask to do more of this because they realize how much it helps them learn. Parents can make choices about which strategies they are going to use for particular behaviors. Allowing parents flexibility in choosing targets of change in their own behavior and in their children's behavior is felt to decrease parental resistance to foreign concepts and increase acceptance.

Learning about Effective Discipline. Child rearing practices of some cultures are characterized by both indulgent affection and harsh punishment (Kapitanoff & Lutzker, 2000). Cultures vary in their styles of discipline, which may be short-term or long-term and may involve physical punishment, embarrassment or shame, withdrawal of love, or consequences such as loss of recreational activity or TV time. Discussion of physical punishment is a highly charged issue. Many parents (across cultures) have used spanking and hitting as their primary form of punishment. Research has shown that ethnic minority parents, less educated parents, and parents from lower socioeconomic circumstances tend to find spanking a more acceptable form of discipline than Time Out compared to middle-income and European-American parents (Corral-Verdugo, Frias-Armenta, Romero, & Munoz, 1995). There is some suggestion that strong discipline, including physical punishment is felt to be important by parents because it will help their children learn to follow the rules and avoid confrontation with possible hostile authorities (Willis, 1992). Therefore, confronting parents with the statement that spanking is not acceptable may cause them to be defensive or combative or to hide the fact they spank. Instead, a culturally responsive delivery of the discipline concepts involves a respectful exploration of parents' goals for discipline including what parents see as the benefits and barriers of spanking compared with other discipline approaches. (See Chapter Eight and Nine on group process for additional discussion.) Such a collaborative approach is a useful way to help parents work through their values and for group leaders to address any misconceptions. For example, parents may think that in order for discipline to work it must involve their children experiencing some physical pain and expressing remorse. Consequently they may think a strategy such as Time Out is too lenient, likely to result in "spoiled" children, and not punishing enough to make children realize the seriousness of their misbehavior, especially if the child does not cry or express sorrow. Group leaders remind parents of the modeling and attention learning principles and help them gain insight into how they may be inadvertently contributing to more aggression in their children if they are overly harsh. Group leaders help parents think through their long-term goals for their children and the kind of relationship they want with them versus their short-term goals. It is important that parents understand that the group leader agrees with their goal to have control over their children's behavior, or for their children not to challenge authority and will work with them to successfully achieve this goal. Because discipline is not a topic that is discussed until the 8th or 9th session, parents and group leaders will have established some trust in their relationship and by this time parents will also have worked hard to build up a positive relationship with their child and will have experienced the benefits of this approach. They are likely to be more open to trying a different approach to discipline, such as logical consequences and loss of privileges, especially if they understand how it will help them accomplish their goal.

Another topic that might be discussed is that despite the cultural acceptability of physical discipline, parents sometimes worry about using this strategy because they know that in some cases it might result in a Child Protective Services referral. Without an alternative to physical punishment, they feel powerless in knowing how to manage misbehavior. Open discussion about this and help with learning new and successful nonphysical discipline approaches can give them the power and control that is important to them in their relationship with their children. However, the group leader must be able to assess when the cultural norm of physical punishment becomes abusive and help parents find alternative and effective approaches.

Spanish Interpreter: *I also sense a lot of frustration about the culture of "no spanking" in America.*

Therapist: *Can you tell me a little more about that? What do you mean by "frustration"?*

Spanish Interpreter: *Well, a lot of the Hispanic parents were raised with the "if you spare the rod, you spoil the child" philosophy, and it worked for them. They're grown up now and they're fine.*

Therapist: *So the parents are feeling that they want to spank their children, but the American culture is not accepting of that?*

Spanish Interpreter: *Yes because they'll get reported to Child Protective Services (CPS).*

Therapist: *So this makes them feel powerless not only in the world but also with their children? So how do we give parents more power and confidence in their parenting? In fact, that might be our goal for the parenting program—how can we help mothers and fathers have more control over what's happening at home and feel confident about their approach particularly with regard to their parenting?*

Vietnamese, Cambodian Interpreter: *Yes, sometimes children learn if you want someone to protect you, call 911. But children don't understand that their parent can protect them more than anybody else. The police they come. They take a report, and then they take the child away and then there'll be more problems for their family. The children don't understand what the consequences are.*

Therapist: *How does that get translated into practice? Are parents afraid to tell you if they're spanking their children? Do they talk about it in parent groups? Or, are they afraid to talk about it because they worry they're going to be reported to CPS?*

Amharic/Arabic Interpreter: *That discussion actually did come up two or three weeks in a row in our parenting group this year. The parents were asking what the rules were for hitting and were looking for some kind of information. They argued a bit about how they felt they should have the right to spank, and how that was the best way to discipline the child. It was an interesting for us to talk about the rules in the U.S .versus their ideals. We would say, "That is one way to parent, but we would like to offer you another way." We kind of danced around the subject trying not to be judgmental, but yet still talking with them a lot. At least three of our four cultural groups talked about all sorts of physical punishment. But they don't know what to do instead of spanking or hitting.*

Helping Parents Think about Long-Term Goals. Group leaders help parents think about the long-term goals as well as the short-term goals for themselves and their children. For highly stressed and socio-economically disadvantaged families it can be hard to think beyond the immediate daily needs at times; however, when therapists help them understand what the advantages of some parenting approaches are for enhancing the future possibilities for their children, in terms of school success or strong attachment to their family and culture or ability to solve future problems by problem solving strategies, this can help parents try something new.

Spanish Interpreter: *Maybe just for clarity, and I think everyone's said this, but you can think of it like, "Balancing the faith to your own culture with the natural acculturation that happens."*

Therapist: *Now, that, I think, is a great goal that we take away from this discussion. These are sort of the difficulties or the barriers that the families face.*

Spanish Interpreter: *Well, that's the rub. Maybe that's the goal, but it's also the tension of how to balance those things, because acculturation is going to happen. But how do we balance that? How do our kids balance that? And how do we balance that when our kids are* *changing faster than we are? Because it's not just a language thing. The kids are also getting the culture at a much faster rate, and so you feel proud that they're getting the culture, while at the same time, that same pride you have scares you. Because it means it's going to take them away from you. And it's going to take them away from their grandparents who maybe are in their home country. And, you know, there's all these kind of tensions around that.*

Therapist: *Yes, kind of the worry that if you do this acculturation thing, what's that doing to your own cultural identity?*

Spanish Interpreters: *Yes, that's probably something that you wake up with every day.*

Principle 4: Work Collaboratively with Interpreters

Selecting Interpreters. If possible, it is ideal to have a trained group leader who speaks the same language as the parents in the group. This avoids the need for an interpreter and facilitates discussion. Unfortunately this often isn't possible, either because of the lack of availability of trained leaders from the relevant cultures, or because families in a group represent several different cultures and language groups. In these cases, groups will need to be run with interpreters. Partnering with carefully selected interpreters who are well-respected leaders from the same communities and cultural backgrounds as parents can provide another avenue of understanding between the group leaders and the families who do not speak the same language as the leaders. By collaborating closely with these interpreters, group leaders have further opportunities to learn more about a particular culture, values, and parenting beliefs. In preparation for leading groups, group leaders and interpreters can have thoughtful and sensitive discussions for how to translate particular parenting strategies across cultures, so that parents understand how the concepts are relevant for achieving their goals for their children. See focus group interview with interpreters on website (Webster-Stratton, 2006).

www.incredibleyears.com/Library/default.asp

Training Interpreters. Before working with the parent groups, interpreters themselves need comprehensive training to understand the key

Interpreters need comprehensive training to understand the key social learning principles underlying the parenting socialization process.

social learning principles (e.g., modeling or attention principles), relationship and child development principles underlying the parenting socialization concepts that underpin the Incredible Years program. Initially, interpreters themselves may find the parenting concepts to be foreign from their own experiences and may be unsure of the translations for particular concepts and words and the value of the skills for their families. Therefore, it is important to take the time to explore these issues with interpreters before starting the group, so that interpreters will be confident and convincing in their translations to parents. For example, in a training workshop I was giving for interpreters from some East African countries, we got stuck on the definition of the word "praise." It was not until I understood that praise was the word reserved for praising God that we were able to select another word (encouragement) for use in describing the importance of parents giving positive feedback to children. In order to help interpreters understand the behavior management concepts underpinning the program, they are encouraged to participate "as a parent" in a parent group first and then practice the strategies they have learned with their own children or with children in a preschool setting. The interpreters' role is not only to translate words, but to help bridge the gap between the different cultures so that parents understand the meaning of the concepts and relevance for their families.

Using Interpreters as Coaches. Interpreters who have had practical experience with the program material (participating in a prior parenting group and practicing the strategies with their own children) will be better able to model and coach the parents. They will also be able to share their own initial barriers to using particular strategies as well as their successes. In many ways, the interpreters also act as coaches for parents providing encouragement, support, and feedback to parents as needed. It is important that interpreters be trained in the collaborative methods of working with parents and the principles of building a positive relationship with them. Helping interpreters understand how to praise parents' efforts and develop a supportive and understanding relationship with them will be key to their success at coaching parents during the group practices as well as their effectiveness at making the weekly calls home. A note of caution is if the interpreter lives in the same community as the parents, it will be important to review the rules of confidentiality and for interpreters to reassure parents they will not divulge parents' personal issues outside the group.

> ***Tigrinya Interpreter:*** *I couldn't believe how the child-directed play idea worked with my child. My 5-year-old comes from school and he has to read a book every day. He didn't want to read with me. He said he wasn't going to read. I said "Okay. Let's do activities instead. Okay the activity is to find 5 fish on the page, and we'll take turns." We did that for hours, and he enjoyed that. And I knew I was promoting his reading skills and enjoyment of books.*

Interpreting the Meaning of the Vignettes. The interpreters are especially helpful in interpreting the meaning of the video vignettes. Even though the video vignettes may not be translated into the language of the parents, the behaviors shown on the tapes are still useful learning because they demonstrate and model the skills being taught such as parents playing and talking with children. The interpreters can use the vignettes to trigger a discussion of what behaviors they saw on the video vignette and help attribute meaning to particular parenting skills demonstrated. Interpreters should be provided with the opportunity to watch each vignette in training workshops before they are shown and translated for parents in the group. Many interpreters find it helpful to use the scripts that are available for each vignette so that they can give their families a brief summary of the content of the vignette just prior to it being shown in the group. After a vignette is shown, the interpreter checks with the families to ensure that they understood the content of the vignette. After this has happened, then the group is ready to process the vignette and its implications for how the parents might interact with their children.

Many interpreters find it helpful to use the scripts that are available for each vignette.

Interpreter Roles

- Provide accurate translations of everything said by all parents and group leaders
- Help parents understand the meaning of concepts in objective and unbiased ways
- Represent the parents' point of view for the group leader and to other parents
- Help leader understand when something isn't understood by a parent and there is need for further clarification
- Help leader understand cultural differences and their relevance for the topic being discussed
- Help parents understand how the IY principles are aligned with their cultural values and goals
- Signal group leader to stop frequently for translation
- Coach and reinforce parents for their efforts in small group practices
- Review video vignettes prior to each group and help parents to process content
- Make buddy calls during the week and encourage parents to do home activities
- Review home activities with parents each week; provide written translations as needed
- Help parents participate in weekly evaluations of sessions and what their learning style is

Interpreter Feedback. As the groups continue, the interpreters meet weekly with group leaders to review content, to give feedback to group leaders on parents' progress, to ask questions about how to respond to particular parent concerns and to plan for subsequent sessions.

> ***Spanish Interpreter:*** *Our group is going great. We have 10 regular participants and attendance has been very regular. People have really engaged I think. We have 2 interpreters for different languages, and we have 2 English speaking people without interpreters, and they add a lot to the group. Our group is feeling very comfortable now. They are really doing the work. You can tell*

> *from their questions that they are really trying it. Real barriers are coming up. For example, one asked, "What happens when my child doesn't want me to do descriptive commenting?" That is really good because they are doing work. They are comfortable bringing up the issues. There is a balance of participation to include everyone to share their ideas. People who are getting interpretations are often a few seconds behind. We have adjusted to wait for them. Then we balance so that the English speaking people are engaged and involved. We try hard to make sure everyone has an opportunity to participate.*

Communicating through Interpreters. As noted above, there are times when the interpreters will be working directly with the parents who speak their languages. For example, three parents who speak Vietnamese may break into a small group to do a practice entirely in Vietnamese, while other groups practice the same skills in other languages. Or, an interpreter may spend 2 minutes orienting her parents to a vignette before the group leader turns it on. At these times, it is not necessary for the interpreter to translate every word that is said, particularly if the translator has been trained and understands the content well.

However, during large group discussions, it is very important that all parent and leader comments are translated. Group leaders will need to learn to pace their presentation of material so that there are pauses for translation. Interpreters should also take responsibility for this, signaling the group leader when a pause is needed. Rather than summarizing for parents, for example, "he did his play homework last week and it went well," the interpreter should speak in the parent's voice, for example, "I played with my child two times last week. She loved the time with me and I was surprised that it went so well." Group leaders should remember to look directly at parents as they are talking, rather than at the interpreter. Remember that complete translation will also allow parents in the group to get to know each other. This kind of word-by-word translation will add time to the group, often doubling the time that it will take to get through the program. However, the added benefits in terms of relationship building between therapists, parents, and the interpreters are invaluable.

Principle 5: Promoting a Supportive Group and Empowering Parents

Building informal and sustainable support networks. Cooperative and collaborative learning in groups results in cross-cultural understanding and eventual friendships. This also leads to parents developing multicultural support systems within their schools and communities. Through the group discussions, parents not only learn about each other's cultural differences, but also discover that they have many issues in common. It can be very empowering for parents to realize that they are not alone in their worries about how to approach a teacher about their child's problem, or unsure how to help with homework, or unable to read the school newsletters. These group discussions will normalize their experiences and empower them to find some ways to approach the problem and will decrease their sense of isolation.

Another way in which group support and positive relationships are nurtured is by pairing up parent buddies in the group who make phone calls each week to share the experiences they have had using some of the strategies they have been learning. Sometimes these buddies may be paired up by language or culture groups. These buddy calls are important in terms of building the support systems within the group and helping parents to experience the value of parental support.

Often ignored is the role of extended family and support systems in maintaining nurturing parenting. In fact, in some cultures child rearing is often done by extended family members who may be the primary disciplinarians (Sutton & Broken Nose, 1996). Therefore, cooperation between family members is important. In our program, partners and family members involved in the children's child rearing are invited to the parent groups. Studies have shown that the presence of a partner or grandparents at parent groups has been found to increase support for married as well as single parents, to result in more lasting effects for children's behavior over time (Webster-Stratton, 1985) and to play an important role in preventing abuse (Lutzker, 1992).

Empowering Parents' Insights and Reframing Their Understanding of Their Child's Developmental Needs. As discussed in Chapter Eight, group leaders draw important parenting principles from the parents' discussions of the vignettes. For example, if a parent observes on the video vignette that the parent's controlling style seemed to stifle the child's concentration or persistence with his homework, then the parent would be given credit for the principle. The leader would summarize, "*Sophie's principle is that encouragement rather than excessive control leads children to be more motivated to do their homework and stick with a difficult task.*" This principle is written down on a flip chart next to the parent's name. The interpreters can translate these on paper for parents who do not speak English. Each week a typed list of the parents' principles is given out to the parents. For parents who do not read, the interpreters can refer to the list each week to verbally review the prior week's key principles, using the parent's name for the principle as the group leader does. The purpose of this approach is to empower parents' insights and give them ownership of the principles they discover. Throughout the discussions, leaders help parents to understand children's developmental tasks such as achieving language skills, drive for exploration and curiosity, developing emotional self-regulation skills to replace aggression, and making friendships. Parents come to see their child's point of view and therapists reframe the parents' negative cognitions triggered by children's misbehavior, which may lead to harsh responses. For example, a child's bid for autonomy or independence may be explained as a key skill for children's eventual success in school, something that could be encouraged.

Each week a typed list of the parents' principles is given out to the parents.

Arabic Interpreter: *Yes. There is a family I'm working with and the dad is bombarding his child. He is sending his child to Koran School six to seven hours every day. He says that he expects his child to be a real Muslim. To do that you have to learn your verses—all of the verses. The boy is not even five years old. He will resent his dad because he's going to see other kids going around having a lot of fun, while he's the one sitting inside learning the verses. The father is kind of unrealistic.*

Therapist: *Perhaps he doesn't understand what is developmentally appropriate for children this age.*

Arabic Interpreter: *Exactly. Like putting your child in a bucket of water and expect that child not to wade.*

Reviewing Weekly Session Evaluations and Making Adjustments According to Learning Styles and Parents' Personal Goals. Culturally relevant practice involves collaborative planning with parents to meet their goals and regular program evaluations to ask parents how they are doing achieving their goals and whether they are experiencing success. After every weekly group session parents complete a session evaluation that asks them to rate their satisfaction with program content, methods, group leadership skills, relevance of video vignettes, and quality of group discussions. Interpreters and group leaders use these evaluations to explore parents' experiences with the learning process. For example, do parents want to view more or fewer vignettes, engage in more discussion or practices, or would they prefer audio CDs of the book rather than written materials? Do they feel the program is being rushed or not long enough? How difficult are they finding the home activities or buddy calls? Group leaders acknowledge that each parent's learning style is different and will be respected. Asking for feedback on the methods that are working well for them (or less well) periodically can help group leaders to make adjustments so that the methods and processes work for everyone. This respect on the part of the group leader for different learning styles is important modeling for the parents and builds group tolerance for accepting differences in learning styles; an approach we hope they will also use with their own children.

Part of the parent program involves asking parents to do some home activities that may include reading a chapter from the IY parent book, or recording their observations of their play interactions, or determining their house rules and routines. Because some of these assignments require reading or writing ability they may be difficult for some parents. Group leaders can offer the option of listening to the chapters on CD for English and Spanish speaking parents rather than reading them and can tailor the other activities so that they are meaningful to every parent. One of the ways that this individual adjustment is done is by asking parents to complete a self-monitoring checklist each week. On this checklist parents determine their own goals for their home activities for that week: be it the reading, observations, or playtime with their children. Thus, parents are making choices regarding what learning approach they believe is most useful and most realistic for them. In the subsequent session, group leaders check to see if they have achieved their personal goals and if not, explore the barriers to achieving them. This process is respectful to different learning styles and acknowledges parents' self-determination regarding what is the best learning method for them.

> ***Therapist:*** *Do you remember in our first meeting we discussed the goal of helping parents to have an alternative to spanking or hitting children? Do you think you were successful with that?*
>
> ***Amharic Interpreter:*** *In our country the discipline we learned was different—harsher, more hitting. I really think the parents and myself as well learned a better way that was more beneficial. They learned to ignore, to take away privileges and to teach them other behaviors –they learned a lot.*
>
> ***Arabic Interpreter:*** *Back home, kids have to listen to and respect parents. We learned to listen to our kids and follow their lead. I've learned that if you listen to them, they will listen to you. At first I was worried and the parents were skeptical because it seemed we were giving the kids all the power and parents less. In the end the parents were surprised that they got more power over their children.*
>
> ***Arabic Interpreter:*** *In one family I interviewed I saw that everyone was involved with the homework. The parent said, "I have never had my kids discussing and sharing ideas, but when you start doing homework, the family has to communicate more.*

Empowering Parents and Helping Children Develop a Healthy Ethnic Identity. Sometimes parents fail to become involved with schools in the traditional ways such as attending parent orientation nights, meeting with teachers, volunteering in classrooms, or joining parent organizations, or knowing how to help their child with homework. Language and possible reading barriers, difficult work schedules,

Parents are encouraged to promote their children's pride in their cultural background by continuing their oral history, by telling them stories using their native language.

multiple jobs, beliefs that parents should not question teachers regarding school matters, prior bad experiences with schools, lack of child care, and lack of understanding how to participate in classrooms or children's homework are all possible barriers to parents' school involvement. Being respectful of cultural diversity means that leaders not only understand the barriers families face but also can empower parents by expanding the meaning of parent involvement to include other ways they can support their children. For example, helping parents understand that they are involved with their children when they encourage their children to stay in school, or when they express their high expectations for their children to succeed, or when they provide consistent open and ongoing communication with their children, and when they provide loving support, pride in their culture and family traditions. Indeed research has shown that higher student grade point averages correlates with maintenance of traditional values, ethnic pride, strong relationships and close social and cultural ties with members of the same ethnic group (Nieto, 1992). Parents are encouraged to promote their children's pride in their cultural background by continuing their oral history, by telling them stories about their childhoods and what it was like for them growing up.

Principle 6: Promoting Home-School Partnerships

Somali Interpreter: *Yes, I'm a single mother, and I go to work, and I have to buy groceries, clean everything. So I have no relationship with the schools or outside. The kids, usually they're learning a lot of stuff outside, and they come to the house, and I don't even have time to sit down and to talk to them and to communicate and to try to understand them. So the kids think the parents don't understand what's going on. The parents understand, but they don't have enough time, and the kids say, "I want to buy this." Maybe the parent cannot afford it. The children think, "My mother doesn't know what's* *going on." So there's a lot of problems, but we're trying to hold as much as we can until they grow up and understand what's going on themselves. So we have a lot of problems— we don't know how to solve. We just keep running and running and do whatever we can.*

Therapist: *So part of it is, with everything you have to do, is lack of time and finances. Are you saying that other people don't understand that? Or, are you saying your children don't think that the mother cares?*

Somali Interpreter: *What I mean, for example, the kids they go to school. Right? As a parent I have to have time to communicate with teachers and schools and keep in touch and know what's going on in the classroom and what the children are learning. Like, sometimes I get a call my child has missed school. I don't get time to go back and follow up, and the teachers think I don't care …*

Therapist: *You mean teachers don't understand all the hundred other things that parents are having to do.*

Vietnamese Interpreter: *So when you come to the U.S., you have to learn how the school system is working. You have to learn step-by-step. So we need, in the parent class, something in the curriculum that explains to the parents how the system works in this country. Because most parents in our country, when a child is in school, think it is the teacher's responsibility. A child's success or lack of success is the teacher's fault. It's not the parent's fault. So parents come here, thinking that way. The parent is only responsible to feed the children, to give them some clothes to wear, and some money to buy toys. And in our culture, the first people we respect are the parents. The second people we respect are the teachers. We also have a proverb, "You are not a success without a teacher. If you want success, you have to have a teacher with you." So the teacher is also not only teaching about how to read and write, but teaching about how to become a good citizen, too. That is in our culture. And so when a parent comes here, if the child does something wrong, most of the time it's blamed on the school.*

Tigrinya Interpreter: *Culture is not the only reason we give all the responsibility to the teacher. Because the family doesn't speak the language, they cannot understand or read the homework for their children. So there's no way they can even be able to help with their school work. So maybe the mother stays home and the father's at work. And they cannot get the help that they need. It's not the parents' fault, because the parent doesn't even understand what's going on or how to solve the problem they have. We don't have that much ability to find out what is happening at school. No one asks us what we need. So we have no choice with that.*

Therapist: *And is that similar in the Chinese culture?*

Chinese Interpreter: *Yes. I have parents tell me, "Oh, my children need to be sent to teacher for discipline. I tell them something at home, they don't listen to me."*

Therapist: *I think we see the parents' sense of powerless coming back to the discussion again. The feeling that children will obey the teacher, but they don't obey parents at home.*

Chinese Interpreter: *Well, there's kind of a reversal here. We have parents in my culture that don't want the teachers teaching their children morals and values. The parents want to do that. In some of these cultures, it's the exact opposite. That's seen as the teacher's job.*

Spanish Interpreter: *Yes, there's a lot of information that gets sent home in English. That's been my experience too. I'm always being asked by parents to translate what comes home from the school. So there's just a lot of breakdown in communication*

Arabic Interpreter: *You know on the home-school thing. My friend, his dad works two jobs, and he comes home and says, "Did you do your homework?" Every night "Did you do your homework today?" "Yeah." "Let me see," said the dad. The kid answered him, "Dad, what do you know about homework?" The father was shocked. He called me and said, "I can't believe my son. Every night,*

> *I ask him, 'Did you do your homework?' I'm assuming I'm doing a good thing, reminding him. Now it's come back to me, I don't have enough tools to ask him, 'How did you do this?' And I don't even have the time to go to school and get the tools so I can show my son the directions to doing his homework."*
>
> *That's the most difficult. The parents do not have enough tools at home to help the children to become competitive like any other children in America and function within school and society. So what we see is that by the time children reach high school, they are often disengaged from their parents. How many immigrant children are successful today? What is the percent of success in every area? It's very small. By the time they reach high school, they end up dropping out. And when you ask them, "Why can't you go back to school? Why can't you do the work for yourself?" They don't want to talk about it.*
>
> **Therapist:** *Oh, I think this is a really important point. I mean, this friend of yours, first of all, he took the first step of showing interest in his son's homework, which was a really important step. Now he's saying, "And then what?" "If I didn't have homework where I grew up or if I can't read the assignment, I'm not sure what to do next." So you are saying parents need some help in knowing how to support their children's learning.*

These interpreters' comments indicate the parents' sense of alienation from their children's school experiences. They reveal that parents may not understand the schools' expectations for how they should be involved in their children's education, either because of different cultural expectations or simply because of language or work schedule barriers. For such parents, the therapists utilizing the Basic IY Toddler and Preschool Parent Programs will spend extra time and focused practice on how to promote their children's school readiness skills such as language development, reading skills and following directions. Even if the parents don't read, they will learn ways to enhance their children's motivation to read and enjoyment of books through interactive reading methods and storytelling. For therapists utilizing the IY School Age Parent program, therapists will spend extra time utilizing the *Supporting Your Child's*

Education and *ADVANCE* programs which focus on how to coach children doing homework as well as ways to collaborate with teachers so they understand how to support their children's learning at home.

Chinese Interpreter: *I just want to make a different point of view from a child's perspective. A child's going to be living here for a long time. They better be adapted to the society. And it's important for the parent to know that keeping their old values is a good thing, but also give them room to adapt to the new culture, where they're going to be living, function, or whatever, contribute to the society. So it's important to be open minded and then be educated in a way that keeps the good values of the old country but, is open to the new things as well. And it's easier for a child. Like in my experience, I feel much better now that my mom actually went back to school to take classes. One day she told me, "Wow, I didn't know that it was this difficult to take classes, go to college." And actually for me to hear her say that, "Wow, now she understands me." Because she has that knowledge, and it kind of fills the gap between the parents and the child as well.*

Therapist: *So you are bringing up a key theme in terms of what we're going to want to think about in terms of how we help families —that is acknowledging the integrity and respecting the culture of each family. At the same time how do we help parents navigate the things that they need to do in order to help their children be successful in this society? I know that our conversations have raised important points that will influence the way we work with parents.*

Advocating For and With Parents. Finally, in addition to empowering parents by helping them realize the essential role they play in their children's emotional, social, and academic development, therapists can also advocate for parents' needs as well as help parents advocate for themselves. For example, a therapist can advocate for schools to provide interpreters for parents for school orientation nights or teacher meetings. They can recommend newsletters that go home be translated in the language of the parent. They can invite teachers to parent groups to explain classroom curriculum or ways parents can support their children's learning at home in order to be successful at school. Together with parents, therapists can communicate with teachers about particular concerns they face in regard to assisting their children with their academic needs.

SUMMARY

It is an immensely rewarding opportunity to bring new perspectives about effective child management parenting practices and child development principles to parents from different backgrounds. Leaders and therapists who have a multicultural perspective will be caring and collaborative in their approach, take time to listen and understand parents, will try to make the material relevant for parents' goals and family circumstances, will recognize the importance of native language, family traditions, and rituals, and will acknowledge and call on parents to share their cultural knowledge during discussions. Collaborating with parents in this way has the effect of giving back dignity, respect, and self-control to parents who may be feeling low self-confidence, stress, and uncertainty about the appropriateness of a parenting program for their family and culture. This collaborative model has the multiple advantages of reducing attrition rates, increasing motivation and commitment, and reducing resistance. Working together in this collaborative way will enhance parents' confidence, build family support systems, and strengthen communities by highlighting that parents' goals for their children transcend culture, thereby providing mutual understanding.

The Incredible Years® Child Dinosaur Social, Emotional, and Problem Solving Skills Program

Despite the clear evidence regarding the efficacy of parent training as a treatment approach, a number of studies have indicated that while parent training results in predictable improvements in child behavior at home, it does not necessarily result in improvements at school and with peers (Eyberg, et al., 2008; Taylor & Biglan, 1998). In our own studies with the Incredible Years parent programs, teacher reports showed that approximately 1/3 of children with conduct problems whose parents received the treatment program continued to have clinical levels of peer problems, classroom aggression and noncompliance two to three years after treatment (Webster-Stratton, 1990b). Approximately 8 to12 years later, 18% of the children had had criminal justice system involvement and 23% major delinquent acts. The majority of teenagers were well adjusted and rates of risky behaviors were in the normal range, according to normative data (Webster-Stratton, Rinaldi, & Reid, 2011). It may be that the failure of parent treatment programs to consistently produce cross-setting generalization and long-term improvements in some children stems from the narrowness of the intervention focus on a single risk factor. Most parent programs exclusively focus on training parents to manage children's social behavior at home rather than helping them to address their children's academic problems at school or relationship and emotional regulation problems with peers. Parent training programs often fail to involve teachers in the treatment plans. In order for sustainable results and generalization across setting or time to occur, treatments must include teachers and children's peer groups so that a common socialization process and language is used across settings.

More sustained results may be achieved when teachers and children are involved in treatment in early years.

The limitations of parent treatment programs led to a second approach to treating children conduct problems; that is, directly training children in social skills, emotional literacy, problem solving, and anger management. The preschool and first school years (ages 3-8 years) are felt to be a strategic time to intervene directly with children who have early onset conduct problems, before they move from the preoperational phase of cognitive brain development to the concrete phase and before negative behaviors and cognitions crystallize. Intervening at this strategic developmental stage may prevent the formation of permanent patterns of peer rejection and alienation, negative school reputations, academic failure and formation of deviant peer group friendships. Therefore, in addition to the IY parent program, it is recommended that the IY child treatment program be offered, particularly for children whose behavior problems are pervasive across the home and school or day care settings. Like the IY parent program, it is important that the IY child treatment program be flexible enough to meet the needs of children with complicated developmental and family profiles. Since young children cannot easily communicate their feelings or worries and the reasons for their behaviors, it is important for therapists to look beyond the aggressive symptoms to the underlying reasons for the misbehavior and address other, less obvious symptoms such as anxiety, depression, attachment problems, or developmental delays. The

skilled therapist will develop a working model for every child and their parents based on the child's biological make up, developmental ability, comorbidity, family background and parenting experiences, and functional analyses of the behavior problems (Kazdin & Whitley, 2006).

The IY child program, which is called *Dina Dinosaur's Social, Emotional and Problem Solving Skills Treatment Program* (aka Dinosaur School) is an evidence-based program that has been shown in three randomized control group treatment trials by the developer (Herman, Borden, Reinke, & Webster-Stratton, 2011; Webster-Stratton & Hammond, 1997; Webster-Stratton, et al., 2011; Webster-Stratton, Reid, & Hammond, 2004) and in one independent replication (Larsson, et al., 2009; Mørch, Larsson, Clifford, Drugli, & Fossum, 2004) to significantly reduce aggressive behavior, internalizing symptoms, strengthen positive parent-child interactions, and increase emotional language and social problem solving skills with peers. For a review of treatment studies see (Webster-Stratton & Reid, 2010) and refer to Chapter Two.

A prevention version of the dinosaur curriculum designed to be offered to whole classrooms 2-3 times a week has also been evaluated with positive outcomes for reducing classroom aggression and promoting social competence and school readiness in high risk populations (Webster-Stratton, Reid, & Stoolmiller, 2008). As noted above, although the presenting diagnoses for the treatment studies was ODD or conduct problems, these program evaluations represent treatment outcomes for children with many other complicated diagnoses and risk factors. This chapter provides a description of the child dinosaur small group treatment model and how it is tailored to address the particular goals of each child so that the intervention is developmentally and therapeutically appropriate. The Leader's manual (Webster-Stratton, 1990, rev 2007, 2012) provides recommended protocols for offering the child dinosaur program to groups of 6 children, ages 4-8, with a primary diagnosis of ODD/ADHD, but is also appropriate for addressing co-morbid problems such as depression, anxiety, attachment difficulties, and language or developmental delays. The program can also be tailored for children who acting out because of issues related to abuse, neglect, or life stress (e.g., divorce). The treatment version of the program is offered by counselors, therapists, or early childhood specialists who have experience treating young children with conduct problems. Groups meet weekly in a mental health setting for 18-22 weeks in 2-hour sessions, ideally in conjunction with the parent program. Parent and child protocols are organized so as to dovetail the content being learned. The dinosaur treatment program can also be offered in hourly pull out small groups twice a week in schools with counselors. The protocols are considered the minimal number of core sessions, vignettes and content required to achieve results similar to those in the published literature. However, the length of the program, number of vignettes shown, and the emphases given to certain components of the program can be expanded or lengthened, according to the individual needs of the children in each group.

OVERVIEW OF THE DINA DINOSAUR SOCIAL, EMOTIONAL AND PROBLEM SOLVING TREATMENT PROGRAM

In order for therapists to deliver the program effectively, it is extremely important to understand the core content of the program, the teaching methods, and the therapeutic process of the program delivery. This program is described in greater detail in the program leader's manual (Webster-Stratton, 2012) and in a summary chapter (Webster-Stratton & Reid, 2005). Therapists with a thorough understanding of the program quickly see that it is designed to allow for tailoring the teaching and learning process, as well as the behavioral goals, to the special needs of individual children in the group.

Content of Program

The next table provides an outline of the core content presented in the specific order listed below for all groups of children. Each dinosaur unit

CONTENT AND OBJECTIVES OF THE DINA DINOSAUR SOCIAL, EMOTION AND PROBLEM SOLVING SKILLS PROGRAM

Making New Friends and Learning School Rules (Apatosaurus Unit)

- Understanding the Importance of Rules
- Participating in the process of rule making
- Understanding consequences if rules are broken ~ time out to calm down for aggression
- Learning how to earn rewards for good behavior
- Learning to build friendships

Dina Teaches How to Do Your Best in School (Iguanodon Unit)

- Learning to listen, wait, avoid interruptions, and quietly put up a hand to ask questions in class
- Learning to handle other children who tease or interfere with child's ability to work at school
- Learning to stop, think, and check work
- Learning the importance of co-operation with teacher and other children
- Practicing concentrating and persisting with activity when frustrated

Wally Teaches about Detecting and Understanding Feelings (Triceratops Unit)

- Learning words for different feelings
- Learning to tell how someone is feeling from verbal and non verbal signs and sounds
- Increasing awareness of nonverbal facial communication to portray feelings
- Learning different ways to relax and calm down (positive imagery, deep breathing, happy places)
- Understanding feelings from different perspectives
- Practicing talking about feelings

Wally Teaches Problem-Solving Steps (Stegosaurus Unit)

- Learning to identify a problem
- Thinking of solutions to hypothetical problems

- Learning verbal assertive skills
- Learning to inhibit impulsive reactions
- Understanding what apology means
- Thinking of alternative solutions to problem situations such as being teased, left out, hit
- Learning to understand that solutions have consequences
- Learning to critically evaluate solutions

Tiny Turtle Teaches Anger Management (Tyrannosaurus Rex Unit)
- Recognizing that anger can interfere with good problem solving
- Using the turtle technique to manage anger
- Understanding when apologies are helpful
- Recognizing anger in oneself and others
- Understanding that feeling anger is okay but acting on it by hitting or hurting someone else is not
- Learning to control anger reactions ~ positive self-talk, visualizations, relaxation methods
- Practicing alternative responses to being teased, bullied, or yelled at by an angry adult or peer

Molly Manners Teaches How to be Friendly (Allosaurus Unit)
- Learning what friendship means and how to be friendly
- Understanding ways to help others
- Learning the concepts of sharing and helping
- Learning what teamwork means
- Understanding the benefits of sharing, helping and teamwork
- Practicing friendship skills

Molly Explains How to Talk with Friends (Brachiosaurus Unit)
- Learning how to ask questions and tell something to a friend
- Learning to listen carefully to what a friend is saying
- Learning to speak up about something that is bothering you
- Understanding how to give a compliment or apology
- Learning how to enter into groups of children already playing
- Learning to make a suggestion rather than give a command

builds on the prior unit and skills, so it is important not to skip units or complete them out of order. However, therapists make developmentally appropriate modifications based on the children's needs in the group. For example, in the Doing Your Best in School unit, groups of very young children (4-5 years) would focus on listening, waiting, and raising a quiet hand, while older groups (6-7 years) would learn to ignore distractions and to concentrate on work. Similarly, as outlined in the subsequent sections, particular content areas can be emphasized for children who have differing sets of behavioral problems and developmental delays.

The next section provides a brief description and rationale for each of the treatment units of the program. Please see the book, *Incredible Teachers: Nurturing Children's Social, Emotional, and Academic Competence* by Webster-Stratton (2012) for more details.

Making Friends and Learning School Rules and How to Do Your Best in School (Apatosaurus and Iguanodon Units)

When working with children with conduct problems, gaining their cooperation and compliance is key to being able to socialize and teach them. Research has indicated that these children are noncompliant about 80-90% of the time a request is made of them by parents or teachers (Webster-Stratton & Lindsay, 1999). Thus, one of the first tasks of this treatment program that is somewhat different from other social skills programs is the emphasis on compliance training procedures. Our initial group sessions focus on the importance of group dinosaur rules such as following directions, keeping hands to selves, raising a quiet hand, using a polite and friendly voice, and listening to the teacher. Rules are demonstrated, role played, and practiced with the children using life-sized puppets. Incentives are given (dinosaur chips) to children for following rules throughout the group sessions. Children also learn that a Time Out to calm down will be a consequence for unsafe behavior and children practice with puppets how to take a Time Out and use calm down strategies. As part of this process, they begin to learn to use self-calming deep breathing and self-talk using the calm down thermometer as a visual cue.

Quiet hands up in class

Wally Teaches about Detecting and Understanding Feelings (Triceratops Unit)

Once the group rules and expectations have been discussed, modeled, practiced, and reinforced, the children are ready to move on to content on emotional literacy. Children with ODD and ADHD often have language delays and limited vocabulary to express their feelings, thus contributing to their difficulties regulating emotional responses (Frick et al., 1991; Sturge, 1982; Blair, Denham, Kochanoff, & Whipple, 2004). They may also have negative feelings and thoughts about themselves and others and difficulty perceiving another's point of view or feelings different from their own (Dodge, 1993). They have difficulty reading facial cues and distort or underutilize social cues (Dodge & Price, 1994).

The first step in the Triceratops Feelings unit is to help children learn to recognize their own feelings as well as the emotional vocabulary to be able to tell others how they are feeling. The second step is to accurately identify and understand others' feelings. Next therapists help them learn how to manage their feelings of anger or disappointment or sadness or frustration by encouraging them to name their feelings, to think differently about why an event occurred, and to respond calmly to situations that cause emotional arousal (e.g., such as being teased or left out). The therapists teach children to use positive self-talk, positive imagery, and relaxation strategies to keep themselves calm. Through the use of laminated cue cards and video vignettes of children demonstrating various emotions, children discuss and learn about a wide range of feeling states.

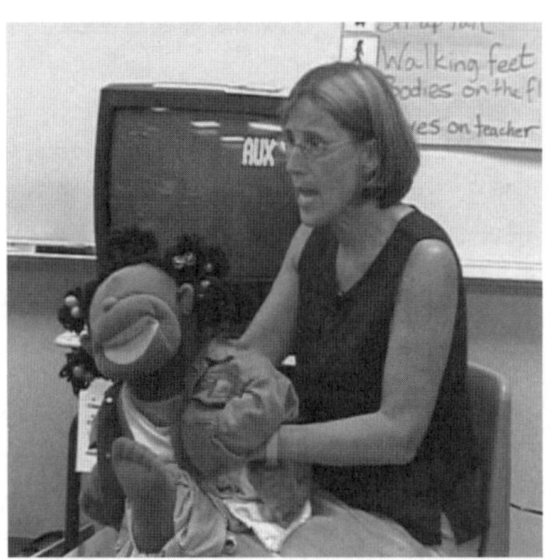

The unit begins with basic sad, angry, happy, and scared feelings and progresses to more complex feelings such as frustration, excitement, disappointment, loneliness, impatience, forgiveness and embarrassment. The children learn to recognize their own feelings by checking their bodies and faces for "tight" (tense) muscles, relaxed muscles, frowns, smiles, and sensations in other parts of their bodies (e.g., butterflies in their stomachs). Matching the facial expressions and body postures shown on cue cards helps the children to recognize the cues from their own bodies and associate a word with these feelings. Next, children are guided to use their detective skills to look for clues in another person's facial expression, behavior, or tone of voice to recognize what the person may be feeling and to think about why they might be feeling that way. Video vignettes, photos of sports stars and other famous people, as well as pictures of the children in the group are all engaging ways to provide experience in "reading" feeling cues. As the children become more skilled at recognizing feelings in themselves and others, they begin to learn empathy, perspective taking, and emotional regulation.

Children also learn strategies for changing negative (angry, frustrated, sad) feelings into more positive feelings. Wally (a child-sized puppet) teaches the children some of his "secrets" for calming down (take a deep breath, think a happy thought). Games, positive imagery, feelings songs and activities are used to illustrate how feelings change over time and how different people can react differently to the same event. To practice perspective taking, role plays include scenarios in which the child takes the part of the teacher, parent, or another child who has a problem. The puppets are used to model how to talk about and cope with different feelings. This work on feelings is integrated into and underlies all the subsequent units in this curriculum.

Detective Wally Teaches Problem-Solving Steps (Stegosaurus Unit)

Children who are hyperactive, impulsive, inattentive, and aggressive have been shown to have cognitive deficits in key aspects of social problem solving (Dodge & Crick, 1990). Such children perceive social situations in hostile terms, generate fewer prosocial ways of solving interpersonal conflict, and anticipate fewer consequences for aggression (Dodge & Price, 1994). They act aggressively and impulsively without stopping to think of non-aggressive solutions or of the other person's perspective and expect their aggressive responses to yield positive results. There is evidence that children who employ appropriate problem-solving strategies play more constructively, are better liked by their peers, and are more cooperative at home and school. Consequently, in this next program of the intervention, therapists teach children to generate more prosocial solutions to their problems and to evaluate which solutions are likely to lead to positive consequences. In essence, these children are provided with a thinking strategy that corrects the flaws in their decision-making process and reduces their risk of developing ongoing peer relationship problems. Children learn a 7-step process of problem solving:

(1) How am I feeling, and what is my problem? (define problem and feelings)
(2) What is a solution?
(3) What are some more solutions? (brainstorm solutions)
(4) What are the consequences?
(5) What is the best solution? (Is the solution safe? fair? and does it lead to good feelings?)
(6) Can I use my plan? and
(7) How did I do? (evaluate outcome and reinforce efforts)

A great deal of time is spent on steps 1, 2, and 3 to help young preschool children increase their repertoire of possible prosocial solutions (e.g., trade, ask, share, take turns, wait, walk away, take a deep breath, etc.). In fact, for the 4-to 5-year olds, these three steps may be the entire focus of this unit. One to two new solutions are introduced in each session, and the children are given multiple opportunities to role play and practice these solutions with a puppet or another child. Laminated cue cards of pictures of over 40 solutions are provided in Wally's detective kit and are used by children to generate possible solutions and evaluate whether they will work to solve particular problems. Children role play solutions to problem scenarios introduced by the puppets, the video vignettes, or by the children themselves. The children are guided to consult the solution kit when a real-life problem occurs. Activities for this program include writing and acting in a problem-solving play, going "fishing" for solutions (with a magnetized fishing rod), and working as a group to generate enough solutions to join "Wally's Problem-Solving Detective Club."

A great deal of time is spent on steps 1, 2, and 3 to help young preschool children increase their repertoire of possible prosocial solutions .

Tiny Turtle Teaches Anger Management (Tyrannosaurus Rex Unit)

Aggression and inadequate impulse control are perhaps the most potent obstacles to effective problem solving and forming successful friendships for children with ODD and ADHD. Without help, these children are more likely to experience ongoing peer rejection and continued social problems for years afterwards (Coie, 1990). Such children have difficulty regulating their negative affect in order to generate positive solutions to conflict situations. Furthermore, there is evidence that aggressive children are more likely to misinterpret ambiguous situations as hostile or threatening. This tendency to perceive hostile intent in others has been seen as one source of their aggressive behavior (Dodge & Coie, 1987; Walker, Colvin, & Ramsey, 1995).

Consequently, once the basic framework for problem solving has been taught, children learn about anger-management strategies. Anger management programs based on the work of Novaco (1975) have been shown to reduce aggression in middle- and high-schoolers and to maintain gains in problem-solving skills (Lochman & Dunn, 1993). Clearly children cannot solve problems if they are too angry to think calmly. The puppet, Tiny Turtle, is used to teach the children a 5-step anger management strategy that includes:

(1) Recognize anger;
(2) Think "stop;"
(3) Take three deep breaths;
(4) Go into your shell, and tell yourself "I can calm down;"
(5) Try again.

Tiny's shell is the basis for many activities: making a large cardboard shell that children can actually hide under, making grocery bag "shells" or vests, molding play dough shells for small plastic figures (the children pretend the figures are mad and help them to calm down in the play dough shells), and making teasing shields. Each of these activities provides multiple opportunities for the therapist to help the children practice the steps of anger management. Children are helped to recognize the clues in their bodies that tell them they are getting angry and to learn to use self-talk, deep breathing, and positive imagery to help themselves calm down. Therapists also use guided imagery exercises with the children (having them close their eyes and pretend to be in a cocoon or turtle shell) to help them experience the feeling of being relaxed and calm.

The situations that the puppets bring to the group are formulated according to experiences and issues relevant to particular children in the group.

Video vignettes of children handling anger or being teased or rejected are used to trigger role plays to practice these calming down strategies. Additionally, the puppets talk to the children about their problems and ask for their ideas about some solutions (e.g., a parent or teacher was mad at them for a mistake they made, being left out of a birthday party, a parent getting divorced, or forgetting their homework). The situations that the puppets bring to the group are formulated according to experiences and issues relevant to particular children in the group. Throughout the discussion of vignettes and role-play demonstrations, the therapists and puppets help the children to change some of their attributions about events. For example, Molly explains, "*Maybe he was teasing you because he really wanted to be your friend but didn't know how to ask you nicely*" or, "*You know, all kids get turned down sometimes when they want to play; it doesn't mean they don't like you*" or, "*I think that it was an accident that he bumped into you.*"

Molly Manners Teaches How to Be Friendly and How to Talk with Friends (Allosaurus and Brachiosaurus Units)

Children with conduct problems have particular difficulty forming and maintaining friendships. Our research, and that of others, has indicated that these children have significantly delayed play skills, including difficulties waiting for a turn, accepting peers' suggestions, offering an idea rather than demanding something, or collaborating in play with peers (Webster-Stratton & Lindsay, 1999). They also have poor conversation skills, difficulty responding to the overtures of others, and poor group entry skills. Consequently, in the friendship program, the therapists focus on teaching children a repertoire of friendly behaviors such as sharing, taking turns, asking, making a suggestion, apologizing, agreeing with others, and giving compliments. In addition, children are taught specific prosocial responses for common peer situations, such as entering a group of children who are already playing, i.e.:

(1) watch from sidelines and show interest;
(2) continue watching and give a compliment;
(3) wait for a pause;
(4) ask politely to join in and accept the response.

As with other new material, children see these friendship skills modeled by the puppets or in video scenario examples and practice using them in role plays and cooperative games.

Selecting children for the groups

When offering the small group child training program for diagnosed children, it is ideal to carefully select the type of children who will be in each group. Typically we recommend no more than 6 children per group. A general guideline for group selection is to include at least one same sex and same age peer for each child (e.g., do not place one girl in a group of five boys or one four-year-old in a group of six-year-olds). However, as long as each child has a peer, we often recommend mixing genders, ages, and diagnoses to make more heterogeneous groups. It is recommended, if feasible, to include two typically developing peer models in each group. This will ensure that there will be children who can help model appropriate social behavior and self-regulation for other children who have more difficulties with conduct problems, hyperactivity and developmental delays. These peer models will also benefit from the program because of the leadership skills they practice, as well as the understanding and empathy they learn for children with different developmental abilities. If peer models are not possible, it can also

Typically no more than 6 children per group are recommended.

be helpful to have a mixed gender group. Even if the girls are diagnosed with conduct and attention problems, we have found that their behaviors present differently enough that a group of two girls and four boys (all with ODD) runs more smoothly than a group of six diagnosed boys. We recommend mixed-age groups (e.g., three four-year-olds and three six-year-olds or two four-year-olds, two five-year-olds, and two six-year-olds), so that older peers can serve as models for younger children. We also recommend that one group is not made up entirely of children with comorbid ODD and ADHD. We have found that these groups have such high levels of distractability and disruption that they are very difficult to run productively.

This learning is interactive, engaging, fun, and paced at the level of the children in the group.

One exception to our recommendation of mixed diagnosed groups is for children with Asperger's Syndrome or some other mild autism spectrum disorders. For these children, we recommend treatment in a group of other children with similar diagnoses, along with typically developing peer models. It is our experience that children with autism spectrum diagnoses may become dysregulated if placed in a group made up of highly hyperactive and aggressive children because of the high level of noise, activity, and physical stimulation. We also believe the inclusion of typically developing children is crucial for these children because of the need for prosocial peer modeling.

Schedule for Two-Hour Session

When children arrive, they begin by engaging in coached play time with their peers. One therapist works to coach these social interactions, reinforcing concepts that children have learned during prior weeks. The other therapist reviews homework that children have brought in, giving them individual attention and encouragement for their efforts. This may be done using one of the puppets and children receive special stamps or stickers on their assignments. This playtime and homework review usually lasts 10-15 minutes, and then the therapists transition the children to a structured circle time to present new content. Although the

dinosaur curriculum is child focused and individualized for different developmental levels or family situations, it is important that structured learning occur in each session. This learning is interactive, engaging, fun, and paced at the level of the children in the group. The goal is to present new ideas or content so children begin to increase their repertoire of ideas and responses. This plan to present new material to children in a structured small group circle time is paired with the idea of taking advantage of teachable moments that occur naturally between the children during the time they are in the group.

During circle time the video vignettes and puppets are both used to present content that is then processed during discussions, problem solving, role play practices, and collaborative learning. After each vignette, the therapist solicits ideas from the children and involves them in the process of problem solving, sharing, and discussing ideas and reactions. To enhance generalization, the video vignettes selected for each of the units involve real-life situations at school (e.g., playground and classroom) and home. Some vignettes represent children behaving in prosocial ways such as helping their teachers, playing well with peers, using problem solving, or anger management techniques. Other vignettes are examples of children having difficulty in conflict situations, such as teasing, arguing, and destructive behavior. The video vignettes show children of differing ages, sexes, and cultures interacting with adults (parents or teachers) or with other children. After viewing the vignettes, children discuss feelings of the characters, decide whether the solutions are good or bad choices, generate ideas for more effective solutions, and role play alternative responses. Although some mild negative video vignettes are shown so that children can show how they would improve the situation, the program uses a far great number of positive vignettes and puppet scenarios than negative examples (about 5 to 1), and children are coached to help solve or resolve any problems that they see in the vignettes. The children are never asked to act out the inappropriate responses, only the positive alternatives.

The first circle time lasts 20-30 minutes, depending on the developmental level of the children. Following this first circle, a snack time provides an opportunity for the therapist to model, coach, and praise prosocial behavior and use of new skills in real life. Children are guided to engage in friendly conversations with peers and therapists and are given responsibility for helping with aspects of snack set-up and clean up. Following snack time, children return to circle time for another structured learning time, and then break into two groups for small group activity time. These small group activities are designed to allow for hands-on practice of the content learned during the lesson. Children might work on a cooperative poster, play a board game that involves turn-taking and waiting patiently, role play solutions using puppets, share art supplies, or make feeling masks. The group ends with another coached play session where therapists coach positive peer interactions. Children also count their dinosaur chips during this time and turn them in for prizes from Dina's special box. During the last 10 minutes of the session, one group leader leaves the group to meet with the parents and give a summary of the session content for the day. Parents are given recommendations for home activities that will reinforce the child's new learning and children have dinosaur homework activities to complete. Parents are asked to sign the home activities, so the therapist knows that the parent is being exposed to the content and helping the child with the assignments. The session ends with closing circle time where children come together, sing, say goodbye to the puppets and give compliments to their friends. Parents are often invited in to observe this last circle.

Group Rules and Schedules

Each treatment group is set up with clear and contingent behavioral expectations that are necessary to manage and teach children with oppositional and aggressive conduct problems. During the first group sessions, rules and expectations are reviewed and role-played. Children participate actively in this process and help to establish the classroom rules. A predictable and routine schedule helps children feel safe in this environment and know what is expected of them. A picture schedule for the group is displayed prominently on the wall, with each segment of the group given its own picture and written heading (e.g., homework review, circle time, small group activity, snack time, play choice time). Each week, one child is given responsibility for tracking the schedule by moving an arrow to point to each activity as it happens. Predictability is also established within the routines and rituals of each group. For example, every circle time lesson starts with familiar dinosaur school songs. Puppets enter the group in a similar way each week and greet the children individually. Video vignettes are always introduced with the "ready, set, action" statement to ensure children are focused. Children are also assigned jobs each week (schedule changer, line leader, snack helper) and these jobs are pictured for them to see easily. Consistency in routines and schedules makes it easier for children to attend to the learning.

IY CHILD GROUP METHODS AND PROCESSES

The group methods and processes for teaching social skills and emotional regulation to young children must be tailored to the children's learning styles, temperament, diagnoses, and cognitive abilities. Within the 4–8 year-old age range, there are vast differences in children's developmental ability. Some children in a group may be reading fluently, other children may not read at all. Some children will be able to grasp relatively complicated ideas, such as how to evaluate possible future consequences of an action while others are operating in the "here and now" with little ability to predict ahead. The dinosaur treatment program provides relevant content areas for the preschool to early elementary school age group. A skilled therapist will then choose developmentally appropriate practice activities to present the material to the child in any given group according to the goals for that child.

However, all groups make extensive use of music, video vignettes, role play practices, child-size puppets, hands-on practice activities, home

All groups make extensive use of music, video vignettes, role play practices, child-size puppets, and hands-on practice activities.

work assignments, letters, and phone calls to parents and teachers. Within these methods, the therapists make individual adjustments according to the needs and developmental status of particular children in their groups.

Using Puppets

The therapists use child-size boy and girl puppets to model appropriate child behavior. There is also a dinosaur puppet (Dina Dinosaur) who is the director of Dinosaur school and teaches school rules and rewards and praises children who are doing well. The puppets, "Wally" and "Molly," help narrate the video vignettes and ask the children for help with common conflict situations that directly reflect the reality of children's issues in the group. For example, Wally (one of the puppets) could be upset about being scolded for getting out of seat at school (ADHD), or, angry because someone took his ball and upset because he responded by hitting that child (emotion regulation problems), or embarrassed and frustrated because he is the only child in this class who cannot read (language and reading delays), or scared of being left at school in the morning (separation anxiety), or worried because he heard his parents are arguing and talking about divorce (depressed), or sad because a family member died, or distressed because he was placed in foster care. It is important for the therapists to use the puppets to individualize these suggestions to meet the needs of children in their groups. The puppets easily engage the children in the process of talking about feelings, thinking of possible solutions or coping strategies, and then role playing these ideas.

In addition to Wally and Molly, a variety of other puppets visit the group. These other puppets help to address diverse problems and living circumstances that children in the group may experience (one puppet may live in foster care, another puppet may have parents who are divorced, another puppet may have a reading disability). Additional puppets can also help to represent diverse ethnic and cultural backgrounds of children in the group. The puppets are an integral part of the program's success as they evoke the children's imaginations. Young children are enthralled with the puppets and will talk about sensitive or painful issues with a puppet more easily than with adults. The puppets quickly become real to the children and are very effective models.

Live and Video Modeling and Role Playing Practice Methods

In accordance with modeling and self-efficacy theories of learning (Bandura, 1989), children using the program develop their skills by watching (and modeling) video vignette examples of key problem-solving and interpersonal skills. Video vignettes provide a more flexible method of training than didactic instruction or sole reliance on role play because they can portray a wide variety of models, situations, and settings for children to watch and discuss. This flexible modeling approach results in better generalization of the training content and, therefore, better long-term maintenance. Further, it is an engaging method of learning for less verbally oriented children, younger children, or children with short attention spans.

Video vignettes and puppet role plays serve as the stimulus for children to talk about, demonstrate, and practice different solutions or feelings or thoughts. For example, a puppet might talk about feeling sad because his father has left home, or feeling frustrated because she can't learn to read, or lonely because no one will play with him. The puppet will ask the children how to respond to this feeling or experience and when the children generate suggestions, they are asked to act them out with the puppet. Role playing provides live modeling opportunities for children to practice new skills and experience different perspectives. With children ages four to six, the role playing can be acted out by a child and the therapist's puppet while the second group leader sits with the remaining children and helps them think of alternative responses. Older children can help develop scripts and put on skits in pairs with one therapist acting as coach.

Practice Activities—Coaching/Cueing/Reinforcing

For each of the sessions, there are a series of activities that can be chosen to practice the skills targeted in that session. For example, a friendship session about sharing is paired with an art project where there are limited supplies and students have to figure out how to share. During a session on cooperation, children are asked to design their own dinosaur incorporating everyone's ideas. In the problem-solving unit children are given a problem and asked to think of and act out as many solutions as they can. The problems can be presented on a colorful cue card or in a problem-solving book. Children who are reading and writing can read the problem and write solutions while non-readers dictate or draw a picture of their solutions. Children are encouraged to look in Wally's detective kit (a box that contains all the solutions that children have learned) for more solutions.

During activity time, children are usually divided into two groups of three children. For some activities, children might be divided along developmental lines with more advanced children doing a harder version of the same activity than less advanced children. Other times, developmental levels may be mixed so that more advanced children can help the younger children. A therapist sits with each group of children and "coaches" and comments on prosocial behavior using social, emotional, persistence, and academic coaching methods. Dinosaur chips may also be earned for friendly behaviors during these activities. Most of the practice activities described in this program also help strengthen academic skills such as writing, reading, sequencing, vocabulary, problem solving, and discrimination skills. Thus, this program enhances academic as well as social competence. During small group activity time therapists also work to coach learning behaviors such as verbal and nonverbal communication skills that include collaborating, cooperating, listening, attending, speaking up, and asking questions. These are key skills for a child to learn academic skills and be successful in the classroom environment.

Reinforcement

A token system is used whereby children earn tokens ("dinosaur chips") for appropriate behavior. These chips are exchanged for stickers and small prizes at the end of the group. Children receive very high levels of praise and the chip reinforcement. As little attention as possible is given to negative behaviors. Much off-task behavior is ignored, and children are redirected or prompted with non-verbal cues. When necessary, children are given warnings of a consequence (loss of privilege) for disruptive or non-compliant behavior, and leaders follow through with the consequence if the misbehavior continues. Aggressive behavior receives an automatic brief Time Out away from the therapist and peer attention in order to provide children a time and place to calm down.

This behavior management process is also manipulated to meet the individual needs of the children in the group. For instance, not all children are earning chips for the same behaviors. Therapists will have somewhat different behavioral expectations for each child in the group and therefore will set different limits accordingly. Some children may be earning dinosaur chips for listening to teachers, following directions, and being cooperative. Other children might be rewarded for prosocial behaviors such as helping, sharing, and giving suggestions. In this way, each child in the group is working on target goals within a system that is clear, developmentally appropriate, has been negotiated ahead of time, and feels fair to all children. Leaders look for ways to make sure that children who are working hard at their individual goals are earning chips at relatively equal rates. If needed, the token system is modified to meet individual children's goals (examples of this are described below).

Collaborating with Parents

At the end of every session, one of the child therapists spends 5-10 minutes explaining the objectives for the child group sessions and the home activities to the parents. If parents are in the parent group, the therapist joins this group to give the "Dinosaur Update." The child sessions are organized to dovetail with the learning in the parent group sessions. For example, when parents have learned emotion coaching they will be asked to use this coaching at home to build their children's emotional literacy. This will occur at the same time the children are

IY Parent and Child Program

Session One	Parent Training:	Introductions, Goals, & Child-directed play
	Child Training:	Making New Friends and Learning School Rules
Session Two	Parent Training:	Child-directed Play
	Child Training:	Making New Friends and Learning School Rules
Session Three	Parent Training:	Academic and Persistence Coaching
	Child Training:	How to Do Your Best in School
Session Four	Parent Training:	Academic and Persistence Coaching
	Child Training:	How to Do Your Best in School
Session Five	Parent Training:	Social and Emotional Coaching
	Child Training:	How to Do Your Best in School
Session Six	Parent Training:	Social and Emotional Coaching
	Child Training:	Understanding Feelings
Session Seven	Parent Training:	The Art of Effective Praise & Encouragement
	Child Training:	Understanding Feelings
Session Eight	Parent Training:	Motivating Children Through Incentives
	Child Training:	Understanding Feelings
Session Nine	Parent Training:	Motivating Children Through Incentives
	Child Training:	Problem-Solving Part 1
Session Ten	Parent Training:	Establishing Routines & Household Rules
	Child Training:	Problem-Solving Part 2
Session Eleven	Parent Training:	Effective Limit Setting
	Child Training:	Problem-Solving Part 3
Session Twelve	Parent Training:	Follow Through with Commands
	Child Training:	Anger Management Part 4 & 5
Session Thirteen	Parent Training:	Ignoring Children's Inappropriate Behaviors
	Child Training:	Anger Management Part 4 & 5
Session Fourteen	Parent Training:	Time Out to Calm Down
	Child Training:	Problem-Solving Part 6
Session Fifteen	Parent Training:	Time Out for Aggression & Non Compliance
	Child Training:	How to be Friendly Part 1
Session Sixteen	Parent Training:	Natural & Logical Consequences
	Child Training:	How to be Friendly Part 2
Session Seventeen	Parent Training:	Teaching Children to Problem Solve
	Child Training:	How to be Friendly Part 3 & 4
Session Eighteen	Parent Training:	Teaching Children to Problem Solve
	Child Training:	How to Talk to Friends Part 1
Session Nineteen	Parent Training:	Review Or Adult Problem-Solving (optional Advance Program)
	Child Training:	How to Talk to Friends Part 2
Session Twenty	Parent Training:	Review and Graduation
	Child Training:	Review and Graduation

learning emotion vocabulary in their small group dinosaur program. Or, parents will be asked to model calm down strategies when they are solving their own problems around the same time the children are beginning to learn ways to self-regulate. When children are learning basic solutions such using their words, sharing, waiting, and helping, parents are asked to coach, praise and reinforce these behaviors at home. The aim is for the language used by the child therapists to also be used by the parents at home. The next table shows how the content for the parent and child groups are coordinated.

Collaborating with Teachers

The child therapists send letters to the children's teachers explaining dinosaur school content and objectives and asking teachers to give positive attention to the targeted behaviors when they occur in the classroom. Every 2-3 weeks the therapists call the teachers and share the strategies they are finding helpful as well as collaborating on the targeted skills to encourage. The therapist may visit the classroom to see the children's behavior in the school setting and to provide support for the teacher's efforts. At this time the therapist and teacher collaborate on a behavior plan for the child with discussion of positive behavioral goals and strategies for meeting these goals.

The therapist and teacher collaborate on a behavior plan for the child with discussion of positive behavioral goals.

TAILORING THE PROGRAM TO ADDRESS CHILDREN'S INDIVIDUAL NEEDS

As outlined in the introduction to this chapter, many children who present for treatment with externalizing behaviors (ODD, ADHD, CD) also experience a variety of other symptoms (e.g., depression, anxiety, mild autism spectrum disorders, or learning and language difficulties) or may be living in stressful circumstances (divorce, foster care). It is important to remember that the effectiveness studies for the Incredible Years treatment programs have been conducted on samples where children presented with the primary diagnoses as ODD or ADHD, and they have not been tested as the intervention for children whose primary diagnosis was anxiety, depression, or autism. However, as noted in Chapter One, the children with ODD and ADHD in these research studies were made up of children with complex and diverse needs and comorbidities. In other words, in addition to their externalizing symptoms, these children showed a full range of other behavioral and developmental symptoms and were experiencing multiple life stressors that complicated the etiology of their diagnosis and treatment response. Therapists working with such children will need to respond and adapt to the broad range of needs of children in their groups. The following sections outline ways that therapists modify and adapt the program with fidelity to meet children's individual needs.

Tips for Tailoring for Children with ADHD

Children with Attention Deficit Disorder (ADD) with or without Hyperactivity (ADHD) have difficulty attending to, hearing, or remembering adult requests, and therefore don't seem to be cooperative. They often have difficulty completing tasks such as schoolwork, homework, chores, or other activities that require sustained concentration. Many children with ADD/ADHD have trouble making friends (Coie, Dodge, & Kupersmidt, 1990). Because of their impulsivity and distractability, it is hard for them to wait for a turn when playing or to concentrate long enough to complete a puzzle or game. They are more likely to grab things away from other children, or disrupt a carefully built tower or puzzle because of their activity level and lack of patience. In fact, research has shown these children are significantly delayed in their play and social skills (Barkley, 1996; Webster-Stratton & Lindsay, 1999). For example, a 6-year-old with ADHD plays more like a 4- year-old and will have difficulty with sharing, waiting, taking turns, and focusing or persisting with a play activity for more than a few minutes. Such children are more likely to be engaged in either solitary or parallel play. If they are in the parallel play stage of development, they will be fairly uninterested in other children and rarely initiate interactions. If they are interested in interacting with other children, they may avoid doing this either because they have experienced rejection in the past or because they don't know how to play appropriately.

Content focus. For children with ADHD, there is a special focus on the content topics of Doing Your Best in School, Emotion Regulation, and Friendship Skills. These three areas address the key skills deficits experienced by most children with ADHD. In the school unit, for the younger children there is a focus on listening, following directions, and persisting with a difficult play activity. Therapists use "persistence coaching" to coach them to stay focused and to keep trying when something is difficult. If they are older there is a focus on concentration, stopping to understand the assignments before doing schoolwork, stopping to check and recheck work, and learning to block out distractions. In the Feelings and Anger Management Units, the focus for these children is on emotional regulation. They learn to relax, recognize signs of dysregulation, and learn to calm down by taking deep breaths, thinking of their happy place and using positive self-talk. In the Friendship Units, these children are taught specific social sequences for situations such as entering a group of children who are already playing, waiting for a turn, learning how to play cooperatively with a peer and how to negotiate the decision-making process with other children and learning how to communicate.

The structure of the group is modified for children with ADHD.

The structure of the group is modified for children with ADHD because of their more limited capacity for sustained attention during circle time and their need for more movement than other children. Therapists introduce more songs, more role plays and physical activities, and more hands-on group activities to keep the attention of children. If the entire group is comprised of children diagnosed with ADHD, the 2-hour format is revised to include three shorter circle time lessons lasting 10-15 minutes instead of two 30 minute circle time lessons. An additional small group activity may be planned and children are often given additional time for coached play activities. If the group consists of children with and without ADHD, the structure is modified to allow those more focused children to work longer on their small group activity while permitting the inattentive children to work on a different activity. Special opportunities to move and be engaged (beyond those provided for the entire group) are set up for children with ADHD. For instance, the child with ADHD may be asked to come to the front of the group to hold a cue card, or be asked to retrieve something for the therapist from the back of the room. The therapist may have the child come sit on his/her lap for a few minutes (this should be contingent on appropriate behavior, rather than as a response to off-task behavior). The child may also be placed in a seat next to the therapist and physical touch (therapist hand on shoulder or arm) may help sustain the child's ability to stay focused.

The ADHD child may be given slightly more physical space than other children and visual boundaries used to delineate the space. For example, a masking tape box might be placed around the child's chair and as long as the child is within the tape boundaries he/she would not be required to be seated with both feet on the floor at all times. It may also be helpful to give the child a sanctioned "wiggle space" to use if it becomes too difficult to stay in the group. This is not a punishment, rather it is a self-regulation space so that the child has an option of a place to go to re-regulate and then come back to the group. This space should also be marked out with a physical boundary and might have nearby a picture of the puppet Wally relaxing, or taking deep breaths as signal to remind children of the calm down steps. Another approach is to ask the child with ADHD who is becoming very distracted to go over to an area of the room where there is a "Show me Five" hand posted on the wall and to put their hand on the poster to help them regain focus. This "Show Me Five" hand cue is a signal with a picture for each finger that indicates the following—eyes on the teacher, ears open, mouth closed, hands to self, and body quiet.

Therapists are coaching, praising, labeling, and reinforcing (with tokens) targeted child behaviors such as waiting, managing impulsivity (e.g., remembering to raise a quiet hand rather than blurting out), staying calm, staying in seat, concentrating, appropriately using wiggle space, and respecting physical boundaries. At first, therapists notice even very short periods of attention, waiting, and calm behavior, and a child might receive a tangible reward such as a token along with praise for sitting in his chair for as short a period of time as 30 seconds. One goal for these children, however, is to help them learn to sustain this kind of attention for longer and longer periods of time. Gradually over the course of treatment, therapists will tailor their rewards, rate of praise and their expectations to extend the children's ability to focus, wait, concentrate, and attend.

It is important to begin to teach children with ADHD to self-regulate and use cognitive strategies and positive self-talk. Initially, adult prompting and visual cues are used to achieve this. For example children are shown a picture of Dina Dinosaur concentrating. Under her picture are the words, "stop, look, think, check." These words are rehearsed out loud with hand motions to accompany each word. Picture cue cards also accompany each word (e.g., stop sign, looking eyes, light bulb symbol, and check mark). Children practice an activity requiring concentrating while the teacher, puppets, or other children help to remember each of the steps, and the steps are repeated out loud with the picture cues. The child can be provided with a picture cue card of Dina concentrating and this card might be placed on her desk at school to remind her of the skill she is practicing. The classroom teacher is asked to periodically walk by and prompt the child to use the concentration steps by tapping the picture. At the end of a period, the child can be asked to reflect on whether they concentrated and followed Dina's steps. They can be provided with self praise or coping statements (e.g., "I did it! I'm good at concentrating," or "I forgot to concentrate this time, but I bet I can concentrate on my next work").

Stop - look - think - check

In the friendship unit, the precise steps for learning how to play with another child are taught, modeled, prompted, and practiced extensively. First, children watch video vignettes of children playing with a variety of toys (blocks, make believe, puzzles, art projects, etc.) and in a variety of settings (playground, classroom), and they are prompted by the therapists to notice how the children on the video vignettes wait, take turns, and share. Then each child practices one or two play skills (which may be modeled by the therapist) with one of the puppets and is reinforced for these behaviors. Next, they are paired up with another child (their buddy) to play with and the therapist prompts, coaches, and reinforces them for using these friendly play behaviors. Sometimes it is helpful to break up the group by taking pairs of children out of the large group to practice their play skills without the distractions of other children in their peer group. After these dyadic practice sessions, the children return to the group for a circle time lesson focused on learning a particular social skill.

Tips for Working with Children with Language or Reading Delays

Approximately 30 percent of children with conduct problems and/or ADHD also have academic problems such as language or reading delays or learning disabilities (Bennett, Brown, Boyle, Racine, & Offord, 2003; Kaiser, Hancock, Cai, Foster, & Hester, 2000; Sturge, 1982).

For children with academic problems there is a special focus on the content topic of Doing Your Best in School. All of the tailoring recommendations suggested for improving the concentration skills of children with ADHD will also be helpful for a child who is struggling academically. Therapists who have a group with children with learning problems will also want to frequently engage in interactive or dialogic reading. This reading style encourages exploration of a book without the sole focus on reading the words accurately. Therapists discuss the pictures with the child by taking turns labeling objects, feelings, or other aspects of the picture, follow the child's lead and interest in the story, and help the child make up alternate endings to the stories, or even act out parts of the story with hand puppets. As children become familiar with particular stories, they may become the storyteller and will read or recite the story back to the therapist. Research has shown that when preschool teachers and parents read dialogically with their children, the children's vocabulary increases significantly (Whitehurst, et al., 1999) as well as their word recognition and motivation to read.

For these children, the link between written and oral language should be emphasized throughout the curriculum. Each visual cue card that presents a new social, emotional, or problem-solving concept has both a picture and a word that describes the concept. Having the group practice "reading" the word on the picture by repeating it aloud, pointing to the word as it is said, and acting out the word at the same time that it is spoken will help children with language delays to associate printed words with spoken words. Small group activities can also be chosen that will reinforce particular academic goals. There are many activities that involve reading and writing that can be adjusted for children with different developmental levels. Using small group activities that target a particular skill area for a child provides a low-pressure time for children to experience success with academic activities that may be difficult for them at school because therapists can provide extra scaffolding to make this learning successful.

Therapists focus special effort on labeling, praising, and encouraging academic behaviors and processes for children with learning problems. Raising a quiet hand, concentrating on work, checking something again, correcting a mistake, trying again, and persisting on a hard task are all examples of behaviors to reinforce. Cognitive processes are also recognized by therapists. Examples of this are: "*I can see you are really thinking hard about your answer.*" "*When it's hard to read, you tell yourself, I can do it if I just look at one letter at a time.*" "*It's great that you stayed calm and asked for help on that work. Did you tell yourself, I can stay calm even though I don't know this word?*"

Children's attachment classifications are not permanent and may become more secure if caregiver relationships become more predictable and comforting.

Communicating with the child's classroom teacher is particularly important for children who are struggling academically. The classroom teacher may be able to share the child's academic goals with the therapist, and in turn, the therapist can share strategies that are working with the child in Dinosaur School.

Tips for Working with Children with Attachment Problems

Children may have ambivalent or avoidant attachment patterns with their biological, foster, or adoptive parents for a variety of reasons (Bakersman-Kranenburg, Van Ijzendoorn, & Juffer, 2003). Insecure attachment may develop because children have experienced abandonment, neglect, death of a parent, trauma, or physical abuse during their early childhood years. It may also occur because parental or caregiver responses have been unpredictable, inconsistent, harsh, and dismissive of children's emotional needs. Children with attachment problems come from a variety of home settings. Some may be living with biological parents, others may be living with relatives, or with adoptive or foster parents. Some children may have lived their lives in one household while others may have been moved either formally (through adoption or foster care) or informally (care by a relative) to other households. Children who have experienced such stressful and inconsistent parenting learn not to trust the world or their relationships with others. Their insecure attachment, in turn, affects how they process information, solve problems, and behave with others. For example, some children with insecure attachment may be angry with adults and oppositional, suspicious, or rejecting of therapist attention or attempts to nurture them. Other children may have an insatiable need for adult attention and be resentful and clingy whenever attention is given to someone other than themselves. Still other children with insecure attachment may have difficulty separating from their parent or caregiver or be frightened of adults and become emotionally absent or disassociated to escape their fears. Children's attachment classifications are not permanent and may become more secure if caregiver and other adult relationships become more predictable and consistent, sensitive to their cues and comforting when distressed (Van Ijzendoorn, Juffer, & Duyvesteyn, 1998).

Particular content focus for children with attachment difficulties will be on the Feelings Unit, as well as the anger management and emotional regulation topics. Content on safety and coping with adults' anger will also be important. Children who have attachment problems may also have experienced inconsistent rules and responses to their behaviors, so knowledge of rules and expectations for their behavior in Dinosaur School will help them to feel safe and more secure in their relationships.

Children who have experienced negative and traumatizing events may experience anger, anxiety, depression, or sadness. In many cases, these feelings may have been ignored or invalidated by caregivers, and the children may be confused by these feelings. Consequently, children may not be able to label or discuss their feelings easily and may also believe that it's not safe to share these feelings with others. Such children often have difficulty managing emotions and frequently express sadness and fears by appearing angry and hostile towards others. For children with attachment problems, extra time is spent on labeling and identifying feeling words. It is important to help children understand that any feeling is okay to have, and to learn that it is how they react to that feeling that is important (e.g., it's okay to be very mad at someone, but it's not okay to hit). It is also important for the therapists to watch for times when children are having positive emotions and to label these emotions (e.g., *"John, you look like you are feeling proud of your new backpack,"* or *"Sally, I see a big smile on your face. I think you are happy to see Wally today."*). Typically children's negative emotions receive much more attention from adults than the positive ones. As children begin to have a larger repertoire of feeling words, then they can begin to express emotion in new ways.

Children with attachment problems also need help to develop coping strategies for managing anger and sadness. Depending on the age of the child, these strategies will be a combination of behavioral and cognitive techniques. For example, specific behaviors that children learn to manage anger are taking three deep breaths, counting to 10, and practicing making their bodies tense and relaxed. Cognitive strategies range from simple statements such as, "I can do it, I can calm down" to more complex cognitions such as, "I'm feeling mad because my sister took my truck, but I'm going to be strong and ignore her. Then I won't get in trouble and I'll prove I can control my anger." Behavioral strategies for managing sadness include telling a safe adult that you feel sad, or finding a fun activity to do. Cognitive strategies involve thinking of happy thoughts or places, giving a compliment to yourself, or telling yourself that feelings can change and even though you're sad now, you will feel better later.

It is important to discuss ways for the child to stay safe and to cope with an adult's anger.

It is important to discuss ways for the child to stay safe and to cope with an adult's anger. Depending on the child's current living situation, these discussions may focus on helping children understand that even when adults are angry, they still love their children or, for a child who is still in a potentially abusive situation, the emphasis should be on identifying when the adults around them aren't safe and to have a plan for what to do when this happens. Children discuss coping strategies to use when an adult is angry with them such as apologizing, giving the adult some time to calm down, and knowing a safe place to go or a safe person to talk to if an adult is very angry at them. A discussion about the fact that sometimes, even though parents love their children, they act in ways that will hurt them can help children talk about these fearful times. Children learn that it's not okay for their parents to do this, and that it means that their parents need some help learning how to calm down and how to take care of them. It is important to understand the child's living circumstances. These discussions will be framed differently if the child is still living with a potentially abusive adult than if the child is living with a foster parent but plans to return home eventually.

For children with attachment problems, it is very important that the parent be as involved as possible in the treatment process. Ideally, the parent should be in a parenting group at the same time as the child is in the child group. If this is not possible, then it is important for the therapist to have regular communication with the parent about the particular goals of Dinosaur School and specific things that the parent can do at home to increase parent–child bonding.

Since children with attachment difficulties may be mistrustful of adults, the puppets are a particularly important teaching method. Children will often warm up to the puppets and talk about things that they wouldn't talk about with an adult. The puppets are also a useful tool for demonstrating appropriate touch. The puppets model that it's important to ask before touching someone (e.g., "Would you like a hug or a hand shake?"). For a child who is inappropriately affectionate, the puppet can model appropriate reactions (e.g., "I'd rather not have a kiss on the lips, but I'd love it if you gave me a hug or a high five."). Children who are suspicious and reluctant to receive adult physical touch or affection may be willing to receive a hug or a handshake or a high five from the puppet. Gradually the puppets will help the therapist to form a bond with a mistrustful child.

Children with attachment problems have difficulty with separations and reunions with their caregivers and other adults. These issues can be addressed by making sure that the puppets and therapists have routine greeting rituals and welcome each child in a personal and predictable way at each Dinosaur School session. If a puppet or a therapist is going to miss a session, children are prepared for this separation in advance, or if the absence is unexpected, children are given a chance to ask questions about why the person is missing and when he or she will be back. Goodbyes are treated in the same predictable way. Puppets and therapists say goodbye at the end of each session, and before the end of treatment, several weeks are spent talking about the fact that Dinosaur school will be ending. The children's feelings about this are explored, and the therapists, children, and puppets discuss ways to cope with feeling sad and keeping in touch. The repeated predictability of greetings and reunions can help to increase children's sense of security with adult relationships. The therapists also help to model these greetings and reunions for parents at the beginning and ending of each group session.

Children with attachment problems who have been blamed or abused by adults in the past may be suspicious of praise. They may respond by rejecting it, getting overexcited, or misbehaving. For example, a child tears up his art paper when his teacher praises him, or a child gets up and runs around the room the instant that the therapist gives her a token for sitting in her chair. It is important to be persistent and generous with praise and reinforcement for these children, even though sometimes children become more disruptive at first. These children are good at training adults to stop praising them, which only reinforces their idea that they are "bad." Therapists may experiment with the way in which praise is given. Instead of exuberant praise, the praise may be given in quiet, personal moments. The therapist may give it quickly, and then deflect attention from the child, so as not to put the child on the spot to accept the praise. Any rejection or arguments that result from the praise are ignored. It can also be effective to give praise to the wary child indirectly, such as giving it to another adult but in a setting where the child will overhear the comment, (e.g., "Carolyn, I wanted to let you know that I'm proud of Simone for picking up all the toys so fast when I asked."). At first, it may be important to pair each praise statement with a tangible reinforcement (a token or sticker). For some children these tangible rewards are more meaningful than praise because they don't trust that adults are sincere with their praise. Gradually they will learn to accept the praise if it is consistent and genuine.

Tips for Working with Children with Internalizing Problems Such as Anxiety and Depression

Internalizing or anxiety disorders encompass a wide variety of conditions such as generalized anxiety disorder (GAD), social or school phobia, separation anxiety disorder (SAD), obsessive compulsive disorder (OCD) and depression. Young children may not recognize these feelings or be able to talk about them with others. Consequently their anxieties may be expressed in symptoms that include crying, clinging behavior, stomachaches, headaches, irritability, and withdrawal. Depressed children may misbehave or even express their sadness in the form of aggressive behavior and angry talk in their interactions with others.

A focus on the feelings, emotional regulation, problem solving, and friendship units will be important for children with anxious or depressed affect. Very often children with anxiety and depression have received a lot of adult concern and recognition around their fearful and sad behaviors. While it is important to ensure that children have the vocabulary and awareness to recognize and discuss these feelings, these negative feelings should be cues for them to implement anxiety management and coping strategies. As mentioned above, these coping strategies will be both behavioral (find a friend, take a deep breath, find something fun to do, use a muscle relaxation strategy, give yourself a reward for

trying) and cognitive (stop the negative self-talk, think of a happy or relaxing thought, give yourself a compliment, tell yourself that you can change your feelings, change anxious self-talk to a coping thought). The emphasis should be on the power that children have to make themselves feel better. In the problem-solving unit, the emphasis can continue to be on children's ability to think of solutions to situations that they find anxiety provoking or that make them sad. Relaxation techniques can be particularly useful for children who are fearful and anxious. The relaxation thermometer is often used to help children manage angry feelings, but can also be used to help children calm themselves when they are scared or anxious. In addition to learning problem solving, another component of the program focuses on friendship skills, play, and communication skills. Since many of these children are socially phobic, they need help in making friends and knowing how to enter in play or to play cooperatively with another child. In the Dinosaur program children have weekly coached practice sessions in play interaction skills with the other children. In addition, children learn and practice communication skills such as how to introduce themselves, what kinds of questions to ask in order to initiate a conversation with a friend, and how to give and receive compliments. Role play and rehearsal within the safety of the group, with the puppets, can provide the practice children need to be brave enough to try these skills out with peers.

As with other issues, the puppets can help to individualize the problems to match children's anxieties or sad thoughts. Wally has a stomachache and is fearful about going to school without his parents, or presenting to his classmates at "show and tell," or making a call to a friend. Molly might be sad because she feels like she doesn't have any friends. The children can help identify the puppet's feelings and then help learn to problem solve coping strategies. Role-play and rehearsal with the puppet will help the children practice the strategies to use for themselves.

Therapists and the puppets can challenge children's expression of negative emotions, especially when they are unrealistic. For example, they can help children understand that it is normal for to sometimes be excluded or turned down. Children can be helped to understand how to respond to this perceived or real rejection and encouraged to try again later.

It is particularly important that the therapists are careful not to inadvertently reinforce children's fears or depression. It is tempting to offer large amounts of comfort or sympathy to a child who is anxious or sad. While there are certainly appropriate times to comfort a distressed child, a child who commonly expresses emotion in the form of anxiety and sadness has most likely learned that these emotions elicit positive adult attention and comfort. A brief reassurance when the child expresses a negative emotion paired with a coping thought can help to break this cycle (e.g., "*I'm glad you told me you're sad. I wonder what activity you could choose to make yourself feel better?*"). In addition, therapists should look for opportunities to praise and give attention and affection when the child is happy, brave, calm, or relaxed (e.g. "*Wow! I'm so impressed with you. You are so brave to come to group all by yourself, and you even look very calm! You must be so proud of yourself to be able to do that. Can I give you a hug?*"). Children who learn that they can cope with their anxious and sad feelings will have increased self-confidence and will not need to seek as much adult reassurance to regulate these feelings.

Parents of these children are helped to reinforce these same skills at home. They are encouraged to minimize the amount of attention they give to worried, sad, and anxious behaviors, and to help reinforce the new coping strategies their children are learning. They can also help to reinforce the other skills children are learning by setting up and monitoring play dates for their children, encouraging them to join school sports or clubs, and by firmly supporting them to participate in activities that are scary. Parents can provide rewards for "brave" behaviors (e.g., going to school, going to bed alone, talking to other children) and can help to celebrate their children's success.

Tips for Working with Children with Developmental Delays

The small group Dinosaur school format is not appropriate for children with severe developmental delays. Children who have very little receptive and expressive language and who are functioning below the mental age of 3 will likely not be able to absorb the content in a way that is therapeutically effective. More intensive intervention, delivered in early intervention school settings is likely to produce more generalization and progress. However, many children with moderate developmental delays have participated in the program with success. For these children all units are important and will need to be presented at the developmental level of the children in the group. The School Rules and Doing Your Best in School units will help establish rules and expectations for school and group behavior. Some of the content on advanced study skills such as concentration may be omitted, depending on the academic goals for children in the group. However, learning to sit in a circle, wait for a turn to talk, raise a hand, look at the teacher, and answer a question will all be useful skills.

The feelings units will begin with recognition of a variety of feeling states in oneself and others. As children's feeling vocabulary increases, coping strategies will be provided for managing negative emotions (happy thought, deep breaths). In the problem solving unit, basic solutions to hypothetical problems will be rehearsed (e.g., wait and take turns, help, share, ask, get parent). Evaluating the consequences of solutions is a more advanced cognitive skill and may not be appropriate for many young and developmentally delayed children. Nonetheless, most children can be helped to make the distinction between positive "thumbs up" and negative "thumbs down" solutions. Children with delays are taught the turtle technique for anger management and learn this in concrete ways, such as actually going under a turtle shell and rehearsing the calm down words to use and the deep breathing steps. In the friendship units the emphasis will be on teaching friendship skills, such as introducing oneself, asking questions, listening, complimenting, taking turns, helping, and sharing.

The basic methods and process will not change for children with developmental delays; however, the delivery should be adapted in some areas to meet the needs of the group. Some children with more severe delays will not be able to wait until the end of a group to trade in tokens for prizes. In this case, offer multiple, more frequent opportunities to trade in chips. Other children may not be able to understand a token economy at all, either because they cannot count or cannot anticipate consequences or the connection between waiting for a certain number of chips and obtaining a prize. For these children, other more concrete and immediate reward systems will be used. For example, the children could earn marbles in a jar for targeted social behaviors, and when the jar reaches a certain level (marked clearly) the group earns a special snack or activity. These children may also benefit from earning stickers or hand stamps given immediately after the positive behaviors occur.

If behavior problems are less severe, it may not be necessary to use a formal tangible reward system. High rates of teacher positive attention and praise paired with varied teaching modalities (puppets, songs, movement games, small group activities, short circle times) may be enough to keep some groups interested and engaged. Spontaneous rewards, such as the first person who is sitting quietly gets to line up first, are very effective with such children.

For children with delays, limited language skills, and short attention spans, it is preferable to offer the program in more frequent, but shorter sessions. For instance, instead of meeting weekly for 2 hours, the group could meet 2-3 times a week for shorter time periods. This provides opportunities for more frequent practice and reinforcement of the behaviors being taught. It is particularly important with delayed (or younger) groups to keep the group lively and to keep the activities varied. Less therapist teaching and group discussion and more active child involvement in role plays, songs, games, and hands-on activities will lead to more learning and engagement. Repetition is also important. Each lesson or concept may need to be presented multiple times. For example, in a typically developing group, children discuss 2 or 3 different solutions in one group (sharing, waiting, helping, and taking turns). In a group for delayed children, several lessons might be spent just on one of the solutions such as "sharing." Each child in the group will do multiple role plays or practices that demonstrate sharing. The vignettes may be shown more than once or extra vignettes showing more examples of sharing are included at subsequent sessions. In addition, extra small group activities practicing sharing activities are planned to reinforce the learning. It is more important that the children learn each social skills concept well than that the curriculum be rushed to cover too many concepts at once. If material is not covered thoroughly, the children will be confused or overwhelmed with new concepts and behaviors. Our model is to make it simple, be sure the language-based instruction is brief and clear, provide multiple opportunities for modeling (with video vignettes) and plan many small group manipulative practice activities.

Helping

All of the concepts presented in Dinosaur School have picture cue cards to accompany the lessons. The use of these visual cue cards will be particularly important for children with developmental delays and with impaired receptive and expressive language development (as is evident in children with autism). These cards should be prominently displayed and referred to frequently each time the concept is discussed or modeled. In addition, children with language delays may need to have their own set of smaller feeling or solution cue cards (velcroed to a portable picture board or key ring) that they can use to communicate with others. For example, if a child wants to use a toy that another child has, the therapists can prompt the child to look for the "share" or "ask" cue card and hand it to the child she would like to share toys with. Or, if the child would like help with an activity, he can be prompted to point to the "help" cue card.

In addition to providing visual cues to promote social interactions and nonverbal communication, therapists, and teachers working with these children will use child-directed descriptive commenting (described in detail in Chapter Four). For these children, the descriptive comments will focus on providing appropriate vocabulary to describe the child's play (in essence, providing the language that the child may not be able to express on his own). This commenting will be balanced between academic/persistence, social, and emotion coaching to support the child's development in all areas. In addition to using pure descriptive comments, therapists will also provide children with appropriate verbal prompts, for example. "You can say: '*Can I have the truck please?*'" or "Tell him: '*I'm not done yet*'" to scaffold the play interactions with language that they may not be able to produce independently. This coaching will help build their school readiness skills and language production.

SUMMARY

In this chapter, we have shown how the *Incredible Years Child Dinosaur Social, Emotional, and Problem Solving Skills Program* can be adapted to treat multiple presenting co-morbid issues, however this is only one part of an intervention approach. Children who present for treatment with conduct problems are likely to be experiencing family circumstances that also contribute to their behavioral difficulties. A comprehensive intervention will always involve parent training to strengthen the parent-child relationship and help parents understand how to coach and encourage their child's emotional, social and academic learning at home. This will be crucial to helping children generalize their skills to other settings and relationships.

Therapists delivering the program must be very familiar with the basic group therapy content, methods, and process and should understand the rationale for presenting each content unit in the recommended order as well as the cognitive social learning principles that are important for working therapeutically with children (e.g., frequent positive attention for social behaviors and emotional regulation skills that they would like to see increase and minimal attention for behaviors they would like to see decrease). With this in mind, the therapist, in conjunction with the parents and classroom teachers, can set individual behavioral goals and develop a behavior plan for each child in the group. Central to this treatment model is the idea that while a specific set of skills are taught in a specific order, the way the skills are taught, the level of sophistication with which they are presented, and the amount of time spent on each content area must depend on each child's behavioral and emotional needs as well as his or her developmental level. In this way, the program can be used in conjunction with the parent program to provide a comprehensive treatment that will help children cope with different situations and circumstances across the home and school settings.

Tailoring the Incredible Years® Parent and Child Programs for Child Welfare Referred Families

The Incredible Years (IY) parenting program is relevant for use with maltreating families with young children. Its focus on nurturing parenting and promoting positive attachment relationships, ongoing monitoring and safety, and family interpersonal and support needs, and reducing children's problems with emotional regulation, social skills, and cognitive development address many of the needs of families involved in the child welfare system. All of the collaborative methods and processes described earlier in Chapter Eight are designed to build support networks and decrease the isolation and sense of alienation commonly found among parents involved in the child welfare system. The collaborative approach aims to enhance parent participation, motivation, and attendance and provides added focus on cognitive restructuring, emotional regulation strategies, and behavioral practice and experiential methods of learning.

For this population, we recommend the parent program be combined with the IY therapeutic child treatment group, which has been described in Chapter Twelve. Because families involved with child welfare services often experience multiple stressors that go beyond parenting issues, it is highly recommended that both the IY BASIC and the ADVANCE programs are offered. The table below is provided to show how the Core IY Parenting Program is adapted for the child welfare population.

ADAPTING THE IY PROGRAM FOR THE CHILD WELFARE POPULATION

Core IY components	IY Fidelity Adaptations
Standard Topics and Protocols for each of 4 Basic Parenting Programs according to age group targeted (2008 versions)	Cover standard topics and protocols; increase focus in key areas: parent-child attachment, emotion and social coaching, parental attributions and self-talk, positive discipline, monitoring, safety-proofing, self-care
Vignette Protocols	Use all core vignettes and add additional vignettes if parents in the group are not mastering material
Program Dosage (18-20 sessions)	May need more sessions to cover core program if groups take longer to understand and master material
Key Group Teaching/Learning Methods (goal setting, behavioral practice, principle building, values exercises, tailoring to meet cultural and developmental issues, home activities)	Increased parent practice and role plays in sessions, develop scripts for language skills and cognitions, more explicit teaching about developmentally appropriate parenting practices, adapt home activities for families without children in the home

Alliance building techniques (collaborative learning, buddy calls, weekly leader support calls, praise to parents, incentives for parents)	All standard alliance building techniques apply to this population; may need increased efforts to engage families (more praise, more incentives, and spending longer to build a trusting relationship between parents and leaders)
Food, transportation, daycare	No adaptations needed, but essential to offer these
Core model does not offer home visits	Add a minimum of 4 home visits to coach and practice parent-child interactions using coach home visit manuals
Core model does not address collaboration with case workers or planning for visitation with children	Train and coordinate with case workers to plan for parent-child visitations. Case workers must understand the core IY topics and parenting strategies to coach families during these visits
Core model suggests use of IY Advance and Child Programs for children with diagnoses or very high risk families	Use additional IY Programs: • Advance Program to teach anger and depression management and problem-solving steps • Child Social, Emotional and Problem-Solving Skills Small Group Therapy Program (Dinosaur School) offered with parent program

THE BASIC PARENT PROGRAM

As discussed in earlier chapters, the Basic Parenting program has four separate versions, each geared towards a different age group (baby, toddler, preschool, school age). Since it may be difficult for parents with histories of abuse and neglect to generalize parenting skills and behavior management principles for one age group to another age group, it is recommended that groups are comprised of parents who have children of roughly the same age. The baby and young preschool children programs are particularly important for the child welfare populations because the rate of maltreatment from birth to 1 year is approximately double the rate for children aged 4 to 7 years. Furthermore, more than three-quarters of all children who die due to abuse and neglect are younger than 4 years (U.S. Department of Health and Social Services Administration on Children Youth and Families, 2006). Ideally, high-risk parents would be offered the baby program as soon as their babies are born, followed by the toddler, preschool, and school age programs as their children reach each developmental age group. Disadvantaged families with histories of child welfare involvement will need ongoing parent support and scaffolding for each stage of their children's developmental transition in order to be able to break the cycle of intergenerational transmission of abuse and neglect. A chronic condition is better treated with a repeated and ongoing dose of multifaceted intervention and is more likely to have sustainable outcomes and prevent future occurrence than a single dose model approach. The core content and objectives of the Basic program are well suited to the child welfare population. The parenting pyramid's foundation with its emphasis on relationship building and positive parenting in

Disadvantaged families with histories of child welfare involvement will need ongoing parent support and scaffolding for each stage of their children's developmental transition in order to be able to break the cycle of intergenerational transmission of abuse and neglect.

the first half of the program builds up parent-child attachment and the positive discipline and limit setting in the second half of the program provides an alternative to harsher discipline styles. The figure below provides a list of the specific aims from each of these categories and can be compared to the content/goals required of mandated parenting programs for this population.

IY PARENT BASIC PROGRAM OBJECTIVES

Strengthen Parent-Child Relationships and Bonding

- Increase parents' empathy towards their children.
- Increase parent knowledge of normal child development and provide age appropriate expectations and sensitivity to individual differences in children.
- Promote consistent monitoring and predictable supervision to keep children safe.
- Increase parents' positive thoughts and decrease their negative attributions about their children.
- Encourage more effective praise and encouragement for targeted prosocial behaviors.
- Promote positive parent-child relationships and strengthen parent-child attachment.
- Increase child-directed play and parent enjoyment of parent-child interactions.
- Help parents to become social, emotion, persistence, and academic "coaches" for their children.

Promote Predictable Routines, Effective Limit Setting, Non-Punitive Discipline, and Problem Solving

- Promote understanding of the importance of predictable schedules, routines, and consistent responses, particularly in regard to separations and reunions with children.

- Teach anger management strategies and affect regulation so parents can stay calm, controlled, and patient when disciplining their children.
- Help parents set realistic goals for their children's social, emotional, and academic behavior.
- Help parents set up behavior plans and develop salient rewards for targeted prosocial behaviors.
- Reduce harsh and physical discipline and promote consistent, nonpunitive discipline.
- Promote children's self-regulation skills by using brief Time Outs to calm down.
- Teach parents to help children manage anger through problem-solving and self-regulation strategies.
- Promote joyful experiences and memories and reduce exposure to adult arguments, violent TV, computer games, and an atmosphere of fear or depression.

ADAPTATIONS FOR PARENTS REFERRED BY CHILD WELFARE

Child-Directed Play and Coaching Skills—Strengthening Parent-Child Bonding and Building Children's Social and Emotional Competence

The programs on child-directed play and academic, persistence, social, and emotion coaching are core components of the IY program and are an especially relevant topic for the child welfare population because of their focus on the parent-child relationship, bonding, and attachment. It is important not to move on to the discipline units until parents begin to understand the concept and language needed for child-directed play, coaching, praise, and incentives and have begun to form more positive relationships with their children. For this population it is recommended that most of the vignettes from the child-directed play and coaching programs be shown (in groups with less challenging populations a subset of the total vignettes is suggested).

For many of these parents, child-directed play and coaching is a foreign skill and difficult language to learn. Many of these parents experienced abusive or neglectful parenting as children and so have not had this kind of nurturing experience modeled for them. Their current relationships with their children may be ambivalent, stressed, and challenging. They also are likely to be feeling unsuccessful as parents, and may believe that their children will not want to spend time with them.

Parents in child welfare groups are provided with many more intensive behavioral practice play experiences.

Parents in child welfare groups are provided with many more intensive behavioral practice play experiences than a typical group. Parents take turns role playing or practicing playing "parent" or "child". Leaders need to simplify skills, develop written scripts and do repeated practices before moving on to more complex parenting. This provides practice with new parenting techniques and gives parents an opportunity to see the world through the perspective of their children, which promotes feelings of empathy for their needs. Parents also have daily home assignments to practice what they are learning. If children are in childcare at the same location as the parenting group, it is ideal to allot some time at the end of each session for parents to practice the new play interaction and communication skills with their children, in the context of supportive coaching and feedback from the group leader. Alternatively, parents can receive this coaching and supervision of their parenting skills during a home visit. A home visitor coach manual is available for use by home visitor coaches or case managers who will help parents practice the skills they are learning with their children. In some cases, home practice assignments will need to be modified with this population if parents do not have their children at home. More attention will be given to modifying home assignments in the process section of this chapter.

The net result of this added emphasis on child-directed play and coaching is the strengthening of a more secure attachment between parents and children as well as more sensitive and responsive parenting and more parental understanding when reacting to their children's behaviors. It also facilitates the strengthening of children's self-esteem; academic, social, and emotional competence; and language skills, which may have been delayed due to prior lack of adequate parent cognitive stimulation and parental language interactions.

Praise and Rewards—Increasing Positive Parenting Skills, Thoughts and Communication With Others

When parents are stressed and depressed, they are less likely to praise and encourage their children or even to notice positive behaviors when they occur. Moreover, they are more likely to be irritated, critical, or angry about minor annoying misbehaviors (Ashman, Dawson, & Panagiotides, 2008; Fergusson & Lynskey, 1993; Levendosky, Okun, & Parker, 1995). At these times, parents need help to identify positive behaviors they want to encourage, to learn the precise praise language to use by recording the scripts and to develop strategies for remembering to praise these behaviors frequently. As with the play principle, parents are helped to understand the impact of praise and positive reinforcement on all relationships (partners, colleagues, family members, friendships, their children's teachers). Finally, in this program they begin to learn about the importance of positive self-talk or self-praise. They rehearse and record positive motivational statements they can use when they find themselves getting negative, such as: "*I am a good parent; I'm doing my best; I can handle this; I will cope; I can stay calm; I can help her learn to control herself; I did a pretty good job talking to my case worker; No one is perfect—I can do this; I try hard.*" Learning to stop negative thoughts, substitute these positive coping statements and use self-praise for their negative self-defeating thoughts is a recurring exercise for this population throughout all the parenting group sessions.

Group leaders also coach these parents constantly with praise and encouragement. They offer surprise rewards for meeting their personal goals and set up planned rewards for doing aspects of the home activities that are difficult. Leaders may set up parent reward charts posted on the wall where parents receive stickers for completing home activities and reading, and participating in practices and problem solving discussions. The leader challenges the parents to earn a certain number of stickers in order to receive special rewards such as clothing, toys and books for their children or self-care items such as lotion, special teas, chocolate and massage or department store coupons.

Positive Discipline—Increasing Children's Sense of Safety and Security

Frequently, abusive parents have unrealistic expectations of their children's behavior. They do not understand that all children disobey about 1/3 of the time and all children whine, cry, tantrum, and are defiant and oppositional at times. In this program, parents are helped to understand that these behaviors are normal and healthy expressions of self-confidence, independence and a biological drive for discovery and exploration. They are also helped to identify the important rules for their family and to keep these to a minimum. They learn to reduce excessive and unnecessary commands and criticisms and to give necessary commands clearly, politely, and calmly without fear of their children's response. The message emphasized is the ability to state a command assertively and respectfully but without negative affect or hostility. Parents learn that yelling and excessive angry responses to child behaviors may inadvertently reinforce the child's misbehavior. This requires parents use self-control strategies and regulate their negative responses. Parents learn to identify positive opposite behaviors that they want to see more of and to give praise, attention, and small incentives in order to increase those behaviors.

Handling Misbehavior—Strengthening Parents' and Children's Self-Regulation Skills

Parents learn to ignore many of the annoying behaviors that children exhibit such as crying, tantruming, whining, arguing, and backtalk. The difference between briefly ignoring an inappropriate behavior and neglecting a child is emphasized with this population. Developmental guidelines define what ignoring looks like and how to keep children safe while ignoring. The key to using a "planned ignore" successfully is that parents learn never to ignore the child, but instead, to briefly ignore an inappropriate behavior. Parents are

The most important part of ignoring is to return positive attention to the child as soon as the inappropriate behavior stops.

taught to stay near the child during ignoring and that the most important part of ignoring is to return positive attention to the child as soon as the inappropriate behavior stops. Parents learn that planned ignoring is only effective when the parent-child bond is strong so the therapist and parents must spend sufficient time on the child-directed play, coaching, praise and the incentive portion of the program to strengthen their relationship before starting this topic. In general, this topic comes after 10-12 weeks spent building parent-child attachment and positive parenting strategies.

Parents are trained to use a *brief* Time Out to calm down as a nonviolent and respectful consequence for aggressive behavior in children 3 to 8 years. Time Out is only 3-5 minutes in duration and is a well monitored period where children learn to regulate their negative emotions. However, the group leader carefully considers parents' readiness to implement Time Out. It is important that parents are engaged in regular play times and have successfully learned to coach and praise prosocial behaviors before starting Time Out. It is also important that parents have learned some personal self-calming strategies before using Time Out. This may mean that they practice numerous Time Out scenarios in the group before initiating this at home. Lastly, parents discuss appropriate ways to monitor their child's safety during Time Out. Parents learn how to teach their children how to calm down in Time Out before having to use it for aggressive behavior by practicing with them some deep breathing and positive self-statements such as, "I can calm down; I can try again." Time Out is not intended as a humiliation experience for the child, rather a time for the child (and parent) to reflect, to calm themselves and to think of a new solution. After a child has completed Time Out, the parent looks for the first opportunity for the child to be successful and to receive positive parental attention, coaching and praise.

Many of the parents have used spanking, smacking or hitting in the past as their primary form of discipline and have experienced physical discipline themselves as children. Some of them have experienced being locked up as children, so will have fears about using Time Out. They usually are unaware of how to use Time Out appropriately or why ignoring strategies work to reduce misbehavior. Therefore, it can be difficult for them to give up spanking or hitting, especially as it often seems to work to get their child to obey in the short run. A variety of practice, discussion, and brainstorming strategies help parents to think about both the short- and long-term advantages of spanking and Time Out. The goal is to have parents discover that in the short term, spanking may help control their child, but its use leads to long-term difficulties for their child in terms of escalating aggression and fear of their parent. In contrast, Time Out, delivered in a respectful and calm way, is difficult for the parent in the short term because so much self-control is required, but in the long run results in more child self-regulation and healthier parent-child relationships. Discussions about spanking in the context of a group of parents who have been referred to the child welfare system will involve the reality that many of these parents are being carefully monitored. It is likely that spanking their children may result in additional consequences from the child welfare system. This provides an additional incentive to use other methods of discipline, but also may add to parents' resentment about being monitored and their helpless feelings if they feel they don't have other discipline strategies to manage misbehavior. Providing parents with a chance to explore feelings of guilt, anger, inadequacy, fear of losing their children, and other emotions that occur during the use of physical discipline can help parents be more receptive to learning new coping strategies. In addition to learning nonviolent discipline approaches, parents learn ways to manage their own anger. These include: (a) recognizing early that anger is building up; (b) deep breathing and muscle relaxation exercises; (c) challenging negative self-talk and rewriting positive self-talk; (d) positive imagery, and (e) taking brief Time Outs themselves. As part of this process, parents develop an "emergency" plan for times when they feel that they cannot handle a situation on their own without losing control. This may involve calling a buddy from the group or a friend, calling the group leader, or some other way of getting support to defuse a situation.

Teaching Children to Problem Solve

The final program in the series is helping parents learn how to teach their children to problem solve in conflict situations. Parents help children learn solutions to try when feeling angry, sad, hurt, or disappointed. They are given books to read to their children about problems they can solve using puppets and make-believe games (Webster-Stratton, 1998a, 1998b, 1998c, 1998d). Parents often find it difficult to teach their children problem-solving skills because they have their own difficulties with problem solving. For this reason, supplementing the basic parenting program with the Advance program (see description below) on adult problem solving is recommended before the program on teaching children to problem solve.

Monitoring, Safety and Home Child Proofing

In order to parent in positive and consistent ways, parents must be monitoring their children. Particularly in the case of neglecting parents, monitoring is a key theme that is discussed in every session. Parents are given information about why they cannot leave children unattended and brainstorm what to do when they feel they have to leave their child. Options for appropriate and safe babysitters and childcare are discussed, and problem solving occurs around barriers. Developmental expectations for monitoring different age children are also discussed. Parents learn about the value of appropriate continual monitoring across the age spans for promoting their children's social and emotional development, safety and sense of security. Parents are helped to see the potential negative outcomes of not monitoring, both for their children and themselves. Other safety issues are covered, with an emphasis on how these issues change for children of different ages and developmental levels. The baby and toddler program place particular emphasis on home child-proofing and parents are asked to complete checklists of things to check in their home and these are reviewed in detail in the sessions. In the school age program monitoring preadolescent children's whereabouts after school, in the evening, and on weekends is emphasized. They are often surprised to learn than ongoing monitoring of adolescents' whereabouts is a way of promoting ongoing attachment in addition to keeping them safe.

Parents learn about the value of appropriate continual monitoring across the age spans for promoting their children's development, safety and sense of security.

IY Group Process and Methods of Engaging Families

Above we discussed ways to tailor the program content to families involved in the child welfare system. In addition to the need for content adaptation or increased focus, other barriers often arise with this population. Below we will highlight some of the group leader group processes and methods that are used to overcome these barriers.

Therapists help parents to incorporate a new cognitive and emotional framework.

Collaborative Process

Parents involved in the child welfare system may be difficult to engage because they are angry about being required or mandated to participate in parent education. The IY parent program model, with its emphasis on collaboration rather than didactic prescriptions and lectures and its non-blaming focus on parent strengths instead of deficits, is designed to counteract parent resistance and passivity. Collaboration implies that parents are actively involved in setting their own goals for themselves and their children and when they do this in groups many parents find comfort in the realization that they are not alone and that other parents

SUPPORTING AND ADVOCATING FOR PARENTS

have similar goals such as "getting child welfare out of their lives" or getting their children back. Because of their sense of isolation such parents find tremendous benefit from talking with their assigned a buddy (another parent in the group) as well as with their group leader each week. This approach builds a support team that serves to diffuse parents' anger, depression and sense of stigmatization. Making new friends and sharing mutual experiences is motivating and supportive for these parents, who often feel alienated and blamed (Coohey, 1996; Hutchings & Webster-Stratton, 2004; Roditti, 2005). Eventually therapists help parents to incorporate a new cognitive and emotional framework of themselves and their parenting and community.

While the collaborative and supportive relationship between parents and therapists is the underlying structure for the IY process of intervention, within this relationship the program's incorporation of motivational concepts such as individual goal setting, self-monitoring, reinforcing motivational self-talk, examination of personal belief systems via benefit and barriers values exercises, peer buddy calls, and group leader coaching helps to empower parents and promote demoralized parents' active engagement with the program. Since all of these methods have been described in Chapter Eight and Nine, readers should look there for basic descriptions of how they are used in the group. In this chapter, we provide specific examples of the particular relevance of a therapy strategy for helping this population of parents to determine and accept responsibility for what they want to achieve within a supportive context.

Benefits and Barriers Brainstorms

The benefits and barriers exercises that introduce each content area are used as a therapeutic technique to help parents articulate and examine their own beliefs about each new topic. This brainstorm also provides therapists with an overview about what parents know and believe about parenting. During the brainstorms, the therapist's role is to reflect, clarify, and extend the points that parents are making. For example, during a brainstorm on the benefits of playing with children a parent might say, "Play makes children happy." The therapist would respond, "*That's a good observation. Parent play makes children happy. Why do you think children are so happy to have their parents play with them?*" This discussion could continue to help parents in the group explore the idea that children value parental attention above all else; that to a child, the parent is the most important person in the world, that getting to play with them is the best "gift" they can offer. This realization can be eye opening for parents who might have felt that their child's demands for attention were irritating and bothersome. Therapists can explore further to ask parents to think about whether playing with their children has any benefits for them. Frequently in the program, parents are encouraged to think about parent-child interactions from both points of view—the parent and the child. This reflection increases empathy for the child as well as helping the parents to see the mutual benefits of a strong-parent child relationship.

Therapists help parents find acceptable solutions to overcome their barriers.

After the group members have explored the benefits of a particular topic, they are encouraged to explore the barriers. This is particularly useful in groups of parents where there is resistance to a specific topic or to the idea of a parenting group in general. By inviting parents to share their concerns and barriers, the therapist is able to diffuse and validate some of the emotional or reluctant reactions that parents might have. During this brainstorm, the therapist listens to each barrier and acknowledges it. This is not a time to dispute the barrier or to try to convince parents that a strategy is worth trying, in spite of the barriers. For instance, a parent might say, "I just don't have the time to play, and when I do play, he just wants to play the same game over and over." The therapist responds, "*So, you're mentioning two really common barriers here. First, it can be really hard to find the time to play when you have so many other things to do just to keep up with day-to-day life. And the second thing you mentioned is that sometimes children's play is a little boring for adults. It really can be hard to patiently sit through 15 minutes of lining up the same cars in a row and then racing them around a track, especially when there is so much else to do.*" Another parent might say, "My child is just so hyperactive and aggressive, that I really don't like playing with him." The therapist responds, "*This is another common barrier. Some children because of their temperament are really exhausting to play with.*

They aren't much fun to be with sometimes." By acknowledging and trying to understand the parents' barriers, the therapist can begin to address the resistance that often comes when a new strategy is introduced. In the barriers exercise, it is understood by the whole group that there are things within the strategy itself or their environment that make the new strategies hard to implement. From here, the therapist moves the group on to the discussion of the content by summarizing the benefits and letting the group members know that they will work to find acceptable solutions to their particular barriers.

Self-Monitoring and Home Activities Incentives

Home activities are an important part of the group learning process, but parents who are reluctant to attend a group will often also be resistant to the idea of being told what they need to do at home. To address this possible barrier, parents are given control over their own home activities. Before leaving the group each week they are asked to write down their commitment to whatever part of the assignment they feel is realistic for them to complete and what their goal will be for the week. This strategy helps parents to take ownership of the learning process and helps to reduce resistance to being told what they must do for homework. At the beginning of the following session, parents record whether they have achieved their goal. Therapists review their progress working on their personal homework goals each week, making encouraging comments and giving them rewards (stickers, special food and prizes) and group applauses for their achievements. In addition, the group therapists ask the parents to share with their buddy or the whole group what home activities they feel most proud of. This exercise is important for this population because it helps them focus on positive successes rather than failures as well as learn how to praise themselves and each other, an important element of building support. During the week therapists phone (text or email if no one home) to see how parents are doing with their home activities and to support their progress.

Parents are asked to share with their buddy their success with home activities.

Balancing Collaboration and Teaching

Therapists balance the need to present basic information that the parents might not know while acknowledging their perspectives, culture and prior experiences.

Although therapists are collaborative, this does not mean that they passively let parents in the group take over the discussion or withdraw from involvement. A skilled therapist will alternate between providing parents with accurate information about child development, encouraging parents' efforts at home, gently challenging or confronting a parents' belief in a harsh or ineffective parenting strategy, and engaging and coaching them in practices of the new skills or thoughts they are learning or to reenact difficulties they have encountered at home. Therapists work to maintain fidelity to teaching the core behavior-management principles, while helping families reflect on how these principles are relevant for their own goals. The therapist balances the need to present basic information that the parents might not know or have unrealistic expectations about while acknowledging their perspectives, experiences and helping them see that different parenting styles can be effective. In some child welfare parent groups, parents may need more basic teaching than in a group of parents with more baseline skills. However, because child welfare parents may be more resistant to the program, the therapist will need considerable therapeutic skill to bond with parents, to highlight the skills that these parents do have, and to empower them to feel as if they can make changes that will benefit their children. In a sense, a therapist working with this population needs to be more directive, more collaborative, more culturally sensitive, and more therapeutically skilled. Thus therapists will need high levels of consultation and support when using this program.

Mediating Video Vignettes and Practices

The video vignettes are a key part of the learning process with this population because they provide the group with a common visual experience to watch and think about and because frequently this population lacks the language, cognitive and communication skills for in depth verbal discussions. Prior to showing a vignette, the therapist provides some information to the group about the vignette ahead of time and prompts the parents to watch for something specific: "*In this next vignette, see what you think about the pace of this mother's play with her child. In particular, I'm curious to hear what you think the child might be feeling.*" Therapists pause the vignettes periodically to find out what parents thought about a particular part of the interaction, "*Before we go on, what feeling do you see in the child's face right there?*" "*Why do you think the child felt that way?*" "*What would you do next?*" This approach helps parents think about the child's perspective as well as enhance their emotional literacy. In the vignette discussions it is important that the therapists encourage parents to notice and discuss effective and positive parenting interactions. This sets the expectation that praising positive aspects of other parents' behavior is important, and that there is usually something good to say about most typical parent-child interactions. In the IY parenting vignettes, most are designed to reflect generally positive parenting styles, and even vignettes that are examples of less effective parenting usually have some positive aspects to them. There is often a tendency for parents involved in the child welfare system to look for what is wrong or to be critical even of vignettes where parents are being positive and nurturing. This likely reflects their experience of feeling judged and criticized for their own parenting. If a group is allowed to offer only critical and negative comments about the vignettes, this will reinforce their idea that others are looking for negative parenting and making judgments of themselves. If several negative comments have been made about a vignette, the therapist might say: "*I think you have all brought up some really important ideas about how this interaction could be improved. Before we move on, I wonder if anyone has noticed anything that this father is doing well?*"

Therapists look for opportunities to take the cognitive learning into active, experiential learning.

Experienced therapists understand that any reaction that a parent has to the vignette is important and can be used in the discussion and learning process. If parents believe that the interaction is effective, then the therapist helps to pull out a general principle from the parents' observations about the vignettes. "*You know, I think I hear a principle there. Julie said that the mother was playing at a faster speed than the child could keep up with—let's call that Julie's Pacing Principle. Often a child needs much more time to explore during their play than we do as adults.*" If parents are uncomfortable or critical with the style of the interaction of the parent in the vignette, then the therapist helps the group to tailor the strategy to fit something positive about the individual parent's style. "*So, it sounds like you think that parent's voice is too sugary and you wouldn't be comfortable saying that. You know, there are so many different ways of letting your child know that you are enjoying them, and it's important to do this in a way that feels comfortable to you. What would it look like if you were going to let your daughter know that you were having fun with her? Can you show me what you say?*" Always, after parents have built up a list of effective parenting strategies, the therapist structures a series of practices to try out the new strategies. For parents referred by child welfare, this is the essence of their learning because it takes the cognitive learning into active, experiential learning.

Building Supportive Relationships

Another form of support is for the therapist to establish positive expectations for change. This population of parents is often skeptical about their ability to change, especially if they see in their behavior a family pattern, for patterns often seem fixed and irreversible. For example, one parent said, "My mother beat me, now I beat my children." In such a case, the therapist must express his or her confidence in the parent's ability to break the family cycle. The therapist can point out each small step toward change, even the step of coming to therapy in the first place, as evidence that the problem is not fixed or irreversible. These parents need to be reinforced through constant positive feedback for each success, however small, and for each change in their behavior or thought pattern, whether or not it results in any immediate change in their child's behavior. In fact, parents are forewarned that usually child behavior doesn't change right away and that children will often resist the change or even misbehave more when they interact in a different way. It can also be helpful to cite examples of other parents in similar situations who have been successful in teaching their children to behave more appropriately because of their persistence using the strategy. For example, the therapist might say, "*You are working really hard to make a change in your parenting while your child is still young. This will help both of you avoid getting into a permanent rut of negative interactions but instead a more enjoyable relationship. Good for you for tackling this now. By consistently and regularly using this coaching approach in your play times, a few months from now you will have a different relationship with your child than you did with your mother."*

Childcare and Transportation

Another barrier to attendance is addressed by providing practical assistance by offering dinner, child care, and transportation for the groups. These are offered in all of our community-based groups, not just to families involved in child welfare, and are rated highly as a strong motivator for families' ongoing participation. Over and over, when families are asked to list reasons for not attending a group, childcare and transportation are among the top reasons listed.

Parents Who Have Lost Custody of their Children

A unique barrier to delivering the IY parent program to the child welfare population is that some of the children in these groups may have been removed from the home to foster care before or during the parent training. While we have discussed some tailoring of the content for this population earlier, these modifications cannot make up for the fact that when children are living with their parents, the parent-child relationship and attachment is built up in the first part of the program and becomes the foundation for later parent and child change and proactive discipline. In the absence of this chance for parents to work directly on the parent-child relationship, IY is still potentially useful training for parents because of its use of video modeling, group support, behavioral rehearsal, and discrete practice experiences during the group sessions. These methods provide an opportunity for parents who are not living with their children to practice, watch and discuss examples

It is highly recommended that parents retake the program after reunification with their children in order to practice their new skills with support.

of parenting interactions. The examples of the DVDs, role-plays, and other group members help to prepare parents for their children's return. If parents regain custody of their children, it is highly recommended that they participate in the program again after reunification. At this time they will be able to apply the skills they have learned, and can receive the support and feedback from other parents and their group leaders during this transition time.

Parents who do not have custody will need extra coaching and more frequent role-plays and practice opportunities during the group sessions. To further provide them with practices, after viewing and discussing a vignette, the vignette can be replayed with the sound track turned off while parents practice using descriptive commenting, coaching and praise language while watching the children shown playing on the video vignettes. Other practices with their children can be set up during visitations or by having the children brought to the clinic for individual coached practices. One IY model currently being tested in New York (Linares, Montalto, MinMin, & S., 2006) is training foster parents and biological parents together in groups; because the children are in day care during these trainings, part of the training includes spending extra time before or after the group sessions for coached practices with the children. Home activities should be modified depending on the parents' access to their children. Parents are encouraged to practice their play and coaching skills with children of relatives or friends. Visitation times with their own children are an ideal time to practice the new coaching and child-directed play skills and communication approaches, and parents can be helped to plan activities to do with their child during visitations and to anticipate their child's response to seeing them after a separation. During sessions parents practice how they will greet their children and how they will separate from them when it is time to leave their visits. It is recommended that the visitation supervisors be trained in the IY program so that their support will be consistent with what parents learn in the group.

It is recommended that visitation supervisors be trained in the program in order to suport parents' practice of the new skills.

The focus for these parents will also be geared to helping them address some of their personal needs for confidence building and enhanced support networks. This is done by broadening their understanding of how the many parenting skills and principles can be extended to other relationships. The following are some examples of ways each of the four main homework topic areas are expanded for parents whose children are in foster care:

Play topic. To broaden parents' understanding of the purpose of play and showing them how it refuels all relationships, they are given the assignment to do something pleasurable for themselves with another adult, such as meeting a friend for coffee, taking a walk with a person they find supportive, or doing something nice for themselves. The idea of nurturing oneself and building supportive friendships begins with this first topic on play. This illustrates the parenting principles of improving parents' depressed and despondent affect by building in some joyful times for themselves. These parents are often surprised when the group leader gives them homework to do something fun for themselves and this caring message immediately helps to dispel some of their resentment for being in the group.

Learning how to successfully ask for support from others is a key skill for parents to learn.

Praise and reward topics. Parents who are able to have telephone contact or visitation with their children rehearse and practice ways to praise their children during visits and on the phone and respond positively to what they are doing in the foster home or at school. To extend their praise homework practice, parents are asked to praise friends, colleagues, store clerks, or other adults they are in contact with. They learn about the importance of praise for building positive support systems. In addition, they learn and practice using positive self-encouragement statements as well as how to set up reward systems for themselves for completing things that are difficult for them to do such as exercising, calling a friend, paying their bills, applying for a job or cleaning the bathroom. Therapists can negotiate an added bonus by providing a fun prize for parents who meet a particular goal they have set for themselves.

Rules, routines and limit setting topics. Parents are encouraged to think about what rules and limits apply to their visitations with their children. They discuss the added stresses of setting limits in the brief time they have with their children, and additional challenges of children who are upset and resentful about the separation. They practice how to communicate their expectations clearly, calmly, and positively when they see their children. In addition to learning about setting limits with children, an emphasis for these parents includes how to apply these same principles to other relationships. For example, in a conflictual partner relationship, a parent might be encouraged to think about something she would like help with (such as cleaning up clothes and newspapers from bedroom floor) and coached in how to communicate this request in a positive and noncritical way. Learning how to successfully ask for support from others is a key skill for parents to learn. They are also encouraged to think about life circumstances that are risky or dangerous to themselves or their children (e.g., an abusive or substance abuse partner). They learn about safe ways to set limits on these behaviors to protect themselves and their children. Finally, setting up predictable routines in their personal lives can be challenging for many of these parents. Many don't have schedules for eating, doing laundry, or self-care or know how to plan their weekly calendars. We recommend giving them calendars, helping them figure out their goals for the day and the week, and coaching them in ways to organize their schedules. Consequently the homework for this topic area is tailored to help them focus on some upsetting aspect of their life that they would like to change, to set a goal, and set up a plan to accomplish this.

Therapists help parents organize their daily schedule with calendars and predictable routines.

Discipline topic. There is an emphasis on identifying situations other than with their children that cause them to be angry or to react, and to plan for anger management strategies to use in these situations. They are helped to identify situations they could ignore or when to take a personal Time Out to calm down and practice self-control strategies such as stress management, deep breathing, positive imagery, and time away to refuel. They learn how to practice disputing negative and irrational thoughts and replacing them with more calming and coping thoughts. While these parents do not have children at home for practicing these skills when children misbehave, there are countless other stress producing situations that they can use to practice these skills in real life.

Group Constellation

Group constellation is an issue to consider when organizing a parent group. A group could consist entirely of mandated parents or could be a mixture of mandated and non-mandated parents. Both kinds of groups have advantages. If all parents in a group have been mandated, the group provides them with support from a number of other families who are experiencing the same challenges. Group members may share the sense of anger, shame or despair about the circumstances that have required them to be in the group. This collective experience may be useful in group bonding and also may lead to group goals and discussions about ways to change parenting interactions to avoid future involvement with Child Protective Services (CPS). On the other hand, a group that consists entirely of parents who are mandated to attend may initially be more difficult to motivate and engage. Also, it may foster parent negativity about being victims of the system rather than focusing attention on effective parenting. The therapist will need to constantly scaffold the group discussions to keep them on a positive and productive track.

One of the advantages of doing the IY program in mixed groups (parents who are mandated combined with those who volunteer) is that parents listen to one another talking about their goals. This gives parents who are mandated a chance to observe other parents openly acknowledging that they want to be a calmer or more positive parent, or to hit and scream less, or to find ways to manage their children's behavior problems. This group disclosure process helps the parents who are mandated begin to realize that other parents have similar issues and are being proactive about finding solutions, regardless of their level of involvement with CPS. It is important that parents' goals for themselves and their children be revisited throughout the program, because this allows all parents to change their views about what they might want to accomplish and to take on more responsibility for their own learning. In some cases, it may be feasible and even ideal for biological parents and the foster parents of their children to attend the same parenting group. This kind of collaboration provides unique therapeutic challenges, but also potentially tremendous benefits for children.

IY Home Visitor Coaching Model

In addition to the IY basic group meetings, we recommend that families referred to child welfare who have their children at home receive a minimum of four home visits to practice the skills taught in the groups. During the visit, the home visitor helps parents to use the skills learned in the group with their children. Home visitors can coach, model, prompt, and support the parent in these practice sessions. Sometimes case managers are already visiting these families anyway, so if they are trained in the IY program it is an opportunity to do in-home rehearsal and reinforcement of skills. A home visitor–coaching manual with session protocols is available, as well as workbooks for parents (Webster-Stratton, 2008). If parents cannot attend the group at all, due to work schedule difficulties, the manual offers protocols for leaders to offer the entire program at home.

It is recommended for child welfare referred families to have a minimum of four home visits to have coached practice with their children, in addition to group sessions.

THE IY ADVANCE PARENT PROGRAM

As described in Chapter Six, the advanced parent program, which focuses on interpersonal issues, is an adjunct parent program that is particularly applicable to families involved with child welfare services because these families often experience multiple stressors that make it difficult for them to focus solely on parenting issues. For example, they often have mental health issues (Burns et al., 2004), elevated rates of depression (U.S. Department of Health and Social Services Administration on Children

Youth and Families, 2006), anger control difficulties (Ateah & Durrant, 2005), and conflictual relationships with partners and other family members that frequently escalate to domestic violence (Hazen, Connelly, Kelleher, Landsverk, & Barth, 2004; Hurlburt, Barth, Leslie, Landsverk, & McRae, in submission). The advanced parent program component addresses many of these issues as they relate to parenting and also to parents' functioning in their adult family environment. Therapists are also responsible for referring parents to other, more specialized treatment programs for substance abuse, domestic violence, or clinical levels depression.

Typically, the advanced program is offered after the basic program and takes another 8 to 9 sessions for a total of 22 to 28 sessions. In the advanced program, parents learn effective communication skills, more ways to cope with discouraging and depressive thoughts, more practice with anger-management strategies, ways to give and get support, and effective problem-solving strategies. However, as we have seen, some of these advanced program themes are woven throughout the basic program. For instance, in every unit in the basic program, there is an emphasis on how the behavior management principles parents are learning can help them cope with their own emotions and their other adult relationships as well as with their child's behavior and emotions. If this is done skillfully and consistently, parents will have some experience with many of these concepts even if the ADVANCE program is not offered after the BASIC program.

THE THERAPEUTIC CHILD TREATMENT GROUP

In addition to the parent group, the therapeutic child treatment group, outlined in Chapter Twelve, is recommended for this population because research has indicated that children who have been neglected or abused have more behavior problems, self-regulation and emotional difficulties, and other developmental disabilities, learning, and social difficulties than typical children (Crick & Dodge, 1994; Fantuzzo et al., 1991; Jaffee, Caspi, Moffitt, & Taylor, 2004; Knutson, DeGarmo, Koeppl, & Reid, 2005). Offering the full length children treatment program (18-22 sessions) in conjunction with the parenting group allows for the possibility of joint parent-child activities where parents are able to practice new skills with their children in some sessions. In mixed groups where at least some parents are living with their children, those who are not living with their children can still be involved in the joint parent-child play sessions. Parents who do not have a child to practice with may be paired up for practice with other parent-child dyads under supervision of the group leader.

Adaptations for Children in the Child Welfare System

Children who have experienced abandonment, neglect, trauma, or abuse during their childhood years often develop insecure, ambivalent or avoidant attachment patterns with their parents or caregivers (Bakermans-Kranenburg, Van Ijzendoorn, & Juffer, 2003). The child groups provide children with a model of secure and healthy adult-child relationships and also teach specific skills that will help the child to navigate other relationships in their lives. See Chapter Twelve for specific adaptations for this population.

SUMMARY

We have discussed how to deliver IY parent and child core program principles and adapt the program with fidelity to meet the needs of intact families referred by child welfare as well as families where the children have been removed from the home. These evidence-based interventions have demonstrated ability to improve parent-child relationships and to build parents' own sense of competence and self-control as well as strengthen their supportive family and community networks and reduce child behavior problems (Letarte, 2010; Webster-Stratton, 2010; 2011). While it is not uncommon for child welfare agencies to seek briefer interventions than the Incredible Years, these families are complex and in the highest risk category for re-abuse and maltreatment if not adequately trained and supported. Data in the parenting literature supports the notion that parenting curricula need to be substantial to produce sustainable effects with challenging populations (Kazdin & Mazurick, 1994). Data from the IY programs have shown that the dosage of the intervention received and fidelity with which it is delivered are directly linked to changes in parenting and child behaviors (Baydar, Reid, & Webster-Stratton, 2003; Eames et al., 2009). Our standard treatment recommendation for child welfare families referred because of abuse and neglect is a minimum of 18 2-hour parent and child group sessions delivered by accredited IY group leaders who have high levels of support and consultation (Webster-Stratton, 2010; 2011).

Parenting curricula need to be substantial to produce sustainable effects with challenging populations.

Parent participation in the full IY program is expected to improve the parent relationship and attachment with their childern, increase parents' sense of competence and self-control, increase the use of positive discipline strategies, predictable schedules and monitoring, and reduce the rates of harsh and physical discipline. Child participation in the full IY child program is expected to improve children's emotional regulation, social skills and to strengthen problem-solving skills as well as attachment and trust with parents. In the long term, we expect that these improvements in parenting and parent-child relationships will lead to lower rates of re-abuse, fewer re-reports to Child Welfare Services and more academically, emotionally, and socially competent children. In order to break the intergenerational cycle of parent-child violence and neglect and child conduct problems, it is also necessary to provide enough training and support to therapists to assure program fidelity with the goal of these children getting the best parenting possible.

Case Example: Targeting Multiple Areas of Risk with a Coordinated Approach

Parent training is often perceived as a narrowly focused behavioral intervention that concentrates exclusively on increasing child compliance and reducing aggressive behavior at home. By now it will have become apparent that parent training interventions are far from simple and involve a variety of theoretical underpinnings and a complex and broad understanding of the individual parents' emotions, cognitions and culture, their relationships both within the family and within the school and community as well as the nature of the children's behavior problems and developmental needs. While many parents of young children seek help because of their noncompliant and aggressive behavior at home, data presented earlier in this book highlight the fact that many of these children are experiencing problems in other settings and also present with a wide range of issues that go beyond their externalizing problems. Thus, the majority of children who receive treatment for ODD/CD exhibit a variety of emotional, behavioral, developmental

For children with ODD/CD and ADHD the most effective treatment will involve the IY parent, teacher, and child programs.

and family difficulties. For young children whose behavior problems are pervasive (i.e., with parents, teachers, and peers), parent training will be most effective when offered in combination with the IY teacher and child training programs (Webster-Stratton & Hammond, 1997; Webster-Stratton, Reid, & Hammond, 2004). This type of comprehensive treatment plan targets multiple risk and protective factors for children with conduct problems across settings and attempts to effect change in all areas of the child's experience. The following case example about Robbie, presented briefly in Chapter One, illustrates a coordinated approach to working with a child with pervasive emotional and behavioral difficulties. In this case, therapists worked with Robbie's parents and teachers as well as directly with Robbie (IY parent group, IY teacher training, and child emotional and social skills dinosaur group) to provide a comprehensive intervention that addressed particular social, emotional, and behavioral goals for Robbie as well as developing a support team for the adults in his life.

CASE EXAMPLE

Intake Information

Donna and Marty were referred to the University of Washington Parenting Clinic by their school psychologist because of difficulties at home and at school with their 4-year-old son, Robbie. Although Robbie was only in preschool, he already had a substantial reputation at the school for his aggressive, oppositional, and inattentive behavior in the classroom and on the playground. His parents felt that since starting school these problem behaviors seemed to be increasing in intensity. At the time that this family came to the clinic, Robbie's teacher had approached his parents and told them that she did not believe her classroom was an appropriate place for Robbie. She had noticed Robbie's language difficulties and told the parents that he did not listen to her instructions, would not sit still during circle time and frequently poked other children and ran away from her when she tried to discipline him. Robbie was regularly being sent to the director's office and on at least two occasions his mother had been called to pick him up early because of his aggressive behavior. This was distressful to Donna because she found it difficult to manage him at home with his two younger siblings and looked forward to a break from him when he was in school.

In addition to these problems at school, Donna and Marty were concerned about his behavior at home. Both parents reported that his problems began as a toddler when he was extremely volatile and aggressive. He had problems from the time he started preschool at 3 years old and had been asked to leave two other settings because of his misbehavior. They reported that he continued to frequently "lose control of his behavior," would hit his sister if he didn't get what he wanted or throw something, engage in extended temper tantrums, refuse to comply with parental requests, and engage in aggressive or destructive behavior. He was difficult to understand and had limited ability to express his needs verbally. Both parents reported feeling helpless to change Robbie's behavior once it reached these proportions. They described their typical parenting style involving verbal reasoning and then angry yelling at Robbie in problem situations, but this merely escalated his misbehavior. They also had tried a number of different discipline strategies (e.g., Time Out, loss of privileges), but Robbie was unresponsive to their efforts. They were often at a loss as to what events had triggered the tantrums and oppositional behavior and described Robbie as having a "Jekyll and Hyde" personality. They were quick to describe Robbie's strengths as well as his difficulties. During his good times, they reported that he was a generous, loving, charming child with a good sense of humor. Robbie had been assessed by a psychologist prior to coming to the clinic and had been diagnosed as having ODD and numerous symptoms of ADHD, but

was just below the threshold warranting formal diagnosis. Prior to coming to the Parenting Clinic, Donna and Marty had enrolled Robbie in a 10-week social skills program recommended by their school counselor, but saw no change in his behavior as a result of the group.

In addition to the difficulties of managing Robbie's behavior, Donna and Marty were quite concerned about the effect that his difficulties were having on his self-esteem. During the year prior to the intake, Robbie had begun saying that no one liked him at preschool and that he was the dumbest kid in his class. They also perceived him as depressed and anxious about school and his lack of friends.

This is a middle-class Caucasian family. Both parents are college graduates, and Marty works long hours as an engineer. At the time of the intake they had been married for 13 years and both reported that their marital relationship was strained over arguments about how to handle his behavior. Marty was drinking more heavily and avoided going home after work because of the stress he experienced there. They also have two other younger children, a daughter who was 3 years old and had no significant behavior problems and a 10-month-old baby. Neither parent reported any mental health issues, although Donna had a history of depression and reported feeling exhausted and tired, and Marty and Donna were both concerned about Marty's use of alcohol as a coping strategy. Standardized measures involving the Beck Depression Inventory (Beck, Steer, & Garbin, 1988), and the Dyadic Adjustment Scale (Spanier, 1976) confirmed moderate scores for depression for the mother and low marital satisfaction for both parents. Robbie's difficulties were putting a significant strain on the family's functioning. Both parents felt that Robbie's problems were their main focus, to the exclusion of other activities and interests. They felt that they no longer had control over their family and were worried that Robbie's behavior was on an irreversible trajectory. They were perplexed by their inability to help Robbie, since they had little difficulty with their daughter. They were worried about the effect of Robbie's aggressive behavior on his sister and were concerned that they were not giving his siblings enough of their attention and that his behavior might cause them to misbehave. In sum, this family told the story of a family "under siege" that we had heard from many of the families described in Chapter Three.

Assessments

In addition to the family functioning measures completed by these families we recommend therapists administer one standardized measure of parenting practices and a parent and teacher report of child behavior problems. Here are some recommendations:

Parenting

Parenting Scale (Arnold, O'Leary, Wolff, & Acker, 1993);
Parenting Practices Inventory (PPI)
See web site
www.incredibleyears.com/Measures/forms_GL.asp
Or,
Parent Stress Inventory (Abidin, 1995)

Child Behavior

Eyberg Child Behavior Inventory (ECBI) (Eyberg & Pincus, 1999) .
Child Behavior Checklist (CBCL) (Achenbach & Edelbrock, 1991)
Child Behavior Checklist for Teachers (TRF) (Achenbach, 1991)
http://www.incredibleyears.com/Measures/forms_GL.asp

See table at the end of this chapter for a summary of key information on Robbie's behavior according to these measures.

Note that in addition to Robbie's externalizing behaviors, his internalizing and attention scores on the parent and teacher CBCL were elevated at intake. Robbie's scores on the Eyberg Child Behavior Inventory (ECBI) were also in the clinical range (Eyberg & Pincus, 1999; Robinson, Eyberg, & Ross, 1980). The ECBI is a 36-item behavioral inventory that provides a total problem score (number of behaviors parents endorse as problematic) as well as an intensity score for those behaviors (how frequently they occur on a 7-point scale). Problem scores of 16 and intensity scores of 142 correspond to the 90th percentile for this measure.

Our school observer visited Robbie's classroom on 4 occasions and coded him in two structured and two unstructured periods using the MOOSES coding system (Tapp, Wehby, & Ellis, 1995). The observer noted that Robbie had great difficulty concentrating. During both structured observations, Robbie was disengaged for the majority of the time (crawling around during circle time, wandering around the room when other children were engaged in structured tasks). During the unstructured observations (on the playground or at lunch) Robbie was aggressive with other children on multiple occasions or engaged in solitary play. The observer's impression was that in the classroom the teacher had given up on Robbie. She ignored all his off-task behavior unless he was overtly disruptive or aggressive at which point she reprimanded him or sent him to the director's office. She seemed to have stopped requiring anything of him socially or academically and gave no attention to him for on-task or positive behaviors when they occurred.

The family was observed in their home for an hour on two occasions before treatment started using the DPICS-R coding system (Robinson & Eyberg, 1981; Webster-Stratton, 1988). During both observations our observer rated Robbie's behavior as very challenging. He was noncompliant to 89% of his parent's commands, and was engaged in ongoing yelling, crying and whining. Because of his language and emotional regulation difficulties he tended to grab or hit to get what he wanted. The coder summary report noted that, *"Donna and Marty are intelligent, thoughtful, considerate parents, but nothing they do is working. They encourage conversation and opinions from the children, but Robbie tunes them out and doesn't respond to verbal instructions. They are completely bamboozled when his response is defiance and noncompliance. It is an awful situation that the parents keep feeding into. He cries over real or imagined hurts and the parents are all over him with asking questions and giving lectures until they finally get angry. The minute they leave, he stops. His sister and the baby get very little of their time because Robbie is the center of their universe. He is controlling the household with his negative behavior. There are no negative consequences for Robbie's behavior."*

Treatment

Treatment began in October, following the assessment period. Robbie and his parents came to the clinic weekly for two hours in the evening for 20 weeks. During that time Robbie attended the IY child dinosaur treatment group with 5 other children (3 boys and 2 girls, ages 4-7) and his parents attended the IY parenting group with the parents of those children.

IY PARENT GROUP

During the initial group session, parents describe their child, their reasons for coming to the clinic and their goals. The parents in this group seemed to form an immediate bond with other parents around the common issues of aggression, noncompliance, inattention, language delays, frustration with teachers' responses and school problems. Many of the parents, and Donna, in particular, described how isolated she felt as a parent of a "problem child." She felt that they could no longer socialize with their friends because Robbie was not able to behave appropriately. She felt judged by other parents and was beginning to feel that she was a "bad parent" because nothing she did worked with Robbie. After the group, Marty privately expressed relief about the other parents in the group. He said, "I can see that this is a group of good, committed parents. They are a lot like we are and are dealing with similar problems." He had been afraid that a parenting group would consist of parents who were clearly parenting badly and that he and Donna would feel out of place. Donna and Marty expressed their goals for Robbie primarily in terms of his self-esteem and their ability to manage his behavior better without fighting. Although they clearly wanted home-life to be smoother, they wanted most for him to be successful in school, to learn to regulate his emotions, and make friends with other children. Donna and Marty were active participants in the parenting group and added thoughtful reflections to the group discussions. In the first session when parents were asked to play with their child at home, they both reported that they didn't enjoy playing with him and felt that they didn't have the time to set aside daily playtimes.

In the child group Robbie was difficult to understand and had limited ability to express his needs verbally. He exhibited considerable oppositional behavior and frequent temper tantrums, often at times when he was unable to find the words to express his wishes or needs. He quickly became frustrated with many tasks or games and moved rapidly from one activity to another, often in a somewhat destructive whirlwind! When asked questions, Robbie would often shut down and refuse to respond, even to questions that he may have had the words to answer.

Child-Directed Play. One important aspect to Robbie's treatment plan was the therapist encouraging Robbie's parents to devote time to playing with Robbie. She helped them work out a schedule where they would alternate days, and would each commit to a 10 minute play time with Robbie while the other parent watched the other two children. Since Robbie's father worked long hours, they decided to do these play times right after dinner. Neither parent was enthusiastic about this idea, but agreed that they would try to stick to the schedule for two weeks and then evaluate whether they felt Robbie was making any progress. During these child-directed play times, they were instructed to use academic coaching to provide labels for objects he used commonly which would help increase his vocabulary and confidence with using language. At the same time, the therapist helped the parents work hard to limit their questions and instructions to Robbie so that he would not feel pressured to have to provide verbal information or follow directions. For example "Wow, Robbie is rolling that train up the hill. Now his train is going under the track. Robbie has a long track, and he is adding, one, two, three pieces to it. Now the track is even longer. He's pushing that blue engine around the corner."

After the first week, Robbie's mother reported that she had managed two play times while Robbie's father helped to get the two younger children ready for bed. While this was only partially meeting their goal, the therapist focused on praising their success. Although Robbie's father had not played with Robbie, the therapist emphasized his instrumental role in making the play times happen since he had taken care of the other children. She asked Robbie's mother to describe Robbie's reaction to these play times. She reported that Robbie seemed to enjoy her attention and her use of descriptive language and would often look up with interest as she was commenting. Occasionally, he would even hold up a particular toy for identification and then would resume his play. Towards the end of each play session, she noticed that he would start to label some of the objects on his own, imitating her descriptive language. Donna was encouraged by his cooperation and enjoyment being with her. She reflected that it had been several years since she had spent any time alone with Robbie, and she was amazed at how much calmer he was without his siblings around. While she had not seen changes in his behavior during the rest of the day, she was willing to continue the play for the next week, and was looking forward to spending more time with Robbie.

The therapist asked Marty to talk about what kind of support he needed to make the play sessions work for him. At first he said that he thought it was more important for Donna to play with Robbie, since she was the one who was with him most of the time. As this discussion continued, however, he shared that he was uncertain about how to respond to Robbie during the play sessions, and that he didn't think Robbie would want to play with him. He described himself as the disciplinarian and said that the children all turned to their mother for comfort and conversation. He expressed remorse at his difficulties in managing his emotions and admitted that often his interactions with Robbie ended in yelling and frustration. The therapist praised him for being courageous enough to share these worries and acknowledged that it can be very scary and uncomfortable to try a new pattern of interactions, even with a child. She asked Marty if he would be willing to practice the descriptive commenting in the group, and he agreed.

Practice Exercises. She assigned Marty a buddy coach for this practice, another father in the group who clearly had had some success with the play sessions during the prior week. The buddy coach's role was to sit beside Marty and whisper descriptive comments whenever he wasn't sure what to say. At first, Marty was very quiet, mostly repeating comments that the coach whispered. As the role play progressed, Marty was able to make a few comments himself. The therapist paused the role play and praised him for his success. She also elicited feedback from the coach and from the parent who was in role as the "child." In this way, Marty received positive feedback from three different sources. She also asked him to report his own feelings about the experience. He said: "I don't think I did a very good job with this. The words don't come out when I want them to, and I'm not sure what to say. But I appreciate hearing that I did okay." Next the therapist explained that even

Coached and supportive child-directed play practices helped the father to engage with his son.

sitting next to Robbie and making just a few comments would be a powerful experience for Robbie. She assured him that even if he couldn't think of any words to say, his attention would have a powerful positive effect on Robbie. She challenged him to find at least one time during the week to take the risk to play with Robbie. Donna said that she would support him and encourage him and that she would take care of the other children when he was playing with Robbie. Together, the parents set the goal to double their play times during the next week, trying to have Robbie have at least two play sessions with each parent.

Over the next weeks, Robbie's parents reported more success with the play sessions. Donna reported how important it was to her that she and Marty were a team in this effort. She reflected on how alone she had felt before the group started, and that knowing they were both doing this, and that they had a structured plan for how to manage the three children was a relief to her. Marty continued to be unsure about his ability to do the coaching, but he did stick to his commitment to do 2-3 play sessions a week with Robbie and was coming home earlier from work. He had trouble articulating what he did or said during the play sessions, but could describe Robbie's positive response and was proud that Robbie asked for more play time with him. The therapist continued to set up frequent practice coaching opportunities during the group, and Marty was a willing participant in these. She found that when she put him in the coaching role (helping another parent), he was actually able to suggest more descriptive comments, perhaps because he was not feeling as pressured. After each practice session, the therapist helped the group to label all the different things that Marty had done or said, so that he would become more aware of all the different positive strategies that he was using.

Descriptive Commenting and Coaching. Persistence and emotion coaching were also an important part of Robbie's treatment plan. In order to gradually increase the amount of time that Robbie spent on a given activity, Robbie's parents were encouraged to identify times when Robbie was focused, calm, working hard and carefully, concentrating, and sticking with an activity even though he was getting frustrated. Robbie's attention span and time spent playing was immediately longer with an activity whenever descriptive commenting and coaching was used, most likely because he enjoyed his parents' attention and wanted it to continue. This provided many opportunities to comment on his persistence. Since Robbie was so easily dysregulated and quick to get angry, attention was given to times when he was calm, regulated, patient and content. When Robbie started to become angry, his feelings were labeled, and then the parent predicted that he would be able to stay calm and try again. (If he trantrumed, he was ignored.) Robbie gradually began to label his own emotions "I'm frustrated!" or "I'm happy" and to use simple calm-down techniques when he was dysregulated (taking deep breaths). Robbie's father shared that he had his own difficulties with anger management, and worked hard to model using self-regulation strategies in front of Robbie. The therapist coached him to label his feelings out loud and then to use self-talk to model a coping response: "I'm feeling really frustrated right now. I am going to take a breath and walk around the room to try to cool off."

The parents spent 6-7 weeks building a stronger relationship with Robbie through regular coached child-directed play times interspersed in 5-10 minute intervals depending on his attention span throughout the day. Since Robbie's mother was not able to devote much one-on-one time to Robbie during the day, the parent group helped to brainstorm ways that she could incorporate this coaching into her daily routine (bath time, meal time, car rides, getting dressed). She reported that it became easier as she practiced, and that she could sometimes coach Robbie and his sister at the same time. For Marty, the coaching felt like a foreign language. He reported that he couldn't think of what to say, and felt tongue-tied as he tried to coach Robbie's positive behaviors and emotions. The therapists continued to have Marty practice during the parent group sessions, providing him with ideas for coaching language to use in these practice role plays. They also recorded the group's favorite coaching statements and typed them onto laminated index cards so that Marty and other parents would have prompts to refer to during their practice play times. Marty reported that he felt silly reading the words from the cards, but was determined to keep trying since he could see that Robbie was responsive to the coaching.

Once the therapist and parents felt they had learned how to use academic and persistence coaching skills successfully, they began to work on social skills which were also delayed, as his play was most often parallel and he did not initiate interactions with other children. In fact, at times when he came into contact with other children during play, he screamed or tantrumed because he believed that they were going to take his toys. If another child had a toy that he wanted, he would grab, hit or scream in an attempt to get the toy for himself. Since Robbie had extreme difficulty playing near other children, the therapist first helped the parents to use social coaching in their individual play with him. The parents were encouraged to model prosocial behavior and label their own friendly behaviors as well as Robbie's appropriate social skills whenever they occurred. If they saw that Robbie was interested in something they were holding they would say, "Robbie, I'd like to be your friend and share this block with you." When Robbie took the block, they said, "I can see I made you happy. That makes me happy." They extended their modeling to imaginary play with puppets and action figures, having the puppets share, ask for turns, and play cooperatively with Robbie. After Robbie became used to the idea that adults would share with him, the therapist helped the parents begin to prompt him to use words to ask for what he wanted rather than grabbing it. For example, "Robbie, I see that you want this train. You can say, 'please can I have the train.'" At first, they did not ask Robbie to reciprocate because the idea of giving up something he was holding was so difficult for him. However, they involved Robbie in simple turn taking activities, for example, "Robbie, would you like to help me build a tower? I'll wait while you put the first piece on. Wow! Now you're waiting while I add a piece. You and I are sharing these blocks and are really taking turns!" Or, when playing with duplos and puppets, the parent using the puppet character would ask Robbie, "Can I have that red block?" If Robbie shared with his parent he would praise his friendly behavior by saying, "You are so friendly to share that with me, I am happy," but if he did not share they dropped the prompt, ignored the refusal and continued with modeling social behaviors and describing actions and feelings. Because of Robbie's immature developmental stage of play, and because of the home stressors, the therapist did not suggest they start peer social coaching until the parents had learned to successfully use all the coaching methods as well as some proactive discipline strategies.

The therapist returned to teaching the parents peer coaching strategies for use when he was playing with another child or sibling in the last few sessions of the program after they had learned some proactive discipline strategies and ways to manage his aggression with his sister.

By week 7 in the program, Robbie's parents were both providing daily child-directed play sessions and noticed that Robbie looked forward to these play times with them. They also reported using some of the coaching methods when he was interacting with his siblings as well as other times during the day such as bath time and getting ready for bed. They were working hard to give attention to his prosocial behaviors and to ignore the misbehaviors they had targeted such as tantrums and yelling. They were beginning to feel more confident about their parenting but were still afraid to take a night out together away from the children for fear he would hit his siblings. Aggression had decreased but was still a concern.

Praise. In this unit, Marty and Donna were encouraged to think strategically about specific positive behavioral goals for Robbie. Although they had experienced success with the play and coaching units, they still had some difficulty formulating their goals in positive terms. At first, when asked, they articulated goals such as "to stop hitting his sister," "quit saying no to everything we ask him to do," "stop running around the house like a wild animal." Other parents in the group had similar difficulties when formulating positive goals for their children so the therapists had parents work in small groups to think of "positive opposite" behaviors for each of the negative behaviors listed. Parents returned from this assignment with goals such as "be nice to his sister," "mind us better," and "behave better around the house." From here the therapist worked with the whole group to make each of these goals into concrete and specific positive behaviors. For instance, she asked, "*What does it look like to be nice to a sibling?*" The parents brainstormed a list of positive and friendly behaviors, thinking back to some of the positive social skills that they had been coaching in the play sessions such as:

Helping parents focus on specific positive opposite behaviors with scripted coaching and praise is key.

"use gentle touch," "use words instead of grabbing," "share a toy." Marty and Donna, were given an assignment to pick one specific positive behavioral goal for Robbie and to work to praise that behavior frequently during the week. Since his aggression towards his sister was one of their prime concerns, they picked the goal of using gentle touch, and keeping his hands to himself. They then were given an assignment to brainstorm a list of specific praise statements they could use to give him positive feedback whenever he was gentle with her. The next week Marty returned and reported that he was surprised by how often he had been able to notice the positive behaviors. He said, "It's funny. I think I thought he was hitting her all the time, but when I think about it, he was maybe hitting 4-5 times a day. That's too much hitting, and we were really focused on that. What I didn't see is that there are actually a lot of times when he's playing with her without hitting. This week, I really tried to notice and praise those times. I think that helped. He still hit when he was frustrated, but I think he's more aware of the gentle touch, and I'm realizing how focused we are on him when he's doing the wrong thing."

Incentives. For Marty and Donna, this same behavioral goal was then linked to a tangible incentive. Because of Robbie's young age and inattentive temperament, the therapist helped them to decide to use small spontaneous rewards rather than a formal incentive system. Donna also acknowledged that it would be hard for her to be consistent with a formal sticker chart because of how hectic she felt her day was. Instead, she filled one pocket with marbles each morning. Whenever she saw Robbie being gentle or using words with his sister, she gave Robbie a marble. She also gave one to his sister, so that the system would feel fair to the two children. The two children loved playing with the marbles and Robbie liked to collect them in a special jar and count how many he had earned. Donna and Marty discussed whether they needed to let Robbie trade in the marbles for a small prize, but decided that, for now, he was very happy with just the marble. The therapist encouraged them to keep the system simple at first, as long as the marble was reinforcing. They also talked about the possibility of modifying the system if necessary, by changing the marble to another small reward (a sticker, hand stamp, raisin, or gold fish cracker), or allowing Robbie to trade in his marbles for a prize.

Parents need support and encouragement to stay calm and stick to their behavior plan.

Since Donna was with the children for much more of the day, she gave out the majority of the marbles. She felt that it was useful to be focusing on both children. She observed, "You know, now that I'm giving marbles to both Robbie and his sister, I think that I might have been missing out on her part in their earlier interactions. In some ways, she is already a little more sophisticated that Robbie is, even though he is older, and I think she was subtly pushing him into being aggressive. Now that they are both getting rewards for being friendly, I think that she is working harder to be nice to him, and he is responding to that. Also, having the marbles in my pocket is a great reminder to me that I need to notice the friendly behaviors. Every time that I put my hand in my pocket, I feel them there and I try to see if I can give one out. It's also great, because I have them with me when we are out in public."

Ignoring. The discipline topics and limit setting units were also challenging for these parents. Both were accustomed to giving many commands to Robbie when he was misbehaving. As noted by our observer during the home visit, this provided Robbie with considerable attention for his misbehavior. Observations indicated that Donna gave a high number of negative commands (more than one per minute) and few clear, direct commands. She seemed uncertain and tentative about limit setting. Both Donna and Marty had initial concerns about the rationale behind the ignoring strategy. Donna was worried that Robbie would not understand what was expected of him if she ignored his behavior and that he would think that she was not responsive to him. She felt that her own mother had not given her enough attention and felt that it was important to respond to all Robbie's behavior. She did, acknowledge, however, that she was unhappy with her current pattern of responses in which she became increasingly more angry, and was willing to try to ignore. Marty felt that ignoring was not a strong enough message for the kinds of disruptive behaviors that Robbie was displaying. He felt that Robbie would feel like he was "getting away with something" if he was ignored. However, like Donna, at this point in the program, Marty was willing to trust the group process enough to agree to give ignoring an experimental try.

Parents are helped to script positive, coping thought statements in order to control their emotional and behavioral responses.

Robbie was very persistent with his whining and tantrums, and both parents needed support and encouragement to stick to their discipline plans. For Donna, this involved teaching her to use calming self-talk (e.g., " I can stay calm, I can handle this") and reframing strategies (e.g., "He will feel safer when he learns there are predictable limits"). With Donna, in particular, Robbie would frequently tantrum and scream loudly, which she found difficult to ignore. When she did ignore, he would also cry and yell that she didn't love him and would become so upset that she worried about whether he would be okay. She was inclined to catastrophize the situation and worry that Robbie's behavior was irreversible and that he was on the path to becoming a delinquent. Donna practiced changing these negative thoughts by substituting coping thoughts such as, "He's knows that I love him, he's just saying that to get my attention." "If I keep ignoring this time, next time he'll know that I mean business." "We can change this behavior." "Robbie is only 5 and if we help him now, he won't become a delinquent."

Marty issued fewer commands but when he did he was very angry and would lose his temper and he had difficulty ignoring Robbie's behavior during the tantrums. The group discussed with Marty the long-term benefits of continuing to ignore and they also helped him to problem solve ways to make sure that Robbie was safe. With encouragement from the group, the therapists, and several role plays where Donna and Marty took turns being Robbie themselves and then reversing roles, they managed to successfully complete several lengthy ignore sequences with Robbie. They began to understand the rationale for ignoring and noticed that the frequency of Robbie's very intense tantrums was decreasing.

Time Out to Calm Down. Robbie's relationship with his parents had improved considerably and he had been learning some more appropriate social behaviors, but there were still times when his behavior was aggressive or unsafe. Since it was clear that Robbie was now attuned to his parents' positive attention, the therapist taught the parents to use Time Out for the aggressive and unsafe behaviors. First, they prepared

Robbie by explaining what behavior would result in Time Out (aggressive or unsafe behavior), where Time Out would be, and how long he would stay there. Next they helped him to practice how to calm down while he was in Time Out, showing him how to take deep breaths, and think of something that made him feel calm and happy (polar bears). Several times when Robbie was calm, he practiced going to Time Out, taking deep breaths, and thinking about polar bears. He was allowed to bring a stuffed polar bear to the Time Out chair as a visual reminder of his happy thought and feeling.

Robbie's parents were coached to minimize the need for Time Out by intensifying their use of praise whenever Robbie was calm, and distractions and redirections whenever they could see his frustrations escalating. They modeled the words he could use when angry at a sibling. For example, "that is my car, please give it back" or, "please don't touch my model."

After the parent group session on Time Out, the parents used this strategy with Robbie several times each day, but his parents noticed that the length of the Time Outs decreased over the course of the week. At first, his behavior was very dysregulated during Time Out, with tantrums that lasted approximately 30 minutes. By the end of the week, he still had several Time Outs in a day, but the tantrums were briefer, lasting about 10 minutes. Over the course of several weeks, the number of Time Outs decreased to 1-2 per week, and Robbie was usually able to regulate his emotions within 5 minutes.The therapist called the parents weekly to check in on how the Time Outs were going, to refine any difficulties and to promote their use of child directed play times, coaching and use of incentives at times when Robbie was appropriate. Incentives such as stickers of polar bears and other zoo animals at this time were increased for staying calm, being patient and sharing with his siblings. Robbie was definitely getting a lot more parental attention for prosocial behaviors than for aggression and misbehavior.

Getting and Giving Support

Donna and Marty talked about one of their goals needing more support and fun time together. They felt they were both exhausted with providing Robbie with so much supervision, coaching, and care he needed that they never had time together without Robbie. When they were home together on the weekends, they tended to argue about Marty's drinking, or about the things that needed to be done around the house. While they had a goal of finding a babysitter for a date night, they did not feel comfortable leaving all three children with a teenage babysitter, and they did not feel that they could afford an adult babysitter for an evening. Robbie's aunt agreed to take the two older children for an afternoon. This allowed his parents to be together with just the baby. She napped for two hours, while they worked on household chores together and then when she woke up, they took her for a walk around the neighborhood. Although this was not a traditional dinner and a movie date night, they found that they enjoyed the companionship of getting some household jobs done together, and were also able to actually talk to each other during the walk, something that wasn't possible when the two older children were with them.

Adult Communication and Problem Solving

The topics on communication and problem solving with each other from the IY Advance curriculum were immensely helpful for Donna and Marty. They found this was a way they could safely talk about Robbie's problems, their goals for him and work together to come up with the parenting strategies they were both going to use. For example, since most of their energy had been focused on Robbie, they had not taken as much time to talk together about other issues or to have some special time with their daughter who they felt was being neglected. After a few weeks using this problem solving discussion format they began to address some of their personal problems and goals. As with the play units, they commented that they appreciated the assignment to spend focused time with each other doing something pleasurable and on the specific problem-solving exercises. Both noticed that as their lives became too busy, they tended to let the play sessions with the children as well as their time with each other slip. When they did this, they found that they were in "reaction mode" with each other and with Robbie. When they were able to turn this around and plan the time to play with the children and talk to each other, they felt more proactive and in control of their family time. With the encouragement of the group, Donna and Marty scheduled some evenings together away from the children, although they felt guilty about this. Eventually they decided this time was important for them and when the parent group was over, they continued to go out together on the night that the group had been held.

Problem Solving with Children

In week 18 of the treatment program after they had learned the problem solving strategies for themselves, they began to coach Robbie in some basic problem solving language. Since Robbie had language delays and inattentiveness, the therapist encouraged his parents to present him with hypothetical problem situations through the use of puppets and toy animals. Because Robbie liked and collected plastic polar bears, his parents used these to talk to him. His mother's polar bear said to Robbie's bear, "I'm so frustrated. I just tried to catch a fish for dinner and it escaped! I'm hungry. What should I do?" Robbie said, "Try to catch another fish." His mother's bear responded, "That's a good idea. I think I need to try again. I'm going to take a breath to calm down. Can you help me?" Robbie's bear helped her to take some breaths and then his mother asked, "Do you think we could work together to catch some fish. Maybe teamwork would help." Robbie agreed and the bears caught a fish together and his mother was able to praise his cooperation. In this way the parents began to introduce the problem solving and feeling language to prepare him for eventual problem solving on his own.

INCREDIBLE YEARS CHILD DINOSAUR SOCIAL AND EMOTIONAL SKILLS AND PROBLEM SOLVING PROGRAM

Robbie was initially resistant to the idea of coming to the child groups. His negative experience with school made him extremely reluctant to participate in any activity that seemed remotely like school. He reported that he hated the children at his daytime school and did not want to meet any new children at night. In addition, because of his attentional difficulties, participating in a two-hour group after a long day in the classroom was a challenge.

During the first several sessions, the child group leaders/therapists allowed children to discuss their feelings about coming to the groups. The leaders had the puppets model that they, too, had been scared or mad when they first came to Dinosaur school, but that they soon started to like the group, and that they made good friends. After this initial processing, the therapist ignored Robbie's complaints about being in the group. Rather, the leaders focused on coaching, praising and giving dinosaur chips for any appropriate behavior that he exhibited. They quickly noticed that while he was reluctant to volunteer answers or participate on his own, if he was asked by the puppet to help another child with a project, he quickly became involved. Initially Robbie sought attention from the other children in the group by being disruptive, silly, and loud. The other children were taught to ignore this inappropriate behavior and to give him privacy until he calmed down. Robbie was also put in charge of helping to monitor other children's friendly and positive behavior. This provided him with an opportunity to receive attention and positive approval from the other children. Children were taught to compliment things that they liked about the other children, and therapists repeatedly pointed out and reinforced every instance of friendly behavior they observed. After 4 sessions, Robbie began to report to his parents that he liked Dinosaur school. Two of the other boys in the group became friends with Robbie, and they began to have some play dates after school. From this point on, Robbie was consistently positive about coming to the group and his parents reported that he seemed happy about a group-peer activity for the first time in his life.

A second issue for Robbie during the child groups was difficulty sitting and attending for more than a few minutes at a time. In this particular group, 3 children had been diagnosed with ADHD, and Robbie had borderline symptoms, so modifications made for Robbie were also used for the other children. The therapists arranged the format of the group such that children had frequent opportunities to change activities and move around. After watching each video vignette, therapists would lead a brief discussion with the puppet and then would have children get up and role play the situation. They continually interspersed sedentary activities with more active rehearsal, music and "hands-on" learning and games to engage the children. Robbie was reinforced for attentive behavior, but the therapist also ignored considerable wiggling and movement if he was engaged in the lesson. Robbie was also allowed to leave the group and go to a "wiggle space" if he was unable to sit still. Unlike Time Out, this was not a punishment, and Robbie could participate in the group discussions from the wiggle space as long as he appropriately raised his hand. At first therapists prompted him to use the wiggle space, and eventually he began to learn to recognize when he needed a break from sitting still. He was given three wiggle passes to use during a session and received a bonus dinosaur chip for using them quietly. As long as the activities changed frequently and the therapists monitored Robbie's attention-level and need to move around, they were able to keep him engaged and on-task. When reviewing DVDs of the sessions, Robbie's problem behavior frequently occurred if he had been sitting for longer periods of time without a break. If a therapist managed to redirect and re-engage him when he first became restless or off-task, the sequence of misbehavior could be diverted fairly easily. Robbie was motivated by earning dinosaur stickers because he knew if he got 8 dinosaur chips, that he could pick a prize from the dinosaur special box. In that box the therapists put some small polar bear and other Arctic animals that they knew would be motivating to him.

IY TEACHER CLASSROOM MANAGEMENT TRAINING

Although Donna and Marty felt they were making progress in terms of their skills at home and their interactions with Robbie, they were experiencing significant conflict with the school. Even after Robbie's behavior began to improve at home, it continued to worsen at school. His teacher was repeatedly requesting that he be removed from her classroom, and Robbie was so unhappy at school that it became a battle just to get him onto the bus in the mornings. Donna and Marty had been called into the school on numerous occasions because of Robbie's behavior. In one instance at recess, Robbie was digging in the dirt with an open paperclip. When the playground assistant requested that Robbie give her the paperclip, he refused and waved it at her. The incident was written up describing the paperclip as a weapon. Since the school had a no-tolerance policy, the school planned to suspend Robbie for three days. Donna and Marty's relationship with Robbie's teacher and with the school director had become quite adversarial. They reported that whenever they met with the director and the teachers, they felt personally attacked, and felt responsible for defending Robbie, even though they agreed that his behavior had been unacceptable. Particularly in the paperclip incident, they felt that if a similar event had occurred with another child, it would not have been handled so severely. In our conversations with the school, it was clear that the teacher and director were frustrated with the parents, with Robbie, and with the difficulty of dealing with Robbie's aggressive and noncompliant behavior on a day-to-day basis. In addition, parents of other children were reluctant to allow Robbie to associate with their children because of his aggressive behavior.

Although this book has not focused on classroom interventions, there is an *Incredible Years Teacher Classroom Management Training Program* (Webster-Stratton, 1994; Webster-Stratton, Reinke, Herman, & Newcomer, 2011) delivered to groups of teachers in 6 day-long workshops spaced monthly throughout the fall and winter of school year. Our data show that in cases, such as Robbie's, where children show pervasive conduct problems across home and school setting, the teacher program adds to the effectiveness of the parent program (Webster-Stratton, et al., 2004). The teacher program parallels topics taught in the parent group such as building positive relationships with students, strategies to promote parent-teacher collaboration and parent participation, the importance of teacher persistence, social and emotion coaching, praise and incentives, proactive strategies to prevent problems, proactive discipline hierarchies, and classroom management approaches designed to increase children's emotional, social and problem-solving skills. As with the parent program, the teacher program is offered as a collaborative venture between the group leader and the teachers and is delivered in a group setting so as to build teacher support teams. Goal setting,

For pervasive child behavior problems, adding the teacher program to the parent program improves outcomes at school.

role-play practices, discussion and self-reflective inventories are used to cover key classroom management strategies (Webster-Stratton, et al., 2011). Teachers are seen as the experts and are encouraged to use each other as resources and supports for solving difficult problems in the classroom. With the group leader's guidance, teachers help each other to make changes at the classroom-level as well as implementing individual behavior plans for the target child. Outside of the training days, therapists and/or IY coaches observe the target child in the classroom, meet with the teachers individually to develop behavior plans, and facilitate meetings with the parents, teachers, and other school personnel (Reinke, Stormont, Webster-Stratton, Newcomer, & Herman, 2012). In addition to the six scheduled days of teacher training, our therapists meet with parents and teachers to develop behavior plans and deal with school issues. At the end of the school year, the therapist works with the parents and teachers to develop a transition plan to document successful strategies for the child's next teacher.

The typical sequence of our treatment program is for the parent and child groups to meet for the first month and then to begin the teacher training after we have established relationships with the families and have worked with the child. It quickly became clear that intervention with the school and teacher would be necessary with Robbie. After the incident with the paperclip, a school meeting was set up with the therapist, the teacher, the director, and Donna and Marty. Ahead of time, the therapist rehearsed with Donna and Marty the importance of beginning the meeting with an acknowledgement of the work that the teacher and school had done on Robbie's behalf. They also agreed to share some of the difficulties they were having with Robbie at home. Lastly, they rehearsed a non-confrontive way to request that the school consider a different alternative to suspension. With the therapist at the meeting to support them, they felt comfortable acknowledging that they knew that Robbie was a difficult child to manage. This helped to establish a bond with the teacher who had been feeling as if Robbie's parents blamed her for all the difficulties that Robbie was having. The therapist also helped discuss with the director that sending Robbie home for misbehavior could actually backfire and be reinforcing for Robbie since he felt so negatively about being at school. Together the teacher, director, and parents agreed that for aggressive behaviors, Robbie would be given a brief Time Out to calm down in the classroom or would lose the privilege of using the classroom computer which he was very fond of. The therapist encouraged everyone to think of the process of making Robbie successful in this classroom as a long-term goal with many small steps. At that meeting the teacher and the parents began to set up a behavior plan to increase home-school communication and to focus on small, positive goals for Robbie's behavior in the classroom. The school also referred Robbie for a speech and language assessment through the school district. As a result of this assessment he began to receive speech therapy twice a week.

Robbie's teacher attended the IY teacher training program when it began in November and observed some of the child group sessions in the clinic. Although she participated actively in the teacher training sessions, she and the parents continued to report that the situation at school had not improved. It began to seem that Robbie had established such a negative reputation in that classroom in the first few months of school that it was hard for his teacher and his peers to view him in a positive light. Another school meeting was set up to discuss the continued difficulty, and it was decided that Robbie might be more successful in the other preschool classroom in the school. Moving a child to a new classroom is quite unusual in our program, but seemed to be the best option in this particular situation. Prior to moving Robbie to the second classroom, a meeting was set up with the old and new teacher, Robbie's parents, and the therapist from the clinic. A transition plan was discussed so that Robbie would begin in the new classroom with a behavior plan in place. This plan focused on a few positive behavioral goals with frequent reinforcement, a wiggle space for times when Robbie was having difficulty sitting still, and a back-up Time Out plan for severe negative behavior. Robbie had been participating very successfully in the child Dinosaur groups at the Parenting Clinic, so feedback from the clinic child therapist was incorporated into the plan. Robbie was able to earn breaks for successfully completing manageable parts of structured tasks. He was also given sanctioned reasons to move around the classroom since it was difficult for him to sit still for long periods of time. The therapist also worked individually with the new teacher to make up the content that she had missed during the first teacher training meetings. The new teacher agreed to attend the subsequent teacher training sessions and the original teacher stayed as well. Since academic, persistence, social and emotion coaching had worked well for the parents, the teacher was trained in this strategy and paid particular attention at first to academic and persistence coaching in order to strengthen Robbie's language skills as well as his attention and persistence with a task. Later in the year they combined this with social and emotion coaching.

This classroom switch worked extremely well for Robbie. His new teacher was able to begin on a more positive note with Robbie. His behavior continued to be difficult, but she had the support of the principal, the therapist at the clinic, and Donna and Marty, so problems were addressed as they occurred. Peer issues were also addressed immediately, and his new teacher made a concerted effort to introduce Robbie to the class in a positive light. As part of his behavior plan he was able to earn chances to assist other children (an activity that had proven to be very reinforcing to him in our child Dinosaur group at the clinic). On the playground, Robbie was initially limited to activities in a smaller, well-supervised area, and through appropriate behavior was able to earn the privilege of expanded recess. Robbie made good progress in his speech therapy, and was soon able to express many more of his ideas with intelligible words.

During the remainder of the year, there were several additional incidents that required Donna and Marty to meet with the teacher and the director. For those meetings, the therapist met with Donna and Marty at the clinic prior to the school meeting and discussed a strategy with them and practiced how they would problem solve with the teacher. Then they attended the school meetings themselves and worked with the school to set up a plan to deal with the problems. This increased their confidence in their ability to deal successfully on their own with the school issues. By the end of the year, the director, teacher, and Donna and Marty had an effective collaborative relationship. In Session 17 of the parent group, which covered the topic of problem solving with teachers, Donna and Marty demonstrated for the group how they used the problem-solving strategies to work with coming up with solutions for Robbie's problems. When our therapist attended the last meeting to discuss a transition plan for the next year, Donna and Marty needed little help to negotiate the best placement for Robbie's 1st kindergarten grade year. Altogether, the therapist attended two initial meetings at the school, and the transition meeting at the end of the year. Therapists from the Parenting Clinic also called Robbie's teacher during the year to check on his behavior plan and update her on the curriculum presented to Robbie in the Dinosaur Group. Although the timing of these meetings was earlier than our usual protocol, the number of meetings was well within the usual range for our other families. The therapist spent slightly more time on phone consultations than for families where school issues were not the main concern.

SUMMARY OF TREATMENT

Robbie's behavior improved at home first as Donna and Marty began to use more effective limit setting, combined with frequent coaching and positive interactions designed to build language and targeted emotion language and social skills. There continued to be explosive incidents throughout the treatment period, but they became less frequent, and Donna and Marty were confident in their ability to handle the problems. The Dinosaur child group quickly became a reinforcing activity for Robbie, and he made some of his first friends in the group. His parents reported that he was proud of these friends and proud of his ability to help them. This was in sharp contrast to his negative feelings about peers and school at the beginning of the year. The school situation was most difficult for this family. The change in the classroom placement along with some initial work in helping the parents and school to work together for Robbie (instead of blaming each other for the difficulties) led to a much smoother school experience for Robbie. As at home, Robbie's difficult behavior and explosive episodes at school continued, but were reported to be less frequent and less intense. In addition, the school and the teacher felt capable in their ability to handle the behaviors and work collaboratively with Robbie's parents to set goals and modify his behavior plan as needed. It is worth noting that a classroom change, such as this one, is rare in the families who participate in our treatment. Our first goal is almost always to make a current classroom situation work for the child and the teacher. However, in cases where a classroom switch is determined to be most beneficial to the child, the goal of the treatment then becomes to make the transition as smooth as possible.

Post Treatment

All observations and reports were collected again immediately post-treatment (6 months after the initial assessment, and 1 month prior to school ending) and 1 and 2 years later when Robbie was in grades 1 and 2 (see Tables 1 and Figures 1 and 2). Over all, Robbie showed fewer behavior problems following treatment, and these changes maintained at the follow-up assessments. On the ECBI, Robbie's behavior was in the clinical range at pretest and in the normal range at post-test and follow-up. On the CBCL, according to parent report, Robbie's scores decreased across time points. It is clear from the scores, however, that he continued to have higher rates of externalizing problems (particularly at school) than other children his age. It is notable that his internalizing CBCL scores dropped to within the normal range following treatment. Robbie's scores on the Attention subscale of the CBCL dropped according to parent report, but remained high on the teacher report. It is also notable that Donna and Marty's stress scores related to parenting issues dropped substantially following treatment, reflecting their reports that although Robbie continued to be a challenging child, they now felt they had the skills and confidence to manage his behavior. They also reported feeling more support in their marriage and they were spending more time together away from the children.

The home observations reflected a much different picture than those at pre-test. Overall Donna and Marty issued fewer commands, and Donna, in particular, drastically reduced her use of indirect or vague commands. Robbie was still noncompliant approximately 60% of the time, but this was a reduction from baseline, and Donna and Marty followed through when Robbie was noncompliant. Interestingly, the biggest change in Robbie's behavior was in his attitude and negative affect. The average number of negative behaviors (whining, crying, yelling, name calling) that Robbie displayed dropped from 43 at pre-

BASELINE, POST TREATMENT AND 1- AND 2-YEAR FOLLOW UP ASSESSMENTS

	Baseline	Immediate Post Treatment	1-Year Follow-Up	2-Year Follow-Up
Mother Report				
Eyberg Prob.[a]	18	11	9	4
Eyberg Intensity	139	118	112	116
CBCL Ext.[b]	71 (98%)	66 (95%)	63 (90%)	58 (79%)
CBCL Int.	61 (86%)	57 (76%)	46 (34%)	43 (24%)
CBCL Attention	63 (90%)	60 (84%)	60 (84%)	57 (76%)
Father Report				
Eyberg Prob.	21	14	7	9
Eyberg Intensity	155	126	117	107
CBCL Ext.	72 (99%)	70 (98%)	71 (98%)	66 (95%)
CBCL Int.	71 (98%)	49 (46%)	53 (62%)	53 (62%)
CBCL Attention	60 (84%)	57 (76%)	63 (90%)	51 (54%)
Teacher Report				
TRF Ext.[c]	78 (100%)	62 (88%)	68 (96%)	71 (98%)
TRF Int.	60 (84%)	51 (54%)	57 (76%)	56 (73%)
TRF Attention	68 (96%)	62 (88%)	67 (96%)	75 (99%)
Classroom Observation				
Ratio of Teacher Praise to Criticals	1.5	7.75	—	
Satisfaction[d]				
Mother	—	6.5	6	—
Father	—	6	5.3	—
Teacher	—	5.7	—	—

a Eyberg Child Behavior Inventory (Robinson et al., 1980)
b Child Behavior Check List (Achenbach, 1991a): T-scores and percentiles
c Teacher Report Form (Achenbach, 1991b)
d IY Treatment Satisfaction measure: 7-point scale, 7=very satisfied

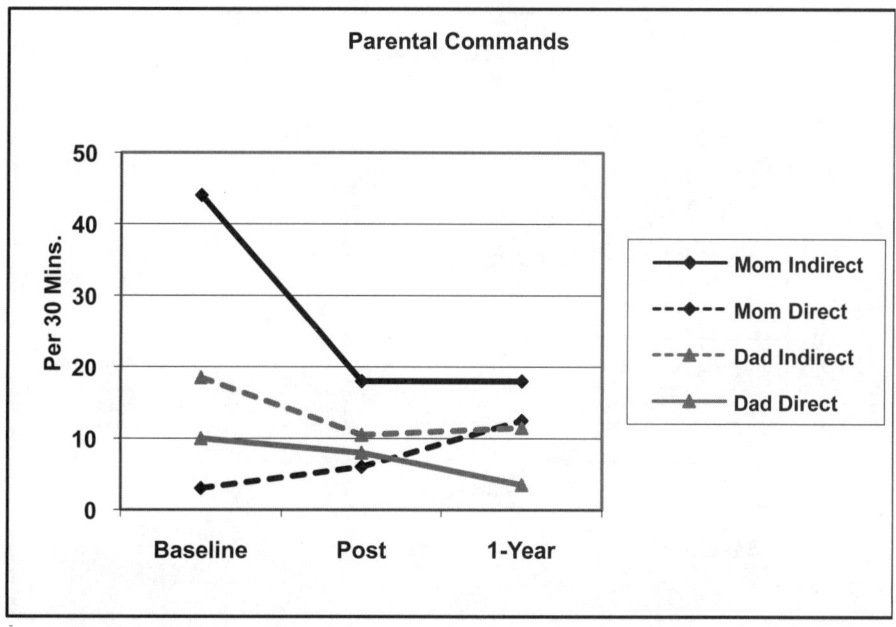

Figure 2.Number of direct (e.g., "Pick up your toys") and indirect ("Wouldn't it be nice if your toys were picked up") parent commands observed at baseline, post-treatment, and 1-year follow up.

test to around 3 at post-test and follow-up. So, although he was still disobeying his parents more than half of the time, he was much calmer and much less dysregulated. This was likely because Donna and Marty were no longer reinforcing these behaviors with attention, but instead were calmly following through with their commands. During one visit, Robbie was given a Time Out for noncompliance. Robbie complained and yelled, but Donna ignored and calmly followed through with the Time Out. When Robbie returned from Time Out, he initially pouted, but received little attention for the pouting and quickly rejoined the conversation in a positive manner. This time the coder's impressions of the visit were, "*These parents enjoy spending time as a family and are very involved in their kid's activities. Donna and Marty appear to have the art of ignoring down. Robbie made negative comments at the start of each visit, but these comments disappeared when he received no attention for them. These parents appear to have good control over both children.*"

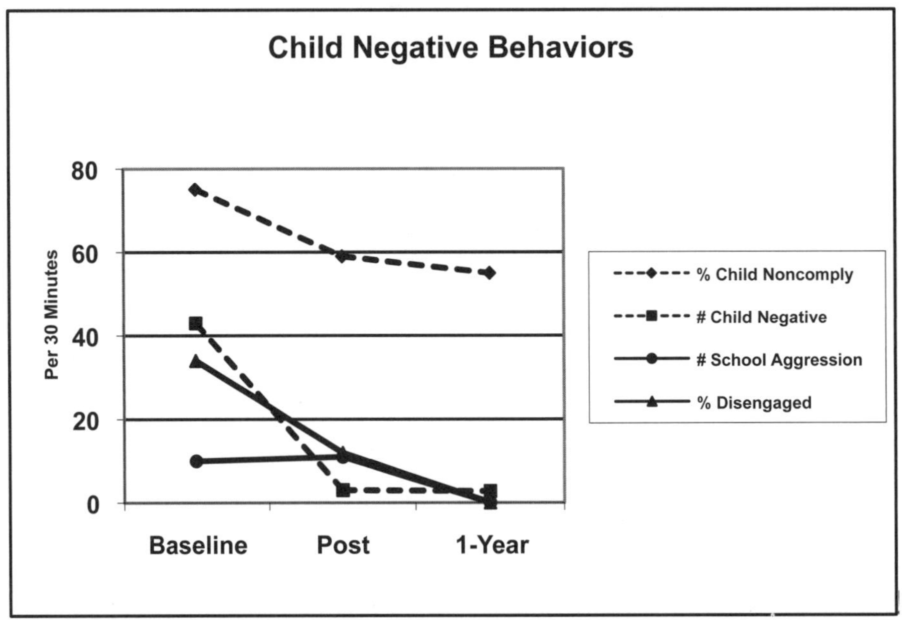

Figure 1.Child behaviors observed at home (dashed) and at school (solid) at baseline, post-treatment, and 1-year follow-up. Percent noncomply: percentage noncompliance to parent commands at home. Number child negatives: frequency of child whining, crying, smart talk, and aggression at home. Number school aggression: frequency of aggressive behaviors to peers or teachers. Percent disengaged: percentage of time that child was disengaged at school.

The post-treatment school observation also showed a different situation than the pre-treatment observation. The independent observer reported that Robbie was somewhat restless and inattentive during the two circle times, but that the teacher ignored the misbehaviors and re-engaged him in the discussion. During structured work time, Robbie finished his work and went to the teacher to receive a sticker. During recess, Robbie was actively engaged in playing with other children. At one point the playing became rough as Robbie and three other children began tossing rocks into the air (although not at another child). A recess assistant intervened and Robbie and a friend were sent to a different part of the playground, where they began to dig a hole. At another recess, he played kickball with friends.

Follow-up Contact with the Family

Although their treatment ended three years ago, Donna and Marty have continued to stay in touch with their therapists at the Parenting Clinic. Over the past three years Robbie has continued to be challenging at home and at school, but his behavior in both settings is more manageable. Donna and Marty report that Robbie's difficult times frequently coincide with times when their schedules are busier than usual, and they have stopped being as consistent with child-directed play times, positive discipline and limit setting. At these times, they make an effort to sit down together and problem solve the situation. They almost always feel capable of making the changes they need to in order to turn the negative cycle around. Occasionally they consult with their therapist about a difficult situation, but at these times they have usually already come up with a reasonable plan of action. There have been 2-3 major incidents at school in the past three years. Each time, Donna and Marty have arranged a meeting with the school and have felt capable of handling the situation on their own. They are on very good terms with Robbie's teacher and the school principal and are comfortable working together with them to plan Robbie's education.

At the 1-year follow-up, when Robbie was in kindergarten, his parents reported that his Individualized Education Plan had been expanded from a speech and language focus to add behavioral goals. In addition to speech, he received resource room instruction for two 40-minute periods a week. He was occasionally sent to the resource room if his behavior was unmanageable in the regular classroom. His parents also reported that he had begun taking Imipramine for a diagnosis of Sensory Integration Disorder. At the 2-year follow-up, Robbie was still receiving resource room assistance and was continuing to take the medication.

Robbie was involved in group activities for the first time and became enthusiastic about Boy Scouts and baseball. He had friends at school and in the neighborhood. He reported that he liked school and liked his teacher.

SUMMARY

Young children presenting with ODD/CD frequently exhibit these problems across settings (home, school, peers). In addition to oppositional and aggressive behaviors, they frequently display symptoms of ADHD and higher than normal levels of anxiety and/or depression. Manualized evidence-based treatments such as The Incredible Years programs that have the flexibility to address issues in all the problem areas can be extremely effective for these children. This child, family, and school received the same content as other parents participating in our groups. In each area, however, the therapist focused the treatment on the issues that were most salient for this case. In this way, the therapist was able to tailor the manualized treatment to the individual situation, with a successful result for the family.

In addition to the individual support provided by the therapists, the group aspect of the treatment was also extremely helpful for this family. Being part of a group of other parents and children with similar issues provided support and confidence. These personal connections with the other families helped to remove some of the stigma and guilt that Donna and Marty felt because of their difficulties with Robbie. Group training can also help parents to become more independent in their problem solving (rather than depending solely on the therapist). Donna and Marty actively participated in the buddy-calls during the group and frequently called other parents for support when they were first implementing Time Out. Even after the group ended, they continued to socialize with other parents and also used them as resources when problems came up. For Robbie, the other children in the Dinosaur Group provided some of his first positive peer relationships. See the behavior plan that was developed for Robbie in collaboration between therapists, teacher and parents.

BEHAVIOR PLAN FOR: ROBBIE

Robbie is having a great time in Dinosaur School. He enjoys the puppets and likes to help other children. He is cooperating well with teacher instructions.

Targeted Misbehavior	Occasion	Desired Behavior	Proactive Strategies and Reinforcers	Consequence of Misbehaviors
1. Robbie sometimes makes inappropriate and disruptive comments during circle time and small group activities.	Circle time & small group activities	Give on task answers and use polite language.	Notice and praise Robbie whenever he gives on task answers, "Wow, Robbie, you were really listening and paying attention, that was a great idea to share." An adult nearby can prompt him to raise a hand or help focus him on the current activity. He responds to rewards for shortterm goals—e.g. a goldfish cracker when he remains on task for a specific period of time. Teach his peers to ignore his low level disruptions. Use the word ignore whenever a child is using disruptive language during class, praise other child for using their ignore muscles. Use persistence coaching when he is focused and on task during a play activity.	Ignore all inappropriate, defiant talk and encourage others to do so too. If he continues to be disruptive, start by giving him redirection-e.g. "Robbie please be quiet so that you can listen." Remind him of the positive consequence for quieting down-e.g. "When your mouth is quiet you'll earn a goldfish cracker." Praise other children for staying calm and ignoring his disruptions.
2. Robbie can be wiggly and impulsive at circle time (rolls around on the floor, gets revved up, etc.).	Circle time	To keep his body calm at circle time.	Have a well-delineated wiggle spot for Robbie at circle time. This may be a carpet square or a taped off space near the circle. Praise Robbie when he is sitting up in that space. Keep circle time content moving forward and interesting and provide plenty of turns for Robbie to participate. Small incentives such as	Ignore mild wiggly behavior and rolling around. If it carries on for long, give a direct command to sit up in his spot and praise compliance.

Targeted Misbehavior	Occasion	Desired Behavior	Proactive Strategies and Reinforcers	Consequence of Misbehaviors
			a hand stamp towards a small prize or privilege may help Robbie stay motivated and attentive for longer periods of time. Praise Robbie whenever he does raise a quiet hand and call on him right away. Involve Robbie as much as possible in circle time by giving him chances to help others, which he likes to do. Praise Robbie for keeping a calm body. If Robbie becomes very dysregulated, prompt him to use a calm-down strategy such as taking 3 deep breaths or walking away for a minute and then trying again. Notice and praise Robbie when he is calm, patient and polite.	
3. Sometimes Robbie does not comply with teacher requests.	Can be any time, happens mostly at small group and transition times	To follow teacher directions.	Praise Robbie for participating in activities and maintaining his focus by rewarding him for short-term goals—e.g. the goldfish cracker challenge. Get Robbie's attention before giving a command. Give simple and direct commands and praise any compliance. Since transitions can be hard for Robbie, give him a warning before a transition is going to occur and give him something to look forward to. "After you take that last bite of snack , you'll get to be our first helper at circle time today." Praise Robbie whenever he transitions smoothly.	Remind Robbie of the positive consequences of following directions, "When you finish cleaning up, you'll get to be the line leader today." If he does not comply with a direct command, give Robbie a warning for a brief time out.

Targeted Misbehavior	Occasion	Desired Behavior	Proactive Strategies and Reinforcers	Consequence of Misbehaviors
4. Robbie is friendly and interested in his peers but often engages in parallel play.	Play time	To engage in and sustain positive play with his peers. To demonstrate friendship behaviors such as sharing, helping, asking for a turn, waiting, and trading a toy.	Have an adult nearby during playtime to coach Robbie's play interactions with other children. Try to get Robbie to notice others nearby engaged in play, for example "Did you see the cool train track Jacob is building?" Teach Robbie the meaning of pro-social behaviors such as asking, sharing, and turn taking. For example, use yourself to model sharing, "Robbie, I'd like to share this car with you. Can you say, please can I have it?" Model asking, "Robbie, could I use your train for a minute? I will give it right back." Label and praise Robbie's participation in any of this—e.g. "Robbie you just shared with me, that was so friendly." If Robbie wants something that another child has, provide him with the words to ask and then praise him for using words.	N/A

Parent involvement: Therapists and teachers will partner with parents to coordinate targeted behaviors to ignore and positive opposite behaviors to coach, praise and give incentives to at home. Positive notes from teacher will be given bonus stickers at home by parents.

Epilogue: Future Directions

When it comes to describing children's behavior problems, nothing seems to have changed very much over the years. Take the following quotation:

> *The children now love luxury. They have bad manners, contempt for authority; they show disrespect to their elders and love to chatter in places of exercise. They no longer rise when the elders enter the room. They contradict parents, chatter before company, gobble up dainties at the table, cross their legs and are tyrants over their teachers.*

This could be a member of the present-day older generation bemoaning the lowering of standards among the youth of today. But, in fact, the complainant, writing in the 5th Century BC, is Socrates. Or take the following quotation from an Egyptian priest, 6,000 years ago: "Our earth is degenerate; children no longer obey their parents." In light of this longevity, can we, today, expect to put an end to children's behavior problems? Certainly not! Children always have, and always will, "misbehave." It is a natural, normal developmental process and in many senses, is a necessary aspect of growing up. Children rightfully resist unreasonable demands from parents. Even when parental demands are reasonable, children have to test out limits and rules, explore and discover consequences on their own, shape their identity and assert their independence by clashing against that of their parents and teachers.

But, of course, there is a difference between developmentally normal limit testing and excessive defiance and behavior problems. As in all things, moderation is a virtue and excess is risky and even dangerous. The conduct problems that typify the children who are the subject of this book are extreme and risky behavior problems. These children exhibit persistent patterns of aggressive and oppositional behavior that lead to significant impairment in their everyday functioning at home or school. Their conduct is considered out of control and unmanageable by their parents and their teachers because of the frequency and intensity with which it occurs. In the preschool years, typical "externalizing" behaviors include noncompliance, aggression, tantrums, and oppositional-defiant behaviors; in the school years problem behaviors include violations of classroom and adult authority such as disruptive behavior, truancy, and delinquent activities (e.g., vandalism, shoplifting). For many of these children, their aggression and negativity place them at increased risk of being rejected by their peers, suspended or expelled from school, academic failure and being abused by their parents. The early onset of these disruptive behavior problems place them at the highest risk for serious adolescent and adulthood problems including drug abuse, violence and involvement with the criminal justice system. Thus early onset conduct problems confer multiple risks: they put children at risk, in terms of blighting their futures; they put parents at risk of abusing, even losing their children into foster care; they put society at risk with the seeds of violence and delinquency they propagate for the future.

The broader context of conduct disorders, problems of violence, criminality, child abuse and sheer misery for countless children and their parents, can seem overwhelming. Yet we who work with children with conduct problems and their families can take heart, for intervention during the early toddler and preschool years is clearly strategic. Successful early intervention can provide parents, teachers, and children with tools to self-regulate and substitute prosocial behaviors and conflict resolution skills for aggressive behavior before this behavior results in peer rejection, deviant peer groups, academic failure and well-entrenched negative reputations. Early intervention, in the critical period when brain development is malleable, can help children form healthy neural pathways that will be present for the rest of their lives. This is also the time when parents and teachers (not peers) are still the primary socialization influences in the child's development. This window of early brain and social development offers promise for preventing the trajectory from ODD to CD.

Early intervention, in the critical period when brain development is malleable, can help children form healthy neural pathways that will be present for the rest of their lives.

If conduct problems have proven so intractable in the past, it is largely because they were viewed as moral problems rather than behavioral, cognitive, and emotional regulation development problems. Or, because we have waited until adolescence to intervene when there has been a cascade of risk factors for which to address. There is little doubt that training parents in how to promote young children's social and emotional competence and reduce behavior problems is the treatment of choice for early-onset conduct problems. Whereas adolescent conduct disorders have proved to be more resistant to traditional psychotherapies, we have seen important developments in the past two decades in the application of cognitive social learning methods in group settings and in individual family casework. Reviews of these parent training interventions are highly promising (Kazdin & Weisz, 2010), particularly when they address the broader family interpersonal issues that impact on parental functioning (e.g., marital communication, depression, stress management, support networks). These broader-based interventions may help mediate the negative influences of family stressors on parenting skills (Dadds & McHugh, 1992; Sanders, Markie-Dadds, Tully, & Bor, 2000; Wahler, Cartor, Fleischman, & Lambert, 1993; Webster-Stratton, 1990, 1994).

It is becoming clear that for children with pervasive (home, school, and peer) problems, treatment needs to aim beyond within-family change, expanding to the child's broader social context of the school and community environment. Given the academic and developmental delays and school behavior problems typical of children with conduct problems, and given the influence of the school environment and teachers on conduct disorders, it is surprising that training programs for parents of children with conduct problems have not, in general, involved teachers as partners with parents in coordinated treatment plans. Typically, teachers are left struggling alone in the classroom with a difficult and noncompliant child who exhibits academic as well as disruptive behavior problems. Moreover, despite the documented links between underachievement, language delays, reading disabilities, and conduct disorders, there have been very few attempts to increase the effectiveness of parent training programs by adding an academic skills training component for parents through school settings. Parents need to know how to help their children with their behavior problems at home, and also with their social and academic difficulties (e.g., reading and writing) at school. In addition, parents need to know how to support their children's teachers' efforts and work with them in partnerships to develop coordinated behavior plans. If parents and teachers can collaborate as a team to help these children with their academic skills, there may be important secondary benefits on emotional regulation and social behaviors.

Parents need to know how to support their children's teachers' efforts and work with them in partnerships to develop coordinated behavior plans.

The treatment research and practice for children with conduct disorders continues to inform and improve treatment outcomes. The role of cognitive influences and parent-child attachment, not only in child therapy but in the understanding of parents' theories and attributions about children and their development (e.g. Belsky & Fearson, 2002; Compas, Phares, Banez, & Howell, 1991; Greenberg, Speltz, & DeKlyen, 1993; Moretti, Holland, & Peterson, 1994; Smith & O'Leary, 1995), has assumed increasing and well-deserved significance in this field. Research into cognition, attachment, and clinical practice utilizing the fruits of discoveries in this area should make for more effective emotional-behavioral-cognitive methods for the treatment of conduct disorders. Research into developmental issues and brain development is another potentially fruitful area of increasing the clinician's success. Any increase in our knowledge of normal cognitive and empathy development, of moral and social reasoning, and child-rearing influences on such development, will feed advantageously into our clinical work.

A vital issue in reaching a larger number of families is the effective dissemination of knowledge about parent behavior management skills. This can be most successfully accomplished through the collaboration of various professionals who work with these families: psychologists, psychiatrists, teachers, nurses, social workers. And it is, in my opinion, within the collaborative model that there is particular scope for improving our service to, and success with families of children with conduct problems: collaboration, that is, with our clients. Collaboration is active, nonblaming, nonhierarchical, and a reciprocal relationship built on trust, respect and open communication. It acknowledges that expertise is not the sole property of the therapist, that parents are experts regarding their children's needs, goals, family culture, and environment. The collaborative model allows therapists to tailor the program content, pacing and methods to parents' culture, individual goals, and children's developmental stage. Even more than other therapeutic models such as that of analyst, collaboration requires a creative touch. Here we have the fascinating but difficult-to-define "mix" of art and science. There is a component that has been shown to be necessary (but not sufficient) in this kind of work; the therapist must be extraordinarily skilled in coping with the resistance to change that characterizes many of the families referred for treatment, for collaboration requires that they actively participate in treatment, not just passively assent to it. Ordinarily, this level of clinical skill requires several years of supervised clinical experience. The use of a collaborative style in teaching and communicating information about behavioral technology is a craft, an amalgam of creativity and

The use of a collaborative style in teaching and communicating information about behavioral technology is a craft, an amalgam of creativity and applied science.

applied science. And it is here that the excitement for such future research lies, in defining, describing, and applying the therapeutic ingredients precisely.

In order to be truly successful in impacting this disorder, our interventions must involve a reduction in professional boundaries and a collaboration process that extends to all the pivotal partners in the lives of children: their parents, teachers, nurses, physicians, psychologists, school personnel such as school nurses and social workers, and, of course, the children themselves. The prospect of such a degree of collaboration is indeed exciting. Moreover, like parents who need support and training to successfully manage these children's behavior problems and to achieve their goals, so do therapists need ongoing support, coaching and consultation to be able to competently integrate all the therapy and cognitive, emotion and behavior change methods and processes discussed in this book.

Therapist support teams will make all the difference to assuring therapy fidelity and to sustainable outcomes.

REFERENCES

Abidin, R. R. (1995). *Parenting Stress Index, Third Edition: Professional Manual*. Odessa, FL: Psychological Assessment Resources, Inc.

Abramson, L. Y., Seligman, M. E. P., & Teasdale, J. D. (1978). Learned helplessness in humans: Critique and reformulation. *Journal of Abnormal Psychology*, *87*, 49-74.

Achenbach, T. M. (1991). *Manual for the teacher's report form and teacher version of the child behavior profile*. Burlington, VT: University of Vermont, Department of Psychiatry.

Achenbach, T. M., & Edelbrock, C. S. (1991). *Manual for the Child Behavior Checklist and Revised Child Behavior Profile*. Burlington, VT: University Associates in Psychiatry.

Ainsworth, M. (1974). Infant-mother attachment and social development: Socialization as a product of reciprocal responsiveness to signals. In M. Richards (Ed.), *The integration of the child into the social world*. Cambridge: Cambridge University Press.

American Psychiatric Association. (2000). *Diagnostic and statistical manual of mental disorders, text revision* (DSM-IV). Washington D. C.: Author.

Arnold, D., O'Leary, S. G., Wolff, L. S., & Acker, M. M. (1993). The Parenting Scale: A measure of dysfunctional parenting in discipline situations. *Psychological Assessment*, *5*(2), 137-144.

Asarnow, J. R., & Callan, J. W. (1985). Boys with peer adjustment problems: Social cognitive processes. *Journal of Consulting an Clinical Psychology*, *53*, 80-87.

Ashman, S. B., Dawson, G., & Panagiotides, H. (2008). Trajectories of maternal depression over 7 years: Relations with child psychophysiology and behavior and role of contextual risks. *Development and Psychopathology*, *20*(1), 55-77.

Ateah, C. A., & Durrant, J. E. (2005). Maternal use of physical punishment in response to child misbehavior: implications for child abuse prevention. *Child Abuse and Neglect*, *29*(2), 169-185.

Baker-Henningham, H., Walker, S., Powell, C., & Meeks Gardner, J. (2009). A pilot study of the Incredible Years Teacher Training programme and a curricullum unit on social and emotional skills in community pre-schools in Jamaica. *Child: Care Health and Development*.

Bakermans-Kranenburg, M. J., Van Ijzendoorn, M. H., & Juffer, F. (2003). Less is more: Meta-analyses of sensitivity and attachment interventions in early childhood. *Psychological Bulletin, 129*, 195-215.

Bandura, A. (1977). *Social learning theory*. Englewood Cliffs: Prentice-Hall, Inc.

Bandura, A. (1982). Self-efficacy mechanisms in human agency. *American Psychologist, 84*, 191-215.

Bandura, A. (1989). Regulation of cognitive processes through perceived self-efficacy. *Developmental Psychology, 25*, 729-735.

Barrett, E. R., & Davis, S. (1995). Perceptions of beginning teachers' needs in classroom management. *Teacher Education and Practice, 11*, 22-27.

Barth, R. P., Landsverk, J., Chamberlain, P., Reid, J. B., Rolls, J. A., Hurlburt, M. S., et al. (2005). Parent-training programs in child welfare services: Planning for a more evidence-based approach to serving biological parents. *Research on Social Work Practice, 15*(5), 353-371.

Bates, J. (1990). Conceptual and empirical linkages between temperament and behavior problems: A commentary on the Sanson, Prior and Kyrios study. *Merrill-Palmer Quarterly, 36*(2), 193-199.

Battistich, V., Schaps, E., & Wilson, N. (2004). Effects of an elementary school intervention in students "connectiveness" to school and social adjustment during middle school. *The Journal of Primary Prevention 24*, 243-262.

Baumrind, D. (1995). Child rearing dimensions relevant to child maltreatment. In D. Baumrind (Ed.), *Child maltreatment and optimal care giving in social contexts* (pp. 55-73). New York: Garland Publishing.

Baydar, N., Reid, M. J., & Webster-Stratton, C. (2003). The role of mental health factors and program engagement in the effectiveness of a preventive parenting program for Head Start mothers. *Child Development, 74*(5), 1433-1453.

Beauchaine, T. P. (2001). Vagal tone, development, and Gray's motivational theory: Towards an integrated model of autonomic nervous system functioning in psychophysiology. *Development and Psychopathology, 13*, 1183-1214.

Beauchaine, T. P., Hinshaw, S. P., & Pang, K. C. (in press). Comorbidity of attention-deficit/hyperactivity disorder and conduct disorder: Biological, environmental, and developmental mechanisms. *Clinical Psychology: Science and Practice*.

Beauchaine, T. P., Neuhaus, E., Brenner, S. L., & Gatzke-Kopp, L. (2008). Ten good reasons to consider biological processes in prevention and intervention research. *Development and Psychopathology, 20*, 745-774.

Beck, A. T. (1979). *Cognitive therapy and emotional disorders*. New York: New American Library.

Beck, A. T., Steer, R. A., & Garbin, M. G. (1988). Psychometric properties of the Beck Depression Inventory: Twenty-five years of evaluation. *Clinical Psychology Review,* 8, 77-100.

Beck, J. S. (2005). Cognitive therapy for challenging problems. New York: The Guilford Press.

Belsky, J., & de Haan, M. (2011). Annual research review: Parenting and children's brain development: the end of the beginning *Journal of Child Psychology and Psychiatry, 52*(4), 409-428.

Belsky, J., & Fearson, R. M. (2002). Early attachment secruity, subsequent maternal sensitivity, and later child development: Does continuity in development depend upon continuity of caregiving? *Attachment & human Development*, 4(3), 361-387.

Bennett, K. J., Brown, K. S., Boyle, M., Racine, Y., & Offord, D. (2003). Does low reading achievement at school entry cause conduct problems? *Social Science and Medicine*, 56(2443-2448).

Bierman, K. L., Coie, J. D., Dodge, K. A., Greenberg, M. T., Lochman, J. E., & McMahon, R. J. (1992). A developmental and clinical model for the prevention of conduct disorder: The FAST Track Program. *Development and Psychopathology*, 4, 509-527.

Blair, C. (2002). School Readiness: Integrating cognition and emotion in a neurological conceptualization of children's functioning at school entry. *American Psychologist, 57*(2), 111-127.

Blair, K. A., Denham, S. A., Kochanoff, A., & Whipple, B. (2004). Playing it cool: Temperament, emotion regulation, and social behavior in preschoolers. *Journal of School Psychology, 42*, 419-443.

Boggs, S. R., Eyberg, S., & Reynolds, L. A. (1990). Concurrent validity of the Eyberg Child Behavior Inventory. *Journal of Clinical Child Psychology, 19*(1), 75-78.

Bowlby, J. (1980). *Attachment and loss: Loss, sadness, and depression.* New York: Basic Books.

Bowlby, J. (1988). *A secure base: Parent-child attachment and healthy development.* New York: Basic Books

Breiner, J., & Forehand, R. (1982). Mother-child interactions: A comparison of a clinic-referred developmentally delayed group and two non-delayed groups. *Appl Res Ment Retard, 3*(2), 175-183.

Brestan, E. V., & Eyberg, S. M. (1998). Effective psychosocial treatments of conduct-disordered children and adolescents: 29 years, 82 studies, and 5,272 kids. *Journal of Clinical Child Psychology, 27*, 180-189.

Brinkmeyer, M. Y., & Eyberg, S. M. (2003). Parent-child interaction therapy for oppositional children. In A. E. Kazdin & J. R. Weisz (Eds.), *Evidence-based psychotherapies for children and adolescents* (pp. 204-223). New York Guilford.

Brody, G. H., Beach, S. R. H., Philibert, R. A., Chen, Y. F., & Lei, M. K. (2009). Parenting moderates a genetic vulnerability facgtor in longitudinal increases in youths' substance use. *Journal of Consulting and Clinical Psychology, 77*(1), 1-11.

Brophy, J. E. (1996). *Teaching problem students*. New York: Guilford.

Brotman, L. M., Grouley, K. K., Chesir-Teran, D., Dennis, T., Klein, R. G., & Shrout, P. (2005). Prevention for preschoolers at high risk for conduct problems: Immediate outcomes on parenting practices and child social competence. *Journal of Clinical Child and Adolescent Pyschology 34*, 724-734.

Brown, A. C., Green, R. J., & Druckman, J. (1990). A comparison of stepfamilies with and without child-focused problems. *Am J Orthopsychiatry*, 60(4), 556-566.

Burns, B. J., Phillips, S. D., Wagner, H. R., Barth, R. P., Kolko, D. J., & Campbell, Y. (2004). Mental health need and access to mental health services by youths involved with child welfare: A national survey. *Journal of American Academy of Child and Adolescent Psychiatry, 443*(8), 960-970.

Camp, B. W., & Bash, M. A. S. (1985). *Think aloud: Increasing social and cognitive skills - A problem-solving program for children in the classroom* . Champaigne, IL: Research Press.

Campbell, S. B. (1994). Hard-to-manage preschool boys: externalizing behavior, social competence, and family context at two-year followup. *Journal of Abnormal Child Psychology, 22*(2), 147-166.

Campbell, S. B., Ewing, L. J., Breaux, A. M., & Szumowski, E. K. (1986). Parent-referred problem three-year-olds: Follow-up at school entry. *Journal of Child Psychology and Psychiatry, 27*(4), 473-488.

Caprara, G. V., Barbaranelli, C., Pastorelli, C., Bandura, A., & Zimbardo, P. G. (2000). Prosocial foundations of children's academic achievement. *Psychological Science*, 302-306.

Carlson, J. S., Tiret, H. B., Bender, S. L., & Benson, L. (2011). The influence of group training in the Incredible Years teacher classroom management program on preschool teachers' classroom management strategies. *Journal of Applied School Psychology, 27*(2), 134-154.

Carr, E. G., Taylor, J. G., & Robinson, S. (1991). The effects of severe behavior problems in children on the teaching behavior of adults. *Journal of Applied Behavior Analysis, 24*, 523-535.

Caughy, M. O. B., Miller, T. L., & Genevro, J. L. (2003). The effects of Healthy Steps on discipline strategies of parents of young children. *Journal of Applied Developmental Psychology, 24*, 517-534.

Cerda, M., Sagdeon, A., Johnson, J., & Galea, S. (2010). Genetic and environmental influences on psychiatric comorbidity: A systematic review. *Journal of Affective Disorders, 126*, 14-38.

Chaffin, M., Silovsky, J. F., Funderburk, B., Valle, L. A., Brestan, E. V., Balachova, T., et al. (2004). Parent-child interaction therapy with physically abusive parents: Efficacy for reducing future abuse reports. *Journal of Consulting and Clinical Psychology, 72*(3), 500-510.

Christenson, S. L., & Sheridan, S. M. (2001). *School and families: Creating essential connections for learning*. New York, NY: Guilford Press.

Cicchetti, D., Rogosch, F., & Toth, S. L. (2006). Fostering secure attachment in infants in maltreating families through preventive interventions. *Development and Psychopathology, 18*, 623-649.

Collins, W. A., Maccoby, E. E., Steinberg, L., Hetherington, E. M., & Bornstein, M. H. (2000). Contemporary research on parenting: The case for nurture and nature. *American Psychologist, 55*, 218-232.

Compas, B. E., Phares, V., Banez, G. A., & Howell, D. C. (1991). Correlates of internalizing and externalizing behavior problems: perceived competence, causal attributions, and parental symptoms. *J Abnorm Child Psychol, 19*(2), 197-218.

Conduct Problems Prevention Research Group. (2002). Predictor variables associated with positive Fast Track outcomes at the end of the third grade. *Journal of Abnormal Child Psychology, 30*, 37-52.

Conroy, M., & Sutherland, K. (2008). Preventing and ameliorating young children's chronic problem behaviors: An ecological classroom-based approach. *Psychology in the Schools*, 46(1), 3-17.

Coohey, C. (1996). Child Maltreatment: Testing the social isolation hypothesis. *Child Abuse and Neglect, 20*(3), 241-254.

Corral-Verdugo, V., Frias-Armenta, M., Romero, M., & Munoz, A. (1995). Validity of a scale of beliefs regarding the positive effects of punishing children: A study of Mexican mothers. *Child Abuse and Neglect, 19*, 669-679.

Cottrell, D., & Boston, P. (2002). The effectiveness of systemic family therapy for children and adolescents. *Journal of Child Psychology and Psychiatry, 43*, 573-586.

Cowen, E. L., Pedro, C. J., & Alpert, G. L. (1990). Relationships between support and adjustment among children of divorce. *Journal of Child Psychology and Psychiatry, 31*(5), 727-735.

Crick, N. R., & Dodge, K. A. (1994). A review and reformulation of social information processing mechanisms in children's social adjustment. *Psychological Bulletin, 115*, 74-101.

Crnic, K. A., & Greenberg, M. T. (1990). Minor parenting stresses with young children. *Child Development, 61*, 1628-1637.

Cummings, E. M. (1994). Marital conflict and children's functioning. *Social Development, 3*(1), 16-36.

Cunningham, C. E., Boyle, M., Offord, D., Racine, Y., Hundert, J., Secord, M., et al. (2000). Tri-Ministry Study: Correlates of school-based parenting course utilization. *Journal of Consulting and Clinical Psychology*, 68, 928-933.

Cunningham, C. E., Bremner, R., & Boyle, M. (1995). Large group community-based parenting programs for families of preschoolers at risk for disruptive behaviour disorders: Utilization, cost effectiveness, and outcome. *Journal of Child Psychology and Psychiatry, 36*, 1141-1159.

Dadds, M. R., & McHugh, T. A. (1992). Social support and treatment outcome in behavioral family therapy for child conduct problems. *Journal of Consulting and Clinical Psychology*, 60(2), 252-259.

Davies, P. T., & Cummings, M. (1994). Marital conflict and child adjustment: An emotional security hypothesis. *Psychological Bulletin, 116*, 387-411.

Deater-Deckard, K., Dodge, K. A., Bates, J. E., & Pettit, G. S. (1996). Physical discipline among African-American and European-American mothers: Links to children's externalizing behaviors. *Developmental Psychology, 32*, 1065-1072.

Decety, J., & Meyer, M. (2008). From emotion resonance to empathic understanding: A social developmental nueroscience account. Development and Psychopathology, *Development and Psychopathology*(20), 1053-1080.

Dionne, R., Davis, B., Sheeber, L., & Madrigal, L. (2009). Initial evaluation of a cultural approach to implementation of evidence-based parenting interventions in American Indian communities. *Journal of Community Psychology, 37*(7), 911-921.

Dishion, T. J., & Andrews, D. W. (1995). Preventing escalation in problem behaviors with high-risk young adolescents: Immediate and 1-year outcomes. *Journal of Consulting and Clinical Psychology*, 63(4), 538-548.

Dishion, T. J., & Piehler, T. F. (2007). Peer dynamics in the development and change of child and adolescent problem behavior. In A. S. Masten (Ed.), *Multilevel dynamics in development psychopathology: Pathways to the future* (pp. 151-180). Mahwah,NJ: Erlbaum

Dishion, T. J., McCord, J., & Poulin, F. (1999). When interventions harm: Peer groups and problem behavior. American Psychologist, 54, 755-764.

Dishion, T. J., Patterson, G. R., Stoolmiller, M., & Skinner, M. L. (1991). Family, school, and behavioral antecedants to early adolescent involvement with antisocial peers. Developmental Psychology, 27(1), 172-180.

Dodge, K. A., & Crick, N. R. (1990). Social information processing bases of aggressive behavior in children. Personality and Social Psychology Bulletin, 16, 8-22.

Dodge, K. A., Pettit, G. S., & Bates, J. E. (1994). Socialization mediators of the relation between socioeconomic status and child conduct problems. Special Issue: Children and poverty. Child Development, 65(2), 649-665.

Dodge, K. A., Price, J. M., Bachorowski, J. A., & Newman, J. P. (1990). Hostile attributional biases in severely aggressive adolescents. Journal of Abnormal Psychology, 99(4), 385-392.

Doll, B., Zucker, S., & Brehm, K. (2004). Resilient Classrooms: Creating Healthy Environments for Learning. New York, NY: Guildford Press.

Drugli, M. B., & Larsson, B. (2006). Children aged 4-8 years treated with parent training and child therapy because of conduct problems: Generalisation effects to day-care and school settings European Child and Adolescent Psychiatry, 15, 392-399.

Dumas, J. E., & Wahler, R. G. (1983). Predictors of treatment outcome in parent training: Mother insularity and socioeconomic disadvantage. Behavioral Assessment, 5, 301-313.

Dumas, J. E., & Wahler, R. G. (1985). Indiscriminate mothering as a contextual factor in aggressive-oppositional child behavior: "damned if you do and damned if you don't:. J Abnorm Child Psychol, 13(1), 1-17.

Duncan, G. J., Dowsett, C. J., Claessens, A., Magnuson, K., Huston, A. C., & Klebanov, P. (2007). School readiness and later achivement. Developmental Psychology, 43, 1428-1446.

Durlak, J. A., Weissberg, R. P., & Pachan, M. (2010). A meta-analysis of after-school programs that seek to promote personal and social skills in children and adolescence. American Journal of Community Psychology, 45, 294-309.

Durlak, J. A., Weissberg, R. P., Dymnick, A., B., Taylor, R. D., & Schellinger, B. (2011). The Impact of Enhancing Students' Social and Emotional Learning: A Meta-Analyses of School-based Universal Interventions. *Child Development, 82*, 405-432.

Dweck, C. S. (1975). The role of expectations and attributions in the alleviation of learned helplessness. *Journal of Personality and Social Psychology, 31*, 674-685.

D'Zurilla, T. J., & Nezu, A. (1982). Social problem-solving in adults. In P. C. Kendall (Ed.), *Advances in cognitive behavioral research and therapy* (Vol. 1). New York: Academic Press.

Eames, C., Daley, D., Hutchings, J., Whitaker, C. J., Bywater, T., Jones, K., et al. (2010). The impact of group leaders behaviour on parent acquisition of key parenting skills during parent training. *Behaviour Research and Therapy, 48*, 1221-1226.

Eames, C., Daley, D., Hutchings, J., Whitaker, C. J., Jones, K., Hughes, J. C., et al. (2009). Treatment fidelity as a predictor of behaviour change in parents attending group-based parent training. *Child: care, health and development*, 1-10.

Edelbrock, C., Rende, R., Plomin, R., & Thompson, L. A. (1995). A twin study of competence and problem behavior in childhood and early adolescence. *J Child Psychol Psychiatry, 36*(5), 775-785.

Egger, H. L., & Angold, A. (2006). Common emotional and behavioral disorders in preschool children: Presentation, nosology, and epidemiology. *Journal of Child Psychology and Psychiatry, 47*, 313-337.

Eisenberg, N. (2005). Age changes in prosocial responding adn moral reasoning in adolescence adn early adulthood. *Journal of Reserach on Adolescence, 15*, 235-260.

Elias, M. J., & Tobias, S. E. (1996). *Social problem solving: Interventions in schools*. New York: Guilford.

Epstein, A. (1992). School and family partnerships. In M. Alkin (Ed.), *Encyclopedia of Educational Research* (pp. 1139-1151). New York: MacMillan.

Evans, G. W. (2004). The environment of childhood poverty. *American Psychologist, 59*(2), 77-92.

Evertson, C. M., & Weinstein, C. S. (2006). Classroom Management as a Field of Inquiry. In C. M. Evertson & C. S. Weinstein (Eds.), *Handbook of classroom management: Research, practice, and contemporary issues* (pp. 3-15). Mahwah, NJ: Lawrence Erlbaum Associates Publishers.

Eyberg, S. M. (1988). Parent-child interaction therapy: Integration of traditional and behavioral concerns. Child and Family Behavior Therapy, 10, 33-46.

Eyberg, S. M., & Pincus, D. (1999). Eyberg child behavior inventory and Sutter-Eyberg behavior inventory—revised: Professional manual. Odessa, FL: Psychological Assessment Resources.

Eyberg, S. M., Boggs, S., & Algina, J. (1995). Parent-child interaction therapy: A psychosocial model for the treatment of young children with conduct problem behavior and their families. Psychopharmacology Bulletin, 31, 83-91.

Eyberg, S. M., Funderburk, B. W., Hembree-Kigin, T. L., McNeil, C. B., Querido, J. G., & Hood, K. K. (2001). Parent-child interaction therapy with behavior problem children: One and two year maintenance of treatment effects in the family. Child and Family Behavior Therapy, 23(4), 1-20.

Eyberg, S. M., Nelson, M. M., & Boggs, S. R. (2008). Evidence-based psychosocial treatments for child and adolescent with disruptive behavior. Journal of Clinical Child & Adolescent Psychology, 37, 215-237.

Fantuzzo, J. W., DelGaudio, W. A., Atkins, M., Meyers, R., & Noone, M. (1998). A contextually relevant assessment of the impact of child maltreatment on the social competencies of low-income urban children. Journal of American Academy of Child and Adolescent Psychiatry, 37, 1201-1208.

Fantuzzo, J. W., DePaola, L. M., Lambert, L., Martino, T., Anderson, G., & Sutton, S. (1991). Effects of interpersonal violence on the psychological adjustment and competencies of young children. Journal of Consulting and Clinical Psychology, 59, 258-265.

Feinberg, M., Neiderhiser, J., Howe, G., & Hetherington, E. M. (2001). Adolescent, parent, and observer perceptions of parenting: Genetic and environmental influences on shared and distinct perceptions. Child Development, 72, 1266-1284.

Fergusson, D. M., & Lynskey, M. T. (1993). The effects of maternal depression on child conduct disorder and attention deficit behaviours. Social Psychiatry and Psychiatric Epidemiology, 28(3), 116-123.

Feshbach, N. (1989). The construct of empathy and the phenomenon of physical maltreatment of children. In D. Cicchetti & V. Carlson (Eds.), *Child maltreatment: Theory and research on the causes and consequences of child abuse and neglect* (pp. 349-373). Cambridge, MA: Cambridge University Press.

Fincham, F. D. (1994). Does marital conflict cause child maladjustment? Directions and challenges for longitudinal research. *Journal of Family Psychology*, 8, 128-140.

Fixen, D., Blase, K., Friedman, R., & Wallace, F. (2005). *Implementation research: A synthesis of the literature*. Tampa, FL: University of South Florida, Louis de la Porte Florida Mental Health Institute.

Forehand, R. L., & McMahon, R. J. (1981). *Helping the noncompliant child: A clinician's guide to parent training*. New York: Guilford Press.

Forehand, R., & Kotchick, B. A. (2002). Behavioral parent training: Current challenges and potential solutions. *Journal of Child and Family Studies*, *11*, 377-384.

Forehand, R., Sturgis, E. T., McMahon, R. J., Aguar, D., Green, K., Wells, K., et al. (1979). Parent behavioral training to modify child noncompliance: Treatment generalization across time and from home to school. *Behavior Modification*, *3*, 3-25.

Forehand, R., Thomas, A. M., Wierson, M., B2ody, G., & Fauber, R. (1990). Role of maternal functioning and parenting skills in adolescent functioning following parental divorce. *J Abnorm Psychol*, 99(3), 278-283.

Forgatch, M. (1989). Patterns and outcome in family problem solving: The disrupting effect of negative emotion. *Journal of Marriage and the Family*, 5(1), 115-124.

Forgatch, M., Patterson, G., & Skinner, M. (1988). A mediational model for the effect of divorce in antisocial behavior in boys. In E. M. Hetherington & J. D. Arasteh (Eds.), *The impact of divorce, single parenting and stepparenting on children* (pp. 135-154). Hillsdale, NJ: Lawrence Erlbaum Associates, Inc.

Fowles, D. C. (1988). Psychophysiological and psychopathy: A motivational approach. *25*, 373-391.

Frick, P. J., Lahey, B. B., Loeber, R., Stouthamer-Loeber, M., Christ, M. A., & Hanson, K. (1992). Familial risk factors to oppositional defiant disorder and conduct disorder: Parental psychopathology and maternal parenting. *Journal of Consulting and Clinical Psychology*, 60, 49-55.

Frick, P. J., Stickle, T. R., Dandreux, D. M., Farrell, J. M., & Kimonis, E. R. (2005). Callous-unemotional traits in predicting the severity and stability of conduct problems and deliqnuency. *Journal of Abnormal Child Psychology*, *33*, 471-487.

Frick, P., Kamphaus, R. W., Lahey, B. B., Loeber, R., Christ, M. G., Hart, E., et al. (1991). Academic underachievement and the disruptive behavior disorders. *Journal of Consulting and Clinical Psychology*, 59, 289-294.

Frick, P., Lahey, B., Hartdagen, S., & Hynd, G. (1989). Conduct problems in boys: Relations to maternal personality, marital satisfaction, and socioeconomic status. *Journal of Clinical Child Psychology, 18*, 114-120.

Garber, J., & Horowitz, J. (2002). Depression in children. In I. H. Gotlib & C. L. Hammen (Eds.), *Handbook of Depression*. New York: Guildford Press.

Gardner, F., Burton, J., & Klimes, I. (2006). Randomized controlled trial of a parenting intervention in the voluntary sector for reducing conduct problems in children: Outcomes and mechanisms of change. *Journal of Child Psychology and Psychiatry, 47*, 1123-1132.

Gorensten, E. E., & Newman, J. P. (1980). Disinhibitory psychopathology: A new perspective and model for research. *Psychological Review, 87*, 301-315.

Gottfredson, D. C., & Gottfredson, G. D. (2002). Quality of school-based prevention programs: Results from a national survey. *Journal of Research in Crime and Delinquency, 39*, 3-35.

Greenberg, M. T., Domitrovich, C., & Bumbarger, B. (2001). The prevention of mental disorders in school-age chldren: Current state of the field. *Prevention and Treatment*, 1-62.

Greenberg, M. T., Speltz, M. L., & DeKlyen, M. (1993). The role of attachment in the early development of disruptive behavior problems. 5, 191-213.

Gresham, F. M. (1998). Social skills training: Should we raze, remodel, or rebuild? *Behavioral Disorders, 24*, 19-25.

Gross, D., Fogg, L., Webster-Stratton, C., Garvey, C., W., J., & Grady, J. (2003). Parent training with families of toddlers in day care in low-income urban communities. Journal of Consulting and Clinical Psychology, 71(2), 261-278.

Grossmann, K. E., Grossmann, K., & Waters, E. (2005). Attachment from infancy to adulthood: The major longitudinal studies. New York: Guilford Press.

Grych, J. H., & Fincham, F. D. (1990). Marital conflict and children's adjustment: A cognitive contextual framework. Psychological Bulletin, 108, 267-290.

Haarachi, T. W., Catalano, R. G., & Hawkins, J. G. (1997). Effective recruitment for parenting programs within ethnic minority communities. Child and adolescent social work journal, 14(1), 23-39.

Hartman, R. R., Stage, S., & Webster-Stratton, C. (2003). A growth curve analysis of parent training outcomes: Examining the influence of child factors (inattention, impulsivity, and hyperactivity problems), parental and family risk factors. The Child Psychology and Psychiatry Journal, 44(3), 388-398.

Hashima, P. Y., & Amato, P. R. (1994). Poverty, social support, and parental behavior. Child Development, 65, 394-403.

Hawkins, J. D., & Weiss, J. G. (1985). The social developmental model: An integrated approach to delinquency prevention. Journal of Primary Prevention, 6, 73-95.

Hawkins, J. D., Catalano, R. F., Kosterman, R., Abbott, R., & Hill, K. G. (1999). Preventing adolescent health-risk behaviors by strengthening protection during childhood. Archives of Pediatrics and Adolescent Medicine, 153, 226-234.

Hawkins, J. D., Herrenkoh., T., Farrington, D. P., Brewer, D., Catalano, R. F., & Harachi, T. W. (1998). A review of predictors of youth violence. In R. Loeber & D. P. Farrington (Eds.), Serious and violent juvenile offenders: Risk factors and successful interventions (pp. 106-146). Thousand Oaks: CA: Sage.

Hawkins, J. D., Smith, B. H., & Catalano, R. F. (2004). Social development and social and emotional learning. In J. E. Zins, R. P. Weissberg, M. C. Wang & H. J. Walberg (Eds.), Building academic success on soical and emotional learning: What does the research say? (pp. 135-150). New York: Teachers College Press.

Hazen, A., Connelly, C. D., Kelleher, K., Landsverk, J., & Barth, R. P. (2004). Intimate partner violence among female caregivers of children reported for child maltreatment. *Child Abuse and Neglect, 28*, 301-319.

Henggeler, S. W., Schoenwald, S. K., Liao, J. G., Letourneau, E. J., & Edwards, D. L. (2002). Transporting efficacious treatments to field settings: The link between supervisory practices and therapist fidelity in MST programs. *Journal of Clinical Child & Adolescent Psychology, 31*(2).

Hinshaw, S. P. (1992). Externalizing behavior problems and academic underachievement in childhood and adolescence: Causal relationships and underlying mechanisms. *Psychological Bulletin, 111*, 127-155.

Hoagwood, K., Burns, B. J., & Weisz, J. (2002). A profitable conjunction: From science to service in children's mental health. In B. J. Burns & K. Hoagwood (Eds.), *Community-based interventions for youth with severe emotional disturbances* (pp. 327-338). New York: Oxford University Press.

Houston, W. r., & Williamson, J. L. (1992). Perceptions of their preparation by 42 Texas elementary school teachers copared with their responses as student teachers. *Teacher Education and Practice*, 8, 27-42.

Hurlburt, M., Barth, R. P., Leslie, L. K., Landsverk, J., & McRae, J. (in submission). Building on Strengths: Current status and opportunities for improvement of parent trianing for families in child welfare.

Hutchings, J., & Gardner, F. (2006). Evaluation of Incredible Years Parenting Program with Sure Start Parents

Hutchings, J., & Webster-Stratton, C. (2004). Community-based support for parents. In M. Hohughi & N. Long (Eds.), *Handbook of parenting: Theory and research for practice* (pp. 334-351). London: Sage.

Hutchings, J., Daley, D., Jones, E. E., Martin, P., Bywater, T., & Gwyn, R. (2007). Early results from developing and researching the Webster-Stratton Incredible Years Teacher Classroom Management Training Programme in North West Wales. *Journal of Children's Services*, *2*(3), 15-26.

Hutchings, J., Gardner, F., Bywater, T., Daley, D., Whitaker, C., Jones, K., et al. (2007). Parenting intervention in Sure Start services for children at risk of developing conduct disorder: Pragmatic randomized controlled trial. *British Medical Journal, 334*(7595), 1-7.

Ingersoll, R. M. (2002). High turnover plagues schools. *USA Today*.

Jacobson, N. S., & Margolin, G. (1979). *Marital therapy: Strategies based on social learning and behavior as exchange principles*. New York: Brunner/Mazel.

Jaffee, S. R., & Maikovich-Fong, A. K. (2011). Effects of chronic maltreatment and maltreatment timing on children's behavior and cognitive abilities. *Journal of Child Psychology and Psychiatry, 52*(2), 184-194.

Jaffee, S. R., Caspi, A., Moffitt, T. E., & Taylor, A. (2004). Physical maltreatment victim to antisocial child: Evidence of environmentally mediated process. *Journal of Abnormal Psychology, 113*, 44-55.

Jouriles, E. N., Murphy, C. M., Farris, A. M., & Smith, D. A. (1991). Marital adjustment, parental disagreements about child rearing and behavior problems in boys: Increasing the specificity of the marital assessment. *Child Development, 62*(6), 1424-1433.

Kaiser, A. P., Hancock, T. B., Cai, X., Foster, E. M., & Hester, P. (2000). Parent-reported behavior problems and language delays in boys and girls enrolled in Head Start classrooms. *Behavior Disorders, 26*, 26-41.

Kaminski, J. W., Valle, L. A., Filene, J. H., & Boyle, C. L. (2008). A meta-analytic review of components associated with parent training program effectiveness. *Journal of Abnormal Child Psychology, 36*, 567-589.

Kapitanoff, S. H., & Lutzker, J. R. (2000). Cultural issues in the relation between child disabilities and child abuse. *Aggression and Violent Behavior, 5*(3), 227-244.

Kazdin, A. E. (1987). Treatment of antisocial behavior in children: Current status and future directions. *Psychological Bulletin, 102*(2), 187-203.

Kazdin, A. E., Esveldt-Dawson, K., French, N. H., & Unis, A. S. (1987). Problem-solving skills training and relationship therapy in the treatment of antisocial child behavior. *Journal of Consulting and Clinical Psychology, 55*, 76-85.

Kazdin, A., & Mazurick, J. L. (1994). Dropping out of child psychotherapy: Distinguishing early and late dropouts over the course of treatment. *Journal of Consulting and Clinical Psychology, 62*, 1069-1074.

Kazdin, A. E. (2002). Psychosocial treatments for conduct disorder in children and adolescents. In P. E. Nathan & J. M. Gorman (Eds.), *A guide to treatments that work* (pp. 57-85). New York: Oxford University Press.

Kazdin, A. E. (2003). Psychotherapy for children and adolescents. *Annual Review of Psychology 54*, 253-276.

Kazdin, A. E. (2005). *Parent management training.* New York Oxford University Press.

Kazdin, A. E., & Weisz, J. R. (2003). *Evidence-Based Psychotherapies for Children and Adolescents*. NY: Guilford Press.

Kazdin, A. E., & Weisz, J. R. (2010). *Evidence-based p sychotherapies for children and adolescents*, 2nd edition. New York: Guilford Publications.

Kazdin, A. E., & Whitley, M. K. (2006). Comorbidity, case complexity, and effects of evidence-based treatments for children referred for disruptive behavior. *Journal of Consulting and Clinical Psychology, 74*, 455-467.

Kellam, S. G., Ling, X., Merisca, R., Brown, C. H., & Ialongo, N. (1998). The effect of the level of aggression in the first grade classroom on the course and malleability of aggressive behavior into middle school. *Development and Psychopathology, 10*, 165-185.

Kendall, P. C. (1993). Cognitive-behavioral therapies with youth: Guiding theory, current status and emerging developments. *Journal of Consulting and Clinical Psychology, 61*, 235-247.

Kim, E., Cain, K., & Webster-Stratton, C. (2008). The preliminary effect of a parenting program for Korean American mothers: A randomized controlled experimental study. *International Journal of Nursing Studies*, 45, 1261-1273.

Kim, E., Choe, H., & Webster-Stratton, C. (2010). Korean immigrant parents' evaluations of the delivery of a parenting program for cultural and linguistic appropriateness and usefulness. *Family and Community Health,* 33(4), 1-13.

Kim-Cohen, J., Caspi, A., Taylor, A., Williams, B., & Newcombe, R. (2006). MAOA, maltreatment, and gene-environment interaction predicting children's mental health: new evidence and a meta-analysis. *Molecular Psychiatry 11*, 903-913.

Knutson, J. F., DeGarmo, D., Koeppl, G., & Reid, J. B. (2005). Care neglect, supervisory neglect and harsh parenting in the development of children's aggression: A replication and extension. *Child Maltreatment, 10*, 92-107.

Ladd, G. W., Price, J. M., & Hart, C. H. (1990). Preschooler's behavioral orientations and patterns of peer contact: Predictive of social status? In S. R. Asher & J. D. Coie (Eds.), *Peer rejection in childhood*. New York: Cambridge University Press.

Lahey, B. B., & Waldman, I. D. (2003). A developmental propensity model of the origins of conduct problems during childhood and adolescence. In B. B. Lahey, T. E. Moffitt & A. Caspi (Eds.), *Causes of conduct disorder and juvenile delinquency* (pp. 76-117). New York: Guilford Press.

Lahey, B. B., Hart, E. L., Pliszka, S., Applegate, B., & McBurnett, K. (1993). Neurophysiological correlates of conduct disorder: A rationale and review of current research. *Journal of Clinical Child Psychology, 22*, 141-153.

Larsson, B., Fossum, B., Clifford, G., Drugli, M., Handegard, B., & Morch, W. (2009). Treatment of oppositional defiant and conduct problems in young Norwegian children: Results of a randomized trial. *European Child Adolescent Psychiatry, 18*(1), 42-52.

Lau, A. S. (2007). *Physical discipline in Chinese American immigrant families:The role of cultural values, contextual stress, and adaptive culture*.

Lau, A. S., Fung, J. J., Ho, L. Y., Liu, L. L., & Gudino, O. G. (2011). Parent training with high-risk immigrant chinese families: A pilot group randomized trial yielding practice-based evidence. *Behavior Therapy, 42*, 413-426.

Lavigne, J. V., LeBailly, S. A., Gouze, K. R., Cicchetti, C., Pochyly, J., Arend, R., et al. (2008). Treating Oppositional Defiant Disorder in primary care: A comparison of three models. *Journal of Pediatric Psychology*, 33(5), 449-461.

Lee, E. (1988). Cultural factors in working with Southeast Asian refugee adolescents. *Journal of Adolescents, 11*, 167-179.

Lees, D. G., & Ronan, K. R. (2005). *Parent management training for solo mothers of children diagnosed with attention deficit disorder: An effectiveness and multiple baseline evaluation*. Massey University, Palmerston.

Levendosky, A. A., Okun, A., & Parker, J. G. (1995). Depression and maltreatment as predictors of social competence and social problem-solving skills in school-age children. *Child Abuse Negl, 19*(10), 1183-1195.

Lieh-Mak, F., Lee, P. W. H., & Luk, S. L. (1984). Problems encountered in teaching Chinese parents to be behavior therapists. *Psychologia, 27*, 56-64.

Linares, L. O., Montalto, D., MinMin, L., & S., V. (2006). A Promising Parent Intervention in Foster Care. *Journal of Consulting and Clinical Psychology, 74*(1), 32-41.

Lochman, J. E. (1990). Modification of childhood aggression. *Prog Behav Modif, 25*(47), 47-85.

Lochman, J. E., & Wells, K. C. (2002). Contextual social-cognitive mediators and child outcome: A test of the theoretical model in the Coping Power Program. *Development and Psychopathology, 14*, 971-993.

Lochman, J. E., & Wells, K. C. (2004). The Coping Power Program for preadolescent aggressive boys and their parents: outcome effects at the 1-year follow-up. *Journal of Consulting and Clinical Psychology, 72*, 571-578.

Lochman, J. E., Boxmeyer, C. L., Powell, N. P., Roth, D., & Windle, M. (2006). Masked intervention effects: Analytic methods for addressing low dosage of intervention. *New Directions for Evaluation, 110*, 19-32.

Lochman, J. E., Burch, P. R., Curry, J. F., & Lampron, L. B. (1984). Treatment and generalization effects of cognitive-behavioral and goal-setting interventions with aggressive boys. *Journal of Consulting and Clinical Psychology, 52*(5), 915-916.

Lochman, J. E., Lampron, L. B., Burch, P. R., & Curry, J. F. (1985). Client characteristics associated with behavior change for treated and untreated aggressive boys. *J Abnorm Child Psychol, 13*(4), 527-538.

Loeber, R., & Farrington, D. P. (2000). Young children who commit crime: Epidemiology, developmental origins, risk factors, early interventions, and policy implications. *Developmental Psychopathology, 12*(4), 737-762.

Loeber, R., Lahey, B. B., & Thomas, C. (1991). Diagnostic conundrum of oppositional defiant disorder and conduct disorder. 100, 379-390.

Lutzker, J. R. (1992). Developmental disabilities and child abuse and neglect: The ecobehavioral imperative. *Behavior Change, 9*, 149-156.

Lynam, D. R., Caspi, A., Moffitt, T. E., Wikstrom, P. H., Loeber, R., & Novak, S. (2000). The interaction between impulsivity and neighborhood context on offending: The effects of impulsivity are stronger in poorer neighborhoods. *Journal of Abnormal Child Psychology, 109*, 563-574.

Lynch, M. A., & Roberts, J. (1977). Predicting child abuse: Signes of bonding failure in teh maternity hospital. *British Medical Journal, 278*, 624-636.

Malecki, C. K., & Elliott, S. N. (2002). Children's social behaviors as predictors of academic achievement: A longitudinal analysis. *School Psychology Quarterly, 17*, 1-23.

Maziade, M., Cote, R., Bernier, H., Boutin, P., & Thivierge, J. (1989). Significance of extreme temperament infancy for clinical status in pre-school years II. 14, 544-551.

McLoyd, V. C. (1990). The impact of economic hardship on black families and children: Psychological distress, parenting, and socio-emotional development. *Child Development, 61*, 311-346.

Meichenbaum, D., & Turk, D. (1987). *Facilitating treatment adherence: A practitioner's guidebook*. New York: Plenum Press.

Menting, B., Van Lier, P. A. C., & Koot, H. M. (2011). Language skills, peer rejection, and the development of externalizing behavior from kindergarten to fourth grade. *Journal of Child Psychology and Psychiatry 52*(1), 72-79.

Milich, R., Hartung, C. M., Martin, C. A., & Haigler, E. D. (1994). Behavioral disinhibition and underlying processes in adolescents with disruptive beahvior disorders. In D. K. Routh (Ed.), *Disruptive behavior disorders in childhood* (pp. 109-138). New York: Plenum.

Miller Brotman, L., Klein, R. G., Kamboukos, D., Brown, E. J., Coard, S., & L., S.-S. (2003). Preventive intervention for urban, low-income preschoolers at familial risk for conduct problems: A randomized pilot study. *Journal of Child Psychology and Psychiatry, 32*(2), 246-257.

Miller, W. R., & Rollnick, S. (2002). Motivational interviewing. New York: Guilford Press.

Mize, J., & Cox, R. A. (1990). Social knowledge and social competence: number and quality of strategies as predictors of peer behavior. *Journal of Genetics Psychology, 151*(1), 117-127.

Moretti, M. M., Holland, R., & Peterson, S. (1994). Long term outcome of an attachment-based program for conduct disorder. *Canadian Journal of Psychiatry, 39*(6), 360-370.

Murrihy, R., Kidman, A., & Ollendick, T. (2010). *Clinician's handbook for the assessment and treatment of conduct problems in youth:* Springer Press.

Najaka, S. S., Gottfredson, D. C., & Wilson, D. B. (2001). A meta-analytic inquiry into the relationship between selected risk factors and problem behavior. *Prevention Science, 2*, 257-272.

Nieto, S. (1992). *Affirming diversity: The sociopolitical context of multicultural education*. New York: Longman.

O'Connor, E., Dearing, E., & Collins, B. A. (2011). Teacher-child relationship and behavior problem trajectories in elementary school. *American Educatinal Research Journal, 48*(1), 120-162.

Offord, D. R., & Bennet, K. J. (1994). Conduct disorder: Long term outcomes and intervention effectiveness. *Journal of the American Academy of Child and Adolescent Psychiatry, 33*, 1069-1078.

Ogg, J. A., & Carlson, J. S. (2009). The self-administered Incredible Years parent training program: Perceived effectiveness, acceptability and integrity with children exhibiting symptoms of Attention-Deficit/Hyperactivity Disorder. *Journal of Evidence- Based Practices for Schools, 10*(2), 143-161.

O'Leary, K. D., & Emery, R. E. (1982). Marital discord and child behavior problems. In M. D. Levine & P. Satz (Eds.), *Middle Childhood: Developmental variation and dysfunction* (pp. 345-364). New York: Academic Press.

Ostrander, R., & Herman, K. C. (2006). Potential developmental, cognitive, and parenting mediators of the relationship between ADHD and depression. *Journal of Consulting and Clinical Psychology, 74*, 89-98.

Paster, V. (1986). A social action model of intervention for difficult to reach populations. *American Journal of Orthopsychiatry, 56*(4), 625-629.

Patterson, G. R. (1975a). *Families: Applications of social learning to family life*. Champaign, IL: Research Press.

Patterson, G. R. (1982). *Coercive family process*. Eugene, OR: Castalia.

Patterson, G. R., & Capaldi, D. (1991). Antisocial parents: Unskilled and vulnerable. In P. Cowan & M. Hertherington (Eds.), *Family transitions* (pp. 195-218). Hillsdale, NJ: Erlbaum.

Patterson, G. R., & Fisher, P. A. (2002). Recent developments in our understanding of parenting: bidirectional effects, causal models, and search for parsimony. In M. H. Bornstein (Ed.), *Handbook of Parenting: Practical Issues in Parenting, Vol 5* (pp. 59-88). Mahwah, NJ: Erlbaum.

Patterson, G. R., & Forgatch, M. S. (1995). Predicting future clinical adjustment from treatment outcome and process variables. *Psychological Assessment, 7*(2), 275-285.

Patterson, G. R., Capaldi, D., & Bank, L. (1991). An early starter model for predicting delinquency. In D. J. Pepler & K. H. Rubin (Eds.), *The development and treatment of childhood aggression* (pp. 139-168). Hillsdale, NJ: Erlbaum.

Patterson, G., Reid, J., & Dishion, T. (1992). *Antisocial boys: A social interactional approach* (Vol. 4). Eugene, OR: Castalia Publishing.

Pettit, G. S., Bates, J. E., & Dodge, K. A. (1997). Supportive parenting, ecological context, and children's adjustment: A seven-year longitudinal study. *Child Development*, 68(5), 908-923.

Piaget, J. (1962). *Play, Dreams and Imitation in Childhood* New York: Norton.

Piaget, J., & Inhelder, B. (1962). *The Psychology of the Child*. New York Basic Books.

Portes, A., & Rumbaut, R. G. (2001). *Legacies: The story of the immigrant second generation*. Berkeley and Los Angeles, CA: University of California Press.

Posthumus, J. A., Raaijmakers, M. A. J., Maassen, G. H., Engeland, H., & Matthys, W. (2011). Sustained effects of Incredible Years as a preventive intervention in preschool children with conduct problems *Journal of Abnormal Child Psychology*.

Quay, H. C. (1993). The psychopathology of undersocialized aggressive conduct disorder: A theoretical perspective. *Development and Psychopathology*, 5, 165-180.

Raine, A., & Venables, P. (1984). Tonic heart rate level, social class, and antisocial class and antisocial behavior in adolescents. *Biological Psychology, 18*, 123-132.

Raine, A., Venables, P., & Mednick, S. (1997). Low resting heart rate at age three years predisposes to aggression at age 11 years: Evidence from the Mauritius Child Health Project. *Journal of the Academy of Child and Adolescent Psychiatary*, 36, 1457-1464.

Raver, C. C., Jones, S. M., Li-Grining, C. P., Metzger, M., Champion, K. M., & Sardin, L. (2008). Improving preschool classroom processes: Preliminary findings from a randomized trial implemented in Head Start settings. *Early Childhood Research Quarterly*, *23*, 10-26.

Reese, L. E., Vera, E. M., & Caldwell, L. D. (2006). *The role and function of culture in violence prevention practice and science*. Washington, D.C.: American Psychological Association

Reese, L. E., Vera, E. M., & Hasbrouck, L. (2003). *Examining the impact of violence on ethnic minority youth, their families, and communities: Issues for prevention, practice and science*. Thousand Oaks, CA: Sage.

Reid, M. J., Webster-Stratton, C., & Beauchaine, T. P. (2001). Parent training in Head Start: A comparison of program response among African American, Asian American, Caucasian, and Hispanic mothers. *Prevention Science*, *2*(4), 209-227.

Reid, M. J., Webster-Stratton, C., & Hammond, M. (2007). Enhancing a classroom social competence and problem-solving curriculum by offering parent training to families of moderate-to-high-risk elementary school children. *Journal of Clinical Child and Adolescent Psychology*, *36*(5), 605-620.

Reinke, W. M., & Herman, K. C. (2002). Creating school environments that deter antisocial behaviors in youth. *Psychology in the Schools*, *39*(549-559).

Reinke, W. M., Stormont, M., Herman, K. C., Puri, R., & Goel, N. (2010). Supporting children's mental health in schools: Teacher perceptions of needs, roles and barriers. *School Psychology Quarterly*.

Reinke, W. M., Stormont, M., Webster-Stratton, C., Newcomer, L., & Herman, K. (in submission). The Incredible Years Classroom Management Program: Using Coaching to Support Generalization to Real World Settings *Psychology in Schools*.

Resnicow, K., Solar, R., Braithwaite, R., Ahluwalia, J., & Butler, J. (2000). Cultural sensitivity in substance abuse prevention. *Journal of Community Psychology*, *28*, 271-290.

Rinaldi, J. (2001). Long-term outcomes of parent training and predictors of adolescent adjustment. *Dissertation Abstracts International*, 62(05), 2498 (UMI No. 3014016).

Robins, L. N. (1981). Epidemiological approaches to natural history research: Antisocial disorders in children. *Journal of the American Academy of Child Psychiatry, 20*, 566-580.

Robinson, E. A., & Eyberg, S. M. (1981). The Dyadic Parent-Child Interaction Coding System: Standardization and validation. *Journal of Consulting and Clinical Psychology, 49*, 245-250.

Robinson, E. A., Eyberg, S. M., & Ross, A. W. (1980). The standardization of an inventory of child conduct problem behaviors. *Journal of Clinical Child Psychology, 9*, 22-28.

Roditti, M. G. (2005). Understanding communities of neglectful parents: Child caring networks and child neglect. *Child Welfare, 84*(2), 277-298.

Rogers, C. (1983). *Freedom to learn for the 80's*. Columbus, Ohio: Merrill.

Rose, S. L., Rose, S. A., & Feldman, J. (1989). Stability of behavior problems in very young children. *Development and Psychopathology, 1*, 5-20.

Rothbart, M. K., & Bates, J. E. (1998). Tempermament. In W. Damon & N. Eisenberg (Eds.), *Handbook of child psychology:vol. 3 Social, emotional, and personality development (5th ed.)* (pp. 105-176). New York: Wiley.

Rothbart, M. K., Ahadi, S. A., Hershey, K. L., & Fisher, P. (2001). Investigations of temperament at three to seven years: The chldren's behavior questionnaire. Child Development, 72, 1394-1408.

Sanders, M. R. (2008). Triple P-Positive Parenting Program as a public health approach to strengthening parenting. *Journal of Family Psychology, 22*, 506-517.

Sanders, M. R., Markie-Dadds, C., Tully, L. A., & Bor, W. (2000). The Triple P-Positive Parenting Program: A comparison of enhanced, standard and self-directed behavioural family intervention for parents of children with early onset conduct problems. *Journal of Consulting and Clinical Psychology, 68*, 624-640.

Sandler, I. N., Schoenfelder, E. N., Wolchik, S. A., & MacKinnon, D. P. (2011). Long-term Impact of Prevention Programs to Promote Effective Paernting:Lasting Effects but Uncertain Processes. *Annual Review of Psychology, 62*, 299-329.

Scarpa, A., Raine, A., Venables, P. H., & Mednick, S. A. (1997). Heart rate and skin conductance in behaviorally inhibited Mauritian children. *Journal of Abnormal Psychology, 10*(6), 182-190.

Schmidt, K., Solanto, M., & Bridger, W. (1985). Electrodermal activity of undersocialized aggresssive children: A pilot study. *Journal of Child Psychology and Psychiatry, 26*, 653-660.

Schoenalkd, S. K., & Hoagwood, K. (2001). Effectiveness, transportability, and dissemination of interventions: What matters when? *Journal of Psychiatric Services, 52*(9), 1190-1197.

Schonfeld, I. S., Shaffer, D., O'Connor, P., & Portnoy, S. (1988). Conduct disorder and cognitive functioning: Testing three causal hypotheses. *Child Development, 59*(4), 993-1007.

Scott, S., Carby, A., & Rendu, A. (2008). *Impact of Therapists' Skill on Effectiveness of Parenting Groups for Child Antisocial Behavior.* London: King's College, Institute of Psychiatry, University College London.

Scott, S., O'Connor, T. G., Futh, A., Matias, C., Price, J., & Doolan, M. (2010). Impact of a parenting program in a high-risk, multiethnic community: The PALS trial. *Journal of Child Psychology and Psychiatry*.

Scott, S., Spender, Q., Doolan, M., Jacobs, B., & Aspland, H. (2001). Multicentre controlled trial of parenting groups for child antisocial behaviour in clinical practice. *British Medical Journal, 323*(28), 1-5.

Scott, S., Sylva, K., Doolan, M., Price, J., Jacobs, B., Crook, C., et al. (2009). Randomised controlled trial of parent groups for child antisocial behaviour targeting multiple risk factors: the SPOKES project. *The Journal of Child Psychology and Psychiatry*.

Sedlar, G., & Hansen, D. J. (2001). Anger, child behavior, and family distress: Further evaluation of the Parental Anger Inventory. *Journal of Family Violence, 16*, 361-373.

Seifer, R. (2000). Temperament and goodness of fit: Implications for developmental psychopathology. In A. J. Sameroff, M. Lewis & S. Miller (Eds.), *Handbook of developmental psychopathology* (pp. 257-276). New York: Plenum.

Seligman, M. (1990). *Learned Optimism*. Sydney: Random House.

Seligman, M. E. P. (1975). *Helplessness*. San Francisco, CA: Freeman.

Shernoff, E. S., & Kratochwill, T. R. (2007). Transporting an evidence-based classroom management program for preschoolers with disruptive behavior problems to a school: An analysis of implementation, outcomes, and contextual variables. *School Psychology Quarterly, 22*(3), 449-472.

Shores, R. E., Jack, S. L., Gunter, P. L., Ellis, D. N., DeGriere, T. J., & Wehby, J. H. (1993). Classroom interactions of children with behavioral problems. *Journal of Emotional and Behavioral Disorders, 1*(27-39).

Shure, M. B. (1997). Interpersonal cognitive problem solving: Primary prevention of early high-risk behaviors in the preschool and primary years. In G. W. Albee & T. P. Gullotta (Eds.), *Primary Prevention Works* (pp. 167-188). Thounsand Oaks, CA: Sage.

Simonsen, B., & Fairbanks, S. (2008). Evidence-based practices in classroom management: Considerations for research to practice. *Education & Treatment of Children, 31*(3), 351-380.

Smith, A. M., & O'Leary, S. G. (1995). Attributions and arousal as predictors of maternal discipline. *Cognitive therapy and research, 19*(4), 459-471.

Snyder, H. (2001a). Child delinquents. In R. Loeber & D. P. Farrington (Eds.), *Risk factors and successful interventions*. Thousand Oaks, CA: Sage.

Snyder, H. (2001b). Epidemiology of official offending. In R. Loeber & D. Farrington (Eds.), *Child delinquents: Development, intervention and service needs* (pp. 25-46). Thousand Oaks, CA: Sage.

Snyder, J., & Stoolmiller, M. (2002). *Reinforcement and coercive mechanisms in the development of antisocial behavior. The family.* . Washington, DC: American Psychological Association.

Spaccarelli, S., Cotler, S., & Penman, D. (1992). Problem-solving skills training as a supplement to behavioral parent training. *Cognitive Therapy and Research, 16*, 1-18.

Spanier, G. B. (1976). Measuring dyadic adjustment: New scales for assessing the quality of marriage and similar dyads. *Journal of Marriage and the Family, 38*, 15-28.

Spitzer, A., Webster-Stratton, C., & Hollinsworth, T. (1991). Coping with conduct-problem children: Parents gaining knowledge and control. *Journal of Clinical Child Psychology, 20*, 413-427.

Stormont, M., Smith, S. C., & Lewis, T. J. (2007). Teacher implementation of precorrection and praise statements in Head Start classrooms as a component of a program-wide system of positive behavioral support. *Journal of Behavioral Education, 16*, 280-290.

Sturge, C. (1982). Reading retardation and antisocial behavior. *Journal of Child Psychology and Psychiatry, 23*, 21-23.

Sutton, C. T., & Broken Nose, M. A. (1996). *American Indian families: An overview*. New York, NY: Guilford Press.

Tapp, J., Wehby, J. H., & Ellis, D. (1995). A multiple option observation system for experimental studies: MOOSES. *Behavior Research Methods, Instruments, and Computers, 27*(1), 25-31.

Taylor, T. K., Schmidt, F., Pepler, D., & Hodgins, H. (1998). A comparison of eclectic treatment with Webster-Stratton's Parents and Children Series in a children's mental health center: A randomized controlled trial. *Behavior Therapy, 29*, 221-240.

Thomas, A., & Chess, S. (1977). *Temperament and Development*. New York: Brunner/Mazel.

Tremblay, R. E., Japel, C., Perusse, D., Boivin, M., Zoccolillo, M., Montplaisir, J., et al. (2000). The search for the age of "onset" of physical aggression: Rousseau and Bandura revisited. *Criminal Behavior and Mental Health, 24*(2), 129-141.

Tremblay, R. E., Mass, L. C., Pagani, L., & Vitaro, F. (1996). From childhood physical aggression to adolescent maladjustment: The Montreal Prevention Experiment. In R. D. Peters & R. J. MacMahon (Eds.), *Preventing childhood disorders, substance abuse and delinquency* (pp. 268-298). Thousand Oaks: Sage.

U.S. Department of Health and Social Services Administration on Children Youth and Families. (2006). Child Maltreatment 2004. Retrieved from http://acf.dhhs.gov/programs/cb/pubs/cm04/chapterhree.htm#age

Valman, H. B. (1980). The first year of life: mother-infant bonding. *British Medical Journal, 280*, 308-310.

Van Izendoorn, M. H. (1995). Adult attachment representations, parental responsiveness, and infant attachment: A meta-analysis on the predictive validity of the Adult Attachment Interview. *Psychological Bulletin, 177*, 387-403.

Wahler, R. G. (1980). The insular mother: Her problems in parent-child treatment. *Journal of Applied Behavior Analysis, 13*(2), 207-219.

Wahler, R. G., & Barnes, P. G. (1988). *Synthesis training as a supplement to parental training with troubled mothers*. Paper presented at the Association for the Advancement of Behavior Therapy, New York.

Wahler, R. G., & Sansbury, L. E. (1990). The monitoring skills of troubled mothers: Their problems in defining child deviance. *Journal of Abnormal Child Psychology, 18*(5), 577-589.

Wahler, R. G., Cartor, P. G., Fleischman, J., & Lambert, W. (1993). The impact of synthesis teaching and parent training with mothers of conduct disordered children. *Journal of Abnormal Child Psychology, 12*, 425-440.

Walker, H. M. (1995). *The acting-out child: Coping with classroom disruption*. Longmont, CO: Sopris West.

Walker, H. M., Colvin, G., & Ramsey, E. (1995). *Antisocial behavior in school: Strategies and best practices*. Pacific Grove, CA: Brooks/Cole.

Walker, H. M., Schwartz, I. E., Nippold, M. A., Irvin, L. K., & Noell, J. W. (1994). Social skills in school-age children and youth: Issues and best practices in assessment and intervention. *Topics in Language Disorders, 14*(3), 70-82.

Walker, J. L., Lahey, B. B., Hynd, G. W., & Frame, C. L. (1987). Comparison of specific patterns of antisocial behavior in children with conduct disorder with or without coexisting hyperactivity. J Consult *Clin Psychol, 55*(6), 910-913.

Webster-Stratton, C. (1981). Modification of mothers' behaviors and attitudes through videotape modeling group discussion program. *Behavior Therapy, 12*, 634-642.

Webster-Stratton, C. (1982). Teaching mothers through videotape modeling to change their children's behaviors. *Journal of Pediatric Psychology, 7*(3), 279-294.

Webster-Stratton, C. (1984). Randomized trial of two parent-training programs for families with conduct-disordered children. *Journal of Consulting and Clinical Psychology, 52*(4), 666-678.

Webster-Stratton, C. (1984;2001;2007). *The Incredible Years Parent Training Manual: BASIC Program*. 1411 8th Avenue West, Seattle 98119.

Webster-Stratton, C. (1985). The effects of father involvement in parent training for conduct problem children. *Journal of Child Psychology and Psychiatry, 26*(5), 801-810.

Webster-Stratton, C. (1985a). Comparison of abusive and nonabusive families with conduct-disordered children. *American Journal of Orthopsychiatry, 55*, 59-69.

Webster-Stratton, C. (1985b). Mother perceptions and mother-child interactions: Comparison of a clinic-referred and a non-clinic group. *Journal of Clinical Child Psychology, 14.*(4), 334-339.

Webster-Stratton, C. (1985b). Predictors of treatment outcome in parent training for conduct disordered children. *Behavior Therapy, 16*, 223-243.

Webster-Stratton, C. (1988). *Dyadic Parent-Child Interaction Coding System—Revised Coding Manual* (Unpublished Manuscript): Unpublished Manuscript, University of Washington.

Webster-Stratton, C. (1989). The relationship of marital support, conflict and divorce to parent perceptions, behaviors and childhood conduct problems. *Journal of Marriage and the Family, 51*, 417-430.

Webster-Stratton, C. (1990). Stress: A potential disruptor of parent perceptions and family interactions. *Journal of Clinical Child Psychology, 19*, 302-312.

Webster-Stratton, C. (1990a). Enhancing the effectiveness of self-administered videotape parent training for families with conduct-problem children. *Journal of Abnormal Child Psychology, 18*, 479-492.

Webster-Stratton, C. (1990b). *The Incredible Years parent training Program manual: Effective communication, anger management and problem- solving (ADVANCE)*. Seattle, WA 98119: 1411 8th Avenue West.

Webster-Stratton, C. (1990c). Long-term follow-up of families with young conduct problem children: From preschool to grade school. *Journal of Clinical Child Psychology, 19*(2), 144-149.

Webster-Stratton, C. (1992). Individually administered videotape parent training: "Who benefits?". *Cognitive Therapy and Research, 16*(1), 31-35.

Webster-Stratton, C. (1994). Advancing videotape parent training: A comparison study. *Journal of Consulting and Clinical Psychology,* 62(3), 583-593.

Webster-Stratton, C. (1994). *The Incredible Years Teacher Classroom Management Training Series*. Seattle, WA: Incredible Years

Webster-Stratton, C. (1998). Preventing conduct problems in Head Start children: Strengthening parenting competencies. *Journal of Consulting and Clinical Psychology,* 66(5), 715-730.

Webster-Stratton, C. (1998a). *Wally Learns a Lesson from Tiny Turtle*. Seattle, WA Incredible Years.

Webster-Stratton, C. (1998b). *Wally Meets Dina Dinosaur.* Seattle Incredible Years.

Webster-Stratton, C. (1998c). *Wally's Detective Book for Solving Problems at Home*. Seattle, WA: Incredible Years.

Webster-Stratton, C. (1998d). *Wally's Detective Book for Solving Problems at School*. Seattle, WA: Incredible Years.

Webster-Stratton, C. (1999). *How to promote children's social and emotional competence*. London, England: Sage Publications.

Webster-Stratton, C. (2005). *The Incredible Years: A Trouble-Shooting Guide for Parents of Children Aged 2-8 Years*. Seattle, WA: Incredible Years.

Webster-Stratton, C. (2006). *Training interpreters to deliver the Incredible Years Parent Program: A cross cultural collaboration*.Unpublished manuscript, University of Washington at Seattle.

Webster-Stratton, C. (2007). Tailoring the Incredible Years Parenting Program According to Children's Developmental Needs and Family Risk Factors In J. M. Briesmeister & C. E. Schaefer (Eds.), *Handbook of Parent Training* Hoboken, New Jersey: John Wiley & Sons.

Webster-Stratton, C. (2008). *Home Visit Coaching and Coaches Guidelines:Incredible Years Basic Parents and Children's Series* Seattle, WA: Incredible Years.

Webster-Stratton, C., & Eyberg, S. M. (1982). Child temperament: relationships with child behavior problems and parent-child interactions. 11(2), 123-129.

Webster-Stratton, C., & Hammond, M. (1988). Maternal depression and its relationship to life stress, perceptions of child behavior problems, parenting behaviors and child conduct problems. *Journal of Abnormal Child Psychology, 16*(3), 299-315.

Webster-Stratton, C., & Hammond, M. (1990). Predictors of treatment outcome in parent training for families with conduct problem children. *Behavior Therapy, 21*, 319-337.

Webster-Stratton, C., & Hammond, M. (1997). Treating children with early-onset conduct problems: A comparison of child and parent training interventions. *Journal of Consulting and Clinical Psychology, 65*(1), 93-109.

Webster-Stratton, C., & Hammond, M. (1999). Marital conflict management skills, parenting style, and early-onset conduct problems: Processes and pathways. *Journal of Child Psychology and Psychiatry*, *40*, 917-927.

Webster-Stratton, C., & Herbert, M. (1993). What really happens in parent training? *Behavior Modification*, *17*(4), 407-456.

Webster-Stratton, C., & Herman, K. C. (2008). The impact of parent behavior-management training on child depressive symptoms. *Journal of Counseling Psychology*, *55*(4), 473-484.

Webster-Stratton, C., Hollinsworth, T., & Kolpacoff, M. (1989). The long-term effectiveness and clinical significance of three cost-effective training programs for families with conduct-problem children. *Journal of Consulting and Clinical Psychology*, *57*(4), 550-553.

Webster-Stratton, C., Kolpacoff, M., & Hollinsworth, T. (1988). Self-administered videotape therapy for families with conduct-problem children: Comparison with two cost-effective treatments and a control group. *Journal of Consulting and Clinical Psychology*, *56*(4), 558-566.

Webster-Stratton, C., & Reid, M. J. (1999, November, 1999). *Treating children with early-onset conduct problems: The importance of teacher training*. Paper presented at the Association for the Advancement of Behavior Therapy, Toronto, Canada.

Webster-Stratton, C., & Reid, J. M. (2010). A school-family partnership:Addressing multiple risk factors to improve school readiness and prevent conduct problems in young children. In S. L. Christenson & A. L. Reschly (Eds.), *Handbook on school-family partnerships for promoting student competence* (pp. 204-227). Seattle Routledge/Taylor and Francis.

Webster-Stratton, C., & Reid, M. J. (2010). Adapting the Incredible Years, an evidence-based parenting programme, for families involved in the child welfare system. *Journal of Children's Services* 5(1), 25-42.

Webster-Stratton, C., & Reid, M. J. (2010). The Incredible Years Parents, Teachers and Children Training Series: A multifaceted treatment approach for young children with conduct problems. In A. E. Kazdin & J. R. Weisz (Eds.), *Evidence-based psychotherapies for children and adolescents, 2nd edition* (pp. 194-210). New York: Guilford Publications.

Webster-Stratton, C., Reid, M. J., & Beauchaine, T. P. (2011). Combining Parent and Child Training for Young Children with ADHD. *Journal of Clinical Child and Adolsecent Psychology, 40*(2), 1-13.

Webster-Stratton, C., Reid, M. J., & Hammond, M. (2001). Preventing conduct problems, promoting social competence: A parent and teacher training partnership in Head Start. *Journal of Clinical Child Psychology, 30*(3), 283-302.

Webster-Stratton, C., Reid, M. J., & Hammond, M. (2004). Treating children with early-onset conduct problems: Intervention outcomes for parent, child, and teacher training. *Journal of Clinical Child and Adolescent Psychology, 33*(1), 105-124.

Webster-Stratton, C., Reid, M. J., Hurlburt, M., & Marsenich, L. (in press). Improving therapist fidelity during EBP implementation. *Psychiatric Services*.

Webster-Stratton, C., Reid, M. J., & Stoolmiller, M. (2008). Preventing conduct problems and improving school readiness: Evaluation of the Incredible Years Teacher and Child Training Programs in high-risk schools. *Journal of Child Psychology and Psychiatry 49*(5), 471-488.

Webster-Stratton, C., Reinke, W. M., Herman, K. C., & Newcomer, L. (2011). The Incredible Years Teacher Classroom Management Training: The Methods and Principles that Support Fidelity of Training Delivery. *School Psychology Review, 40*, 509-529.

Webster-Stratton, C., Rinaldi, J., & Reid, J. M. (2010). Long Term Outcomes of the Incredible Years Parenting Program: Predictors of Adolescent Adjustment. Child and Adolescent Mental Health, 16(1), 38-46.

Weissberg, R. P., Kumpfer, K. L., & Seligman, M. E. P. (2003). Prevention that works for children and youth: An introduction. *American Psychologist, 59*, 425-432.

Weisz, J. R., Donenberg, G. R., Han, S. S., & Weiss, B. (1995). Bridging the gap between laboratory and clinic in child and adolescent psychotherapy. Special section: Efficacy and effectiveness in studies of child and adolescent psychotherapy. *Journal of Consulting and Clinical Psychology, 63*(5), 688-701.

Weisz, J. R., Huey, S., & Weersing, V. R. (1998). Psychotherapy outcome research with children and adolescents: The state of the art. *Advances in clinical child psychology, 20*, 49-91.

West, S. G., & Aiken, L. S. (1997). Towards understanding individual effects in multiple component prevention programs: design and analysis issues. In K. J. Bryant, M. Windle & S. G. West (Eds.), *New Methodological Developments in Prevention Research: Alcohol and Substance Abuse Research*. Washington, DC: APA.

White, J., Moffit, T., Earls, F., & Robins, L. (1990). Preschool predictors of persistent conduct disorder and delinquency. *Criminology, 28*, 443-454.

Williford, A. P., & Shelton, T. L. (2008). Using mental health consultation to decrease disruptive behaviors in preschoolers: adapting an empirically-supported intervention. *Journal of Child Psychology and Psychiatry*, 49(2), 191-200.

Willis, W. (1992). *Families with African American roots*. Baltimore, MD: Paul H. Brooks

Wilson, S. J., & Lipsey, M. W. (2007). School-based interventions for aggressive and disruptive behavior:Update of a meta-analysis. *American Journal of Preventive Medicine*, 33(2), 130-143.

Zeanah, C. (1996). Beyond Insecurity: A Reconceptualization of Attachment Disorders in Infancy. *Journal of Consulting and Clinical Psychology*, 64, 42-52.

Zisser, A., & Eyberg, S. M. (2010). Treating oppositional behavior in children using parent-child interaction therapy. In A. E. Kazdin & J. R. Weisz (Eds.), *Evidence-based psychotherapies for children and adolescents* (Vol. 2nd ed, pp. 179-193). New York: Guilford.